When Parties Fail

Edited by

Kay Lawson and

Peter H. Merkl

When Parties Fail

Emerging Alternative

Organizations

PRINCETON

UNIVERSITY

PRESS

Published by Princeton University Press, 41 William Street,
Princeton, New Jersey 08540
In the United Kingdom: Princeton University Press, Guildford, Surrey

Library of Congress Cataloging in Publication Data will be
found on the last printed page of this book

ISBN 0-691-07758-4
ISBN 0-691-10242-2 (pbk.)

This book has been composed in Linotron Sabon

Clothbound editions of Princeton University Press books
are printed on acid-free paper, and binding materials are
chosen for strength and durability. Paperbacks, although satisfactory
for personal collections, are not usually suitable for library rebinding

Printed in the United States of America by Princeton University Press,
Princeton, New Jersey

Designed by Laury A. Egan

CONTENTS

PART VII. CONCLUSIONS

PART I | Introduction

ONE

Alternative Organizations: Environmental, Supplementary, Communitarian, and Antiauthoritarian

KAY LAWSON AND
PETER H. MERKL

The phenomenon of major party decline, often remarked in the context of the American political system, is becoming increasingly apparent in other political systems as well. All over the world, single-issue movements are forming, special interest groups are assuming party-like status, and minor parties are winning startling overnight victories as hitherto dominant parties lose the confidence of their electorates.

Contemporary scholarship has, however, only begun to document this development. As yet we know very little about the causes of major party decline. We do not know if major parties are failing because they are ideologically out of touch with their electorates, poorly organized, underfinanced, badly led, nonaccountable, corrupt, overwhelmed by unethical or fanatical competition, unable to rule effectively, or some combination of these factors. And we have very little data to substantiate or refute any of the propositions implicit in these speculations.

We know even less about the organizations that are emerging to take the place of declining major parties. It may be that the institution of party is gradually disappearing, slowly being replaced by new political structures more suitable for the economic and technological realities of twenty-first-century politics. But little has been done to explore the political organizations that are emerging—to distinguish altogether new forms of organization from those that are simply new manifestations of familiar forms of assemblage, or to separate apparently permanent additions to the political arena from those that are merely epiphenomenal. Ecological and antinuclear issue groups, ad hoc coalitions, "flash" parties, neighborhood committees, and religious movements abound, but we have little idea which circumstances produce which forms of alternative organization, for what purposes, and for what duration.

Finally, we have learned almost nothing about why major parties sometimes survive even when threatened by powerful alternative organizations, nor why others are able to revive after a period of crisis and decline. The elasticity and staying power of some parties despite difficult conditions and aggressive challenges from other groups have been as surprising as the rapid decline and fall of others seemingly well protected and unthreatened by serious competition.

When Parties Fail is a collection of case studies designed to address these questions and fill this gap in our knowledge and understanding of contemporary political organizations. In eighteen cases the authors consider both the conditions associated with major party failure and the nature of an alternative organization that has emerged: its relationship to the existing party structure, its own internal structure, its social composition, its goals and ideological foundations, how its program and activities differ from those of the conventional parties, what evidence there may be of its successful appeal, and its prospects for further development.

Our primary emphasis is on the new organizations, but only as they form in the present context of major party failure. Parties have failed before, and new organizations have emerged to take their places, but normally such developments are country-specific and can be readily explained in terms of local histories of political decline and renewal. Today, however, the phenomenon is of wider dimensions, and it is clearly worthwhile to bring together studies of its various manifestations, to look for patterns, and to identify that which is unique.

Yet what does it mean for a party to fail? Although nearly all our authors concurred that major parties are faltering, and that it was time to give the new parties and movements attempting to take their place the systematic attention called for in the design of this book, they found themselves less able to agree on where exactly to post "failure" on the slope of major party decline. Should it be, as most believed, at the point where major parties are no longer able to perform the functions commonly assigned them in the society in question, e.g., structuring the electoral process, representing and aggregating all significant group interests, organizing government and formulating policy? Or should it be, as Richard Rose and Tom Mackie argue, only at the point where a major party disappears altogether and no comparable successor party forms to take its place? Or should it be someplace in between? Furthermore, how long must the signs of major party decrepitude endure for observers to be sure that an organization really has failed? If there are signs of major party reform and revitalization during the period when the organization is not carrying out its appointed tasks in the expected way and is in danger of being replaced by alternative groups, is it fair to speak of failure—especially if those efforts at renewal eventually pay off? Frank Wilson, using the example of France during the 1970s, sees this as the very antithesis of failure; Rose and Mackie would clearly agree; others would not. Our solution to this lack of agreement was a simple one: we asked each author to include his own definition of party failure early in the chapter. As indicated, nearly all, including the editors, decided that major parties fail when they do not perform the functions they are expected to perform in their own society; that they may eventually be able to resume work at earlier or higher levels of proficiency does not change the fact of their having failed in the past. On the other hand, there was unanimous agreement, often indicated in comments in the individual chapters, that the Rose/Mackie and Wilson perspectives on party failure also have merit, especially as documented by those authors. In short, tempting though it may have been to command our international team of authors to march to exactly the same tune, dressed in exactly the same analytical garb, we decided that accommodating this minor difference of opinion would be more likely to help us get to our destination: the best possible understanding of a complex phenomenon.

It is complex, as becomes even more clear when we turn away from the failing major parties to their would-be surrogates. Dissatisfaction with the world's major parties is widespread, but the exact nature of that discontent, and the action it prompts the disaffected to take, vary widely. This diversity, and the relatively recent formation of most of the alternative organizations discussed by our authors, make categorization risky and the assignment of labels probably premature. While acknowledging that this is so, we have nevertheless found it convenient and heuristically productive to assign each of the organizations studied here to one of four types: Environmentalist, Supplementary, Communitarian, and Antiauthoritarian. Although our categories are tentative, and one or two of the groups could conceivably be shifted from one category to another, we have been reassured by the authors' own satisfaction with the typology we have imposed, and the conviction of each that his own group has been properly assigned. We turn now to an examination of each of these in turn.

ENVIRONMENTALIST ORGANIZATIONS

The environmentalist organizations are the organizations formed in response to today's "New Politics." They have an agenda which includes not only protection of the physical environment but change in the political environment as well. They address such issues as peace, feminism, and participatory decisionmaking, in addition to the more familiar environmental issues of toxic waste, acid rain, and destruction of the biosphere. They are determined to leave behind what seem to them the outdated class or communitarian struggles of the dominant parties. Their leaders and members see the older parties as stubbornly irrelevant, dangerously out of touch with problems that cry out for political solutions. These organizations are characterized by the determination of their members to take direct, personal action in the struggle to bring about change. Traditional party structures are not democratic enough for their tastes; they have sought to establish more egalitarian procedures by assuring that meetings will be open to everyone, that no one will assume the role of "leader" for more than a brief period of time, and that all points of view will be fully discussed.

Six environmentalist organizations are discussed in this volume. To begin with, Donald Schoonmaker discusses one of the world's best-known alternative groups, the Green party of West Germany, and shows us how the rise of an ecological and neutralist movement is now presenting the German voter with zero–sum lifestyle and symbolic issues and attracting enough support to disrupt the established patterns of that nation's postwar party system. A similar agenda, and a similar threat, has been offered by the Swedish Environmentalist party since it emerged in 1981 to threaten the basic bipolarity of Swedish five-party politics. Evert Vedung explains why this party's actual vote in the 1982 elections fell far short of early polls and why it is, at least for the time being, no longer a serious challenge to a system that has been a model of stability for several decades.

In the next essay, Angelo Panebianco examines the Italian Radical party, which was revived from decades of slumber by its decision to address the salient new issues—a decision that enabled it to play a role as a meaningful alternative in that nation's electoral panoply of parties for the first time in its postwar history. This party has maximized its impact on the Italian political system by taking up the environmentalist issues one by one, all but converting itself into a single-issue pressure group for each campaign.

In the next three essays, the authors show us what happens when the environmentalist alternative organizations take the form of activist groups rather than parties, and operate on the local scene rather than in national electoral politics. Robert Sorensen explains how citizen action groups in the Swiss cities of Basel and Zurich use protests, propaganda campaigns, and direct lobbying to fight for "life-style" environmental issues, disdaining both party politics and the use of violence as means to

achieve their ends. In a different context, Raffaella Nanetti traces the role
a coalition of neighborhood organizations has played not only in pursuit
of similar goals but also in hastening the decline and fall of the last dominant metropolitan political party machine in the United States, the Democratic party of Chicago. In the process she discusses the conditions in
which this new form of political organization is likely to prosper and its
potential for institutionalization as a permanent alternative to the old-
fashioned party machine. As a final example of the extraordinary power
of nonmaterial motives to shape political activism outside the normal
party structures, David Apter reviews the rise of the Sanrizuka movement
in Japan, a group that emerged when the Japanese government displaced
two hundred farm families in order to build a large inland airport, causing
not only the farmers but propeace, antinuclear, anti-United States and environmentalist forces to band together in a citizens' participation movement which neither the ruling Liberal Democratic party nor the opposition Communist and Socialist parties have been able to contain or placate.

SUPPLEMENTARY ORGANIZATIONS

The organizations that fall into this second category have, for the most
part, more familiar agendas. The issues that matter to them are issues that
have appeared on other people's political agendas since time immemorial,
such as how to lower taxes or how to assure adequate government attention to the needs of a particular group in the body politic. What characterizes these groups is not their conviction that the issues they address are
new, nor that they themselves constitute a community sharply distinct
from all others (see the following section), but simply their belief that at
the present time there is no way to compel the existing parties to pay adequate attention to them. They seek supplementary representation, and in
order to acquire it they create their own new organizations. Three examples of alternative organizations formed out of the impulse to achieve supplementary representation are presented here.

In our first example, Geoffrey Pridham shows how Britain's two major
parties have moved closer to their "class cores," and how this has had the
effect of persuading some of their more moderate members that they can
no longer be adequately represented by existing parties. This phenomenon
has been particularly marked on the left, where leading representatives of
Labour's moderate wing have formed a new organization to supplement
the choices open to the British voter. The Social Democratic party has sometimes been deliberately vague about the exact issue content of its program, but its criticisms of the far left and far right place it determinedly in

the British political center and make it thereby a new natural ally of the Liberal party.

By way of contrast, Denmark has produced a supplementary party with a much more specific agenda: the Progress party was formed to offer an alternative to those who were frustrated by what seemed to them to be the excessive and intransigent commitment of the major parties to programs of social reform that came at too great expense to the taxpaying middle class. Mogens Pedersen is not certain that this is a case of major party "failure" but describes the part this taxpayers' movement played, under the dynamic leadership of Mogens Glistrup, in bringing about the Danish electoral earthquake of 1973, when the five major parties in the nation each lost between one-fourth and one-half their previous strength in Parliament.

In the United States, the failure of the major parties to protect and advance certain values and interests with the fervor their proponents believe they deserve has come in a period of general party decline and post Watergate campaign finance reforms that have combined to suggest that here those in need of supplementary representation would do best to form not a new party but a new kind of group, the political action committee. Frank Sorauf describes the PACs, "organizations that collect and spend resources (usually cash) to influence election outcomes" and that some now believe threaten to take the place of American parties altogether.

COMMUNITARIAN ORGANIZATIONS

Communitarian responses to party neglect are not a new phenomenon: party politics has never successfully aggregated the interests of every religious, racial, ethnic, or caste community in any nation and the nonaggregated have often been ready and willing to form separate political movements to battle for their rights. In periods of major party decline, it is to be expected that communitarian alternative organizations will be both more plentiful and more persistent. Four authors treat a total of six such groups in Part IV of this book.

To begin with, Myron Aronoff provides a semiotic/phenomenological analysis of the Israeli religious sect Gush Emunim (Bloc of the Faithful), a politico-religious group organized to struggle for literal fulfillment of biblical promise, with particular emphasis on widening the extent of Israel's territorial domain. Next is Peter Pulzer's study of three British communitarian groups. The Scottish Nationalist party and the Welsh Plaid Cymru both formed on nationalist grounds, whereas the National Front is based on race (or, one might prefer to say, on racism).

Of all the communitarian groups included in this book, the National Democratic party of Alabama has perhaps been the most successful in accomplishing its goals, although the party itself has, not unrelatedly, suffered considerable losses in membership and support. Hanes Walton shows us how this party helped black Alabamans take a meaningful role in their state's and nation's politics for the first time, even when battled at every step of the way by one of the nation's most bitterly resistant white supremacist state parties. Dramatic shifts in national racial attitudes and reforms of the electoral system worked to the new party's benefit.

Finally, as Ronald Herring clearly demonstrates, an important component in the success of the Communist party in the Indian state of Kerala has been its strong support from communities degraded in both social and economic terms by the fusion of a dominant caste-class system. Formed by splinter left factions within the Congress party movement, the success of the Communists electorally in Kerala suggests reasons for exceptions to the general rule of Congress hegemony—despite programmatic failures—in most of India.

ANTIAUTHORITARIAN ORGANIZATIONS

Where others focus on a limited range of issues or the interests of a particular group, the antiauthoritarians direct their attention to "the masses," to the rights and interests of the people at large, especially when these are denied by the selfish rule of a narrow elite. It is not surprising that all three of our antiauthoritarian cases have made their appearance in hegemonic party systems heavily backed by (and in one case eventually replaced by) military leadership. What is perhaps surprising is the role that military leadership has played in encouraging the development of the alternative organization in the third case, that of Ghana.

In his study of the Polish Solidarity movement, Zvi Gitelman examines the failure of the Polish United Workers' party, despite its seeming monopoly of power, and the rise of Solidarity to its dramatic climax, noting that the declaration of martial law of December 1981 appears to have been as much a coup against the party as against Solidarity, by then greatly weakened not only by government repression but by its own uncertainty about the kind of alternative it wished to offer: one limited to strong and independent trade unionism or one that offered the Polish people a full populist agenda.

Liang-shing Fan and Frank Feigert discuss the Taiwan Independence Movement and Tangwai [Those Outside the Party], two Taiwanese movements challenging the dominance of that nation's political system by the

Kuomintang and by "mainlanders," i.e., those who came uninvited to the island with Chiang Kai-Shek. Fan and Feigert analyze the emergence of these two movements as indicative of the "inability of the existing party system to accommodate to stress, internal and external."

The People's Defense Committees of Ghana have been brought to life by a different kind of military leadership, one determined to establish not only more efficent and more honest, but also more popular, government than that new nation has known either before or after independence. Jon Kraus carefully traces the ambiguities these groups must operate within: established by nonconstitutional leadership, denied legal status, opposed by a powerful array of special interests, and yet somehow still expected to save the Ghanaian people from the evil effects of the very force that keeps their progenitor in office: the arbitrary and authoritarian exercise of power.

Major Parties Do Not Always Fail

As the above cases make clear, major party failure in this era of general party decline is seldom absolute. The major parties are visibly weaker, are losing votes, and sometimes even lose power, either to other parties in the legislative arena or to other groups in the political system—but so far they have not given up altogether (with the possible exceptions—among our cases—of the Daley machine in Chicago and the white supremacist Democrats in Alabama). They remain very much on the scene, and no study of the related phenomena of major party decline and the formation of alternative organizations would be complete without an examination of the durability of some major parties in this period of stress. Two essays—one a case study and the other an exploration of the fortunes of numerous parties over time—help us make such an examination.

The case Frank Wilson studies is France. Despite successive challenges from a variety of alternative political organizations in the 1960s and 1970s, the French party system has "refused to fail"—the activities of the parties, and the electoral response to those activities, continue to shape the course of French politics. The parties may change dramatically (as in the recent rise of the National Front and decline of the Communist party), but nonparty alternative organizations have little impact. Wilson identifies five factors that make major parties "better able to resist the challenges of alternative groups and organizational decay."

In the broadest study of our collection, Richard Rose and Tom Mackie use electoral results from the national beginnings of nineteen Western nations to explore the conditions under which individual political parties are likely to persist intact or with marginal adaptation, to undergo structural adaptation producing new parties more or less strongly identified with their defunct progenitors, or to disappear altogether. As noted earlier, these authors use a more rigorous definition of party failure than that found in the other essays—for Rose and Mackie, a party "fails" only if it disappears entirely. This approach permits them to offer a useful reminder that what sometimes appears to be a case of party failure may be merely a marginal modification or a structural change in which a party adapts, sacrificing something in organizational continuity for the sake of expected benefits. Of the parties they examine, the median party is one that persists with marginal modifications; only 23 percent disappear completely and 33 percent persist completely intact.

THE BROADER VIEW: LINKAGE AND PARTY SYSTEMS

We begin and end this volume with two essays of our own, in which we attempt not only to provide an overview but also to evaluate the meaning this present proliferation of stronger alternative organizations has for internal systems of linkage between citizen and state and for the overall nature of party systems. In the first, Kay Lawson examines the cases for evidence that major party decline is related to a failure of linkage, and that the degree of success attained by the alternative organizations is owing to the degree to which they fill the linkage void left by the major parties. Her case-by-case analysis leads to unexpected findings, as she discovers distinctly different answers for the four kinds of alternative organizations included in this book. These results prompt her to a further elaboration of linkage theory, a recognition that linkage is possible without political organizations, and a concluding argument that democratic linkage is not.

Peter Merkl questions the impact made by the emergence of these new organizations on different established party systems. He points out that when dissidents find it necessary to form new organizations rather than merely switch loyalties, there is a strong suggestion that not merely individual parties, but whole party systems, may have failed. On the other hand, the new groups are unlikely to have sufficient strength to effectuate significant change in the systems they repudiate. Also proceeding case by case, Merkl offers a close examination of the varying impact alternative organizations have on different kinds of party systems, and concludes with a provocative discussion of the possible wider use of what we may call an alternative to alternative organizations: the initiative and referendum.

In the pleasant and stimulating tasks of gathering and editing these essays, the editors have had the encouragement and support of many individuals and institutions. We particularly wish to thank Mattei Dogan, Samuel Eldersveld, Haruhiro Fukui, Richard Harris, Kent Jennings, Seymour Martin Lipset, Dwaine Marvick, and Peter Nissen for their interest and advice. We are also very grateful to the Hutchins Center for the Study of Democratic Institutions, the Council for European Studies, and the Chancellor's Office of the University of California at Santa Barbara for making possible a two-day conference in Santa Barbara. Over half the authors represented here were able to attend, twelve papers were presented, other distinguished scholars joined in our discussions, and by the end of the second day the consensus was clear: the questions we began with were important and deserved to be examined more systematically. Now that we and our authors have completed our work on this volume, we trust that others will agree with that evaluation. We hope they may also find that we have at least made a creditable beginning to a task that many others must help us complete.

TWO

When Linkage Fails

KAY LAWSON

The essays in this volume make it clear that there are many different kinds of organizations emerging to challenge existing major political parties, that they make their appearance in all kinds of systems, and that they achieve varying degrees of success. Is there any pattern to this development in contemporary politics? What causes such organizations to appear? What causes them to endure—or to fade away?[1]

One way to answer such questions, as Peter Merkl ably demonstrates in the final essay of this book, is to consider major party failures and the emergence of alternative organizations in systemic terms, exploring what happens when the phenomenon takes place in different kinds of party systems and in different kinds of political systems. Another way, and one that will be followed in this chapter, is to consider the phenomenon in linkage terms, asking whether the emergence and the durability of such groups are in some fashion related to the failure of the major parties and the success of their would-be successors in providing adequate and acceptable means of linking citizen to state.

LINKAGE

Linkage is both an old and a new concept in political science. It has been used for some time to describe two practices which at first seem to have nothing to do with each other. It is being used now not only in a sense which subsumes both older meanings and shows their relationship, but which also incorporates the more mundane and familiar meanings of the word "link." In this latter sense, linkage offers a new way of looking at political reality, but one that builds on—and indeed is very largely built of—entirely familiar elements. Because it is easy to imagine, when encoun-

[1] The author wishes to thank David Apter and Peter Merkl for their careful review of this chapter and useful suggestions for its improvement.

tering something familiar within something new, that the something new is really just another name for the something old that one recognizes within it, it is worthwhile to begin this essay with an explanation of these old and new usages of linkage.

For most political scientists, the most familiar usage of "linkage" is that developed by V. O. Key, and carried forward by Norman Luttbeg, and by Heinz Eulau and Kenneth Prewitt, among others (Key, 1964; Luttbeg, 1974, 1975; Eulau and Prewitt, 1973). For Key, linkage means simply "the interconnections between mass opinion and public decision," and most of the others seem to agree, using the term to focus their readers' attention on such intermediaries between citizen and state as groups, parties, opinion polls, and elections. Eulau and Prewitt use the term slightly differently. They are interested in the relationship between citizens and local councilmen, but they tend to use the term "linkage" to cover merely the various acts of citizen participation in that relationship—responsiveness to that participation is held to be a different thing, something provided by "representation." It would make better sense, of course, to treat both participation and representation as subsumed under "linkage"— links have two ends—and then to explore the nature of the connection between the two. Nevertheless, despite these semantic problems, Eulau and Prewitt come closer than any of the others to opening up the nature of the linkage connection itself. The others, including Key, prefer to focus on the agencies of connection and assume that if we understand what they do, we will understand that they have created something that may be called, at least metaphorically, "a link." Used this way, "linkage" has little more theoretical substance than an earlier and comparable metaphor, "transmission belt."

For students of international relations, on the other hand, "linkage" refers to the ways decisions and events in one nation may trigger decisions or events in another. In this sense it refers to "a state's policy of making its course of action concerning a given issue contingent upon another state's behavior in a different issue area," or, more simply, "the practice of tying a concession by one party to a concession by the other" (Stein, 1980; Hamilton, 1981). The two states' actions are said to be "linked," but here again, the usage is largely metaphorical.

In both cases, however, the metaphor "works"—a link is "a connection, usually with a connotation of interaction," and in both these situations a connection is being established between two different elements (citizens' wishes and elite decisions, one nation's decisions and another's) in such a way as to produce reciprocal if not equal impact.

Furthermore, one author, James Rosenau, has made an effort to push the concept beyond metaphor, identifying political links as those that take place between different levels of aggregation (a level of aggregation is usually a geographic unit—local government, state government, national government, international politics—but may also be a unit of organization—city councils, pressure groups, parties, movements, legislatures, bureaucracies, regional bodies, United Nations agencies). Rosenau has also at least begun the exploration of what is going on inside the link by identifying two linkage processes: penetrative (actors from one polity or "level of aggregation" participate in the political processes of another) and reactive (responses are made in one unit to actions initiated in another, made without transfer of actors). And finally, although he developed these ideas as international relations theory, Rosenau saw the wider applicability of the concept, recognizing that "a virtually endless number of levels can be used as the basis for inquiry." Yet despite this most auspicious beginning, Rosenau has failed to see the wider implications of the concept, and has now shifted his attention elsewhere (Rosenau, 1969, 1973, 1974).

What wider implications? Why is it important to push one's way further through the metaphor? What will we find when we get there?

To answer that, it will be helpful to back up a little further and take a yet wider look at our subject, and then to narrow our focus sharply, applying this new usage of linkage to political parties and alternative political organizations.

When we back up, the view is at first overwhelming. After all, everything political happens through an interactive connection, and most of these are established between different levels of aggregation. All the functions political scientists have identified (a) as normally necessary for the continued operation of a social system, and (b) as being performed in whole or in part by politics must be performed in the context of an interactive connection. Participation, leadership recruitment, allocation of resources, the creation and propagation of values, the control of behavior (through the control of force and/or through educative communication) all require the creation of connections between different levels of aggregation. Creating linkages is itself an extremely important function of politics.

To say that the making of links is a function that contributes to the carrying out of other functions is not in itself amazing; the reverse is also true (e.g., it helps to have leaders when it is time to create new connections). But there is a difference between this function and others: to a considerable extent, the creation of links has been a hidden function of politics, hidden because it is everywhere, taken for granted, no more (perhaps less) remarked than the walls of the room we meet in, the screen on which the television image appears. The explicit conditions of linkage have so far acquired only a partial, almost ghostly visibility—and that only in the two areas where it is hardest to establish and maintain them satisfactorily: between citizen and state and between nation and nation. The work of acquiring an understanding of how linkage is established and maintained is most advanced in the study of links between citizen and state, and in particular in the study of the role of political parties in creating that linkage.

This is not because the leaders and activists of parties are personally dedicated to the creation of linkages between citizen and state (although some may be). What they seek is power, and they seek it by attempting to place one or more of themselves in positions of responsibility for performing some of the system's more crucial functions. They want to be the ones who provide what opportunities for participation may exist, who allocate resources and values, who direct the use of the instruments of force and education—and who create (and maintain) links among a wide range of levels of aggregation. To achieve this end, they must present themselves as capable in these domains. They encourage (or pretend to encourage) grass-roots participation and they present more or less clearly designed programs regarding the allocation of resources and values and the exercise of control. But their strongest suit is linkage, and in particular, linkage between citizen and state. Citizens seek some way to interact with the larger political system, influencing how it carries out its functions. The leaders of governments depend on being able to connect themselves to the loyalty and energies of citizens. Parties succeed by helping both accomplish their ends—or appearing to do so. The political party is the one agency that can claim to have as its very raison d'être the creation of an entire linkage chain, a chain of connections that runs from the voters through the candidates and the electoral process to the officials of government. As I have shown in an earlier work, this chain of linkage may take one of four possible forms, or a combination of two or more such forms (Lawson, 1980). The form a party adopts depends on which of the other functions of government its most active members prioritize: participation, policy responsiveness, resource allocation, and/or control (coercive or educative) of behavior. The basic choices are as follows.

Participatory linkage. The party provides participatory linkage when it serves as an agency through which citizens can themselves participate in government. They do this by shaping the party's program, choosing its candidates (or even becoming candidates themselves), and, most importantly, by holding elected representatives responsible to the party program (by controlling ballot access, and specifically by being willing to deny renomination to disloyal incumbents). Such parties have strong grass-roots organizations and are internally democratic procedurally.

Electoral linkage. The party provides this kind of linkage when its leaders control the group's elected representatives, both by controlling ballot access and by requiring prospective candidates to promise, and in the case of incumbents, demonstrate, responsiveness to the views of rank-and-file party members. In this case, those views are independently (and sometimes inaccurately) determined by the party leaders. If grass-roots party structures exist, they are oligarchically controlled, and party activists are mobilized only for electoral chores (registering new voters, canvassing, getting out the vote).

Clientelistic linkage. The party acts as a channel for the exchange of votes for favors. Grass-roots structures are boss-ruled or nonexistent.

Directive linkage. The party is used by those in government office to maintain control over the behavior of citizens. At all levels, from grass roots to national office, the party is an agent of education, or of coercion, or of both.

As noted, these types of linkage by party are not mutually exclusive; indeed, in actual practice, it is rare to find a political party that does not provide more than one form of linkage. The two more common combinations are: (1) Representative-democratic: emphasis on electoral linkage, with some elements of other types; (2) Authoritarian: emphasis on directive linkage, with some elements of other types.

ALTERNATIVE ORGANIZATIONS AND LINKAGE

Because parties claim to provide linkage to the state, and often demonstrably do, it is interesting to consider if the decline in support for major parties and the emergence of alternative organizations are somehow related to major party failure, and alternative organization success, in providing a particular kind of linkage. Two hypotheses come readily to mind.

Hypothesis No. 1: Alternative organizations emerge when major parties fail to provide acceptable forms of linkage.

Hypothesis No. 2: Alternative organizations endure when they succeed in providing the kind of linkage hitherto lacking in the political system.

The essays in this volume provide a wealth of data for testing these hypotheses. We can get a clearer notion of the role played by success or failure in providing linkage in the emergence of alternative organizations by probing each of our cases for answers to the following questions:

1. What is the preferred or expected form of linkage in the political system under study? This question acknowledges that what constitutes a linkage failure in one system may be very different from what it takes to fail in another system. Politically active persons in different political systems have different expectations regarding what kinds of linkage their

parties will provide. Sometimes these expectations change over time. Sometimes new and different groups become politically active and develop their own, different demands for linkage. Linkage failure may thus be a failure to maintain a preferred or at least expected form of linkage, a failure to provide a newly demanded form of linkage, or a failure to provide the usual form of linkage to those newly entering the political arena. These considerations lead us to the second question.

2. What evidence is there that the usual form of linkage either is not being provided or is no longer acceptable (at least to some persons)? If the answer to this question is "none," the case must be set aside: studying linkage will be of no use here. But if there is any such evidence, it makes sense to proceed with the remaining questions.

3. What evidence is there that the major parties are responsible, in whole or in part, for the linkage failure?

4. How well does the alternative organization fill the linkage void? In particular:

a. Is there anything in the way the alternative organization began that increases its potential as a group able to provide the desired linkage?

b. Does the group's internal structure improve its linkage capacity?

c. Do the organization's issue stances or ideological dogma address the linkage problems identified?

d. Is there anything unique about the group's leaders that make them particularly fit for satisfying felt linkage needs?

e. Does the group attract the kind of members most dissatisfied with previously existing forms of linkage?

f. Is there anything about the group's tactics that makes it particularly good at filling the linkage void?

5. Finally, what signs are there in the answers to the foregoing questions that the alternative organization will or will not endure, and are these signs consistent with other indications of its longevity?

ENVIRONMENTALIST ORGANIZATIONS AS
LINKAGE ALTERNATIVES

These questions produce interestingly different answers when addressed to the four sets of alternative organizations identified in this volume: environmentalist, supplementary, communitarian, and antiauthoritarian. We begin with the environmentalists.

Traditional forms of linkage. The German Greens, Swedish Environmentalists, Swiss citizen action groups, Italian Radicals, Chicago Neighborhood Coalition, and Japanese Sanrizuka movement all developed in political systems where some form of democratic political linkage has normally been provided. There is, however, a clear dividing line between the first three cases and the remaining three. In the German, Swedish, and Swiss cases, democratic linkage has tended in the past to take the form of electoral linkage, via a class-based multiparty system, combined with considerable opportunities for participatory linkage, via mass party organizational structures or, as in the case of Switzerland, via frequent use of the initiative and the referendum.

In Italy, Japan, and Chicago, on the other hand, the emphasis has been on clientelistic linkage, via factions brought together in a ruling coalitional machine (the Italian Christian Democrats, the Japanese Liberal Democratic party, and the Chicago Democrats under both Daley and Byrne); in these three systems, machine leaders have frequently determined policy matters with minimal regard for popular concerns.

Dissatisfaction with current linkage patterns. In all six systems, we find increasing evidence that the traditional linkage patterns are no longer satisfactory to some members of the citizenry. Electoral linkage based on class-linked issues is not satisfactory to those who want policy that will address environmental-development issues (ranging from concern over changing neighborhood quality to fear of unrestrained nuclear development), and the very limited opportunities for participatory linkage are no longer acceptable to those who have become increasingly disturbed about patterns of discrimination based on personal characteristics (sex, race) and are eager to take greater part themselves in the decisionmaking process.

Major party linkage failure. These are concerns the leaders of the major parties have been very slow to address. They are used to exercising power in certain ways and find it difficult to believe any change is necessary (a belief that may or may not prove to be well founded). The leaders of the dominant German, Swedish, and Swiss parties are all accustomed to (a) seeking policies designed to maximize economic growth and national defense, and (b) maintaining discriminatory and organizational barriers to would-be competitors for their power. The leaders of the powerful Italian DC, Japanese LDP, and Chicago Democrats have these same habits plus one more: (c) satisfying supporters by the clientelistic distribution of patronage. They have therefore all failed (because they have refused), at least temporarily, to address these new linkage demands.

The new organizations as alternative forms of linkage. In several respects, the alternative organizations that have emerged in each of these nations—the German Greens, the Swedish Environmentalists, the Swiss citizen action groups, the Italian Radicals, the Japanese Sanrizuka movement, and the Chicago Neighborhood Coalition—have characteristics that should permit them to fill the linkage void left by the major parties. They are all of quite recent origin, and thus presumably truly free to address new issues (although two—the German Greens and the Japanese Sanrizuka movement—have interesting roots in earlier groups). They have all established structures which permit the widest possible grass-roots participation. They all address the issues the major parties have failed to treat satisfactorily either in their own programs or in actual practice. None has developed a single strong enduring leader, but this is consistent with their emphasis on participatory linkage; in fact, by establishing collective leadership bodies, the Swedish Environmentalists and the Swiss citizen action groups are perhaps most in keeping with the new linkage needs in this respect.

The membership ranks of all six groups are limited in number, and even the German Greens have never taken more than 8 percent of the vote—and, of course, voters are not all members. However, all six appear to have been able to serve as a focal point for those persons in their societies for whom such issues are paramount: in none of the six systems is there serious competition from comparable organizations for the same clientele (although in some cases other types of parties or groups have adopted some of the same agenda, at least formally; note, for example, the antinuclear plank of the Swedish Communist party and the response of that nation's Center party to the Environmentalist challenge). Finally, all six have shown themselves remarkably adept at developing the necessary means for attracting the attention of the media (usually heavy reliance on demonstrations).

The prospects of the alternative organizations. If these groups are so good at filling the linkage void in their respective systems, does this mean that they are likely to endure? To expand? For the present in all cases the signs seem negative. All six organizations address interests held, so far, only by narrow minorities within their respective societies. In several cases the nation's electoral system (note the 4 percent barrier in Sweden, for example) makes it extremely difficult to penetrate the political arena. Expansion thus seems unlikely, and without expansion, durability must also be in question. Furthermore, should these groups achieve some success (expansion), they would probably be even more likely to disappear: the major parties in all six systems are still strong enough to be able to move out and make these groups' issue stances their own if that is what they must do to stay in power. (In the Chicago case, the national Democratic party provides the larger cradle in which the local party can and probably will survive until even it finds ways to move, at last, with the times.) In sum, the members of the environmentalist organizations may succeed in giving their ideas greater credibility, either as a replay of earlier and in some ways similar efforts to effect radical change (note especially Apter's prediction that the Sanrizuka movement will form a part of Japan's already well-established "radical inheritance") or as watered-down additions to major parties' platforms. But the organizations themselves seem unlikely to endure, and even less likely to grow and prosper.

SUPPLEMENTARY ORGANIZATIONS

We turn now to alternative groups formed by those who have found that the matters they care most about have, for one reason or another, been moved off the major parties' agenda. Rather than accept that fact as irreversible, they have made an attempt to establish new organizations that will give them greater influence. They are less concerned with putting forward new ideas than finding a new home for time-honored values or interests that the major parties now fail to incorporate in their programs—or at least fail to serve with the desired levels of fervor and conviction. Our examples here are the Social Democratic party of Britain, the Progress party of Denmark, and the numerous political action committees of the United States.

Traditional forms of linkage. In the United States, Great Britain, and Denmark, the traditional pattern of linkage has been electoral linkage via political parties whose candidates were held reasonably responsive to the policy demands of their supporters. In both Great Britain and the United States the major parties were broad-based "catchall" parties; in Denmark five parties routinely caught and represented an equally wide range of interests. In all three nations, as new interests formed, their proponents were usually able to find suitable homes somewhere within the party system.

Dissatisfaction with current linkage patterns. That which most distinguishes this group of alternative organizations from the others is the nature of their members' dissatisfaction with prevailing patterns of linkage. Discontent in this case has focused not on the traditional pattern of linkage, but on its loss. Moderate leftists in Britain, single-interest proponents in the United States, and angry taxpayers in Denmark found their interests receiving less and less attention. Ever-increasing expenditures on welfare and other "unnecessary" luxuries for persons other than themselves (consider, for example, the response to the Danish program to support the arts) did not constitute satisfactory responses to their needs, but neither did the right-wing programs that seemed to require too much of them and too little of others when trimming entitlements or improving military preparedness. They were not unhappy with the kind of linkage that had traditionally been available in the system; they were unhappy that it seemed less and less available to them.

Major party linkage failure. The institutions that had provided these disappointed activists with electoral linkage in the past were the major parties, and in all three nations the major parties were in decline, at least as servants of these particular interests. In the United States, the adoption of the party primary system and the advances made in the communications and electronics industries stimulated the growth of individual candidate organizations at the expense of the regular party organizations. In Denmark and England, the media personalization of politics was accompanied by an economic crisis that stimulated the major parties to offer classical conservative or Socialist remedies, remedies that might appeal strongly to the "class cores" of each, but that offered very little to the disaffected interests under consideration here. In the United States, the parties could not, and in Denmark and England they would not, pay the same attention as they had in the past to their needs.

The new organizations as alternative forms of linkage. In Great Britain and Denmark, where parties remained significant forces in the political system, it is appropriate that the supplementary organizations formed as new party challenges to the major parties (Labour and the Conservatives) from whom they drew their leadership. On the other hand, in the United States, where the institution of party was itself coming into serious question, it made more sense to abandon the idea of party altogether if what one wanted was a new way to maintain an old bond with government. The American PACs differ from all the other alternative organizations considered in this volume in that in this case thousands of new groups have emerged to take over a key linkage role of major parties, i.e., holding elected representatives accountable to (some of) their supporters.

(In both Denmark and the United States, changes in the electoral system facilitated the birth and development of the new organizations: changes in the boundaries of Danish municipal and county units and in that nation's principles of nomination made it easier for new parties to win adherents, and the rules of the new Federal Electoral Commission stimulated the growth of PACs in the U.S. The SDP, on the other hand, has been hindered from the outset by an electoral system that makes it all but impossible for a minor party to gain major party status.)

The pragmatic focus of the new groups on finding a supplementary means of bringing influence to bear is apparent in their organizational apparatuses, which are designed to allow the leaders to lead with minimal constraint by the membership: none of the three has shown much interest in the trappings of intragroup democracy. Nor do any of the three present the world with a broad program of issues based on a clear ideology: most

PACs are single issue, the Danish party is nearly so, and the SDP refuses to give substantive content to its version of "social democracy." The leaders of all three tend to be independent notables, while members exercise little or no control and are typically few in number. All three have shown themselves to be effective in attracting media attention when they wish to do so; the American PACs have been the most effective in acquiring and distributing funds to their chosen candidates, and the SDP has made the greatest effort to develop the political alliance as a means to accomplish its goals.

The prospects of the alternative organizations. The success of these groups in filling a linkage void in their societies has been uneven, and so must be any predictions regarding their capacity to endure. At present writing the strongest and fastest growing of the three are the American PACs, groups that have formed not only as alternatives to the major parties that no longer adequately attend to their members' interests, but as powerful alternatives to the institution of party altogether. The weakest appears to be the SDP, boldly aspiring to major party status. But it must be acknowledged that for this group of organizations success or failure does not seem to depend so much on providing the right kind of linkage as on other, extralinkage factors. The PACs are succeeding because loopholes in American campaign finance laws make them the natural outlet for powerful energies. Despite some success in recent elections, it is possible the SDP will nevertheless fail because British electoral law makes it almost impossible for minor parties to expand, whereas the more accommodative Danish electoral laws had much to do with the capacity of the Progress party to remain on the scene. These three cases suggest that it is not enough for an alternative organization to find the linkage need and fill it by originating in the appropriate setting and adopting the correct internal rules, issue stances, leadership style, membership range, and action tactics; in order to prosper, it must also be blessed with the right institutional context.

COMMUNITARIAN ORGANIZATIONS

We consider next a kind of alternative organization that has been around since the world's first countergroups were formed: the organization that is formed by the members of an ethnic or religious community in an effort to protect their rights in a larger society. Here we include Israel's Gush Emunim, Britain's Scottish National party and Welsh Plaid Cymru, Alabama's National Democratic party, and the Communist party of the state of Kerala in India. Does the study of these groups as alternative linkage agencies improve our understanding of their strength and viability?[2]

Traditional forms of linkage. Despite the obvious differences among the traditional linkage patterns of Britain, Israel, Alabama, and Kerala, these four political systems have had in common a tendency to give short shrift to those who sought public policy that would be in keeping with their communal identities. Here, too, the group divides in two parts: the Scots, the Welsh, and the uncompromising Jews of the Gush Emunim live in systems that have given them the same rights granted others but refused them the special policies they felt entitled to demand; the Alabama blacks and the untouchables of Kerala, on the other hand, live in systems where they were treated differently from more privileged majority populations and often denied basic human rights. In the first three cases the traditional pattern was one of electoral linkage; in the other two cases it was a combination of clientelistic and directive linkage, the latter characterized by a strong measure of coercion. In all, major parties served as the dominant agencies of linkage.

Dissatisfaction with current linkage patterns. The members of most of these groups became significantly more dissatisfied with traditional patterns of linkage when they encountered what we might call the cessation of progress. In India, the government's dependency on the support of large landowners caused it to halt its program of land reform. In Israel, devout Jews were distressed to see political principles begin to take ascendancy over religious dogma at a time when the nation should, they believed, be moving steadily toward fulfillment of biblical promise. In Scotland and Wales, unemployment, job insecurity, and high prices were ending a period of relative prosperity when the Scottish National party and Plaid Cymru began to attract greater support. And in Alabama, improving national attitudes on racial matters were unable to penetrate that state's rigid adherence to the doctrine of white supremacy. In short, when it began to seem that long-standing obstacles to progress would not, after all, be removed, a shared sense of outraged communitarianism led to serious dissatisfaction with existing patterns of linkage, and a determination to effect change for the better.

Major party linkage failure. In every case, it was clearly the dominant major party that was held responsible for what the affected groups perceived as linkage failure. Members of the Gush Emunim saw the Israeli

---

[2] The Kerala case fits least comfortably in the category of communitarian, since the Communist party there has always included, as Herring makes clear, several elements besides the Untouchables. My comments here refer to the party to the extent that the inclusion of that important component gives it a significant communitarian element.

Labor party becoming increasingly secular and patronage oriented; Scottish and Welsh nationalists were dismayed by the disappointing performance of Britain's Labour party as champion of their cause; and one of the key tactics employed by both the Indian Congress party and the Alabama Democrats to maintain themselves in power was vigorous enforcement of policies of communitarian oppression.

The new organizations as alternative forms of linkage. If new organizations are to fill the unmet linkage needs of an underrepresented or oppressed community, the first requirement is that their founders find a sheltering home for their birth and infancy. Otherwise, the group is likely either to be coopted by a stronger organization, or made subject to the same (or worse) tactics of oppression that already burden their prospective members. What information we have suggests that the groups under consideration here met that requirement: the Gush Emunim began within the supportive setting of Israeli religious schools, and the Scottish and Welsh nationalist groups began in the heartlands of the communities whose interests they espoused. Similarly, by working through the Communist party rather than forming their own organization, the Kerala untouchables benefited from what legitimacy that party had earned in its earlier struggles against colonial rule.

With regard to internal organization, it seems reasonable to suggest that communitarian alternative organizations will be likely to sacrifice procedural democracy to the need for unified action, in order to make the best use of relatively few actors. However, except for some comments on the settlement secretariats set up by the Gush Emunim, we have very little information about how the parties conduct their internal affairs. We are on better ground when it comes to the next variable: issue stances and ideology. Given that the linkage void that must be filled is the major party failure to address the needs and wishes of the members as a distinct community, we can confidently expect the communitarian alternatives to go to the other extreme, and speak of little else. Here the evidence from our cases is rich and supportive: the Scottish party campaigns on the theme of Scottish self-government, Plaid Cymru on maintaining the Welsh cultural identity, the Gush Emunim on Israeli irredentism as a religious duty, the NDPA on black rights, racial consciousness, and black pride; and the Kerala Communists on the need for greater land redistribution to the poor and oppressed.

The ability of communitarian leaders to provide the missing links to the political system will be enhanced if they give evidence of having qualities particularly cherished in their communities; the Kerala CP leaders' reputation for self-sacrifice, Rabbi Kook's mystic devotion to the holy cause for which he battled, and the NDPA leaders' political freshness (contrasted to the cooption of some earlier black leaders by the white supremacist Democrats) are all cases in point. As far as we can tell, the membership of these groups is drawn from the appropriate populations—it is interesting, however, that both British nationalist parties have been unable to attract more than a minority of the groups whose interests they claim to represent.

Forming an exclusive communitarian organization represents, in itself, a major tactical choice: the group has decided it can do better on its own than as one interest among many in a more heterogeneous organization (with the exception of the Kerala untouchables, who are in fact part of a more heterogeneous group). Beyond that fundamental decision, the tactics communitarian organizations employ are likely to depend on what is available to them in the society in which they must function. Thus the British, Indian, and Alabaman organizations have taken the form of parties and have concentrated on running candidates for office. Gush Emunim provides an interesting exception: disdaining the fully available opportunity to wage electoral battle openly, it uses illegal settlements, attention-getting marches, and strategic alliances with factions in other parties (which its members are free to join) to pursue its ends.

The prospects of the alternative organizations. When we consider the relative strength and durability of these organizations, it appears that the leaders of the Gush Emunim may have understood a rule the others would do well to follow: organizations representing minority interests last longer when they do not seek political power in their own names. Groups that do not follow that rule may well find success to be self-limiting. In Pulzer's view, once they gained a few concessions from the British government, the Scottish and Welsh groups began to decline. Herring suggests that in Kerala those who prosper on lands CP militancy made theirs often lose interest in a party of the disadvantaged and turn to Congress, a party that promises to expand rather than redivide the national pie. And Walton notes that when the actions of the National Democratic party of Alabama inspired white moderates to form their own independent Democratic party, helped force the state's regular Democratic party to abandon much of its racist rhetoric, and brought black control over several county governments in the black belt, the NDPA, no longer the black activist's only hope, was allowed to sink into near oblivion.

On the other hand, Aronoff believes the Gush Emunim, which never openly takes political power, is strong and growing stronger, and has helped legitimize radical nationalism and hawkish views in contemporary Israel. Of course, the conclusion we have drawn from such examples may prove shortsighted: if the linkage interests of the group's members are, in the long run, better served by brief but intensive full participation in the political arena, it may well be worthwhile to sacrifice the lesser good of organizational durability.

ANTIAUTHORITARIAN ORGANIZATIONS

Our final group, the antiauthoritarians, consists of organizations that are founded on behalf of all the people in a nation during a time when a narrow elite maintains authoritarian control. Two of the four we explore in this volume, Solidarity of Poland and the Taiwanese Independence Movement, have the normal characteristics of such groups: their leaders are in direct opposition to the military rulers of the state; the groups themselves are illegal and must operate clandestinely. A third, Taiwan's Tang-wai, operates on the border of legitimacy, maintaining a careful pretense of nonpartisanship. The fourth, the People's Defense Committees of Ghana, is unusual, because in this case it is the elite itself that has created them, and that seeks to combine populist grass-roots structures with authoritarian rule at the center. Once again, we seek linkage explanations for political change.

Predecessor forms of linkage. Poland and Ghana are in such conditions of flux, and have been so for so long, that it would be misleading to speak of "traditional patterns of linkage" in these two cases when we examine the forms of linkage in effect in each state prior to the evolution of the alternative organizations considered here. Linkage to the state in pre-Solidarity Poland was largely directive linkage via the Communist party, although a strong religious heritage meant that in practice the church was sometimes used as a secondary, even if badly crippled, intermediary in the effort to achieve a modicum of policy responsiveness on the part of the regime. Nonmilitary figures who sought access to decisionmaking powers were invariably severely repressed. And in Ghana pre-PDC linkage patterns changed from year to year, as coups and civilian takeovers alternated in bewildering succession and the nation watched indigenous leaders treat democratic principles with as little regard as their colonial predecessors had done. In Taiwan, on the other hand, even though some cosmetic changes have recently been made, the system has scarcely altered in the past forty years: the ruling party and its partner, the military, control all five branches of government, and linkage to the state means obedience to their directives.

Despite the variety apparent in these regimes, in all three the earlier forms of linkage had one important quality in common: they were all highly coercive, and only subelites were in a position to obtain minimal policy responsiveness from those in power.

Dissatisfaction with current linkage patterns. One of the sadder lessons of comparative politics is that widespread dissatisfaction with the performance of government is by no means a guarantee that efforts will be made to bring about a positive change. On the other hand, when a poorly performing government's performance gets even worse, rapidly and visibly, long-felt grievances provide the base on which seemingly sudden movements for change erupt. Such eruptions seem particularly likely when increased oppressiveness coincides with economic decline. Thus the triggering developments in Ghana were accelerated abuses of power by the military and a fall in cocoa prices, and in Poland the visible corruption of party leaders combined with an ever more difficult domestic economy.

The situation Fan and Feigert describe in Taiwan seems very different at first glance: the economy is prospering, and in tolerating the existence of the Tangwai, the ruling elite has at least the appearance of being slightly less repressive than heretofore. However, the government has suffered a significant setback in recent years, one that the Taiwanese know is likely to bring with it a far less prosperous and liberal future: it has proved unable to prevent the recognition of the People's Republic of China by the United States. The subsequent revised agreements between the United States and Taiwan mean that in the not-too-distant future Taiwan will be unable to defend itself against mainland takeover, a change that will bring with it the inevitable decline of economic well-being and probable further invasion of personal liberties. Thus in Taiwan, as in Ghana and Poland, dissatisfaction with current patterns of linkage is based on recently heightened economic and civil libertarian discontent, with the important difference that in this case the discontent has more in it of apprehension of the future than assessment of the past.

Major party linkage failure. Since the military rules (or is a major partner in the ruling junta) in all three nations, does it make sense in these cases to look for signs of major party failure? The question almost answers itself: the existence of military rule is itself nearly always a sign of party failure. In addition, in none of these nations have parties been effective agencies of linkage. Ghana's experience of parties during civilian regimes had persuaded most of her citizens that they were divisive, excessive, and self-interested institutions, with poor or nonexistent links to those they claimed to represent (a belief that may have been exaggerated, since in fact the two major parties did maintain some important ethnic and regional bases of support and some equally important organizational linkages). The Taiwanese KMT stayed in power in part by refusing to allow electoral contests wherever the person in office was orginally chosen by a mainland China constituency (it would not be "fair" to the people of that constituency, who are now, according to official Taiwanese dogma, unable to exercise their rights of suffrage), and the two minor parties hitherto allowed to contest where elections are permitted are recognized by the populace as minipuppets of the regime. And in Poland, it was signs of the growing distrust of the ruling Communist party, as workers' participation in the party apparatus steadily declined and poll data made clear the concomitant decline in popular trust in all institutions of government, that brought the military to power. In all three states the parties have not been held uniquely responsible for the unacceptable state of affairs—see in particular Kraus's alternative hypotheses for Ghana—but they were heavily implicated.

The new organizations as alternative forms of linkage. In order to form under an oppressive government, alternative organizations must meet one of three conditions: they must form with that government's consent, as did the Ghanaian PDCs and the Tangwai; they must form in secret and remain underground, as did the Taiwan Independence Movement; or they must be so powerful right from the beginning that their repression is impossible, the route Solidarity attempted to follow by making its presence felt first in massive strike activity.

What the Taiwanese, Ghanaians, and Poles sought were agencies of linkage that could bring them fairer economic rewards and freedom from oppression by authoritarian regimes—however, that oppression has not always been conceived of as a denial of the basic rights of Western democracy. Ghanaians sought personal freedom on their own, not Western, terms, and this is reflected in the internal organization of their alternative structures: the Ghanaian PDCs have not been concerned to establish procedural rights for their members. On the other hand, Solidarity has been firmly committed to the widest possible participation in a far-reaching network of decentralized units. We have little evidence of the internal organization of the two Taiwanese groups.

All three groups directly address grievances against authoritarian rule in formulating issues that will appeal to the multitudes they claim for their constituency: the Taiwanese movements seek a more open party system and ethnic equality, the PDCs stress the need to root out government corruption and carry out the government's policies fairly, and Solidarity promises to find a way to serve the values of nation and religion while advancing democracy and Socialism. Our authors tell us very little about their leadership, but all three have apparently succeeded in attracting broad memberships composed in very large part of those they mean to serve.

Groups that seek to provide some form of nonauthoritarian linkage within authoritarian systems must be extremely adroit in their choice of tactics. The Ghanian PDCs fit their means to the ambiguity of their status, opening new opportunities for participation to some while removing and punishing others with little or no regard for the niceties of due process. The Taiwanese Independence Movement wisely conducts most of its operations overseas and the Tangwai do their best to maintain the façade of nonpartisanship, but neither group has been able to save several of its leaders from imprisonment and execution. Solidarity has found that its hope of substituting moral for military force was overly optimistic; Gitelman suggests that the group's greatest weakness has been its lack of control over the instruments of force.

The prospects of the alternative organizations. At present writing, Solidarity is all but defunct, neither the Tangwai nor the Taiwanese Independence Movement have achieved significant standing in their nation's politics, and there is no good reason to predict a longer future for the PDCs than for any of Ghana's experiments with new forms of political organization. On the other hand, the aspirations these groups address are unlikely to be taken up by the Taiwanese or Polish ruling forces, and Rawlings himself is prevented by the pluralist demands of trade unions, market women, farmers' groups, the military, and an economic bourgeoisie from making the PDCs into a more effective instrument of populism. So long as this is the case, even if these organizations disappear, others like them are likely to spring up in their place: the linkage failures their existence attests to are among the most bitter and enduring, and the least likely to find resolution through established channels. In this case the mere commitment to ending that impasse, however unlikely the chances of success, ensures these groups a greater longevity than their accomplishments to date might seem to warrant.

THE FRUITS OF LINKAGE FAILURE AND SUCCESS

Our inquiry into these seventeen cases has given us the answers to linkage-related questions and these answers in turn give us the means to test the hypotheses with which we began: (1) alternative organizations emerge when major parties fail to provide acceptable forms of linkage, and (2) alternative organizations endure when they succeed in providing the kind of linkage hitherto lacking in the political system. The evidence strongly supports the first hypothesis and almost equally strongly contradicts the second.

In all the cases examined here, we have found clear signs of linkage failure, and have been able to show that the major parties were held at least partially responsible for that failure. Furthermore, in every case, the alternative organization has emerged in a context appropriate for a group seeking to fill the particular society's linkage void, and has adopted most of the organizational characteristics that would fit it to play that part. The evidence is strong enough to permit us to add Hypothesis 1a: when organizations alternative to major parties emerge, they will take the form that best suits them to fill the linkage void left by the major parties. There are some minor exceptions, but on the whole Hypothesis 1a is also substantiated by these data.

On the other hand, there is very little evidence of any causal link between the new organization's prospects for longevity and its success in filling the linkage void. Hypothesis No. 2 is contradicted by every set of cases, and contradicted differently by each. All six environmentalist organizations capably address unmet linkage needs, but the more successful they are, the more likely they are to disappear, given the continued strength of other parties in the system and those parties' probable readiness to provide at least some of the policies and practices sought by these groups if that is what it takes to stay in power. The three supplementary groups all address a felt linkage need with the appropriate organizational accoutrements, but the probable durability of one (the American PACs) and brevity of the others (the Danish Taxpayers and the British Social Democrats) appear much more closely related to external institutional variables than to the degree of skill with which each addresses linkage needs.

Similarly, the four communitarian organizations we have examined focus on the issues and adopt the forms appropriate for the angry and alienated minorities they represent, but only one, the Gush Emunim, seems likely to endure. For the others, even minimal success in achieving linkage goals, such as obtaining some minor concessions for their members from those in power, seems to lead to a diminuition of support. The more promising prospects of the Gush lend the only whisper of legitimacy to Hypothesis No. 2: there is a suggestion that this group's staying power is related to its choice of linkage tactic, that is, to its decision to take no direct part in electoral battles but to work by methods of direct confrontation that keep interest high and emotional commitment intense.

The antiauthoritarians contradict Hypothesis No. 2 from the opposite direction: these groups appear to be among the least successful in filling the linkage void they find in their systems, yet their very failure may ensure their continued existence. The linkage needs they address are so desperate that any group that shows some promise of meeting them may find enough support to remain on the scene, no matter how far short its performance comes of that promise.

In sum, although major parties' linkage failures may lead to the formation of alternative organizations well designed to fill the linkage void thus produced, the ability of these organizations to prosper and endure seems at least as dependent upon external variables—the nature of other parties, other institutions, and popular attitudes—as upon factors within their own control. Looking at alternative organizations as substitute agencies of linkage between citizen and state helps us understand where they come from, but we must turn to other system variables to understand where they are going.

CONTRIBUTIONS AND CONNECTIONS

The concept of linkage has helped us understand the cases; now it is time to ask: what can the cases tell us about the nature of linkage? What insights do they provide that will deepen and enrich our understanding of political linkage, and, thereby, of the nature of political development?

"Insights" may be too bold a term, at least to begin with. What these case studies offer us in regard to the question of political linkage may more properly be termed initially simply as "reminders." First and foremost, they remind us that political linkage is not always provided only by parties. Second, they remind us that political linkage is always linkage between junior and senior units: e.g., the individual and the party, the party and the state, the individual and the state. Third, they renew our awareness that it is possible to have a linkage relationship that is unsatisfactory to one or both partners and that such dissatisfaction may lead to severance of the linkage bond. And fourth, they help us bear in mind that linkage exists only when the two units in the relationship each contribute something to the other. The interaction that takes place in the exchange of these contributions establishes a connection: that connection is the linkage between the two units.

The fourth reminder—that connections require contributions—bears further investigation. The decline of major parties in the present era suggests that we need to think more about these connections, and be more alert to what is going on when they form, when they function well, when they falter, and when they rupture and break.

However, once we do begin this effort—to open up and understand the connections that are made in the linkage chain between citizen, political organization, and state, and to identify the contributions each must make—we inevitably find ourselves reaching beyond functional analysis. Functional analysis is often a key first step in figuring out what it is that must be studied in order to understand any political phenomenon, but it never gives very much help in the actual exploration. Linkage is properly seen as a function that takes place in all political systems. But when we attempt to understand how that function is actually performed between any particular levels of aggregation, we find ourselves reaching for a mode of analysis that is more complex, more dynamic, and more capable of encompassing the movement of forces through the political arena, the ways they combine, and the impact they have on institutions, policies, and human lives. We find this more dynamic model in systems analysis. Treating the citizen-political organization-government linkage chain as a political subsystem—i.e., combining functional and systems analysis—gives us the analytical framework we need for the job of opening up the linkage connections that are made between citizen and state and identifying the *contributions* that create those connections (see Figure 2.1).

Three sets of connections (kinds of links) form the political linkage chain: the connection between individual and political organization, that between political organization and state, and that between individual and state. In each set, the connection is formed by contributions from both partners. What is it that each contributes—or might contribute? We begin with the first set, individual and organization.

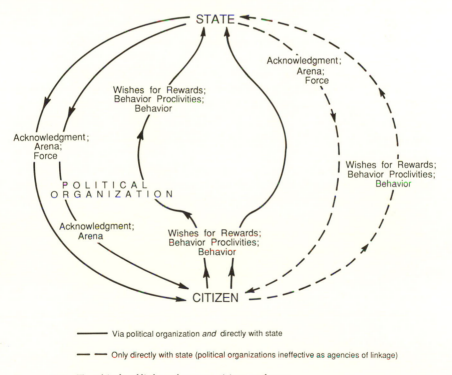

FIGURE 2.1   Two kinds of linkage between citizen and state.

The contributions individuals may make to intermediate political organizations are of three kinds: (1) individuals express (contribute) wishes regarding the rewards they would like to obtain from the state, either for themselves individually, for their groups, or for the polity as a whole; (2) individuals show a proclivity for certain kinds of political behavior, i.e., show a readiness to act in the political arena either by participating (helping to determine programs and candidates, carrying out organization activities, etc.), by bargaining (exchanging votes, money, time, etc., for policy responsiveness or desired clientelistic relationships), or by obeying (learning and following directives); and (3) individuals actually engage in participatory, bargaining, or obeying behavior. (These distinctions are necessary: wishing for rewards is different from wanting to act a certain way; wanting to act a certain way is different from actually acting.)

The organization, on the other hand, may offer individuals (1) acknowledgment of their wishes by incorporating them in its program, its choice of candidates and/or its activities, and (2) an arena in which the kind of action for which the citizens have a proclivity may be practiced. Whether the ensuing linkage should be labeled participatory, electoral, clientelistic, directive, or some combination of types will depend on the exact nature of the contributions made by both sides.[3]

With respect to the second link, that between organization and state, the contributions political organizations may make to the state are: (1) the wishes expressed by organization officials regarding the rewards they would like to obtain from the state, either for themselves individually or for the supporters they represent (in the latter case, the officials may seek different rewards from those the supporters seek for themselves); (2) the behavior proclivities of officials (to participate, by becoming the personnel who do the work of the state; to bargain, by exchanging votes or electoral support for votes or electoral support; and/or to obey, by learning and following directives); and (3) the actual behavior of officials.

In return, the state may offer the political organization (1) acknowledgment of the wishes of its officials by incorporating them in its program; (2) an arena in which the kind of action for which the official has a proclivity may be practiced, and (3) the use or threat of force to compel behavior different from that for which the official has a proclivity.

We come now to the third link, that between individual and state. This kind of link may be established in one of two ways. Where political organ-

---

[3] This formulation takes us well beyond the now-hackneyed trichotomy of the material, solidary, and/or purposive motives of group members. Clark and Wilson, 1961. Although individual motives for joining can still usefully be characterized in those terms, such a classification says very little about what kind of behavior members will be ready to engage in and will in fact engage in, and nothing at all about what the organization itself will be willing to do to acknowledge those motives and make that behavior possible.

izations are effective agencies of linkage, the link between citizen and state will be formed at least in part via those organizations. In this case, individual citizens make their contributions to the organization (as above), but also directly to the state (same contributions), the organization makes its contributions to the state (as above), and the state makes its contributions both to the organizations (as above) and directly to the individuals. This last set of contributions (by the state directly to the individuals) may take the form of acknowledging citizen wishes by incorporating them in policy and/or providing an arena for "acting out" behavior proclivities—or the state may refuse to make either of these contributions, and attempt to substitute as its contribution the real or threatened use of force to compel the citizen to behave as it (the state) desires.

On the other hand, where political organizations are ineffective as agencies of linkage, the link between individual and state may be established without them. In such cases the individual may contribute wishes and behavior proclivities only directly to the state (i.e., without intermediary), and the state may respond by contributing, as in the previous case, acknowledgment of individual wishes (by incorporating these in policy), an arena for "acting out" behavior proclivities, and/or the real or threatened use of force.

These two kinds of linkage between citizen and state are diagramed in Figure 2.1. By laying out these relationships in system terms, Figure 2.1 also helps us see that political links depend on the combination of two or more of the six contribution variables—Wishes for Rewards, Behavior Proclivities, Behavior, Acknowledgment, Arena, and Force and that in such linkage relationships the junior partner's contributions will be one or more of the first three, while the senior partner's contributions will be one or more of the second three.

The quality of any nation's political life depends, it may be argued, on the substantive content of these six contributions, and the connections thus established between junior and senior partners in the linkage chain. What do junior partners in the political system want to obtain, want to do, and do? How and to what extent do senior partners provide the sought-for rewards and enable the activity—or respond instead with force or the threat of force as they pursue their own, unlinked agenda? Comprehensive answers to these questions would take us far beyond any limited inquiry into the linkage role of parties and other organizations.

THE FUTURE OF POLITICAL ORGANIZATIONS

In the realm of scholarship, theory and data can sometimes provide their own example of the reciprocal dynamics of linkage at work, as each contributes meaning to the other, enriches the other, and enables the other to contribute yet more to the connection between them—a connection the scholar, both contributor and observer, hopefully labels "understanding."

Thinking about linkage has helped us understand our cases better; reviewing them has in turn helped us understand the components of linkage better; and now we find ourselves turning the other way once again, applying theory to data. In this book our approach is to assume that when major parties falter, alternative organizations will emerge to attempt to take their place, and either succeed in doing so or manage to stimulate the repudiated parties (or yet other organizations) to take up the gauntlet thus thrown down. In either case, linkage via effective political organization will, we have tended to assume, sooner or later be restored.

However, our exploration of the connective nature of linkage has reminded us (see Figure 2.1) that individuals may be linked to the state directly, without working through political organizations that in turn establish linkages with the state. Given the nature of our project, we have no examples of this possibility among our cases, but we readily call to mind numerous regimes in which political organization outside the state is effectively prohibited. Political organizations are dispensable, and this is true even in those states where they now seem most entrenched. They may falter, they may fail, they may cease to exist.

This may seem a matter of small concern to those who are weary of the political battle and ready to trust their fortunes to any Bonaparte who seems mysteriously in tune with an equally mysterious general will. It may not trouble those who believe with Michels that "he who says organization says oligarchy" and are therefore willing to accept a less differentiated world composed only of leaders and led. But those who are not quite ready to abandon the democratic ideal as either unnecessarily conflictual or impossibly equalitarian, have reason to contemplate the possible disappearance of the political organization with serious concern. We can have linkage without such organizations, but we cannot have democratic linkage.

This last statement is not accepted by everyone. Some would argue that today's modern citizen, well educated, well informed, and above all well equipped with the electronic means to convey his or her opinion on any subject at any time to anyone, can play the role of the true democrat as never before, without need for any intermediaries (Margolis, 1979). However, it can be argued with at least equal plausibility that the need for political organizations is greater today than ever before, thanks to the changes that have made us both less and more capable of ruling ourselves without them.

The first point is simple and familiar: we are less capable of ruling ourselves without benefit of intermediaries now that the candidates for our vote are persistently presented to us with the greatest sophistication of the advertising art and the least of that of philosophy. The second is less obvious, and at first seems contradictory. Our improved standards of literacy and general education, and our greater and better informed attention to issues of substance, have made us better able to choose among the candidates presented for our approval without needing a party boss or group messiah to tell us what to do. Yet the very qualities that seem to free us from the need for political organizations have the effect of pushing those who would rule by manipulation to develop greater and greater skill in doing so. Furthermore, when those who rule by such methods are no longer able to fool enough of the people enough of the time, their next step may well be to drop the charade of pseudo-democratic institutions altogether. In a land of isolated self-sufficient citizens, control of the means of force may be all that is required to bring about the substitution of open oppression for manipulative control.

The alternative is to save the political organization, be it major or minor, old or new, and to use it as the means to establish democratic linkage that works in contemporary terms. The environmentalists' quest for new rewards and a more participatory arena, the supplementarians' refusal to accept political rustication without a fight, the communitarians' eagerness to find a role in the political world that permits them to maintain a cherished identity, and the populists' ardent search for an equalitarian social system—all these pose linkage needs that cannot be bargained away in issueless catchall parties or pigeonholed in organizations formed on antediluvian lines of class cleavage. Nor can they be forever talked away in the media, or turned away by electoral system trickery. They will have to be acknowledged, addressed, aggregated, compromised, and finally brought into the national arena step by step, link by link. Only political organizations can do that work, whether operating as broad-based programmatic coalitions that accommodate these needs in their own wide arms or as narrower units that win a fair share of access to legislative bodies in which their voices can be heard. And only those nations whose institutions are wise enough and whose values are generous enough to accommodate such organizations will be able to ensure at least a measure of democratic linkage between citizen and state.

REFERENCES

Clark, P. B., and J. O. Wilson. 1961. Incentive systems: A theory of organizations. *Administrative Science Quarterly* 6: 129–66.

Eulau, H., and K. Prewitt. 1973. *Labyrinths of democracy: Adaptations, linkages, representation, and policies in urban politics.* New York: Bobbs-Merrill.

Hamilton, J. A. 1981. To link or not to link. *Foreign Policy* Fall:62–81.

Key, V. O. 1964. *Public opinion and American democracy.* New York: Knopf, 409–558.

Lawson, K., ed. 1980. *Political parties and linkage: A comparative perspective.* New Haven: Yale University Press.

———, G. Pomper, and M. Moakley. 1986. Local party activists and electoral linkage. *American Politics Quarterly* 14: 345–75.

Luttbeg, N. R. 1974. *Public opinion and public policy models of political linkage.* Homewood, Ill.: Dorsey Press.

———. 1975. Assessing the influence of public opinion, an overview: Elections and parties as linkages. In *Public opinion,* ed. S. Welch and J. Comer. Palo Alto, Calif.: Mayfield Publishing, 409–531.

Margolis, M. 1979. *Viable democracy.* New York: Penguin Books.

Rosenau, J. N. 1973. Theorizing across systems: Linkage politics revisited. In *Conflict behavior and linkage politics,* ed. Jonathan Wilkenfeld. New York: David McKay.

———. 1974. *Citizenship between elections.* New York: Free Press.

———, ed. 1969. *Linkage politics.* New York: Free Press.

Stein, A. A. 1980. The politics of linkage. *World Politics* 33: 127–44.

PART II | Environmentalist Organizations

THREE

The Challenge of the Greens to the West German Party System

DONALD SCHOONMAKER

It is almost impossible to bring together under one name this variegated collection. Peaceniks and neutralists, environmentalists and friends of nature, nuclear opponents and protectors of life, anticommunists and anticapitalists, internationalists and national pacifists—"Reds" of all shadings from Salon-rose to Mao purple. To all of these forces only two things were crucial: protest against present political and economic relationships and the feeling that the time for a new beginning was ripe and favorable (Bieber et al., 1982).

The national Green party and various "Greens"[1] on the Land (state) and local level are gradually changing the political and cultural landscape in West Germany. Their challenge to the established parties has already had significant consequences since the appearance of the first "Green" party in a small town in Lower Saxony in 1972. They have accelerated a fragmentation already under way in the Social Democratic party, driven the Free Democratic party from its long-held position of coalition-balancer in many Land legislatures and, in fact, have replaced them as the third party in several states. They have also clearly affected the rhetoric of the Christian Democratic party on environmental matters and on the need for moral and cultural reform. Brushed aside continually as a motley crew of ecological romantics, naive peaceniks, and unruly populists, the Greens have steadily increased their power in many local elections as well as in six West German states. They have a disproportionate influence among

[1] I am using the term "Greens" to refer to the Green party which was founded as a national party in 1980 and to related allies, such as various alternative parties. There is no clear organizational structure connecting these various political forces concerned about ecology, peace, and democratization. Green parties on the local level sometimes compete against each other, and the nature of the tie between Land (state) Greens and the national party is quite loose. The complexity of this movement/party will not be resolved by any simple definition. On this matter, see Raschke, 1982: 323–34; for a description of various Green alliances and patterns of fractionalization in the recent decade, see Deutsche Presse Agentur, 1982.

younger, educated, middle-class activists—a postmaterialist intelligent-sia—and after obtaining a meager showing of votes in the 1980 Federal election (1.5 percent), they gained entry to the Bundestag in the 1983 Federal election with 5.6 percent of the total vote.

It is not just in the Federal Republic that major political parties have experienced difficulties in the last decade. Both Samuel Huntington and Samuel Beer have expressed doubts about the adaptability of mass parties in industrialized democracies, especially to the opportunity offered by the participation expansion of the 1970s. Huntington describes the causes for increased participation and expresses serious reservations about the response of the key institution: "The core participant institution, the political party, appears to be verging on a state of institutional and political decay. . . . Unless there is a clear-cut reversal of current trends, however, parties do not appear to be likely mechanisms for structuring the higher levels of participation which should characterize postindustrial society" (Huntington, 1974: 175).

Beer's analysis, which derives from the context of contemporary British politics, is also applicable to postindustrial democracies. He sees technocratic and populistic impulses as inherent strains in a culture of modernity. Unbalanced assertions of the values of scientific rationalism bring on Saint-Simonian technocratic politics while "a romantic revolt in politics" leads to a populism that "embodies a hardly less exaggerated expression of democratic values."[2] Beer's description of the havoc brought to the Labour party by the "romantic populists" is further evidence that some parties will have hard times coping with modern-day decentralists, a theme of significance for West Germany and the Greens. Finally, a recent and most telling essay on the challenge to parties and other established institutions has been offered by Suzanne Berger in her discussion of "Politics and Antipolitics" (Berger, 1979: 27–50).

Berger's theme is the growing politicalization of everyday life and the decay of parties. There is a "vast new wave of collective activity outside of traditional political institutions, while antiparty and antistate attitudes continue to increase. The 'failed connection' between parties and the new political forces is seen as a lack of adaptability for political systems while the alternative is hardly less appealing" (Berger, 1979: 40). Berger's argument has not gone unanswered (Wilson, 1982), and there are others who feel that parties pitch and roll—and sometimes disappear—but that modern mass democracy is impossible without them.

---

[2] Beer, 1982: 11. Beer's definition of populism is worth noting: "By populism I mean an exaggerated assertion of the values of radical democracy. These views are individualist, participatory, majoritarian, and egalitarian with regard to power rather than rewards."

Almost all of these students of postindustrial politics have drawn from Ronald Inglehart's perceptive work, *The Silent Revolution* (Inglehart, 1977), which describes the causes of increased and unorthodox political participation, the high likelihood of widespread elite-challenging activity, and the rise of postmaterialist politics in Western democracies. The Greens in West Germany are essentially a vehicle of postmaterialist politics, and their critique of state, party, and political culture should be understood as part of this large protest movement in industrialized democracies.

The Greens are first and foremost a party of democratic renewal. Even though their label connotes environmental concern, the impulse to reform the society and political system according to populist ideals—in Beer's use of the term—is the center of gravity of this political force. And so the following questions must be raised: will the party and its allies bring about a revitalization of democracy or pluralistic stagnation; will the Greens serve as an early warning system for necessary long-term changes or will the party merely serve as a vehicle for utopian cranks who want to *épater le bourgeois*; how will the Greens affect the established parties, the present arrangement of pluralism, the political culture, and the overall constitutional democracy; how do unconventional, direct-action politics work in a system at home with conventional representative institutions; and finally, is this Green movement/party a flash in the pan, or a political force of staying power?

We need to add some additional questions to our essay, for we are particularly interested in the theme of why some of the major parties in West Germany have failed to respond to the opportunities of citizen participation in the late 1960s and the 1970s. Party failure is something more complex than the obvious disappearance of a complex institution which had previously contested seats and exercised power. In this essay, we look at several aspects of possible party failure which include the following:

— being unable to "handle" tough issues such as budgets, pensions, unemployment, or environment
— losing votes in elections on a steady basis
— failing to recruit new, younger members
— being unable to integrate dissident forces
— losing power in legislative bodies or in coalitions
— losing legitimacy as a result of scandals
— losing the ability to shape the major issues on the political agenda

Party failure can occur on various levels in a federal system like the West German government, and it is significant that the Green challenge springs from an active grass-roots movement, while the major parties seem to suffer from the sluggishness of overcentralized bureaucracies (Raschke, 1982: 9–31).

Our theme in this analysis is that the rise of the Greens represents an inability of the party system to accommodate itself to new issues and a failure on the part of the Social Democrats and Free Democrats to accommodate to the New Left politics of the 1970s. All of the major parties felt that the grass-roots citizen initiatives and local environmental groups were merely episodic protest groups whose voters, sooner or later, would return to the "catchall" parties. The evidence points in another direction. But first we need to set out the context of the challenge of these new and unconventional political forces.

THE CONTEXT OF THE CHALLENGE

For observers of West European politics, the West German party system has performed with surprising efficiency in the first three decades since 1949. Without engaging in exaggerated rhetoric, it was possible to say that the West Germans had created a "political miracle" besides the vaulted economic miracle in the post-World War II period. The pluralistic stagnation of the Weimar party system had been superceded in the Second Republic by two large "people's parties," appealing to broad and diverse strata in the electorate, and a third party, the Free Democrats (FDP), which operated as a restraint on the right-clericalism of the Union parties (CDU/CSU) or the left-egalitarianism of the Social Democrats (SPD).

The constitutional engineers responsible for the West German constitution, the Basic Law, had reached general agreement on a representative democracy—and certainly not a plebiscitary democracy should be constituted. The people should have regular opportunities to choose their representatives, but referenda and other forms of direct democracy were to be avoided. The historic memories of Weimar and the Third Reich cast their shadows. There was ready support for the type of democracy espoused by Joseph Schumpeter: regular competition between elites in which the electorate played a rather retiring role. The electorate pointed in a general direction at election time, but widespread discretion was to be left to party elites. Bonn was to be a party democracy not a populistic democracy.

These concepts about West German democracy were hardly the subject of public debate for the first two decades of the smooth-running parliamentary system of the Bonn Republic. But the late 1960s ushered in a raucous and active student movement aimed at widespread democratization which challenged the assumptions of the founders of the Basic Law. The participatory revolution of the late 1960s and 1970s was not content with a staid representative democracy with merely elite-supporting opportunities. New forms were sought by younger political activists. Brandt's exhortation to "risk more democracy" did not fall on deaf ears. In a very real sense, this call to participation was to bring difficulties to the Social-Liberal coalition (SPD–FDP) just as it was assuming national power.

The Brechtian aphorism, "Erst kommt das Fressen, dann kommt die Moral" [first comes the fodder, then the ideals], used by writers to describe the changed focus from economic and security concerns to quality of life concerns, does not quite capture Brecht's cynicism about value-oriented behavior, but it does highlight the paradox that affluence and well-being can generate satisfaction and stultification as well as disaffection and protest. In West Germany, over thirty years of steady economic growth has provided an "expansion of secondary and higher education, the growing size and diversity of the mass media, and discontinuities in the life experiences of large numbers of people" (Inglehart, 1977: 7). This means an expanded middle class of younger, educated people, a segment of which is inclined toward elite-challenging, rather than elite-supporting political behavior, is at hand. This postwar and postmaterialist generation has played a crucial role in the origins and expansion of Green politics. Electoral data suggest that the activists for local and Land Green parties, unlike those of any of the other parties, received disproportionate support from younger, middle-class, educated citizens. The success of the Greens has not been in establishing a mass party but in developing a sophisticated network of dedicated party workers who feel a strong bond of loyalty and cohesion. The failure of the major parties shows up clearly here. A loss in recruiting young voters, a loss of talented activists, and for the SPD and the FDP, a loss of political power were some of the obvious consequences.

In effect, we are working backward from the astonishing electoral successes of the Greens, locally and nationally, to identify the forces shaping its early development. Although the following generalization needs some qualification, the Greens of today, especially the leadership cadre, are essentially those who were active in the student revolt of the 1960s, and in the SPD party work and citizen initiatives of the 1970s. The cadres from the SDS (Students for Democratic Socialism), the APO (extraparliamentary organization), and the JUSOS (Young Socialists, youth affiliate of the SPD) have distinct postwar generational markings. The election initiatives and the citizen initiatives extend beyond the young generation of postmaterialists to include a wider swathe of the middle class, particularly supporters of the SPD and the FDP. Already in the late 1960s and the early 1970s, the signs of party failure were apparent. The new Green and alternative parties, as well as the citizen initiatives, were borrowing recruits, especially

new blood, from the established parties. One way to examine the historical roots of the Greens is to cast a glance back to the formative experiences
of its present party activists and supporters.

THE STUDENT MOVEMENT

There is little doubt that the student movement[3] of the 1970s helps us
understand the present Greens. Dinne of the Bremen Greens, Hasenclever
of the Baden-Württemberg Greens, Fischer of the Hesse Greens, and Petra
Kelly of the Bavarian Greens all received their baptism rites into grass-
roots politics in the late 1960s. In a recent Bundestag debate, Fischer, a
Green member from Hesse who is one of the party leaders, noted: "Indeed, I belong to a first generation which could really break with fascism.
The 1968 movement created an identity which offered us an exit from the
misery of German history but which left us homeless at the same time"
(Sontheimer, 1984: 2).

The critique of representative democracy (Shell, July 1970: 653–80)
and the party system developed by leftist intellectuals and students has
changed in some respects, but the essential point has remained: parliamentary democracy, which relies exclusively on established political parties to define the public will, is inadequate. The student movement set
forth a vision of a new polity and society, and it extended the range of political actions (Barnes and Kaase, 1979: 38). Sit-ins, go-ins, demonstrations, occupations of buildings, marches, and various acts of civil disobedience were part of the new repertoire of political tactics. It is all too
obvious that the shift from elite-directed to elite-challenging political actions which characterized much of the 1970s received its impetus from the
student movement.

Willy Brandt's successful reelection as chancellor in 1972 helped defuse
a considerable amount of dissatisfaction and dissent, and the student activists of the earliest decade, as well as many of the enlarged student population of the 1970s, were no doubt encouraged by Brandt's appeal for
West Germany to "risk more democracy."

In addition, rapid economic growth, the oil crisis, and extensive social
change in West Germany, such as plans for nuclear power plants, brought
about a redefinition of the younger generation's political style; that in turn
spawned a motley coalition of strange bedfellows which brought the
Greens to more deliberate political action. This new coalition consisted of

---

[3] This part of the essay is an updating of part of my earlier essay, "The New Left and the
West German Party System: Is the Opposition Waxing?" Third International Conference of
Europeanists, Washington, D.C., April 29–May 1, 1982.

many middle-class citizens who felt that they were not being consulted about decisions that affected their homes and working environments. Part of the citizen disenchantment which caused a disaffection from the major parties came from a failure of consultation between the party apparatus and the issues increasingly tied to "growth and progress." Without noticing it, the sacred cows of the 1960s—growth at all costs—became fallen idols in a time of increased participation. The student *march through* the institutions became linked with a wider segment of the middle class in an attempt to *work through* the institutions and to change political values at the grass-roots level.

CITIZEN INITIATIVES

Nowhere is the inability of the traditional political parties to reach citizens and to connect them to decisions of public policy more obvious than in the proliferation of citizen initiatives in the 1970s and 1980s. Udo Bermbach notes: "In the summer of 1977 there were approximately 50,000 civic initiative groups in the German Federal Republic which were able to jointly mobilize more members than all the political parties put together. Of these, roughly 1,000 civic initiative groups with well over 300,000 individual members had joined the supra-regional Federal Association for Civic Action in Protecting the Environment" (Bermbach, 1980: 227).

A critical building block for the Green parties, local, regional and national, has been the network of citizen action groups. In some states, for example Lower Saxony and Baden-Württemberg, a close look at the Green party structure reveals a dense network of various types of citizen action groups. There is no adequate historical account of the complex interplay between the student activists of the 1960s and the middle-class activists in many cities and localities. We know that seemingly spontaneous organizations captured the imagination and the political energy of a sizable number of citizens who were simply fed up with the traditional parties. In addition to reacting to the particular issues that often provided the flash point for action—the construction of a nuclear plant, the enlarging of an airport runway, or the destruction of a historical site—many of these citizens regarded the parties as unwilling surrogates too tied into the status quo. The political culture was being transformed into a more participatory one with calls for decentralization, debureaucratization, and for the extension of the spheres of decisionmaking to the general citizenry. But the traditional parties seemed unable to respond. As one observer has pointed out: "The parties are largely inclined to look upon initiative groups as disagreeable groups who do not comply with institutionalized control and discipline" (Bermbach, 1980: 234).

The parties were hamstrung. They could no more turn away from their philosophy of extensive economic growth as the chief talisman of progress than they could embrace the unconventional methods of promoting public issues through demonstrations. They were perplexed and angered by continual legal challenges to the technocratic civil servants who received their cues from the established parties. In the mid-1970s, the leaders of the traditional parties saw their power waning, but most felt, or hoped, that the protest groups would follow the usual surge and decline cycle.

But recent research on the citizen initiative (*Bürgerinitiativen*) movement indicates that this activity is hardly a passing fad but rather represents a significant extension of the participant role in the West German political culture (Helm, 1980: 30). Jutta Helm notes that: "in 1973, about 2.0 million citizens were active or had recently been active in citizen lobbies. This figure assumes additional significance in view of the fact that only 1.8 million citizens are members of all political parties. Moreover, whereas 12% of all respondents in a representative survey indicated their willingness to be active in political parties, 34% said that they were willing to join a citizen lobby" (Helm, 1980: 576).

The membership of these grass-roots organizations is, at the same time, a profile of the educational and occupational structure of the Green party. The citizens are predominantly middle class, with especially strong representation from what has been termed the "new middle class" (Loewenberg, 1978: 20). The membership is composed mainly of educated, urban, well-to-do citizens with a healthy sprinkling of students. Workers are underrepresented while civil servants, especially teachers and salaried white-collar employees, are overrepresented.

A heightened concern for the effects of public policy decisions on the environment shows up in the most recent research on citizen initiatives. These organizations are distributed over various concerns as follows (Helm, 1980: 576):

I. *Environmental issues*

Environmental protection	17.0%
Traffic	12.0
Urban planning	8.0
Historic monuments	2.5
Urban renewal	3.6

II. *Social and cultural issues*

Nursery schools and playgrounds	16.0
School issues	8.0

Marginal groups (convicts, slumdwellers, gypsies, foreign workers)	7.0
Tenant issues	5.5
Youth issues	5.0
Communal facilities (swimming pool, etc.)	4.0
Cultural affairs	3.3
III. *Narrow groups interests*	5.0
IV. *Commercial interests*	2.0

It is mainly this concern for environmental protection that has brought together traditionally conservative forces—churches, farm organizations, nature and hiking clubs (akin to the Sierra Club)—with the middle-class educated activists who usually lean to the left. The coalition has been further strengthened by the issue of nuclear energy. The oil crisis of 1973 not only reminded citizens of the scarcity and expense of energy sources, it encouraged the economic and political forces promoting nuclear energy. In this instance, the farmer and protector of nature linked up with the citizens who, in addition to being concerned about the environment, were dubious about the legitimacy of state power to build nuclear power plants. One writer calls this issue the linchpin of the Green movement, the antinuclear coalition (Pilat, 1980).

The massive demonstrations against the building of nuclear facilities began at Whyl in 1975 and continued for the next six years; some have been organized by citizen initiative groups and some by the federal or peak organizations of the citizen initiative movement, the BBU. Most of the demonstrations have been peaceful, which points to the nonviolent political style of the citizen initiative groups. The overwhelming tactics of most groups include persistent negotiation and consultation, petitioning for public explanation of policy made or about to be made (hearings), and full utilization of all legal procedures which affect public decisions (Nelkin and Pollack, 1981: 172). A theme that has not been satisfactorily explored in the context of recent West German politics is the positive uses of legalism by citizens against bureaucrats in the interest of sharing authority.

By the beginning of the 1980s, the Green movement was poised for a national party organization. The citizen initiative movement had galvanized a sizable number of young citizens, recruited disillusioned established party members, and developed the groundwork of an interlocking network of political action groups which felt that the winds of democratization and decentralization were in their sails. The traditional parties were slowly realizing that an increasingly large number of very active citizens were putting the brakes on further industrialization. The critique of unplanned industrial growth, the fear of technology run amuck via nuclear power, and the desire to democratize societal and political institutions were issues the major parties responded to in cautious fashion. What critique of their society were the Greens offering? What solutions were being suggested?

THE "GREENPRINT" FOR THE FUTURE

> Our politics is determined by the view that the ecological errors can only be solved through democratic means—that is, with the active assent of the people. We must set about seeking a solution to the crisis soon if we want to prevent an undemocratic solution (Party Preamble of the Green party, June 1980).

The central issues for the Greens are not the despoliation of nature, the pursuit of growth at all costs, or the consequences of increasing industrialization. Those are ends, and the lever that must be grasped relates to means. The crucial problem is the concentration of power in the economic, political, and cultural spheres of life in the Federal Republic. And since this is *the* issue, the main solution is radical democratization in the sense of deconcentration and decentralization. The Greens may have a label that denotes environmental concern and respect for nature, but their central focus lies in liberal attitudes against accumulations of power. Robert Dahl notes in a recent work that "liberalism, and in particular liberal ideas about democracy, were formulated in opposition to concentrated power," and that the "hostility of liberalism to concentration of power runs deep" (Dahl, 1982: 105). Obviously, the Greens solution must concentrate on means compatible with their ideals of human development, but they also attack the ends or goal of their society. The ends, the very idea of progress, are called into question. The critique of the Greens begins on the system level (actually suprasystem when foreign policy is included), focuses on important institutions, and levels off on the issue of moral and civil development. The criticisms show a remarkable fit with the postmaterial critique discussed by Inglehart in his generational analysis, while the solutions offered by the Greens reflect the sketch of a creative and imaginative architect rather than that of an experienced engineer: the vision is there but the mechanics are lacking.

The major values supporting the Green party's conception of an alternative view of society and politics are ecological, social, grass-roots democracy, and nonviolence. Let us consider the greenprint under each of those headings.

PRINCIPLES: Our politics is *ecological* because it gives due priority to the preservation of the natural basis of life for us and future genera-

tions, and directs itself to the needs of people and their creative capacity. It sets itself against the exploitation of humankind and nature
within the competitive capitalistic economy and in the existing centralized planned economy (Party Preamble of the Green party,
adopted, Dortmund, June 1980).

The Greens are concerned about limiting growth in an industrialized society, and the true significance of this active minority of the late 1970s may
be its suggestion to "reach for the brakes"[4] when you do not know where
you are going. The culprits who mindlessly step on the accelerator include
a too powerful state, the structures and values of capitalism, and the well-
organized interests of corporate pluralism which have a stake in present
policies. The ecological model is essentially organic. It thinks in terms of
cautious growth, decline, and renewal. The linear view of progress aided
by technological improvement is utopian thinking to the Greens. Some
scientific and technological advances are too dangerous to be of use, and
nuclear energy is in that category. The promotion of decentralized, soft-
energy alternatives is a prominent aspect of the Green program. The
Greens are critical of capitalism, but they are not calling for the nationalization of the means of production nor are they recrudescent Luddites
wanting to smash factory machines, computers, or robots. They want to
deconcentrate economic power and prevent monopolies and megaorgan-
izations which play the tune of increasing production. One prominent
Green leader has noted: "In any case, I want to make it clear that humans
come first, and, after that, the economy" (Kelly, 1982: 240). The ecological message has an obvious conservative tone to it if you forget that it is
quite radical to question monopoly economic power, the positive use of
nuclear energy, or a view of progress based on technological advance. The
ecological component of the party preamble is wary of "the machine in
the garden" without the admonition of a witless return to nature of the
early romantic movement.

> *Social,* because we feel that people can only confront the crisis when
> their autonomy and free development can be realized in common, to-
> gether with others in harmony with their environment. We uphold
> the view that the upheavals which the solutions to the ecological cri-
> sis may bring should not be made a burden to the working people, the
> disadvantaged, and the handicapped of this society (Party Preamble
> of the Green party, June 1980).

[4] Offe, 1982. Offe notes that Marx likened revolutions to locomotives in world history,
but Walter Benjamin wrote that perhaps it is entirely different. A radical party can also promote preservation.

There is a tension between the ecological and social wings of the Green movement and party, and it is reflected in the fractionalization within the Greens, in debates at party conferences, and in the policy accent of different Land organizations. Which should receive priority, economic or ecological needs? Contrary to Petra Kelly's assertion, many Greens are concerned about jobs and feel that one should use "emergency brakes" with caution. Social values for the Greens include opportunities for education, concern about minorities, sensitivity to the prison conditions and social benefits for the aged, awareness of the numbing effect of monotonous factory tasks for many workers, and acting as a surrogate for the many groups in industrialized politics who received short shrift because of skewed pluralism.

Some of these groups which pursue themes of emancipation are very active within Green parties on the local, state, and national level. There is a clear feminist wing within the Greens, led by Petra Kelly, which calls for equality of opportunities for both sexes and, in Kelly's words, an end to a system in which the "people still holding power are the old men dedicated to economic growth and more armaments (Kelly, 1982: 28).

It is not easy to square the circle here. Guaranteeing both security and equality is costly. The egalitarian and social wings of the national Green party have bridged their differences with proposals for the heavily handicapped, for reductions in the workweek without loss of pay, and for directing the unemployed toward environmental protection projects. But the true binding force for the Greens, a key value for the postwar materialists, is the vehicle of grass-roots democracy. Here participation politics in the first person speaks to present problems, conducts a dialogue with the historical legacy, and points the way to a worthwhile future.

> *Grass roots*, because we stand for direct democracy. Through this method, decisions about public affairs will be the most effectively understood. This form of democracy allows itself to work best more on the local level. We reject the ever-grasping bureaucracy which leaves the citizen helpless against increasing arbitrariness and the growing abuse of power by the economic and state machinery (Party Preamble of the Green party, June 1980).

The cure for the ills of democracy is more democracy, and more democracy for the Greens means a deep suspicion of state power, a belief that parties and parliamentary institutions are badly in need of reform, and a conviction that democracy from below will serve individual and system development. The elite democracy of the Parliamentary Council, shapers of the Basic Law, with its traditional promotion of a narrow representative democracy is rejected. The graffiti on a wall in West Berlin, "Staat, hau ab!" [State, beat it!] is more anarchist in spirit than the Greens' message, but the reliance on direct democracy is no minor point (Berger, 1979: 33). The antipathy to economics of scale carries over to large bureaucratic power blocs in the public sector, and the solvents against massive organizational power are seen as decentralization and deconcentration.[5] Trying to repeal the Weberian tendencies of bureaucracy and the iron laws of Michels is no small task, but the Greens have set this chore for themselves. The antibureaucracy animus is powerful among the Green populists. It leads to a condemnation of anonymous power where "things are in the saddle," rockets on the launching pads, and nuclear plants in woods primeval without personal accountability or even popular consultation.

The institutions of West Germany also fall short by the radical democratic benchmark used by the Greens. The parties are seen as extended instruments of the state, fed by public finance, and tethered to powerful groups of economic interests. In fact, the failure of the parties is caused by their immobility, their ties to special interests. The criticism of the powerful catchall people's parties, whose inclination toward consumer-voters in the center makes them cautious and incapable of reform, is nothing more than a polemical version of Otto Kirchheimer's essay of some decades ago (Kirchheimer, 1966: 237–89). In fact, Kirchheimer's barely disguised jeremiad against the West German established parties has merely been extended by the Greens and other critics (Hasenclever, 1982a: 309–22; Raschke, 1982: 9–31). The charge of myopic vision and overall rigidity applies to the parties and to the overprofessionalized politicians (Huber, 1981). The parties are penetrated by well-organized national interests, and the final negotiation on crucial decisions takes place not in the Parliament, but in the executive-bureaucratic matrix, far from opposition control and criticism (Willers, 1982: 172; Katzenstein, July 1980). Therefore, not only is there a need for more direct democracy to complement representative democracy, but parliamentary democracy must be revitalized by making the corridors of power more accessible (Block, 1982: 146–58). Whether a new party—even if it calls itself "an antiparty party" or "a party unlike the others"—with the aid of a grass-roots movement can make a difference in West German democracy, is the essence of the Green experiment currently underway. The Greens view the party as an extension of the movement. The movement or grass-roots basis is the primary locus of power [*Standbein*], and the parliamentary organization provides

[5] Nullmeier in Raschke, 1982: 342–58. "The 'more,' 'larger,' and 'centralized' political challenge of the '50s, '60s, and early '70s is yielding to the small, simple, and local as the political challenge of the '80s," p. 342. For a critique of the impractical aspect of this aim of the Greens, see Eschenburg, 1982, and Berger, 1979: 40.

amplification (and provocation) of local concerns [*Spielbein*] (Hasen-clever, 1982a: 309–22).

> *Nonviolent,* because only in a nonviolent society can the domination of one person over another and the power of one against the others be abolished. In a time which is characterized by the politics of violence and the threat of violence, we support a variety of forms of nonviolent resistance (Party Preamble of the Green party, June 1980).

What are the limits of dissent in a constitutional democracy, and what are the boundary lines for citizen expression of discontent? For most West Germans, the vote will exhaust their dissatisfaction or approbation. For the Greens, the theme of nonviolent action has domestic and foreign policy implications. Nothing has been debated more heatedly among the Greens than the applicability of civil disobedience to political change. The West Berlin Alternative List, a Green affiliate on the left of the spectrum, speaks against organized violence but for a wide range of actions in the category of civil disobedience. The Baden-Württemberg Greens have detailed the conditions for civil disobedience much more specifically. This is obviously an area where the unconventional political tactics of the postwar generation rub most abrasively against the older generation's concept of law and order. Petra Kelly's comments on civil disobedience give an indication of the tension between the Greens' mode of operation and the traditional political culture and its attitude toward techniques of change: "The more local and regional techniques of civil disobedience and nonviolent resistance develop, the more citizen action groups and self-administrative models are formed, then we will be all the closer to a really democratic society" (Kelly, 1982: 29).

Nonviolence also means disarmament, a desire to detach West Germany from military alliances, a call to make the Bundeswehr strictly a defensive army, and approval of forms of social civil resistance on a decentralized basis instead of standing armies (Szabo, 1983). The Greens identify strongly with third world countries and their struggle for development. Interpreting imperialism as a form of violence, they bemoan the "overarmed, underdeveloped, and overpopulated world" (Verheugen, 1982: 237) to which the superpowers cater.

Some of the critics of the Greens claim that their politics are reminiscent of the notorious Morgenthau plan which called for a demilitarized, nonindustrialized Germany after World War II. This overstates their case. They are opposed to NATO and they are interested in preventing West Germany from being squeezed between the East-West conflict. Once again, spokesperson Kelly has characterized the Green position in a short phrase: "We are not an antimissile movement, but a demilitarization movement operating beyond the Cold War bloc powers which seeks solidarity from grass-roots movements for disarmament in East and West" (Kelly, 1982: 34.)

Finally, the Party Preamble of the national Green party does not specifically state what is already clear to most Green supporters. Humankind is at the center of their reforms. Suzanne Berger is correct in writing that those decentralizing reformers reject economic, technological, and sound determinisms in favor of the primacy of imagination, will, and political activity as critical human activities (Berger, 1979: 33). The "new" individual will restrain Faustian passions and control overactive Promethean twitches because of a respect for the natural environment and a concern for future generations. Raising this goal makes it understandable why the Greens see politics as an opportunity for changing values just as much as it is for gathering votes and controlling power. A new political force seeks a new political culture.

The Shakers and Movers of the Greens

The shakers and movers responsible for the Greenprint are an extraordinarily diverse set of political activists. The major formal statement of political ambitions was developed at the Dortmund Conference in June of 1980, but the founding men and women of the Green party had been debating contentiously since the earlier party conference in 1979. Who were some of these innovators and political gadflies? On the right of center, Herbert Gruhl, former CDU Bundestag member and author of *A Planet is Plundered,* looked for a coalition of ecologists with moderate Socialists and a platform calling for limits on rapacious economic growth. He left the party soon after its founding because of disagreement with the anticapitalist wing.

Rudolph Bahro, exiled émigré from the German Democratic Republic, Marxist theoretician, and cultural innovator, proved to be a gifted speaker. His ideal coalition, which would promote a "revolution of consciousness," was a Green and Red formation of leftists and ecologists, with the Green as the linchpin for the left and right.

Petra Kelly rivaled Bahro as a dynamic speaker, and her major aim included a radical democratic Oeko-Pax [ecology and peace] movement. Her critique of the traditional parties was the sharpest, and her espousal of a new role for women in society suggested that she had little hope that her former party, the SPD, would satisfactorily reduce male domination of party posts.

Wolf-Dieter Hasenclever, a physics teacher and former SPD party activist from Baden-Württemberg, spoke for the antinuclear coalition and for a style of politics that was critical and constructive rather than confrontational. A member of the nondogmatic left, Hasenclever saw the Green coalition engaged in consciousness-raising as well as looking for a share of political power. In an interview in 1980 he stated:

> The question of the value system is especially important. The values of the capitalist industrial society are thoroughly imprinted with the view that "to have more" is decisive for society's norms. Whoever has the highest income is the most prestigious fellow; the city that invests the most in public transport or building streets is the most successful city; the state with the highest export quota has reason to be proud. That is a value system based on materialism. We have to give it up. We have to come to a value system focused on *being* and not *having*, on inner values—love, healthy social relations, peace in an environment of wholeness (Hasenclever, 1980).

The founders of this party, shaped from as diverse a political spectrum imaginable within and beyond the Federal Republic's relatively colorless parties, had few clear goals in the electoral arena. The traditional parties seemed uninterested in their political agenda and disdainful of their bumptious political style. The distance from grass-roots politics to national elections proved to be all too short.

From Grass-Roots to National Elections

Two seemingly unrelated events, which occurred in the late 1960s and the early 1970s help explain how the Green movement culminated in a national Green party at the end of the decade. One event was, as we noted earlier, Willy Brandt's exhortation in 1969 to "risk more democracy," and the other was the formation of the first Green environmentalist party in a small town in Lower Saxony in reaction to the explosion of chlorine gas. Brandt's emphasis on extending democracy to political and social institutions encouraged an already burgeoning number of rebellious citizens, especially among the young and the more educated middle class. The small organizational embryo of the environmental party in Lower Saxony (Salchow, 1980) indicated that citizens felt a need to go beyond the established parties to make their case. The environmentalists and the extraparliamentary opposition connected on the issue of grass-roots politics and many of the key activists were the young intelligentsia. Thus, the dynamics of generational politics changed its locus from the universities and large urban demonstrations to election initiatives, citizen initiatives, and to local and Land parties where it helped contribute to diverse and diffuse coalitions. It led eventually to the founding of a national Green party contesting seats for the Bundestag.

Most Green party activists agree that the antinuclear demonstrations of the 1970s acted as a flash point that turned many citizen initiatives to coalitions of parties (Hasenclever, 1982a: 309–22). Certainly, the rapid growth of the 1960s produced many urban citizen initiatives, but the antinuclear demonstrations, replete with full media coverage as police battled demonstrators, brought many citizens to their feet. City and county successes for the Greens eventually led to participation in Land elections. In June of 1978 the first test came in Hamburg and Lower Saxony, and the ground began to shake a bit under the traditional parties. In neither Land did the Green coalition get above the 5 percent hurdle that you must "vault" to get into the parliament, but in both elections, the Green share of the vote eliminated the Free Democratic party from the Parliaments. From 1978 until 1983, the Greens, with great consistency, drew votes away from the Social Democrats and the Free Democrats, and either eliminated the FDP from the Parliament or replaced it as the third party. Each of the Land elections has a particular set of circumstances, but let us consider the success of the Green party in early 1980 in Baden-Württemberg, a sizable Land with a moderate to conservative tradition, a wide diversity of occupations and classes, and a high degree of rural-urban differences (Oberndoerfer and Mielke, 1980a). The demographic and voting patterns here were to be repeated, with variations, in other Land elections:

1. Most of the vote for the Greens came disproportionately from the eighteen to forty-four age group compared to the other parties.
2. The Greens clearly took votes away from the Free Democratic Party in certain cities, e.g., Freiburg (a university town), and it took younger voters away from all the established parties.
3. The Green voters were highly educated. "A very strong correlation exists between the degree of education and the share of the vote for the Greens."
4. The Greens did especially well in three university cities and were strong in South Baden where the sensibilities of the voters toward environmental matters had been sharpened by conflicts over nuclear plants at Whyl and Fessenheim.
5. The Greens achieved their best results in districts of high mobility with students, salaried workers, and civil servants (teachers and academics).
6. The Greens did especially poorly in worker districts. Their lowest percentage was in Mannheim II (3 percent), a worker's district.

7. The Greens did better with rural workers than urban workers.
8. Religious preference seems to have had no special correlation with a Green vote.
9. The Greens were favored in districts with a low vote. "With increasing participation, their portion of the vote declines. In those cases it can be surmised that the Greens—a typical protest movement with highly motivated followers—had largely exhausted its voting strength" (Oberndoerfer and Mielke, 1980a).

ALLIES AND BEDFELLOWS

The Green success in Baden-Württemberg was a surprise to supporters as well as to the traditional parties. An earlier victory in Bremen had been seen as a fluke of city-state politics (the first entry of the Greens in a *Land* parliament), and the founding of the national party in January 1980 through highly polemical debate convinced many that the party would not outlive its birth. A hint of the ideological splintering and disunity emerged from the national party campaign conference in Dortmund in June. Herbert Gruhl, a former Christian Democratic member of the Bundestag and conservative author of ecological persuasion, quit the party when he was rejected by the party delegates. August Haussleitner, leader of the Bavarian party, withdrew his candidacy because of disclosures about his Nazi past. Olaf Dinne, leader of the Bremen Greens, walked out, disappointed with the influence of the Communist delegates. Ideologically, the "black" Greens (strong conservatives), "red" Greens (Communist or Socialist), and "brown" Greens (Nazi background) made for strange bedfellows along with the overwhelming majority of undogmatic New Leftists.[6]

The Green movement, which had campaigned since its founding in diverse localities against the national parties, now had become a national party ready to contest a federal election. The answer to the question, was it party or movement, was that it was both. The national Greens hoped to draw on the citizen initiative organizations, and the local and Land organizations. The attempt to shape a reasonably coherent organization with a modicum of unity in the presence of diverse political viewpoints showed how difficult it was to form a party of a "new type."

For example, we have concentrated on the Green parties in this essay, but the Greens are often joined in electoral alliances with alternative par-

---

[6] New Left is really quite the same as postmaterialist. The Old Left believed in and promoted economic expansion and growth, it accepted organizational discipline and hierarchy, and it worked through bureaucratic structures. It was not against state power if it could be captured. Inglehart, 1977.

ties which have separate identities. And in Berlin and Hamburg, the parties which stand for Green goals designate themselves as the Alternative List or the Green Alternative List. In general, it can be said that Alternative List parties have a stronger anticapitalist orientation. The fear of reckless economic growth damaging the environment is not just the key concern, but is usually linked to a structural criticism of capitalism. The Green parties of Baden-Württemberg and Lower Saxony have a center of gravity that is more ecological and radically democratic than anticapitalistic. The opposition to nuclear energy and unrestricted growth, and the feeling that only extensive democratization and decentralization would loosen rigid bureaucracies still comprised the kernel of the Greens idea. How did this party fare in the federal elections of 1980 and 1983 running against the establishment?

The Greens polled 1.5 percent of the national vote in 1980 which kept them out of the legislature. In March of 1983, they polled 5.6 percent of the vote and obtained twenty-seven seats. It was the first time in almost twenty-five years that a new party, a party of ecology, peace, and extended democratization, was able to jump the 5 percent hurdle. In retrospect, the low vote in 1980 shows considerable tactical maneuvering for the ideological Green voters. Survey research shows a large number of Green voters supporting the Social Democrats and Schmidt to prevent Franz Josef Strauss (Murphy et al., 1979) from a possible chancellorship. Between 1980 and 1983, the Green parties extended and consolidated their strength in local and Land elections. They had no "lesser evil" to favor in 1983, and they faced the challenge of a Social Democratic party, now in opposition, in competition for a space on the left.

Obvious continuities between the two federal elections fit our early description of Green supporters. Age and education are the crucial demographic variables.[7] In both elections, the Greens drew their support disproportionately from first voters and younger voters, and a much larger percentage of their total voters, in comparison with the other voters, came from the eighteen to forty-four range. The postwar successor generation was speaking to a younger age cohort. There was stronger representation from the salaried middle class with a predominance of support from the social professions (teachers, social workers) and very little support from the working class. Green voters in these Bundestag elections were more apt to be secular than religious, and the parties which were losing voters to the Greens were the Social Democrats and the Free Democrats. The So-

[7] The 1980 data came from Oberndoerfer and Mielke, 1980a and Infas, "Die Bundestagswahl vom 5. Oktober 1980, Bad Godesberg"; the 1983 election data are from Guellner, 1983, and Kaltefleiter, 1983; also *Der Spiegel*, March 14, 1983.

cial Democrats are a political force in decline on the national and local level, and the Greens have accelerated this decline which dates from the mid-1970s (Guellner, 1983). Caught between the embourgeoisement of the workers and the "postbourgeoisement" of the young intelligentsia, the Social Democrats, as Guellner notes, "chased workers from the party, drove away the middle class, and failed to tie postmaterialists to their standard" (Guellner, 1983: 28).

We have cited a variety of reasons why the success of the Greens represents a failure for the major parties, especially the SPD and the FDP. An extensive catalog of factors undermining FDP and SPD electoral support has been documented recently[8] which points to traditional party problems at the Land level (Schmollinger, 1983). In Berlin and Hamburg, the SPD and FDP lost support because of involvement in local scandals. In both of these electoral arenas, speculation in housing schemes and in other financial arrangements alienated voters from their traditional party. The gains of the Greens were partially a result of party personnel "on the take": "Corruption and speculative deals in housing have compromised the big parties, particularly the Social Democrats, in cities like West Berlin and Hamburg, and have made it very difficult for young people to live decently" (Vinocur, 1982).

The removal of the Strauss factor of 1980 and the grass-roots work between 1980 and 1983 brought the Greens a place in the Bundestag (Guellner, 1983: 24). The increased support in the first vote (direct seat), usually considered the all-weather voters, suggests that the kernel of the Green party is growing. In the last decade, a time of belt-tightening for the social state and high unemployment, the postmaterialist Greens have used the movement to capture a small share of legislative power. Supporting economic policies that Theo Sommer of *Die Zeit* calls "stone age," and foreign policies that frighten party elites at home and abroad, this party holds all-weather supporters. Inglehart's response to the question—don't postmaterialists turn to grubby Philistines in hard times—is based on cross-polity data but fits the Bonn Republic quite well:

> As Postmaterialists aged, they moved out of the student ghetto and became a predominant influence among young technocrats, contributing to the rise of a "New Class." They furnish the ideologies and core support for the environmental, zero-growth and anti-nuclear movements; and their opposition to those who give top priority to reindustrialization and rearmament constitutes a distinctive and persisting dimension of political cleavage (Inglehart, Dec. 1981: 880).

[8] For an excellent analysis of Land elections in Berlin, Lower Saxony, Hessen, Bavaria, and Hamburg, see *Zeitschrift fuer Parlamentsfragen*, Feb. 1983.

West German activist Greens would consider Inglehart's use of the word "technocrat" as an epithet, but many of the student protesters have become civil servants, managers, and politicians. It is rare to have radicals with such well-established pension rights, but many Greens are in that category.

THE GREENS IN OFFICE

"I believe that the first and young voters and the powerless women want a fundamental opposition." Petra Kelly, Federal Chairwoman of the Greens, Member of German Bundestag, 1982.

"The Green parliamentarians of Baden-Württemberg reject the position of fundamental opposition." Wolf-Dieter Hasenclever, Green member of Baden-Württemberg Parliament, 1982.

One of the scenes at the opening of the West German Bundestag in early 1983 gave many established politicians a chance to relax in their chairs. Apprehensive about the stylized unconventionality of the new Green members of the Bundestag, they were relieved to see Marie Luise Beck-Oberdorf, a speaker for the Greens, advance to the podium and present newly elected Chancellor Kohl with an evergreen branch. The next day these same politicians read what this Bundestag member had said to Kohl: "I cannot congratulate you. The evergreen expresses our concern about the dying woods." The Greens are now represented in six Land parliaments and in the Bundestag. The difficulty of making generalizations about their participation as legislators stems from the diversity of the Green parties and their techniques, the very short period of time of their parliamentary work, and the paucity of empirical data. Nevertheless, there is sufficient evidence to assess whether the Greens will choose more of the extra-, anti-, or proparliamentary techniques to accomplish their objectives.[9]

[9] The best recent collection of essays by Green members of various local parliaments is in Mettke, 1982c. In this volume, the noteworthy essays are: Martin Jaenicke, "Parlamentarische Entwarnungseffekte? Zur Ortsbestimmung der Alternativbewegung," 69–81; Ernst Hoplitschek, "Partei, Avantgarde, Heimat-oder was? Die 'Alternative Liste fuer Demokratie und Umweltschutz' in Westberlin," 101–19; Martin Mombaur, "Im Parlament und auf der Strasse: Die Doppelstrategie der gruenen Niedersachsen," 135–45; Thea Bock, "Mit diesem Staat ist Keine Natur zu machen, Der Weg der Gruenen-Alternativen ins Hamburger Parlament," 146–58; and Peter Willers, "Den Tiefschlaf der Altparteien Stören: Vom Auf und Ab der 'Gruenen Liste' in Bremen," 259–78. Hasenclever's essay in *Buerger und Parteien*, ed. Raschke, is excellent. Finally, a critique based on a thorough empirical study of the speeches of Green parliamentarians is Scharping and Hofmann-Goettig, 1983. A reply to this criticism is Murphy, 1983.

Though we have no detailed study of the demographic characteristics of the Green parliamentarians in the local, Land, and national parliaments, it is clear that the generational characteristics that we have described for the party activists and supporters are in evidence. Once again, the average age of those legislators is far below that of any of the other parties. Second, there is a preponderance of teachers and professionals with academic training (Remmers, 1982; Hoffman, 1983). The argument can be made that by age, education, and professions the Green legislators would have a sensitivity to Germany's historic legacy (Lipset and Dobson, 1972). A small number of the Green parliamentarians have working-class and trade-union backgrounds, and quite a few were active in the APO, the JUSO's, citizen initiatives, and the SPD at an earlier time.

Extending the movement to a party wing has occurred with much hesitation. Many of the Green activists are aware of the essay by Josef Leinen, federal chairman of the committee for citizen initiatives, about why the Green garb does not fit a national party (Leinen, 1980). But, the Greens, mindful of their reach for a "party unlike the others," hope to combine the benefits of a party with the close contact to the grass roots which a movement offers. These benefits include breaking through the media block by having formal membership in a legislature; bringing issues before Parliament which usually fall through the cracks; acting as a surrogate for underrepresented groups (consumers, women, prisoners, "future generations"); encouraging voters to articulate protest; and exercising forceful criticism as an opposition party. (Jaenicke, 1983.) The Greens see themselves as the "yeast in the dough," and they are well aware of the Parliament's function as an amplifier for "consciousness-raising." But there is a dilemma as to how the opposition role should be played or what emphasis should be given to the parliamentary possibilities listed above. Some of the Green legislators are intent on protecting their political chastity through strict and fundamental abstinence from coalitions which would offer a chance to govern. In Hamburg and in Hesse, the Greens, holding the key to a majority in each Land, participated in coalition talks but raised very difficult demands. A new election in Hamburg produced a majority for the Social Democrats and left some workers with a view of the Greens as contributing to ungovernability.

The new party also has a serious obligation to its promise of internal party democracy which includes:

1. The rotation principle. Legislators should rotate on a regular basis. Two years of a four-year term is often recommended.
2. The imperative mandate. The legislator must consult with the grass-roots organization before making decisions.

3. Only one office in party affairs at one time.
4. Partial acceptance of salary with the rest going to the party.

While those rules may undercut Weber's prediction of inevitable professionalization, they also have clear disadvantages. Rotation opens the way for new ideas, but decreases the value of continuity and experience (Hasenclever, 1982a). Maintaining a vigorous communication with the grass-roots organization and keeping a special line open to the citizen initiatives have proven to be difficult ideals to realize. This mode of operation requires inordinate patience for parliamentarians and assumes a wide range of knowledge on the part of the citizenry. It is a challenge, however, that a populist group cannot avoid and has led to serious disunity in some Green organizations (Willers, 1982).

As we pointed out earlier, the Greens see West Germany as a country with a skewed pluralism which favors powerful, bureaucratized groups, and which prevents needed reforms. The Green response to these ever-present cartels, which have always flourished in Germany, is to raise a voice in the streets and in Parliament (Mombaur, 1982: 135–45). An assessment of Green efforts to redress the configuration of pluralism shows notable successes in many localities and Land parliaments (Helm, 1980: 580; Bock, 1982: 146–58) and some accomplishment in getting issues on the level of national policy debate. Environmental issues are no longer brushed aside so quickly by the major parties, and serious attention is focused on the nuclear problem, foreign and domestic.

Drawing up a balance sheet on the performance of the Greens at this juncture might seem premature, but evidence suggests that the Green parties in Lower Saxony and Baden-Württemberg have offered valuable criticism, recommended policy initiatives, and, in general, have been accepted as serious and informed parliamentarians. Hamburg has lively socialist and ecological factions under the Green umbrella, and they certainly can be credited with redirecting the legislative agenda toward environmental issues. The Greens of Hesse and Bremen have had difficulties fitting themselves into the West German concept of a working parliament. Both Land parties have a tradition as provocateurs rather than as working journeymen, and their contributions to parliamentary debate have not been assessed highly. West Berlin's Alternative List is the hardest to categorize. It is most experimental and diligent in maintaining the connection between the party and the grass roots, in its discussions, in the practice and limits of nonviolence and civil disobedience, and in its quixotic combination of competence and Chaplinesque satire to accomplish its aims (*Deutsche Presse Agentur*, Sept. 1982). The major criticism which has been directed toward the Greens in power has been their inability to specify concrete details for their policies or to offer detailed criticisms of the proposals of the major parties (Scharping and Hofmann-Gottig, March 1983: 319–416; Hort and Kannengiesser, Feb. 26, 1983). A noted journalist who has followed the Greens from movement to party has said, "Never in history has a party produced so many policies so quickly which are so little connected" (Bieber, Sept. 10, 1982). There are varieties of gadflies, and the Green species is seeking its role. Physics teacher and parliamentarian Hasenclever makes a preliminary comment on the Green experiment: "For the Greens as a party there remains a fundamental difficulty. On the one hand to be part of an extraparliamentary movement places rigorous demands of doctrine, direct action, and spontaneity on the party; and on the other hand, to raise the claim to represent competent policy alternatives in competition with the other parties and the population in concrete and credible fashion" (Hasenclever, 1982b: 111).

This is one of the major dilemmas. The other refers to the juxtaposed quotations from Kelly and Hasenclever on the problem of coalition-making or cooperation with the traditional parties. Kelly's view of the Greens as an antiparty party leaves no doubt that she would rather have the new party fail than to succeed with any of the other parties. In a very real sense, she represents the purist position which comes close to eschewing a constructive role in parliamentary affairs. Hasenclever's position is essentially a reformist one, and though he has no illusions about being "swallowed whole" by the SPD, he still thinks in terms of coalitional tactics. Rudolph Bahro's pronouncements on Green strategy are becoming difficult to categorize. He has persistently advocated "hands off" from any SPD overtures because he sees the party as basically committed to economic growth with little concern for environmental effects. But his recent speech at a conference of the Greens had him advocating an alliance with conservative forces (Bieber, 1983). There is no easy solution to the conflict of whether to cooperate with the major parties or not, but the Greens may eventually decide to share power with a party they have been castigating fiercely, and that may begin a new chapter for this loosely integrated party (Bieber, Sontheimer, and Spoerl, 1983: 3).

CONCLUSIONS

The challenging force of the Greens, a hybrid movement/party, has not produced a serious change in the West German party system, but it has hastened the decline of the Social Democrats. It is also causing the Free Democrats to look more searchingly, not only for their raison d'être but also for their voters, and it may well stimulate a sizable majority of Union voters in the next decade on the national level. Contrary to several speculations about the decline of parties in West Germany (Raschke, 1982: 9–31), this political system is essentially a party state in which party influence *and* party control are both increasing, though not in a counterbalancing fashion. The Green challenge to the other parties is a test of their attentiveness to criticism and their tolerance for unconventional tactics (parliamentary and otherwise). However frenetic and short-lived their national role may be, the local level will feel the Green wave for some time to come (Guellner, 1983; Harenberg, 1982: 36–50).

The Greens now affect the calculations of all parties, but most especially the Social Democrats who have changed from a catchall people's party to a party in decline, catching fewer folks on the left and right. There is a generational irony here for, in many ways, the Greens are the hyperactive, undisciplined, and unconventional progeny of the early postwar Social Democrats. Many of the current foreign policy ideals of the Greens come from the 1950s SPD, and many Green party leaders are former members of the party. The Greens, in effect, are carrying forth one strand in the Social Democratic heritage (Merkl, 1980: 35) with their own particular generational and postmaterial stamp.

But the midlife identity crisis of the Social Democrats (Loewenthal, Dec. 1981: 9–10) has not been caused only by the movement/party spawned by it. Almost two decades ago, Otto Kirchheimer lamented the loss of opposition of the left as the Social Democrats followed Herbert Wehner's tactic of "power through embracing" their opponents. Kirchheimer saw West German democracy in decline with the atrophying of the vital functions of control and criticism. The Social Democratic move toward the center in its change from a class party to a mass party did open a space on the left, and the events of the late 1960s and 1970s created a Green movement/party to fill that space. The Social Democrats accomplished significant reforms in domestic and foreign policy, but they also leaned center right (where the voters were) while their ideals and other factors encouraged social reform movements on the left. The push from power in late 1982, confirmed in the March 1983 national election, is more a result of long-term trends than just the emergence of a national Green party and could well lead to regrouping for this major party.

Speaking about West German parties in general, Gerard Braunthal, in his book on the SPD (in power from 1969 to 1982), states: "The cyclical rise of protest movements—many anti-establishment—adds substance to the argument that the German parties experience periodic crises because they are unable or unwilling to provide a conduit for single-issue claims made upon them" (Braunthal, 1983: 296). He tempers this criticism by clearly delineating the factions in the SPD which have tried to span the industrial and postindustrial issues, between the Old Left and the New Left. But his overall comment helps to put the issues of party failure in perspective. The SPD may have failed to meet the challenge of the Greens in the last decade, but Braunthal's historic perspective notes a remarkable continuity of this party, with a century of decline and revival, experience with ideological and factional schism, and longtime strengths in states and municipalities. The Greens have challenged the grass-roots base and recapturing it will not happen quickly.

The Greens usually attract Free Democratic as well as Social Democratic voters, and the Free Democrats have been hurt most decisively by the Greens on the local and Land level (Verheugen, 1982). This could affect coalitionmaking in many Land parliaments as the FDP goes right or left while holding to center, and the Greens have hardly exhibited any coalitionmaking capability. The difficulty of assessing the contest between the Greens and the FDP lies in the size and political ambidextrousness of the new middle class. But the Green generational cadre has continued to add first and young voters, and the FDP recruitment has not (Guellner, 1983; Kaltefleiter, 1983). The more pragmatic Greens realized that in the early 1980s the center was consolidating while the left was fragmenting. A raucous and unconventional postmaterialist movement/party may well provoke a mobilization of materialist voters in the coming decade (Lipset, 1981: 251–99).

The Greens have helped revitalize the West German party system, but their impact also raises some perplexing issues for the Second Republic. They have helped integrate potentially disaffected young voters, and they have provided an organizational vehicle which moves ahead while balancing radical democratic imperatives with the demands on parties as "fighting machines." They have forced a rethinking of the central value of progress in industrialized societies, and they have urged a cautious, albeit radical, approach to nuclear energy and nuclear weapons: "nein, danke!" Other West German parties and other nations must take the Greens into consideration, and that could stimulate less hackneyed problem-solving. Diversifying the options for an electorate increasingly concerned about political decisions while providing expansive opportunities for "arcing" associations on the local and Land level are positive development for the party system and for a democratic society.

The dark lines in the shadow cast by the Greens are also clear. Theodor Eschenburg has expressed concern about the lack of respect for the constitutional order (Eschenburg, 1982). The dilemma here is acute, for the generational party wants civil disobedience and the use of "nonviolence" emblazoned on its shield, while the older generation is apprehensive about these tactics. Here, as in other matters, the past is in the present. The evaluation of the Greens as an effective opposition party is mixed. A lack of informed criticism, and a tendency to lean on puffed-up rhetoric instead of detailed suggestions are part of the problem, as is the reluctance to help in coalitionmaking. The call for extensive decentralization may be a laudable way to develop opportunities for human development, but in an ironic way, it could lead to reprivatization and arrogant particularisms (Kramer, 1983).

If the Greens are underinstitutionalized in their political style and structure, perhaps that is a helpful corrective to powerful and overinstitutionalized political parties. The evidence that we have examined indicates that party failure occurs because the party simply ignores citizen demands on issues which are perceived as crucial. The lack of consultation on such issues as modernized missiles, nuclear power plants, or local planning certainly led to political actions beyond the established parties.

Certainly the Greens are no second empire *Wandervögel*, nonpolitical dropouts from industrial society. The Greens take political activity quite seriously, and the emergence of this postmaterialist movement/party—one of the largest and most politically organized in the industrialized democracies of today—sets up a series of conflicts with the established political forces which will not be easily resolved. These include arguments between materialist and postmaterialist political parties, and arguments within parties, as in the Social Democratic party; between advocates of state leadership in policy and planning and decentralists wanting to "slim" down national public power; between those exploring the limits of dissent and those fearful of the uncertainties of public disorder; and between one generation promoting a "grass-roots politics" ideal of direct democracy, and another quite satisfied with representative democracy with regular elections and elite discretion.

It is very likely that in expanding the participant role in West German politics, the Greens will help change the democratic system into a mixture of forms not unlike the mixtures that have developed in other polities. The fear of direct democracy is part of the German historical legacy, but the constitutional consensus is deep and supple enough now to tolerate experiment.[10] The Green parties are part of the continual democratization of West Germany which has been encouraged by economic growth and channeled by flexible institutional forms like federalism, the electoral law,

[10] Switzerland, France, the United States (especially individual states of the West and Middle West), and the Scandinavian countries have experimented with combinations of direct and representative traditions with mixed results: elements of direct democracy are both useful antidotes to the feelings of powerlessness in modern bureaucratized societies and, sometimes, instruments of innovative force. See Henry Ehrmann's discussion of referenda in Ehrmann, 1982.

and current reforms of local government. In the broader sweep of contemporary German history, the Greens are adding an important chapter to the effective exercise of power by the middle class. Having missed an opportunity in 1848, they were bought off in the second empire and frightened into a dictatorship by the economic insecurity and polarized politics of Weimar. The bourgeois of the first several postwar decades created the affluence and constitutional framework that has, in turn, engendered a politically active gadfly within the system.

Green is the color that suggests renewal in nature and an absence of ripeness. Both attributes apply to this movement/party. The renewal sought is on an individual and system level. (Mansbridge, 1980.) Politics in the first person is asserted as part of a mission to shape a new political culture and to reshape old political structures. The absence of ripeness suggests that part of the Greens—certainly a minority—has a cavalier attitude toward the issues of public order, and a disdainful view of "bounded conflict." Major party failures helped the Greens develop their grass-roots support, but the fractionalization, policy disputes, and personal conflicts in the leadership of this new party could make the recent "greening" of West Germany a very transitory phenomenon. In the coming years, West Germany will experience political actions quite unlike these of earlier decades, ranging from all forms of civil disobedience and protest demonstrations to Gandhian tactics of nonviolence. It is an unsettling type of politics, but it is unavoidable as part of the "rhetoric" of an ongoing dialogue: "Erst kommt das Fressen, dann kommt die Moral, and nachher kommt die Erfahrung."[11]

APPENDIX I

Party Preamble of the Greens

Adopted, Dortmund, June 1980

What do the Greens want?
We want to offer reasonable and necessary alternatives in all political areas.

The dominant politics is determined by the viewpoint that only constant growth can guarantee the living standard and the quality of life. On the contrary, we Greens say that the qualitative living standard is deceptive, and, in reality, the quality of life is diminishing.

Against the existing one-dimensional growth policies, the Greens offer a program whose goal is the restoration or the preservation of the well-being of humankind. According to our view, only this goal should "grow":

[11] A variant on Brecht: first comes the fodder, then the ideals, and after that, experience.

This goal is supported by four points:
economy and the world of labor
peace in the world
environment and nature
man and society

With our program in these areas we contest the viewpoint that we are only a "single-issue party" which concentrates exclusively on the environment. On the contrary, an ecological politics can only become a reality when all essential areas of human existence in our society and in the entire world are taken into consideration. This is, therefore, absolutely necessary because the ecological crisis is a global crisis which through the worldwide accumulation of nuclear material in the military sphere is further aggravated.

Our politics is determined by the view that the ecological crisis can only be solved through democratic means—that is, with the active assent of the people. We must set about seeking a solution to the crisis soon if we want to prevent an undemocratic solution.

Principles:

Our politics is *ecological* because it gives due priority to the preservation of the natural basis of life for us and future generations, and directs itself to the needs of people and their creative capacity. It sets itself against the exploitation of humankind and nature within the competitive capitalistic economy and in the existing centralized planned economy.

—*Social*, because we feel that people can only confront the ecological crisis when their autonomy and free development can be realized in common, together with others and in harmony with their environment. We uphold the view that the upheavals which the solutions to the ecological crisis may bring should not be made a burden to the working people, the disadvantaged, and the handicapped of this society.

—*Grass roots*, because we stand for direct democracy. Through this method, decisions about public affairs will be the most effectively understood. This form of democracy allows itself to work best more on the local level. We reject the ever-grasping bureaucracy which leaves the citizen helpless against increasing arbitrariness and the growing abuse of power by the economic and state machinery.

—*Nonviolent*, because only in a nonviolent society can the domination of one person over another and the power of one against the others be abolished. In a time which is characterized by the politics of violence and the threat of violence, we support a variety of forms of nonviolent resistance. Such types of resistance are, for example, civil disobedience and active social resistance.

REFERENCES

Almond, G., and S. Verba. 1963. *The civic culture*. Princeton: Princeton University Press.

Baker, K. L., R. J. Dalton, and K. Hildebrandt. 1981. *Germany transformed: Political culture and the new politics*. Cambridge: Harvard University Press.

Barnes, S., and M. Kaase, eds. 1979. *Political action: Mass participation in five Western democracies*. Beverly Hills: Sage Publications.

Beer, S. H. 1982. *Britain against itself: The political contradictions of collectivism*. New York: W. W. Norton.

Berger, S. 1979. Politics and antipolitics in Western Europe in the seventies. *Daedalus* 108: 27–50.

Bermbach, U. 1978. On civic initiative groups. In *Elections and parties*, ed. Kaase and von Beyme. Beverly Hills: Sage, 227–42.

Beyme, K. von. 1982. Krise des Parteienstaats—ein internationales Phaenomen? In *Buerger und Parteien*, ed. J. Raschke. Opladen: Westdeutscher Verlag, 87–100.

Bieber, H. 1982. Deutschland soll ergruenen. *Die Zeit*, Sept. 10.

———, M. Sontheimer, and G. Spoerl. 1984. Abschied von den Bluetentraeumen: Usingen und die Folgen: Die Gruenen wagen die Teilhabe an der Macht. *Die Zeit*, Jan. 27.

———, M. Swelien, and G. Spoerl. 1982. Deutschland soll ergruenen: Umweltschuetzer und Kernkraftgegener, Ultralinke und Konservative: Von der Anti-Partei zur dritten Partei. *Die Zeit*, Sept. 10.

Bock, Thea. 1982. Mit diesem Staat ist keine Natur zu machen, der Weg der Gruenen-Alternativen ins Hamburger Parlament. In *Die Gruenen*, ed. J. Mettke. Reinbek bei Hamburg: Rowohlt, 146–58.

Brandt, W. 1981. Wir brauchen die Oeffnung. *Die Zeit*, Dec. 11.

Braunthal, G. 1983. *The West German Social Democrats, 1969–1982: Profile of a party in power*. Boulder: Westview Press.

Buerklin, W. 1981. Die Gruenen und die "Neue Politik": Abschied vom Dreiparteien system? *Politische Vierteljahresschrift*, Dec., 359–82.

Conradt, D. 1980. Changing German political culture. In *The civic culture revisited*, ed. G. Almond and S. Verba, Boston: Little, Brown, 212–72.

———. 1983. The 1983 federal election: A preliminary analysis. Paper delivered at A.P.S.A., Chicago.

Dahl, R. A. 1982. *Dilemmas of pluralist democracy: Autonomy vs. control*. New Haven: Yale University Press.

———, ed. 1971. *Political oppositions in Western democracies*. New Haven: Yale University Press.

———. 1971. *Polyarchy: Participation and opposition*. New Haven: Yale University Press.

———, ed. 1973. *Regimes and oppositions*. New Haven: Yale University Press.

Dahrendorf, R. 1969. *Society and democracy in Germany*. Garden City: Doubleday.

Deutsche Presse Agentur. 1982. Gruene Parteien und Wahlergebnisse in der Bundesrepublik. *Hintergrund: Archiv- und Informations-material*, Das Gruene Spektrum, Teil II: Sept. 13.

Edinger, L. 1977. *Politics in Germany*. Boston: Little, Brown.

Ehrmann, H. 1982. *Politics in France.* Boston: Little, Brown.

Ellwein, T. 1982. Politische Verhaltenslehre heute. In *Buerger und Parteien*, ed. J. Raschke. Opladen: Westdeutscher Verlag, 1204–16.

Eschenburg, T. 1982. Ungeduld mit dem Rechtsstaat. *Die Zeit*, Sept. 3.

Frankland, E. G. 1983. Interpreting the "Green" phenomenon in West German politics. Paper delivered at the American Political Science Association Meeting, Chicago.

Greiffenhagen, M., S. Greiffenhagen, and R. Praetorius, eds. 1981. *Handwoerterbuch zur politischen Kultur der Bundesrepublik Deutschland.* Opladen: Westdeutscher Verlag.

———, and S. Greiffenhagen. 1979. *Ein schwieriges Vaterland: Zur politischen Kultur Deutschlands.* Munich: List Verlag.

Grosser, A. 1971. *Germany in our time.* New York: Praeger.

Guellner, M. 1983. Zwischen Stabilitaet und Wandel: Das politische System nach dem 6 Maerz 1983. *Die Zeit*, March 6.

Guggenberger, B. 1980. *Buergerinitiativen in der Parteiendemokratie.* Stuttgart: Kohlhammer.

———. 1982. Buergerinitiativen: Krisensymptom oder Ergaenzung des Systems der Volksparteien? In *Buerger und Parteien*, ed. J. Raschke. Opladen: Westdeutscher Verlag, 190–203.

Habermas, J. 1979. *Stichworte zur geistigen Situation der Zeit.* Frankfurt: Suhrkamp Verlag.

Harenberg, W. 1982. Sicherer Platz links von der S.P.D.? Die Waehler der Gruenen in den Daten der Demokratie. In *Die Gruenen*, ed. J. Mettke. Reinbek bei Hamburg: Rowohlt, 36–50.

Hasenclever, Wolf-Dieter. 1982a. Die Gruenen und die Buerger—ein neues Selbstverstaendnis als politische Partei? In *Buerger und Parteien*, ed. J. Raschke. Opladen: Westdeutscher Verlag, 309–22.

———. 1982b. Die Gruenen im Landtag von Baden-Württemberg: Bilanz nach zwei Jahren Parlamentspraxis. In *Die Gruenen*, ed. J. Mettke. Reinbek bei Hamburg: Rowohlt, 101–19.

Heclo, H. 1981. Toward a new welfare state. In *The development of welfare states in Europe and America*, ed. A. Heidenheimer and P. Flora. New Brunswick: Transaction, 383–406.

Helm, J. 1980. Citizen lobbies in Western Germany. In *Western European party systems*, ed. P. Merkl. New York: Free Press, 576–96.

Hesse, J. J. 1982. Buerger und Parteien auf lokaler Ebene: Die Kommune als Ort der gesellschaftlichen und politischen Integration? In *Buerger und Parteien*, ed. J. Raschke. Opladen: Westdeutscher Verlag, 235–48.

Hoefl, H. 1982. Oekologie in Lederhosen: Gruensein in Bayern. In *Die Gruenen*, ed. J. Mettke. Reinbek bei Hamburg: Rowohlt, 59–68.

Hoffmann, W. 1983. Der neue Bundestag: Solche und andere Gruene. *Die Zeit*, March 11.

Hoplitschek, E. 1982. Partei, Avantgarde, Heimat—oder was? Die Alternative

Liste fuer Demokratie und Umweltschutz in Westberlin. In *Die Gruenen*, ed. J. Mettke. Reinbek bei Hamburg: Rowohlt, 82–100.

Horacek, M. 1982. Zwischen uns und den Etablierten liegen Welten: Die Gruenen im Frankfurter Rathaus. In *Die Gruenen*, ed. J. Mettke. Reinbek bei Hamburg: Rowohlt, 120–34.

Hort, P., and W. Kannengiesser. 1982. Zwischen Marktwirtschaft und gruener Utopie. *Frankfurter Allgemeine*, Feb. 26.

Huber, J. 1981. Wer soll das alles aendern: Die Alternativen der Alternativbewegung. Berlin: Rotbuch Verlag.

———. 1983. Basisdemokratie und Parlamentarismus. In *Aus Politik und Zeitgeschichte*. Bonn: Jan. 15.

Huntington, S. 1974. Post-industrial politics: How benign will it be? *Comparative Politics*, Jan., 163–92.

Inglehart, R. 1977. *The silent revolution: Changing values and political styles among Western publics*. Princeton: Princeton University Press.

———. 1981. Post-materialism in an environment of insecurity. *American Political Science Review* 75, 880–900.

Jaenicke, M. 1982. Parlamentarische Entwarnungseffekte? Zur Ortsbestimmung der Alternativbewegung. In *Die Gruenen*, ed. J. Mettke. Reinbek bei Hamburg: Rowohlt, 69–81.

Kaack, H., and R. Roth. 1980. *Handbuch des deutschen Parteiensystems: Struktur und Politik in der Bundesrepublik zu Beginn der Achtziger Jahre*, Band 2: *Programmatik und politische Alternativen der Bundestagsparteien*. Opladen: Leske Verlag & Budrich GmbH.

Kaase, M. 1982. Partizipatorische Revolution—Ende der Parteien? In *Buerger und Parteien*, ed. J. Raschke. Opladen: Westdeutscher Verlag, 173–89.

Kaltefleiter, W. 1983. Eine kritische Wahl. *Aus Politik und Zeitgeschichte*. Bonn: April 19.

Katzenstein, P. 1980. Problem or model? West Germany in the 1980s. *World Politics*, June.

Kelly, Petra. 1982. *Frankfurter Rundschau*, Oct. 11.

Kirchheimer, O. 1966. Germany: The vanishing opposition. In *Political opposition in Western democracies*, ed. R. Dahl. New Haven: Yale University Press, 237–259.

Kornhauser, W. 1959. *The politics of mass society*. Glencoe: Free Press.

Kramer, J. 1983. Letter from West Germany. *New Yorker*, Dec. 19.

LaPalombara, J., and M. Weiner, eds. 1966. *Political parties and political development*. Princeton: Princeton University Press.

Lauber, V. 1983. From growth consensus to fragmentation in Western Europe: Political polarization over redistribution and ecology. *Comparative Politics* 15: 329–50.

Leinen, J. 1980. Effektive Lobbyarbeit wichtiger als einige Abgeordnete. *Frankfurter Rundschau*, Nov. 5.

Lepsius, M. R. 1974. Sozialstruktur und Soziale Schichtung in der Bundesrepublik. In *Die Zweite Republik*, ed. R. Loewenthal and H.-P. Schwarz. Stuttgart: Seewald Verlag, 263–88.

Lipset, S. M., and R. B. Dobson. 1972. The intellectual as critic and rebel. *Daedalus*, Summer.

———. 1981. The revolt against modernity. In *Mobilization, center-periphery structures and nation-building: In commemoration of Stein Rokkan*. Ed. P. Torsvik, Bergen, Norway: Universitetsforlaget, 451–99.

Loewenberg, G. 1978. The development of the German party system. In *Germany at the polls: The Bundestag election of 1976*, ed. K. Cerny. Washington: American Enterprise Institute, 1–28.

Loewenthal, R. 1970. *Der romantische Rueckfall*. Stuttgart: Verlag Kohlhammer.

———. 1979. *Gesellschaftswandel und Kulturkrise: Zukunftsprobleme der westlichen Demokratien*. Frankfurt: Fischer Taschenbuch Verlag.

———. 1974. *Sozialismus und aktive Demokratie: Essays zu ihren Voraussetzungen in Deutschland*. Frankfurt: S. Fischer.

———. 1981. Identitaet und Zukunft der Sozialdemokratie: Lassen sich die "Aussteiger" integrieren? *Die Zeit*, Dec. 11.

Mansbridge, J. J. 1980. *Beyond adversary democracy*. New York: Basic Books.

Maslow, A. H. 1954. *Motivation and personality*. New York: Harper & Brothers.

Merkl, P. 1980. West Germany. In *Western European party systems*, ed. P. Merkl. New York: Free Press, 21–60.

Mettke, J. 1982a. "Auf beiden Fluegeln in die Hoehe": Gruene, Bunte und Alternative zwischen Parlament und Strasse. In *Die Gruenen*, ed. J. Mettke. Reinbek bei Hamburg: Rowohlt, 7–25.

———. 1982b. Das Kruezberger Modell: Stadtrat Orlowsky und das gruen-rote Buendnis. In *Die Gruenen*, ed. J. Mettke. Reinbek bei Hamburg: Rowohlt, 51–58.

———, ed. 1982c. *Die Gruenen: Regierungspartner von Morgen*. Reinbek bei Hamburg: Rowohlt.

———, and H. D. Degler. 1982. "Wir muessen die Etablierten entbloessen wo wir koennen." In *Die Gruenen*, ed. J. Mettke. Reinbek bei Hamburg: Rowohlt, 25–35.

Mombaur, M. 1982. Im Parlament und auf der Strasse: Die Doppelstrategie der gruenen Niedersachsen. In *Die Gruenen*, ed. J. Mettke. Reinbek bei Hamburg: Rowohlt, 135–45.

Mueller-Rommel, F., and H. Wilke. 1981. Sozialstruktur und postmaterialistische Wertorientierungen von "Ökolisten." *Politische Vierteljahresschrift*, Dec., 383–397.

Murphy, D. 1982. Bibliographie. In *Buerger und Parteien*, ed. J. Raschke. Opladen: Westdeutscher Verlag, 359–66.

———. 1982. Gruene und Bunte—Theorie und Praxis, alternativer Parteien. In *Buerger und Parteien*, ed. J. Raschke. Opladen: Westdeutscher Verlag, 323–41.

———. 1983. "Alternative" Politik und "Sozialdemokratische" Kritik. Einige

Anmerkungen zum Beitrag von Scharping und Hoffmann-Goettig. In *Zeit-schrift fuer Parlamentsfragen*, March, 146–53.

————, F. Rubart, F. Muller, and J. Raschke. 1979. *Protest: Gruene, Bunte und Steuerrebellen*. Reinbek bei Hamburg: Rowohlt.

Narr, W. D. 1982. Andere Partei oder eine neue Form der Politik? Zu Zerfall und Stabilitaet des bundesrepublikanischen Parteiensystems oder den Erfolgs-chancen der Gruenen. In *Die Gruenen*, ed. J. Mettke. Reinbek bei Hamburg: Rowohlt, 242–71.

Nelkin, D., and M. Pollak. 1981. *The atom besieged: Extraparliamentary dissent in France and Germany*. Cambridge: MIT Press.

Nullmeier, F. 1982. Dezentralisation—eine Alternative zum etablierten System? In *Buerger und Parteien*, ed. J. Raschke. Opladen: Westdeutscher Verlag, 342–58.

Oberndoerfer, D., and G. Mielke. 1980a. Die Parteien behielten ihr Profil. *Die Zeit*, Oct. 10.

Oberndoerfer, D., and G. Mielke. 1980b. *Die Landtagswahl 1980 in Baden-Wuerttemberg*. Freiburg: Seminar fuer Politische Wissenschaft.

Offe, C. 1982. Reaching for the emergency brakes. *Die Zeit*, Aug. 20.

Pilat, J. F. 1980. *Ecological politics: The rise of the Green Movement*. Beverly Hills: Sage Publications.

Powell, B. B., Jr. 1982. *Contemporary democracies: Participation, stability, and violence*. Cambridge: Harvard University Press.

Pross, H. 1982. *Was ist heute deutsch?* Reinbek bei Hamburg: Rowohlt.

Raschke, J. 1982. Einleitung. In *Buerger und Parteien*, ed. J. Raschke. Opladen: Westdeutscher Verlag, 9–31.

Rau, J. 1982. Naehrboden fuer rechtsautoritaere Kraefte: Die Gruenen aus der Sicht der S.P.D. In *Die Gruenen*, ed. J. Mettke. Reinbek bei Hamburg: Ro-wohlt, 179–96.

Reichel, P. 1982. Parteien und politsche Kultur in Deutschland. Ein Rueckblick. In *Buerger und Parteien*, ed. J. von Raschke, Opladen: Westdeutscher Verlag, 101–20.

Remmers, W. 1982. Gruen—eine Konservative Grundhaltung. Die C.D.U. und die Alternativen. In *Die Gruenen*, ed. J. Mettke. Reinbek bei Hamburg: Ro-wohlt, 197–216.

Rochon, T. R. 1983. Political change in ordered societies: The rise of citizens' movements. *Comparative Politics* 15: 351–73.

Rose, R. 1980. *Do parties make a difference?* Chatham, N.J.: Chatham House Publishers.

Rosenstein, M. 1978. *Buergerinitiativen und politisches System: Eine Auseinan-dersetzung mit soziologischen Legitimationstheorien*. Lahn-Giessen: Focus-Verlag.

Salchow, R. 1980. Die Gruenen: Von Buergerinitiativen zur Bundespartei. Ham-burg: Deutsche-Presse Agentur.

Sartori, G. 1976. *Parties and party systems: A framework for analysis*, vol. 1. Cambridge: Cambridge University Press.

Scharping, R., and J. Hoffman-Goettig. 1983. Alternative Politik in den Landes-parlamenten? Ideologiekritische Inhaltanalyse von 300 Redebeitraegen "gruener" Parlamentarier. In *Zeitschrift fuer Parlamentsfragen*, March: 146–53.

Schmollinger, H. 1983. Die Wahl zum Berlin Abgeordnetenhaus vom 10. Mai, 1982. *Zeitschrift fuer Parlamentsfragen*, Feb.

Shell, K. 1970. Extraparliamentary opposition in postwar Germany. *Comparative Politics*, July, 653–80.

Sontheimer, M. 1984. Zuchtmeister der Gruenen; Zynisch, drastisch unentbehr-lich; Joschka Fischer, parlamentarischer Geschaeftsfuehrer: Streiter fuer eine Realpolitik. *Die Zeit* Jan. 20.

Szabo, S., ed. 1983. *The successor generation: International perspectives of post-war Europeans*. London: Butterworths.

Verba, S. 1965. Germany: The remaking of German political culture. In *Political culture and political development*, ed. L. Pye and Verba. Princeton: Princeton University Press, 130–70.

Verheugen, G. 1982. Wer einmal wechselt, kann es wieder tun: Die F.D.P. und die Gruenen. In *Die Gruenen*, ed. J. Mettke. Reinbek bei Hamburg: Rowohlt, 217–41.

Vinocur, J. 1982. Germany's season of discontent. *New York Times Magazine*, Aug. 8.

Weil, F. 1981. Post-fascist liberalism: The development of political tolerance in West Germany since World War II. Ph.D. diss. Harvard University.

Willers. P. 1982. Den Tiefschlaf der Altparteien stoeren: Vom Auf und Ab der "Gruenen Liste" in Bremen. In *Die Gruenen*, ed. J. Mettke. Reinbek bei Hamburg: Rowohlt, 159–78.

Wilson, F. 1982. When parties refuse to fail. Council of European Studies Confer-ence, Washington, D.C.

Zeitschrift fuer Parlamentsfragen, Analyses of Land elections, Feb. 1983.

FOUR

The Swedish Five-Party Syndrome and the Environmentalists

EVERT VEDUNG

A Remarkable Debut

When the Institute for Market Investigations, one of the largest public opinion institutes in Sweden, routinely published its poll for April-May 1982, it caused a political sensation. Seven percent of those polled indicated they would vote for the recently formed Environmentalist party in the general election in September. The number was significant because it was well above the 4 percent necessary to gain a foothold in Parliament. It was remarkably high for an organization only a little more than six months old. Surprisingly, the newcomer was running even with one of the two parties currently in cabinet position, the People's party.[1]

In the next poll by the same institute (abbreviated IMU in Swedish) for May-June, the maverick still attracted 6 percent of the potential voters. The scores could not simply be denounced as accidental.

For granting me time to ask questions for this paper, I wish to extend my thanks to Per Gahrton, Jill Lindgren, Roland von Malborg, Ralph Monö, and Ragnhild Pohanka, all prominent members of the Environmentalist Party. I am particularly indebted to Eva Sahlin, who, besides being a knowledgeable and patient interviewee, has been helpful in supplying various kinds of sources. Ove Joanson, Tommy Möller, and Erik Åsard have provided me with information that has been difficult for me to access. Mats Bäck and Olof Petersson offered some precious observations on the manuscript. I also express my gratitude to M. Donald Hancock, who suggested the topic to the editors of this volume and gave them my name, to my sister-in-law Lena Dahlström-King, who at an early stage ameliorated my English, to Ulla Magnusson who provided some perceptive suggestions on the content, to Joseph Heffernan and Dagmar Hamilton for valuable comments, and to Elspeth Rostow, Dean of the Lyndon B. Johnson School of Public Affairs at the University of Texas at Austin, for providing me the most excellent working conditions during the 1982–83 academic year that I spent in this well-managed and academically outstanding institution.

[1] The Environmentalist party—Miljöpartiet—was founded on Sept. 19, 1981, exactly one year before the 1982 election. For its emergence, see Weinberg, 1982: 17ff., and Gahrton, 1980.

Political pundits began to speculate whether the electorate, for the first time in decades, would vote a sixth party into Parliament. Was the inherited five-party system after all not as firmly grounded as it was generally thought to be? Would an unseasoned challenger, embracing an anti-growth, ecological, propeace, no-nukes, feminist, and decentralist political philosophy, create a situation similar to what the West Germans were experiencing with the emergence of the Greens? Would the new party break up the stiff Socialist/Non-Socialist pattern of Swedish party politics? That the party would elicit support among former People's party and Center party voters seemed fairly obvious. But would the party also attract previous Communist voters, contribute to the disappearance of the latter from Parliament and thereby drastically reduce the chances for a Social Democratic comeback in cabinet position?

Certainly, a sudden change in some opinion scores for an obscure little party raised important questions. To understand their real significance—the scope of the sensation—we must take a closer look at front lines and confrontation patterns in the Swedish party system.

THE SWEDISH FIVE-PARTY SYNDROME

The party systems of the 1960s reflect, with few but significant exceptions, the cleavage structures of the 1920s. . . . An amazing number of parties which had established themselves by the end of World War I survived not only the onslaughts of Fascism and National Socialism but also another world war and a series of profound changes in the social and cultural structure of the policies they were part of.

At least superficially, this statement by Seymour Martin Lipset and Stein Rokkan in an overview of cleavages in Western political systems, is as applicable to the Swedish constellation of five competing parties in 1982 as it was when the political sociologists presented their famous observation fifteen years earlier (Lipset and Rokkan, 1967: 50f). The five-party configuration, as it existed in the beginning of the 1980s, emerged at the end of World War I in the wake of the accomplishment of universal and equal suffrage from men and women and a fully consummated parliamentary system of government. Since the early 1920s, the number five has assumed the guise of a mystic, Pythagorean number in Swedish party politics.

Although fairly old and stable, the five-party syndrome—in the sense of an ingrained, long-lived institutional pattern—has not always dominated Swedish political life. In the early years of this century, the country was actually a two-party state. The struggle between Conservatives and Liberals on the extension of suffrage rights and on Norway's position in the union with Sweden dominated the scene. This balance changed when universal and equal manhood suffrage to the second chamber (and maximization to forty the number of personal votes in elections to local assemblies forming electoral colleges for the First Chamber) was decided upon in 1907–1909 and applied for the first time in the 1911 election. At that point, the Social Democratic party began its phenomenal rise from obscurity to stardom. The bipartite pattern was succeeded by a tripartite division.

The roots of the Conservative party go back to several agrarian, protectionist, nationalist, and generally conservative parties that had emerged in Parliament during the latter quarter of the nineteenth century. A country-wide party was formed in 1904.

The Liberal national organization is two years older than its Conservative counterpart. It was preceded by a loose grouping in Parliament, which became organized as a parliamentary party in the year 1900. The Liberal organizations were rooted in the enfranchisement, temperance, and nonconformist popular movements that had emerged during the latter half of the nineteenth century.

The oldest of the three is the Social Democratic party, which was founded in 1889. However, it was not until 1906 that Social Democratic members of Parliament formed a parliamentary party.

The first sign of a weakening of the three-party structure came in 1913 with the formation of the Swedish Agrarian party. One year later, it was followed by another farmers' party, the Agrarian party. In 1917, each of the two young farmers' organizations won their first seats in Parliament. In 1921, finally, the Agrarian party was born through a merger of the two farmers' parties.

Simultaneously, a development had begun within the ranks of the Social Democrats which culminated in the formation of a Communist party. In May 1917—a few months before the October revolution in Petrograd—a group of leftist dissenters, ousted from the Social Democratic party in February, organized the Left Socialist party. In 1921, after changing its name to the Swedish Communist party, it was made a section of the Communist International. Left Socialists opposing the Bolshevization soon returned to their former Social Democratic home.

The current situation with five parties represented in Parliament—a Communist, a Social Democrat, a Liberal, an Agrarian, and a Conservative party—has been developed and clearly visible since 1921.

The prevailing pattern of five competing parties has persisted for so long that people seem to regard it as an ingrained, unalterable syndrome.

A look at its sixty years of existence reveals, however, that it has not been entirely unshakable.

In Figure 4.1, a sketchy overview is provided of the emergence and development of the five-party system. The broken line dividing the chart into a pre- and post-1921 era marks the birth of the modern five-party constellation. The tendency toward further disintegration seems stronger in Figure 4.1 than it actually has been, because parties are not differentiated with respect to their strength in Parliament. To rectify this impression, the development of organizations which have perished or have not been able to win any places in Parliament by running in elections is indicated by various kinds of dotted and broken lines. The designations of the current big five are given in capital letters at the bottom of Figure 4.1, which offers a vivid picture of the strong trend toward fragmentation of the far Socialist left. The proliferation of minute factions was particularly obvious between 1921 and 1937, and after 1967. The post-1967 split-off parties have all failed in the electoral arena. The last of the Communist splinter organizations to win places in Parliament through a general election was the Socialist party in 1936. There have been a few other insignificant disturbances of the neat five-party pattern. The Liberal party split into two factions in 1923 but was united under the present People's party label in 1934. Since 1964, the Christian Democratic party has tried in vain to gain seats.[2]

In a long-range context, these aberrations from the five-party standard emerge as minuscule disturbances which may be safely overlooked. What might seem remarkable in a comparative perspective is that the Swedish five-party system succeeded in avoiding the disruptions and weaknesses that occurred in many other European countries in the 1970s. There was definitely no counterpart in Sweden to the dramatic shake-up that happened in Denmark in 1973, when the new antitax Progress party of Mogens Glistrup swept upon the political scene and in one stroke became the second largest party in the country or, for that matter in Norway, where a parallel antitax party had less success but still found its way into the Storting (see Pedersen, Chapter 10, this volume).

It was against this background of an exceptionally enduring, sixty-year-old five-party arrangement that the remarkably high public opinion scores from the new Environmentalist party appeared and elicited such inordi-

[2] On the development of the party system, see Särlvik, 1974: 372ff.; Back, 1966: 13ff.; Thermaenius, 1935: 13ff.; for the portion on the Communist party, see Rydenfelt, 1954: 46ff.; Sweden is included as a case in the highly informative account in Berglund and Lindström, 1978. For general presentations in English of Swedish political life, see, e.g., Anton, 1969; Hancock, 1972; and Elder et al., 1982.

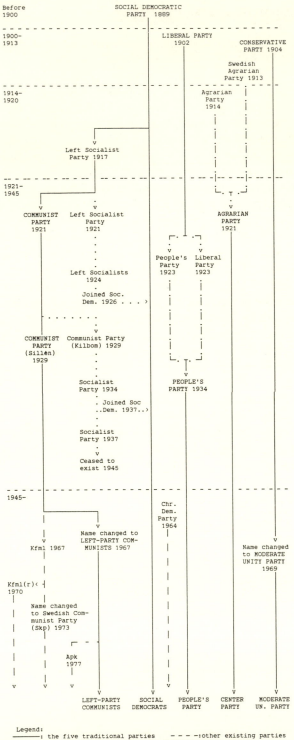

```
Before                      SOCIAL DEMOCRATIC
1900                          PARTY  1889
- - - - - - - - - - - - - - - - - - - - - - - - - - - - - - - -
1900-                              LIBERAL PARTY
1913                                 1902                CONSERVATIVE
                                                        PARTY 1904
                                                 Swedish
                                                 Agrarian
                                                 Party 1913
- - - - - - - - - - - - - - - - - - - - - - - - - - - - - - - - -
1914-                            Agrarian        |
1920                             Party           |
                                 1914            .
                                                 |          |
                                                 |          |
                       v                         |          |
                 Left Socialist                  |          |
                 Party 1917                      |          |
                                                 |          |
- -  - -  - -  - - -- - - - - -  - - - - - - -|- - - -|- - - -
1921-                                         L. T .J
1945    ┌                 .                     .
        v                 v                     v
     COMMUNIST    Left Socialist             AGRARIAN
     PARTY        Party                      PARTY
     1921         1921                       1921
                          .        ┌. .┐
                          .        v   v
                          .    People's Liberal
                          .    Party   Party
                 Left Socialists 1923  1923
                 1924              .     |
                 Joined Soc.       |     |
                 Dem. 1926 . . . >  |     |
                          .        |     |
        . . . . . . .     .        |     |
                 .                 |     |
     COMMUNIST    Communist Party  |     |
     PARTY        (Kilbom) 1929    L. T .J
     (Sillén)         .              v
     1929            .           PEOPLE'S
                 Socialist       PARTY 1934
                 Party 1934
                 . Joined Soc
                 ..Dem. 1937..>
                 Socialist
                 Party 1937
                 v
                 Ceased to
                 exist 1945

- - - - - - - - - - - - - - - - - - - - - - - - - - - - - - -
1945-                            Chr.
                                 Dem.
        |                        Party
        |        v               1964           Name changed
        |    Name changed to      |             to MODERATE
        v    LEFT-PARTY COM-      |             UNITY PARTY
     Kfml 1967 MUNISTS 1967       |             1969
        |                         |
        |                         |
Kfml(r)< ┤                        |
1970     |                        |
  |   Name changed                |
  |   to Swedish Com-             |
  |   munist Party               |
  |   (Skp) 1973                 |
  |       ┌ -                    |
  |       |                      |
  |      Apk                     |
  |      1977                    |
  |       |                      |
  v       v    v        v        v       v        v        v
         LEFT-PARTY  SOCIAL   PEOPLE'S  CENTER    MODERATE
         COMMUNISTS  DEMOCRATS PARTY    PARTY     UN. PARTY

Legend:
————: the five traditional parties    - - -:other existing parties
-.-.-.: nonexisting precursors to the traditional five parties
.......: other nonexisting parties
```

FIGURE 4.1 Development of the Swedish Five-Party System.

nate attention from certain strata of the Swedish public in the spring of
1982.

THE ONE-DIMENSIONAL CHARACTER OF SWEDISH POLITICS

A second tenet that intrigued the media was that the Environmentalist
party might possibly represent a small challenge to another staple of political life in Sweden: the rallying of the parties along one and only one
ideological continuum—the well-known left-right dimension.

Modern Swedish politics is exceptionally one-dimensional. Philosophically, parties align themselves along one single scale, the left-right axis.
This line of conflict concerns the economic struggle between capital and
work, employers and employees, capitalists and proletarians. It also bears
upon the rift between sellers and buyers, owners and tenants, lenders and
borrowers, and contributors and beneficiaries. Parties to the left aspire to
use the powers of government to mitigate, if not put an end to, what is
considered economic exploitation of the worker, to strengthen the position of the consumer against the producer, or ameliorate the lot of the tenant in relation to his landlord. Parties to the right argue that there is no
role for government in the economy, because state intervention hampers
the natural play of the market forces, diminishes freedom of individuals,
and inhibits their initiative and incentive to work.

The left-right dimension, then, summarizes positions on a wide array of
public policy issues concerning, e.g., the degree of government influence
over private enterprise, public or private ownership of the means of production, planned versus market economy, larger or smaller redistribution
of material wealth, more or less extensive social policy programs, and
larger or smaller public sector (Lipset and Rokkan, 1967: 91f.; Harmel
and Janda, 1982: 26ff.).

The actual location of the five major parties along the left-right axis is
illustrated in Figure 4.2.

This mapping of the parties is based upon public statements on policy
goals and means on the elite level (cf. Särlvik, 1974:425). It does not pic-

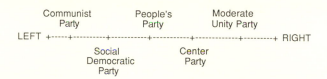
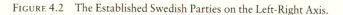

FIGURE 4.2   The Established Swedish Parties on the Left-Right Axis.

ture attitudes that may prevail in the mass electorate. Neither does it show the exact distance between the parties, only the rank order among them.

The location of the parties on the axis has not been entirely stable over time. The People's party and the Center party have changed philosophical position in relation to each other throughout their history. In the 1920s, the Agrarian party was more to the right than the two then-existing Liberal parties. This changed in conjunction with the Great Depression, when the Agrarians in 1933 initiated their close cooperation with the Social Democrats. The new pattern prevailed in the 1940s and 1950s. From the beginning of the 1970s onward, however, it is probably correct to put the Center party slightly to the right of the People's party. It is this situation that is depicted in Figure 4.2. Things may change once more now that the People's party seems to be turning right again.

In the context of the usual left-right cleavage, the Environmentalist party seemed to represent something new and untried. Its concern with ecological goals, decentralization of government, and small-scale technological development did not easily fit into the classical left-right pattern. The new perspective was noted by journalists and received a great deal of media coverage in the early summer of 1982.

Another characteristic of the new party that attracted public attention was its potential threat to a third long-standing feature of the Swedish political scene: the alignment of the parties on the left-right scale into a Socialist and a non-Socialist bloc. The predominant two-bloc pattern of Swedish politics in the 1970s is represented in Figure 4.3.

To start from the left, the Socialist bloc is characterized by a dwarf-giant relationship.[3] The role of the pygmy is performed by the Communists. Since the Great Depression, they have usually commanded only between 4 and 6 percent of the popular vote in general elections. The Social Democratic party is the perpetual giant of Swedish party politics, generally hovering between 44 and 47 percent of the electorate since 1932.[4] The dwarf-giant relationship is made visual in Figure 4.4. The diagram shows the strength of the five Swedish parties computed as a mean of percentage gained in all elections between 1932 and 1979. We may notice, for instance, that the mean support of the Communists has been 5.1 percent as compared to 46.2 percent for the Social Democrats.

During most of the period since the Russian Revolution, the relation-

[3] On cleavages in Swedish politics on the elite level, see Petersson, 1979: 94ff.; Back and Berglund, 1978: 17ff., 132, 157; Berglund and Lindström, 1978: 16ff.; Birgersson and Westerståhl, 1979: 39ff.
[4] With regard to the distribution of votes on different parties, I have strictly followed conventions found in *Statistical Abstract of Sweden* (Statistisk Årsbok för Sverige), published annually by the National Central Bureau of Statistics, Stockholm.

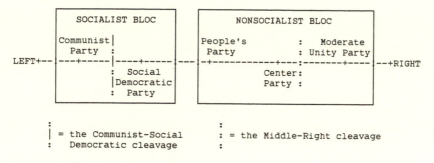

```
       SOCIALIST BLOC              NONSOCIALIST BLOC

     Communist|                 People's        :     Moderate
      Party   :                  Party          : Unity Party
LEFT+--|---+-----|----+-----|---  -+-----------+---:-------+----|--+RIGHT
               :  Social                     Center:
               |Democratic                   Party :
               :  Party
```

```
     :                              :
     | = the Communist-Social       : = the Middle-Right cleavage
     :   Democratic cleavage        :
```

FIGURE 4.3   The Two-Bloc Constellation.

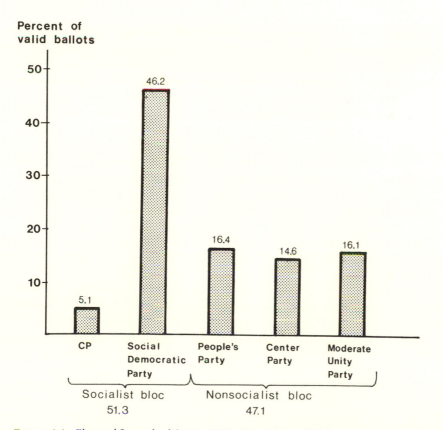

FIGURE 4.4   Electoral Strength of the Established Five Parties, 1932–79.

ship between Socialists and Communists has been similar to what the Bible tells us about Cain and Abel. Organized cooperation has never existed between them. The historical rift on democracy and the role of the Soviet Union has been too deep. To lump the two parties together into a Socialist bloc would, under such circumstances, be entirely unwarranted. This traditional cleavage is indicated by a vertical line in Figure 4.3.

Since the late 1960s, however, a rapprochement has occurred between the two arch rivals. The growing inclination of the Communists to denounce the dictatorship of the proletariat and the leading role of the party of Lenin and Stalin have been important steps that may lead to the emergence of a Socialist bloc. Since the new, fully proportional system for distribution of seats was introduced in 1970, Communist deputies have tended to support Social Democratic governments in most critical situations in Parliament.

Like its Socialist counterpart, the non-Socialist bloc has emerged gradually. Less cohesive and influential, it is made up of three parties instead of two. In contrast with the situation in the Socialist camp, all three parties are potentially equal in strength. This, too, is visualized in Figure 4.4.

A lineal descendant of the old Liberal party, the People's party still refers to itself as "Liberal." The Center party has retained an agrarian base and subscribes to an environmentalist and decentralist philosophy. The Moderate Unity party represents the right wing of Swedish politics. It is the strongest champion of private enterprise and free market economy but has also long ago accepted the basic tenets of the welfare state.

No anti-Socialist party has been able to gain an equally strong position in its bloc as the Social Democrats among the Socialists. In the period after 1932, none of them has ever won more than 25 percent of the votes in a general election.

Furthermore, none of them has been permanently stronger than the others for the entire period since 1932. As far as electoral strength is concerned, they have shifted positions among themselves almost every decade.

From 1932 to 1946, the Right party (in 1969 renamed the Moderate Unity party) was the strongest member of the bloc. At most, it reached 23.5 percent of the electorate in this period. The situation changed in 1946 in favor of the People's party. Until 1968, this Liberal party was the leading non-Socialist force and the main challenger of the Social Democrats. Reaching a summit in 1952, it obtained 24.4 percent of the vote.

After 1968, the People's party declined and for the first time the Center party took the lead in the bloc. The party drew 25.1 percent of the popular vote in 1973. After the Center party assumed cabinet office in 1976 but failed to halt the futher development of nuclear energy, the internal power situation within the non-Socialist bloc once again changed dramatically. This time, the Moderate Unity party gained strong momentum and obtained 20.3 percent of the vote in the 1979 election. In the summer of 1982, it was the largest party in the non-Socialist alliance.

The non-Socialist bloc of the 1970s has emerged only stepwise since the completion of mass democracy and parliamentarism in 1917–18. The latter epic changes were brought about by a coalition of Social Democrats and Liberals, while the Conservatives were bitterly opposed. The constitutional issue solved and democratic rules of the game set, political interest moved toward social issues. With this shift, the classic cooperation between Social Democrats and Liberals ended. The latter came out somewhere in between the Social Democrats on the one hand and the Conservatives and the new Agrarians on the other. The old two-bloc period was succeeded by what may be loosely termed a Social Democrat/Liberal/Agrarian-Conservative three-block era.

This period ended in 1933 when the Agrarians—not the Liberals—made their surprising deal with the Social Democrats on crisis policies. In the periods 1936–39 and 1951–57, they actually collaborated with the Social Democrats in cabinet office.

In the 1960s, in turn, this period of red-green collaboration was followed by a period of efforts on behalf of the Center party and the People's party to form a Centrist alliance, in opposition to Social Democrats as well as to Conservatives. This tendency toward a rift between the right and the middle is indicated by a dotted vertical line in Figure 4.3. The rally toward amalgamation of the two parties in the middle ended in a failure at the 1973 meeting in Uppsala when rank-and-file members of the Center party rejected the idea of a merger.

Contrary to what many people seem to believe, it was not until the 1970s that the option of a non-Socialist three-party government became a realistic alternative in Swedish politics.[5]

In light of the sometimes rigid division into two opposing camps that characterized Swedish politics in the beginning of the 1980s, the Environmentalist party might develop into an unpredictable joker in the political poker game. Its leadership expressly denounced traditional bloc politics and promised to vote from issue to issue. What would happen to old allegiances if this weird party, against all odds, really made it to the national Parliament? Questions like this also lurked behind the growing attention

[5] For the vicissitudes of party strength and patterns of confrontation, see Bigersson and Westerståhl, 1979; Back and Berglund, 1978; Berglund and Lindström, 1978; Bäck, 1980; Särlvik, 1974: 372ff., 381ff.; and Särlvik, 1977: 74. Trends toward "cooperation in the middle" are analyzed in a forthcoming study by Tommy Möller.

devoted to the party in the wake of the IMU polls for April, May, and June of 1982.

THE SOCIAL DEMOCRATIC DOMINANCE OF THE EXECUTIVE

The sudden rise of the Environmentalist party also posed a potential threat to the prospect of the Social Democrats regaining power. Along with the five-party system, the salience of the left-right dimension, and the strong tendency toward two-bloc partition, the Social Democratic dominance of the executive is one of the most conspicuous features of modern Swedish party politics. Since the Great Depression, this party alone has almost consistently controlled the executive branch of government. Every national cabinet between 1932 and 1976 has been dominated by them. It is true that in the years 1936 to 1939, and 1951 to 1957, the country was governed by Social Democratic-Agrarian (Center) coalition cabinets. It is also true that during World War II, all political parties except the Communists formed a grand coalition, a unity cabinet. These periods excluded, however, all cabinet officials have been taken only from the large Social Democratic party. The sole exception to the general rule of Social Democratic control of the executive during this thirty-four year era is the so-called vacation cabinet, fashioned by the Agrarians, which managed to stay in office for one hundred days in the summer of 1936.

Table 4.1 shows the development between 1932 and spring 1982. (This can be studied in Birgersson and Westerståhl, 1979; Bäck, 1980; and Berglund and Lindström, 1978; for a more in-depth discussion of different alternatives to government formation in Sweden, see Ruin, 1968.)

Given the previous dominance of the Social Democrats, the outcome of the September 1976 election was widely noted throughout Scandinavia and the rest of Western Europe. What numerous non-Socialists had dreamt of for decades suddenly had materialized: the Socialist bloc suffered a narrow but clear defeat in a national election and the non-Socialist forces captured a majority of the seats in Parliament. The joy was great among the non-Socialists (for the election of 1976, see Petersson, 1977 and Holmberg, Westerståhl, and Brazén, 1977). As a consequence of the election, a new, three-party, center-to-right coalition cabinet was formed. This government was unique in modern Swedish history. For the first time ever, the non-Socialist triplets succeeded in negotiating a cabinet, leaving room for all three of them and commanding a majority of the seats in Parliament. They united behind Thorbjörn Fälldin, the sheepfarmer from the northern woodlands, leader of the Center party. The new government was

TABLE 4.1   Government Parties in Sweden, 1932–1982

Party in Cabinet Position	Period of Time
Social Democratic party	September 1932–June 1936
Agrarian party	June 1936–September 1936
Social Democratic party Agrarian party	September 28, 1936–December 12, 1939
Social Democratic party People's party Agrarian party Conservative party	December 12, 1939–July 31, 1945
Social Democratic party	July 31, 1945–October 1, 1951
Social Democratic party Agrarian party	October 1, 1951–October 31, 1957
Social Democratic party	October 31, 1957–October 8, 1976
People's party Center party Moderate Unity Party	October 8, 1976–October 18, 1978
People's party	October 18, 1978–October 12, 1979
People's party Center party Moderate Unity party	October 12, 1979–May 5, 1981
People's party Center party	May 5, 1981–

NOTE: The Agrarian party changed its name to Center party in 1957. The Right (Conservative) party changed its name to Moderate Unity party in 1969.

greeted with inordinate expectations and, among political adversaries, dark apprehensions.

From the outset, the novel coalition was ridden by deep disunity on the most pressing policy issue of all, nuclear energy. During the election campaign, Fälldin had led a strong crusade against nuclear fission and publicly promised time and again that nuclear power would be abolished before 1985. The People's party and the Moderates, however, came out strongly in favor of nuclear energy. Serious attempts were made to negotiate a compromise, but they all failed. The cabinet dissolved over this issue after only two years in office (Leijonhufvud, 1979; Vedung, 1979).

In October 1978, the People's party, the smallest in the non-Socialist pack, assumed cabinet office on its own (Petersson, 1979). In the election one year later, the non-Socialists once again succeeded in winning the confidence of the electorate. Their triumph, however, could not have been smaller. They gained 175 parliamentary deputies as compared to 174 for the Socialists.

Again, the non-Socialists decided to form a three-party government. This renewed attempt to unify the non-Socialist parties into a cabinet coalition did not fare much better than the experiment three years earlier. After two years, the Moderate cabinet officers resigned because of disagreement on a tax issue. The People's party and the Center party continued in power (Hadenius, 1981).

Two major political questions in the early summer of 1982 were would the Social Democrats in the September elections take their coveted revenge for the disappointing defeats in 1976 and 1979? And would the four non-Socialist governments between 1976 and 1982 turn out to be only a small parenthesis in a prolonged row of Social Democratic cabinets?

Guidance could be sought from the polls. Those conducted by IMU, referred to earlier in this essay, revealed a pattern displayed in Figure 4.5. It seemed obvious, earlier in the year, that the Social Democrats would regain cabinet position. In February 1982, they were as high as 48 percent and the Communists scored 4.5, i.e., somewhat above the 4 percent required by the constitution for winning seats. This meant a comfortable Socialist majority and a strong Social Democratic government for the next three-year parliamentary period.

But in June the outcome seemed more doubtful. True, the Social Democrats still scored a high 45.5 percent. But the Communists had fallen to 3 percent in April-May and 3.5 percent in May-June, i.e., below the constitutional vote hurdle. The non-Socialists scored only 41 percent in all. Six percent of the interviewees declared themselves in favor of the Environmentalist party. If these numbers were turned into parliamentary seats, the Environmentalist party would gain a pivotal position between the two blocs in the new Parliament. The implications of this for the formation of a future government were far from clear. However, it might well mean that a Social Democratic cabinet would not represent the most expedient way out (IMU's so-called polls on voter sympathies, Institutet för Marknadsundersökningar, Stockholm).

Other studies seemed to corroborate the results of the IMU polls. In March and April 1982, an opinion survey was carried out in the munici-

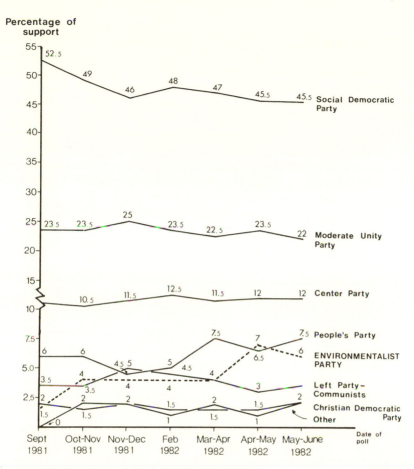

FIGURE 4.5   Party Strength in the IMU Polls in 1981–82.

pality of Lund, an area dominated by Sweden's second oldest university. People were asked how they would vote in the upcoming election.

The findings were striking, almost unbelievable. In an election to Parliament, the Environmentalist party would not only surpass the 4 percent mark but gain more support than the Center party and break even with the People's party (6 vs. 5 and 6 percent respectively). In the municipal election, the Environmentalist party would be even more successful. It would amass more votes than the Center party and the People's party (8 vs. 7 and 7 percent respectively) and acquire a pivotal position between the two blocs (*Sydsvenska Dagbladet*, May 19, 1982).

Several factors, however, contradicted a future development toward a pivotal position in Parliament for the Environmentalist party. The most experienced polling organization in the country, SIFO, consistently published much lower scores for the party than IMU. As a matter of fact, SIFO crammed all parties without representation in Parliament into one single heap labeled "other parties." Under this heading, then, were grouped not only the Environmentalist party but the Christian Democratic party and various Communist splinter groups as well. In spite of this, only between 3.5 and 5 percent of those interviewed by SIFO between March and July 1982 indicated that they would vote for parties other than the traditional five (see the so-called Election Barometers from Svenska Institutet för Opinionsundersökningar—SIFO—Stockholm). This probably meant that the Environmentalist party would not pass the 4 percent limit and that the Socialist bloc would gain a clear majority of the seats.

Two Earlier Attempts to Break the Five-Party Syndrome

History spoke strongly against the newcomer. Since 1936, no sixth party had been able to shatter the five-party syndrome by winning seats in a parliamentary election. Figure 4.6 offers a view of the total backing of minute challengers in national elections since 1932. The Socialist party, the last party outside the big five to capture seats in Parliament, is treated separately in the diagram. The figure shows that after the Socialist party lost seats in the 1940 election, it was not until 1964 that efforts to break the five-party syndrome regained some momentum. Since 1964, new political organizations have been formed as reactions to two perceived failures in the established party system. This may also be seen in Figure 4.1.

First, the alleged neglect of Christian values by the traditional five parties resulted in the formation of the Christian Democratic party in 1964. It attempted to exploit the religious axis, a cleavage base different from the left-right continuum. The party came out strongly against secularization of education in Sweden's all-encompassing system of public schools and the alleged disregard of Christian values in Swedish public radio and television. It demanded stronger support of the family and rejected free abortions.[6] Although the Christian Democratic party has participated in every national election since 1964, it has not been able to attract more than, at best, 1.8 percent of the popular vote.

Second, within the far Communist left, the latent tendency toward or-

---

[6] The booklet *The Christian Democratic Party in Sweden* contains a short summation of the party program. See also Adaktusson and Winerdal, 1979, and Sandström, 1979.

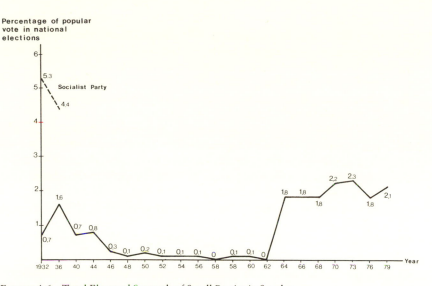

FIGURE 4.6   Total Electoral Strength of Small Parties in Sweden.

ganizational permutation had become manifest again in the 1960s. Policy changes in the Communist party released a chain of reactions that in a decade would quadruple the number of Communist parties in the country. The new organizations may be ordered under the heading "the abysmal left," a phrase coined by Left-Party Communist leader C. H. Hermansson.

In the latter part of the 1960s, the Swedish Communist party began to pursue a more revisionist policy, denouncing the dictatorship of the proletariat and envisaging a peaceful transition to Socialism. To mark this tendency toward Left Socialism, the name was changed in 1967 to the Left-Party Communists. The metamorphosis provoked dissent within the militant left wing of the party and led to the formation of the Marxist-Leninist Communist League, or KFML for short. The KFML was connected with Lenin and Stalin but also with Mao and the Chinese Cultural Revolution. Several factors seemed to favor it: the student revolt in May 1968, the growth of a large, well-organized Vietnam movement, and the sudden wave of illegal strikes that swept the country in 1969–70. However, it experienced a devastating blow in its first election in 1970, obtaining only a microscopic 0.4 percent of the valid ballots.[7]

In October 1970, a few weeks after the election, a minority splinter group within the KFML broke away to the left and formed the Communist

[7] Statistical Abstract, 1971: 393. For a historical account of the KFML, see Rosin, 1978: 46ff.

Party of Marxist-Leninist Revolutionaries, shortened in Swedish to
KFML(r). The "(r)s"—meaning the revolutionaries—attempted to build on
the Communist International tradition between 1924 and 1934, con-
densed in slogans like "Social Democracy is Social Fascism." In 1973, the
remaining majority of the KFML appropriated the designation Swedish
Communist party (SKP) that the Left-Party Communists had abandoned
in 1967 (Pettersson, 1978: 83ff.).

Both of these Communist organizations have been outright failures in
the electoral arena. Although the SKP in 1973, 1976, and 1979 won only
0.4, 0.3, and 0.2 percent of the popular vote, the KFML(r) fared even worse
(Statistical Abstract, 1974: 393 and 1977: 417; Official Statistics of Sweden, General Elections, 1979, pt. 1: 17).

In spite of the break-away of the KFML in 1967, the internal struggle
within the Left-Party Communists continued. Tension between modern
left Socialists and traditional friends of the Soviet Union grew into a ten-
year-long trench warfare. On February 28, 1977, the Workers'-Party
Communists (APK) finally was formed by three orthodox, neo-Stalinist local sections of the Left-Party Communists. It was also joined by two of the
latter's parliamentary deputies. The new party proved unsuccessful in the
1979 elections, losing its two seats and attaining only a paltry 0.2 percent
of the popular ballots (Official Statistics of Sweden, General Elections,
1979, pt. 1: 17; Olsson, 1978: 181ff.).

In the summer of 1982 it could be concluded that none of the attempts
in the last forty years to challenge the inherent stability of the five-party
structure had been successful. How could that fact be explained? At least
part of the explanation could be found in various institutional obstacles
to change.

STRUCTURAL BARRIERS AGAINST UNREPRESENTED PARTIES

Throughout the years, three structural hurdles have worked against the
ascendancy of newcomers to the national, parliamentary scene. They may
be referred to as the constitutional barrier, the funds barrier, and the media barrier.

Although proportional in theory, constitutional obstacles have always
been inherent in the Swedish electoral system. In the bicameral parliament
that existed until the end of the 1970s, the First Chamber was elected indirectly by members of county councils and city councils of cities not included in any county. The term of office was eight years, and only one-
eighth of the chamber was elected each year. This system provided some
overrepresentation for large parties. The Second Chamber was elected di-

rectly every fourth year. Even the proportional distribution of seats in that chamber worked against very small parties.

In the constitutional reform of 1969—first applied in the 1970 election—the bias against smallness was formalized into a new, although not too harsh constitutional barrier. Of the 350 seats in the novel unicameral parliament, 310 were allocated over the 28 territorial constituencies. These permanent seats were distributed proportionally among the contending parties. To counterbalance discrepancies arising from the results of the geographical constituencies, the remaining 40 seats were allocated to secure full proportionality between voting strength and representation in Parliament. To be eligible for these 40 seats, however, parties had to gain at least 4 percent of the total national vote. If they did not pass the 4 percent vote hurdle, they were completely barred from parliamentary representation unless they happened to obtain at least 12 percent of the ballots in a single constituency. However, this only entitled them to seats according to the normal system of distribution in the territorial constituencies, not from the national pool. In certain unhappy circumstances, a party could then reach the 12 percent limit but still not win a seat, because there were no permanent seats left to be conquered in the constituency (Särlvik 1974: 383).

The funds barrier is tied to the technical construction of the party financing arrangement developed by the national legislature in the late 1960s. The amount of public grants received by each party is proportional to the number of seats held by it in Parliament. This means that only parties that have won representation in the legislature are eligible for full participation in the governmental scheme of financial support. This obstacle is all the more important since the extent of public party support is quite substantial. And it is strengthened by the fact that the public subsidies programs established by counties and cities also support represented parties only. Although the seat threshold in counties is only 3 percent of the total vote and there is no percentage hurdle in local elections, the financial rules disfavor beginners (Gidlund, 1983: 11ff., 231ff., and 269ff.).

The media barrier stems from the fact that the rules governing the allocation of time on government-owned radio and television are tied to the 4 percent hurdle. Only parties that have passed that mark and gained seats in Parliament are allowed by the Swedish media authorities to participate in specifically designed election programs. This does not mean that small parties are entirely barred from radio or television. They may receive coverage in newscasts where common rules of newsworthiness are applied and, consequently, where there is no quota system. However, it does mean that they are excluded from an important sector of programs that enjoy considerable popularity among Swedish watchers and listeners.

Together, the constitutional barrier, the funds barrier, and the media barrier put unrepresented parties in a very unfavorable competitive situation compared to that of the traditional five parties.

Now, what political philosophy was the Environmentalist party going to sell to the people of Sweden in an attempt to overcome the institutional obstacles and establish a beachhead in Parliament? In answering this question, emphasis will be placed on what the new party considered the most important ideological failures of the inherited parties and party system.

FIRST ACCUSATION: THE GROWTH FAILURE

The fundamental philosophical point of departure for the Environmentalist party is couched in the accusation that the pursuit of material growth is the worst failure of the present political system. Growth is the overriding goal of all established parties, the Communist and Center parties included. It constitutes a commonly accepted frame within which all political struggle in the country takes place. This push toward sustained growth of the GNP may be referred to as the growth failure. In the theoretical frame proposed in Kay Lawson's essay in the present volume, the Environmentalist stricture is an accusation of a presumable electoral linkage failure. Established parties are not willing to provide the kind of "green," postmaterialist ideological linkage that is needed.

According to the Environmentalists, continued pursuit of material growth will widen and deepen the present crisis of the system. They are persuaded that adverse effects of growth in many cases far outweigh the sum of the beneficial ones.[8]

Nuclear power is the best example of an area where benefits of increased material production are far less significant than the associated risks and drawbacks. To the Environmentalists, nuclear fission is inextricably associated with a ruthless exploitation of the earth's resources, continued industrial growth, and a society built upon highly centralized, large-scale technologies and institutions. What is desperately needed now, they argue, is the development of small-scale, decentralized, local, and robust solutions to societal problems. Furthermore, a large reactor core meltdown may happen, releasing enormous amounts of deadly poisonous radioactivity into the open air. Tremendous research efforts notwithstanding, there is absolutely no safe way of storing high-level radioactive

---

[8] This can be extracted from the official program of the party, published as a separate brochure, but also in the above-mentioned *Nu kommer Miljöpartiet*, 135ff. See also Per Gahrton's contribution to *Nu kommer Miljöpartiet*, 29ff., and my notations from a speech on the party by Per Gahrton at the Swedish Agricultural University, Uppsala, on Dec. 2, 1982.

wastes from nuclear power plants. And plutonium obtained from reprocessing can be used to fabricate nuclear arms. No one can guarantee with absolute certainty that nuclear power is devoid of these three risks. For these reasons, the Environmentalist party strongly embraces a no-nukes policy (pages 2 and 7 in the party program).

SECOND ACCUSATION: THE FAILURE OF A PERVERTED RISK PHILOSOPHY

Another modern technology—the use of pesticides and fertilizers in industrial agriculture—may illustrate the second basic fallacy of the political philosophy of the conventional parties: their stand on risks and risk assessment. Traditional Swedish parties tend to argue that novel technologies and new chemical substances should be employed as long as they have not been proven dangerous. This view is vehemently denounced by supporters of the Environmentalist party. The burden of proof must be reversed, they argue. Potentially dangerous technologies and substances must be proven to be without risk before they can be put to common use. In addition, the burden of proof should be heavier on those who want to market the innovations, and the risk to the community should be virtually nonexistent (Per Gahrton's 1982 speech).

The pursuit of continued material growth, measured in terms of increased GNP, and a perverted risk philosophy are then—according to the Environmentalist party—the main substantive philosophical failures of the traditional parties in Sweden.

THIRD ACCUSATION: THE NUCLEAR POLITICS FAILURE

However, the party system has also failed in a much more immediate sense. Most active members of the young party reacted with growing disappointment to the way the nuclear power issue was handled by the Center party at the end of the 1970s. They had a very hard time accepting the fact that the no-nukes alliance lost the 1980 national referendum on the issue. And they felt contempt and anger for the Social Democrats, who were accused of creating two pronuclear options in the referendum instead of one to avoid an antinuclear landslide.

The unidimensionality of Swedish politics and the pervasiveness of the two-bloc pattern have been underscored earlier in this chapter. The ascendancy in the later 1960s and early 1970s of the new environmental and ecological concerns, particularly the issue of nuclear power, put these traditional features under some stress. The relative positions of the parties on the nuclear issue strongly diverged from the Socialist-non-Socialist bloc pattern. Hereditary foes such as the Social Democrats and the moderates, but also the People's party, came out as strong advocates of nuclear energy. Although supporters at the beginning, the Communist party and the Center party turned and became decidedly antinuclear between 1973 and 1975. It might be suggested that a nuclear-antinuclear dimension was added to the conventional left-right axis. The new situation is depicted in Figure 4.7.

From Figure 4.7 it is obvious that a four-bloc pattern was substituted for the established two-bloc model on the issue of nuclear power. Along with the Socialist and the non-Socialist bloc, two new nuclear and antinuclear blocs emerged. The four-bloc tendency is exaggerated in Figure

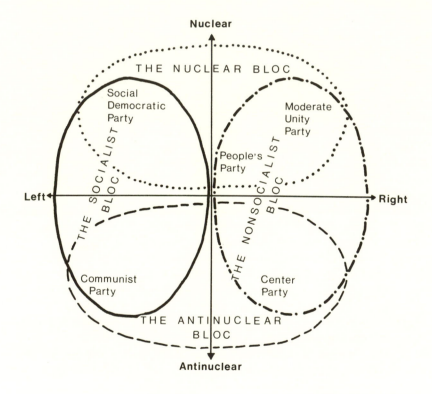

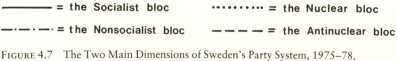

FIGURE 4.7   The Two Main Dimensions of Sweden's Party System, 1975–78.

4.7. The left-right axis was by far the most important one. However, nuclear power created new tensions in the party system, which cannot be explained by reference to the left-right continuum alone (Vedung, 1979: 169ff; Vedung, 1980: 109ff, from where the figure has been adapted).

The nuclear-antinuclear confrontation may be conceived of as part of a more comprehensive growth-ecology dimension. This line of struggle concerns the rift between a political philosophy that generally stresses the beneficial consequences of continued, sustained material growth—more jobs, better housing, better food for lower prices, better transportation, a higher standard of living in general—and one that cannot accept such adverse effects of continued growth as the ruining of the scenic recreational areas through mining, building of oil refineries and construction of airports, highways, or hydroelectric dams; the devastation of fertile agricultural land by the expansion of cities and suburbs; the destruction of natural habitats for fish, birds, and mammalian animals through drainage and filling of wetlands, or the threats to human health and well-being through the dispersion of biocides and pesticides in agriculture and forestry.

This is not the left-right dimension because the issues do not concern the distribution of wealth or influence among those who have more and those who have less. Instead, they bear upon what kind of welfare all of us should have and what our level of welfare should be. The growth-ecology dimension covers issues regarding the level and type of welfare, whereas the left-right dimension concerns the distribution of welfare among members of society.

As early as the end of the 1960s, there were signs of an emerging growth-ecology dimension among Swedish political parties. It seemed that the traditional party system was responsive to several prevailing environmental concerns. Socialists who were against nuclear energy and hostile toward further construction of hydroelectric power plants in wild rivers could vote Communist. Non-Socialist environmentalists could vote for the Center party. There was no great need for an ecological party. But the situation would soon change.

In the 1976 national election, the antinuclear stance of the Center party elicited support from numerous members of the Environmentalist grass-roots movements which had surfaced around 1970. It contributed more than anything else to the narrow victory of the non-Socialists and created the preconditions necessary for the formation of the first pure non-Socialist cabinet in thirty years.

Optimism reigned within the environmental movement. Activists were confident that the Center party would do everything in its might to phase out nuclear power. However, the party commanded only 24 percent of the electorate and felt compelled to compromise with the other two, pronuclear non-Socialist parties in order to assume cabinet position. During the next two years, the Center party was forced to compromise time and again to save the precious, three-party, non-Socialist government. Some progress was made for the antinuclear cause, but nuclear energy was far from shut off, and its further growth was not even brought to a clear stop. Antinuclear people began to believe that contributing to non-Socialist unity was more important to the Center party than fighting nuclear energy.

Even so, numerous Environmentalists again voted for the Center party in the September 1979 election. They could see no realistic alternative. But there was a growing sense that the policy of the Center party in cabinet position had not favored the antinuclear cause in the expected way (Ralph Monö, Ragnhild Pohanka, and Eva Sahlin, all former convenors in the party's political committee, in interviews in July and August 1982). However, earlier that year the situation for nuclear power changed considerably in Sweden. In the beginning of April, a few days after the Three-Mile Island accident, the staunchly pronuclear Social Democrats suddenly announced they would take a more cautious approach. They agreed to the old claim of the Center and Communist parties to hold a national referendum on nuclear power. The other parties followed suit. The referendum was to take place after the parliamentary election in September.

The referendum was held on March 23, 1980, and resulted in a defeat for the antinuclear movement (see Table 4.2). The antinuclear activists had difficulty accepting the defeat. Equally disappointing was the way it came about. The politicking which had taken place before the referendum, when the parties had been negotiating the phrasing of the alternatives to be put forth, caused dismay and outright anger. That two "pronuclear" alternatives were offered instead of one was considered an outrageous tactical speculation by the Social Democrats. For all practical purposes, their option (No. 2) was identical to the one supported by the moderates (No. 1), with the exception of an additional section on public ownership of the nuclear power plants. The antinuclear activists claimed that the latter demand had been consciously inserted to force the moderates to frame an option of their own.

The part common to the two pronuclear alternatives was also a cause for anger. Both included an initial statement that nuclear power would be phased out. However, before the close-down would come about, six more reactors that were either finished or under construction, in addition to the six reactors that were already in use, would be put into operation to diminish dependence on foreign oil. The so-called "nuclear elimination" of these two alternatives obviously implied more than doubling the actual Swedish nuclear capacity. The wording of the "pronuclear" options was

TABLE 4.2   Results of the Nuclear Referendum, March 23, 1980

Options	Supporting Parties	Number of Valid Ballots	% of Valid Votes	Turnout
No. 1.	Moderate party	904,968	18.9	
No. 2.	Social Democrats	1,869,344	39.1	
No. 3.	Center party Communist party Christian Democrats	1,846,911	38.7	
Blank ballots		157,103	3.3	
TOTAL		4,778,326	100.0	75.6

OPTION NO. 1. Nuclear power is to be phased out. . . . To reduce our dependency on oil . . . at most twelve reactors which are now in operation, completed, or under construction are used. There must be no further expansion of nuclear power.

OPTION NO. 2. Nuclear power is to be phased out. . . . To reduce our dependency on oil . . . at most twelve reactors which are now in operation, completed, or under construction are used. There must be no further expansion of nuclear power.

The main responsibility for the production and distribution of electricity must be in public hands. Nuclear power stations and any other future installations of importance for the production of electricity must be owned by the state and the municipalities.

OPTION NO. 3. "No" to the continued expansion of nuclear power.

The phasing out of the six reactors now in operation within a period of, at most, ten years.

looked upon as dishonest double talk to keep lukewarm antinuclear people in line.[9]

The material-growth failure of the political system, combined with the failure of the Center party to halt nuclear power and the failure to dismiss the issue once and for all in the 1980 national referendum, created the conditions necessary for the emergence of an ardently antinuclear, anti-growth, proecological, prosmall-scale and decentralist Environmentalist party in September 1981.

A few years ago, the question was often raised why a Glistrup tax-revolt party—analyzed by Mogens Pedersen in the present volume—had not emerged in Sweden in spite of the fact that our taxes were at least as high,

[9] Maintained by Ralph Monö, Ragnhild Pohanka, and Eva Sahlin in interviews in July and August 1982. A rendering in English of the alternatives in the referendum can be found in Statistical Abstract, 1980: 428.

or maybe even higher, than those of our neighboring Denmark. One probable reason offered was that Sweden's non-Socialist parties had not been able to wrestle power out of the hands of the Social Democrats—in government since 1932—and in cabinet position clearly demonstrate their inability or unwillingness to reduce taxes in the way their Danish brothers had. People longing for lower taxes could still hope that a change would come once the non-Socialists gained power. The reasonable thing to do was to concentrate on the left-right cleavage and hope that the non-Socialists would finally win. There was no need for a new, tax-revolt electoral organization.

This explanation can be viewed in light of one of the two prime hypotheses concerning the emergence of new parties offered by Kay Lawson in Chapter 2. Alternative organizations are formed, she argues, when major parties fail to provide acceptable forms of linkage. Couched in these terms, the Swedish non-Socialist parties offered the form of ideological electoral links on the tax issue that their Danish counterparts had failed to maintain.

The same force seems to have contributed to barring the appearance of new parties in France as well. In that country, however, it was the right that had been in power for a long time while in Sweden it was the left. "The preoccupation with the left-right battle drew attention away from the challenges of alternative organizations at election time," Frank L. Wilson writes in his essay on France in Chapter 19.

But the situation in Sweden would change in 1976. For the first time in forty-four years, the non-Socialist parties came to power. They managed to win the 1979 election as well. And yet, no tax reform turned up. When a proposal finally was presented in 1981, it turned out to be a compromise between the Center party, the People's party, and the Social Democrats. This was too much for the Moderates. Sensitive of the formation of the Progress party in Denmark and fearful that something similar might happen in Sweden, they refused to accept the compromise and left the second three-party coalition. This move paved the way for a great surge in support for the Moderates in the polls and a corresponding weakening of the Center and People's parties. In conclusion, we might say that Sweden has not seen the emergence of any tax-revolt party because the appropriate electoral linkage is purportedly still offered by one of the traditional parties.

But the Swedish political system offers even better support for Lawson's linkage hypothesis on the emergence of new organizations. There is certainly a kind of electoral linkage failure behind the formation of the Environmentalist party. In power, the Center party failed to provide the kind of ideological, postmaterialist electoral linkage that the would-be founders of the Environmentalist party wanted to have. It failed to demonstrate responsiveness in real action to the ecological, particularly antinuclear, views of some rank-and-file party activists and voters. This failure is certainly one factor behind the emergence of the new green party in Sweden.

FOURTH ACCUSATION: THE FAILURE OF CENTRALIST PARTY STRUCTURE

To pursue an antigrowth policy according to ecological principles—an ecopolicy for short—in clear-cut confrontation with the entire political establishment of Sweden, the Environmentalist party has organized its work in an utterly decentralized fashion. Decentralization and local influence are key words in its theory of political organization.

Supporters of the Environmentalist party argue that traditional parties have failed completely to build up organizations allowing for real influence from below. Party congresses, nominally the highest policy organs in all five parties, convene only at two- or three-year intervals.[10] Party boards and, particularly, party leaders have been given extremely powerful positions. This is especially true of parties in office. While exerting strong influence on substantive policy, party leaders also make most of the decision on appointments. They determine who will be included in the delegation to the United Nations, in the most important policy commissions, or appointed to the boards of administrative agencies. The concentration of power in the hands of the party leaders creates a conformist, top-down political climate within the parties (Per Gahrton in his speech of Dec. 2, 1982).

The Environmentalist party has resolutely decided to fashion a new type of antihierarchical and decentralized internal organization. Three tenets emerge as particularly important.

The congress, the highest decisionmaking body of the party, convenes once a year. The intention is, of course, to increase the possibility of the grass roots to influence the leadership of the party.

Another striking idea is collective leadership. The counterpart to the executive committee of the established parties, the political committee, has no chairman or party leader in the traditional sense. Leadership is collective among the eleven members of the committee. Convenorship—a no-

---

[10] The Center party is exceptional with an annual congress.

tion which is preferred to leadership, or chairpersonship—is rotating. In the beginning, "convenors" and "deputy convenors" were elected for only three months at a time. At the end of this brief period, they had to resign and were replaced by other members of the committee. Although convenors are responsible for practical matters with respect to committee meetings, they do not, however, necessarily act as chairpersons during the sessions. Through this rotation arrangement, the founders of the Environmentalist party wanted to assure that influence would be shared by all members of the political committee and to prevent the emergence of a strong and self-sufficient party leader.

After the September 1982 election, however, there has been a clear tendency to elect convenors for somewhat longer periods of time. There seems to be a growing opinion in the party in favor of appointing convenors for one and a half years, at least during elections years.[11]

A third feature, considered antiauthoritarian within the Environmentalist party, is sex equality. For every committee there is a gender quota of six women to five men. This rule has been introduced to impede male dominance.

The national council, which convenes between the congresses, also exhibits some antihierarchical tenets. The council consists of one deputy from each regional party in the twenty-eight constituencies for the Parliament election, all members of the political committee, and representatives from the other committees. However, committee members have no right to vote in the national council. Again, the idea is, of course, that power should be delegated to the regional deputies and not centralized in the party's national bodies.[12]

Sincere attempts are undoubtedly made to implement the fundamental decentralist spirit in all bodies of the party. This philosophy is also of extreme importance for the party's view on how parliamentary work should be handled.

FIFTH ACCUSATION: THE FAILURE OF AN EMASCULATED PARLIAMENT

According to the Swedish constitution, the people are the source of all power and Parliament is the representative of the people. Parliament is, consequently, the highest decisionmaking body in the nation. In fact,

[11] Interview with Jill Lindgren, Jan. 17, 1984.

[12] For this section, see, for instance, Bervå et. al., 1983, and Eva Sahlin's and Inger Paulsson's contributions to *Nu kommer Miljöpartiet*: 63ff., 67ff.

however, most decisions are made long before the issues reach Parliament, and party leaders, particularly those holding major cabinet positions, exert strong influence over them. The Environmentalist party wants to counteract this concentration tendency and "decentralize" power to where it rightly belongs, Parliament.

Important policy programs are prepared by policy commissions, appointed by the cabinet. These task forces provide an arena for compromises between various affected interests. In crucial cases, commissions are made up of politicians from the party or parties in cabinet office and from the parliamentary opposition. Experts from the affected national administrative agencies as well as area specialists from policy institutes, universities, and other institutions of higher learning are included. Advocates for those interest groups and interest organizations which presumably will be affected by the upcoming policies are also included on the commissions. This means that commission proposals usually are well anchored among the interested parties before being disclosed to the public. Compromises are struck and decisions are taken at a very early stage in the policymaking process.

Another striking feature of the Swedish policy process is the consultation procedure. The suggestions of the commissions are sent to numerous interested parties for written reactions. These parties usually include national government agencies, county and municipal governments, major interest organizations, institutions of research and higher learning, and professional associations.

On the basis of the commission scheme and the consultations, a cabinet proposal is worked out. To secure a majority in Parliament, the cabinet may do some negotiating with other parties and make some additional changes in the proposal. Parliament then usually accepts the cabinet bill without major changes. Says Per Gahrton, one of the founding fathers of the Environmentalist party: "Parliament is nothing but a 'powerless chatterbox.' "

Again according to Gahrton, the party's most eloquent spokesman on this issue, all major substantive decisions must be made in Parliament, not in policy commissions, in the cabinet, or simply by party leaders. Party discipline must be weakened, bloc politics softened or, even better, thrown on to the rubbish heap. Members of the Parliament must put less emphasis on prior deals and listen more to arguments and debates on the floor. However, the strategy for affecting a major change in this area is not yet well developed.[13]

[13] See, e.g., Gahrton, 1980: 84ff., and his 1982 speech.

Sixth Accusation: The Failure of Professionalized Politics

To counteract the tendency of making politics a lifetime profession, the Environmentalist party is determined to create a new breed of nonprofessional, amateur parliamentarians.

As it is now, members of Parliament are full-time politicians. Even worse, being a politician is the only occupation many of these public officials have ever known. This is unacceptable, the party argues. A nine-year limit must be set for Parliament assignments to ensure some healthy rotation among its members.

Members of Parliament also often have multiple assignments. Not only are they members of the national Parliament but members of municipal and county legislatures and executives as well. The Environmentalist party wants to put a stop to this. A party member holding a seat in Parliament must not have a seat in municipal or county assemblies or executive committees.

Another solution to the problem of multiple assignment and professionalization would be to make it possible for a member of Parliament to have a leave of absence which would enable him to work outside the national legislature. Leading members of the Environmentalist party have been pondering the idea that two persons—one man and one woman, of course—should be elected to each seat in Parliament. Work-sharing would then be possible and professionalization and concentration of power would be counteracted.[14]

The 1982 Election Failure and Its Causes

At long last, election day was at hand. Would the Environmentalist party be able to fulfill the expectations created by the IMU polling scores in spring and early summer? The answer was no, a very clear no. As it turned out, the party attracted only 1.65 percent of the votes nationally and gained no seats in Parliament. Its score was even lower than that of the Christian Democratic party, which obtained 1.86 percent and made its best election ever. Once more, the five-party syndrome had consolidated its position.

Whether the Environmentalist party failed or not is, of course, arguable. It failed in the sense that it fell short of what many people had reason to expect and that it did not pass the 4 percent constitutional limit.

[14] Party program: 16. See also Eva Sahlin's and Inger Paulsson's chapters in *Nu kommer Miljöpartiet*: 63ff., 67ff.

The prevailing situation in the Swedish Parliament emerges from Table 4.3.

The two best constituencies of the Environmentalist party were Gotland with 2.3 percent, and the city and county of Stockholm with 2.2 percent each. Its worst constituency was the northernmost of them all, Norrbotten, with only one percent of the vote.

In some local elections, the Environmentalist party fared somewhat better in that it succeeded in gaining seats. In 96 of Sweden's 294 municipalities, it won a total of 129 seats. The highest percentages were in Haninge (5.8) and Nynäshamn (5.2) immediately south of Stockholm, and in Lund (5.2) (Statistiska Meddelanden Be, 1982:8; 7f., 36ff.).

Why did the Environmentalist party receive only a paltry 1.7 percent of the total vote? Why did the party fall short of the magical 4 percent mark? We may, of course, explain this failure by referring to the two remaining institutional obstacles confronting small parties in the Swedish political system: the media barrier and the funds barrier. If the Environmentalist party had been allowed to compete with the others on the same terms in the monopoly media, and if the rules concerning eligibility for state funds had been less discriminating against small parties, it might be argued that the outcome would have been more favorable for the challenger.

A third probable cause of the poor outcome may be found in the way the 4 percent hurdle is used in political propaganda. Established parties that seem to be dangerously close to it, use it as a reason to vote for them.

TABLE 4.3 The 1982 Distribution of Votes and Seats in Parliament

Party	Percentage	Seats
Left-Party Communists	5.6	20
Social Democrats	45.6	166
Socialists, Total	51.2	186
People's party	5.9	21
Center party	15.5	56
Moderate Unity party	23.6	86
Non-socialists, Total	45.0	163
Christian Democratic party	1.9	—
Environmentalist party	1.7	—
Other	0.3	—
Small Parties, Total	3.8	—

And to some extent, the strategy seems to work. More importantly in our context, it is exploited by established parties as an argument against supporting an inexperienced beginner. A vote for a tiny competitor is regularly denounced as a *thrown-away vote*, because the party probably will not reach the 4 percent limit anyway. This mechanism was routinely used against the Environmentalist party in its first electoral campaign. The prospects of the thrown-away-vote device were greatly enhanced after the IMU and SIFO election prognoses were published in the media on September 16 and 17. Both revealed that the Environmentalist party was well below the 4 percent cutoff point. The IMU showed 2.9 percent support while SIFO predicted that only two out of one hundred people would actually cast a vote for the party. From this, the media immediately seemed to have concluded that the party would not stand a chance on September 19 (*Dagens Nyheter*, Sept. 16, 1982, and *Svenska Dagbladet*, Sept. 17, 1982). Consequently, during the very last days of the election campaign, no journalist paid any attention to the party and its candidates. This silence probably strengthened the thrown-away-vote factor.

A fourth cause is the organizational factor. The party was founded on September 19, 1981, only—and exactly—one year before the election. This is too short a time to build up a strong party organization which can get across to the voters with a new message.

A fifth, antibloc factor could also have been active. The party consistently refused to be included in either of the two traditional Swedish political blocs. Instead, it argued that it would take a stand from issue to issue in Parliament. Swedish voters are so used to the predominance of the left-right struggle and the concomitant pattern of bloc politics that they cannot fully grasp and subscribe to such an independent attitude. This may also have contributed to the fiasco in the election.[15]

Sixth, the Environmentalist party was exposed to tough competition on its own home turf, the field of ecological concern. That the Center party and, to a lesser extent, the Communist party would marshal all their strength to fight the threat posed by the "green" challengers could not have come as a surprise. More astonishing was the strong competition from the Christian Democrats, which in the campaign came out as astute advocates of a clean and pristine environment. The Environmentalist party, consequently, had obvious difficulties in finding a philosophical niche it could claim as its own.

Finally, the election of 1982 was dominated by worries concerning Sweden's deteriorating economy. Neither the Environmentalist party nor any-

---

[15] A similar explanation for the failure of newcomers is offered by Wilson in his chapter on France in the present volume.

one else succeeded in doing what the Center party had achieved in 1976: making environmental issues—particularly nuclear power—a major theme in mass media and in the campaign in general. The philosophy of ecology was clearly overpowered by the philosophy of growth in the campaign.

In the late 1970s and the beginning of the 1980s, it seemed obvious that the postwar era of unmatched economic growth was over. Industrial stagnation coupled with the energy crisis and a growing deficit in the balance of trade resulted in a weakening of public interest in the environment. "We cannot say no to every source of energy." "Sweden must get on its feet again." "We must get our industry going." Appeals like these abounded in the election of 1982, particularly in Social Democratic propaganda. All this fashioned a political climate in which appeals of decentralization, small is beautiful, and concern for the environment were less effective than they probably would have been three or six years earlier.

REFERENCES

Adaktusson, L., and A. Winerdal. 1979. *Spelet om de kristna väljarna* (The Christian voters' game). Stockholm: Harriers.

Anton, T. 1969. Policy-making and political culture in Sweden. *Scandinavian Political Studies*, 88–102.

Bäck, M. 1980. *Partier och organisationer i Sverige* (Parties and organizations in Sweden). Stockholm: Liber.

Back, P.-E. 1966. Det svenska partiväsendet. *Samhälle och riksdag* 2: 3–153. Stockholm: Almqvist & Wiksell.

———, and S. Berglund. 1978. *Det svenska partiväsendet* (The Swedish party system), Stockholm: Almqvist & Wiksell.

Berglund, S. and U. Lindström. 1978. *The Scandinavian party systems: A comparative study.* Lund: Studentlitteratur.

Bervå, J.-E., et al. 1983. *Miljöpartiet: En studie av organisation och lederskap* (The environmentalist party: A study of organization and leadership), project work in administration, Stockholm School of Economics, mimeo.

Birgersson, B. O. and J. Westerståhl. 1979. *Den svenska folkstyrelsen* (The Swedish government by the people). Stockholm: Liber.

The Christian Democratic Party in Sweden (booklet).

Dagens Nyheter (The Daily News), Stockholm.

Elder, N., et al. 1982. *The consensual democracies? The government and politics of the Scandinavian states.* Oxford: Robertson.

Gahrton, P. 1980. *Det behövs ett framtidsparti* (A futures party is needed). Stockholm: Prisma.

———. 1982. *Speech on the Environmentalist party*, the Swedish Agricultural University, Uppsala. Dec. 2, annotations by Evert Vedung, Uppsala.

Gidlund, G. M. 1982. *Partistöd* (Public subsidies of Swedish political parties). Stockholm: Liber.

Hadenius, A. 1981. *Spelet om skatten: Rationalistisk analys av politiskt besluts-fattande* (The tax game: rationalist analysis of political decisionmaking). Stockholm: Norstedts.

Hancock, M. D. 1972. *Sweden: The politics of postindustrial change.* Hinsdale, Ill.: Dryden Press.

Harmel, R. and K. Janda. 1982. *Parties and their environments: Limits to reform?* New York: Longman.

Holmberg, S., J. Westerståhl, and K. Brazèn. 1977. *Väljarna och kärnkraften* (Voters and nuclear power). Stockholm: Liber.

Institute för Marknadsundersökningar (Institute for Market Investigations, IMU), Polls on voter sympathies. Stockholm: mimeo.

Johansson, L. 1980. *Kärnkraftsomröstningen i kommunerna* (The nuclear power referendum in the municipalities). Lund: Studenlitteratur.

Leijonhufvud, S. 1979. *Ett fall för ministären* (The downfall of a cabinet). Stockholm: Liber.

Lindgren, J. Interview, Jan. 17, 1984.

Lipset, S. M. and S. Rokkan. 1967. Cleavage structures, party systems, and voter alignments: An introduction. In *Party systems and voter alignments: Cross-national perspectives*, ed. S. M. Lipset and S. Rokkan. New York: Free Press, 1–64.

Möller, T. 1985. Nonsocialist cooperation, forthcoming Ph.D. thesis. Uppsala University.

Monö, R. 1982. Interview, June 18.

Nu kommer Miljöpartiet: Om Miljöpartiet av miljöpartister med det officiella partiprogrammet. 1982. (Now comes the Environmentalist party: On the Environmentalist party with the official party program). Stockholm: Timo Förlag.

Olsson, S. E. 1978. VPK 1968–1978: Mellan socialdemokratin och "vänstern" (VPK 1968–1978: Between the social democracy and the "Left"). In *Utanför systemet: Vänstern i Sverige 1968–1978* (Outside the system: The left in Sweden 1968–1978). Stockholm: Rabèn & Sjögren.

Petersson, O. 1977. *Valundersökningar, Rapport 2, Väljarna och valet 1976* (Election studies, report 2, the voters and the election 1976). Stockholm: Statistiska centralbyrån.

———. 1979. *Regeringsbildningen 1978* (The cabinet formation in 1978). Stockholm: Rabèn & Sjögren.

Pettersson, L. 1978. På jakt efter en proletär identitet (In pursuit of a proletarian identity). In *Utanför systemet: Vänstern i Sverige 1968–1978* (Outside the system: The left in Sweden 1968–1978). Stockholm: Rabèn & Sjögren, 83–120.

Pohanka, R. Interviews, June 22, July 1, 1982.

Rosin, B. E. 1978. "KFML/SKP: för ett parti i folkets tjänst" (KFML/SKP: For a party in the service of the people). In *Utanför systemet: Vänstern i Sverige*

1968–1978 (Outside the system: The left in Sweden 1968–1978). Stockholm: Rabén & Sjögren, 46–82.

Ruin, O. 1968. *Mellan samlingsregering och tvåpartisystem: Den svenska regeringsfrågan 1945–1960* (Between unity government and two-party system: The Swedish government issue 1945–1960). Stockholm: Bonniers.

Rydenfelt, S. 1954. *Kommunismen i Sverige: En samhällsvetenskaplig studie* (Communism in Sweden: A social science study). Lund: Gleerups.

Sandström, A. 1979. *KDS—partiet bakom fromhetsvallen* (KDS—The party behind the piety barrier). Stockholm: LT's förlag.

Särlvik, B. 1974. Sweden: The social bases of the parties in a developmental perspective. In *Electoral Behavior: A Comparative Handbook*, ed. R. Rose. New York: Free Press, 371–434.

———. 1977. Recent electoral trends in Sweden. In *Scandinavia at the polls: Recent political trends in Denmark, Norway, and Sweden*, ed., K. H. Cerny. Washington, D.C.: American Enterprise Institute, 73–129.

Statistisk årsbok för Sverige (Statistical Abstract of Sweden). Stockholm: The National Central Bureau of Statistics.

Statistiska Meddelanden. Be 1982: 8, Stockholm: The National Central Bureau of Statistics.

Svenska Dagbladet (The Swedish Daily).

Svenska Institutet för Opinionsundersökningar (Swedish Institute for Opinion Research, SIFO). *Election barometers.* Stockholm: mimeo.

Sydsvenska Dagbladet (South Swedish Daily).

Thermaenius, E. 1935. *Riksdagspartierna,* in the series *Sveriges Riksdag* 2: 17. Stockholm: Riksdagen.

Vedung, E. 1979. *Kärnkraften och regeringen Fälldins fall* (Nuclear power and the resignation of the Fälldin government). Stockholm: Rabén & Sjögren.

———. 1980. Kärnkraften och partisystemet i Sverige (Nuclear power and the party system in Sweden). *Politica* 1: 108–39.

Von Malmborg, R. 1984. Interview, Jan. 13.

Weinberg, G. 1982. Hur miljöpartiet växte fram (The emergence of the Environmentalist party). In *Nu kommer Miljöpartiet: Om Miljöpartiet av miljöpartister med det officiella partiprogrammet* (Now comes the Environmentalist party: On the Environmentalist party with the official party program). Stockholm: Timo Förlag, 17–27.

FIVE

The Italian Radicals:
New Wine in an Old Bottle

ANGELO PANEBIANCO

The history of the new Italian Radical Party (RP), a party that emerged during the sixties and seventies, is instructive from several points of view. First, it will help us understand some essential aspects of political transformations in Western postindustrial societies. Its history, indeed, is also interesting from the theoretical point of view. In many ways, the political history that follows seems to confirm Max Weber's theory on the role of charismatic power (*Economy and Society*, 1968). Weber's view was that institutionalized organizations led by traditional or rational-legal authorities were constitutionally unable to stimulate significant social and political change. Innovation requires the presence of the "revolutionary power" that, according to Weber, could find expression only in charismatic authority (Bendix and Roth, 1971; Eisenstadt, 1968). Weber's analysis, when applied to parties and party systems, implies basically that only *new* political parties—which, being new, are more frequently of the charismatic type—can actually challenge the existing order, or at least introduce new issues into the "political agenda" of the community and promote significant changes in the structure of political conflict.

Furthermore, the case of the RP shows that the rise of a new political protagonist, and challenger to the established parties, depends mainly upon the presence of a *stalemate* situation within the political system at that particular moment. In the absence of certain features that have been characteristic of Italian democracy since World War II, the RP would hardly have been able to penetrate the political system, or at least its impact and challenge would most certainly have been weaker and more circumscribed than they proved to be. After an initial period of difficulty and confusion, furthermore, other political actors will adopt strategies aimed at neutralizing and reabsorbing the challenger, which is what the established parties tried to do to the RP after the election of 1979.

The case of the RP is also instructive because it reminds us that the success of a charismatic party depends not so much on the general evolution of a given political system but rather on the strategic choices of that party's leadership. Even after having achieved considerable success, a political party of this kind may find its political credibility compromised if, for example, its leadership embarks upon a new political project that does not have strong public support. What is more, if its leadership persists in that direction as a matter of conscience (*Gesinnungesthik*), which, according to Weber, is typical of charismatic movements, the potential crisis of that group can deepen. The decision of the leaders of the RP, after the election successes of 1979, to introduce famine in underdeveloped countries as a new issue into the political agenda and to make its pursuit the main goal has progressively weakened the political credibility of the RP. Observers generally believed that public opinion could not be mobilized on this issue.

In more general terms, we can say that the political successes or failures of political organizations depend to a large extent on the personality of their leaders and the role they have assumed. This is only partly true in the case of the more bureaucratic organizations whose leaders maneuver by preestablished rules and who need to negotiate with a plurality of elements within the organization (Mayntz, 1976; Bacharach and Lawler, 1980), which limits their freedom of choice. On the other hand, this principle holds for small nonbureaucratic organizations whose rank and file does not strongly influence the leadership, such as the RP.

NEW POLITICS, OLD POLITICS

In recent years, when analysts have tried to describe the characteristics of European "new politics," they point to the Radical party (Hanning, 1981). But the RP is like a double-headed Janus: it shares many of the characteristics of the "Greens" and other political organizations which came out of the current of so-called "antipolitics"[1] in Europe and the United States. But in other respects it differs in that it has some political, cultural, and organizational affinities with the traditional European radical parties, e.g., *les radicaux de gauche* in France. From a political-cultural point of view the RP represents a synthesis of the old libertarian-democratic tradition and the themes of emerging postindustrial politics. The importance attributed to direct democracy—the RP is often called the "party of the referendum"—the use of the techniques of nonviolence (hunger strikes, civil disobedience), the many political crusades it has un-

[1] The expression "antipolitics" is used here in the meaning of Berger, 1980. The emergence of antipolitics issues and movements seems to be influenced by the postmaterialistic values of postwar European generations. Inglehart, 1977.

dertaken (sexual liberation, antimilitarism, ecology) and, lastly, the *utopian* dimensions of its message, associate this actor clearly with the "new politics," so much so that it has served on several occasions as a model and reference point for other "alternative" groups and organizations in Europe. Other features, however, make it the direct heir of the nineteenth-century libertarian-democratic tradition:[2] its anticlericalism, its opposition to repressive penal laws and the defense of freedom and civil rights. It attributes to Parliament a central role in representative democracy that direct democracy, in the radical perspective, cannot replace but only integrate. In the functioning of the state, it sees the rule of law as a requisite of civilization and rejects the more authoritarian attitudes exhibited by the traditional left.

As I shall try to prove, this political-cultural synthesis,[3] together with a political pragmatism that on various occasions has concentrated all the energies of the party toward specific issues—divorce and abortion above all in the sixties and seventies; disarmament, famine in the world, and opposition to nuclear power plants in more recent times—help explain the persistent disparity between the very small organizational size of the party (see Table 5.1 for membership) and the remarkable political and electoral successes it has often achieved.[4] Summing up, we can say that the role

[2] The radical-democratic tradition in Italy goes back to the middle of the nineteenth century, to the struggles of the first Partito d'Azione, a left-wing group of the Risorgimento, and to the ideological influence of Carlo Cattaneo, one of the first theoreticians of Italian radicalism. In the last decades of the nineteenth century, a Radical party was born. Its most famous leader was Felice Cavallotti. This party led the left opposition in Parliament and in the country at large until the end of the century, when it was overshadowed in popular support by the Socialist party. After the First World War, and up to the advent of facism, Italian radicalism was connected mainly with the names of Piero Gobetti and Gaetano Salvemini. During the fascist era, the main heir of nineteenth-century radicalism was Giustizia e Libertà, a clandestine political group, founded by Aldo Rosselli and other antifascist intellectuals. After the fall of fascism (1943), the merger of Giustizia e Libertà and other political groups gave rise to a new Partito d'Azione that was dissolved in 1947. In 1955 the first Radical party of the postwar period was founded. That party was the direct precursor of the "new" Radical party founded by Marco Panella and other young politicians in the early sixties. On nineteenth-century radicalism, see Galante Garrone, 1973. On the history of the second Partito d'Azione (1943–47), see De Luna, 1982.

[3] This synthesis is reflected in the composition of the RP elite: some of the national leaders come from the student struggles of the early sixties, mainly connected with the traditional issues of Italian radicalism. Other leaders are from the antimilitarist, feminist, and ecological struggles of the late sixties and seventies.

[4] During twenty years and more of political activity, the leaders of the Radical party achieved legalization of divorce, abortion, and conscientious objection to military service, all by working as a pressure group. During the seventies, furthermore, the RP left quite a strong impact on public opinion—about issues such as the legalization of "light drugs," and the defense of sexual and ethnic minorities. Opposition to the illegal role of the intelligence services in Italian politics, against the installation of nuclear power plants, against hunting, industrial

TABLE 5.1   Membership of the Radical Party,
1972–1983

Year	Number
1972[a]	1,300
1973[b]	—
1974[b]	—
1975	1,635
1976	3,827
1977	3,280
1978[c]	1,900
1979	3,309
1980	3,091
1981	2,968
1982[d]	2,300
1983	3,500 (September)

NOTE: In more general terms, the small size of the Radical membership results from three main factors: (1) the very high level of the entrance fees; (2) the fact that the party's membership is *not* renewed automatically every year; (3) the fact that only people who pay the whole entrance fee are classified as members.

[a] There are no reliable data on membership size for the 1962–71 period. As a result, we concluded from direct testimonies that there were no more than one hundred Radical members until the end of the sixties.

[b] For 1973 and 1974, again, there are no reliable data.

[c] The drop of membership in 1978 was the effect of a political decision. In 1978, a temporary "closing" of the party's organization was decided upon as a protest against the "regime."

[d] Between 1981 and 1982, the entrance fees became four to six times more expensive.

played by the Radical party in the Italian political system has been the result of a combination of four fundamental factors:

1. The characteristics of its leadership.
2. The inability of the established parties to implement a fully functioning democracy.

pollution, political corruption, repressive criminal laws, and against the army and the idea of strategic balance were other highlights.

3. The changing political attitudes of large sectors of the electorate brought about by certain postindustrial transformations that, from the seventies on, overwhelmed the Italian establishment.
4. The institutional fragmentation of the political system that for a long time has allowed the RP to utilize many "antiregime"[5] institutional resources.

The leadership characteristics will be discussed in the next section. Let us now examine those aspects of the Italian political system that help us explain the reasons behind the emergence of a political actor with the features of the Radical party.

Sociocultural Modernization, Cleavage Structure, and *Partitocrazia*

Since World War II, Italian society has been characterized by a persistent discrepancy between economic and cultural developments and the political-institutional structures, between an extremely dynamic socioeconomic system which encouraged dramatic changes in the cultural attitudes of large sectors of Italian society and a "paralyzed" political system. Postwar Italian history is, above all, the history of a great transformation, of the extremely rapid and therefore, to a certain extent, traumatic transition from a predominantly agricultural society to an industrial one in the fifties and sixties. At the same time, it is also the history of a highly fragmented and polarized political system,[6] with a poor performance record, persistent government instability, and political stalemate with no turnover of government elites, not to mention the reciprocal veto actions among the principal political actors. While Italian society under-

[5] The expression "antiregime" has a special meaning here. In fact, according to the meaning generally accepted by political scientists (Sartori, 1976), the RP is not an antisystem party. In their messages and in their political practice, they support the republican constitution, parliamentary democracy, and the rule of law. However, the radicals define themselves as an "antiregime" force because in their view, the traditional parties have built a political system very different from the prescriptions of constitutional law, that is, they have transformed the Italian system into a formally democratic but de facto authoritarian "regime."

[6] The Italian party system has been described as an "extreme and polarized system" (Sartori, 1976), characterized by strong ideological polarization due to a fragmented political culture. In terms of a spatial model, the distance between the opposition poles of the left-right continuum is great, and there is a large number (eight, nine) of "relevant" parties which have a "coalition potential" and/or a "blackmail potential." There is a center party, or group of parties in the "center" of the left-right continuum, while the opposite poles are occupied by "antisystem" parties, in the perception of the majority of voters, which cannot be part of any systemic coalition.

went a dramatic modernization process, becoming at the beginning of the seventies, at least to a certain extent, a postindustrial society (Paci, 1982), the political system was unable to keep pace, that is, to produce significant political innovation at the required rate. The result has been, until recently, that one party, a confessional party of populist orientation strongly tied to the Catholic Church, the Christian Democrats (DC), are the dominant party in every coalition attempted since the end of the war.[7]

Furthermore, and largely because of the absence of change in the government elites, the political system has been unable to bring about reforms either in the socioeconomic field or in the state structure. Forty years after the fall of the fascist regime, for instance, the judiciary of the Italian state still depends to a large extent on the laws of the authoritarian period. Many parliamentary bills, with the aim of modernizing the political institutions, therefore were destined never to become law. For many political analysts (Galli, 1975; Pasquino, 1982), the absence of government turnover is the main cause of the generalized phenomenon of political corruption, of the authoritarian attitudes of some state organs, the inefficiency of the public economy, and of the persistent inability on the part of the government to deal with the economic crisis.

From the birth of the democratic regime, this government elite has itself been face to face with the Communist party (PCI), the strongest opposition party. For a long time (until its recent ideological revision),[8] the PCI was understood by the majority of voters to be an antisystem party. Because of the powerful internal and international vetoes against participation by the PCI in national governments, it could never offer a credible "pivot" for an alternative coalition. As a result, during the fifties and sixties, the PCI adapted itself to the stalemate political situation we have described, always on the lookout for compromises and tacit agreements with the government parties. Long before the "rationalization" of this trend in the strategy of the "historical compromise,"[9] the PCI was actively involved in

[7] Since the end of the war, these government coalitions followed each other: "center" coalitions (during the fifties) in which the partners of the DC were the small center parties, the Republicans (PRI), Liberals (PLI), and Social Democrats (PSDI); center-left coalitions (in the sixties and seventies), in which the Socialists (PSI) became part of governments still dominated by the DC; "national solidarity" governments (1976–79), that is, the DC, PSI, PSDI, PRI with the external support of the PCI, and "five-parties" governments (DC, PSI PRI, PSDI, PLI), with the PCI formally in opposition. The same coalition, for the first time with a Socialist premier, was formed after the 1983 elections.

[8] After some years of slow movement in that direction, the PCI has formally broken its alliance with the CP (USSR) as a consequence of the coup d'état in Poland. On the features of the PCI that always distinguished it from the more orthodox PCF, see Blackmer and Tarrow, 1975.

[9] The strategy of the historical compromise, that is the proposed alliance between the PCI

informal parliamentary cooperation with the government majority, mainly in the parliamentary committees (Cazzola, 1974; Di Palma, 1977).

While the PCI presented itself to the mass public as a "revolutionary," Stalinist, pro-Soviet organization, its informal cooperation with government parties formed a stable system of political exchange and, thereby, strengthened the dissociation between "visible" and "invisible" politics (Sartori, 1976): a dissociation, that is, between the official politics of "hard" ideological confrontations among the principal actors, between Communists and anti-Communists, and the daily reality of highly pragmatic and invisible compromises between these same actors.[10] The absence of a credible alternative to DC governments, the high level of "visible" ideological conflict, and the "invisible" collaboration between government and opposition opened up the way to what is called, in a traditional Italian polemical expression, the *partitocrazia*. Partitocrazia means the "degeneration" of a party-based democratic regime (Panebianco, 1978; Pasquino, 1982) and the tendency of parties to control all the principal aspects of social life, thereby reducing their public "accountability," becoming de facto no longer responsible for their actions before the citizens.

In more specific terms, partitocrazia is distinguished by two different, but related factors:

1. The "penetration" or colonization of state organs (bureaucracy, judiciary system, public firms, etc.), mass media, and other crucial sectors of social life by political parties.
2. A "distorted" relationship between government majorities and the opposition; relations are *conflictual* on the visible level and *collaborative* at the invisible, a phenomenon which, for historical reasons, is called in Italy *trasformismo*.[11]

---

and DC and, secondarily, with the PSI, was promoted by the Communist leader, Enrico Berlinguer, in 1973. The basic idea was that a left-coalition government was impossible in Italy—"51% of the seats in parliament is not enough for a stable reform-oriented government in Italy"—and that a grand coalition (among PCI, DC, and PSI) was the only way available for transforming Italian society. After 1976, the "national solidarity" government, with the PCI behind the majority, may be considered an unsuccessful attempt to make up the grand coalition of Communist strategy.

[10] One of the fundamental causes of this "informal" system was the traditionally centralized administrative structure which is controlled by governmental parties. Consequently, its extreme need for central government resources for its local administrations wherever it was in power (mainly in the so-called "red belt" of central Italy), compelled the PCI to cooperate informally with the DC.

[11] Historically, the expression "trasformismo" meant a system of parliamentary relations defined by the absence of clear lines of separation between majority and opposition, a system originally based upon the cooptation of opposition representatives by the government ma-

With regard to the first point, we can conclude that the Italian political system, and the society at large, faced in the fifties and sixties the following situation: while the state, as in all other industrial countries, expanded its area of intervention in the social processes, the government parties expanded their own spheres of influence *within* the state (unlike other industrial countries).[12] A principal catalyst of this process was the political stalemate among the parties, the absence of rotation in the government's elites. Regarding the second point, the relations between the majority and the opposition were influenced both by the formally revolutionary and antisystem features of the PCI—permanently excluded from entering the official government majority—and by the colonization of the state, led by the Christian Democrats. In fact, this process obliged the PCI to adapt itself to the situation, thereby creating a stable neotransformist parliamentary system.

During the seventies, these features of the political system became more and more evident for the following reasons: (1) the birth, in 1970, of the regions, the intermediate level between the central state and local government (regional government had been established by the constitution but had been postponed for more than twenty years); (2) the electoral victory of the PCI in the regional and administrative elections of 1975 (a 7 percent gain); (3) the electoral growth of the PCI in the general elections of 1976 and its consequent entry into the government majority—the so-called "national solidarity" era of 1976–79.

With the establishment of the *regioni*, the "theaters of exchange" between political forces became more numerous, and new opportunities for "party colonization" became available. In 1975, the PCI gained control of many local and regional administrations. Nearly half of the Italian population and the main metropolitan areas were now governed by the Communists. Finally, with the grand coalition of "national solidarity," once more directed by the Christian Democrats with the external support of the PCI, the traditional trasformismo of the parliamentary game was on the

---

jority. This system began officially in 1876 when the so-called Historical Left came into power. The relations between the PCI and the governmental parties after World War II were defined, by analogy, as "neotransformist." Pasquino, 1973. The inability of the political system to produce real "adversary," conflictual relations between majority and opposition in the Parliament is one of the main features of partitocrazia. Originally, the word "partitocrazia" was used mainly by right-wing political writers, who polemicized against the rise of modern mass parties. The radicals gave this term a "left-wing" connotation. Panebianco, 1978.

[12] Originally, the main sector of the parties' expansion within the state apparatus were the public industries. Subsequently, the "hidden" party control extended to the financial system, to the magistracy—or at least, to a great part of it—to the mass media, to cultural organizations, etc.

point of giving birth to an open, "consociational democracy."[13] The failure of this political experiment was the product of many circumstances— economic crisis, terrorism, etc.—but its main cause was a simple fact forgotten by the Communist leaders when they elaborated the strategy of the historical compromise. They forgot that a society of large size and high social and political mobility does not possess the prerequisites of stable consociational regimes.

After 1979 and the defeat of the PCI in the general elections of that year, the political system returned to a stalemate situation. At that point, the PCI changed its official strategy. Its new "goal" became the so-called "democratic alternative," a left-wing government coalition against the DC which in the end was rejected by the Socialists. However, parliamentary relations remained exactly the same as before: the PCI continued to cooperate with the government majority in the legislative process.[14] Its continued role in the "national solidarity" majority of 1976–79 and ideological revision (the severing of the traditional link with the USSR), moreover, transformed the PCI into a "respectable" partner for the other political actors. From then on, cooperation with the PCI in Parliament and local governments became openly acceptable for the government's parties. Its strong position in local governments was confirmed by the administrative elections of 1980 and combined with the traditional strong centralization of the administrative system (Cassese, 1983) to make informal cooperation between the "official" majority and the "official" opposition indispensable. On the one hand, the extreme centralization of the bureaucratic system means that all the financial and other resources needed by the local periphery are controlled by the central bureaucracy and national government. On the other hand, the divisions and endemic conflicts within the government majority necessitate the parliamentary cooperation of the PCI. The rationale of the political exchange is quite clear: the PCI offers the government a pseudo-opposition in Parliament in exchange for the resources that the party needs in order to govern the periphery.

The result is a rather original political structure. During the seventies, the Italian political system departed progressively from the logic of an

[13] On the failure of attempts at consociational democracy in Italy, see Pappalardo, 1980.

[14] On the basis of data collected by the "Parliamentary Research Center," a study center close to the Radical party, during the 1979–83 legislature, the PCI has voted together with the majority of the government on 70.6 percent of the laws passed; it abstained in 16.6 percent of the instances and voted against the government only in the 12.8 percent of the cases. Inside the parliamentary committees, the percentage of the PCI's votes against the government goes down to 5.2 percent. It should be noted that this parliamentary behavior occurred while the PCI was officially in the opposition and proposing a "left alternative" to the governments led by the DC.

"extreme and polarized" party system. At the same time, this system had never been a democracy based on alternative parties or coalitions on the Anglo-Saxon model, nor a consociational democracy. Rather, the Italian political system changed in a different, very peculiar manner: it became an *establishment* (Panebianco, 1983) where a very high level of visible ideological and political conflict among its principal actors goes hand in hand with a sophisticated and quite invisible (to the mass public) system of political bargaining and exchange among these same actors.

Cleavage Structures

Let us look at the Italian political system from the point of view of its cleavage structure (Rokkan, 1970): in this respect, in postwar Italy, the political dynamics has been influenced by four fundamental cleavages with differing intensity at different periods. Some of these cleavages have historical reasons, some are of more recent formation.

1. A *center-periphery* cleavage, due to deep economic and territorial disequilibria (Bagnasco, 1977) and, above all, to the historical division between north and south in its many features and dimensions: state industrialization of the south, clientelistic politics, and periodic upheavals mainly from the right wing against the government. (Graziano, 1980; Tarrow et al., 1978.)

2. A *class* cleavage: a traditional left, both at the political level (Communists and Socialists) and at the union level, confronts the center-right parties and employers' organizations. In reality, the situation is more complex with the division within the left (between Communists and Socialists) and the long presence of the Socialists in the national governments. There is also the entry of the PCI into the majority of the "national solidarity" period, the populist features of the Christian Democratic party (and the Catholic trade unions),[15] and, last but not least, daily cooperation between the left and the center-right in Parliament. All this implies that class divisions in Italy do not correspond exactly to the political divisions between government and opposition. On the contrary, the class divisions cut *across* differing political forces both in government and in parliament.

3. A *state-church* cleavage, well symbolized by the *Concordato*, the agreement between the state and the Catholic Church which was drawn up during the fascist regime and maintained by postwar democratic gov-

---

[15] The trade-union structure in Italy is very fragmented. Besides a myriad of right-oriented or nonpolitical small trade unions, there are three big unions (connected to one another by a confederative agreement): the CGIL, bound to the PCI, the CISL, mainly DC-oriented, and the UIL of the Socialists (PSI).

ernments. Until a few years ago, the privileges that the Concordato guaranteed to the church had an effect, both on state laws—divorce and abortion law, public morality, religious teaching in public schools, the religious presence in public hospitals, etc.—and on the conspicuous financial and economic power that the state reserves to the church in Italy. If we add the presence of a semidominant political party of the confessional type, the permanent overlap between anticlerical and antigovernment attitudes in large sectors of the population (Barnes, 1971) becomes easily understandable.

4. Finally, an *establishment-antiestablishment* cleavage: that is, large sectors of the population exhibit hostile attitudes toward the entire political class. This cleavage is a byproduct of two phenomena: as in other Western countries, it is the result of deep transformations in the political attitudes of some sectors in Italian society (mainly young people and women) toward "antipolitics" attitudes and behavior. (Inglehart, 1979.) It is a reaction to the overbureaucratization of political life and to the drastic changes (demographic, in the job structure, in the education field, in the communication system, etc.) that the social system has undergone. Secondly, this cleavage is also the result of an old—and specifically Italian—problem, namely, a permanent "legitimation deficit" of a political regime whose features we have described: government instability, low political innovation rates, trasformismo, and a state colonized by parties. But the existence of a cleavage does not automatically translate into a conflict, or a set of conflicts over specific issues, within the political arena. A latent cleavage turns into an active one only if there is an elite which can put the relevant issues on the political "agenda." Before the emergence of the Radical party, neither the state/church cleavage nor that of establishment-antiestablishment found a channel of expression in the traditional political elites.

Instead, the major opposition party (the PCI), on the one hand, avoided conflicts with the church because of its "consociational" strategy toward the DC. On the other, the established parties would never raise issues connected with the establishment–antiestablishment cleavage. No traditional party, of course, could deal with the antipolitics issues. And no traditional party would raise the partitocrazia issue, i.e., the problems connected with the degeneration of Italian democracy, because all the traditional actors were involved in this system. In this sense, the established parties can be said to have "failed." Twenty years ago, the Radical party became the political actor that initiated the politicization of these two cleavages. It did so for three reasons: (1) As an outsider, the Radical party was an entirely new actor, without any connections within the established party system. (2) As a "pure" party of opinion, without any links to the material interests of the various occupational groups, social classes, or class fragments, it was free to do so. (3) Its political culture—the synthesis specified earlier between the democratic-radical tradition and postmaterialistic values—allowed it to do so.

This feature of the RP—a "pure" opinion party—helps to explain many aspects of its political behavior. Lacking any "organic" connection with specific social groups, the RP is an organization that does not "articulate" or "represent" material interests. Rather, it tries to mobilize people on the basis of political values, no matter what their position in the system of social stratification may be. As an opinion party, the RP also has great freedom to maneuver because of its independence from material class or specific group interests. For the same reason, its political support among the public is permanently unstable and fleeting. The parliamentary behavior of the RP gives a clear indication of its character as an opinion party: from 1976 until recent times, no draft bill presented by the RP has involved the interests of specific occupational groups. In the last two or three years, there was a partial change in that attitude because the RP began an entirely new crusade for the material welfare of the retired poor. At the same time, it is true that political support for the RP is not completely independent of status and social class. In both the 1976 and 1979 elections, the Radical voters came mainly from the highly educated middle class of urban areas. Young people and women, however, were also strongly represented. Empirical research has shown that the Radical members, too, came mainly from these social sectors (Teodori et al., 1977; Ignazi and Pasquino, 1982). We can say that until recently, at least, the Radical support was coming mainly from the sociocultural groups more sensitive to postmaterialistic values. From this point of view, the analogy with the German Greens is quite evident (Bürklin, 1981). More recently, both the struggle against "hunger in the world" and for the improvement of the welfare of old people may have diversified the Radical clientele.

The two cleavages mentioned present many points of intersection and overlap in the Italian case. It was precisely for this reason that the Radical struggle for divorce and abortion made the state-church cleavage politically relevant and, at the same time, mobilized women's groups together with a more general movement of the postmaterialistic type for sexual liberation.

The overlap between these two cleavages explains much of the larger impact of the Radical crusades of the seventies. Because of its double dimension, the establishment-antiestablishment cleavage, moreover, showed a great potential for mobilizing against partitocrazia not only the traditional sectors of society—as with the referendum against the use of public campaign funds for parties in 1978—but young people and women who are more receptive to a postmaterialist message. The effect was the very strong impact of the Radical appeal on differing social classes and age groups. The ability to influence such heterogeneous social sectors explains why the Radical party, which usually was perceived as a left-wing party (proposing, for instance, a left-wing government against the DC), succeeded on various occasions to find a catchall audience: its political messages were able to influence simultaneously very different sectors of public opinion on the left, in the center, and even on the extreme right[16] of the left-right continuum.[17]

RADICAL POLITICAL ACTION

In order to distinguish it from the Radical party of the nineteenth century and from the political group of the same name which operated from 1955 to 1962, the Radical party is usually called the "new" Radical party. It was formed at the beginning of the sixties (1962) by no more than one hundred people, mainly university students.[18] The original goal of this small group was to reintroduce into the Italian political agenda the anticlerical and libertarian issues of the old historical radical left which was always a very small minority of the Italian political scene. The principal model of the group was Giustizia e Libertà, a left-liberal antifascist move-

[16] The Radicals traditionally receive some audience on the extreme right wing because of their particular position on the problem of neofascism. Following the liberal tradition and unlike all other left-wing parties, the Radicals have always defended the right of all citizens, neofascists included, to freedom of speech and association, and the "equal dignity" of neofascists as with all other political groups.

[17] The relation between Radical politics and position on the left-right continuum is complex and ambiguous. With respect to certain issues such as the PCI's choice of a left-wing "democratic alternative" to the DC coalitions, the RP stands at the extreme left pole of that continuum. However, on many other issues, particularly those connected to the establishment/antiestablishment cleavage, the RP places itself *outside* the left-right continuum. This phenomenon explains its ability to exert an influence on the most politically heterogeneous sectors of the population. In the 1979 elections, for instance, the Radicals gained votes not only from former PCI and PSI voters but also from neofascists (MSI) and some Center party voters.

[18] Officially, the new RP was born between the fall of 1962 and the spring of 1963, immediately after the breakup of the political group of the same name. In 1962 the "old" RP dissolved itself and a large number of its members joined the PSI and PRI, with the purpose of supporting the new center-left government. Only a small wing of the "old" RP, the "radical left" (no more than one hundred members) refused to accept the end of the RP. They inherited its name and preferred opposition to center-left governments and a left-coalition "alternative" to the DC. The members of the "radical left" (afterwards RP) came mainly from university politics, that is, from student associations of the *laïque* tendency, neither Communist nor Catholic, operating during the fifties.

ment of the prewar period. One of the most prestigious former leaders of the movement, the economist and political writer Ernesto Rossi,[19] was, until his death, a sort of "nume tutelare" (a moral inspirer) of the group. From the very beginning, the leader of the group was Marco Panella. Panella came from university politics.[20] With the moral support of Ernesto Rossi, Panella became the real founder of the new party and also the leader who chose from very early on to integrate the old issues of the libertarian-radical tradition with the new issues that in recent times we have learned to call "antipolitics."[21] From the beginning, the group adopted a strategic orientation which favored a "left alternative" to the DC governments and antiestablishmentarian causes.[22]

For the Radical party, 1967 was a year of crucial importance. It was then that the group, consisting of roughly one hundred members, held its first national congress, during which it formulated the articles of its statute, valid to this day: internal organization based on a federal model, annual congresses based on the example of political parties in Britain, direct election of the federal secretary from the floor of the congress, and an "open" structure allowing access to external leagues and associations of

[19] Ernesto Rossi (1897–1967) had been one of the most prestigious personalities of Radical antifascism. He was arrested in 1930 and served nine years in prison as an opponent of the regime. One of the founders of Giustizia e Libertà and the Partito d'Azione, after 1955 he became a member of the "old" RP. In the sixties, he supported and encouraged the "new" Radical party.

[20] In 1957, as president of UNURI, a university student association, Panella and his group launched a political operation which had some influence in national party politics at the time. He led the merger of laïque university students with Communist students into a unique organization. The method followed on that occasion—the organization of alliances on topical problems among the various political sectors—became a constant of the Radicals' political style. From divorce to abortion, and on to the struggle against hunger in the third world, the Radical technique always consisted of assembling ad hoc groups and forces of the most different political colors.

[21] From the beginning, in fact, the new RP characterized itself as the organizer of many political campaigns on sexual liberation, antimilitarism, etc., that had very little to do with historical Radicalism, especially not with the more moderate Radicalism of the fifties. Teodori et al., 1977.

[22] Back in 1959, on the occasion of a controversial article concerning the "old" Radicals that appeared in a Communist daily newspaper, Marco Panella declared himself in favor of a deep "renewal" of the left-wing parties and a left-coalition alternative to the DC. Renewal and transformation of the left, and left-coalition governments were the main strategic issues around which the new RP was built and continue today to be important. Moreover, from the beginning, the RP defined itself as the party of "socialist renewal," a definition involving continuous attention to the internal dynamics of the PSI, a party perpetually divided between its libertarian tendencies and clientelistic attachment to the government on the one hand, and recurrent attempts at a transformation in the Socialist direction, on the other, through pressures from outside the party. The campaign for a Socialist renewal became more vigorous after the birth of the French PS from the ashes of the old SFIO of France.

the single-issue type. In fact, the organizational structure that came out of the 1967 Congress had parallels with the French Radical-Socialist party, according to Maurice Duverger's description, and, for different reasons, with the Labour party in Great Britain. Other aspects of its organizational structure are unique. During the first years that followed the congress, the statutory charter adopted by the Radical party proved important in that it contributed toward the formation of an extremely flexible organization completely free from bureaucratic rigidity, thus facilitating a plebiscitary type of leadership.

Highly original in the party statute of 1967 was the "limited contract" aspect of party membership. Membership was to be renewed every year subject to acceptance of the contents of the general motion of the annual congress. Since the Radical congress motions bound its subscribers only on a limited number of political campaigns on specific issues—to be managed between one annual congress and the next—the practice of *double* membership began: members of other parties were allowed to register as long as they agreed with the annual motion. The "limited contract" and double membership answered different needs: first, they presented the image of a very pragmatic, anti-ideological party which did not tie people to "comprehensive" ideological "choices of life" but only to very specific political issue campaigns. Second, they made it possible for a very small group engaged in certain civil rights campaigns to enlarge its recruitment basis (see Teodori et al., 1977; Gusso, 1982). In the years after 1967, it often happened that other parties' members—mainly Socialists, but also Liberals and sometimes neo-Marxists and members of extreme left groups—were also tactical co-militants. Other statutory features that served to distinguish the RP polemically from the traditional mass parties were the predictable division and autonomy between the parliamentary delegates (not yet existent in 1967) and the party, and the prohibition of rewarding people with offices at any level in contrast to party bureaucracies of traditional organizations. There were also no rules relating to parliamentary discipline on the principle that the deputy represents the people's will and *not* that of the party, and finally a lack of disciplinary measures or committees, or the like.

In 1966, the Radicals had formed the Italian League for Divorce (LID), with Panella as president. The idea was to give institutional form to the struggle for the introduction of divorce in Italy, which had been the main objective of the party for some time. LID was the first formally "external" group federated to the Radical party, a tactic that the party was to use time and time again in the future. From 1966 until the introduction of divorce under pressure from LID in the early 1970's,[23] the Radical party di-

---

[23] Under the pressure of the Radicals, in 1960, a first project for the legalization of divorce

rected its activities entirely to this campaign. Practically no distinction could be made between LID and the Radical party, and this fact led many contemporary political observers into thinking that the Radicals were quite simply a "pressure group" on civil rights issues, or even a single-issue movement. Worth noting at this stage is that from 1967 to 1974, the year of the divorce referendum, the Radical party remained a small group, reaching only 1,000 members at the Turin Congress (1972), while the membership of LID grew so that it became a broad opinion movement, with the support also of the Socialist party and other lay parties.[24]

The divorce issue was most important for the future of the Radical party for the following reasons: there emerged, as a byproduct of the divorce campaign, a singular way of conducting politics which the Radical party has not abandoned to this day. What distinguishes the RP's behavior is its capacity to concentrate all its efforts on only a few specific issues there and then as it takes them up. It called itself a *political party*, but its methods were those of single-issue movements. Furthermore, the success of the divorce referendum, to which even the PCI was forced to give its support, was a clear demonstration that the left wing could gain majorities on civil rights issues and defeat the Right and the moderates. The Radical party maintained that civil rights issues could serve as the standing point for an alternative political coalition to the Christian Democrats and the church. For strategic reasons, the PCI was against the Radical position, which explains the fact that relations between the two parties have been very strained ever since.

During the 1970s, using LID as its model, the Radical party founded many single-issue associations and "federated" movements: the League of Conscientious Objectors (LOC); the Women's Liberation Movement (MLD), the first feminist group in Italy; CISA, an organization which

---

was officially presented in Parliament by a Socialist deputy. Later, this project was fused with an analogous Liberal (PLI) project. The law was approved by Parliament in 1970. The immediate reaction of some Catholic groups supported by the church led to a campaign for popular signatures (the constitution prescribes 500,000) in order to arrange a popular referendum on divorce. This referendum took place in the spring of 1974, and the supporters of divorce won with 60 percent of the valid votes over the antidivorce forces led by the DC. Actually, the electoral campaign for divorce was led by the PCI *obtorto collo* [with twisted neck], after many unsuccessful attempts to come to an agreement with the DC and the church.

[24] By proposing a "renewal" of the Socialist party, the RP created a fairly stable if informal alliance with some Socialist leaders and many grass-roots Socialist militants. To a large extent, the history of the relations between the RP and PSI is interwoven with the history of the internal struggles among the main PSI factions. To some extent in particular, it relates to the history of fights between the two pro-Communist factions whose leaders were, respectively, Riccardo Lombardi and Francesco De Martino, both hostile to the Radicals and their struggles, and the two anti-Communist factions, led by Pietro Nenni and Giacomo Mancini, which favored the Radical campaigns.

openly practiced illegal abortions as part of its campaign for an abortion law; FUORI, the gay association; the *Amici della Terra* (the Friends of the Earth); the Disarmament League, and others.

In the meantime, the Radical party, which at that time had no representatives in Parliament,[25] resorted to referendums in order to force the ruling groups to come to terms with such issues. In 1974, the Radicals failed to gather the 500,000 signatures necessary for the initiation of eight referendums.[26] In 1975, the Radicals attempted a referendum for the legalization of abortion,[27] this time successfully. The political class was forced to pass at least a fairly restrictive law in 1978, partially permitting abortion, but thereby blocking the referendum itself. The referendum campaigns that followed brought about a referendum for the abolition of government financing of political parties (1978) and for the abolition of the so-called "Legge Reale" for internal security, a law which gave much more power to the police and which the RP considered unconstitutional.[28] There followed more referendums on other issues of political and constitutional importance (1981).[29]

[25] In 1972 the Radicals called the general elections of that year antidemocratic. They burned the ballot papers in a public square at the beginning of the electoral campaign mainly as a protest against the state television policy of excluding political minorities from free electoral broadcasts.

[26] Among referendums proposed in 1974 were the abrogation of the Concordato, the legalization of abortion, the rescission of some military laws and penal laws for "crimes of opinion" (victimless crimes). Many of these referendums were proposed again in the following years.

[27] The gathering of popular signatures for legalization of abortion started in the spring of 1975, and was organized by the Radicals and by the MLD, the Radical feminist association, a few months after the arrest of some Radical leaders who had denounced themselves for the illegal termination of pregnancies. These two events had a strong impact on public opinion and on the birth of a feminist movement which was just beginning to evolve in 1975 as a genuine collective movement.

[28] In both referendums, held in the spring of 1978, the RP found itself practically alone against all other parties. Obviously, the disparity of forces determined the actual defeat of the Radical positions. Anyway, the fact that 23 percent of the voters were in favor of the abrogation of the Legge Reale and 43.7 percent were voting for the abolition of public financing for the parties was unanimously recognized as a heavy "moral" defeat of all traditional parties. However, those two referendums were the only survivors of a "package" of eight for which the Radicals had collected the necessary signatures during 1977. The support for some of these referendum proposals, such as that for abolition of mental hospital laws, declined because Parliament meanwhile passed laws on these specific issues. Some of them (Concordato, crimes of opinion, etc.) were declared "inadmissible" by the Constitutional Court.

[29] In 1981, four Radical referendums were held: complete liberalization of abortion, abolition of life sentences, abolition of gun licensing, and the "demilitarization" of customs officers. On that occasion, the Radical proposals were abruptly defeated, never reaching more than 10 to 12 percent of popular support for each referendum. Some observers have

The RP adopted the strategy of the 1974, 1978, and 1981 referendums in an attempt to wake up Parliament. The inertia and immobility of the parliamentary institution was due to the political equilibrium that had been established among the forces, rendering it incapable of bringing about any really significant or important changes. In this period, Panella also initiated nonviolent protest. He repeatedly practiced civil disobedience—in 1975 for example, he was arrested for smoking marijuana in public places—and long hunger strikes protesting the curtain of silence that (state) television had drawn over Radical activities, and the repressive laws, etc. As time went on, the effect these actions had on public opinion grew progressively more dramatic.

In 1976, the Radical party participated in the general elections for the first time and four Radicals entered Parliament, one of whom was Marco Panella. During the next three years, the Radical party was even more in the public eye and, now in Parliament,[30] they carried on the same campaigns which for years they had conducted outside Parliament. They distinguished themselves also within the left as being the most uncompromising opponents of the tacit alliance between the Christian Democrats and the Communists. In the 1979 elections, the Radicals gained 3.4 percent of the vote, a percentage the new commentators unanimously called a truly fine achievement. From 1979 until the present day, the main issues the Radicals have dealt with have been famine in the third world, antimilitarism, opposition to nuclear power plants, and old people's welfare, each addressed in their characteristic style.

Among the main Radical initiatives of this period were the following: an international "manifesto" on hunger, signed by at least fifty Nobel prize winners from around the world; the organization of an annual "Easter March" against hunger in Rome with thousands of people—this march has been repeated every year since 1979; and most importantly, the draft of a bill which would oblige Parliament to save at least three million people in the third world from famine. That project was signed by hundreds of Italian mayors of all political tendencies, by many Catholic priests, and by many prominent intellectuals. On two occasions, this Radical project was discussed by the Italian Parliament. In both cases, the gov-

---

ascribed the beginning of the crisis in the Radical party to this defeat. The referendums were part of a "package" of ten, including those against nuclear power plants and for the abolition of hunting, proposed by Radicals and nearly all declared inadmissible by the Constitutional Court. After the sentence, the Radicals hinted at illegal pressures on the court by some governmental parties.

[30] Since their first entry into Parliament in 1976, the Radicals established the method, never since abandoned, of parliamentary rotation: the replacement of deputies, at midterm of the legislature, with new ones.

ernment majority refused to draw funds from the military budget in order to finance the hunger project. The Catholic Church, the historical and traditional antagonist of Radicalism, on those occasions was the strongest external supporter of the Radical initiative.

Radical Organization and Leadership

The RP represents the unstable marriage of two differing organizational principles: a formally libertarian structure—direct participation of members, no delegates at the RP national congresses, direct election of central organs, complete absence of internal disciplinary mechanisms for party members and for members of Parliament—combined with a charismatic type of organization in the Weberian sense of the word. Although Panella has led the Radical party from the beginning, he has rarely held any formal position in it. Surprisingly enough, from 1972 until 1981, the year in which he became party secretary, Panella was not even a party member. The relationship between Panella and the miniscule group of subleaders and disciples who follow him is clearly of the charismatic type.[31] The distinctive feature defining an organization's charismatic nature is the symbiotic tie-in between its leader and its organizational identity. This is most certainly the case with the Radical party. The majority of both the sympathizers and the general public are united in believing that the Radical party *is* Marco Panella.[32] The tension that exists between the libertarian organizational structure and the charismatic principle is due to the fact that charisma always signifies a high centralization of power. We can thus conclude that there is a fundamental contradiction within the organizational structure of the RP, a contradiction that does not exist in authoritarian charismatic parties in which the formal power structure coincides with effective power, as with the Nazi party's *Führerprinzip*, or "democratic centralism" among the Leninist sects.

There is, therefore, continuous tension between the formal power structure (libertarian) and the effective power structure (charismatic), which accounts for the fact that internal conflict within the RP has always been quite high. We see on the one hand a great deal of power concentrated in

[31] On the organizational characteristics of charismatic parties, see Panebianco, 1982.

[32] From the end of the seventies, all public surveys reveal two constant features in the relationship between the RP and public opinion. First, there is the great "popularity" of Marco Panella who on several occasions turned out to be one of the most popular leaders after the president of the republic, Sandro Pertini. Secondly, there is a strong discrepancy between the number of Radical voters and the very high number of people who sympathize with the Radicals without voting for them.

one person, the party leader—90 percent of the membership regularly vote for him and his proposals at the annual national congresses—while, on the other hand, there exists a democratic-libertarian formal structure which permits anyone who wants to become leader to try the game. There are no institutional mechanisms present within the system that can either suppress or placate conflict. This is the fundamental difference between the RP and bureaucratic political organizations such as the Communist party in which conflicts are, at least to a certain extent, deflated or smoothed over and therefore as a matter of course kept under control by means of its bureaucratic apparatus. Within the RP, which does not possess these means, the leader can exploit his enormous popularity within the rank and file while also exploiting the fact that public opinion identifies him with the party itself. This is why the history of the RP, right from the start, has been a history of battles of the kind described above with splinter groups formed by a series of aspiring leaders all of whom are regularly defeated by Panella at the national congress.

To take an overall view of the situation, we can conclude that the complete freedom of action—as in the choice of issues, strategies and even day-to-day tactics—allowed the original leader of the party is a direct function of the low level of institutionalization of the organization.[33] Despite the large political audience it has acquired, above all from the mid-seventies onward, the party is in fact still very small[34] and totally devoid of bureaucratic tendencies. The Radical party has been entitled to state funding of political parties since 1976, the year in which it obtained parliamentary representation, but the money is not used for the practically nonexistent party machine. Instead, nearly all of it is turned over to the information sector. The RP has tried to counter mass-media censorship by establishing its own national radio station (Radio Radicale) which absorbs most of the public funds which RP has at its disposal. Given these circumstances, the organization of the party remains extremely fragile and there are no signs of bureaucratization. Many of the conflicts which have taken place within the RP, above all in recent years, have involved mem-

[33] On the institutional theory, see Selznick, 1957, and Huntington, 1968. For an application to the case of party organizations, see Panebianco, 1982.

[34] According to organizational sociology (Haldrich, 1979), the *size* of an organization is often a variable manipulated by the leaders. In the case of the RP, the very large disproportion between the smallness of the party and its large *audience*—for instance, in 1979 the RP with its 3,309 members gathered 1,259,352 votes—is a phenomenon that depends to a large extent on a "Malthusian policy" on membership. The logic of this policy is quite clear: conspicuous growth of the membership would have involved a further increase of conflicts inside the party.

bers pressing for a stronger organization, but these attempts have been regularly defeated by the party leader.

DEGREE OF FREEDOM OF LEADERSHIP

There exists, in fact, an inverse relationship between the level of institutionalization reached and the freedom of action the leadership possesses. If the level of institutionalization is high, the bureaucratic apparatus is very large and strong. Its leaders' freedom of action will be heavily conditioned by an organization of imposing dimensions and by a series of bureaucratic imperatives. When the level of institutionalization is low, as is the case with the RP, the opposite is true: there are no organizational restraints, or very few, on what the leadership can do. This is why the Radical party shows no signs of what Michels called "goal substitution" or, rather, the tendency that the survival of the organization may become a goal in itself. Low institutionalization implies that the official goals of the party, as dictated by its leader, are not "distorted" or altered by organizational mechanisms as such. In this kind of party, the organization is not and cannot become an end in itself. The low level of institutionalization within the RP, maintained over its twenty plus years of activity, is closely connected to its charismatic nature. It is the end result of a successful policy adopted by its historical leadership which has blocked all attempts on the part of internal opposition elements to bring about what Weber defined as the "routinization of charisma."

If we are to understand the role the RP has played in Italian society, we must consider the relationships the party has traditionally established between itself and the various movements it has either directly brought into existence or indirectly favored by means of its political activities, such as gay movements, women's liberation, ecological and antinuclear energy associations, antimilitarist associations, movements for the rights of the "ailing," of ethnic minorities, etc. Given its organizational characteristics, not to mention the persistent refusal on the part of its leadership to bureaucratize the party, the RP has always managed, on each occasion, to establish its cultural hegemony over the groups concerned but without ever, or hardly ever, "hegemonizing" the policy or organizational levels. The relationship between the RP and such movements normally develops as follows: first, the RP gives rise to the movement, bringing it into being by means of its political action, as was the case with LOC, FUORI, MLD, etc. At the same time, the RP lends the movement its considerable political and cultural resources. As the movement emerges into the social context, it frees itself of its Radical leadership and becomes an institutionalized organization, as with LOC; or it splits up, forming a series of groups which no longer have ties with the RP, as with the feminist associations; or it turns into a pressure group, as with FUORI, and directs its political requests to the left-wing parties in general. To sum up then, we see that the RP has been and is responsible for the birth of antipolitics movements and maintains their leadership in this primary stage. If the movement is successful and manages to gain widening support, it tends to institutionalize itself, and the traditional left, especially the Communist party, takes control of it, or at least tries to.

The innovative, *dynamic* part of the process is therefore dominated by the RP, the following *static* phase, characterized by bureaucratic management, is dominated by the traditional left. In this sequence of events, one can see the difference between a charismatic organization which, by refusing to bureaucratize itself, maintains the freedom of movement necessary for bringing about new political issues, but also lacks the political and organizational resources necessary for managing the stage of development that follows, and the bureaucratic organizations of the traditional left. The latter cannot bring up "innovative" lines but can instead, during the second phase, "manage" what has already been created.

We now have the elements for understanding the principal differences between the Radical party and other new European political movements, leaving aside the undeniable affinities between the two. The differences between the Radicals and the German Green movement, for instance, are of two types: structural-genetic and cultural. From the genetic point of view, the difference is quite clear. The Green movement was born out of a process of aggregation or federation involving a large number of groups from all over West Germany. This explains to a great extent the sharp ideological differences between various sectors of the German Greens. These differences are reflected in the plurality of its leaders. In Italy's case, the Radical party was formed by a small group which was politically and ideologically extremely homogeneous and gathered round a single leader. We can also say that the German Greens came out of a process of territorial *diffusion* while the Radicals are the result of territorial penetration (Eliassen and Svaasand, 1975).

The second difference, as we have already mentioned, can be explained in terms of the cultural synthesis the Radical party represents between the antipolitics issues and the democratic and libertarian tradition. As far as the Greens are concerned, by contrast, the political culture of their movement is definitely more heterogeneous. Some sectors of the Green movement have in fact taken the Italian Radicals as their model and have taken from them not only some specific topics for intervention but also some fundamental politicocultural characteristics. Other sectors of the Green movement have gone in different directions: they have blended, or attempted to blend, antipolitics, postindustrial issues with the ideological tradition of the Marxist left: the green-red tendency which today seems to dominate the Green movement in Germany. The cause of this fundamental difference may be attributable to the fact that, while the Italian Radicals, due to their origin, were completely extraneous to the New Left and the student movements of the late sixties, many leaders and militants of the Green movement have come out of that experience and have therefore adapted the neo-Marxist ideology of the movements of the sixties to the priorities of "political ecology" and other new issues.

Conclusions

Once the initial phase of inertia and disorientation had been overcome, the established parties reacted to the Radical challenge, particularly after 1979, by adopting various counterstrategies.

The PCI had major difficulties because of the failure of the "historical compromise" strategy in the mid-seventies. It responded to the Radical challenge by considerably modifying its own political line in a "catchall" direction and trying to adapt the new issues that had been monopolized up to that moment by the Radicals to traditional working-class interests. On ecology, for example, the PCI created the League for the Environment, an ecological organization formally independent of PCI but actually ancillary to it. Similar organizations were devised for the problems of homosexuals, of the feminists, etc. At the same time, the PCI tried to take the "hegemony" on pacifist and antimilitarist groups away from the Radical party, promoting an intense mobilization against the installation of the cruise missiles at Comiso, Sicily.

While the PCI was trying to reabsorb the Radical challenge by taking possession of some issues that were traditionally Radical, the government parties followed a different tack with different instruments and at different times. During the 1976–79 legislative session, the Radicals launched many obstructive bills, against the special penal laws on terrorism, against the increase in public financing of the parties, against increases of the military budget, etc. These negative initiatives were exploited by the progovernment press, that is, practically the entire Italian media, to attribute the image of an "antisystem" party to the Radicals. This operation was shared both by the DC, which was alarmed in part by the effect of the Radical struggle for the "starving" on the Catholic electorate, and the PSI, which wanted to get rid of a dangerous competitor. The PSI carried out its strategy to politically liquidate the Radicals by influencing the mass media under its control and, above all, by playing on the tensions and inner contradictions of the Radical party itself. During 1982, the PSI succeeded in bringing about a small split within the Radical parliamentary group, taking some Radical deputies into its own ranks.[35]

From 1980 on, the parties in power, thanks to their influence on state television and on the daily press, also succeeded in imposing a curtain of silence over most Radical initiatives. With the collaboration of the PCI, which furnished the president of the chamber of deputies, the parties in power also reduced the spaces of institutional maneuver that the Radicals had managed to utilize in the past. This was accomplished by modifying the parliamentary rules as a punitive measure against the minorities, and by urging the Constitutional Court to adopt a restrictive view on referendums. The end result of these complicated counterstrategies, together with the defection of Radical deputies to the ranks of the PSI, was a widely held belief, dating from 1981, that Panella's leadership was weakening and that the Radical party was entering its final crisis. From that moment on, various quarters predicted the imminent disappearance of the Radical party. Aside from the countermoves of the established parties, other factors played a role in the crisis of the Radical party at the beginning of the eighties. Most important was a substantial strategic failure: the elections in 1979, paradoxically, meant not only the electoral success of the RP but also its failure to conquer and transform the PSI in a radical direction. From the beginning of the seventies, this had been the strategic aim of the party and was continuously repeated in the public speeches of the Radical leaders. Only a profound transformation of the PSI, led and "hegemonized" by the Radicals, they argued, could have renewed the left, changed the political system, and opened the way to an alternative government to the DC. The model was, in some ways at least, an analogy to the transformation of the old SFIO by Mitterrand. During the seventies, this appeared to be a realistic design, because the Radicals exerted very strong political and cultural influence on the PSI and their struggles represented a fundamental pole of attraction for many Socialist militants and voters.

The remarkable 1979 electoral success of the RP was not sufficient to trigger a crisis within the PSI and thus permit the Radical conquest of it. Increasing hostility between the two parties ensued instead. Given the failure of that plan, the RP entered upon a period of strategic hesitations, and its political isolation within the left increased as Socialist hostility was added to the traditional Communist attitude toward Radicalism.

[35] Altogether, five Radical deputies of the national Parliament, and one of the European Parliament, passed to the Socialist ranks during 1982, while two other deputies went to the PCI. At the time of the general elections in 1983, only one of these ex-Radical deputies succeeded in being reelected on a Socialist ticket.

A further reason for the Radical crisis in the early eighties was the nature of the main issue to which the RP had now turned—the need to help the starving of the world. At first, the RP seemed conspicuously successful on the international level. The Radicals were able to involve the European parliament in this subject and they had acted, moreover, as a privileged intermediary of the FAO and other international organizations. At the national level, they moved the Parliament, on several occasions, to public debates about the issue. The Radicals themselves succeeded in swaying a large part of public opinion. However, it soon became obvious that the struggle about starvation in the world, precisely because of its inherent characteristics, would not mobilize people with the same intensity as did former Radical struggles (divorce, abortion, etc.). There were objections, several times, inside the Radical party, but Panella refused to give up on this issue, even in the face of the progressive weakening of public support shown by the polls on the Radical party.

On the eve of general elections, in 1983, many political observers thought that the RP was politically and electorally "liquidated." But this was not true. The Radicals instead launched a double attack: they presented their own electoral lists and took part in the electoral campaign and yet, at the same time, advocated abstention as a way of opposing the partitocrazia. In spite of this divided official position, the RP achieved 2.3 percent of the popular vote and eleven seats. Thanks to its propaganda, the number of abstentions and blank and spoiled ballots also increased considerably. In the administrative elections of 1980, the Radicals had not participated and had advocated abstention, with the result that the RP remained a party with representation at the national but not at the local level. In 1983, the presentation of candidates and, at the same time, an official position in favor of popular abstention at the polls, was a combination officially justified by the fact that only in this way was it possible for the RP to participate in the free public television electoral broadcasts. One of the RP seats won in 1983 went to a neo-Marxist intellectual, Antonio Negri, a former leader of an extreme-left group (Autonomia), accused of complicity with terrorists, and imprisoned since 1979 without trial. The Radicals introduced his name into their lists in order to protest against excessive periods of "preventive incarceration" before a regular trial, in Negri's case four years. Negri's election brought him parliamentary immunity and hence automatic release from prison. Public opinion was deeply divided on this case.

It is hard to tell what the future holds for the RP. A new and considerable period of instability of electoral behavior in Italy seems to open the door to any possibility. Perhaps we shall witness the eventual defeat of this pure opinion party without links of any kind to specific social groups, perhaps a huge growth of its ranks. The general evolution of the political system to a large extent will be responsible for the outcome. There was a strong increase in "protest" voting against the traditional parties with the elections in 1983: an increase in abstentions, a rising vote for small protest parties. The weakening of the traditional "hinge" of Italian politics (the DC) brought the heavy electoral losses of the DC without the emergence of an alternative "hinge"—the PCI also had some losses, however contained—which may have opened a new phase of instability and uncertainty characterized by polarization and fragmentation. In 1983, the extreme wings gained and so did the small, intermediate parties. However, whatever the future of the RP may be, the changes it has brought into Italian politics, both in political style and policy content, are here to stay for a long time.

REFERENCES

Bacharach, S. B., and E. J. Lawler. 1980. *Power and politics in organizations*. San Francisco: Jossey Bass Publishers.

Bagnasco, A. 1977. *Tre Italie*. Bologna: Il Mulino.

Barnes, S. H. 1971. Modelli spaziali e l'identificazione dell'elettore italiano. *Rivista Italiana di Scienza Politica*: 123–43.

Blackmer, D. L., and S. Tarrow, eds. 1975. *Communism in Italy and France*. Princeton: Princeton University Press.

Bendix, R., and G. T. Roth. 1971. *Scholarship and partisanship: Essays on Max Weber*. Berkeley: University of California Press.

Berger, S. 1980. Politics and anti-politics in Western Europe. *Daedalus*, Winter: 27–50.

Bürklin, W. 1981. *The "Greens" and the "new politics": Goodbye to the three-party system?* Florence: European University Institute.

Cassese, S. 1983. *Il sistema amministrativo italiano*. Bologna: Il Mulino.

Cazzola, F. 1974. *Consenso e opposizione nel parlamento italiano*. Milan: Giuffre.

De Luna, G. 1982. *Storia del Partito d'Azione*. Milan: Feltrinelli.

Di Palma, G. 1977. *Surviving without governing*. Berkeley: University of California Press.

Duverger, M. 1951. *Les partis politiques*. Paris: Colin.

Eisenstadt, S. N. 1968. *Introduction to Max Weber, On charisma and institution-building, selected papers*. Chicago: University of Chicago Press, ix–lvi.

Eliassen, K., and L. Svaasand. 1975. The formation of mass political organizations: An analytical framework. *Scandinavian Political Studies* 10: 95–120.

Galante Garrone, A. 1973. *I radicali in Italia (1849–1925)*. Milan: Garzanti.

Galli, G. 1975. *Dal bipartitismo imperfetto alla possibile alternativa*. Bologna: Il Mulino.

Graziano, L. 1980. *Clientelismo e sistema politico*. Milan: Franco Angeli.

Gusso, M. 1982. *Il Partito Radicale: Organizzazione e leadership*. Padua: Cleup.

Haldrich, H. E. 1979. *Organizations and environment*. Englewood Cliffs: Prentice-Hall.

Hanning, L. 1981. The Italian Radical party and the "new politics." *West European Politics* 4: 267–81.

Huntington, S. H. 1968. *Political order in changing societies*. New Haven: Yale University Press.

Ignazi, P., and G. Pasquino. 1982. *Da partito-movimento a partito-istituzione?* Bologna: Il Mulino.

Inglehart, R. 1977. *The silent revolution*. Princeton: Princeton University Press.

———. 1979. Political action: The impact of values, cognitive level and social background. In *Political action: Mass participation in five Western democracies*, ed. S. H. Barnes, M. Kaase. London: Sage Publications, 343–80.

Mayntz, R. 1976. Conceptual models of organizational decision-making and their applications to the policy process. In *European contributions to organizational theory*, ed. M. Sami Kassen. Amsterdam: Van Gorkum, 114–25.

Paci, M. 1982. *La struttura sociale italiana*. Bologna: Il Mulino.

Panebianco, A. 1978. Le risorse della partitocrazia e gli equivoci della partecipazione. *Argomenti Radicali* 2: 26–41.

———. 1982. *Modelli di partito: Organizzazione e potere nei partiti politici*. Bologna: Il Mulino.

———. 1983. *I partiti politici italiani fra centro e periferia*. Archivio ISAP, Milan: Giuffre.

Pappalardo, A. 1980. La politica consociativa nella democrazia italiana. *Rivista Italiana di Scienza Politica* A: 73–123.

Pasquino, G. 1973. Il sistema politico italiano fra neo-trasformismo e democrazia consociativa. *Il Mulino* 22: 549–66.

———. 1982. *Degenerazione dei partiti e riforme istituzionali*. Bari: Laterza.

Rokkan, S. 1970. *Citizens, elections, parties*. Oslo: Universitetsforlaget.

Sartori, G. 1976. *Parties and party systems*. New York: Cambridge University Press.

Selznick, P. 1957. *Leadership in administration: A sociological interpretation*. New York: Harper and Row.

Tarrow, S., et al., eds. 1978. *Territorial politics in industrial nations*. New York: Praeger.

Teodori, M., P. Ignazi, and A. Panebianco. 1977. *I nuovi radicali: Storia e sociologia di un movimento politico*. Milan: Mondadori.

Weber, M. 1968. *Economy and society*. Berkeley: University of California Press.

SIX

Civic Action Groups in Switzerland: Challenge to Political Parties?

ROBERT C. A. SORENSEN

Switzerland provides a rich context in which to examine the workings of the political parties of a society in two respects: on the one hand, a particularly prominent position is held by political parties in Switzerland given institutionalization of historical efforts to bridge a variety of linguistic, confessional, class, and regional lines of cleavage and to assure stable and effective government;[1] on the other hand, institutions are available on three geopolitical levels—community, canton, and nation—for direct citizen participation, not only in the election of government officials, but also in decisionmaking on matters of substance and policy through initiative and referendum.[2] The balance between these two dimensions endows Swiss politics with a unique character referred to by some as "semidirect democracy" (e.g., Meynaud 1969). Given the institutions of direct democracy through which the citizenry may vote without reference to party affiliation and given a longstanding tradition of creating a federal executive through a "grand coalition" of the country's major parties, political parties in Switzerland might be seen to suffer a sort of institutionalized qualification of their ability to represent popular concerns and engage in interparty competition. In comparison with the roles of political parties in other advanced industrial democracies, these limitations might be perceived as an a priori case of party failure or a situation which in the long run might erode the existing ties between the parties and the Swiss

The author gratefully acknowledges the financial support of the Conference Group on German Politics, The Center for the Study of Federalism at Temple University, and particularly the Fritz Thyssen Foundation of Köln, West Germany, which enabled him to conduct the research related to this essay. (Unless otherwise indicated, translations are by the author of this essay.)

[1] Much of the literature deals with the "consociational democracy" theme. See, for example, Steiner and Obler, 1977, and Steiner, 1974. In German there is Gruner, 1977.

[2] A good overview is given by Aubert, 1978.

people. In fact, trends of change, especially over the past decade, have engendered growing speculation about the viability of the Swiss constitutional system and, particularly, of the role of the parties in it: declining participation in the elections for the national legislative body has suggested diminishing voter interest in the established parties; repeated popular rejection, through referendums, of policies approved by elected officials leads to conjecture that the Swiss lack confidence in their representatives and government; a rising number of popularly introduced initiatives and referendums further casts doubt on the people's faith in the existing political parties to raise and resolve issues of concern; and declining turnout on initiative and referendum issues has suggested diminished voter interest in public matters in general.[3]

This essay will examine five instances of protest groups organized in the cities of Basel and Zürich in the mid-1970s, whose activist members virtually unanimously perceived the political parties of Switzerland to be unresponsive and ineffective. These groups were distinguished by their predominantly "grassroots" character, without major involvement from any established interest group or political party, and their orientation to the general citizenry as a support base, as opposed to any group limited in terms of ideology or political party affiliation. They fit the "post-materialist" categorization suggested for them in this volume on the basis of the "quality of life" issues they were established to deal with, their emphasis on unconventional, direct action tactics, and their egalitarian and solidary form of organization. In addition to these characteristics of new issues and enhanced personal involvement in politics, these groups are distinguished quite simply in the element of vocal opposition they infuse into a context otherwise accented by an orientation to cooperation and consensualism among the major political parties in Switzerland. The issues which motivated the individuals involved in these groups might well have been the objects of political party activity, in and out of government institutions, yet the activists perceived the issues to be inadequately addressed and the parties to be inadequately attentive. The broad concern of this essay is to explore the nature of the relationship between the civic action groups and political parties. The yield of the analysis suggests that the protest groups did not represent efforts to generate new political parties. Neither, however, are these groups to be understood in terms of conventional interest groups or typical organizations sponsoring initiative and referendum campaigns. Instead, they point to pursuit of a particular understanding of citizen participation and democracy which, while challenging the effec-

---

[3] The landmark writing on these concerns was done in 1964 by the Swiss Max Imboden, 1971. More recently, related topics have been discussed by Gruner, 1978.

tiveness of existing political parties and governmental structures, would act as gadfly to the institutions of popular interest aggregation, articulation, and government, rather than as a replacement. This essay provides an overview of the workings of parties in Switzerland and the response of the people to the parties. Case studies of five civic action groups will then allow an analysis of the relationship between the parties and the new instances of popular activism.

ARE PARTIES FAILING IN SWITZERLAND?

The role exercized by political parties and their elites in Switzerland is a fundamental element of Jürg Steiner's substantial work on that society, *Amicable Agreement Versus Majority Rule* (1974). Given a highly segmented society, stability is sought via a strong orientation to consensualism among elites. Steiner uses Gerhard Lehmbruch's term, "amicable agreement" (Lehmbruch 1974: 70–89), to refer to the preeminent pattern of decisionmaking in Switzerland which he saw in 1974 as a fundamental alternative to the "majoritarian model."

> In the majoritarian model there is no concern for enlarging the agreement beyond the number required to win. Whenever a majority is reached, a vote is taken and the majority position wins. In the model of "amicable agreement," discussion goes on until a solution is found that is acceptable to all participants in the decision-making process. If a vote is taken, the purpose is only to ratify a commonly accepted decision (Steiner 1974: 5).

The significance of this approach lies in the efforts made by public officials in Swiss government to take into consideration as much as possible the expressed and anticipated concerns of popular representatives, government administrators, political parties, and interest groups.

The outstanding example of this cultivated consensualism in Switzerland is the unusual federal executive, the Bundesrat (Federal Council), made up of seven members with collective responsibility. The seven are selected via a "magic formula" which has been consistently applied since 1959: two members drawn from each of the three major Swiss parties, plus one member from a fourth.[4] The executive is elected by the two

[4] The parties and their percentages of the seats in the National Council as of the elections of 1983 are: (1) Free Democratic party (or Radicals), 27.0 percent; (2) Christian Democratic party, 21.0 percent; (3) Social Democratic party, 23.5 percent; and (4) Swiss People's party, 11.5 percent. The four parties received 83 percent of the seats with 77.5 percent of the popular vote.

houses of the Federal Assembly, the popularly elected Nationalrat (National Council) and the indirectly elected Ständerat (Council of States), for a four-year term of office which is not subject to interruption. Presidency and vice-presidency of the Federal Council are rotated annually among members, and only on the rarest of occasions is reelection to the executive refused to a member who chooses to embark on another term. The result is an executive of a presidential rather than a parliamentary sort in that the body is not accountable to a parliamentary majority during its term, and its all-party makeup (i.e., including all of the major parties) largely rules out open partisan conflict within it which, if present, might impede or even rule out smooth functioning of the body.

The institutions of direct democracy further foster interparty cooperation in the Federal Assembly, as well as in the Federal Council. The facts that all proposals for constitutional amendments must, even if legislated, be submitted to national referendums, that all ordinary legislation is susceptible to popular challenge through the right of the voters and the cantons to generate an "optional referendum," and that the people and the cantons have the right through the national initiative to call for constitutional amendments, work to associate all major political parties more closely with a governing function as opposed to a competing or opposition function. The point is not only that legislation may be challenged or proposed by some sector of the populace, but that political party representatives dissatisfied with government or parliamentary action may sponsor an initiative or referendum campaign: hence there is a premium on gaining maximum agreement, reinforced by the realistic recognition of manifold differences of interest in the society (Gruner 1978b: 351–52). Given that the Federal Council is not dependent on a parliamentary majority during the course of its term and that the parties in the Federal Assembly tend to be more cantonal organizations than national ones in view of the powerful localist forces in this federal society, "there is generally no strong discipline in Swiss parties" in the Federal Assembly (Steiner 1974: 69–70). All of this contributes to relatively low levels of interparty conflict.

This situation is further supported by well-institutionalized mechanisms for consultation with interest group representatives, another major potential source of referendum challenge. The inclusion of interest group representatives in "expert committees" that contribute to the development of legislative proposals and extended communications with them through a "notification process" (*Vernehmlassungsverfahren*) is designed to assure the greatest possible agreement before the passage of law in order to avoid later challenges (Sidjanski 1974: 106–11; Reich 1974: 117–26). Byproducts of the process are close identification between party and interest group representatives and, more significantly, the overshadowing of political parties by close ties between interest groups and representatives of the federal bureaucracy. As early as 1969, Eric Gruner wrote that "The parties are ending up in the rear-guard across the line in their race with the interest groups" (Gruner 1977: 179):[5] "Hence the impression that only the government [Federal Council], the administration, and the interest groups take part in the big decisions of Swiss politics any more. If Swiss democracy is to function fruitfully in the future, then the parties urgently need to gain increased value."

Steiner notes, however, that "the principle of amicable agreement is not applied universally throughout the political system of Switzerland," and that "the Swiss party system can . . . be termed non-competitive only in the sense that amicable agreement is the prevailing pattern of conflict regulation" (Steiner 1974: 42–45). The parties included in the federal executive maintain a right to oppose government policies either in parliamentary votes or through the referendum procedures. Representatives of a party included in the Federal Council have on occasion attacked department (i.e., cabinet) heads from other parties in that body. Furthermore, the strong tradition of cantonal autonomy frequently results in pronounced independence of cantonal parties from national leaders of the same party in the executive or the Federal Assembly (Steiner 1974: 37–42).

Although "channels of communication" do exist through which opposition to government policy can be articulated by political party representatives, Steiner points out that practice usually falls short of potential. The major Swiss parties are generally in agreement with government policies rather than in opposition.

> The political system of Switzerland is thus fundamentally different from the classical model in which, according to Dahl, "opposition is so sharply distinguished that it is possible to identify unambiguously *the* opposition." Dahl finds the largest deviations from this model in the United States and Switzerland. In the United States it is "never easy to distinguish 'opposition' from 'government'; and it is exceedingly difficult, if not impossible to identify the opposition" (Steiner 1974: 48–49).

Steiner adds that "the demands of the individual parties never differ strongly. . . . [They] all conform to the system in that they adhere to the

---

[5] This comment and the following reference were both published in the 1969 edition of Gruner's book and kept in the second, expanded edition printed in 1977 under the same title. The page reference is p. 179 in both cases.

fundamental democratic principles. The consensus does not stop here, but it is extended to a more or less perfect agreement about the ends to be achieved on all important issues." The upshot of this analysis would appear to be a relatively low level of interparty competition and party-based opposition to the national government, even in the freedom of action Steiner describes beyond the limits of the preeminent model of conflict resolution, amicable agreement. As a result, the salience of parties in terms of their ideological and policy difference is reduced. The corresponding limitation of the role of political parties has been seen by some as constituting a failure of sorts, i.e., with regard to the articulation of popular interests and prospects of innovation vis-à-vis government policies and recognized problems of political conflict. Citing Erich Gruner's sense of the function of political parties, Rudolf Schilling concluded in 1973:

> that the existing parties are simply not or no longer or only in part "spiritual families" and "filter-organizations" that make the people "politically efficacious." Today a large part of the people stands apart from the parties, maintains a deep mistrust towards them, in fact, and has by no means the opinion or the hope of being able to become politically efficacious by joining a party.
>
> The good name of the parties is under attack. Only a few citizens still believe that parties are groups which can make participation in politics possible for them (Schilling 1973: 90).

In a different article drawing on the same study, Sidjanski notes that 74 percent of the populace regards the role of political parties as being "rather important" (a category made up of "very" and "fairly" important), while only 8 percent regards them as "not so important" or "not important at all." Only 45 percent of the sample, however, judged the degree of influence of parties to be "just the right amount," while those of a differing view were divided equally between 14 percent who saw parties as having "too much influence" and 14 percent who felt they had "not enough influence." Twenty-seven percent of the respondents were categorized as "don't knows" (Sidjanski 1974: 115–16). While parties are clearly perceived as important, the indicators of satisfaction with their performance suggest that in this context, at least, a more discriminating conclusion might be called for than Sidjanski's perception of overall contentment noted above.

Another point is the ostensible contentment of the Swiss writers, including some who decry the "political inertia" evidenced by the pronounced continuity in the makeup of the Federal Assembly and the Federal Council in the face of societal change. Roger Girod cites urbanization, changing patterns of employment, and a general increase in the level of affluence in

Switzerland as factors in contrast with the persistence in the relative strengths of the political parties of the country on all levels of government. Girod perceives the conservative political culture of the Swiss and the broad acceptance of this traditionalism by the successor generations as explanatory variables (Girod 1976: 215–22).

In their examination of the relevance of a "left-right dimension" to political party identification and perceptions of party character among Swiss voters, however, Sidjanski and Inglehart tie the extant, enduring party system, and patterns of representation, to the largely untroubled dimension of *conventional* social-economic issues. Issues of outstanding controversy in the past decade, however, have tapped a new dimension unrelated to the basic left-right alignment of the major parties. Analysis of two controversial "traditionalist" parties recently established over the issue of foreign workers in the country provides an example of societal conflict along lines unrepresented in the established party system (Inglehart and Sidjanski 1976: 225–42). The authors perceive a novel "cosmopolitan-traditional" dimension of popular political attitudes with relevance to new lines of political conflict over questions of "life style" distinct from conventional economic issues.

> Conceivably, such life-style issues may play an increasingly important role in future Swiss politics. . . . The left-right continuum has little relationship to the issues that have been most controversial in recent politics. . . .
>
> If noneconomic issues remain central, the major parties will be faced with a difficult choice. As one alternative they may attempt to maintain consensual government based on the present broad establishment coalition—in which case the terms left and right would tend to become simply conventional (and increasingly outdated) labels. This strategy might minimize overt political conflict; but it would also tend to minimize the significance of public influence through the electoral process. This tendency is already well advanced, as is suggested by the fact that the Swiss public shows one of the world's lowest rates of participation in national elections, with a turnout generally below even the American rate (Inglehart and Sidjanski 1976: 240–41).

On the basis of their special interest, in this article, in the nationalist, antiforeigner miniparties, Inglehart and Sidjanski conclude: "The existence of a political cartel may tend to dampen the advocacy of social change, but under present conditions its most important consequence may be that it hinders the development of a reactionary movement—which might otherwise have considerable potential for growth" (ibid.).

The "reactionary" issue in this case, however, is primarily important as one illustration of a political issue not addressed by the established parties and the left-right dimension. Henry Kerr notes that voters differing in their identification with the left and the right tend to agree on issues of traditional class conflict such as the fairness of income distribution in Switzerland and the desirability of government intervention in the housing sector. They show disagreement, however, on issues such as confidence in the country's current political leadership and the equality of treatment given by political leaders to citizens of different socioeconomic status. Kerr notes that these developments would appear to lend support to the Inglehart thesis of emergent support of "postmaterialist" values among particular population groups in advanced industrial societies (Kerr 1975: 71–81).[6] But this evidence is on voter attitudes. It is not clear that the parties have taken cognizance of changing popular concerns.

One indicator of diminishing popular attachment to the parties may be the declining level of participation in elections for the National Council. The record over the past two decades shows a pronounced downward trend (*Statistisches Jahrbuch* 1982):

1955	70.1%
1959	68.5%
1963	66.1%
1967	65.7%
1971	56.9%
1975	52.4%
1979	47.9%
1983	48.9%

In a study published in 1977, Leonhard Neidhart and Jean-Pierre Hoby asked their national sample to judge the following statement: "Elections don't change anything in our politics anyway." A slim majority of 52 percent responded that this was "generally" and "absolutely" not true, while 42 percent replied that this statement was "in part" or "completely" true, with 5 percent without judgment. Greater doubts concerning parties and the parliamentary system, however, were revealed in more specific questions. As to the statement that "What is decided in our parliaments has generally already been resolved in some committee," 62 percent of the respondents believed it "in part" or "completely" true, while only 23 percent believed it "generally" or "absolutely" not to be the case, with 15 percent without judgment. That "Almost only representatives of special interests sit in our parliaments" was found to be "in part" or "com-

---

6 The reference is to Ronald Inglehart, *The Silent Revolution*.

pletely" true by 70 percent of the respondents, with only 18 percent rejecting the notion as "generally" or "absolutely" not true (Neidhart and Hoby 1977: 120, 186).

Several writers have noted what they consider a surprisingly high level of persons with no political party identification in Switzerland. In the study by Sidjanski et al., Kerr notes that up to 35 percent of the sample profess no party identification. In 1980, Schmidtchen suggests a level of close to half of the Swiss electorate (Kerr 1975: 52; Schmidtchen 1980: 367–70). Neidhart and Hoby found that only 12 percent of their respondents were members of a political party. Fifteen percent would consider joining a party if recruited, but 73 percent ruled out the prospect under any circumstance. A general index of orientation to political parties was constructed on the basis of responses to four separate questions. The findings showed only 21 percent of the sample to be "positively" or "generally positively" inclined toward the parties, with 54 percent indicating negative feelings, and 26 percent offering no judgment (Neidhart and Hoby 1977: 112–17).

A further indication of popular disinterest in the political parties is revealed in a distinct degree of discrimination among Swiss voters between the different forms of institutional participation available to them, as revealed in the Sidjanski study. A not unsubstantial sector of the sample indicated greater readiness to participate in local elections and local and national voting, at the expense of participation in the elections for the National Council. This tendency was understandably pronounced among respondents who indicated a lack of confidence in the political parties of Switzerland, as indicated by approval of the following statements:

1. Our parties are concerned with the voters only when it is a question of getting their leaders into important positions.
2. Since we have initiatives and referendums, political parties are not so important here (Roig 1977: 164–67).

INITIATIVES AND REFERENDUMS

As noted above, participation in initiative and referendum votes is a dimension of Swiss politics in which citizens may take part without reference to political parties. The votes are on proposed constitutional amendments and ordinary legislation. Still, in contrasting Switzerland's "referendum democracy" to the parliamentary systems prevalent in Europe, the Swiss writer Max Imboden cited the main role of political parties as being to guide the people in their voting choices, rather than competition for election to office. Concerned with a decline of partisan involvement in voting, Imboden chastised the Swiss parties for neglecting this responsibility in a landmark critique of Swiss politics published almost two decades ago (Imboden 1971: 298–300). The last decade has seen the distance between parties and populace, in the context of the initiative and referendum votes, only widen. In 1977, Neidhart and Hoby noted the diminished "mobilization potential of intermediary organizations." With regard to federal voting, one-third of those interviewed in their national study reported reliance on the Federal Council for their voting decisions, but only one-eighth on the recommendations of the political parties, a level falling short of the reliance on combined media sources (newspapers 12 percent and radio and television 12 percent). Almost one-fifth of those interviewed replied that one could not rely on anyone for such advice (Neidhart and Hoby 1977: 118).

Declining popular participation in voting has become one of the most controversial topics considered by Swiss political writers. Jean-François Aubert records 295 referendums and 125 initiatives during the period between 1848 and 1978 (Aubert 1978: 43–45). The average percentage of those voting has declined steadily during that period and the subsequent four years (*Statistisches Jahrbuch*):

1880–1913	58%
1914–44	61%
1945–59	54%
1960–69	43%
1970–78	42%
1979–June 6, 1982	40% (18 plebiscites)

Already in the sixties, Max Imboden warned that the institutions of direct democracy no longer fit the contemporary needs of popular participation in terms of form, timing, choice, and applicability, and thus were losing their "relative importance" in the Swiss political process (Imboden 1971: 279). By 1975, the Zürich journalist, Hans Tschäni, reexamined the main points of Imboden's argument and concluded that the term "crisis" might better describe the Swiss situation than "malaise" (Tschäni 1975). Neidhart and Hoby wrote in 1977 that only 40 percent of their respondents claimed regular attendance at the polls, of which almost two-thirds were motivated by "duty," in contrast to a bit more than one-third made up of interested and engaged voters. The remaining 60 percent of those who were eligible to vote but did not broke down into three groups of roughly equal size on the basis of the following clustered "motivation structures" for nonparticipation: lack of political interest, a sense of incompetence vis-à-vis current political questions, and a feeling of impotence with regard to the potential of actually having political impact (Neidhart and Hoby 1977: 73–77). Concerning the statement, "When a national initiative doesn't please the authorities, they table it ('auf die lange Bank schieben')," 69 percent of those interviewed were in full or partial agreement, while only 24 percent disagreed in part or completely. When asked to judge the comment that "Many people think that voting generally doesn't achieve much of anything," 57 percent agreed fully or in part, while only 36 percent disagreed in part or completely (Neidhart and Hoby 1977: 136–38, 179).

In paradoxical contrast to declining participation in initiatives and referendums and an apparent decline in the public's respect for the institutions of direct democracy, the last decade has seen an increase in the number of efforts to generate initiatives. Kurt Eichenberger acknowledged a particularly high level of legally accredited initiative and referendum campaigns in 1978 (forty-seven, with an additional twenty-three in process of gaining status), but chose not to perceive the situation as one of a "crisis of governability" or a "flood of demands that might be impossible to deal with or that might destroy the institutions [of direct democracy and government]. On the one hand this high number [of prospective votes] is an expression of a very considerable need for innovation and an 'innovation-deficit,' and on the other of the celebrated fact that feelings of distress and wishes for change should be brought forth from the midst of the people in an orderly procedure" (Eichenberger 1977: 318–33, esp. 323, n. 14).

Perhaps mirroring a diminution of the appeal of the established parties, there has also been a marked increase in the initiative and referendum campaigns sponsored by nontraditional agents—ad hoc organizations rather than the more conventional interest group or political party sponsors. While the referendum traditionally was a route for established interests to challenge innovative policies of the government and legislature, and the initiative an instrument for minority interests (such as political parties excluded from the collegial executive) to draw publicity to their concerns and demonstrate public support (even if insufficient for voting victory), increasingly often in the last decade, voting campaigns have been organized by grass-roots coalitions (Steiner 1974: 203). In a broad study of the "myth and reality" of direct democracy in Switzerland, Jean-Daniel Delley writes that popular lack of trust in the interest groups and the major political parties has contributed to this new trend: "the activity of ad hoc committees bringing together persons who have decided to act in a particular area, without reference to a party or an organization, has developed at an accelerated rate since the end of the 1960s" (Delley 1978: 73).

The expansion in the number of unconventionally sponsored electoral campaigns during the 1970s was also characterized by increasing attention to unconventional voting issues. As opposed to relatively limited and technical issues, themes which may be understood as falling closer to the "quality of life" dimension of the Sidjanski-Inglehart discussion referred to earlier increasingly became the targets of voting campaigns.[7] As one oft-cited Swiss analyst noted critically, "It is not primarily so much a question of rulemaking for them, that is, of general and abstract regulation, as of involvement and interference in government and administration, specifically at those places where it seems particularly vital ("es mehr ans Läbige geht") or where, from their point of view, the final decisions are made ("die Weichen gestellt werden") (Huber 1976: 25). Eichenberger notes:

> Instead, as up to now, primarily to the making of law, plebiscitary access is being sought to licensing, to administrative-legal sanctions, to measures of commercial policy, to the construction project, to the laying out of streets, and to the development of educational curricula. It is not at all so much the "fundamental," the "principal," the "super-dimensional" which are the aims of popular democracy today, but much more that which is close to the skin, immediately visible, precisely contemporary, and about to happen (Eichenberger 1977: 323).

Beyond the increase in number and variety of initiative and referendum campaigns, Eichenberger calls attention to an additional new trend of most direct relevance to this essay, "the imitation of free-form citizen-initiatives, as they have appeared in the Federal Republic of Germany and [which] in Switzerland still represent legally foreign constructs" (ibid.). These grass-roots groups, of the sort to be examined more closely later in this essay, were intent not only on conventional direct democracy but also (and sometimes exclusively) on lobbying, pressure-group activities, and direct interaction with government officials in a manner generally alien to the Swiss political experience. The term used to refer to such groups was that given to comparable ones in West Germany, where institutions of direct democracy are nonexistent on the national level and present on state (Land) and local levels in only a limited number of cases: *Bürgerinitiativen* (citizen initiatives). The existence of such "civic action groups" in Switzerland has been seen to imply a potential failure of both the institutions of popular democracy and the political parties. Schmidtchen writes: "The Swiss party system stands at the limits of its potentials for popular representation. Symptoms are not only the growing divide between political de-

---

[7] Examples beyond the foreigners issue cited above are highway and traffic planning, automobile-free Sundays, nuclear power, environmental protection, and historic preservation.

mands and trust in the parties, but also movements outside of the political party landscape. The civic action groups (*Bürgerinitiativen*) can only be interesting because the parties can no longer represent specific problems in specific and in part local areas of the society" (Schmidtchen 1980: 384). Schmidtchen does not see these civic action groups as hostile to the party system, but neither does he feel they are concerned with strengthening it. Jean Kellerhals writes of "distrust aimed towards the large voluntary organizations (the trades unions or political parties)," "due both to their bureaucratic pattern and their inertia, which do not allow them to act as rapidly as one would hope," as having contributed to the emergence of new " 'explosion' movements, spontaneously formed and without a structured framework" (Kellerhals 1974: 249). And while calling for more moderate demands upon the state, Federal Chancellor Karl Huber admits, "The rise of the so-called civic action groups (*Bürgerinitiativen*) shows that the question for new forms of participation is being raised" (Huber 1976: 26–32).

UNCONVENTIONAL POLITICAL PARTICIPATION

As startling an ostensible discrepancy as such civic action groups might seem to represent on the political landscape of Switzerland, their potential was noted in the same 1972 study keynoted by Sidjanski's generally optimistic assessment. In the same volume, Charles Roig cited the existence of "a category of citizens whose fundamental reaction seems to be a 'rejection' of all that is institutionalized and official in political life. We have called these citizens 'activators' (*actionnistes*) on the basis of the very clear preference that they show for direct and mass action. They represent about 30% of the electorate, which is not negligible" (Roig 1977: 185–86).

Steiner and Obler contributed a warning signal as well, in a subsequently published article on consociationalism in Switzerland: "The positive feedback process between more consociational decision-making and less hostility may break down in the long run. Consociational decision-making seems to have the tendency to reduce the innovative capacity of a political system and render effective political participation difficult at the mass level. These two effects may cause frustrations and, ultimately, even the outbreak of new violence" (Suter 1976).

Criticism, in very strong language, of the viability of conventional participation in Swiss institutions for the purposes of bringing about changes in government policy was published by a cofounder of a controversial grass-roots antinuclear power group: "Our democracy has abdicated.

What remains? Direct action" (Wiener 1978). The grass-roots groups which emerged in Switzerland throughout the 1970s provided for some a new, albeit different, source of confidence in the condition of Swiss democracy. In a piece entitled, "Who out there is speaking of a democracy which has fallen asleep?" Edmond Tondeur argued that the "new forms of expression of political will should neither be underestimated nor prematurely declared heretical" (Tondeur 1975). The Basel philosopher Arnold Künzli wrote that "since the ensconced stability of the institutionalized society cannot otherwise be broken up, the citizen has begun to rebel outside of the institutions."

> Abstention from voting and elections and citizen action groups are two sides—one passive and one active—of one and the same civic rebellion against a democratic system that doesn't function any more, which attempts to legitimize its sclerosis as stability. With the citizen action groups and similar efforts, we are dealing with novel, noninstitutionalized social grass-roots processes, which might be able to help us to a new understanding of democracy (Künzli 1976).

That the civic action groups conflicted with conventional Swiss politics in their grass-roots character and, more significantly, in their inclination toward unconventional activism and civil disobedience, is evidenced by the following commentary:

> Professor Künzli is right when he calls for an overcoming of political apathy and speaks and writes of the need for expanded popular involvement. But why in the devil must this happen "outside of the institutions"? Rebellion leads very quickly into so sharp a contradiction to the tradition-stamped society that pressure and counterpressure result in a whirlpool which even the most reasonable government may no longer be able to guide along reasonable lines (Suter 1976).

On the other hand, Rudolf Schilling sees the grass-roots groups in large part as potential restorers of vitality to the political institutions of Switzerland—and, in particular, the parties.

> The parties must once again become what they were: groups which represent public interests and not special interests. . . .
> This tendency can only be encouraged if as many as possible new grass-roots groups organize themselves and become strong, as it were, in competition with the parties. . . . Only in this way can the parties be forced to rediscover their proper role and become strong

again as parties instead of being mere appendages of interest groups (Schilling 1973: 92–93).

FIVE CIVIC ACTION PROTEST GROUPS

The concern of the analysis of five civic action protest groups which follows is how, if at all, the new orientation toward grass-roots participation differs from conventional political participation in Switzerland and what implications it may entail for political parties. Three hypotheses of particular relevance will be considered: (1) that the new activism is being carried out by individuals alienated from the existing political parties; (2) that the new activism will engender abnormal levels of conflict, as well as illegality and even violence; (3) that the new activism will lead to the creation of new political parties.

The grass-roots protest groups examined in this essay were selected from a number of relevant instances of protest in the cities of Basel and Zürich with one common denominator: membership was unbiased by any criterion and particularly not by any particular political perspective or group affiliation. Accordingly, these groups were all established by collections of quite diverse concerned citizens, without the sponsorship of any established interest groups or political parties.

The Committee for the Preservation of the Old City (CPOC) (Komitee zur Erhaltung der Altstadt) was founded to oppose plans of the city-canton of Basel to renovate publicly owned, neglected old buildings in the heart of the city for upper-income tenants. The second group, the Committee for the Rescue of the Horburg Quarter (CRHQ) (Komitee zur Rettung des Horburgquartiers),[8] emerged when Baselers in an area already disturbed by heavy automobile and truck traffic learned that key streets were to be widened and trees and gardens lost to accommodate a feeder route to an urban highway. The Nonviolent Kaiseraugst Action (NKA) (Gewaltfreie Aktion Kaiseraugst) was established by citizens of the metropolitan area of Basel in opposition to planned construction of a nuclear power plant at Kaiseraugst, in the neighboring canton of Aargau. The Action for a Livable Zürich (ALZ) (Aktion Wohnliches Zürich) organized in response to a decision of the cantonal government to purchase property in a residential neighborhood and tear down quaint old houses in order to build a modern archive building. Finally, the Nonviolent Milchbuck Tunnel Action (NMTA) (Gewaltfreie Aktion Milchbuck-Tunnel) opposed the

---

[8] Three of the following case studies are drawn from an earlier publication of this writer. See Sorensen, 1981.

construction of a major highway tunnel under one of the city's mountains. A short description of the history of each group follows.

The Committee for the Preservation of the Old City (CPOC) in Basel was formed by fifteen people in March of 1976 in response to the recommendation of the city-canton executive that forty publicly owned properties be renovated. Confronted with a declining tax base in the city's limited geographical area, the government proposed a subsidized move for current residents, largely retirees, students, and other low-income individuals, to allow renovation of the buildings into higher-quality, higher-rent, family apartments. The ancient façades of the structures would be retained. Early in April, the cantonal parliament accepted the plan (*NZ*, March 13 and 17, 1976).

On April 22, CPOC announced its plan to gather signatures for institution of a referendum vote to challenge the parliament's decision. The group's challenge was based first of all on the questionable basis of the project in terms of generally accepted professional standards of historic preservation and social as well as aesthetic concerns of city planning. Particular exception was taken to the prospect of creating a "Disneyland," luxury habitat at the expense of the elderly and other low-income residents. Criticism was also aimed at the closed process through which construction plans had been developed as well as the very high cost of the project and the resulting high rents of apartments and shops made available. (Such financial concerns have been the most certain source of perennial popular rejection of government projects in Switzerland.)

> The preservation of ancient structures is a historic task which cannot steer clear of social consciousness; the outside and inside of a historic building constitute a unity; renovation should be undertaken not against, but with the inhabitants; the old city belongs to all people, not only a privileged class—it should not "represent," it should live; we demand openness in planning—this calls not only for clearly formulated guidelines, but also alternatives.[9]

From the over 100,000 eligible voters in the city, 4,500 signatures were collected, three times the number required to start the referendum (*BN*, June 25, 1976).

In the ensuing months, CPOC waged a referendum campaign that was only mildly unusual. The effort was unconventional, however, in its rejection of a plan supported by all of the major political parties of the canton,

---

[9] Komitee zur Erhaltung der Altstadt, "Argumentationskatalog für den Abstimmungskampf," unpublished group memorandum.

objection to the particular approach and ends of the plan in spite of agreement that the buildings were in need of renovation, and the diversified makeup of its grass-roots membership. Still, group actions were modest and proper out of respect for public opinion. Visits to residents of the houses in dispute were made to document and publicize their needs and hopes, a debate was sponsored between CPOC members and government representatives, and information was made available to the public through leaflets and street stands (*NZ*, Sept. 30, 1976).

On September 27, 1976, official results of the vote showed the CPOC campaign to have been defeated by 47 votes. Corrected information gave CPOC a 305-vote margin of victory, 29,609 to 29,304. Concerned by the closeness of the outcome, the head of the cantonal justice department instituted a recount and, on September 28, announced a victory for the government, after all, by a margin of 77 votes (*BN*, Sept. 28, 1976). Convinced of the impropriety of the recount, CPOC lodged formal protests, first with the cantonal parliament, then with the federal courts—in both cases to no avail. In spite of strong feelings of disappointment, members of the group resigned themselves to accept the status quo (*AZ-Basel*, Oct. 8, 1976).

The Horburg Quarter of Basel is a densely populated, working-class neighborhood adjoining Ciba-Geigy, one of the city's three multinational chemical firms. Early in 1975, residents of the neighborhood submitted a petition to the government of the city-canton requesting alleviation of congestion on Horburg Street, one of the area's major routes, through the redirection of truck traffic via streets in industrial areas. On June 11, the government announced plans for a widening of Horburgstrasse to accommodate four lanes, at the expense of trees and green areas, ostensibly in support of public transportation. Fearing instead that Horburgstrasse had been designated as an urban highway feeder route that would bring more traffic, noise, and pollution into the area, the citizens founded the Committee for the Rescue of the Horburg Quarter (CRHQ).[10]

> The association plans the rescue of the quarter from any influences that might injure the quality of life in the Horburg Quarter; at the same time it means to serve as a source of strengthened communication among inhabitants of the quarter.

> The means for the accomplishment of this goal include publicity work of all kinds, such as, for example, distribution of information

[10] Komitee zur Rettung des Horburgquartiers, "Verbreiterung Horburgstrasse—Nein!" a pamphlet published by the Committee for the Rescue of the Horburg Quarter (CRHQ) on Dec. 1, 1975.

material, the organization of meetings and neighborhood parties, etc.[11]

Officials of the cantonal construction department refused to meet with CRHQ or to give them access to the plans for the proposed construction. On September 13 and 14, CRHQ sponsored a neighborhood party and press conference to publicize its cause. In anticipation of consideration to be given to the government's proposal by the city-canton's parliament, CRHQ announced: "You must consider a measure which came into existence through disregard of the most elementary democratic rules. The immediately affected inhabitants of the quarter had no opportunity to express their response to the planned widening of the Horburgstrasse through any notification process (*Vernehmlassungsverfahren*), in spite of the fact that they frequently made an effort to gain it."[12] When the parliament met to deal with the government's proposal on September 25, members of CRHQ threw flyers from the gallery and displayed posters. The proposal was sent to a special committee for further study. Perceiving an effort to allow public attention to fade, CRHQ subsequently organized a "protest-promenade" (*Demonstrations-Spaziergang*) during the afternoon rush hour on October 22, at which some one hundred participants competed with heavy traffic to make their point (*NZ*, Oct. 23, 1975; *BN*, Oct. 23, 1975). Toward the end of 1975, a twenty-six-page brochure publicized the cause, and in March of 1976, when unknown individuals put up counterfeit street signs to show that traffic could easily be rerouted around residential areas, CRHQ representatives showed up to demonstrate and distribute a new neighborhood newspaper while the police restored the status quo.

On May 19, the parliamentary committee published its report. A seven to six majority recommended that the plans be returned to the government for reconsideration. The minority vote recommended a "partial widening." The CRHQ announced it would seek a referendum against the project, if approved in full, and was particularly bitter about the minority report: a "partial widening" was to cost under two million francs and would thus not be liable to a referendum challenge. When the proposal came before the parliament on October 21, however, the government stated its willingness to withdraw it for the purposes of a "creative pause" in the city planning process. By a large majority, and with no objections, the cantonal parliament supported this decision. The committee claimed

---

[11] From the "Statutes of the Association 'Committee for the Rescue of the Horburg Quarter,' " ratified by a plenary meeting of the group on July 9, 1975.

[12] Letter from the CRHQ to members of the Basel-City cantonal parliament, Sept. 1975.

a triumph on the basis of popular pressure and the threat of a referendum campaign (NZ, Oct. 22, 1976).

The Nonviolent Kaiseraugst Action (NKA) was founded in December 1973, by about twenty people from the metropolitan Basel area who were opposed to plans for an atomic power plant to be built some ten miles from the city in the neighboring canton of Aargau.[13] Repeated demonstrations of support for the project from the government of Aargau and the federal government had frustrated a variety of protests from local residents and the governments of the adjoining cantons of Basel-City and Basel-Countryside. Petitions to various levels of government and court action yielded no satisfaction to the project's critics.[14] In March 1975, even without a construction license for the nuclear portion of the plant, the power company began excavation work at the site.

On April 1, members of the NKA illegally occupied the property.

> The nonpartisan Nonviolent Kaiseraugst Action and its affiliated groups limit themselves for the achievement of their goals to nonviolent means. To these belong: full information and enlightenment of the population, a prerequisite for self-determination; political actions such as petitions, initiatives, and parliamentary interpellation; demonstrations and protests; noncooperation such as strikes and boycotts; and civil disobedience such as tax strikes and occupations. By all of these actions, objects are not to be damaged, if possible, and under no conditions should persons be physically harmed. Neither is the opponent personally attacked, but only his position and function.[15]

Members of the group had spent hundreds of hours in regular meetings during the preceding weeks debating the pros and cons of alternative strategies. A commitment existed to allow all participants full opportunity to voice their views and to create the maximum possible sense of solidarity among those involved.

At major demonstrations on April 6 and 26, 16,000 and 18,000 people temporarily joined the "occupation" to register their sympathy and offer popular legitimacy to the "full-time" protestors. The NKA and other groups which had joined the occupation had instituted democratic procedures for decisionmaking among all present via a "plenary assembly," which gave its support to the following demands:

---

[13] For an excellent case study, see Schroeren, 1977.

[14] A useful chronology may be found included in *Expertengespräche zur Frage der Atomkraftwerke in der Region Basel—Ein Bericht der Verhandlungsdelegation*, 1975.

[15] NKA, "Grundsatzerklärung der Gewaltfreien Aktion Kaiseraugst," leaflet dated April 29, 1975. See also, "Gewaltfreie Gewalt," *Die Weltwoche*, April 9, 1975.

1. a halt to construction for one month, to allow for negotiations during this time over the questions in dispute; 2. a specified and binding schedule for negotiations; and 3. no changes of any kind on the property [to be abandoned] during the negotiations—including construction of a fence [around the site] or demolition of the structures set up by the occupiers.[16]

By early June, representatives of the federal government and the power plant construction company agreed to these demands. On June 11, 1975, the protestors gave up the occupation. The product of negotiations between the NKA and their opponents was formal hearings dealing with radiation, safety, meteorology, energy needs, alternative energy sources, and the licensing process for nuclear power plants. The hearings and related negotiations continued for the next several years, and the NKA had reason to credit itself with success, but could not claim a final victory (*NZ*, April 1, 1976). In the meantime, however, demands for a renewal of militant action led to a schism in the group in late 1975 and a virtual halt to group activity. The more radical element hoped to keep alive the tactic of direct action and to maintain the commitment of the antinuclear activists. The other faction gave priority to a national initiative designed to achieve a federal constitutional amendment that would effectively ban construction of nuclear power plants. This initiative was voted on by the Swiss people on February 15, 1979, and rejected (*AZ-Basel*, July 28, 1975; *NZ*, Sept. 13, 1975).

The Action for a Livable Zürich (ALZ) was established in the summer of 1973 when the cantonal government announced its intention to purchase property and demolish six houses in a residential neighborhood noted for its early-nineteenth-century Biedermeier atmosphere. Five residents of the threatened houses, as well as some twenty-five other people of the "most diverse political, social, and professional circles," made up the core of activists. Members of the group called to the public's attention the particular mix of living facilities—small workshops, stores, gardens, and trees—that would be irreparably damaged by construction of the planned cantonal archive facility and the development that would probably ensue (*NZZ*, Nov. 13, 1974; *TA*, June 29, 1973). The ALZ was also upset that the government decision had occurred without public hearings or publication of studies which had been done of the project, including two negative ones from the landmark commission; but it was primarily angered by the discovery that the canton had offered the owner of the property, who happened to be an architect, the design job for the center. Residents were star-

[16] Cited in: *Expertengespräche*, 1975: 116. See also, "Kaiseraugst: Abbruch," *National Zeitung* (NZ), June 9, 1975.

tled when scaffolding equipment appeared at the houses out of the blue. The "call to action" of the ALZ included the following concerns:

> We are not against the construction of a state archive facility. But we are against the fact that the state wants to house its past in a location, of all places, where it must destroy the past to do so—and not only the past, but also contemporary city life. . . .
>
> We ask how serious the officials are with their advocacy of a "livable" city when they themselves continually offer support for the destruction of "livability."
>
> We expect from the "public hand," particularly in the case of public construction plans, more openness in the planning process and we demand better coordination and cooperation for all those involved in the planning process—and affected tenants belong to this group, too (*Die Tat*, June 29, 1975).

Beyond a call to the public for signatures in support of their causes, the ALZ generated interpellations to be taken up in the city legislature and the cantonal parliament. Should the latter body ultimately approve the plan, the ALZ threatened to pursue a referendum against such an expenditure of public funds. Nonetheless, in March of 1975, the cantonal parliament approved the 15-million-franc funding for the project. On March 18, the ALZ announced a drive to start a referendum, and within forty-five days, 16,000 signatures had been collected, 11,000 more than legally required. The committee sponsored demonstration marches, information tables throughout the center of the city, a neighborhood party (*Quartierfest*), and an art exhibition of works "for the cause" in support of their activities. An opposing group, Friends of the State Archive, was established that characterized the members of ALZ first as "nostalgics" and then as "fellow travelers of the extreme left and right." The referendum was held, throughout the canton of Zürich (named the same as the city) on December 7, 1975. (It was to be a cantonal archive.) The vote was 171,000 against and 96,000 for, with a turnout of 41.3 percent (*NZZ*, Dec. 8, 1975). The ALZ had triumphed. Nonetheless, six months later, the owner of the property decided to tear down the houses in question and build new apartment buildings privately. As noted in a newspaper account, "as far as the private apartment building, that is now to appear in the place of the state archive project, is concerned, there will be no vote" (*TA*, May 19, 1976). The ALZ members no longer had any recourse.

The Nonviolent Milchbuck Tunnel Action" (NMTA) in Zürich was established on March 30, 1976, to oppose the construction of an urban highway tunnel. The group introduced itself in a brochure entitled "Stop the highway construction—it is not too late!" and made reference to the damage already done to the city:

> The population watches this destruction of our city with irresolution and inactivity; ignorance, indifference, and resignation, as well as the duplicity of those who allow themselves to be called "the representatives of the people" have led them to this condition along with training to an understanding of democracy which limits itself to keeping one's mouth shut and accepting whatever comes.
>
> Democratic forms must be created which would allow those affected, those interested, and those "in sympathy" to influence the planning process at all times. . . . Neither the parliamentary institutions nor those of direct democracy (die politischen Volksrechte) such as initiatives and referendums are sufficient to realize this demand (GAM, 1976).

The tunnel was to provide one of two branches in a Y-shaped expressway cutting through the center of the city which some of the founders of the NMTA had been fighting for several years. Objections to the tunnel were tied to its cost, the noise which would result from increased traffic, the destruction of residential areas, and the expected increase in land values and rents in the inner city. Beyond these grounds, however, the activists considered the insistence of cantonal authorities on construction of the tunnel and the highway project to be evidence of a flagrant disregard for the will of the majority of citizens in the city. Although such a majority had expressed its opposition to the "Y-highway" in an initiative vote held in 1974, the vote had been held on the cantonal level because the highway was a cantonal project. Since a cantonal majority had not been achieved for either rejection of the highway or an alternative plan suggested by the government, planners declared the vote a victory for the original highway plan (Schweingruber 1976).

Members of the NMTA saw their group as a last-ditch attempt to stop the citywide construction plans. A new effort, open to unconventional forms of protest behavior, was to be generated, and the organization and decisionmaking of the group were to cultivate the democratic values ostensibly neglected in the official policymaking process. The founders of the NMTA were explicitly concerned with avoiding the failures other citizens groups had experienced. Their stated goal was to create an environment in which the largest and most diverse collection of people could communicate with each other openly about issues and strategies and make decisions with the support of an overwhelming majority of those participating (GAM 1976: 33–36).

On April 1, the cantonal authorities announced plans to begin demolition of houses at the site of one of the two mouths of the tunnel. Four days later, supported by a decision of their plenary assembly, fifty members of the NMTA occupied one of the houses overnight until 250 policemen forced them to leave. On April 12, the construction site at the other end of the tunnel was found flooded with water. Responsibility for the sabotage was claimed by a hitherto unknown, and otherwise anonymous, Action Group for More Swimming Pools (*Die Tat*, April 4, 1976; *Tagblatt*, April 7, 1976; *TA*, April 13, 1976). The nineteenth of April brought another twelve-hour "occupation" of houses threatened with demolition, and on May 10 the machinery and equipment of the demolition crews were again briefly taken over. In both cases, police action led to dispersal of the demonstrators; in the second case, twenty-four individuals were arrested (*NZZ*, April 15, 1976; *AZ-Freier Aargauer*, April 21, 1976; *Die Tat*, May 10, 1976).

None of these incidents drew broad support from the general public. The sporadic instances of civil disobedience failed to gain the popular legitimation given in the case of opposition to the planned reactor at Kaiseraugst. Debate over the militant tactics, however, provoked factionalism and withdrawals from the NMTA. Following the demolition of all of the controversial buildings at one mouth of the disputed tunnel-to-be, activity in the protest group lost momentum. Some activists turned their attention to one more cantonal initiative, "For a Zürich Without Expressways," which was defeated in a vote held on March 13, 1977 (*NZZ*, March 14, 1977).

What Kind of Challenge to the Political Parties?

The research in Basel and Zürich was designed to examine the motivations of participants in these unconventional forms of citizen activism. The method offered the opportunity to look in close detail at the concerns and ambitions of the activists relevant to the three hypotheses noted at the beginning of the section on the case studies. "Core activists" to be interviewed were selected through a combination of reputational and "snowball" techniques: names were gathered from newspaper accounts, interested observers such as journalists, and from group participants. Between seven and thirteen persons were interviewed from each group. Demographic data from the forty-nine activists in the five groups do not provide any outstanding grounds for differentiating among them. All five sets of "core" activists were made up almost exclusively of individuals from a relatively evenly distributed age span from twenty to forty years, with university degrees or experience, and were preponderantly men. In almost all cases, they were employed as professionals, e.g., lawyers, journalists, city planners, and teachers. The activists revealed a very high degree of confirmation of the postmaterialist values posited by Inglehart. Priority was given to the societal goals of giving "the people more say in important governmental decisions" and "protecting freedom of speech" over those of "maintaining order in the nation" and "fighting rising prices."[17] All of the respondents expressed relatively high degrees of satisfaction with their jobs and incomes along with relatively strong levels of dissatisfaction with "the way democracy is functioning in Switzerland" and "the kind of society Switzerland is today."

There was also a marked continuity in concerns and objectives among members of all five groups in spite of the variety of issues in question. Respondents revealed a high degree of alienation from the major parties of Switzerland. In fact, participation in or trying to influence the politics of any party was almost unanimously rejected as a means of achieving the goals of the groups. Absent in all cases was support for either a general illegal or violent attack on society or violence against individuals, although a clear readiness to engage in unconventional forms of political activity and civil disobedience was manifest. At the same time, there was no support demonstrated for the establishment of a new political party or pursuit of electoral politics. The preeminent theme expressed by core group members was that of creating a participatory experience which would allow those involved to deal with the issue in question in the context of a new dimension of political community and personal activism. Primary emphasis was placed on information, communication, and participation in pursuit of group solidarity for all involved.

Although more than half of the activists interviewed reported regular participation in the national elections, almost all stated they had no party identification. The same high percentage of the respondents perceived the political parties as lacking in influence with regard to the issues of controversy and, moreover, as indifferent and unhelpful to the concerns of the protest groups. The major parties of Switzerland were seen as too small to have any impact. In all five cases, the nonpartisan nature of the protest group was perceived as a fundamentally desirable quality. It was associated with the realization of a true grass-roots orientation, transcending party differences tied to an irrelevant competition. A conscious indifference to the dimension of political parties was seen as conferring a quality of legitimacy on the new political community. It is not particularly startling that the first hypothesis entertained above, that the new activism in

---

[17] Inglehart, 1977: Appendix A contained the questionnaire used in a 1973 survey in Western Europe.

Switzerland is being carried out by individuals alienated from the major existing political parties, should be largely unchallenged by the available data.

What of the second hypothesis? It has been reported that incidents of illegality, certainly, and even violence against machinery and building, did occur. But do the civic action protest groups reveal a pronounced and sustained turn toward illegality and violence in a society which prides itself in orderly political processes? To ascertain the attitudes of respondents vis-à-vis unconventional forms of political action, interview questions followed a format used by a team of social scientists in a major contemporary crossnational study of political behavior.[18] The respondents were asked to state their degree of approval, under "conceivable circumstances," or disapproval of: (1) petitions; (2) lawful demonstrations; (3) boycotts; (4) rent strikes; (5) blocking traffic; (6) unofficial strikes; (7) occupation of buildings; (8) damaging property; and (9) violence against persons.[19]

What the interview responses revealed is a bit surprising. The activists in all five groups showed no significant differences in the judgments of the protest behaviors cited above. The overwhelming majority, in all five cases, gave full approval to the potential justifiability of protest behaviors one through seven. A minority in all five cases gave tentative approval to "damaging property," while "violence against persons" was virtually unanimously rejected.

In the cases of three out of the five civic action groups, activity was fundamentally compatible with the conventional Swiss laws for direct democracy. The campaigns led to government action to avoid a referendum in one case (Horburgstrasse), positive government action in response to a referendum victory in another (Action for a Livable Zürich), and to a lost referendum in the third (Basel-Old City). In all three cases the groups accepted the outcomes of their campaigns. In none of these cases was there advocacy of violent acts. This was the case even though a large proportion of respondents in these groups expressed potential approval under conceivable circumstances of illegal acts or civil disobedience.

In the two cases in which incidents of illegality and violence were pronounced, applicability of the institutions of direct democracy was complicated if not ruled out by a strong mismatch between the geographical location of those affected and the pertinent levels of voter and government jurisdiction. The nuclear power plant objected to by citizens from the metropolitan Basel areas was to be built in the neighboring canton of Aargau,

[18] The Technical Appendix of Barnes and Kaase, 1979, explains the construction of the variables used in the study.

[19] Raising questions on illegal behavior in this research was a sensitive matter since those interviewed had actually been participants in the protest groups.

where jurisdiction was held by voters and officials of the community at Kaiseraugst and the canton of Aargau, as well as authorities of the federal government. The highway system opposed by citizens of the city of Zürich was under the jurisdiction of voters and authorities of the full canton of Zürich and, again, federal officials.[20] In these two cases, incidents of illegality and violence (against property) did take place. In one instance they marked the end of the effort, as support for the cause was thereby seriously eroded, both within and without the group (Milchbuck Tunnel). In the second case (Kaiseraugst), illegal trespassing received widespread and long-term support from within and without the group.

The activists interviewed may in the majority have given potential approval, under conceivable circumstances, to illegal acts, and some reported potential approval of violence—but illegal acts were the exceptional cases and were sustained for several weeks only in a particularly complex but popular cause. Thus these cases of grass-roots activism generally did not entail high levels of conflict involving illegality or violence, even though a high degree of potential tolerance for such conflict was indicated and alienation from the political parties of Switzerland was substantial. The second hypothesis entertained above, that the new activism would engender abnormal levels of conflict, as well as illegality and violence, must be in large part rejected. In all of the groups, a widely accepted sense of right and wrong as well as a concern for the reactions of the general public delineated, albeit to a varying degree, a boundary between acceptable and unacceptable tactics for the protest groups.

There was virtually no support among respondents for the idea that a strong sense of animosity toward government officials had motivated participants in the protest groups. While unconventional acts were acceptable, the atmosphere of experiences reported had been one of practicality rather than sensationalism or impassioned militance. In all five groups, and especially in the Kaiseraugst and Milchbuck Tunnel cases, however, the majority of respondents found fault with the potential of the institutions of direct democracy. Government officials can delay the occurrence of a vote for lengthy periods (*Schubladisierung*) and, in the case of an initiative, always have the opportunity to present an alternative proposal (*Gegenvorschlag*) to the voters which may result in confusion and main-

[20] In contrast, it should be noted, the decisionmaking power for the issues raised by CPOC and CRHQ in Basel was located with the citizens and authorities of the city-canton alone. In the case of the ALZ of Zürich, funding for the proposed cantonal archive opposed by local activists had to be voted on by the entire canton. In this case, however, the voters outside of the city backed the local concern on various grounds, including a parsimonious inclination and a wariness of appropriations for development of the cantonal capital and the perceived neglect of outlying regions.

tenance of the status quo.[21] Votes can be lost because of an infelicitous wording of the resolution; in addition, votes always have to be cast in a simple yes or no form, ruling out more differentiated viewpoints; and all too often, people other than those directly affected hold the majority of the votes, or people affected by some issue are without recourse given particular geopolitical boundaries. Virtually all respondents, including those who had "won the battle, but lost the war" in the fight to save the Biedermeier neighborhood in Zürich, acknowledged some value in the rights of direct democracy but admitted profound reservations concerning the prospects of exercising these rights to achieve their aims. Sponsoring initiative and referendum campaigns may have provided a basic context for the involvement of most of the activists, but it was clearly not the only motivation for participation in the civic action groups. What evidence is there that another was to challenge political parties and, perhaps, to create new ones?

In no case did respondents indicate any sentiment in favor of establishing a new political party. Apart from their expressed high feelings of alienation from existing parties, the activists expressed low levels of confidence in the electoral system and the system of representative democracy in general. Rather than anticipating gaining control of the reins of government at any level, most of those interviewed were concerned essentially with the cause that had led to the creation of their group and foresaw an end to their activity at the time in the future when the issue was ultimately resolved, one way or the other. Virtually all of the activists disclaimed any kind of ideological framework underlying their involvement. Participation in the protest group was grounded in a strong sense of having been affected personally by the issue at hand and an equally powerful need to do something about it. More fundamental than this perception, however, was an incentive for participation which consistently appeared to predominate among the motivations of the activists. This was the desire to create and then maintain, for the duration of the controversy, a novel dimension of active community participation. For the majority of those interviewed, this concern came virtually to overshadow the issue which had originally triggered activist involvement. Such a community was to be open to all interested individuals and emphasize a revitalization of political consciousness and personal involvement. An unconventionally personal and activist appeal to the broader community and a direct involvement with the authorities responsible for policy and decisionmaking via

[21] The variety of means authorities have of influencing the workings of procedures of initiative and referendum votes along desired lines is discussed in Schweingruber, 1976, as well as in the brochure, GAM, 1976.

publications, demonstrations, and participatory events, including civil disobedience, represented further departures from the conventions of popular political participation in Switzerland. The details of the issue and its ramifications were to be made understandable to those directly affected. A context for deliberations and debate free of traditional and misleading social and political cleavages as well as inhibiting organizational hierarchies was to be created.

The group was to serve as a clearinghouse of information and as a vehicle for the aggregation and articulation of interests, but primary emphasis was on supporting the participatory experience of the core activists rather than creating a broader constituency or rationalizing the workings of the group to maximize efficiency or fine-tune relations with persons outside. While all respondents saw the openness of their groups to all interested persons as a good quality, there was virtual unanimity as to the desirability of having no more than fifteen to thirty persons actively involved. While contacts with political parties, interest groups, or other grass-roots organizations were generally perceived as potentially useful, this orientation was overshadowed by the view of most respondents that efforts to form outside alliances would distract and detract from the participatory experience of the core group. Most respondents admitted that more concern for hierarchy and structure might have led to better coordination of group meetings and activities, but the overwhelming consensus was that attention to this dimension would have risked inhibiting participation and creating unwanted oligarchies or hardening of natural leadership patterns. Development of a platform or ideology beyond attention to the specific concern that had brought together the group was seen as a threat to the issue- and action-based unity that had been achieved. The resulting protest groups were amorphous, the patterns and duration of participation unpredictable. But that is how the activists wanted it to be.

The nature of these civic action protest groups, therefore, must be described as one of informal, loosely structured pressure groups rather than potential political parties, with a role as stimuli to parties, complementary to them as opposed to standing in direct competition or opposition to them. It is important to note that this status is by choice, showing a popular desire for a form of participation different from that of political party involvement. In some ways, this choice is as potent, however, if not more so, as a choice for party status. The civic action groups remain free of electoral concerns and official, parliamentary propriety, and free to be more direct and, potentially, embarrassing in their dealings with authorities than a "Green party" of West Germany, for example, might be able to afford to be, over the long or even the short term. Material discussed in this essay would suggest that if some of these Swiss activists did organize a new party on the national level such as the Green party of West Germany, strong tensions would exist between the fundamental commitment to a particular kind of unstructured communitarian participation and the normal requirements of running an inevitably larger, more formal organization geared toward electoral and parliamentary or governmental participation.

The civic action groups need not necessarily represent a failure of the major parties or the party system; rather, they point to the need to clarify just what roles the parties will play, given recent changes in Swiss society. These changes may be understood in terms used by Lawson and Merkl in the introductory and concluding chapters of this volume. Newly distinct, postmaterialist subgroups of the population are looking for new "rewards" and new "arenas" for participation in the context of novel forms of activism. The groups suggest changes in political linkage functions between individuals and political organizations and between both individuals and organizations *and* the state: most significantly, to use Lawson's terms, attention is shifted from "electoral linkage" to "participatory linkage." In terms of Merkl's concerns, furthermore, there is evidence among the activists of a degree of alienation from the conventional political system as a whole—the party system and the system of initiative and referendum—illustrated in declining voter turnout and diminished support for major parties. No major party was seen as a viable vehicle by the activists and no effort was made to ally with or found a new small party.

Participants in the five groups studied made it clear that for them involvement in the civic action groups represented the most appealing and important possible context of political activity. Implied is particular interest in the dimension of "participatory linkage" perceived by these individuals to be deficient in the organizations of the major parties of Switzerland—and in the conventional workings of the initiative and referendum processes as well. The primary emphasis on an activist, egalitarian, and small-scale context for participation allows greater flexibility in the pursuit of postmaterialist issues and action strategies. While the roles of political parties may not be eliminated by such participation, it entails an obvious challenge in terms of the appeal of the parties and their relevance for the Swiss population. In addition to being inadequate as contexts for popular participation, the parties were generally seen by the activists as inert and out of touch with their concerns, shackled to an administrative state primarily responsive to major societal interest groups and the inherent momentum of the governmental bureaucracy. If the parties continue to lose their roles as popular representatives in the electoral, parliamentary, and governmental processes and as advisers for popular decisions to be made in the context of initiative and referendum elections, can their total irrelevance be far removed? Clearly, the fundamental challenge for political parties is to restore popular interest and support for programmatic organizations which compete for election to legislative and executive positions and take appropriately distinct and perceptible stands on election issues, as well as legislative and policy issues. Among various means to this end, more political party attention to the types of specific issue cases which motivate participation in civic action groups is required. Under such circumstances, the role of political parties in Switzerland might be reinvigorated through interaction with grass-roots groups, which would continue to find their reason to exist on the basis of the particular kind of participation they entail, beyond their roots in specific issue-tied controversies.

What the civic action groups offer in terms of a participation mechanism for a small group with a specific interest on the local level may be impossible for parties to offer in contemporary advanced industrial societies—even in one as small as Switzerland. The specific nature of this "linkage connection" is even less compatible with the context of conventional political party organization and activity than a new "Green party" environment. A fundamental point is that this particular form of participation is a goal in and of itself, *as well as* a means of attempting to accomplish change in society. That these groups are small and, in most cases, of limited duration should not be perceived as a sign of their failure or of the likelihood of limited prospects for groups of this type in the future. Disappearance of the group upon achievement of its goal need not be tied to goal achievement or political party adaptation, and dissolution of the group without goal achievement need not reflect failure if concerns about the form of participation have been as important as those about the specific issue conflict in question. Whether successful or not in terms of goal achievement, the small size, limited duration, and sporadic quality of the civic action protest groups are inherent in the nature of the phenomenon. In this sense it is less duration than the frequency of occurrence of the civic action protest groups that is the sign of the popularity and the future prospects of such activism.

The material presented here draws on the case of Switzerland, with its distinctive institutions providing partially separate realms for political party activity and popular direct democracy. It may, however, be in some respects a preview or parallel to what lies ahead for other advanced industrial societies in which political parties have come to be assimiliated into the process of administration, at the cost of representing popular concerns, and segments of the population are increasingly politically active at the grass-roots level. If the civic action groups represent a genuine popular desire for new forms of popular political participation, political parties need to develop means of connecting with the new phenomenon, rather than recoiling from it, rejecting it, or criminalizing it as dangerous or illegal. In the place of concern for the destabilizing effect of departures from the status quo, there should be recognition of the constructive side of increased citizen involvement for the revitalization of complex democracies.

There is no question, however, that the communitarian, activist ethos of the civic action groups examined in this essay can be seen to be tied to traditional values deeply rooted in the specific case of Switzerland. The cases of unconventional behavior and even those of illegal protest considered above were efforts to maintain, under circumstances perceived as unresponsive and even undemocratic, a community-based, popular decisionmaking function. Writers on Switzerland frequently note direct, communal democracy as the historical foundation of politics in that country (Gasser 1976; Siegfried 1956; Baker 1974). This is a function influenced but never controlled by political parties, yet one they have become more and more removed from, as indicated in this essay. It is also a function that has become increasingly difficult for Swiss citizens to perform. Urban growth and more concentrated population density and infrastructure development have appeared as increasingly influential factors during the past two decades, particularly relevant to the metropolitan areas of Basel and Zürich. A neighborhood concern is now more likely to be insufficient to draw the attention of city or cantonal voters, and citizens in one area are more likely to be concerned about developments in a neighboring area across legal boundaries beyond which they have no recourse to decisionmaking processes. In the absence of popular bodies, agents, and institutions with authority to deal with localized or regional issues, the civic action protest groups represent new "communities" of politically active citizens. The local, communal context of Swiss democracy is recreated in a different form as the basic component of the protest groups analyzed in this essay.

REFERENCES

Aubert, J. F. 1978. Switzerland. In *Referendums*, ed. Butler and Ranney.
AZ-Basel. 1975. An der Parteipolitik scheiden sich die Geister. July 28.
————. 1976. Wird der Zahlensalat vor Bundesgericht entwirrt? Oct. 8.
AZ-Freier Aargauer. 1976. Polizeieinsatz am Milchbuck. April 21.
Barber, B. R. 1974. *The death of communal liberty. A history of freedom in a Swiss mountain canton*. Princeton: Princeton University Press.

Barnes, S. H., and M. Kaase. 1979. *Political action. Mass participation in five Western democracies.* Beverly Hills: Sage Publications.

Basler Nachrichten (BN). 1975. Gegen mehr Lärm und Abgase. Oct. 23.

BN. 1976. Nein zum Markthof—knappes Nein zur Altstadtsanierung! Sept. 27.

BN. 1976. Wir brauchen keine Luxuswohnungen. June 25.

Budge, I., and I. Crewe, eds. 1976. *Party identification and beyond.* New York: Wiley.

Butler, D., and A. Ranney, eds. 1978. *Referendums.* Washington, D.C.: American Enterprise Institute.

Delley, J.-D. 1978. *L'Initiative populaire en Suisse. Mythe et réalité de la démocratie directe.* Lausanne: Editions L'Age d'Hommes.

Eichenberger, K. 1977. Zusammen- und Gegenspiel representativer und plebiszitärer Komponenten im schweizerischen Regierungssystem, *Zeitschrift für Parlamentsfragen,* Oct. 8: 318–33.

Esman, M. J., ed. 1977. *Ethnic conflict in the Western world.* Ithaca and London: Cornell University Press.

Expertengespräche zur Frage der Atomkraftwerke in der Region Basel—Ein Bericht der Verhandlungsdelegation. 1975. Liestal.

GAM, Gewalftfreie Aktion gegen den Milchbuck-Tunnel. 1976. *Baustop am Y— noch nicht zu spät! Die chronique scandaleuse einer 20 jährigen Fehlplanung.* Zürich.

Gasser, A. 1976. *Staatlicher Grossraum und Autonome Kleinräume.* Basel: Social Strategies Publishers Co-operative Society.

Girod, R. 1976. Phänomen Schweiz: Sozialer Wandel, politische Beharrung. *Schweizer Monatshefte* 56: 216–22.

Gruner, E. 1977. *Die Parteien der Schweiz.* Bern: Francke Verlag.

——. 1978a. *Ist der schweizerische Staat zerstörbar?* Bern: Haupt.

——. 1978b. The political system of Switzerland. In *Modern Switzerland,* ed. J. M. Luck. Palo Alto, Calif.: Society For the Promotion of Science and Scholarship, 351–52.

Die Helvetische Malaise. 1971. In *Staat und Recht,* ed. H. Imboden. Basel and Stuttgart: Helbing und Lichtenhahn.

Huber, H. 1976. Die Ursachen der Initiativenflut. *Neue Zürcher Zeitung,* Jan. 20.

Huber, K. 1976. Indifferenz und Resignation in der direkten Demokratie. *Documenta* 2: 26–32.

Inglehart, R. 1977. *The silent revolution.* Princeton: Princeton University Press.

——, and D. Sidjanski. 1976. The left, the right, the establishment and the Swiss electorate. In *Party identification,* ed. Budge and Crewe, 225–42.

Kellerhals, J. 1974. Voluntary associations in Switzerland. In *The nature of voluntary action around the world. Voluntary action research,* ed. D. H. Smith. Lexington, Mass.: Lexington Books, 1974, 231–50, esp. 249.

Kerr, H. 1975. Electeurs et forces partisans. In Sidjanski et al., 1975: 71–81.

Künzli, A. 1976. Der rebellische Bürger und die *stabile* Gesellschaft. *Badener Tagblatt,* Jan. 10.

Lehmbruch, G. 1974. A non-competitive pattern of conflict management in liberal democracies: The case of Switzerland, Austria, and Lebanon. In McRae, 1974: 70–89.

McRae, K. D., ed. 1974. *Consociational democracy. Political accommodation in segmented societies.* Toronto: McClelland and Stewart.

Meynaud, J. 1969. *La Démocratie semi-directe en Suisse.* University of Montreal.

Nationalzeitung (NZ), 1975 and 1976.

Neidhart, L., and J. P. Hoby. 1977. *Ursachen der gegenwärtigen Stimmenabstinenz in der Schweiz.* Zürich: Ein Forschungsbericht im Auftrag der Justizabteilung der eidgenössischen Justiz- und Polizeidepartments, 186, 290–91.

Neue Zürcher Zeitung (NZZ), 1974, 1975, 1976, and 1977.

Reich, R. 1975. Notes on the local and cantonal influence in the Swiss federal consultation process. *Publius* 5: 117–26.

Roig, C. 1975. La stratification politique. In Sidjanski et al., 1975: 155–86.

Schilling, R. 1973. *Die Demokratie der Teilnahme.* Zürich: Schulthess.

Schmidtchen, G. 1980. Repräsentiert der Nationalrat die gesellschaftlichen Probleme der Schweiz? *Zeitschrift für Parlamentsfragen,* Nov. 11: 336–85.

Schroeren, M. 1977. *Z. B. Kaiseraugst.* Zürich: Schweizerischer Friedensrat.

Schweingruber, B. 1976. Y—eine Stadt wird betrogen. *Das Konzept,* April 20.

Sidjanski, D. 1974. Interest groups in Switzerland. *Annals of the American Academy of Political and Social Sciences* 413: 106–11.

———. 1976. The Swiss and their politics. *Government and Opposition* 11: 320–21.

———, C. Roig, H. Kerr, R. Inglehart, and J. Nicola. 1975. *Les Suisses et la politique.* Bern: Herbert Lang.

Siegfried, A. 1956. *Switzerland. A democratic way of life.* New York: Duell, Sloan and Pearce.

Sorensen, R.C.A. 1981. Participation and protest in Switzerland: Three cases of grass-roots activism. *Laurentian University Review* 14: 81–96.

Statistisches Jahrbuch der Schweiz. Basel: Birkhauser Verlag.

Steiner, J. 1974. *Amicable agreement versus majority rule. Conflict resolution in Switzerland.* Chapel Hill: University of North Carolina Press.

———, and J. Obler. 1977. Does the consociational theory really hold for Switzerland? In M. J. Esman, 1977: 324–42.

Suter, H. 1976. Wird uns der Bürgeraufstand retten? Bietet die Partizipation "Basisgruppen" einen Weg zur Überwindung politischer Apathie? *Luzerner Tagblatt,* March 9.

Tagblatt. 1976. Belagerer an der Nordstrasse zum Rückzug gezwungen. April 7.

Tagesanzeiger. (TA) 1973, 1976.

Die Tat. 1975. Aufruf der Aktion Wohnliches Zürich. June 29.

———. 1975. Polizeieinsatz gegen Hausbesetzer. May 10.

———. 1976. Gegen Häuserabbruch demonstriert. April 4.

Tondeur, E. 1975. Wer spricht da von der "eingeschlafenen Demokratie"? *Tagesanzeiger,* May 3.

Tschäni, H. 1975. *Demokratie auf dem Holzweg.* Zürich: Artemis.

Weltwoche. 1975. Gewaltfreie Gewalt. April 9.

Wiener, D. 1978. Unsere Demokratie dankt ab. Was bleibt? Die direkte Aktion. *Basler Zeitung,* Jan. 14.

SEVEN

Community Groups
as Alternative Political
Organizations in Chicago

RAFFAELLA Y. NANETTI

It is difficult to pick up a book on American political parties that does not discuss the decline or failure of the party system. There is an abundance of empirical and impressionistic data available which show that party identification among the electorate is down (Burnham, 1975), party leaders' ability to choose candidates for public office has diminished (Kirkpatrick, 1978), and the role of party organs in aggregating and formulating public demands is definitely on the wane (Ranney, 1978). Nevertheless, Saloma and Sontag (1972) and others have identified a countervailing trend which points to the increased desire of the electorate to participate in the selection of candidates for national and local office though the primary process. We have also seen the rise of political action committees (PACs) (Crotty and Jacobson, 1980) that made a definite impact on the 1980 and 1982 elections. At the local level, voluntary associations continue to pressure for an opening up of the political process (Simpson, 1979).

The contradictory nature of the literature on American political parties makes it difficult to decide whether the phenomenon of party decline is caused by the failure of the party system (that is, lack of ideological competition between the parties, initial ante too high for new parties to emerge, difficult requirements for voter registration, leadership recruitment too cumbersome, etc.) or if the problem lies with the specific parties in question (that is, antiquated procedures and programs of the Democratic and Republican parties). Without doubt, the two traditional American parties have experienced a decline in both power and effectiveness, and there seems to be no immediate solution to their crisis (Ladd, 1982). In addition, the political system does not seem to be able to encourage the development of alternative parties (as, for example, in West Germany

* The research for this essay was supported by the School of Urban Planning and Policy of the University of Illinois at Chicago. Particular thanks go to Augustin Olivera who helped in the research.

with the Greens, Great Britain with the Social Democrats, or in Italy with the Radicals), nor have the existing parties given signs of the spontaneous type of regeneration undergone by the Socialist party in France. Instead, the United States provides an example of a case where the decline of the traditional parties has given rise to nonparty political alternatives—for example, PACs, single-issue movements, personalized electoral machines, lobbies and interest groups, voluntary citizen organizations, etc.—that are slowly absorbing functions previously carried out by the parties. At the local level, strong political party organizations that had provided the basic building blocks for the parties at the state and national levels have practically become extinct.

The party under scrutiny here is the local Democratic party organization in Chicago (and Cook County) which, until recently, seemed to have avoided the fate of all other big-city parties (Rakove, 1975). In other words, the Chicago experience with the machine is unique in that it has been perpetuated much longer than was the case in other American cities. But the Chicago Democratic party is now suffering from the same ills that brought about the general decline of political party organizations in the rest of the United States.[1] The fate of the machine in Chicago is not a portent of things to come in other cities but instead the last replay of party organizational demise that has already happened elsewhere. What is new, however, is the nature of the alternative groups that are coming to the forefront as replacements.

The city of Chicago has historically been a political arena dominated by one party. Until 1931, the dominant political force was the Republican party. After the 1931 election of the Democrat Anton J. Cermak as Chicago's (only foreign-born) mayor and the Democratic sweep of local and national offices in the 1932 elections, the Democrats became in Chicago what Giovanni Sartori (1976: 192–201) has called a "predominant party" (that is, the party always wins but still continues to participate in a potentially competitive electoral process). The present essay will look at how and why the Democratic party organization lost its role of *predominance* through its inability (or unwillingness) to continue to perform the basic functions of an urban political machine. The resulting vacuum is being filled by other groups and institutions. An illustration of the alternatives to the political machine is provided by an analysis of the 1981 struggle over the formulation of the North Loop Redevelopment Program.

[1] Using the classification scheme developed by Rose and Mackie, the case presented by the Democratic party in Chicago is not one of the party disappearing but rather of undergoing a major change in structure and identity.

Party Functions and the Democratic Machine

As stated by Lawson (1980: 3), "Political parties can be put to almost any political or governmental purpose." In pluralistic societies, however, they usually perform six main functions. Three of these are characteristic of the role of "parties-in-the-electorate": (1) demand aggregation, articulation, and transmission; (2) leadership recruitment, selection, and promotion to public office; and (3) citizen education, mobilization, and participation in the political process.[2] The other three functions are more concerned with the presence of the "party-in-government": (4) policy formulation and decisionmaking; (5) conflict adjudication over policy decisions and administration; and (6) service delivery and resource allocation to the party faithful.[3] Works on the Chicago Democratic machine have always stressed the latter party-in-government functions (and especially service delivery and resource allocation) in describing the fundamental nature of the "spoils" system in maintaining the party organization. The party-in-the-electorate functions are seen by the machine as subordinate but necessary to keep the party's monopoly over resource allocation. For Edward Banfield (1967: 237), the distinguishing characteristic of the party machine is the jobs, graft, and favors that it can produce for the purpose of attracting political support. "A 'machine' is a party of a particular kind, one which relies characteristically upon the attraction of material rewards rather than enthusiasm for political principles."

Kathleen Kemp and Robert Lineberry (1982) emphasize that machine politics are viable when the policy outputs or rewards are "divisible" or "non-zero sum"—that is, the party has at its disposal a sufficient amount of resources that can be spread among a wide number of clients without ever appearing to be exhaustible. The machine is characterized by the classical clientelistic exchange pattern where patrons with an abundance of scarce resources come into contact with a population that has a great need for resources and few scruples about exchanging principles for favors. A necessary condition, then, for machine politics is a citizenry amenable to manipulation by the agents of the party. As expressed by Thomas Guterbock (1980: 6–7) in a recent study of the Chicago machine,

> In a material exchange model, the communities which support the machine are anonymous, atomistic slums characterized by social disorganization. The absence of shared standards and effective sanc-

---

[2] These three functions of the "party-in-the-electorate" correspond to the participatory and electoral linkages described by Lawson.

[3] The three functions of the "party-in-government" are reflected in Lawson's clientelistic and directive linkages.

tions in such settings means that even though some residents may hold democratic ideals, they have little incentive to act in accordance with their values. In this environment the party agents are able through their service activities to generate a network of obligations which people repay by voting as they are told. The relationship of the voter to the precinct captain is face-to-face but essentially utilitarian and "segmental" (i.e., narrow in its functional scope). The relationship is built around the exchange of specific material incentives for votes. Because of this lack of resources the voter values the bucket of coal or other small favors he receives, and because of this lack of community ties he has no support for any attempt he might make to arrive at his own electoral choice. The machine supporter is materially motivated and responds to material incentives.

For an effective political machine to exist, it must have available to it: (1) a significant amount of resources to be distributed among its clients; (2) exclusive control over resources and decisions affecting their allocation; (3) a vast army of potential clients ready to enter into the negotiation for the exchange of votes for scarce resources; (4) the lack of a sense of ideological principles and/or identification with community solidarity on the part of the clients; and (5) the freedom to seek electoral support from all potential voters, irrespective of race, ethnic origin, religion, or class considerations. These conditions slowly began to erode in the post-World War II period as the city's socioeconomic structure was transformed. Guterbock (1980) found that the "resources-for-votes" exchange model did not stand up to the political realities of his north side ward in the 1970s. Instead, the voters were much more willing to exchange their votes for political and social commitment and a desire for securing the protection of the local community. Voters were developing a sense of common solidarity. Even more telling are the results of Kenneth Mlandenka's study (1982) of the correlation at the ward level between the Richard J. Daley vote for mayor in the 1973 and 1967 elections and the distribution of recreational facilities, fire protection services, teacher/pupil ratios in the public schools, and garbage collection services. He concludes (1982: 155) that "There is no evidence that the pattern of service distribution in the city is a consequence of rational political calculations about who should win and who should lose in the struggle over finite resources. Instead, distributional outcomes are largely a function of party decisions, population shifts, technological changes, and reliance upon technical rational criteria and professional values."

Mladenka's evaluation is supported by more impressionistic studies (Preston, 1982; Brune, 1981) of the black community in Chicago during the last twenty years. Despite the crucial nature of black support for the Democratic machine in the postwar period, blacks were not rewarded with better services, more patronage, higher level administrative jobs, political influence, or a halt to police brutality and discrimination. The pattern continued under the Jane Byrne administration even though her victory in the 1979 Democratic primary was substantially based on a black revolt against the previous mayor, Michael Bilandic. A similar fate (and an even greater exclusion from political patronage) has befallen the Hispanic community (Belenchia, 1982).

THE DECLINE OF THE MACHINE

The machine's increased alienation from the black, Hispanic, and progressive white communities under Richard J. Daley was a product of the attempt to keep white ethnics and working-class voters from fleeing to the suburbs.[4] It has been argued that in the 1950s and 1960s white support for the machine was given in return for the physical isolation of the black ghettos. Mike Royko (1971: 137) writes that in the first eight years of the Daley administration:

> Containing the Negro was unspoken city policy. Even expressways were planned as man-made barriers, the unofficial borders. The Dan Ryan, for instance, was shifted several blocks during the planning stage to make one of the ghetto walls. Proposals to scatter public housing, thus breaking the segregation pattern, were killed by City Hall. The city's rule was that no public housing could go into a ward without the alderman's consent. Housing for the aged was kept out of white wards because it might attract old Negroes.

The black proletariat and middle class supported the machine, under the leadership of the powerful black committeeman William Dawson, in the belief that they would eventually reap the same benefits previously allocated to successive waves of white immigrants. The Democratic machine's and City Hall's unsympathetic response to the rise of black consciousness and social mobilization in the 1960s meant that the black community's *turn* was indefinitely postponed.[5] As a consequence, there was a dramatic falling off of black votes for machine candidates in mayoral elections. Preston (1982: 96) has demonstrated that the turnout in both black mid-

[4] As it turned out, these were the three voting blocs that gave Harold Washington the victory in the 1983 mayoral election.

[5] "Our turn" was the most potent slogan that mobilized the black community behind Washington's candidacy.

dle-class and working-class wards for Chicago mayoral elections was half of what it was for presidential elections: 38.2 percent versus 71.5 percent in the 1971–77 period. Thus, by the end of the 1970s, the political rationale for the presence of black support for machine candidates had been substantially weakened. The decline of black enthusiasm for machine candidates reflected the breakup of the racial and socioeconomic alliance that at the beginning of the 1930s had brought the party to a position of predominance in the city.

In the immediate post-World War I period, Chicago's ethnics were aroused by the xenophobic activities of the Klan; they were adamantly opposed to the limitation of personal freedom imposed by Prohibition; and they protested strongly the Johnson Act of 1924 that placed strict quotas on eastern and southern European immigration. The original Cermak majority that defeated the Republicans in 1931 was constructed on issues strongly felt by the city's working-class and ethnic communities. It is argued by Allswang (1971: 124–25) that the Depression had less of an impact on changing the voting patterns of Chicago's ethnic community than did the more personal issues of the 1920s in consolidating the new Democratic voters' identification with the party's programs and policies at the national and local levels.

The Democrats proceeded into the post-Roosevelt era with a solid coalition that brought together disparate groups ranging from the city's intellectual-academic community to the poorer sections of the working class. The party's national image and leaders (for example, Adlai Stevenson and the Kennedy brothers) continued to balance the more conservative course embarked on by the Cook County party organization when it endorsed Daley in 1955.

The contradictions between the national mood of the Democratic party and the outlook of the Chicago leadership began to surface during the 1960s and were brought to a head through a series of events in 1968–69. The immediate catalysts were the Martin Luther King assassination and the Democratic convention held at Chicago's Conrad Hilton hotel. Richard J. Daley, reflecting the antiprotest mood of the white core of the Democratic machine and a staunch supporter of President Johnson's Vietnam policy, issued "shoot to kill" orders to the police in response to the disorders sparked by the King assassination and unleashed a "police riot" (as defined by the Kerner Commission) against the war protesters and pro-Eugene McCarthy forces at the convention. The gap between the national and local levels of the Democratic party was further widened in December 1969 with the murder of Black Panther leaders Fred Hampton and Mark Clark by a Chicago police squad led by the machine's State Attorney, Edward Hanrahan.

Hanrahan's unsuccessful reelection bid in 1972 registered the machine's first political defeat at the hands of the black community. The year 1972 also saw the definitive break between the local party organization and the national Democratic party leadership when local, independent Democratic alderman William Singer successfully ousted the Cook County Democratic party delegation from the presidential convention. The decision was upheld in 1974 by the U.S. Supreme Court, and it served to put the machine on notice that it was no longer the sole voice for Chicago Democrats.

The views held by the rebel group of white, independent antimachine activists were reflective of the ideas that had become predominant in the national Democratic party in the post-1968 period. In explaining his reason for running for election as an independent, William Singer spoke about the "enormous reservoir of people who wanted to do something after 1968" (Rakove, 1979: 365). Dick Simpson (1979: 3) describes the flowering of the neighborhood government in the 44th Ward as the product of a marriage between political philosophy and a movement for change.

> Living in Chicago in the late 1960s we revolted against the leadership of Richard J. Daley and a remote national government under Presidents Lyndon Johnson and Richard Nixon. Our wing of the general movement for change in the country focused first on the electoral arena. We defeated the machine, at least in local contests, on a platform of more citizen participation. Having taken power, we redesigned local government to fulfill our promises to the electorate.

Blacks were also no longer willing to give the city administration the benefit of the doubt and wait patiently for their turn to access the machine's patronage. Community groups which had come into existence in the black areas on the heels of federally funded redevelopment projects began to assume a greater political orientation. After 1972, the machine could no longer present itself as the sole or even most legitimate spokesman for Chicago and Cook County Democrats. Its core support became increasingly identified with those who looked at the past when white ethnics were the numerically dominant sociopolitical force rather than facing up to the city's current racial and economic problems. William Grimshaw (1982: 72) has observed that whereas "the classic machine had relied on a contiguous mass of black and white low-income inner-city wards for its primary support, the new party (i.e., 1970–1979) receives the vast bulk of its support from the city's most racially threatened white wards." In the 1975 and 1977 mayoral primaries, the incumbent mayors (Daley and Bilandic) received less than half of the black vote in comparison to the 75 percent to 80 percent black support that had been a tradition in previous elections. The most telling result that bore witness to the lack of success of the machine in maintaining the confidence of black voters was the attempt in 1976 of the party to dump Congressman Ralph Metcalfe for his strong criticism of police brutality against blacks. Running as an independent against a black machine candidate, Metcalfe carried practically all of the 400 precincts in his district for an overwhelming electoral triumph. For the first time, blacks revolting against the machine were successful in defeating its candidate *and* electing an independent Democrat. The result was to be repeated in the 1979 and 1983 mayoral primary and aldermanic elections.

In the last two mayoral election campaigns, the Democratic machine was no longer perceived by many black and a growing number of white voters as having adequately carried out basic party functions—that is, it had not adequately aggregated, articulated, or transmitted political demands to policymakers. Those of the white ethnic sectors in the southwestern and northwestern parts of the city had been given precedence over the demands of the black and Hispanic residents. Leadership recruitment and selection remained hopelessly skewed in favor of white ward leaders. The party tried to prevent the introduction into party discussions of the new ideas and policies that were making headway in the Democratic party at other levels and areas in the country. Even more galling, however, was the machine's complete failure to function in an evenhanded manner as a party-in-government. It refused to open up the selection of alternative policies and administrative procedures and to open bidding in the awarding of city contracts. Daley and Bilandic maintained decisions within the confines of a small group of associates (Byrne referred to them as the "evil cabal" in her 1979 campaign). Any conflict that arose over the course or content of public policy was always handled as a matter to be settled personally by the mayor. And the mayor's word was law in the City Council which, until 1983, never engaged in any discussion of public policy or exercised its power of oversight with regard to city administrative practices and procedures.

The machine was no longer able to perform effectively as a party-in-government because it had lost three of its component features. First, local elites saw their power of discretion over local resources reduced. Monetary flows from the state and federal governments were increasingly accompanied by controls limiting the amount of local manipulation that could be exercised. The increased unionization of city and county employees also served to reduce the flexibility enjoyed by the leadership in controlling the patronage army. Teachers, transport workers, police, and firemen all obtained job security and freedom from political pressures through union contracts. The 1979 Shackman decree issued by Judge Nicholas J. Bua, prohibiting the city from firing employees for political reasons, spread job security to city workers. At the top rungs of the administration, the increased need for qualified professionals made wages and expertise, rather than political clout, the determining factors in hiring. Thus, in the span of a few years the major underpinnings of the vast patronage army at the beck and call of the mayor were substantially dislodged.

Second, despite the city administration's attempt to keep whites within the city, there had been a change in Chicago's population. White flight to the suburbs reduced the size of the pool of potential clients coming from the ranks of less educated white ethnics who looked to public jobs as the primary source of employment. Those who replaced the whites—blacks and Hispanics—were not given the same access to public resources. They had to find employment in the private sector. Private-sector employment also characterized the white professionals and white-collar workers returning to the city. The returnees served to increase pressure on city services by demanding them as a right acquired through the payment of taxes and residence rather than as a favor for voting Democratic.

Third, in the 1970s there was a general move toward a more ideological content in Chicago politics and a greater emphasis on direct forms of citizen participation. The level of political consciousness among minority groups grew as a result of the black and Hispanic empowerment movements and in reaction to the deterioration of their schools, housing, social services, and job opportunities. At the same time, the new white voter was no longer willing to delegate political decisionmaking or representation to the Democratic party committeeman or precinct captain/worker. The desire was strong for true grass-roots organizations, and the machine was in no position to respond.

The Cook County Democratic party has no provisions in its rules or traditions for direct citizen participation. Its raison d'être is to provide control of the voting base by the leadership. The latter decides party policies, chooses party candidates, and allocates resources. The only time that the leaders have to touch base with the electorate is during the election campaigns for public office or ward/township committeeman. Otherwise, the top rungs of the party are hermetically sealed off from the citizenry. The ward offices do not operate as community centers for discussion and activity. Responsibility for maintaining contact with the electorate is delegated to an appointed precinct captain and precinct workers who are normally on the public payroll and view precinct work as an integral part of job security. The precinct worker is not responsible to the registered Democrats in the precinct because they do not have any role in selecting him.

He is accountable only to the ward committeeman who appointed him in the first place and who could have him fired from his city job. Under such an arrangement there is no incentive for the precinct worker to be a conduit to the party for citizen demands, nor does the organization provide any form of direct participation of citizens in party affairs. Therefore, the Democratic party organization has not operationalized to any degree the participatory linkage described by Lawson. The party base is effectively excluded from shaping the party's program, choosing its candidates, or holding elected party officials accountable to the wishes of Democrats.

The nature of the Chicago machine is illustrative of the American model of party organization which never moved in the direction of formal membership that is characteristic of European mass parties (Duverger, 1954: 71). American parties have defined themselves as essentially electoral machines focused on mobilizing voters during election campaigns.[6] When voters in Chicago advanced demands to participate in the formulation of policies and other facets of party activity, the party treated such requests as hostile actions that had to be ignored or defeated. It was in response to this type of political vacuum and negative reactions that neighborhood organizations began to blossom across the city and slowly incorporated the linkage functions that the party was ignoring. The shift in the public's attention and support of neighborhood groups first became evident during the course of the 1981 North Loop controversy.

The net result of the decline of the machine's performance as a governing party was that it started to lose elections. Before 1968, the machine had rarely lost an election for alderman and never an election for mayor, but by 1979 the monopoly over the city's elected offices and electoral linkage function had quickly eroded. The first failures were defeats suffered at the hands of white liberal insurgents like William Singer and Dick Simpson. Next, the black voters began to dig in their heels against machine candidates. In 1982–83 this pattern of increased independence from the machine also appeared in the city's Hispanic neighborhoods. The definitive sign of a severe crisis was registered in the 1979 Democratic mayoral primary when the incumbent mayor and machine candidate was defeated by an independent antimachine Democrat. In 1983 the second consecutive defeat of the machine's mayoral candidate proved that 1979 had represented a watershed in Chicago politics. The challenge to the dominance of the machine was not coming from another party but from within the party fold, and it was finding its organizational base in previously nonpolitical organizations such as neighborhood groups that were slowly being sucked

---

[6] V. O. Key (1964: 347) describes party machines as pressure groups which try to get candidates elected to public office.

into the vacuum left by the party's retreat from its traditional functions and voting base.[7]

THE JANE BYRNE ERA AND THE NORTH LOOP CONTROVERSY

Jane Byrne's victory in the 1979 election sent shock waves through the Chicago political establishment. Immediately after the election, the new mayor made a few antimachine moves and continued to patronize community groups whose support had been instrumental during the campaign. She nominated a blue ribbon transition team to rethink the organization of city government and propose a thorough restructuring.[8] But it soon became clear that more than being antimachine, the new mayor was anti-Daley.

In the first few months, Byrne lashed out at the old Daley powerbrokers and personally attempted to remove close associates of Daley's son, Richard M. Daley, from the city payroll. Another aspect of the anti-Daley strategy was to undermine the notion that the old guard, despite all of its faults, knew how to govern—that is, Chicago was "the city that worked." It was in this context that the independent Democratic mayor revealed that the school board's budget had an enormous deficit which under Daley had been disguised through a sleight of the accountant's pen: two sets of books were kept on school expenditures. One was for public display; the existence of the other was known only by a few members of Daley's inner circle.[9] The subsequent scandal shook the business and financial community's confidence in the city. The New York bond rating for the city of Chicago bonds immediately dropped, thereby forcing the city to pay higher interest rates for the bonds that it had to float to bail out the school

[7] It is not clear whether Epton's 48.4 percent in the 1983 mayoral election has been completely flushed out of Chicago's political system. However, it is of interest to note that in 1984 Ronald Reagan received "only" 34.7 percent and incumbent Republican senator Charles Percy 30.5 percent of the vote in Chicago. Of even greater significance was the strong victory of Richard M. Daley over his Republican challenger, Richard Brzeczek (ex-police chief under Byrne) in the race for state's attorney.

[8] The transition team was headed by Louis Masotti of the Center for Urban Affairs of Northwestern University and included professors from Northwestern and the University of Illinois at Chicago, officials from banks, research organizations, and large community groups.

[9] As recounted by Grimshaw (1982: 71), Daley was reported to have said in 1975, in countering Governor Dan Walker's contention that there was not enough money in the state budget to support a series of education appropriations that Daley wanted: "You can make a budget say whatever you want it to say."

system. All of this was presented as the legacy of the Daley and Bilandic administrations.

Groups that supported Byrne during the electoral campaign soon found out that the new mayor had changed her mind on a number of issues. Municipal employee trade unions had enthusiastically welcomed the maverick candidate's endorsement of the principle of collective bargaining for city employees. But once in office, Jane Byrne stalled in carrying out her promise to recognize the elected representatives of the police and firefighters as legitimate bargaining partners, and the unionization of other municipal employees remained stalled during the Byrne administration.

Even though the regular Democratic machine emerged from the 1979 election in a weakened state, it sought to immediately reconcile its differences with the new mayor, and the reconciliation proved to be quite easy. Before being ousted in 1978 as Commissioner of Consumer Sales, Weights, and Measures for alleging a kickback scheme as part of the city's approval of a taxi fare increase, Byrne had been a member of the Democratic machine, holding the position of vice-chairman of the Cook County Democratic party. Richard J. Daley had personally picked Byrne in 1968 to represent the female voters in the Cook County Democratic party Central Committee. Her removal as commissioner (and then as member of the Central Committee) had not changed her organizational views on the machine. Jane Byrne remained a machine politician and her election in 1979 set the stage for her triumphant return to the party fold. After a brief series of spats, she made her peace with the machine's leaders in the City Council.[10] Her assumption of total control over the party was consummated in March 1982 when she succeeded in getting Edward Vrdolyak elected chairman of the Cook County Democratic party's Central Committee, but her rapprochement with the machine was reflected by a number of decisions prior to 1982 which signaled that "machine style" politics had returned to City Hall—the resignation of the head of the transition team, the dropping of plans to reorganize city government, and the resurrection of policies from the former Daley-Bilandic administrations.

The most notable of the recycled policies was the North Loop Redevelopment project which promised to bring into Jane Byrne's fold Chicago's wary business and trade-union leaders. The massive construction program called for by the project would generate thousands of jobs for the unions, and developers would benefit from a whole range of tax abate-

---

[10] In a truly bizarre turn of events, in 1980 Edward Burke ran as Jane Byrne's and the machine's candidate for state's attorney against Richard M. Daley, whose candidacy was supported by the old coalition that had elected Byrne in 1979. Daley defeated Burke by a two-to-one margin and then went on to defeat by the narrowest of margins the incumbent Republican Bernard Carey who was also cursed with Jane Byrne's blessing.

ments, financial subsidies, and improvements and amenities to be provided by the city. Tax abatements were of utmost interest to the local business community because Chicago was the only major city that had not used tax incentives to attract or keep business in the downtown area.

The North Loop project in 1972 had been the brainchild of a business group, the State Street Council, and in 1973 it became a part of the larger development proposal also advanced by a private group, the Chicago 21 Plan for the Central Communities of Chicago.[11] Mayor Daley had put the project in the hands of Arthur Rubloff, Chicago's real estate magnate and the city's chief private developer. The purpose of the project was to revitalize the northern part of the Loop through the total demolition of the existing buildings and the creation of a modern office building complex. However, since the Rubloff plan proposed the destruction of some of Chicago's most historically significant buildings, the public outcry over the implications of the proposal finally killed it. Attention was then turned to changing the plan by focusing on a major flagship hotel (rather than office buildings) and maintaining some, but not all, of the architectural landmarks.

In 1977–78 the Hilton Corporation began negotiating with the Bilandic administration on what was at first one (1978) and then two (1979) blocks of the total eight-block area of the North Loop. At the time of the negotiations, the city applied to HUD for $25 million of federal Urban Development Action Grant (UDAG) money to acquire and prepare the site for a "generic hotel" to be built by a group of investors without ever specifying that Hilton was the only prospective occupant. On the UDAG application the city specifically stated that tax abatements would not be sought for the project if federal funding was provided. As was common practice in Chicago, the site was never discussed with any other interested party, no provisions were made to open the construction process to competitive bidding, and the names of the investors who would be the real owners of the hotel and the main beneficiaries of the tax abatement were never revealed. The deal had all of the earmarks of the "honest graft" so aptly described by Plunkitt of Tammany Hall (Riordin, 1963: 3) and so much a part of machine politics (Key, 1974: 360–63).

By the time HUD made the announcement in January 1979, awarding $8 million to the city to develop the site, it was clear that the ante had been raised. The city was going to use the UDAG funds plus an additional $55

---

[11] The Chicago 21 Plan was published in 1973. Though it received the sponsorship of the city, it was proposed by the Central Area Committee, a group composed of the heads of only the most prominent corporations, financial institutions, utility companies, and large department stores present in the Loop. No smaller store, merchant association, civic group, consumer group, or others were represented in the committee.

million from Continental Bank to purchase, clear, and prepare the two-block area where the hotel was to be constructed. Once the site was ready, the city would sell it for $50 a square foot, not far from where the Hyatt chain had paid $400 a square foot for a less attractive location.[12] Even that was not enough. The group of investors and Hilton wanted more.

NEIGHBORHOODS AND CIVIC GROUPS ORGANIZE

For a long time the implications of the North Loop project for the city's tax base and the political maneuvering by the mayor had generally not been a major topic of conversation by the media or by citizens at large. At the March 1978 public hearings on the Urban Development Action Grant proposal—the public forum where the UDAG application had to be aired—black and white groups from the south and west sides of the city objected to the use of such a vast amount of money to develop the downtown area while steps were taken to cut back funds earmarked for the neighborhoods. The other group concerned about redevelopment in the North Loop was composed of architectural preservationists organized under the Landmarks Preservation Council. Preservationists had reacted strongly to the Rubloff plan to demolish large parts of the North Loop which contained a dozen architecturally significant buildings, including landmarks on the federal National Register of Historic Places.

During the 1979 primary, candidate Byrne had made the North Loop project a campaign issue. She had come out against it as a waste of taxpayers' money that could be better spent in the neighborhoods. Transition team papers had been prepared and publicized which indicated a change in priority with development programs targeted for areas from the Loop.[13] Three months after the election, the mayor changed her views. On

[12] The difference between the $50 and $400 a square foot for the hotel parcel was as much as $61,250,000. Jared Schlaes, a local real estate consultant, stated at the public hearings held on the North Loop project in November 1981 that prime land in the Loop had been selling for $700 and even $1,000 a square foot. Thus, the real value of the sale of land at the city-designated price could have been well in excess of $100 million.

[13] In addition to a thorough evaluation study of city agencies, the work of the transition team concentrated on the analysis of two related issues which had been the core of Byrne's campaign: the deteriorating economic conditions of the city and the widespread public and private disinvestment in many of the city's neighborhoods. One of the reports, "Jobs and the Economy," stressed as "priority concerns": (1) high unemployment and concentration of low income, particularly among minorities and in certain neighborhoods; (2) deterioration of the tax base and disinvestment in many city neighborhoods; and (3) a continued deterioration of commercial strips and convenience shopping in many neighborhoods. A second report, "Neighborhood Revitalization," was based on the premise that the "weak link in our

the heels of the Continental Bank's commitment of funds, Byrne began to mobilize her office to move forward on the other requests that had been made to the previous Bilandic administration. The investment group behind Hilton assumed the position that it would not proceed with the hotel complex if the city did not succeed in securing a thirteen-year tax abatement.

In the spring of 1980, a Cook County ordinance was passed to permit new commercial buildings throughout the county, including the city of Chicago, to be assessed at 16 percent of market value (the same as for homeowners) rather than the existing 40 percent for commercial property. The lower assessment was to continue for thirteen years after which the property would be reassessed at the 40 percent rate. A key provision was that the final word on the abatement would be up to the county tax assessor (who in this case was Thomas Hynes, a political ally of Richard M. Daley). In addition, public hearings had to be held before a tax break could be granted, and the applicant had to prove that the development could not take place without the abatement. On May 20, 1980, the city and Hilton signed a contract that obligated the city to tear down fourteen buildings in the immediate vicinity of the proposed hotel, seek the consent of Hilton before constructing anything new in the North Loop, and petition the tax assessor for the tax abatement. The contract, in effect, gave Hilton and investors veto rights over the entire eight-block North Loop redevelopment project.

Given the city's failure to produce a comprehensive plan for the area, the revelation of the contents of the Hilton contract set off a strong reaction from a number of neighborhood groups on the city's north side. The property tax committee of the Lake View Citizen Council (LVCC) and the education committee of the Northwest Community Organization (NCO) began to consider the implications of the tax abatement on property taxes for homeowners and the financial problems of the school system. An impact study conducted by independent researchers (Lyons and Mahan, 1981) predicted that, as a direct result of the tax abatement, local taxing bodies would loose $37.7 million a year and $490.7 million over the thirteen-year period.

In August 1980 the city made its formal request to Hynes for the tax abatement. The assessor initially rejected the request, based on the lack of full information on the ownership of the North Loop parcels and the identity of the investors, opposition to the discounted land prices that would be paid for the prepared sites, and the lack of a comprehensive plan for the

economic chain is the neighborhoods: Chicago has typified a 'top down' approach to neighborhoods."

area. While the city prepared the answers to these objections, the neighborhood groups used the time to mount a full-scale drive against the city's request. The delay was also welcomed by the assessor because it permitted him to wait for the results of the Cook County State Attorney's race. The victory by Richard M. Daley over the machine candidate in the primary (Edward Burke)[14] and incumbent Republican Bernard Carey (also backed by Byrne) provided Tom Hynes with added leverage on the North Loop. It also gave citizen groups the possibility of maneuvering between the two groups (Daley versus Byrne) struggling for control of the Democratic party. For the first time in decades, the mayor did not control all of the other major Democratic officeholders and party officials in the city or the county.

The neighborhood groups moved to exploit this split within the ranks of the Democratic party. In their view, the granting of the tax break would have shifted the power to grant tax relief from the tax assessor to the mayor's office. The city could then pick and choose its business clients and control a new form of patronage—that is, distributing tax abatements to its friends in business—that had the potential of being more effective in influencing the course of politics in the 1980s than the distribution of a bucket of coal or garbage can covers. A commonality of interests was thus established between the anti-Byrne forces within the Democratic party and the insurgent neighborhood groups. Both forces were interested in preventing the growth of the patronage pool available to the mayor and her machine allies.

In addition to neighborhood groups, more elitist "civic" organizations began to emerge in opposition to the city's handling of the North Loop project. In November 1980 the Civic Coalition Task Force on the North Loop was created under the leadership of a lawyer/developer particularly interested in saving the downtown theaters from demolition and the president of the Chicago Bar Association. The Task Force brought together twenty diverse civic groups, from the exclusive City Club to the NAACP, the League of Women Voters, and watchdog groups such as the Better Government Association. What troubled the Task Force was that the project was moving forward without a comprehensive plan, without open bidding on the Hilton and other North Loop parcels, and without the possibility of any public input into the decisionmaking process.

A parallel demand to open up the planning process with regard to the North Loop began to be voiced by NCO and LVCC in February 1981 through their efforts to put together a Chicago-wide coalition of community groups in opposition to the tax break. While the Task Force preferred

[14] Burke was a member of the "evil cabal" described by Byrne in 1979.

to be in opposition to the city's North Loop proposals on technical and preservationist grounds, the neighborhood groups ventured into the political arena, bringing up the issue of the allocation of public resources and the search for means to redirect public policy. The neighborhood position was that the North Loop project could go ahead without tax incentives. Financial resources available to the city should be directed toward the neighborhoods rather than to another downtown development which could easily leverage private capital. The neighborhood groups also argued that the Hilton project was an attempt by the mayor to assemble a coalition of real estate interests that subsequently would be marshaled in support of her next mayoral race. The pressure mounted against the mayor's proposal with the formation in March 1981 of the Campaign Against the North Loop Tax Break by a coalition of community organizations.

THE CAMPAIGN AS AN ALTERNATIVE POLITICAL ORGANIZATION

Chicago's social history is rich in both grass-roots and elite (civic) voluntary associations. One needs only to recall the settlement house service organizations. Yet, a strong degree of fragmentation and aloofness has characterized the commitment of these various groups to the city's political process. Until 1981 it was hard to find examples of coalitionbuilding across territorially based community groups. The starting point for the creation of a citywide coalition was the fragmentation and breakdown of the Democratic machine. The party clearly displayed its inability to perform its functions of conflict adjudication, demand aggregation, citizen mobilization, policy formulation, and service delivery. The coalition of community groups and civic organizations was now in a position to openly challenge the party on what had previously been its exclusive turf: the political arena.

To determine the viability of organizations like the Campaign Against the North Loop Tax Break as an alternative to the Democratic machine in Chicago, we must analyze its structure, goals, strategies, and prospects for the future. The role of the Campaign in the North Loop controversy illustrates how neighborhood groups can develop a more direct political role in light of the machine's growing weakness.[15]

One of the first considerations to be taken into account is the territorial

---

[15] The argument being made here is that community groups operating on a citywide basis can function as "local PACs" and quasi-party organizations in forming ad hoc coalitions and mobilizing citizen support to address issues that are deeply felt by the community and which the Democratic party is unable or unwilling to address.

reach of community groups in the city. Neighborhood groups cover the more densely populated areas of the city and can speak for about three-fourths of the city's population. When the Campaign was organized, this became a significant point of leverage over the city and county administrators. When Hynes met with representatives of the Campaign, he acknowledged their political strength and promised that the tax incentive would not be approved without a full public discussion and hearings on the issue.

Structurally, the Campaign was a coalition of neighborhood umbrella organizations that cover areas roughly equivalent to the seventy-seven "community areas" which have been used since the 1930s to subdivide the city. In contrast to the Democratic party, these umbrella groups do have viable grass-roots organizations (that is, do provide for participatory linkages to the citizenry) in the form of smaller neighborhood territorial units. Membership is first defined in relation to the more immediate neighborhood unit and secondly to the umbrella organization. Members simultaneously join both organizations and pay membership dues that give them voting and participatory rights in both organizations. All of these organizations have functioning leadership bodies that are periodically elected by the membership. The organizations have regularly scheduled meetings, and the membership can participate in the formation of group policies and strategy choices through specific issue committees. Many of the community groups and issue committees sent representatives to speak and make decisions on their behalf within the Campaign. Membership in the Campaign was open to all interested groups, and it kept growing throughout the fight over the North Loop.

The Campaign's agenda was determined by a coordinating committee composed of designated group representatives. The committee acted as a clearing house where issues were first raised and recommendations were developed for consideration by the member organizations and, more importantly, by general Campaign meetings. Mass meetings were used by the Campaign to dramatize its concerns and focus media attention. Motions in the coordinating committee and general meetings were adopted on a majority basis, but in most cases decisions were consensual in nature.

A few organizational decisions which were made at the beginning turned out to be extremely useful. One was the idea to have an "administrative" apparatus capable of carrying out the background work needed to bring forward the deliberations. The administrative staff was provided by the Housing Agenda (an activist group within the Illinois Public Action Council) rather than by one of the territorially based groups in order to avoid the hegemony of any one organization in the Campaign, and the staff was composed of full-time professionals rather than volunteer workers. The experience, dedication, and reliability of the staff were crucial in pulling together and holding on to diverse member groups and assuring them a flow of timely information.

A second key decision was the establishment of working linkages with the Civic Coalition Task Force through selected individuals who became members of the steering committees of both organizations (i.e., Campaign and Task Force). In this manner valuable information was shared by the two groups. The Campaign gained access to technical expertise that it otherwise would not have had while the Task Force received mass support for its historic preservationist claims. Ultimately, the ability to identify and work toward a common purpose and program on the North Loop strengthened the complementary strategies of the grass-roots Campaign and the Civic Coalition Task Force.

During the period of initial growth and activity, the Campaign did not attract the interest of Chicago's Democratic party. The diverse nature of the two organizations provided little reason for contact. Party ward committeemen or precinct captains paid no attention to Campaign-sponsored events in their wards. Had the machine been capable of carrying out the demand aggregation function, it would have monitored the growth of this citizens' movement in order to take appropriate action (for example, cooptation) at the opportune time. The control that Byrne tried to reestablish over the party did not extend uniformly down to the precinct level where party organizational forces remained split between the Daley and Byrne camps.

From the beginning, the Campaign had two sets of objectives. The first was the short-term goal of defeating the Mayor's North Loop proposal. Its second goal was longer range in nature: to change Chicago's style of politics and decisionmaking in the direction of increased public control and a broader definition of the public interest. The Campaign elaborated proposals for the North Loop which did not have a specific physical design content but did outline a specific process of how decisions should be made. Its program incorporated the principles of comprehensive planning, public participation, and open bidding to be adopted by the city in the North Loop and in future projects.[16]

The first test of the Campaign was, therefore, to establish citywide public support in favor of the short-time objective of modifying the city's North Loop proposal. Critical to the objective was the choice of strategy. The strategy that was followed combined high media visibility, in-depth

[16] The three principles became known as the "three Os": overall planning, open process, open bidding. They formed the common ground for action with the Civic Coalition Task Force.

studies, wide publicization of the implications of the city's development proposal, and the search for externally allied groups. The actual size of the community group support and, ultimately, the decision of the city to drop its request for a tax abatement suggest that the strategy succeeded. How was the Campaign's strategy implemented?

The Campaign was able to keep alive the public's sentiment against the tax break through the spring and summer of 1981. In preventing an immediate decision on the city's request, other groups whose interest were immediately affected were given sufficient time to mobilize. In August 1981 a group of North Michigan Avenue hotel owners organized under the heading of the Property Conservation Council in opposition to what was interpreted as the city's preferred treatment for one hotel chain (Hilton). The council financed a study on the potential profit margin of the new Hilton hotel which came to a conclusion much different from that reached by the city's consultants. Thus, when the public hearings were held on November 14 and 16, 1981, an overwhelming coalition of community, civic, and business groups was organized against the tax abatement. Assessor Hynes announced on December 9, 1981, that he would reject a flat tax break but instead would tie any reduction of taxes to the eventual profitability of the hotel. After a month's delay, Hilton pulled out of the deal with the city and decided that it would be more economical to rehabilitate the existing Conrad Hilton rather than build a new hotel under the conditions stipulated by the tax assessor.

An Evaluation of the Campaign

Using the six indicators cited earlier for the functioning of political parties, it is possible to analyze how well the Campaign succeeded in approximating the activities of a full-fledged political organization. *Demand aggregation* signifies the ability of the organization to reflect public sentiment and provide the means for analyzing the impact of policies on public welfare. The Campaign performed this function quite well with regard to the North Loop controversy. It was instrumental in voicing public outrage over the city's "honest graft"; it analyzed the impact of the tax break in terms of school funding and other public services; and it pointed to the ripple effect that the development project would have on downtown revitalization and the structure of property taxes in the city of Chicago.

Citizen mobilization refers to the size of the mass following mobilized, the means selected to express the organization's positions, and the involvement of members in the decisionmaking process. Here again, the Campaign receives high marks because it was able to mobilize diverse socioeconomic groups on a citywide basis. During the course of the struggle, a wide range of individuals and groups participated in different forums to express the Campaign's preoccupations and state its positions.

With regard to *policy formation*, the Campaign succeeded in bringing the citizenry in direct contact with the public officials (that is, tax assessor through scheduled meetings and city officials during the course of the hearings) involved in making the final decision. It presented well-prepared testimony (community positions and technical analysis) that went to the heart of the issues. The Campaign also suggested alternatives to the current plan, urging a greater mix of commercial, residential, and cultural uses in the North Loop.

The Campaign's *conflict adjudication* role was one of the crucial aspects of its activities. It forced out into the open the conflict between the Byrne and Daley camps in the Democratic party and different groups in the business community (hotel operators, retailers, entertainment establishments, etc.) over the plans for the North Loop. Because of the Campaign's activities, this conflict could not be settled behind closed doors in the mayor's office.

The Campaign did less well in *service delivery* and *resource allocation*. It did not succeed in gaining any immediate material benefits for the individuals and groups active in the Campaign, though it did provide a considerable amount of symbolic rewards. Neighborhood groups were courted by the media and eventually given credit for having defeated "the biggest real estate deal ever conceived."

Notwithstanding the success on the North Loop tax abatement issue, the question remains whether neighborhood organizations operating through the Campaign achieved the long-term goal of changing the way public policy is made in Chicago. The answer must of necessity be speculative in nature, but there have been numerous events since the rejection of the tax abatement proposal, suggesting that neighborhood and civic groups in Chicago will continue to have influence.

It must be remembered that a precedent was set with the Campaign and that the monopoly of the Democratic party over citywide politics has been broken. The rejection of the city's request for tax abatements for the North Loop represented a watershed for public policymaking in Chicago. For the first time in the city's history, neighborhood groups and civic organizations were able to seize the political initiative against the mayor's office and the Democratic party. The public and media reaction demonstrated that these groups had a tremendous reservoir of credibility in voicing citizen concerns and speaking for the public interest. There is ample evidence that the Campaign built on organizational strength that had been in existence for a long time in many of Chicago's neighborhoods. The political clout of the LVCC in the 44th Ward is just one example of how grass-roots neighborhood organizations filled the vacuum left by the machine at the local level and are basically in a better position to respond to the increased demand for citizen participation in neighborhood and city affairs.

If the Campaign or similar coalitions are to grow and expand, they must gain access to tangible rewards for the community. The machine must be eliminated as the gatekeeper for the distribution of services and the allocation of resources. The Campaign was by its very nature a temporary coalition to fight one issue on behalf of the citizens. But there is no reason why a citywide organization of community groups cannot be institutionalized on a permanent basis as an alternative type of participatory and decisionmaking body. The opposition to such a body remains political—that is, to be found among the city's elected officials (mayor and aldermen)—who see the formalization of neighborhood power as a direct attack on their roles as political representatives.

CONFIRMATION OF PARTY DECLINE: THE 1983 ELECTIONS

The results of the 1983 Democratic primary (February 22) and general elections (April 12) provided ample evidence that the decline of the Democratic party had achieved crisis proportions. Despite the backing of the party organization, a $10 million campaign fund, and the mobilization of an army of city workers, the incumbent mayor came in second with 33.5 percent of the vote in the Democratic primary. Thirty-six percent of the vote gave Harold Washington the victory. Byrne's poor showing represents the lowest percentage that the official Democratic candidate for mayor has ever received. Michael Bilandic in 1979 was the first to dip below the 50 percent mark. The 1983 result showed that the Bilandic loss was no fluke and that the party was no longer able to rally a majority of the voters behind its candidate for the city's most important public office.

The problem was further highlighted in the mayoral general election when white Democratic voters abandoned the black Democratic candidate in a pell-mell rush to vote for a white man, even if he was a Republican. A parallel and even more serious display of party disintegration was provided when a number of Democratic party committeemen and aldermen crossed party lines to back the Republican candidate. These developments brought home the message that, for both white party leaders and voters, a candidate's race was more important than his party affiliation. White Democrats' reluctance to vote for Washington showed that the three party-in-the-electorate functions have been reduced (as is suggested above) to the aggregation of demands for racial segregation, the recruitment of white leaders for public office, and the exclusion of blacks from the top echelons of city government.

The attempt to use racial fear as a political ploy had been a part of the Byrne primary campaign. The mayor had gone out of her way in 1982 to antagonize the black community by appointing whites to posts previously held by blacks on the school and public housing boards. The hope was that these moves would shore up her standing among whites in the racially homogenous southwest and northwest sides and thus undermine political support for Richard M. Daley and entice a black candidate to enter the race.

The strategy failed because the party's white linkages with the voters—precinct captains and workers—remained divided between the Daley and Byrne camps; the black "plantation" vote—that is, susceptible to pure clientelistic considerations such as jobs and handouts—proved to be much smaller than expected; and the ex-mayor did not do as well as expected among Hispanics. Washington was able to galvanize the black community behind his candidacy based on a program of extensive reforms and redistribution of power. Not surprisingly, his program also found significant support in Hispanic and white middle-class communities.

In the general election, the Republican candidate, Bernard Epton, refined the Byrne strategy. Given the sense of racial panic that gripped the white ethnic community, Epton's candidacy was presented as the "last chance" for whites to keep blacks from taking over City Hall and all of Chicago. However, the racial polarization strategy failed once again because a number of Hispanics and whites came out in support of Washington's commitment to reform.

The racial nature of the primary and general election campaigns served to accelerate the demise of the Democratic party organization. The cadre infrastructure for the party went from a pre-1983 conservative and white-power orientation to activists from the traditionally excluded and progressive groups in the city. The net result of the transformation is that the party-in-the-electorate will have to be rebuilt from the ground up, and the cooperation of neighborhood organizations will be crucial.

The 1983 campaign also put to rest much of what was left of the party-in-government functions. Washington consistently campaigned on the desire to eliminate patronage and the spoils system. The issue became moot when Judge Nicholas J. Bua ruled in March 1983 that the city and county had one year to eliminate politically motivated hirings and harassment of municipal workers. It will be some time before a new Democratic party emerges from the ashes of the 1983 campaign. But it is clear that the era of the monolithic Chicago Democratic machine that was capable of fulfilling a wide variety of political functions and servicing diverse ethnic and racial groups is over. In the summer of 1983, the Democratic party and City Council split into two camps: a minority of twenty-one lakefront and black aldermen supporting the mayor and a majority, machine block of twenty-nine aldermen led by the Cook County Democratic party chairman, Edward Vrydolyak. The division was temporarily patched up during the 1984 election campaign and was instrumental in maintaining intact Democratic party seats in the House of Representatives and electing Illinois's second Democratic senator, Paul Simon.[17]

Despite these temporary truces, the trajectory of machine fortunes has tended to point downward while that of community groups continues to rise. One case in point is the creation in February 1984 of the Save Our Neighborhoods Save Our City Coalition (Nanetti, 1986) by two large neighborhood umbrella organizations—Northwest Neighborhood Federation and Southwest Parish Federation—in two large white ethnic areas of the city for the purpose of addressing five important housing and urban development issues. The expressed goal of the new group is to become the promoter of a citywide, multiracial neighborhood movement that can fill the political policy vacuum left by the demise of the machine. Another example is provided by the success of the second citywide coalition—the Chicago 1992 Committee—put together by neighborhood groups to fight the proposed 1992 World's Fair. Therefore, the course of events since 1981 suggests that the Campaign Against the North Loop Tax Break was the first in a series of citywide neighborhood coalitions coming to the forefront in Chicago politics to assume the political linkage functions that the Democratic party no longer performs.[18]

References

Allswang, J. M. 1971. *A house for all peoples*. Lexington, Ky.: The University of Kentucky Press.

Banfield, E. C. 1961. *Political influence*. New York: Free Press.

Belenchia, J. 1982. Latinos and Chicago politics. In Gove and Masotti, 1982: 118–45.

[17] Simon received 68.8 percent of the vote in Chicago and had majorities in forty-three of Chicago's fifty wards.

[18] It is interesting to note that one of the key demands of the Save Our Neighborhoods Save Our City Coalition (which addresses the point of the Campaign's lack of tangible rewards to distribute to its members) is to decentralize all city decisions on planning, capital investment, and social services to neighborhood planning boards and set up a "neighborhood fund" to be used for neighborhood economic development and improvement projects. Contributions to the neighborhood fund would be provided by developers of downtown Loop projects as part of a downtown-neighborhood linkage development program.

Brune, T. ed. 1981. *Neglected neighborhoods.* Chicago: Community Renewal Society.

Burnham, W. D. 1975. American politics in the 1970s: Beyond party? In *The American party systems,* ed. W. N. Chambers and W. D. Burnham. New York: Oxford University Press, 308–57.

Crotty, W. J., and G. C. Jacobson, 1980. *American parties in decline.* Boston: Little, Brown.

Duverger, M. 1954. *Political parties.* New York: John Wiley & Sons.

Gove, S. K., and L. M. Masotti, eds. *After Daley: Chicago politics in transition.* Urbana, Ill.: University of Illinois Press.

Grimshaw, W. J. 1982. The Daley legacy: A declining politics of party, race, and public unions. In Gove and Masotti, 1982: 57–87.

Guterbock, T. M. 1980. *Machine politics in transition.* Chicago: The University of Chicago Press.

Kemp. K. A., and R. L. Lineberry. 1982. The last of the great urban machines and the last of the great urban mayors? Chicago politics, 1955–77. In Gove and Masotti, 1982: 1–26.

Key, V. O. 1964. *Politics, parties, and pressure groups.* New York: Thomas Y. Crowell.

Kirkpatrick, J. J. 1978. *Dismantling the parties.* Washington, D.C.: American Enterprise Institute.

Ladd, E. C. 1982. *Where have all the voters gone?* New York: W. W. Norton.

Lawson, K. 1980. Political parties and linkage. In *Political parties and linkage: A comparative perspective,* ed. K. Lawson. New Haven: Yale University Press, 3–24.

Lyons, A., and T. Mahan. 1981. Some potential impacts of the North Loop tax break in Chicago schools (mimeo.).

Mladenka, K. R. 1982. The urban bureaucracy and the Chicago political machine: Who gets what and the limits of political control. In Gove and Masotti, 1982: 146–58.

Nanetti, R. Y. 1986. Living with change or the threat of it: Neighborhood maintenance strategies in Chicago. In *The urban caldron: Adapting land use planning to social and demographic change,* ed. J. DiMento, L. Graymer, and F. Schnidman. Oelgeschlager, 103–14.

Preston, M. B. 1982. Black politics in the post-Daley era. In Gove and Masotti, 1982: 88–117.

Rakove, M. 1975. *Don't Make No Waves . . . Don't Back No Losers.* Bloomington: Indiana University Press.

———. 1979. *We Don't Want Nobody Nobody Sent.* Bloomington: Indiana University Press.

Ranney, A. 1978. The political parties: Reform and decline. In *The new American political system,* ed. Anthony King. Washington, D.C.: American Enterprise Institute, 213–47.

Riordon, W. L. 1963. *Plunkitt of Tammany Hall.* New York: E. P. Dutton.

Royko, M. 1971. *Boss: Richard J. Daley of Chicago.* New York: E. P. Dutton.

Saloma III, J. S., and F. H. Sontag. 1972. *Parties*. New York: Alfred A. Knopf.

Sartori, G. 1976. *Parties and party systems*. New York: Oxford University Press.

Simpson, D. 1979. The philosophical basis of neighborhood government. In *Neighborhood government in Chicago's 44th ward*, ed. D. Simpson, J. Stevens, and R. Konen. Champaign, Ill.: Stipes Publishing Co., 3–29.

EIGHT

Sanrizuka: A Case
of Violent Protest in
a Multiparty State

DAVID E. APTER

Violence is the "disordering" side of politics. The mediation and prevention of violence is a primary task of any state. In democracies the causes
of such disorder are commonly regarded as pathologies the most serious
of which either reveal some kind of injustice or result from the malfunctioning of representative institutions. Knowing how to deal with the more
serious pathologies is difficult in part because it is very difficult to link protest and violence directly to injustice or institutional unresponsiveness.
(There is no "justice quotient," the variation of which will predict the outbreak of violence.) Nor is it possible to gauge when political temperatures
will rise to a point where violent protest seems likely to break out. One
reason for the lack of indicators is the weakness of current explanatory
theories. Highly generalized structural ones lead to overkill conclusions.
Those concerned with individual psychological variables are mostly devoid of interpretive understanding. They treat circumstance and situation
as residuals. It is precisely on these residuals that the present study focuses.

The concern is with a particular form of citizen protest that I will call
extrainstitutional, i.e., it expresses itself outside normal linkage channels.
In the case I will examine, the issues are by no means fleeting. Indeed, the
movement has lasted over a period of twenty years. Its causes and effects
and the role violence has played in it need to be analyzed over time. Its
durability is all the more surprising since it has occurred in Japan, one of
the most successful examples of a democratic multiparty state.

Analytical materials will be drawn rather arbitrarily from two different
sources. One, political economy, emphasizes how violence can result from
marginalization, in this case of small farmers driven into the labor force
by deliberate governmental design. The other, deriving from structural-
ism, indicates how this experience of violence can be translated into special languages, symbolism, speech acts, and semiotics. The two very different ingredients come together in the events occurring at an old imperial

crossroads in rural Chiba, and which is the present site of the new Narita International Airport.

Confrontation between farmers and police at this site escalated over time. As it did so, it led to increasingly generalized and polarized views about a number of important social and political questions. Some pertained to the negative social consequences of Japan's economic policies. Others were about Japan's role as an international power. So powerful was the symbolism evoked by such confrontation that very diverse protest coalitions were effectively united. For some in the opposition, the construction of the airport led to a rejection of the democratic polity, posing challenges to the authority of the state itself (Apter and Sawa, 1984).[1]

Although the facts are straightforward enough, the story is complex. Perhaps the best place to begin is not at the beginning but at the crossroads itself and at a mass rally held in Sanrizuka Park on March 28, 1982, by farmers of the Hantai Domei, the Sanrizuka-Shibayama Opposition League Against the New Tokyo International Airport, their militant allies and supporting groups. Clad in face masks, helmets, and "combat" dress, surrounded by antiriot police in full regalia, and under police observation from circling helicopters, the leaders read the following statement to the assembled crowd:

> The whole world faces now a grave crisis of imminent war—nuclear war; the human being is now threatened with holocaust and total annihilation. An urgent demand for peace expressed in antiwar, antinuclear protest is becoming more and more common, not only among the Japanese people but also among people all over the world.
>
> We, members of the Opposition League and those who are rallying around it, have been fighting for seventeen years against the construction of Sanrizuka military airport under the banner of "Stop war! Fight for peace!" in diametrical, violent confrontation with the state power.
>
> Now that antiwar, antinuclear struggle is gaining momentum anew, we feel it our duty, as ones [sic] fighting in Sanrizuka—a fortress of people's struggle of the whole of Japan—to fill responsible positions in this struggle (Apter, 1982).

In the audience were representatives of a variety of citizen groups, as well as students, trade unionists, members of the Chiba branch of the locomotive union, and, of course, followers of sects manning fortresses in

[1] This study was made possible by funds from the Japan Foundation and the Center for International Studies, Yale University. The research represents a collaborative effort with Nagayo Sawa, coauthor of the book from which part of this material is taken.

the area. Waving huge banners and massed flags imprinted with slogans attacking the airport, imperialism, and militarism, the leaders proclaimed the most peaceful intents. Sanrizuka Park, the staging area, is itself of some significance. It is the last remnant of an old imperial estate whose lands once comprised a good deal of the terrain on which the present airport is constructed. While the rally was going on, planes were taking off and landing every few minutes from the one runway the government has been able to build, although passengers remained totally oblivious to what was happening just a few thousand yards away. Even though the two crossroads, the airport and Sanrizuka, are cheek by jowl, those who use the first neither know—now would most of them much care—what happens at the second. It is at the second, Sanrizuka itself and its environs, where people care very much about the first, either for or against. The more they care, the more serious the protest. The more serious the protest, the greater the tendency to violence. The more violence, the more polarization between the movement and the state, and the more passionate their ideological differences.

The protest itself began as a simple conflict of interests between the farmers in the area of Chiba Prefecture designated for the construction of the New Tokyo International Airport and the government. The first site selected in 1965 was Tomisato, some sixty-six kilometers from Tokyo. The original decision aroused such spontaneous reaction that the site was changed to Sanrizuka, a few kilometers away, a more thinly populated area where imperial land was available. Again there was protest. This time the government refused to give way. Violent confrontations occurred. In 1967 the movement, which until then consisted of farmers, was joined by New Left sects and became increasingly radicalized.

As confrontation became more bitter, violence escalated as did mutual estrangement between those protesting against and those favoring government policy. As other issues became joined to the original protest, principles became more important than interests. A variety of groups from all over Japan came to regard existing laws as repressive, representative institutions as unresponsive, and political leaders and senior civil servants unaccountable at best and coercive at worst. Lack of an effective political opposition also contributed to the sense of frustration. The Communist party, which initially supported the farmers, tried to use them for its own purposes. The Socialists were largely ineffective in a system controlled and dominated from the start by the Liberal-Democratic party (Cole, Totton, and Uyehara, 1966). Given the circumstances—the lack of consultation, ineffective due process, inadequate power of local governments, and an ineffective opposition in Parliament—the statement read at the rally becomes less surprising. As violent protest continued, this movement, like many others, came to demand a place in history, and in heroic moral terms. The more it did so, the more it was able to establish a common front with other groups representing many different expressions of public grievance. What makes this movement particularly special is not the magnitude of its claims, but the place and role it came to occupy in the protest politics of Japan.

THE SANRIZUKA MOVEMENT

This small place with its few inhabitants came to be taken seriously as a surrogate for the most abstract and pressing moral concerns. So Sanrizuka, a rural pocket of Chiba Prefecture, could become a "fortress of people's struggle" whose leaders would claim responsible positions in that struggle. Eventually the Sanrizuka movement accumulated such a variety of principles that it seemed to represent a fault line for all forms of citizen protest, something volcanic, a shifting terrain where all other cleavages joined to form a concrete disjunctive community in a "mobilization space." As it gained momentum, the movement converted considerable numbers of citizens into partisans on one side or the other and created a wider circle of public opinion willing to suspend judgments instead of automatically supporting the government position. People became less passive, more interested and alert. On the fringes they were passionate (Apter, 1979).

The movement was composed of three components. The first and original group consisted of farmers and their households, divided into those living in the environs of Sanrizuka itself, in neighboring hamlets and villages where the main agricultural product is vegetables, and those in nearby Shibayama where the main product is rice. The Sanrizuka area came under the general administration of Narita City, Shibayama under the general administration of Shibayama Town. The farmers' movement or Hantai Domei had representatives in both the Narita City Assembly (including the secretary-general of the movement) and the Shibayama Town Council. Both supported the movement and both reversed their support under pressure from the Chiba Prefecture government which shares responsibility with the Airport Authority and the Ministry of Transportation for acquiring land and keeping the peace, under the LDP government.

Although the first stage of the airport has been built, protest continues over construction of the second. On the original site where the airport is today, all villages, farms, woods, etc. have, of course, disappeared and the original inhabitants dispersed. Families inside the second stage site have dwindled to twelve. The main farmers' support remains Shibayama where the inhabitants are concerned with problems of land use, ecology, irrigation, and other factors affected by so large an undertaking as the airport. Together the Sanrizuka-Shibayama Hantai Domei consists of about 120 households of which a dwindling number continue to be active in the struggle with the authorities.

The second component of the Sanrizuka movement consists of radical militant sects living in fortresses and solidarity huts on land made available by farmers, or on airport land on which construction has not yet begun. Some of the members are cadres living more or less permanently in these huts and fortresses. Others come part time from universities and jobs to help the farmers protest, and to work for them in the fields. Some have married into farm families. Some have been fighting for as long as twenty years alongside the farmers.

A third component consists of supporting groups belonging to sects with larger networks. Some of these sects are very powerful, such as Chu-kaku-ha which originally, like many others, split off from the Japan Communist party and came to prominence during the student struggles in 1960, led by the student organization, Zengakuren. These supporting networks not only provide funds for the movement and supporters, but help rally support in trade unions like Chibadoro, the Chiba branch of the locomotive union on which supplies of fuel to the airport depend (Scalapino, 1967).[2]

Until recently, control of the movement rested with the farmers. However, as the number of farmers has declined (and as the mood in Japan shifts to the right), farmers have split into two groups. The sects which originally came to the area to support the farmers and confront the government (while their own main bases remained outside) find that as their outside support erodes, their stake in Sanrizuka increases. They have no other place to go.

The loose organization of the Hantai Domei has been both a strength and a weakness. The death by cancer of an exceptional president in 1979 left something of a vacuum at the top. The tough old farmer who replaced him as acting president was subsequently forced to resign under pressure from some of the sects which charged him with collaborating with the airport authorities. Several other key members of the Hantai Domei had to resign as well. For a time the movement was dominated by the secretary-general, who ran it from his headquarters in a kimono shop. But as he

[2] Chukaku-ha, together with its ally, Chibadoro, has been responsible for continuing acts of sabotage, not only of the airport, but also of other facilities such as the Japan National Railways.

came to favor Chukaku-ha over Fourth International and other sects, he became less effective as a liaison person between farmers, sects, and supporting groups. Eventually the farmers split into two Hantai Domei groups, one favoring coalition with Socialist sects including Fourth International, and the other favoring Chukaku-ha and its allies.

The power of the movement always depended heavily on personalities. It survives mainly because of its strength in tiny village and hamlet organizations. In such bodies, support comes from women, elders, youth, and other groups. A few key figures, survivors in every sense of the word, keep the struggle alive. It takes only a small number of dedicated people to mobilize outside support. In this activity the sects are crucial.

So small, fragile, and divided an organizational structure gives no hint of what this movement has been able to do nor the extent to which a stalemate continues at the airport. Even though the first round of violent confrontation came to an end in May 1978 when the airport opened for business, delays, overruns, security and the like have resulted in astronomical costs. The airport, which was supposed to open in 1970, remains only partly constructed. It continues to be controversial for a number of reasons, not all of them having to do with farmers or sects. Businessmen and other travelers complain that the airport is too far from Tokyo. It takes too long to get there and back. There are traffic delays. It is inconvenient. It also remains vulnerable to attack by militants. Indeed, the government's plans to complete both a fuel pipeline and a Shinkansen or bullet train have been thwarted by confrontations and sabotage.

Militants and farmers have maps showing every conduit of the airport, and all the facilities, rooms, control points, etc. In the last outbreak of major violence, they entered through the sewer system and hid there overnight. The next morning they went to the top of the control tower, smashed equipment worth millions of dollars, and hoisted a red banner out the window, thereby delaying the opening by several months.

Indeed, from 1967 until the airport opened in 1978, the movement was widely seen as a metaphor for struggle, the airport serving as a surrogate for the "one-party" state, a state which in turn served as a symbol of imperialism and militarism, and a potential instrument of nuclear holocaust, so particularly an issue in Japan. Immediate events of violence on the site served as reminders of these and other issues of wider significance. Previous loyalties to the state came to an abrupt end when old people invaded the hall during ceremonies celebrating the handing over of the imperial estates at Sanrizuka to the government airport authorities. A fight against government teams of surveyors invested the terrain itself with a kind of independence, Sanrizuka becoming a world partly outside the jurisdiction of the state. Watchtowers and fortresses were built by farmers and militants on lands the government wished to acquire for the airport, and attacks against them by government police came to represent the defense of the "revolution." Taking over the airport control tower just before the airport opened in March 1978 showed that the defenders could take over the commanding heights of power. Each of these events came to be seen as a logic of history in common with the logic of revolutionary movements elsewhere, as I will try to show.

The movement became a mixture of action and story in which the protagonist represented an enduring alliance of small farmers (all grandfathers and ex-soldiers who fought in the Second World War) and militants from New Left sects of postwar Japan. Their movement, lasting for a whole generation, raises broad questions about the limits of party politics in the absence of an effective opposition and the substitution of factional politics of the LDP in its place. It also suggests how concern over some of the more negative aspects of modern industrial life manifests itself politically. Even in a successful society like Japan, progress has its victims. What this case suggests is some of the costs as well as the benefits of economic transformation. It is the other side of the corporate Japan, "Japan as number one" as Ezra Vogel puts it (Vogel, 1979). For if Japan today is a monument to discipline, intelligence, and hard work, and its political leaders have served as shrewd guides to effective policy, as always there is another side to the story.

THE ISSUES

The airport, not yet complete but functioning, stands athwart the old crossroads at Sanrizuka where the emperor once owned large estates, experimental farms, and a horse ranch dating back before Tokugawa times. The landscape, sufficiently beautiful to have earned the reputation of being the Barbizon of Japan, was a place of much local pride and affectionate nurture over many generations. The transformation of it (and the farms and villages adjacent to it) into a runway and terminals, converted the terrain itself into a metaphorical landscape. The government decision to put an airport there transformed the entire area into metaphors of organicism, fertility, nature. It also retrieved another "history"—or better, a "memory"—which, underlying all this charm, summoned a bitter legacy of struggles between peasant and lord, tenant and landlord. As "history," both have their place in this movement.

Traditions aside, there is wide agreement within the movement that the airport irrevocably destroys certain values essential to life itself. Hence the original question of self-interest was the farmers' defense of their land, their private property, their patrimony. As conflict continued, self-interest became the most trivial part of the movement which saw itself as an alternative politics, setting itself against the general drift of society. It represented a minority view, of course. All the more reason that as a protest army, it marched up the hill of principle so quickly. And once confrontations occurred, and violence (in which a few were killed, thousands wounded, and more thousands arrested), it became virtually impossible for the government to convince people to pack those principles up and march right down again to the practical world of bargaining and negotiation.

And not only for reasons of confrontation and alternative views of life. There were specific and directly significant political issues involved. We have already mentioned several: the dominance of the Liberal Democratic party, the weakness of the legitimate opposition, the lack of effective due process, the inadequacy of local government, the absence of appropriate consultative mechanisms and procedures outside elite circles, to name a few. As a result of this movement and others like it, many political changes have occurred. Local governments have learned better how to protect local interests. National government has had to take responsibility for the negative effects of economic growth which in the name of progress resulted in pollution and environmental disaster. Today the worst effects of both are being mitigated. It took movements of this kind and extrainstitutional protest to force the government to act (Tsurumi, 1979).

Nevertheless, these are changes in practice more than in organization or principle. The government still has no institutionalized way to deal with movements of this kind, especially at a local level. In Japan, perhaps more than in other democracies, it is very difficult for the government to deal with them without confrontations. Lack of effective institutional development at the bottom is also made worse by the lack of effective opposition parties at the top. Both circumstances contribute to extrainstitutional protest as a strategy of opposition. The government's chief weapons remain secret negotiations and private manipulation; but movements like this one take every possible precaution—from mutual surveillance to self-criticism—against such tactics. They treat as traitors those who would favor negotiation or compromise. They react immediately against those who suggest temperate solutions. Indeed, this movement has been reluctant to back away from the largest principles to accommodate the most practical needs of the farmers themselves, a practice which in the end will prove to be its undoing.

In the end, the farmers of the Hantai Domei will be forced to give up lands needed to finish the airport. Nor can they ignore financial compensation from the government and offers of alternative lands which the government promises to provide. After all, farmers have responsibilities to their own households as well as to those in the movement. It is for this reason that the movement has tried to involve whole families, including wives and children, in active protest. For the group just outside the airport area, irrigation is the crucial issue, and offers by the government to support new irrigation schemes have already so reduced the number of Hantai Domei farmers that all know that the government will win. If they want to preserve their way of life, they will need government help in order to do it.

But this movement has been much more than a farmers' movement, although farmers were at the core of it. It has served as a lightning rod for protest movements all over Japan: antinuclear, environmental, peace, those protesting discrimination against Koreans in Japan, or against a pariah caste like the Burakamin. Through its links with the seventeen supporting New Left sects, the movement also fights against the presence of American forces and nuclear ships and facilities. Together, farmers and sects maintain some thirty-three fortresses and solidarity huts scattered about the airport. They continue to confront the fences and watchtowers of the airport authorities, sometime nose to nose, or eyeball to eyeball.

The View from Above

From a government perspective, the issue is completely different. The airport was part of a more important decision reached by the Japanese Cabinet in 1960 which emphasized industrial over rural development in a program popularly dubbed "income doubling." Its principal objects were to reduce the size of those sectors of the economy which were relatively inefficient and where income was lagging behind more productive sectors by diverting the labor force into needed and better-paying occupations. Regarded by government as a forward-looking program of general economic and social improvement, it also marked Japan's coming of age as an industrial power, and a way of putting firmly behind her the legacy of defeat in the war, and the long years of poverty and reconstruction which were its aftermath. With this changed policy, the new airport was decided upon in part to handle the increased commerce projected. It also was to be a symbol of the new role Japan would play in the world (Lockwood, 1968; Androuais, 1984).

Not until 1965 was a site decided on. The problems involved in site selection, the decision made and politics of its implementation tell us a good deal about the working of Japanese political life, both parliamentary and bureaucratic. The selection took a long time because of party politics, factional patronage struggles within the ruling Liberal Democratic party, and also for technical reasons. With only 15 percent of the land of Japan arable, virtually every proposed site for so large an undertaking simply had to be controversial. Even if assessments of relative costs and benefits were limited to technical matters, the political consequences could not help but stimulate hard bargaining and dirty politicking within the governing LDP. So complex were the issues in these terms that those in charge forgot those not directly involved in making the decisions. They ignored the local people themselves.

Nor did the government believe that opposition would endure. Despite the political embarrassment caused by confrontation, officials had plenty of reasons for self-congratulation. Under the guidance of the Liberal Democratic party, the government had gone from success to success, and not only in economic but social terms. The LDP politicians had a sense of their own sureness, expertise, and, through factions and party bosses, a degree of openness to public need that enabled them to mediate problems rather than legislate solutions. From their perspective, the problem of the airport was technical rather than political, despite the opposition from below. The airport was the largest single project ever undertaken by the Japanese government, and those responsible were more concerned with its complex organizational, jurisdictional, and decisional aspects. Hence, while officials could be sympathetic to the farmers' plight, they believed the airport to be a self-evident public good. Modern industrial Japan needed an additional facility to serve metropolitan Tokyo and the industrial-petro-chemical complex which much of Chiba Prefecture had become. The government was perfectly willing to negotiate terms with farmers, but not to compromise on the airport itself. When militants appeared on the scene, such negotiations became almost impossible. For the government, the militants were the cause of the difficulties. They were the ultimate subversives.

At the first site chosen, Tomisato, farmers protested so violently that the government gave it up and secretly moved the new site to Sanrizuka, a more thinly populated area. Much of the land already belonged to the Imperial Household. The government assumed that the opposition would be less strong and effective. It considered the site change a tribute to its own flexibility since, after all, officials had responded to public outcries at Tomisato.

There was, to be sure, a good deal to this view, although it was not the way it appeared to threatened farmers for whom the lack of consultation was outrageous—an act of aggression against them and their way of life. But clearly there was principle on the government side as well. In line with its industrialization policy, it wanted to drive small farmers off the land

and into the industrial labor force in order to raise incomes, something the government regarded as a self-evident benefit to all. However, both militants and farmers alike interpreted this as an example of how state capitalism negates democracy, generates a surplus by means of primitive accumulation, creates an industrial reserve army, and generates a class struggle between capitalists and farmers. Hence what was a confrontation over competing interests from the perspective of the government became a class struggle from the standpoint of the movement.

The latter also saw the state as a bureaucratic capitalist agent of both U.S. and Japanese imperialism with the new airport being built mainly to serve U.S. needs in Vietnam. As the struggle with the government evolved, the movement became more and more heroic, epic, and remarkable both in its own eyes and to a widening circle of admiring supporters. It gathered such strength, momentum, and outside support that over the years almost a million people came to this place to protest. It was a tocsin for the "AMPO" generation, fighting against Japanese remilitarization and changes in the United States-Japan Treaty. Within this increasingly radical alliance, the broadest principles were married to the most immediate concerns in a rhetoric reflecting and appropriate to the escalating violence of the confrontation with the government.

SANRIZUKA AS A "MOBILIZATION SPACE"

A key factor was indeed violence. The combined opposition sought to isolate the airport physically by means of the fortresses constructed around it at key points. Mobilizations served not only to focus on specific issues but were occasions in which surveyors, architects, builders, engineers, indeed the airport workers themselves, were transformed from instruments of construction to destruction, their activities despoiling the land, the patrimony, the sacred soil itself. Displaced grave sites became violations of ancestral property. Wounds and deaths were final expressions of desecration. The Airport Authority, which had the central responsibility for building and running the airport, became not only an instrument of an insensitive bureaucracy of which one might approve or disapprove, but an agency of government serving as a comprador and partner of the United States, the highest stage of imperialism, the capitalism of a United States-Japan alliance for remilitarization. So a moral architecture was created within this crossroads, this confrontational space which intensified as the bulldozers cleared the land of its trees, houses, farms, and people. The combined opposition fought back with Molotov cocktails and sticks. Old women sprayed the police with night soil and chained themselves to trees. Bunkers were built underground. Watchtowers were built to the sky.

Violence was endowed with legitimacy, and legitimacy with violence. The incidents were not isolated from other protests in Japan and they need to be seen in the context of a retrievable legacy that goes back a long way before this movement (Smith, 1959). Prototypes can be found in earlier turn-of-the-century conflicts brought about when Meiji governments sought rapid industrialization and fostered militarism (Bowen, 1980). Some farmers came from a tradition which, antibourgeois, was imbued with the spirit of the "warrior-peasant" and which had more in common, at least originally, with the tradition of the radical right, with its nostalgia for the rural hamlet and its hostility to Meiji industrialization and urban embourgeoisement. Others had been members of the Japan Socialist party or the Japan Communist party. This dual tradition, the one associated with the class struggle, the left, and the other the unity of the rural community, the right, has been combined today in an endogenous radicalism which is essentially nondoctrinaire but highly militant. It constitutes a specific ideology constructed out of the events in which farmers and militants have themselves participated, what we will call a "mytho-logics."

Here, then, is one secret of why this movement became important despite its small size. It retrieved an inheritance which was originally divided between left and right, yet which stemmed from some of the same original causes, and combined them around a common set of problems, a political economic problem represented by Japan's successful pursuit of an innovative capitalism which has allowed her to surpass the USSR in economic power and to become the world's second industrial force. It retrieved too a tradition in which those who become marginalized in the process become the concrete manifestation of all those others in society penalized in one way or another by development. So the ideology drew upon an ensemble of grievances, few of which could be rectified by prevailing means of legitimate party, interest, and factional politics.

In this case there is even more hidden under the surface, including a radical version of Protestant Christianity in which religious pietism revealed itself not in textual exegesis but in living out as a practice the precepts of disciplined Christian corporatism within which a unique degree of individualism was allowed, an alternative to the primacy of group affiliation so characteristic of Japanese social life. (In this there was a specifically Tolstoyan strand.) Christianity also retrieved earlier links with the left. From the pre-World War One period to the beginnings of the Japan Communist party, it was common for students to become Socialists after an initial involvement with Christian precept under circumstances of specific protest and mobilization, not so different from this case (Smethurst, 1974).

There is, then, a complex radical inheritance. Some groups trace their origins to Marxist study groups which, attracting people to the study of texts, made some of them into virtual monks, provided them with "safe" houses, and divided them by sects in which doctrine became all important. Most of the sects involved in the Sanrizuka movement derive from breakaway movements, mainly from the Japan Communist party from 1956 on (Scalapino and Masumi, 1962; Scalapino, 1967). Japan's was the first New Left, and its rise and success on university campuses, and its own historic 1968, when it took over the main tower of the University of Tokyo, were noted throughout the world.

The consciousness of such multiple retrievals by participants was a very significant aspect of the struggle itself. Just as every year the storming of the control tower is commemorated by a mass rally serving as an occasion to enunciate principles of antistate action, so the control tower event was itself an explicit reminder of an internal struggle in which a key tower had been destroyed by the riot police in Sanrizuka, which in turn was a reminder of the storming of the tower at Tokyo University itself. The iconography is explicit. The symbolism is understood by all. Each event overlaps with others to constitute a structure behind a narrative, a structure which can itself refer to the logic of arguments against the state. Retrievals, then, lead to projections in the form of a "mytho-logics."

These symbolic displays were hardly lost on the authorities. They too understood what was going on. They were deeply disturbed by the link between farmers and militants. The government regarded the alliance between farmers and militants as unholy. While farmers might have a just cause, since their livelihoods were at stake, militants did not. When the latter encouraged the farmers to build fortresses and underground bunkers, this was outright rebellion. To oppose the airport on grounds of ideological principle was to oppose the legitimacy of the state and to challenge the authority of the government itself.

In a sense the government was right. But the question it could not answer was how militants were able to radicalize farmers so successfully. Even more curious was how those on the fringe of society could generate such widespread support. How did it happen that old women subservient in many ways to their men, became the most radical in their actions? Why did old people, who could be expected to regard matters from the sidelines, prepare to commit mass suicide on the grounds of the imperial estate as a protest against construction of the airport there? Why, after the farmers initiated the first violence, did they elect a president who was an artist, a militant Christian, and something of a local intellectual? If such a fellow saw himself as a Christ standing in the field (*Standing in the Field* was the title of one of his books) and invoking Christian precept, he was just a crank from a government perspective. Tomura may in his own mind have represented a logic of revolution which he claimed was inspired by the example of Christ's martyrdom, but it was very hard for the government to take him seriously (Tomura, 1975). For that mistake they paid dearly. For it was Tomura who, after being beaten by the riot police, brought in the militant sects and made them into his disciples.

Above all, what the government could not understand was that under the surface of the events themselves, principles other than those made explicit in confrontation were being enacted—the continuity of the society, the unity of opposites involved when farmers and militants joined forces, a sense of immortality resulting from that unity, a rejuvenation when youth and aged came together which made violence celebratory. When farmers revived the hamlet with its more egalitarian tradition, and organized the Hantai Domei around women, elders, youth, and other corps, they captured the imagination of many because this seemed so essentially Japanese. Even the fortresses built by militants had as their prototypes the sect houses and original study groups of early radical days. In the struggles that followed, farmers saw the fortresses as World War Two bunkers against the enemy, while militants regarded them as the equivalent of underground peasant fortifications in Vietnam.

These, then, are some of the ingredients of a conflict which gave an ideological dynamism to a movement which was very different from its ostensible issues and causes. Moreover, the episodes of violent confrontation were understood in precisely this complex way by a much larger audience, so much so that the little crossroads of Sanrizuka became a "mobilization space."

A mobilization space is a particular terrain in which groups converge to confront an "outside" force. Each contributes its own issues and grievances to the whole and thus escalates the principles on which the confrontation is based. In this case, the terrain was the imperial crossroads. It served to retrieve old grievances. Within it new projections were projected. Each confrontational event added particularity to the ideology, enabling the movement to generate its own mythology out of the events, its heroes and martyrs, speaking to a wider audience, and translating the sequence of experiences into a narrative which struck the sensibilities of those not directly involved. The narrative illustrated a logic of what was wrong. The events were epic, the stuff of which myths are made. Since I want to suggest some reasons why this happened and use this case to draw some more general conclusions relating extrainstitutional protest to ideology, let me clarify certain key assumptions.

Ideologies become effective when they enable events to symbolize "deep structures." Their narration as "history" retrieves. Their representation as text projects. With interpretation, action becomes necessity, necessity becomes morality, and morality becomes logical—that is, normative. Required are "transformations," changes of meaning; in this case: from a "terrain" or place to a surrogate for a field of forces, from an ecology of functional relations to a moral architecture, from leadership to messianicism, from interests to principles, from principles to necessity (Ricoeur, 1967). Let me discuss some of these a bit further.

From place to surrogate. Sanrizuka was not a place where traditional life had been preserved as if in a museum. The farmers living there and in the hamlets and villages around the crossroads were not peasants but small-scale agro-businessmen, concerned with the market, investment, mechanization of farming techniques, government agricultural policy, and the like. They were voters involved in rural cooperatives and active participants in the polity. Not a few were bosses and local officials in the Japan Socialist party and the Liberal Democratic party. The days when they were a small semiindependent yeomanry, with some being tenants and others landlords, disappeared rapidly after the 1947 reforms which gave everyone land. Moreover, changes in farming had been associated with the imperial estate ever since Meiji times. Sanrizuka was not a pocket of traditionalism fighting progress. It had been and was a place where shrewd farmers innovated and had become highly efficient. They were not poor and they were good farmers (Dore, 1978).

Hence the selection of the site for an airport did not pose traditionalism against modernity, or peasant revolt against the state, but one kind of modernism against another: commercial agriculture as a way of life against the internationalization of industrial activity. Each side, farmers and government, represented two sides of the modernity coin. The one side was agro-business. The other side was industrialization. The latter would create irrevocable alterations in the actual conditions of social life, as had already occurred in Chiba Prefecture (pollution, ecological change, etc.) and dislocate and displace the population, pushing farmers into the industrial labor force. The farmers then came to represent "society," the state, bureaucratic capitalism. The airport became the surrogate for the state. The Sanrizuka crossroads was the surrogate for society. The confrontations by farmers were designed to create a no man's land around the airport, erecting fortresses, etc. to isolate the state from society until it could become more responsive to society's needs as they defined them. The field of forces explicitly engaged by this included anti-Vietnam, antipollution, environmental, and a variety of citizen protest groups, the most important of which were associated with the Hiroshima peace movement on the one hand and the Minamata movement on the other (Smith, 1978).

From functional ecology to moral architecture. By ecology, what is meant is the understanding of a space in terms of its functional relationships, land and water, irrigation and crops, the social ecology which follows from it, farmers, merchants, etc. to the political ecology of interests which generate political participation. Perhaps the best exposition of the politics of an ecological terrain is in the work of Stein Rokkan and his associates, showing how institutional politics work as a reflection of "ecologies" in this ramified sense of the term. Ecological politics is essentially bargaining politics within well-defined institutional frames (Rokkan, 1970). Translate the terrain into a moral architecture and it is precisely the bargaining aspect which drops out in favor of a mobilization aspect using or prone to use extrainstitutional means. This translation occurred in Sanrizuka when the airport was seen to be an excrescence on the actual land itself, changing the agro-businessman into the protagonist of a way of life which was self-legitimizing.

Here retrieval becomes important. The imperial estate itself was a place where artists used to come from all over Japan, and where visitors in the spring would witness the cherry trees in bloom. The landscape itself, especially around Sanrizuka and in Shibayama, was charming and miniaturized, with small meandering roads, ribbonlike lanes leading out to meadows or rice paddies. Not that the entire landscape was bucolic; far from it. There were the beginnings of urban sprawl, and a network of fast transportation. But the Sanrizuka crossroads still led out to hamlets and villages, some very old, some dating from Meiji times, some populated by "pioneers," ex-soldiers who had built up their farms from scrub land. The social ecology constituted a network of "mediations," funerals and weddings, three-generation families, in which modernity facilitated rather than threatened social life.

The airport violated this space, this way of life. The nature of its transport was seen as the ultimate aggression. In this battle of the two crossroads, hamlets and villages, solidarity huts and fortresses, and towers and underground bunkers came to represent a moral architecture, the hamlets and villages representing a superior moral existence based on nurture and cultivation in contrast to the careless ruthlessness of the runways and buildings of an airport and of the industrialization, pollution, ecological disaster they represented. The solidarity huts and fortresses were the defense points against all this. The bunkers burrowed into the land as a sacred soil, the defenders going underground while the towers claimed the sky, the rain, the weather, against not only airplanes but against the monopoly of the sky held by the American armed forces which controlled the airways. The battle between the Sanrizuka crossroads and the airport was thus a battle between civility and ruthlessness, peace and war. Farmers in their headbands, women in their baggy pants and straw hats, militants in their helmets peopled those constructions and arrayed themselves against the glass, steel, and concrete of the airport itself. It is in this explicit physical sense that Sanrizuka constructed a moral architecture, all the more compelling because the airport was ringed with two linked chain fences, topped with electrified barbed wire, a dry moat between, and guard towers constructed with electronic surveillance equipment; nearby were barracks for thousands of riot police, all to be attacked by staves, spears, sticks, stones, Molotov cocktails, excrement, and other instruments of a "people's war."

From leadership to messianicism. A moral architecture is a function of a special language. The language cannot be entirely written. Nor can it be exclusively articulated in public places. Both are important, text and articulation, but neither is sufficient. What is needed is a language able to convert retrievalism into projection and use events to illustrate a logic, a logic to endow the events with symbolic power. An agent is required, one who seems to speak not on his own but simply as a vessel, a container for what everyone understands and shares but cannot voice, not a leader but a mythic spokesman. In this movement it was Issaku Tomura, the insider-outsider, the Christian whose little church became the moral center of the movement, the Christ who stood in the fields, and by his austere personal conduct, his compassion, and his reserve seemed to be the essential Japanese. His grandfather had come to Sanrizuka to build new kinds of farm equipment for the experimental farming being undertaken there. He himself knew all the farmers because he sold them farm equipment from his shop in Sanrizuka. But he was also an outsider who had been opposed to the Second World War, who made modern sculptures out of old equipment parts, and who stood aloof from local-interest politics. Indeed, it was this latter factor which made him the only candidate to lead the farmers' movement. Given all the other divisions and factionalism which divided the farmers, his capacity to be one of them while being above them made him a unique figure.

It was Tomura who turned the events themselves into a language of violence. When the riot police brought in bulldozers to clear the land, remove villages, and do the necessary survey and construction work, Tomura turned this into an invasion of the cosmological space of the "authentic" Japan. He saw it as governmental contempt for the people, a lack of respect, and more, for he insisted that parliamentary government did not and could not represent the people's interest. It was not only the failure of due process, of effective local government, and other aspects of democracy which he found wanting, but for him capitalism and parliamentary government were ultimately contradictory. It was this view which enabled him to embrace radical militants whose behavior would have otherwise offended him, for he was in his outrage a deeply conservative man, like the farmers themselves.

Language and moral architecture were molded by Tomura's simple but persuasive biblical rhetoric into a set of slogans which could be hung from towers and worn on headbands. The militants built a huge tower called a Farmer's Broadcasting Tower which was to enable messages to be shouted to all the participants, and to the four quarters of the cosmological, almost Confucian space which constituted its natural heaven, and to the world of journalists, photographers, and above all, to television cameramen who came rushing to the site when the tower was attacked by water cannon, bulldozers, and cranes. In this way, the instruments of construction were converted into weapons of destruction at the hands of a government composed of riot police and bureaucrats who fought against farmers whose weapons were their farm implements, and who sang folk songs, and grieved over their lands (Austin, 1962).

It was Tomura, then, who was more than a leader. He was a messiah who described the fall, and promised grace through resistance, devotion to the cause, and moral discipline. By bringing in the militants, he thought he could not only provide reinforcement for farmers and outside support for the cause, but through their concern for the future, find a solution, a new way of life.

From interests to principles. In the end, however, no matter how shrewdly articulated, symbolism and its political expression as myth and logic—or its embroidery as retrieval and projection—will have only a transitory effect unless locked into some kind of stable picture of the world as it is and the world as it ought to be. For Tomura, and for the Han-tai Domei and its militant allies, there could be no hard and fast ideology. There were too many differences between them for that, and, in a movement so small, too many personalities. What was required were principles broad enough to be considered as unifying moral aims, and capable of inspiring lofty convictions on the one hand, but which provided for experiments, alternative routes to a final solution. For farmers and their children this meant seeking ways to live out principles in new modes of farming. Hence the movement spawned a variety of concrete experiments, organic farming, a small collective group called the "One-Pack Movement," and several others (Apter and Sawa, 1984). Most of these were efforts to reduce the vulnerability of the individual farmer and to make farming attractive to the next generation. They not only sought new and different modes of personal living through joint or collective enterprise, but also a principled alternative to commercialization and capitalism.

There was good reason for trying to enunciate "practical" as well as abstract principles. To convert abstraction into real life is to drive out precisely those pressures to convert principles into interests and to bargain, a goal which was the main hope and strategy of the government. The government never saw the matter as one of principle but only interest, and watched with bewilderment as the principles piled up, one on top of the other, in a crescendo of antagonism against the Liberal Democratic party and its policy. But it assumed that in the end, interest would win over principle, given patience, craft, and manipulation. In turn, the government failed to sufficiently recognize that it too had principles, of a public interest kind. It was also not prepared to convert opposition into a basis for reforms at the local government level, and for the provision of more effective due process, procedures, not to speak of other institutional arrangements and safeguards for private citizens, that we associate with virtually every functioning democratic system. It was the bureaucrats who refused to see this, more than the politicians, some of whom were caught in the middle, like the governor of Chiba Prefecture. Hence the more the Sanrizuka movement spoke in the name of principle and the more public sympathy was aroused—both by the confrontations and issues themselves—the more the government tried to convert principle into interest. It succeeded in buying out a large number of farmers. But it made itself appear corrupt and corrupting in the eyes of many. When the weak articulate principle against the strong and a David takes on a Goliath, the political consequences are rarely those intended.

From principle to necessity. Indeed, it was precisely because of the government's success with so many of the farmers that those who remained in opposition came to represent an embattled moral force, the inner Japanese, whose wishes should have been "mediated" by government rather than "corrupted." Farmers and militants were able to touch on a wider sense of public discomfort over precisely the larger issues which had been troubling many Japanese before the movement actually began, concerns over what kind of society the new Japan should properly become. Surveys taken at the time this movement began and conducted by the Office of the Prime Minister, indicated troubled responses to the question of Japan's future role in the world, and as a world power. Today Japan is more confident of its place. In the mid-1960s the question of government, the relationship to the United States, the problem of militarism were complex and troubling. No one can calculate the consequences of nuclear holocaust like the Japanese. Memories were shorter then than today. Despite friendship and admiration for the United States and a frenetic adaptation of many American things to fit local ways, there was much that troubled the Japanese about Americanization, not least of which was the Vietnam War itself.

The movement offered a logic to this ambiguity. In the pursuit of industrialization, a way of life was to be shut down. Small farmers were to be driven into an industrial reserve army. The class struggle that was occurring in Vietnam and had occurred in China, was not recapitulating itself among the small farmers. Primitive accumulation was the precondition of bureaucratic finance capitalism. Polarization, visible in confrontation, constituted the visible aspect of this class struggle. Socialism would begin in the rural sectors and spread to the urban centers where fighting had already begun in the universities. The alliance between militants and farmers would win over the workers, especially the teachers and the railway workers who had been radicalized by the Japan Communist party but would break away from it because of its conservatism. What these principles articulated, then, was not the necessity *for* revolution, of favoring it, but the necessity *of* revolution, of doing it—a necessity with parallels to the great revolutions of the past, and most particularly the Russian, Chinese, and Cuban. All began small. All were in accordance with history. Principle revealed necessity. Theory was action. Action was theory. So went the logic of necessity.

We should probably end our discussion here. It was apparent that despite the success of the movement in preventing the airport from being completed, necessity was wrong, principles were faulty, the messianicism was overblown, the moral architecture hollow, and the terrain in the end just a terrain. Today there is squabbling within the movement. Tomura is dead. Most of his successors have been expelled. The farmers are deserting the movement. The sects fight on because they have no place else to go. The public is no longer concerned.

But this would perhaps miss the different ways in which this movement and others like it are important. I now want to show how and why this movement—one more in a history of protest movements which cannot win on their own terms—like the others, will leave more than just a memory or a trace. Such movements are events which reinforce a language of protest, one able to provide authenticity to protest and a continuing base for extrainstitutional activity and the legitimization of violence. Because of this capacity, the Sanrizuka movement, and others like it, have had permanent effects on Japanese politics.

SANRIZUKA AS A "SEMIOTIC" SPACE

Precisely because it was a mobilization space, Sanrizuka was also a "semiotic" space (Eco, 1979). Events were "read" like an epic narrative, a tale that seemed to come down from the old times (which it of course retrieved) and also as a logic of projection, a theory, for confrontation was a necessity. So the Sanrizuka struggle itself forms an underlying layer for other future events. My assumption is that despite the triviality of the circumstances bounded by the terrain of the two crossroads, they became part of a more fundamental and ongoing debate about the character, design, and moral purpose of modern society itself, posing the problem of the limits of democracy and, indeed, the limits of the state. Representing enduring and perennial themes—the last becoming first, society against the state, the weak becoming strong, interest being converted to principle—Sanrizuka reinforces a radical logic with a set of informing acts (Apter, 1985). By defining a larger cosmological space, underground to a sacred soil, above ground to the sky itself, and within the space, a moral terrain, it shows how a real architecture and a moral one confirm each other.

Sanrizuka represents a battle which continues at the center of "developmentalism" itself, for the process no longer seems as benign as it once did. As the social overhead costs of industrialization increase rather than decline, even this small struggle contains the larger question of what development means for the state. It raises questions, too, about how development itself changes society. For the farmers resisted becoming marginals, functionally superfluous people, whose existence becomes an embarrassment, a problem only now becoming significant in other parts of the labor force as technology changes.

Finally, Sanrizuka suggests that underlying the logic of necessity is a logic of exchange which offers the basis of an exchange of meaning. By seeking necessity in the event, the airport becomes not simply a surrogate for a state, but a metonymy for a theory of the state. Opposition to it is not simply protest but revolution. In the end, as already indicated, the momentum of "revolution," even when it fails, can be perpetually reinvoked in succeeding protests, with previous events an inheritance embodied in a language which passes for rationality itself.

The way this can happen is illustrated by this struggle. Each of the main episodes became punctuation marks in a text and a narrative, a story read by the public with considerable attention and an instruction which some at least took seriously. The narrative of events is composed of specific violent occasions: the outer rim land survey, the transfer of the imperial estate, the first and second expropriation struggles, the control tower takeover. Each constituted battles in a war against the state, complete with accounts of violence as well as rituals of sacrifice. There is principle here as well, and within narrative and text, instructions deriving from and defined by each episode. The first, the outer rim land survey, was widely understood as a metaphor of rape and a metonymy of state capitalism. The second, the transfer of the imperial estate, was both a metaphor of betrayal and a metonymy for primitive accumulation. The first and second land expropriations were seen as metaphors of violence and death and

metonymies of marginalization and polarization. The final violent episode, the control tower takeover, was a metaphor of transcendence, a cap-
turing of the commanding heights, and a metonymy for revolution, the
revolution this movement hoped to accomplish. In turn, the episodes constituted a history, a narrative of the struggle and a text representing a radical theory, violation of local and private space, illegitimate conveyance,
polarization, the creation of an industrial reserve army, and the legitimization of the struggle. Such a theory is designed to convince and persuade.
More, it becomes a logic of necessity, impelling action. So a semiotic space
is filled and ideology becomes a form of "instruction."

What is the instruction? The rape of the land, the ending of farmers' obligations to the state, the violation of the sacred body of society itself, all
require that selfless resistance which will prevent the state, as a ruthless
superlandlord and an instrument of imperialism, from having its way.
Yeomen must fight to prevent their conversion into marginals even more
debased than tenants in the old days. In this way each episode forms with
the others as a structure of explanation and a theory of the antistate, as
Figure 8.1 suggests.

At its outer limit, the conversion of each episode into metaphorical and
metonymical "deep structures" suggests a universal dynamic appropriate
to revolutionary movements elsewhere. In more specific terms, we see first
a unity of opposites between farmers and militants, opposite in age and
occupation and unified by an almost familial and ideological embrace.
Second, there is the set of contradictions which sets revolutionary episodes
in motion—Japaneseness versus Americanization, marginals versus state
capitalism, society versus the state, and of course the stage for all these,
Sanrizuka versus the airport. Finally, there is the search for that mass support which will lead to a disjunction in which the parliamentary state will
give way to citizen participation and collective enterprise.

Some Consequences of the Movement in Japan

A mobilization space does not always become semiotic. When it does,
it creates its own power, a mytho-logics, which when it works can have a
persuasiveness which defies number. It generates commitment. It moti-
vates action. The question is, however, to what purpose. I now want to
suggest that even if the consequences of this movement in Japan have been
slight in terms of institutional changes, it has stimulated considerable political learning. Both government and private citizens' groups have learned
a good deal from the Sanrizuka struggle. People have become much more
willing to fight against what appears to them as government arbitrariness.

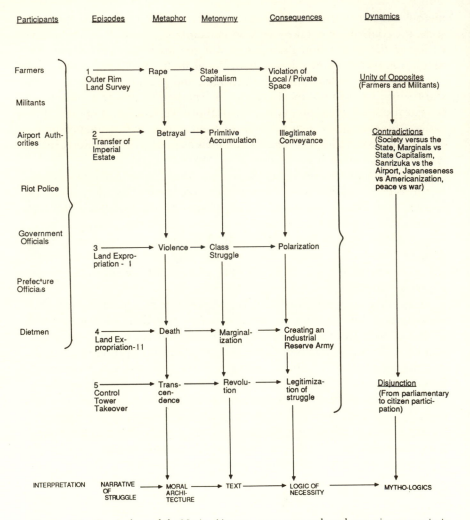

FIGURE 8.1   Sanrizuka and the Narita Airport—two crossroads and a terrain as a semiotic space.

They have been encouraged to join forces with other opposition groups and appeal to public opinion in ways perhaps lacking in Japan in the past. In effect, a moving equilibrium of opposition coalitions has been possible, despite the single-party dominance of the Liberal Democratic party and the relative impotence of the opposition parties. Indeed, the latter depend for survival on their ability to mediate various forms of extrainstitutional protest, making compromise more palatable. One might argue that in Japan, institutional opposition derives some of its functions from extrainstitutional activity rather than by making such activity superfluous, its more conventional and traditional role.

In turn, the government itself has learned how to be more shrewd, to anticipate political problems, and to avoid conflicts of this kind by taking necessary preliminary steps, most specifically by widening the scope of consultations and blurring a little the boundaries of bureaucratic jurisdictions. Moreover, local authorities are becoming more adept at bargaining with the national government. So is the private sector. As all sides have learned to bargain more efficiently, they prevent the translation of interests into principles, the creation of a mobilization and semiotic space, and the formation of a mytho-logics in which ordinary solutions become virtually unacceptable.

Moreover, in other circumstances like the Osaka International Airport case, the government has allowed consultation to take place while preserving the dignity of all those involved. For if we can single out one factor as most immediately consequential in converting Sanrizuka into a mobilization space, it was that the government deeply offended the farmers' dignity. It ignored their wishes in the decisional process. It ignored their efforts to protest by constitutional means. It attacked them when they refused to give up.

Indeed, it was the ultimate indignity of the farmers' position which gave the movement its original moral force and rallied public opinion and sympathy. Even those who disapproved of the tactics of confrontation and violence saw the government as reprehensible and came to understand why, from a farmer's standpoint, ordinary bargaining and mediation rules and the conventional processes of party and interest group politics were the cause of the problem rather than the solution. Government efforts to coopt leaders of the movement, or to compromise them on the matter of compensation, were taken not as illustrations of government flexibility but of duplicity, moral laxity. Hence, farmers established themselves as the "party of principle" against a government defined as a "party of expediency" and by so doing appealed to a broad spectrum of liberal and Socialist sympathizers.

As for militancy, the point of no return was crossed after Mr. Tomura, the president of the Hantai Domei, was badly beaten by the riot police. After that it was the state itself which became the target. The new agenda for the movement became not merely an amendment of the decision to build the airport at Sanrizuka but a rupture in the relations of power; not an extension of political coverage but an alteration in the rules of politics. In such circumstances, grievances convert to ideology, issues that are plural become singular, clienteles intersect, and link up as networks, and individual "speech acts" become systems of action.

Above all, then, the government today tries to avoid just that kind of activity which will generate militancy. Since the control tower takeover, it has refrained from provocative acts. It has not proceeded with dispatch to the next phase of the construction. It has avoided confrontation.

In terms of the actual issue itself, the construction of the airport, each side has won something and lost something. Today the airport is in use despite its truncated quality. More than 30,000,000 passengers have used it since it opened in 1978. Fighting continues over the second phase, although the tactics have changed and it is the government which now eschews violence even though it seems determined to press on and complete the construction. Moreover, there are now doubts that the airport will ever be completed as envisaged. Indeed, it may be becoming partially obsolete. Government has won in the sense that it has a functioning airport at Sanrizuka. But the cost has been very great and the victory partial.

Farmers and militants have also won a partial victory. The government has been forced to accede to the principle that small farmers should not be obliterated by state policy. Militants have found in Sanrizuka a semipermanent staging area, an arena of action, a stage for confrontations, which some believe will continue to "reveal" the fundamental contradictions of state capitalism in Japan. Rightly or wrongly, they have successfully endowed the issues with a more fundamental significance, a matter of the state versus a sector of society whose embedded symbolic value in Japan is part of the tradition of "Japaneseness." They have attached the universality of their ideologies to the particularities of a society in continuous change, and transformed a conflict of rural versus industrial interests into a problem of marginality, functional superfluousness, and the social overhead costs of development itself.

In Japan the Sanrizuka movement came to represent the most generalized expression of all postwar extrainstitutional protest, including the anti-Vietnam War movement, the peace movement, the antinuclear movement, etc. Around this struggle and within the confines of its mobilization space all the problems of capitalism and bureaucratic power have been articulated, and then made into something more, a semiotics of protest going well beyond its concrete substance. So much so that for some, the

Sanrizuka movement is the defining case of citizen protest in Japan. For others it was less important, simply one among many protest movements and a minor tune played in a major key. Both assessments have merit. There is a sense in which its importance has been less in terms of the impact it has had on the larger drift of Japanese politics and society than how it reflects the ambiguities of the drift itself.

SOME LARGER IMPLICATIONS

So much for the implications of the movement in Japan itself. What about the wider problem, the problem of the state when confronted with extrainstitutional protest? What this movement suggests is that as developmental change generates increasingly high social overhead costs, more and more interests are offended, and more and more people are adversely affected. The problem is not, nor can it be, opposition itself. Any exercise of power is bound to generate some opposition. No one at the top, even those who appear most impervious to demands made from the bottom, would argue that in today's world sovereignty itself can offer the privileges of sole jurisdictions. Even centralized power is diluted by the actual forces and geometries of organized political groups. Some pluralism and accountability always exists.

The problem is that even in Japan, whose economic success is second to none, the fit between growing political resources and public needs is becoming unstuck. The dilution of centralized authority through regularized forms of accountability, what we mean by "institutionalized" politics, the elaboration of which in terms of regular instruments of popular political participation is the special virtue of democracy, does not enable a sure and identifiable public interest to prevail. This means that democracy itself is in growing trouble. For only in a democracy does the legitimate exercise of power depend on participation—a participation which, moreover, not only accepts the principle of opposition but makes it the dynamic factor within a state in which citizen rights are broadly as well as specifically defined and applications of coercion limited. Such opposition is constitutionally provided for along with appropriate channels and instruments for its expression. In contrast, extrainstitutional opposition, or protests which take place outside such channels and by other means, are disturbing, irresponsible, dangerous and aberrant, a kind of pathology.

Such a view is necessary, especially in a democratic state. Any system which in the last analysis depends on accommodation and mutual deferences must maintain a clear boundary between legality and illegality, proper and improper behavior, and the respect for authority itself. Yet it should not be entirely forgotten that virtually all the mechanisms and instruments of politics and the ways and means and scope of representation and participation, all of which appear to make extrainstitutional protest redundant, themselves originated with one or other aspects of such activity. What we call democracy, then, is a result of extrainstitutional protest which produced institutional modifications. Electoral reform, expansion of the franchise, the right to organize in trades unions, the basic protection of individual liberties—all have experienced as part of their specific history and evolution some degree of extrainstitutional origins and force. The democratization of access to power, the widening of political participation, indeed the evolution of democracy, are bound up with such activities. Accomplishment should not blind us to the continuing need for such kinds of opposition, at least to the degree that they lead to corrective modifications within the principles of democracy itself.

Equally, we ought not to be blinded to what has changed. The increasing articulation of opposition issues, in principle, can lead to the formation of an oppositional space, extrainstitutional in character, part mobilization, part semiotic, in which institutional adaptation and government response make things worse instead of better. We may be reaching a point where governments have already accepted responsibilities and obligations beyond their means of effective discharge. If so, it will be increasingly difficult for governments to make the necessary amendments in policy and adaptations in institutional structure to render necessary changes politically acceptable. As this becomes so, movements of this kind pose the question of the limits of the state itself.

What this suggests is, in part, the need for renewed speculation on classic themes, the problem of system and jurisdiction, accountability and responsiveness, and perhaps a renewed concern with alternatives of sovereignty and power than those currently available. We say "movements of this kind" because they press fundamental principles in a way which cannot be ignored and whose political acts can have wide repercussions of the sort described (i.e., when groups organize around the belief that they cannot effectively utilize prevailing and organized structures of political participation in order to affect government policy).

For another part, we need to utilize new concepts for the analysis of ideologies, more structuralist perhaps, more phenomenological as well, to understand the dynamics of behavior, language, and interpretation that these movements generate. Analyses like Pierre Bourdieu's *Outline of a Theory of Practice* in the first instance or Paul Ricoeur's *The Symbolism of Evil* are perhaps too rarely read by those willing and able to go to the field to study such matters firsthand. Indeed, for the examination of such issues, the heavy weapons of modern survey and computer analysis may play us false, for what they show us as empirical reality may be further away from certain truths than a view of the moon looking through the wrong end of a telescope.

While this is not the place to argue such issues, what I have tried to suggest is this. The older and more obvious solutions to the problem of extrainstitutional protest, namely to widen the circle, expand the system, and include inside more effectively those who are currently left out, are becoming more and more difficult to employ. Moreover, mobilization movements which construct a semiotic space are very difficult to absorb. If our analysis is correct, and governments are in increasing difficulty over how best to deal with responsibilities already incurred, then further increases in such responsibilities are likely to be counterproductive, adding more layers of institutional indigestion and adding to the bureaucracy and to government by committees so that they will be less accountable rather than more, and less efficient in catering to public demands. The danger is that institutional accommodation of a kind bound up with the evolution of democracy itself may now produce an opposite effect. No ready solutions are at hand. Governments try to deal with the problem as best they can, vacillating between giving in and holding firm, hoping by these means to locate those strategic points at issue where mediation can occur without threats to the basic structure of politics. But such circumstances are increasingly frustrating on all sides, with each pointing the finger of recrimination at the other, a condition under which events provide the circumstances for confrontation, violence, and the formation of those mobilization spaces which have semiotic impact and consequence.

If these assumptions are correct, offended groups will have few options if they already lack power, so that the only real alternative to passivity and compliance is force or the threat of force. But as soon as violations of legal and institutional limits of politics are advocated by a movement, no matter how small it is or insignificant, and a signal goes out to those in authority—an alert—events can easily take on these wider semiotic proportions. There is a quickening of concern all around. Beyond a certain point such circumstances in a democratic state invite not simply extrainstitutional protest but the extreme version of it which involves terrorism, the semiotic of death and transfiguration, a phenomenon which captures the greatest publicity and involves the smallest and most extreme groups. As long as the public is repelled by their activities and clienteles remain limited, terror remains the semiotics without the mobilization. But terrorism also tries to reverse the order and go past a semiotic space defined as a symbolism of violence and convert citizens into a network of counterelites, mobilized out of the ensemble of those increasingly alienated from prevailing institutional politics. The aim is the conversion of such counterelites into counterclienteles, the two forming that revolutionary mobilization which is the specter haunting all democratic governments.

Movements like the one in Sanrizuka stand between terrorism, which is proscribed, and more ordinary citizen protest. Raising issues that are not easily negotiated, such movements reject the ordinary processes of political bargaining and accommodation. To the extent that they touch on fundamental issues of principle, they must be taken seriously enough to enable political learning to occur on all sides, and to stimulate a review of issues in terms larger than immediate instrumentalities. Such movements renew interest in old themes: How to respond to extrainstitutional protest, how to separate legitimate grievance from illegitimate, how to sense deeper structural concerns, and how to decide what it is necessary to defend. If extrainstitutional protest is part of the natural inheritance of democracy itself, today its extreme alternative—terrorism—prejudices that inheritance. If between protest and terror there is a huge gap, it will repay us all—scholars and politicians—to listen, learn, and try to accommodate to those groups far away from the commanding heights of politics and society, and concern ourselves especially with those becoming marginalized and estranged. The spokesmen for the Sanrizuka movement who proclaimed at their rally that "the whole world faces now a grave crisis" could have added to their list of potential catastrophies, the democratic state itself. For in the end, like everything else, it is just a representation, just an idea—one of the better ones.

References

Androuais, A. 1984. Le processus de restructuration de l'économie japonaise. In *Japon, le consensus: Mythe et réalités*, ed. Bouisson and Faure. Paris: Economica, 395–428.

Apter, D. E. 1979. Notes on the underground: Left violence in the national state. In *The state*, ed. S. R. Graubard. New York: W. W. Norton.

———. 1982. *Fight*. Tokyo: Moblization for Sanrizuka and Doro-Chiba.

———. 1985. The new mytho/logics and the specter of superfluous man. *Social Research* 52: 269–307.

———, and N. Sawa. 1984. *Against the state*. Cambridge: Harvard University Press.

Austin, J. L. 1962. *How to do things with words*. Oxford: Oxford University Press.

Bourdieu, P. 1977. *Outline of a theory of practice*. Cambridge: Cambridge University Press.

Cole, A. B., G. O. Totton, and C. H. Uyehara, eds. 1966. *Socialist parties in postwar Japan*. New Haven: Yale University Press.

Dore, R. P. 1978. *Shinohata: Portrait of a Japanese village*. New York: Pantheon Books.

Eco, U. 1979. *A theory of semiotics*. Bloomington: Indiana University Press.

Lockwood, W. W. 1968. *The economic development of Japan*. Princeton: Princeton University Press.

Norman, E. H. 1965. *Soldier and peasant in Japan*. Vancouver, B.C.: University of British Columbia.

Ricoeur, P. 1967. *The symbolism of evil*. Boston: Beacon Press.

Rokkan, S. 1970. *Citizens, elections, parties*. Oslo: Universitetsforlage.

Scalapino, R. A. 1967. *The Japanese Communist movement*. Berkeley: University of California Press.

———, and J. Masumi. 1962. *Parties and politics in contemporary Japan*. Berkeley: University of California Press.

Smethurst, R. J. 1974. *A social basis for prewar Japanese militarism*. Berkeley: University of California Press.

Smith II, H. D. 1972. *Japan's first student radicals*. Cambridge: Harvard University Press.

Smith, R. J. 1978. *Karusu: The price of progress in a Japanese village*. Stanford: Stanford University Press.

Smith, T. C. 1959. *The agrarian origins of modern Japan*. Stanford: Stanford University Press.

Tomura, I. 1975. Ten years of struggle: Sanrizuka and its links with Asia. *AMPO: Japan-Asia Quarterly Review* 7: 39–44.

Tsurumi, K. 1979. Aspects of endogenous development in modern Japan. Part 3, Man, nature and technology: A case of Minamata. Tokyo: Institute of International Relations, Sophia University.

Vogel, E. 1979. *Japan as number one*. Cambridge: Harvard University Press.

PART III | Supplementary Organizations

NINE

The Social Democratic Party in Britain: Protest or New Political Tendency?

GEOFFREY PRIDHAM

Problems, Questions, and Approaches

How does one set about assessing a brand new political party—especially when it has so far shown contradictory signs of success, ranging from a dramatic breakthrough overtaking both major parties electorally during the course of 1981 to a modest third-party position in the 1983 election, followed by a variable performance between these two positions and continuing uncertainty regarding its future as an actor on the British political scene?

The British Social Democratic party (SDP), founded in March 1981 as a breakaway from the Labour party, has, in alliance with the Liberal party, performed effectively as a protest party, harnessing disillusionment with the performance of the two major parties in government. But is it succeeding in establishing itself as the convincing and legitimate exponent of a new political tendency?

Whether the SDP will prove to be merely a flash party or will instead take a more permanent place in the British party system may ultimately rest on whether or not the constituency-based majority form of electoral system, which has been highly discriminatory against third or smaller parties, is reformed. However, any overall assessment of the significance of the SDP—whether its career is of short or long duration—must also confront the meaning of the "failure" of the establishment parties, and hence the possible "success" of any new party. This definitional point is all the more necessary here because by common judgment the SDP has, at least in the first few years of its existence, been considerably dependent on the negative impact of the Labour and Conservative parties.

The main point about the term "party failure" is that it is invariably relative, and that, accordingly, it may appear in different versions. For instance, it may mean in the short term the failure to achieve national office or in the intermediate term the inability to implement policy or ideological goals. Parties may rise and fall electorally, especially in this period of volatility; they may even disappear, although this is more likely to be as organizational and electoral entities, while the ideological tendency they represent may come to be taken over by a successor party (the "new parties for old" syndrome). However, any complete appraisal of parties failing must take account of their role societally as well as institutionally, although here there is some danger of one-dimensional judgments. The "failure" or indeed "success" of individual parties may be explained to a significant extent by social change, but one key variable must always be their adaptability or lack of it. In short, party failure in any absolute or quasi-absolute sense, is a rare phenomenon and almost certainly attributable to exceptional circumstances, such as the very evident failure of a political system, or the traumatic impact of a calamitous war.

For our purposes here, the principal distinction will be drawn between cyclical or temporary and structural change in party systems. The former is short lived and usually implies a return to the starting point, even though the underlying causes of change may remain (e.g., social change and/or disillusionment with governmental performance). This is usually because established parties manage eventually to adapt. Structural change in party systems normally refers to significant new directions or turning points in the balance of strength between individual parties which then become consolidated. That is, they feature some degree of permanence where new or sometimes preexisting small parties challenge the dominance of older parties, and are wholly or in part successful. The result may be either the substitution of one political force by another, or a more open competitive game marked by instability. Institutional arrangements, and especially the nature of the electoral system, may possibly condition the full expression of such structural change, at the parliamentary as distinct from the popular level; in the case of cyclical change this may be one attributable reason why it did not become structural.

There are several possible ways of approaching the analysis of a new party phenomenon such as the SDP. One approach is the historical, but the problem here is that by definition a new party will have very little history. One can look at its development since its recent beginnings, and draw some (possibly tentative) conclusions, but it is more instructive with this approach to relate the new party to longer-term trends in the party system. In the present case, this approach is all the more necessary and is indeed essential considering the very novelty of the SDP. Can one say that the SDP/ Liberal Alliance is filling a political space vacated by the "extremism" of the two major British parties? Have conditions long been developing which merely require the concrete presentation of a political and electoral alternative, or is that too simple an answer?

There is also the broad comparative approach. In the case of the SDP, three versions of this approach are possible.

1. The comparative approach may be cross-national. Similar developments, notably electoral dealignment and the appearance (sometimes sudden) of new political parties, have occurred in many other West European democracies over the same period since the late 1960s. It may then be considered how far these factors or conditions are applicable in the British case. This approach provides pointers, but leads to no definitive conclusions.

2. Another comparative approach is to focus on the typology of the SDP. This may tell us something significant about its intrinsic strengths and weaknesses, and therefore its potential as a political force.

3. A final comparative angle may be called thematic, in that various hypotheses relevant to the general problem of emergent political parties may be tested against the example in question. To some extent these touch on the typological aspects, but they involve a higher or deeper level of analysis. How do the Social Democrats relate to ideologies and political movements in general? Where do they stand exactly in the political spectrum of the British party system, or is the concept of the "center" a chimera? The answers to thematic questions like these help us determine whether the SDP is beginning to represent a new political tendency or is merely a protest party.

These various historical and comparative approaches individually provide clues about this new British political force, so that it is reasonable to adopt them all together. The aim of this essay is to do precisely that, concentrating on the SDP's formative phase, and then to draw conclusions by way of identifying the key determinants which should positively or negatively affect its further development.

CHANGING PATTERNS IN THE BRITISH PARTY SYSTEM: A COMPARATIVE PERSPECTIVE

There are many West European experiences of structural change, and these have been concentrated in the period since the late 1960s. In several countries, cases of declining dominance on the part of long-established or long-term governing parties have occurred (e.g., Social Democratic parties in Scandinavia), although weakening electoral support may combine with coalitional change or the effects of the electoral system in "exaggerating" trends (e.g., the Socialist triumph in France in 1981) that produce new directions in party systems.

West European democracies have exhibited more frequent changes of power owing to growing electoral volatility and the harsh economic climate in which the capacity for parties to perform in government has been severely reduced. During this same period, social-structural and/or political-cultural changes of importance have occurred with basic effects on party systems in several countries. Another significant development, common to most European countries, has been the appearance of post-materialist political values or the "New Politics," as it is often called. The overall result of these various developments has been to create greater fluidity, unpredictability, and instability in party systems than at any time since 1945, and thereby more potential openings for new political forces to make an impact.

In very many instances, new parties have in fact done that. Notable cases have been the entry onto the political stage of regionalist parties, ecologist parties, miscellaneous protest parties, and breakaway parties on the political left. It is obviously the last of these forms of protest which offers the closest analogy for the British case. Relevant cases include the Danish Center Democrats (launched in 1972 by a Social Democratic deputy, in protest against his party's alleged move to the left), the Dutch DS '70 (Democratic Socialists, formed in that year as a similar ideological protest against the left's growing control of the Dutch Labor party) and historically the Italian PSDI (Social Democrats who split from the PSI in 1947 over Socialist cooperation with the Communists). A characteristic of these new formations has been their ideological identification as centrist rather than moderate left. Electorally, they may have taken their place in the structure of their party systems but as minority parties. There has been no dramatic "breaking of the mould," at least as their direct achievement.

Social-structural transformation has tended to weaken the intensity of traditional class affiliation and thereby the electoral base and appeal of established parties, particularly those on the left. However, the actual impact of new parties challenging the old in this situation depends—apart from their own intrinsic strengths—on a variety of conditions in the party-political environment: the extent of sociopolitical cleavages, the degree of polarization between political forces, and the conditions of party competition, including the number and type of rival parties as well as their relative ability to respond to social and political change. Particularly significant is the exact relationship between ideological movement in parties, economic distress and social-structural change (Alt, 1979). Looking at the period from the late 1960s into the 1980s, we discover that the salient quality is the presence of virtually all possible determinants of structural change in party systems where an overriding part in crystallizing this process of change is played by economic factors. This is notably the case with Britain.

Aside from the obvious conclusion that the United Kingdom is by no means unique in experiencing significant change in its party system, comparatively speaking it becomes clear that in this particular case almost all of the common causes of structural change are present and have existed long enough to be considered a trend: electoral volatility (certainly), party organizational fragmentation (yes, recently), the existence of an ideological void (yes, both parties and especially Labour have moved away from a "catchall" electoral approach), demographic or social-structural change (yes, with the decline of the traditional occupations and class cohesion), the occurrence of traumatic political events (in Northern Ireland, though not really elsewhere), and above all the politically corrosive effects of economic crisis.

Such basic change in the party system has become a strong focus of academic work on British politics since the mid-1970s (Finer, 1980; Drucker, 1979; Kavanagh, 1977). Looking more closely at this development, it becomes apparent that the two-party system strictly exists if at all only at the parliamentary level, with the electoral system as the remaining key determinant, and even that parliamentary two-party system has come under greater challenge. The overall decline in dominance by both Labour and Conservatives may be documented by their combined share of the whole electorate: from 80 percent in 1951, through 74 percent in 1959, to 56 percent in October 1974 and 61 percent in 1979 (Crewe et al., 1977: 130). This decline in the two-party dominance has hardly been reflected in parliamentary representation. The total of Liberal seats at Westminster during the period from 1951 to 1979 ranged from six (as in three elections in the 1950s) to fourteen (February 1974—with a drop to eleven in 1979). However, the total parliamentary representation for all parties other than the major two has risen from the range of zero to six from 1951 to 1970 to twenty-three, twenty-six, and seventeen in the elections of February and October 1974 and 1979 respectively (indicating the small Liberal increase in seats but notably the rise at that time of the SNP).

Electoral volatility has been a distinct trend from the 1960s. This is demonstrated, for instance, in the growing tendency for by-elections to register strong swings against the party in government. Governing parties began to experience one-term periods in office. What is significant is the upsurge in by-election successes for the third party, as in the Liberal gains of 1972–73, and those of the SDP/Liberal Alliance of 1981–82. Work on electoral volatility has emphasized partisan dealignment through a process of weakening intensity in traditional party identification, shown, for example, in how supporters of the major parties, particularly Labour, have decreasingly accepted their main tenets and policies (Crewe et al., 1977: 129–90). According to one study, the number of "very strong" Conservative and Labour identifiers together has fallen from 40 percent in 1964, through 39 percent in 1970 and 26 percent in 1974, then 20 percent in 1979 (*The Times*, March 21, 1981). At the same time, the vote for the Liberals—although they have benefited more than before from this erosion of two-party support—has continued to lack a substantial hard core of voters and to be essentially volatile (considerably more so than the Labour or Conservative vote), largely negative (as the party exploited public rejection of the major parties), and based on little active backing of Liberal policies (Alt et. al., 1977).

The party competition scene at the national parliamentary level has not, however, changed dramatically, although events like the minority Labour government of 1974 and the Lib/Lab Pact of 1977–78 have suggested that the future of single-party governments is more uncertain. The political, economic, and societal bases for the concentration of electoral support behind the two major parties of Labour and the Conservatives have progressively weakened, a process of change that has accelerated since the 1960s, leaving the electoral system as the principal, if not the last remaining, prop for two-party politics.

Nevertheless, it does not follow that because a potential is created it will automatically be exploited successfully by any new political force. It is here that we turn to the SDP to examine its strengths and weaknesses, in order to assess its capacity to make a major and lasting entry onto the British political stage. Or will it, on the contrary, turn out to have performed a very impressive but short-lived walk-on part?

THE FORMATION OF THE SDP
AND ITS ALLIANCE WITH THE LIBERALS

Before turning to look at the typology of the SDP, it is necessary to make some general introductory points about its founding and early development. Also, while this study concentrates on the SDP itself, it must be remembered that from the very beginning it has had a close relationship with the Liberal party.

Inevitably, the SDP's own development has been strongly influenced by this relationship in various ways—in its structure, its formulation of policy, and even in the choice of its first party leader. Not surprisingly, too, the SDP's very identity as a separate political party has been affected—problematically—by the need to create itself virtually from scratch (requiring self-demarcation) while at the same time forming the Alliance. Yet, the majoritarian nature of the British electoral system made close electoral cooperation essential: two center-type parties could not afford electoral rivalry in the British system.

It must not be forgotten that while the Social Democrats are a new political force, at least as an organizational entity, the Liberals are an established party with a long historical tradition, even though they have played a secondary rather than central role in British politics since they ceased to be a major governing force more than half a century ago. Apart from posing certain problems of adjustment in the Alliance, this difference of identity and tradition complicated any ideological definition of the center force it represented—that is, the two parties taken together. "Social Democracy" was a new ideological label in British politics, but what did it really mean in substance? Old ideological wine decanted into new political bottles?

The SDP's self-presentation and self-image as a "new" force in British politics should not be dismissed too arbitrarily, not least because its very identity has revolved around that belief. Its rationale in the eyes of its leaders (unless they are thoroughly cynical), its activists and members and, presumably to some significant degree, in the eyes of the voters has been its "newness." At the press conference launching the SDP in March 1981, Roy Jenkins commented: "We offer not only a new party, although it is that, but a new approach; we want to get away from the politics of outdated dogmatism and class confrontation; we want to release the energies of people who are fed up with the old slanging match." Furthermore, it was the newness and hence news value of the SDP which above all explained the intense media coverage it received throughout 1981. The extent of the SDP's actual novelty will be examined critically in the subsequent sections of this essay.

New political parties often employ a negative motive to justify their emergence—in fact, the negative may be stronger than the positive point of reference in the early stages of development. In the case of the British SDP, the overriding negative motive was antipathy towards the Labour party. This was no surprise, for all of the founding "Gang of Four" were former Labour ministers.[1] All of the SDP MPs save for one ex-Tory were ex-Labour during the 1979–83 Parliament, while several prominent SDP organizers had also left the Labour party. The anti-Labour motive was pronounced in its influence on structural arrangements and discussion

---

[1] The "Gang of Four" were Roy Jenkins (formerly Chancellor of the Exchequer and Home Secretary), Shirley Williams (former education minister), David Owen (former foreign secretary), and William Rodgers (minister of transport). Jenkins's career break with Labour had been cushioned by his four years in Brussels, as president of the European Commission.

within the early SDP, but even more interesting is the question whether this negative motive is so compelling that it pushes the SDP across the ideological spectrum eventually to a distinctly centrist if not center-right position. On the other hand, the British SDP might settle into an ideological space in line with most West European Social Democrats, i.e., on the center-left, a position perhaps facilitated by the strong pro-Europeanism of its leaders.

The prospect of a new "radical center" force was first raised by Roy Jenkins in a lecture at Dimbleby in November 1979. The following year witnessed a slow-motion breakaway from the Labour party of some prominent and otherwise unknown MPs at Westminster, and then in January 1981 a Council for Social Democracy was created. The council served as the brief precursor to the political party—the SDP was formed in March 1981. Additional MPs moved across from the Labour party to the SDP, and by early 1983 the new party had thirty representatives in Parliament.

At the parliamentary level, the compelling motive for founding or joining the SDP and leaving Labour was essentially ideological (covering a variety of specific motives ranging from basic differences over policy and changes in the Labour party's structure, strengthening the position of the extraparliamentary wing and hence the left within it, to personal friction and much "bad blood" arising from conflicts with constituency and other parliamentary colleagues). However, the actual founding of the SDP including the timing of its launching was strongly influenced by two other factors: the persistently optimistic indications of its potential voting appeal, and the attitude of the Liberals as prospective alliance partners.

There had been poll evidence of strong potential interest in, if not demand for, a "center party" before the SDP was founded, and even before the Dimbleby lecture. As far back as 1972, a poll commissioned by *The Times* indicated that a center force linking Jenkins-led Labour moderates with the Liberals would be likely to cut deeply into the Labour party's electorate, by 44 percent. In January 1980, the same paper that had been monitoring potential center-party support (and also promoting its cause), published a detailed survey showing continuing strong sympathy for a center party (54 percent would welcome the formation of a center party, combining the interest in differently composed versions of it), although there was also a fragmentation of this passive consensus when it came to the possibility of actually voting for one version over another (*The Times*, Jan. 17, 1980). The most popular version—an alliance of moderate/right-wing Labourites plus Liberals—was preferred by only 23 percent. Other interesting leads provided by this poll (carried out only six weeks after the Dimbleby lecture) were: that a center party would draw roughly equally from voters of both major parties, that 42 percent would support the Liberal party if it "had a reasonable chance of winning the election," and overwhelming support for the idea of electoral reform (72 percent favored introducing a system based on proportional representation). A little more than a year later, when the Council for Social Democracy had just been formed, support for the above-mentioned formation had risen from 23 percent to 39 percent, most of the new support coming from disenchanted Tories (*The Times*, Feb. 9 1981). As in the 1980 poll, there was a strong feeling that the two major parties were moving too much to their respective extremes, though more with respect to Labour than the Conservatives, while nearly six out of ten believed "the present political system no longer works properly." There was still no clear consensus on the right solution, although 37 percent thought that a new Social Democratic party would "win quite a lot of seats" at the next general election. In other words, the concrete presence for the first time of an emerging center force had begun to crystallize opinion compared with earlier polls, but there were still some uncertainties and a waiting on events.

It is important to note that the Liberals, and in particular their leader David Steel, played a formative role in the creation of the SDP. Steel was partly instrumental in persuading Jenkins, with whom he had a close political association, that a separate Social Democratic party would in combination with the Liberals have a better chance of challenging the electoral dominance of the two major parties than if the Jenkinsites were to join the Liberal party directly. Liberal pressure also came, both privately and publicly, in urging prospective Labour defectors, including the Gang of Four, to act sooner rather than later.

The Liberal interest in such an alliance was in a way obvious, as it accorded clearly with the strategic aims of David Steel. Steel had long been an advocate of an alliance or coalition involving the Liberals, who in his view had tried unsuccessfully for a realignment of party forces in opposition for twenty years and should now try it through a governmental role (Steel, 1980: 36). The Lib/Lab Pact of 1977–78 was regarded by Steel, though less wholeheartedly by his party, as a step in this strategic direction even though its immediate political dividends were limited (ibid., chapter 11). In other words, the Liberals had to overcome the obstacle of the British majority electoral system by circumventing it from within, through an alliance with, or gaining some leverage over, one of the other parties. The idea of turning the voting system on its head through a dramatic electoral breakthrough seemed unrealistic, and at best a long-term prospect based on continued growing electoral volatility, so that the Liberals' very early reaction to the idea of a "center party" after the Dimbleby lecture was one of skepticism about its possible electoral impact and also concern, within Liberal ranks though less on Steel's part, that such a new party might duplicate (i.e., rival) the Liberals' political space. However, should the new party—in combination with the Liberals—gain momentum and take off, then the way might be open for the third-force breakthrough that had so far eluded the Liberals standing alone. That was the strategic calculation of Steel, though this was obviously not revealed in his positive though guarded response to the Dimbleby lecture in 1979.

A party alliance is likely to be reasonably durable and presumably arises when both participants see a sufficient balance of mutual benefits—that is, they complement each other and the sum total of their efforts produces greater advantages for both than had each pursued a separate political role. There were certain mutual benefits evident from the start which helped to consummate the SDP/Liberal relationship. As one newspaper correspondent noted about the Alliance: "Mr. Steel had gained a lot of Indian chiefs with an unknown number of Indians; Mr. Jenkins and the Limehouse Gang had gained a lot of Indians in the constituencies to justify the chiefs' feathers they wore" (David Wood, *The Times*, Feb. 15, 1982).

The SDP, top-heavy as it was, could offer several prestigious or popular political figures with governmental experience which the Liberals had previously lacked; while the Liberals had a larger grass-roots following with a background of campaigning, especially in local politics. The clinching factor which, however, gave momentum to the Alliance from the outset, and more than anything else cemented it and enabled it to overcome some serious internal problems (such as friction between the two parties over the allotment of parliamentary candidates and reservations especially among Liberals about the Alliance), was the potential and actual electoral appeal of the Alliance. This trend in popularity held out a real prospect for governmental power, and that, to say the least, had a politically aphrodisiac effect on both parties. The SDP/Liberal Alliance was set on course for a full-scale party alliance—moving from electoral cooperation through policy coordination to the quest for a shared role in government—and is the first real example of this in postwar British politics. This experiment has not been without internal difficulties, some of them considerable, both between and within both parties in the Alliance (Pridham, 1983).

For the SDP, the greatest problem has been establishing its own identity while working out the Alliance with the Liberals. This difficulty is due in part to the sheer time and attention spent on arrangements with the Liberals (notably in devising and implementing schemes for sharing out constituency seats) at this formative stage of SDP's development, inevitably preventing it from concentrating on its own affairs. More seriously, there has been a contradiction between these concurrent exercises. In contrast with the Liberals, who have a long and proud tradition as a party, the Social Democrats have lacked any identifiable tradition. They attach themselves to Social Democracy which has a respectable tradition in continental Europe, but enjoys no distinct roots in British politics, even though it is akin to the "Butskellite" consensus[2] to which both Labour and the Conservatives had adhered in government during the 1950s and 1960s. David Owen has written: "We discussed among ourselves many names of the new party, Democratic, Radical, Democratic Labour, even Independent Labour, but we always came back to the Social Democratic tradition, to the need to relate to an existing political philosophy. . ." (*The Observer*, June 20, 1982). Roy Jenkins has, however, admitted: "I hesitated over whether it was a good label, not because I thought it was inaccurate or damaging, but I thought it sounded a bit heavy and pedagogic, and alien in British terms" (*The Guardian*, Nov. 24, 1981). The problem of establishing a new political tradition was compounded by the effort to do so while allying with another, established party. Political parties invariably include in their armory of identity resources negative points of reference vis-à-vis all other political forces, but it was impossible for the SDP to demarcate itself from the Liberals at this formative stage. The SDP, therefore, faced from its origins an identity conundrum which appeared insoluble.

There was yet another factor peculiar to the SDP's origins that hamstrung its efforts to establish its identity and hence its image. The SDP, at least in its initial stage of development, was highly dependent on circumstances outside its own control. One of these was the tendency of both major parties to move to their own ideological extremes. What would happen if they both began to moderate their policy lines, as Kinnock has attempted with Labour since 1983? In a booklet on local campaigning, one SDP councillor commented early in 1982 on the SDP's "extraordinary momentum" during the previous year:

> Of course, the Labour and Tory parties have helped us enormously in that task. By stubbornly sticking to dogmatic and heartless policies, Mrs. Thatcher has succeeded in making her administration the most unpopular since the War. The Labour Party continues to commit mass suicide, slowly and in front of television cameras. Together, they have opened up a vast vacuum in the political spectrum which we have been able to occupy. The danger is that this fortuitous cir-

[2] "Butskellism" was the term used to apply to the significant if not considerable overlap in basic policy positions at this time between the two major parties, e.g., over the mixed economy, in a desire to create a more equal society, and in an attachment to political liberalism. The word amalgamated the names of R. A. Butler (a major figure in the Conservative party and very influential in its policy formulation) and Hugh Gaitskell, leader of the Labour party.

cumstance may not continue. Indeed, both parties show signs of moving back towards the centre . . . (Forester: 5).

A second external factor was the SDP's special relationship with the media. During the first year of its existence, the SDP enjoyed an intensive honeymoon period with the media. The SDP was attractive not only because of its very newness and its appeal to the media's partiality for possible dramatic future events (would it in fact "break the mould" of British politics, to use the SDP's own catch phrase), but also because the new party harmonized with the media's largely centrist values—it was "culturally proximate" for media people (Seymour-Ure, 1982: 433-34). The extensive coverage with which the SDP was blessed turned it into an "issue" itself, and hence contributed in no small way to the momentum of the party during this year. To quote one assessment of the SDP's relationship with the media: "perhaps media coverage is the first part of the mould to be broken, and the SDP should not for this purpose be thought a minor party at all" (ibid.: 442).

For all these reasons, the SDP fully earned the label of "media party." On the other hand, the assumption in this argument of a somehow passive reliance on outside factors can be carried too far. The SDP sought and skillfully cultivated the attention of the media from the start, successfully using professional show business techniques to announce the formation of the new movement in March 1981. The honeymoon ended—rather abruptly—when the SDP and the Liberals fell into open conflict over the share-out of parliamentary candidates in January 1982, a conflict which coincided with the beginning of the slump in the Alliance's electoral appeal. This controversy induced a bout of adverse coverage in the media, with some lasting damage to the SDP's image—the "nice people's party" was apparently indulging in "Tammany Hall behavior." In any case, the newness of the SDP was bound to fade eventually in the eyes of both the media and the public. The SDP's image is extremely vulnerable and volatile, as indeed is its electoral appeal; the uncertainty of its media image derives from the fact that its identity has lacked clarity and solidity. To establish more accurately the extent of this problem, the discussion will now turn to a more detailed examination of the SDP's structural, programmatic, and electoral characteristics.

THE SDP: WHAT TYPE OF PARTY

Certain characteristics of the SDP have emerged from the preceding discussion. Just to repeat: it adhered to the Social Democratic tendency, although it showed early signs of being more centrist than moderate left; it presented itself as a new political force with "radical" prospects; there was much truth in its being a "media party" (distinctly more so than the Labour and Conservative and even the Liberal parties) rather than one which could rely more autonomously on its own organizational resources; and it suffered from identity problems not least because of its umbilical link with the Liberals.

These features must be subjected to further questioning. For instance, any discussion of the new party's "Social Democracy" cannot be complete without taking into account internal differences over its ideological direction—which, of course, in turn inhibited its search for its own identity. What exactly is "new" about the SDP—that is, apart from the newness of its existence as a party in British politics? Is its newness merely rhetorical in an effort to exploit discontent with the established parties? The effect of the Alliance relationship with the Liberals on the SDP's own development should be investigated more precisely. There are additional aspects that need attention. What is the nature and extent of the party's structure? Where does it stand on policy issues? What is the breadth and depth of its electoral support? Furthermore, any overall assessment of the SDP as a type of political party has to identify the balance of priorities accorded each of these features (e.g., the SDP may have a program, but is it a programmatic party?), and may establish how far such characteristics influence each other (e.g., in what way does the SDP's ideology color its structural life?).

STRUCTURE. The SDP has made a deliberate effort to provide for unconventional structures and procedures in line with its self-presentation as a new political force, but how far has the reality of party life accorded with structural formality? There is invariably a basic deviation, if not dichotomy, between reality and formality in party structural relationships. Ideology and structure can come together since parties of the left are usually more articulated structurally and more bureaucratic than those of the right in parliamentary democracies. An examination of the SDP's structure should therefore also tell us something about its broader characteristics as a type of political party. The following discussion will look briefly at the motives behind its structural development, and then at both the formality and the reality.

The overriding motive was the negative one of self-demarcation from the Labour party, structurally—and, implicitly, ideologically. On the part of several SDP leaders, this motive was compulsive and focused on the question of internal party democracy or participation. It is revealing here to look more closely at the specific views held by SDP leaders, who dominated much of the debate on this matter. In an interview with "Weekend World" in November 1981, Roy Jenkins stressed: "After all, one of the things which the great row in the Labour Party's been about . . . is the desire to make MPs delegates, automatically just answering to instructions received from elsewhere, and this may put members of the government in the same position. It's a revolt against that which has been one of the factors leading to what is effectively now the break-up and decline of the Labour Party" ("Weekend World," Nov. 29, 1981). Contained in this is an elitist outlook which at the principled level at least conflicted with the idea of real internal party participation in policy formulation. On the other hand, Shirley Williams, less of an elitist by temperament than Jenkins, emphasized more participatory features in an article she wrote at the time of the SDP's founding, and also echoed another line of criticism toward her old party. According to her, the SDP: "will be a party of individual members. We shall not accept the affiliation of trade unions or businesses. . . . The use of the trade union block vote to elect a party leader who might become the Prime Minister of Britain was for the three of us who signed the Limehouse Declaration the immediate though not the sole issue which precipitated our breach with the Labour Party. So, the new party will be transparently democratic" (*The Times*, March 26, 1981). As a value, this anti-Labour motive was transmitted downward to activists, if it was not already held by them. The *SDP Newsletter*, an information sheet circulated to activists, had this to say about policy formation: "The principal advantage of our approach is that it involves the ordinary member directly and sensibly in policy making and avoids the resolution-type approach typical of, for example, the Labour Party" (*SDP Newsletter*, 1981: 3). An indication that this negative motive was often simply a gut reaction to Labour rather than one necessarily based on a positive organization concept was given by one SDP MP: "Nor does a determination to reject the practices of the Labour Party—admirable if this had meant the rejection of the old party prejudices—become anything other than silly if, in fact, it results in no more than administrative decisions about not having an annual conference because Labour has one, or not basing local parties on the constituencies because Labour does so, or disparaging local party members who were formerly active workers in the old parties" (Tom Ellis, SDP MP, letter to *The Times*, June 5, 1981).

Looking at the early structure, we can see various features which obviously aimed at making the SDP different from the other parties: the idea of a collective leadership, the appointment of a business-style party chief executive, the provision of finances almost entirely from individual subscriptions and avoiding affiliation fees or company donations, the larger area rather than constituency party as the local unit, the preference for a "rolling" conference in three cities across the country, and the idea of postal ballots among members on policy matters. There was a certain self-consciousness about these provisions, as, for instance, in Shirley William's comment that "our collective leadership, which will remain throughout this interim period, and perhaps beyond if the membership so wishes, challenges the conventional pyramid structure of the old parties" (*The Times*, March 26, 1981). Nevertheless, behind this structural differentiation could lie specific reasons in addition to the rejection of traditional party procedures. Of the original features, it was the area party structure which received the most attention, not least because the other parties had been based at the grass-roots level on constituency associations. Each SDP area party covered up to seven parliamentary constituencies. This structure was intended to facilitate cooperation with the Liberals, particularly on the share-out of parliamentary candidacies, as well as to prevent a recurrence of the "domination" of small constituency parties by "cliques" (as the SDP saw the Labour party). Otherwise, the SDP possessed structural features analogous to those encountered in the other parties: the national committee (party organization executive), the consultative assembly (annual conference), the parliamentary committee of all MP's in the House of Commons, and of course the leader (Roy Jenkins was eventually elected in July 1982 by a postal ballot of all members).

What was this structure like in reality? The SDP is only four years old at the time of writing, but various clues may be gained from its early organizational development. Some of the unconventional features proved more difficult to put into operation than expected. The area party structure has with some local variation been a cumbersome unit, particularly as the large territory has made it difficult to mobilize members, and has often caused resentment among them. The "rolling" conference seemed more of a gimmick than a practicable proposition; and attendance was much lower in 1982 than in 1981 at the height of the SDP's popularity; in 1983 it was abandoned altogether in favor of the conventional party conference in one location. The idea of a collective leadership has effectively been abandoned as a strict practice. The Gang of Four have continued to be viewed and esteemed within the party as its cofounders. Together they determined SDP positions and policy while the party structure was being fully established, and all four acquired official positions: Jenkins as leader, Williams as president, and Owen and Rodgers as vice-presidents. But the need for electoral appeal, as well as media expectations and practical convenience, such as simplifying relations with the Liberals, strengthened the focus on the figure of Jenkins in the initial phase. This may be said all the more in the case of David Owen, who became SDP leader in the summer of 1983. His dominance in the party has led to the virtual disappearance of the original collective leadership.

One characteristic of the party structure as a whole is its centralization. This has been evident in the organizational control of the party headquarters in Cowley Street in London, over such matters as membership recruitment, but more generally in the deliberate dominance of the national politicians with regard to policy formulation. The latter raised the problem of conflict with the party principle of internal democracy and membership involvement. According to the SDP constitution (ch. VI, sec. E), the election program and policy in general would be based on a policy statement adopted by the Council for Social Democracy (the 450-odd-member "parliament of the party," meeting at least thrice annually) and prepared by the Policy Sub-Committee (both MPs and non-MPs, with a controlling majority of the former). The principle of wider participation was, however, recognized in the provision: "the Policy Sub-Committee shall circulate provisional draft statements of policy to all area parties and regional committees for comment and shall take such comments into account when preparing final draft statements for submission to the Council" (VI/E/6). In practice, there has been some pressures from middle-level elites for effective participation, as at the Kensington constitutional convention of the SDP (February 1982) when they demanded a one-member-one-vote system of electing a leader, and then at the council's first meeting (October 1982) when a platform proposal for a statutory approach as the first stage of the party's income policy was rejected. These may be significant pointers to a future trend, but meanwhile the party structure has been very centralized. This caused friction with the Liberal party because the structural contrast between the Alliance partners (local autonomy is strongly rooted among the Liberals) added to the complications of dividing constituency seats.

Party membership and finance are usually fair indicators of the health of a party. On both counts, the SDP may be said to be weak rather than strong. In the first few weeks after its founding in March 1981, there was a dramatic mushrooming of membership registration (43,588 in the first ten days alone), but this soon leveled off with the total climbing gradually to 78,000 by early 1982. This high point hardly made the SDP a mass party (even the Liberals had considerably more with a claimed membership of 180,000), and in any case it declined to about 65,000 by autumn of 1982, to 60,000 by the summer of 1983, and 50,000 by early 1985 because some enthusiasm had waned by the time the issue of membership renewal arose. This membership deficit has naturally created financial problems. The major parties are also short of cash, but they can rely on either trade-union or big business donations, while the SDP faced the awesome prospect of having to organize and finance an electoral machine from scratch. Following the general election of 1983, the staff at national party headquarters was reduced drastically from fifty-three to twenty-eight on grounds of financial necessity.

Nevertheless, the SDP has developed a national party structure with some novel features in a relatively short time. While the predominant motive had originally been negative in rejecting the procedures of the established parties, notably those of Labour, the SDP's structure began to acquire some life of its own. It was, however, distinctly top-heavy: at its lower reaches effective activity was limited by a numerically weak membership, tight control by the national headquarters, and by the fact, initially, that key activists tended to be "political virgins" rather than hardened professionals.[3] The SDP was organizationally vulnerable, so that its slump in electoral support during 1982 occasioned doubts about its staying power. In conclusion—and it must be an interim judgment—the SDP can be classified structurally as a centralized party with low articulation, top-heavy in political weight but with some participatory features. One might even say, with some justification, that it was "notable-led" in view of the limited size of its membership, the predominance of middle-class professionals among it, and in particular the special role of the Gang of Four.

IDEOLOGY AND PROGRAM.   Where does the SDP stand in the ideological spectrum of British politics, and what is meant by "the Center"? Does it have a program? What are its positions on issues, and can it in any way be said to be a programmatic party? The answers to these questions throw significant light on the party's identity, and consequently show how much depth there may be to its newness.

One difficulty in defining party ideology is that some political forces deny they are "ideological," although it may be said—not perversely—that the degree of willingness to be described as ideological is itself an indicator of the nature of a party's ideology. On this basis, the SDP stands revealed as a political party on the side of being reluctant rather than willing to espouse its ideology. Public statements from SDP leaders, coupled with interviews by this author, have regularly revealed a knee-jerk aversion to being placed within the conventional left-right spectrum and toward "ideology" as such. Roy Jenkins has on more than one occasion referred disparagingly to what he calls "the disease of manifestoitis" in British politics; David Owen commented in a public lecture that the SDP

---

[3] According to an ORC survey published by "Weekend World" in November 1981, 67 percent of SDP members had not previously belonged to another political party.

"reflects thankfully that the new party members, most of whom have never belonged to a political party before, have not adopted the old stereotyping of what were supposedly left and right attitudes" (David Owen, Woodcock Lecture, Leicester University, Jan. 14, 1982). There has been much talk in SDP circles about the party's representing an "approach" rather than an ideology, but what does this mean? Roy Jenkins has spelt out his aversion to "manifestoitis" in a radio broadcast: "I will feel very bound by things that we have committed ourselves to, which is one reason why I'm very loathe to commit ourselves to too many things, because I think politicians make promises too easily and then find them hanging round their neck, and I'm anxious that we shouldn't promise the world . . . (we should) be cautious about detailed policy commitment" (interview with "Weekend World," Nov. 29, 1981).

Some clue to the SDP's ideology should be provided by its actual self-placement, when pressed, in the political spectrum. "Party identity," like ideology with which it is intrinsically linked, is in the first instance perceived by those involved in a party. There was much debate in the press during 1981–82, reflecting divided internal thinking within the SDP, as to whether it would turn into a "mark two Labour party" (i.e., moderate left) or a "center party." The four leaders contributed to this debate, though somewhat confusingly, with their own individual versions of where the SDP stood. Jenkins originally introduced the idea of a new party in the 1973 Dimbleby lecture as being of the "radical center," and has gone on record several times as saying that he has "not used the word 'Socialist' for years"; Rodgers described the SDP early in 1982 as being "firmly on the non-ideological centre-left"; while Shirley Williams at the time of the party's founding expressed her dislike of the term "center," and said she could live with "moderate" but liked "radical" (also used frequently by Owen). In their famous open letter to the Labour party in August 1980, the then "Gang of Three" (Owen, Rodgers, and Williams) had rejected the idea of a "Center party" for it "would lack roots and a coherent philosophy." But they were writing without Roy Jenkins, who must be seen as an unrepentant centrist, and his leadership was likely to move the party's programmatic position rightward from center-left.

The alliance with the Liberals also creates pressure for centrist positions to be adopted. The Liberals have quietly expressed their antipathy toward a "mark two Labour party" model for the SDP, so that this is increasingly unlikely. There have been visible signs that the SDP is moving away from and even disowning its Socialist inheritance, as in David Owen's expunging of the term "Socialist" from the shortened paperback edition of his statement of political philosophy, *Face the Future*, apparently under pressure from the party membership (Stephenson, 1982: 175).[4] What also emerges from looking at the attitudes of the Gang of Four is an internal division over the party's ideological direction, which surfaced publicly despite the blandness of the SDP's image.

The SDP has, nevertheless, officially adopted the Social Democratic tendency, so it remains to be seen how much this choice has filled out programmatically. Evidence has been provided in the generalized form of principles and policy guidelines. A number of official pronouncements have been issued, such as "The Declaration for Social Democracy" (January 1981—also known as the Limehouse Declaration), "Twelve Tasks for Social Democrats" (March 1981, published to coincide with the party's launching), and "A Fresh Start for Britain" (June 1981, a joint statement of both Alliance parties). One might add that the draft constitution contained a concise "statement of principles," that the SDP has issued a series of discussion papers on policy positions, and that three of the Gang of Four (not Roy Jenkins) have written books outlining their policy thoughts: Shirley Williams, *Politics is for People* (1981); David Owen, *Face the Future* (1981); and William Rodgers, *The Politics of Change* (1982).

This corpus of various statements, some long, some unbelievably brief, is difficult to qualify as a whole, as the works range from pamphlets—usually spiced with a good dose of anti-Labourism—to more speculative accounts of current political issues or broader philosophical questions, as in the books (David Owen's runs to 526 pages). It seems unlikely that any of the three books—the most detailed and explicit statements in the list above—will act as the kind of programmatic stimulus or bible that Crosland's *The Future of Socialism* did for the Labour party in the 1950s and 1960s. It is their role as possible indicators of the SDP's programmatic direction, rather than their publication or existence, which should really count. The Limehouse Declaration spoke of the SDP's desire to attract "all those who are committed to the values, principles and policies of Social Democracy," but what did that mean in the British context? One party publication, David Marquand's "Russet-Coated Captains: the challenge of Social Democracy" (one of the SDP's Open Forum Papers), attempted to establish some guidelines. Marquand begins by stating that "in politics, as in wine-tasting, content matters," and goes on to argue that there was a Social Democratic tradition in the United Kingdom long before the SDP was founded. It was an amalgam, according to him, of Fabian Socialism

---

[4] According to the same ORC survey published by "Weekend World," 65 percent of SDP members preferred to see the SDP as a "party of moderate reform" against 34 percent who preferred to see it as a "party of radical change."

(i.e., reformism), "New Liberalism" (the commitment to freedom but with the state playing a role in social policy), and "Tory Democracy" (i.e., Butlerism). Thus, Marquand, a close political ally of Jenkins, gives the game away that the SDP's version of Social Democracy is really Butskellite centrism. It is interesting that, while the party has stressed its newness, programmatically it is somewhat *déjà vu*. It has even been cruelly suggested that what the SDP offers is "a better yesterday."

It was, therefore, not surprising that the SDP proved bashful in translating its ideological approach into specific policy proposals. The SDP was for some time on the defensive about accusations that it had no policies, a charge made in the media and also by the major parties as one of their means of countering the challenge from the SDP. There were further considerations behind the party's deliberately low policy profile, notably electoral, for specific proposals could be divisive both within the party itself and among its voters, seeing that at the time (1981) it was drawing heavily from both Labour and Conservative supporters. On the other hand, a variety of pressures came to operate in compelling the SDP to declare its position on policies, and these tended to increase with time: The SDP's parliamentary party had to respond to Government decisions; media exposure, especially during by-elections, forced several SDP leaders (notably Jenkins and Williams) to formulate specific positions in an ad hoc fashion during the campaigns; persistent demands from the Liberals that the Alliance should be given policy content, underlining how much more programmatic they were than the SDP in their emphasis on policy; and, crucially, a growing awareness that after all the new party's credibility might suffer if the accusation about its "lack of policies" became common currency. Early surveys suggested that the SDP electorate was notoriously ignorant about its party's policies, and hinted that the SDP might begin to lose some of its electoral shine because of its hesitation over policies (*New Statesman*, March 5, 1982).

In fact, the claim by the SDP that it needed time to develop its policies was true. It took time for its special policy committees to produce consultative documents (in the form of "Green papers"), and it took more time to elaborate common positions with the Liberals, notably through two joint policy commissions on constitutional reform and employment and industrial recovery. Certain policy differences did materialize between the two Alliance parties, as over the emphasis on economic growth, the degree of devolution, nuclear energy and particularly defense (the SDP was decidedly Atlanticist, the Liberals included a strong unilateralist wing). On the other hand, certain SDP positions were clear from the beginning, especially in external relations (unqualified support for the European Community as well as NATO) and in its preference for a mixed economy. During the course of 1982, other positions were formulated, sometimes as joint proposals with the Liberals: on electoral reform (advocating the single transferable vote system), for a human rights commission, on employment, on reform of the trade unions, and in support of industrial democracy. Since then, the SDP can hardly be accused of lacking detailed policy proposals.

However, there is an essential difference between the functional production of proposals on this or that policy by a party and its self-presentation as a programmatic force, that is, relating single-issue commitments to a solid and coherent program in a way that establishes its identity. The SDP has achieved the former goal, but has so far failed to measure up to the latter requirement. This is not an easy achievement for a new political party, all the more so in this case since "the Center" has in British politics been more a certain attitude of mind—on closer examination an incohesive one—rather than a systematic body of political thinking. The conclusion here is that in the political spectrum the SDP stands in a centrist position (reasonably close to that of the Liberals) and not a moderate left one; and that it is not a programmatic party if that means giving a distinct priority to the formulation of a detailed and comprehensive program. Does the SDP simply offer Butskellism rehashed—taken out of the political cupboard, relabeled, tarted up, and presented to the voters in sexy wrapping—or will it eventually, if and once it becomes established as a party, begin to lay down roots as a distinct political tendency?

ELECTORAL SUPPORT.   Looking at the SDP's reluctant attitudes toward policies and policy as such, one could surmise that it was basically an electoral party (i.e., one whose overriding concern is to win votes). In a sense, it could hardly help being so, considering the electoral momentum behind its founding and the high electoral performance that blessed its first year of existence, not to mention the time pressure coming from its first general election—foreseeably, at the latest in 1984, though conceivably any time before then.

The SDP established its reputation—dramatically—through its breakthrough in a series of by-elections during 1981, coupled with continuously encouraging forecasts in the opinion polls. In the three by-elections in which it participated during 1981, the Alliance (the SDP provided the candidate in two, the Liberals in one) achieved a vote ranging from 40 percent to 49.1 percent, with considerable swings from both major parties (from Labour ranging from 21.8 percent to 24.9 percent; from the Conservatives from 24.2 percent to 27.5 percent) and an increase over the Liberal vote in the 1979 general election ranging from 29.5 percent to 33.9 percent (*The Times*, March 27, 1982). This level of support suggested that the existence of the Alliance increased the credibility of both component parties as election winners, thus generating additional support. (*The Times*, July 18, 1981). Trends in local by-elections through 1981 indicated a comparable level of support for the Alliance, with it winning overall two out of three contests (*The Times*, Dec. 30, 1981; *New Statesman*, Jan. 1, 1981).

The year 1982 told a very different if not contrary electoral story: a range of voting support in (seven) by-elections down to 8.2 percent to 33.4 percent, with an increase in the Liberal vote of 1979 ranging from 8.2 percent to 26.7 percent. The opinion polls, which had in 1981 indicated a level of support for the Alliance fluctuating around 40 percent, now dipped to around 30 percent and even lower, sometimes less than 20 percent. Results in local by-elections confirmed the same story of a decline in electoral appeal, though there was some evidence of an ability to maintain a position just below 30 percent. Clearly, therefore, the SDP/Liberal Alliance was as much a victim as a beneficiary of electoral volatility in Britain. In view of the majoritarian form of electoral system, this was at best a vulnerable and at worst a dangerous position to hold.

The reasons for this turnabout in the Alliance's electoral fortunes were not difficult to locate. At a visible level, the end of the media honeymoon in early 1982 was relevant, since media coverage affects turnout and consequently the chances of the parties if they were particularly advantaged by that (which the SDP was). The excitement engendered by the 1981 by-election campaigns because of the Alliance's impact produced a turnout only 4.3 percent to 9.7 percent below that for the preceding general election in the said constituencies (unusual for British by-elections); but during those held in 1982 the decline in turnout ranged from 15.4 percent to 30.2 percent (with the exception of 0.6 percent in the Hillhead election when Jenkins was the Alliance candidate) (*The Times*, Oct. 30, 1982). There was much truth in the statement of one journalist that "the SDP/Liberal Alliance lives and dies by the opinion polls . . . it grows because it is growing; or declines because it is already thought to be dying" (Hugo Young, *Sunday Times*, Oct. 17, 1982).

The key problem was that dealignment was not followed by realignment (i.e., a stable new direction for voting behavior), nor was that possible in so short a time. Seen in a long-term perspective, the Alliance—notably the Social Democrats—were obviously benefiting from the erosion of Labour's support since the 1960s, but every indicator suggested that whereas the Liberals had electoral precedent and some local activity to build on, support for the SDP was volatile and extremely vulnerable to less favorable circumstances. The new party's disastrous showing in the local elections of May 1982 (during the Falklands War) illustrated this vulnerability only too well. The volatility of the SDP's appeal had been underlined by the last-minute switches to Jenkins in both his by-elections at Warrington in July 1981 (when he nearly won) and at Glasgow, Hillhead in March 1982 (when he was successful in winning a seat in Parliament).

The thinness of commitment among Alliance supporters was established by survey evidence about their low degree of party identification, certainly lower than that for the major parties. In April 1981, according to Gallup, while 35 percent of the Conservatives said they were very or fairly close to their party and 28 percent in Labour's case, the figures for the SDP and the Liberals were 17 percent and 13 percent respectively (*Daily Telegraph*, April 16, 1981). That was a very short time after the formation of the SDP, but the figures almost a year later were not much different. The Gallup polls during January-April 1982 averaged out for the same category: 31 percent Conservatives, 31 percent Labour, 12 percent SDP, and 13 percent Liberals. (Figures provided by Ivor Crewe in a paper given at the Contemporary British Politics Workshop, Political Studies Association Conference, April 1982.) Conversely, the figures from the same source for those prospective party supporters "not close to any party" were: Conservatives 47 percent, Labour 50 percent, Liberals 68 percent, and SDP 71 percent.

A further indication of the same feature marking Alliance support has been the weak or unclear policy profile of the SDP, in particular among its voters. The level of their knowledge of the party's policy positions was markedly low, including a distinct tendency to identify these positions incorrectly (*New Statesman*, March 5, 1982). Even with the contours of its policy stands becoming clearer, the SDP is not guaranteed any stability in its voting support. A survey of Marplan published in September 1982 showed that Alliance supporters were overwhelmingly consumer-minded—that, is, they were much readier than Labour or Conservative supporters to shop around if the policy mixture on offer failed to attract them. On nine of the eleven issues named, more than a third of intending Alliance supporters said they would consider switching if dissatisfied (see Table 9.1).

In conclusion, the SDP/Liberal Alliance emerged electorally during 1981–83 as essentially a protest party—though on a larger scale than any previous third party since the war—with no significant signs of becoming in any way a new political tendency with a predictable electoral base. The electorate of the SDP/Liberal Alliance is a highly volatile one and hence its performance so far holds out no foreseeable chance of a permanent change, at the electoral level, in the British party system. This volatility means basic uncertainty about the Alliance's electoral future even after the national election of 1983 (when together the Liberals and the SDP won 26 percent of the vote), especially in view of the electoral system and the dra-

TABLE 9.1   Policy Issues and Switching Potential of Alliance
Supporters

For each of these issues, please say whether you would consider
switching your vote, or not voting at all, if your present party's attitude
on the issue turns out to be different from your own.

	Total	Con	Lab	Lib/SDP
Defense spending	27	23	26	35
Nuclear arms	34	27	34	50
In or out of EEC	29	23	30	39
Referendum on EEC	23	18	21	33
Inflation and unemployment	34	24	35	48
Prices and incomes	20	15	19	28
Nationalization	27	25	25	38
Less tax even if less social services	26	18	28	36
Less tax even if less industrial aid	22	17	21	29
Electoral reform	20	14	17	32
Trade unions: change or leave alone	26	23	23	36

SOURCE: *The Guardian*, Sept. 23, 1982.

matic difference it can make to the shifting of party support within the 30
percent range. It also means that the major parties can draw back support
from the Alliance, depending on the intensity of public disaffection with
their performance in government and opposition. Even though the Alliance's performance electorally was impressive between 1981 and 1983,
and it proved more capable than the Liberals had previously been of vault-
ing the barrier of the electoral system, nevertheless, the strong dependence
of the Alliance on a combination of favorable circumstances means that
this performance level does not alter the main conclusion.

CONCLUSIONS

Returning to the broad theme of this essay and of this book, it can be
said that since "party failure" in the United Kingdom is not absolute—the

situation of the 1970s and foreseeably of the 1980s cannot be described as exceptional historical circumstances amounting to manifest system failure—then "success" could hardly be absolute for any new party. There are significant signs of structural change in the British party system—longer-term trends, notably the dealignment of the Labour vote—but nevertheless, future developments might also prove that overall party change will have been more cyclical than structural. In this case, the SDP will have been a cyclical (i.e., temporary) beneficiary of such change. But inevitably, there are uncertainties about the eventual outcome.

To what extent do these uncertainties give encouragement to the SDP or provide possible opportunities for it? This study has attempted to evaluate the nature and role of a new political party in the first few years of its existence, and this naturally limits the validity of any early assessment. But patterns have emerged, and it is possible to make reasoned calculations. The record of the SDP so far illustrates one general lesson, which may well be applied to other countries where established parties have "failed" and new ones have arisen to challenge them: the success of the latter does not follow automatically or even straightforwardly from the weakness of the former, for there are many intermediary variables which may or may not be conditional on the performance of the new party in question. But let us turn to answering the question contained in the title of this essay.

Any estimation of whether a new political force is merely a protest party or amounts to a new political tendency must be comprehensive. Although any such judgment on the British SDP has to be a tentative one, different signs from its early development allow for an informed estimate. Electorally, the SDP is still rather more a party of protest—on a mass scale—though fluctuatingly so. It has channeled growing disillusionment with the operation of the political system in the United Kingdom, but voting support for the SDP has been more negatively motivated, with little indication of positive support for it as such. Its electorate is above all highly volatile. Ideologically and programmatically, the SDP is again more of a protest party—as yet, at least—than a distinctly new political tendency. Its self-presentation as a "new" political force has expressed first and foremost its self-differentiation, if not self-demarcation, from the major political parties, notably Labour, but there has not been sufficient indication of how it stands programmatically as a whole.

Ideologically, the signs are that the SDP will develop into a centrist rather than moderate left party, but "centrism" is incohesive as an ideology in Britain, while for electoral and attitudinal reasons the SDP has been hesitant, and earlier evasive, about its policy approach. This creates serious problems for its identity as a political party. Structurally, the SDP has already developed many distinctive or recognizable features, but it cannot in this respect be described as a mass party. Its early emphasis on its structural development underlined how much it saw itself as a prospective political tendency, but it has been slow to develop the stronger organization that would provide backbone and stability for the functioning of a true mass party. Finally, the SDP must be judged in conjunction with its alliance with the Liberals. Here the basis for the new center force's future operation has been created.

For the SDP to develop into a new political tendency, certain conditions relating to potential structural change in the British party system would have to be satisfied. The main achievement of the SDP so far—apart from the creation of its alliance with the Liberals—has been an initial electoral breakthrough, but this must revive and maintain itself, even though that is highly dependent on a continuing combination of favorable circumstances: continuous and positive media treatment, plus the failure of the major parties to move back toward the center. Second, the SDP has benefited in its birth from a partial fragmentation of the Labour party, but this has taken a very limited form. In terms of political weight, this fragmentation has been top-heavy: it has largely focused on the national parliamentary level and then only among some, by no means all, of the Labour right wing, although there has been some replication (again limited) of this process among Labour local councillors and party activists. A more serious split within one or both of the major parties would undoubtedly help the SDP and the Alliance and give it a more viable future. Thirdly, the most essential requirement for stabilizing the SDP's future role—and possibly its survival—as a new political force is basic reform of the electoral system. Only that would help to counter the uncertainty arising from the volatility of its electorate. Meanwhile, any assessment of the SDP/Liberal Alliance's chances of "breaking the mould" must, in light of the preceding discussion of its operation during its formative phase, be a skeptical one—in line with similar experience elsewhere in Western Europe.

As a final conclusion, just two points. First, it is clear from this study that the "failure" of the old and the possible "success" of the new are certainly interdependent, even if not exclusively so. That is, factors which determine the one almost certainly help to determine the other, though not necessarily more favorably, taking, for instance, the crucial factor of electoral volatility. Part of the story is something of a "both sides of the same coin" argument. Second, the chance of success for new political forces depends ultimately on the nature of the real problem facing the country in question. The economic and hence political crisis in Britain may be really a case of poor governmental performance though of long duration. If so, the SDP, together with the Liberals, is likely to remain one among several actors on the stage of British parliamentary politics. Indeed, the SDP is a much more conventional political party than it makes out, and it is without doubt system-supportive. Should, however, the situation in Britain develop into one of real system collapse, then the SDP and the Alliance are hardly likely to be regarded as offering a radical alternative to what has preceded.

Altogether, with reference to the problems addressed by this book, it may be clearly stated that a failure of electoral linkage, especially on the part of the Labour party, gave birth to the British SDP and that the party has sought to address this failure through its ideological stance. As such, it is a straightforward case of a supplementary linkage alternative, and this perhaps helps to explain its conventional nature. And yet it has presented itself as a "radical" new force denoting protest. The SDP cannot be described in any way as an obvious vehicle for expressing new or typical postindustrial concerns; rather, it is a matter of bland protest against trends of left-right polarization in British politics. This mixture of the conventional and the SDP's self-proclaimed "radicalism" lies, together with doubts about its programmatic substance, at the heart of its identity problem. It is especially for this reason that the vacating of ideological space by the major parties does not guarantee the survival and endurance of this new party. The best that can be said about the signs on this question is that they indicate uncertainty rather than a definite or likely outcome either way—negative or positive. On the one hand, declining class identity and reduced partisan identification, as well as general disillusionment with— or at least fairly brittle support for—the governmental performance of the two alternating parties, provide a potentially strong opportunity for the SDP and its Alliance partner, the Liberals. On the other hand, this opportunity may well be restricted or even countered by the electoral system which buttresses the established parties, not to mention that continuing concentration on traditional political concerns possibly favors the latter in responding to the SDP challenge.

REFERENCES

Alt, J. 1979. *The politics of economic decline: Economic management and political behavior in Britain since 1964.* Cambridge: Cambridge University Press.

Alt, J., I. Crewe, and B. Sarlvik. 1977. Angels in plastic: The Liberal surge in 1974. *Political Studies* 25: 343–68.

Bradley, I. 1981. *Breaking the mould? The birth and prospects of the Social Democratic party.* Oxford: Martin Robertson.

Crewe, I., B. Sarlvik, and J. Alt. 1977. Partisan dealignment in Britain, 1964–75. *British Journal of Political Science* 129–90.

Drucker, H. M. ed. 1979. *Multi-party Britain*. London: Macmillan.

Finer, S. E. 1980. *The changing British party system, 1945–79*. Washington, D.C.: American Enterprise Institute.

Forester, T. N.d. Campaigning in the local community: How to win local elections. *SDP Open Forum Paper No. 6*.

Josephs, J. 1983. *Inside the Alliance: An inside account of the development and prospects of the Liberal–SDP Alliance*. London: John Martin Publishing.

Kavanagh, D. 1977. Party politics in question. In *New trends in British politics: Issues for research*, ed. D. Kavanagh and R. Rose. London: Sage, 191–219.

Marquand, D. 1981. The case for coalition. Unservile stage papers (Liberal Publication Department), No. 28.

————. N.d. Russet-coated captains: The challenge of Social Democracy. *SDP Open Forum Paper No. 5*.

Pridham, G. 1983. Not so much a programme—More a way of life: European perspectives on the British SDP/Liberal Alliance. *Parliamentary Affairs* 36: 183–200.

SDP, *Constitution of the Social Democratic party*.

Seymour-Ure, C. 1982. The SDP and the media. *Political Quarterly* 53: 433–42.

Steel, D. 1980. *A house divided: The Lib/Lab and the future of politics*. London: Weidenfeld and Nicolson.

Stephenson, H. 1982. *Claret and chips: The rise of the SDP*. London: Michael Joseph.

Zentner, P. 1982. *Social Democracy in Britain: Must Labour lose?* London: John Martin Publishing.

TEN

The Defeat of All Parties:
The Danish Folketing
Election, 1973

MOGENS N. PEDERSEN

THE PROBLEM: FAILURE OF ALL PARTIES?

It had never been as cold in Christiansborg, the seat of the Danish parliament, as it was in December 1973. The unpleasant winter weather, combined with drastic restrictions on the use of oil for heating purposes, made the indoor climate almost arctic. As one observer noticed, this "halfway arctic staging matched the political atmosphere perfectly" (Ninn-Hansen, 1974: 241). The newspapers depicted the political scene in no less dramatic terms. The Folketing election of December 4, 1973, was described as a "landslide election," an "electoral earthquake." A leading Conservative newspaper wrote about the "ghastly election" that had made a new politician, Mogens Glistrup, "the victor of the election on a basis of massive protest among the voters" (*Berlingske Tidende*, Dec. 5, 1973). These descriptions could easily be multiplied, since all incumbent politicians and their media apparatus were in a state of shock, and therefore often reacted in dramatic ways.

In contrast, the political climate in Denmark before 1973 had been described as quiet and stable. Political scientists used to classify the Danish political culture as "homogeneous and secularized" (Almond and Verba, 1963). The political system was a "consensus system" (Eckstein, 1966), and the party system was described as a "working multiparty system" (Rustow, 1956). What had happened in Danish politics, "where hardly anyone raises his voice and the rhetoric of revolution finds few admirers" (Dahl, 1970: 4), since even calm observers would use big words, and the international press for a time would treat Danish politics and the 1973 election as an important event?

The author wishes to acknowledge the help provided by VW-Stiftung as well as by European University Institute. Many colleagues have given their advice. Special thanks go to Hans Daalder, Leiden, and to Gunnar Sjöblom, Copenhagen.

The answer becomes evident, when the basic results of that election are recapitulated (see Table 10.1).

TABLE 10.1   Distribution of Seats in the Folketing before and after the 1973 election

| Party | No. of Seats | | |
	Before	After	Loss (%)
Social Democrats	70	46	34
Radical Liberals	27	20	35
Agrarian Liberals	30	22	27
Conservatives	31	16	48
Socialist People's party	17	11	35
Communists	—	6	
Justice party	—	5	
Center Democrats	—	14	
Christian People's party	—	7	
Progress party	—	28	
Total Number of Seats	175	175	

A look at these figures makes it clear why the initial reaction among Danish politicians was one of shock, and why subsequent analytical writings still use colorful words to describe this "cataclysmic election" (Fitzmaurice, 1981: xxii).

In terms of the arithmetics of the party system, it is no exaggeration to speak about a landslide election. The preelection Folketing was composed of five parties, four of which dated back to the nineteenth century.[1] Only the Socialist People's party was a relative newcomer, formed in 1959 as a splinter party from the—in 1973—apparently defunct Communist party. The four "old" parties dominated the scene at the time. They had commanded about 95 percent of the electoral support during the interwar period, and in the 1950s and 1960s they still polled almost 90 percent of the vote. Due to the strictly applied principle of proportional representation, they also completely dominated the Folketing. The first important observation to be made is that all parties lost in the election, losses ranging from

[1] For descriptions of the traditional Danish party system, the reader is referred to Damgaard, 1974. The individual parties are portrayed in Wende, 1981, and in Fitzmaurice, 1981.

27 percent to 48 percent. More than a third of the members of the Folketing were replaced by new politicians.

The all-encompassing defeat also meant that it was not only the incumbent governing party, the Social Democratic party, that lost, but also all opposition parties, parties on both flanks of the Social Democrats. The hardest beating was taken by the Conservatives.

The magnitude of the change is considerable. In terms of aggregate electoral volatility, the 1973 election ranks highest among all elections in Western Europe since the Second World War (Pedersen, 1979, 1983), and electoral as well as legislative fractionalization rose to the highest point ever in Danish politics, as five new parties were grafted on to the party system.

One should, however, be careful when interpreting these numerical properties of the party system. Thus, it should not be forgotten that two of the victorious parties were in fact old-timers in Danish politics. The Communist party had been represented in the Folketing from 1932 to 1960, the Justice party from 1926 to 1960. After thirteen years out in the cold, they returned, partly carried by the wave of protest, and the political and social unrest that had arisen in Danish politics since the late 1960s. Although they had survived due to their small nuclei of faithful followers and members and due to their clear-cut and uncompromising ideologies, they had also succeeded in revising their public images. In the case of the Stalinist Communist party as well as in the case of the Georgeist Justice party, it is highly probable that the modest electoral success was due to a principled and unrelenting opposition to European integration and to Denmark's joining the EEC.

Apart from these parties, three brand new parties entered Parliament. The Christian People's party had been formed in 1970 with the major purpose of objecting to "moral decay and cultural nihilism," in the words of its founders (Andersen, 1975: 31). The liberalization of pictorial pornography and the liberalization of abortion, two measures that had curiously enough been passed by a bourgeois tripartite government between 1968 and 1971, were the two major events that triggered the formation of a "religious" party in Denmark. Due primarily to internal factional conflicts, the party had been deprived of electoral support and representation in 1971, but in 1973 it gained a modest hold, entering Danish politics as a predominantly bourgeois party, but a party prepared to cooperate in any coalition as long as the major goals of the party would be furthered.

The Center Democrats, the second new party, can in some ways be considered a brand new party, but in other ways it was a familiar creature. It was founded a few weeks before the 1973 election by a prominent, if maverick, right-wing Social Democrat, Erhard Jakobsen, who broke away from his old party after a long history of dissident behavior. The party was, however, not just another splinter party. It cast itself as a new party without a traditional program, but with an intended no-nonsense stand on burning issues for the middle classes. Thus, it was defending private property rights without rejecting the basic principles of the welfare state. Cultural issues were cultivated: the Center Democrats strongly criticized the alleged left-wing abuses in the state-controlled electronic media, in the universities, schools, etc. Just like the Christian People's party, the Center Democrats projected themselves as a party prepared to support governments and to enter coalitions as long as it was beneficial to the attainment of the basic goals of the party, be they short term or long term.

The third and by far the largest of the new parties that entered the Folketing in 1973 was the Progress party. It was a peculiar form of party, especially in its early days. If by a party we understand a "political group identified by an official label that presents at elections, and is capable of placing through elections, . . . candidates for public office" (Sartori, 1976: 63), then the Progress party was, of course, a party. But as a new party, it lacked many of the other characteristics of European parties, such as, e.g., members and organizational structures. It saw itself not as a party but as a popular movement, the "Progress Army," marching against "The System," and against the "Old Parties." The ideological thinking within the new party cannot be reduced to a simple formula, but it can be said that it included a criticism of existing parties for being outdated. According to this view, parties belong to societies in which deep cleavages are present, not to societies like the Danish in which the notion of social classes and cleavages had become obsolete. The reigning Social Democratic party was made a special target for the rhetorics of the leader of the party, Mogens Glistrup. He often made the point that the Social Democrats had been good enough in their time, but that the party was now as superfluous as all other old parties. In line with this thinking, the Progress party on several occasions during the first years of its existence cast itself in the role as a successor of the Social Democrats, even to the point that it took over some of the Socialist symbols, songs, etc.

We will not pursue the description of the new parties much longer. Enough has been said to form the conclusion that these new parties, with the possible exception of the Communist party, differed considerably in style, outlook, and ideological inclination from the older parties. An examination of the social composition of their electorates would also have revealed that the new parties, and in particular the Progress party, were not at all linked to social classes in the same way as the old ones were. The Progress party, as a matter of fact, attracted voters from all strata, with the exception of public employees; more than any other party, it reflected the occupational composition of the population at large, with the result that the party was able to boast in its propaganda materials that it was the second largest working-class party.

The character of these parties suggests that a major realignment took place in Danish politics in 1973. The older parties had been closely linked to the social structure: manual workers were overwhelmingly Social Democrats, farmers tended to be Agrarian Liberals, employers and white-collar employees would often vote Conservative, and the Radical Liberals traditionally attracted two categories of voters, the smallholders and the urban intelligentsia. This linkage had existed since the "freeze" of the party system that occurred between 1910 and 1920 (cf. Lipset and Rokkan, 1967), and although the bonds were weakening during the 1960s, it was with the election of 1973 that they were almost cut. A comparison of class voting in 1957 and in 1973 is quite revealing. It shows that the relative number of workers voting for the Social Democrats declined from 80 percent to 39 percent; in the rural population the share of Agrarian Liberals decreased during the same period from 79 percent to 50 percent, and the Conservatives who were supported by 39 percent of all employers in 1957 were down to 9 percent in the dramatic election in 1973 (Worre, 1979).

It was at the time—and still is—tempting to interpret the 1973 election and its dramatic outcome as an act of punishment: the voters protested against and punished those parties that had shared the responsibility for government in preceding years. It was not just one party that had failed—it was the entire pre-1973 party system, government as well as opposition, that was blamed for failures.

The remaining sections of this essay will scrutinize this interpretation by discussing a number of explanations of the electoral upheaval. We will build up a weak factor theory that purports to explain the outcome of the 1973 election and at the same time also accounts for the deadlock that has characterized Danish politics during the years that have passed since 1973.

Two Strategies of Explanation

There is no lack of suggestions, explanatory sketches, and singular generalizations concerning the 1973 election. As a matter of fact, the process of understanding all the why's started on the very election night, when flabbergasted politicians and political commentators had to face the reality of defeat or understand electoral success. At the time, the result was often interpreted as an aberration, and several prognostic statements suggested a return to "normalcy." Five elections later, the interest should, however, turn toward understanding the situation as one of fundamental realignment in Danish politics.

With a slight simplification, we may say that two explanatory strategies have been pursued by those who have tried to come to grips with this complex problem. One strategy, mostly pursued by Danish political scientists, has consisted in a gradual buildup of partial explanations, couched in purely domestic terms. Others have tried to understand the phenomenon in the broader context of comparative politics, i.e., attempted to sort out explanatory factors that are unique and then contrasted them with factors that pertain to a larger set of Western political systems. A few comments will be made about each of these strategies, their possibilities and their shortcomings.

To a considerable extent, the Danes' learning process has focused upon the rise of the Progress party. It sometimes looks as if the proper understanding of the 1973 election and its aftermath is tantamount to a valid analysis of the basis of electoral support for this new party. Often the perspective is even narrower, concentrating on understanding the reasons why a considerable fraction of the working class and the petit bourgeoisie were attracted by the appeals of the party.[2]

Such analyses often provide important suggestions, but they do not add up to the most satisfactory explanation. For one thing, they have demonstrated the complexity of partisan change. For each social category that contributed to the growth of the Progress party, a separate explanation apparently is called for. More important, the breakthrough of the Progress party was only part of a wider uprooting in the electorate. There is a lack of parallel studies of the other new parties as well as of the unexpected revival of older parties like the Communist party and the Justice party. It is plausible that an analysis of these latter phenomena would show that they are as elusive and complex as the former.

Some scholars have approached the problem from the opposite angle by asking why and how the Social Democratic party lost a considerable amount of support in 1973, most notably within the working class. Several authors have stressed that it is difficult to understand the decomposition of the party if one does not include an analysis of the strategic policy decisions made by the Social Democrats while in office, especially during the period 1966–68 and 1971–73. Thus it has been suggested that the handling of housing policy was of crucial importance for Social Demo-

[2] For a summary of some of these attempts, see Wickman, 1977.

crats' losses to the Socialist People's party in 1966 and to some of the new parties in 1973 (Esping-Andersen, 1978, 1980).

In comparison, the fate of the older bourgeois parties is neglected. The performance of the tripartite government (1968–71) has not yet been analyzed in terms of expectations, goals, and actual performance, but it is common knowledge that an important key to the outcome of the 1973 election and the ensuing leadership crises within the Agrarian Liberal party and the Conservative party may be found in such an evaluation. As is the case with the Social Democrats, the failure of the other older parties must to a considerable extent be interpreted as a response to strategic policy decisions made by these parties in government as well as in opposition.

In conclusion, it ought to be said that such analyses may contribute to an understanding of the 1973 electoral outcome, but that neither a study of the conditions of success, nor of defeat, will provide more than a partial understanding. It must be remembered that five parties lost and five other parties, most of them new, won. Thus *explanandum* is a complex pattern of format change, unique among Western party systems. The complexity becomes even more puzzling, when it is remembered that a genuine realignment happened: for six consecutive elections during the 1970s and 1980s the 1973 format has survived despite considerable electoral volatility. *Explanandum* apparently is a fundamental realignment in a multiparty system.

The second research strategy has consisted of attempts to analyze these phenomena in comparative terms. The search is directed toward the identification of unique factors inherent in the Danish situation that may account for a unique sequence of events. The critical part of such analyses, i.e, the attempts to weed out from the explanatory model all those factors that are more or less common to a larger group of party systems, is, of course, as important as is the search for the unique factors.

Among comparative analyses the least rewarding are those that are encapsulated in grander attempts at typologizing (e.g., Sartori, 1976; Lijphart, 1977; Heisler, 1974). These studies are focusing on other problems; at best they provide suggestive discussion points (e.g., Sartori, 1976: 150–51); they sometimes are outdated and therefore misleading (e.g., Lijphart, 1977: 110–11). Older theories about the development of party systems, like the affluence/embourgeoisement hypothesis (Lipset, 1967) or the "catchall" hypothesis (Kirchheimer, 1966) are not too helpful in general or in particular with regard to understanding the most recent development in Denmark (see e.g., Wolinetz, 1979).

Among comparative analyses, that of Harold Wilensky is most important (Wilensky, 1975, 1976). In his attempt to understand the conditions of so-called tax-welfare backlash, he puts heavy stress on the visibility of taxation and the rate of change in taxation as catalysts of backlash. He refers explicitly to the Danish case.[3]

This analysis has been further refined by Hibbs and Madsen (1981), whose comparative analysis deserves attention. They see the source of backlash in developments in the taxation structure as well as in the expenditure structure of the government budget. Rapidly rising, highly visible, general revenue taxes are considered the most important long-run cause of backlash, while the gross level of taxation does not seem to contribute to an explanation. In the short run, a catalyst for backlash in Denmark apparently was the increasing divergence between growing pretax income and decreasing posttax earnings, the real take-home pay (cf. also Rose and Peters, 1978). They further suggest that labor-intensive, government-supplied services which easily give rise to complaints about inefficiency, bureaucratic red tape, and overpayment of civil servants are more likely to cause political trouble than public utilization of cash transfers.

Although this is a rather convincing analysis of the background for the electoral uproar in 1973, two complaints have to be voiced. The first is that the analysis is troubled by an unclear and ambiguous definition of the dependent variable, welfare-state backlash. What the authors are accounting for is the emergence on the political scene of the Progress party, no more, but probably somewhat less. As we have seen, explanandum is a more complex phenomenon, and therefore this analysis also belongs to the group of partial analyses. Second, the authors are more successful in accounting for the unique 1973 situation than for the subsequent stalemate within the party system, another deficiency shared by most other analytical attempts.

In conclusion, we have to stress that the massive release of electoral energy in 1973 was caused not just by one factor, but by a wide variety of factors. For the sake of convenience, these factors can be grouped into four categories. First to be mentioned are a number of *long-term* social-structural as well as political factors that had been operating in Danish society for years, but which evidently assisted in bringing about the electoral outcome. Second comes another group of *shorter-term factors*, mostly related to the strategic choices and policies of parties during the late 1960s and early 1970s. The electoral upheaval itself was triggered by *short-term, catalytic phenomena*, which, in an interplay with unique *facilitating structural conditions*, produced the outcome.

It may be too demanding to suggest that these four groups of factors are the necessary and sufficient conditions for an electoral landslide like the Danish in 1973. One should rather say that these four types of explana-

---

[3] Consult also the perceptive, if superficial, analysis in Heidenheimer et al., 1975: 246–51.

tory factors constitute a minimal framework for understanding the phenomena.

Long-Term Factors of Change

The Danish social structure since the middle 1950s has undergone a profound transformation. It is an open question, how many parallels can be found in Western Europe; in most other countries the social structure has changed significantly, but a case can be made for the argument that the shift from industrial society to the "service society" has taken place more rapidly in Denmark than in most, if not all, other European societies. A few key figures will indicate the amount and the timing of this structural transformation.

The service-rendering sector of the economy grew from approximately 35 percent in 1950 to almost 60 percent at the end of 1970. During the same period, the percentage of the population within the once dominant agricultural sector decreased from approximately 27 percent to a tiny 8 percent. The balance between urban and rural population shifted significantly as a result of this development. In social-class terminology the redistribution is no less impressive—with the "middle-class" population growing out of all bounds, while the working class and the entrepreneurial class are contracting in absolute as well as in relative terms. The balance within the highly amorphous and heterogeneous middle categories has tilted too: in 1950 the relationship between public and private middle-class employees was 3 to 7, while at the end of the 1970s it was more like 5 to 5 (Andersen, 1979: 117).

That traditional bonds between classes and parties would become less strong as this development progressed is commonplace, but the effects upon the party system are far from easy to discern, since they involve not only effects upon the voters, but also effects upon the parties as strategic actors. A perceptive observer of Danish politics analyzed the 1973 outcome in these terms (Bendix, 1974: 19): "too late it dawned upon the so-called old parties, that their electoral basis in distinct social categories and thus also income-groupings had crumbled away due to technological developments in society. In a way the old parties are suspended in the air, representing something which no longer exists, viz. a structure of occupations and interests which dwindled away in the period after the Second World War. . . ."

This is a convincing interpretation, but one which is difficult to test. Static analyses of the changing social structure are numerous, and so are analyses of the distribution of various population groups on parties. But such analyses do not allow inferences about effects of the changing social structure upon the electorate. The only truly dynamic study which has been carried out did in fact detect a certain, albeit not very strong, structural effect, thus suggesting that the erosion of the voters' allegiance to the older parties has at least partly been due to rapid socioeconomic change (Jarlov and Kristensen, 1978).

Rokkan and Lipset (1966) convincingly argued that the party systems "froze" about 1920 along the basic cleavage dimensions prevalent at that time (cf. Damgaard, 1974). In Denmark these dimensions were the urban-rural cleavage and the class cleavage. Since the 1950s the proportion of the electorate that would belong to each of the four quadrants of the party space produced by crossing these two dimensions has changed so much that it would be rather strange if the party system had not undergone considerable transformation.

Concomitant with the deteriorating bonds between the voter, "his" social class, and "his" party has been a pronounced tendency within the parties to experiment with new types of electoral appeals, coalitions, etc. Since appeals to the traditional target group no longer suffice if the individual party wants to sustain its electoral strength, all parties in the years before 1973 were involved in a process of strategical and tactical revision. Each of the five incumbent parties changed coalition partners, or was preparing for such shifts of commitments. In several cases—e.g., in the late 1960s when the Radical Liberals reversed their traditional alignment with the Social Democratic party—the new strategy paid off so well that other parties were tempted to look for new partners, at least in the sense that the cultivation of short-term issues became more common than had been the case before. "Catchall" tendencies were highly visible in most parties before 1970. But even if this is the case, social-structural change does not provide us with a neat and simple explanation of the realignment. The crucial task for those who want to understand recent changes in the party system in the light of changes in the social structure does not consist in demonstrating *that* a relationship exists; rather it consists in the more demanding assignment of estimating *how large* a part of the radical transformation can be accounted for in terms of a social-structural transformation that is extensive, but maybe no more extensive than that encountered in other political systems which did not experience *their* 1973 election.

In addition to the deterioration of socioeconomic bonds between voters and parties, there also exists circumstantial evidence for another related process that might undermine the "classical" party system. A creeping loss of support for the government and for the politicians as political leaders is probably the best way to characterize this development. It did not surface very often during the 1960s, but when it did, it always came as a surprise. Since this aspect is not often discussed, we will dwell on it for a little while. Studies of the so-called popularity functions of the parties during the pre-1973 period suggest that Danish voters behaved like voters in other political systems, i.e., held the government responsible for the changing economic situation (Paldam and Schneider, 1980). A certain decline in the popularity of each government through its life cycle can also be traced in semiannual commercial opinion polls on this issue. But apart from these "standard" outlets of praise and criticism, there were a number of incidents in which public opinion was dramatically different from the policies of the government, and in some cases even from that of the entire Folketing. We will briefly review a few of these incidents.

In 1953 the referendum had been introduced in the new constitution as a device that could be put to use under various conditions. The bourgeois opposition, using one of these provisions, called a referendum in 1963 on a set of land reform bills that had been passed by the Folketing. The government bills were heavily defeated. The significance of this event was not the retarding effects of the referendum, but the considerable discrepancy between the distribution of voters in the referendum and in previous and subsequent elections. The lack of fit between the parties in Parliament and the participants in the referendum of 1963 becomes interesting in light of later events.

Some years later—in 1969—the story repeated itself. A proposal to lower the voting age to eighteen was put to a referendum as required by the constitution. The lowering of the voting age had been proposed by the Social Democrats and other parties to the "left" of the bourgeois tripartite government, but in the final "free" division on the proposal, a number of government supporters even sided with the left-wing parties, carrying the bill through Parliament with a comfortable majority. In the referendum, in which 64 percent of the voters participated, an overwhelming majority (50 percent of all registered voters) voted against the proposal. This outcome was widely interpreted as a reaction against the turbulence of the youth revolt of 1968–69 and as a defeat of the left parties, but again the lack of fit between the majority opinion in Parliament and in the electorate takes on a special significance when considered in connection with the election of 1973 (Riis, 1969; Nielsen, 1970; Svensson, 1978).

The most conspicuous example of a situation which reveals a misfit between the opinion of political leaders and voters is, however, an incident that happened in 1965. In 1964 all parties in the Folketing except the small right-wing party, the Independents, had passed a bill which created a new scheme of economic support for the creative arts. For some reason, this decision had not been much noticed by the daily press, and there was no hint at the time that the voters disagreed with the politicians. But when in early 1965 the new government agency entrusted with the administration of the program distributed its first stipends to artists, a public uproar rose in a few days. Throughout the press, acrimonious criticism was expressed; at a large number of factories, petitions were signed by thousands of workers. After a few days, several politicians started to back down from their earlier supportive positions, and heavy political pressure was put on the Social Democratic government, which in due time also decided to cut back somewhat the amount of money to be allocated.

This chain of events was at the time widely interpreted as a revolt, in which the man in the street reacted against the cultural elite and against the political elite. It takes on a special interest, since it has been demonstrated that later support for the Progress party came from the same categories of voters, from the same geographical locales, and even in many cases from the same individuals, who had been active in 1965.[4]

On the preceding pages some of the long-term factors of structural change and protest potential have been sketched, and it has been suggested that there were several forewarnings before 1973, even if these were not acted upon in strategic terms by the parties.

Equally important, however, are a number of relatively shorter-term factors operating in Danish politics during the late 1960s and early 1970s. Since some of these factors—especially those related to taxation levels and rates—have been identified and discussed widely in the literature, the discussion here can be brief.

SHORTER-TERM FACTORS OF CHANGE

During the four or five years preceding 1973, far-reaching reforms occurred in Danish politics. Some of these reforms were carefully planned and carried out; others were "just happening." It is no exaggeration to say that Danish politicians made more and deeper attempts to change the fabric of Danish life during these few years than they had done at any earlier stage in modern Danish history. A few of the more significant reforms ought to be mentioned and discussed.

A major municipal reform was undertaken in 1970. The number of primary municipalities was reduced from more than 1,100 to 275, and the number of counties was equally reduced from 23 to 14. With such extensive revisions of the boundaries for a number of political activities, one

---

[4] Unfortunately, no social scientists have as yet studied the sequence of events of the Kunstfondsdebat. Kastrup and Lærkesen, 1979, contains a well-documented and rich analysis from the perspective of the humanities.

should expect that relations between voters and parties would change. We do not know much about such effects, but it is plausible that the net result was a weakening of the emotional bonds between voters and parties. At the same time, a major reform of the electoral districts and constituencies was carried through, resulting in an increase in the size of units. The electoral reform also introduced new principles of nomination that made it more difficult to predict election outcomes in personal terms. Turnover of members of Parliament did, of course, reach a peak in 1973, but it had already increased considerably in the preceding election in 1971 (Pedersen, 1981).

For all the importance of the municipal and electoral reforms, the tax reform was, however, in terms of conflict potential even more important. A number of scholars have pointed at the rapid increase in taxation, and especially in the highly visible general income taxation, as a primary source of public dissatisfaction. The "Glistrup-curve" has become a household term (e.g., Wilensky, 1976: 19). One ought, however, to be aware that the tax reform was a complicated reform, and that its effects upon the minds of voters must have been very diverse. What happened, in brief, was that a political decision had been made in 1967 to switch to a new formula of tax collecting, the pay-as-you-earn formula. This change created administrative problems, and for that reason had to be postponed one year; it did not take effect until January 1970, when the tripartite bourgeois government was in power. This postponement created a great deal of confusion, especially since it was evident that even after the postponement the switch would not be totally successful. A simultaneous change of taxation principles, from taxation of the family unit to taxation of the individual adult, did not make the reform easier to implement and furthermore made for considerable criticism from feminists, who considered this part of the reform less than ideal.

Since the tax reform was introduced in such a way that it tended to stimulate individual economic activity, it was also deemed necessary to increase taxation in order to control the economy.[5] This increase was, however, also made necessary by other costly reforms carried out by the tripartite government. The final result is well known: an increase in tax revenue from 33 percent of GNP to 44 percent in three years, even though the government tried hard to control the growth of the public sector.

The point has been made that there were other reforms initiated before 1973, and especially during the period between 1968 and 1971, which

---

[5] The year 1969 was made a so-called "tax-free" year, meaning that income earned during 1969 was only taxed if it surpassed the income of adjacent years with a certain percentage. This arrangement created a certain incitement for individuals to earn—and probably also spend—in excess of the normal level.

were not totally successful, and which drew heavy criticism from various categories of citizens. A former minister in the tripartite government in a candid analysis has admitted that "the greatest mistake of this government was that it aspired to compete with earlier governments with regard to the introduction of as many and as large reforms as possible" (Ninn-Hansen, 1974: 86). Apart from the tax reform and the municipal reform (which was also ridden with problems of implementation), one could mention the liberalization of pornography, the liberalization of the right to have an abortion, the radical legislation of university government, etc. These reforms, plus some failed reform attempts,[6] were met by criticism in large segments of the population. Many traditional supporters of the government parties found these too far-reaching. On the other hand, the Socialist opposition often attacked the government for not going far enough. Polarization increased not only among parties in Parliament, but also among the voters and the politicians. It continued even after the election of 1971, when a Social Democratic minority government took over from the unfortunate tripartite government. Nor did this shift reverse the critical trend in the population.[7]

It is not the intention to discuss here in any detail the political history of the period immediately before the 1973 election. Enough has been said to warn against too simplistic explanations of the Danish case. What happened was not just a tax-welfare backlash. It is more to the point to say that the outcome of this election also reflected a punishment of all those parties which in rapid succession had been in government position, and which had all to some extent failed to meet the expectation of their core voters.[8] To interpret the events of 1973 as a manifestation of protesting taxpayers is at best tantamount to only a partial explanation of the success of only one of the five winning parties.

CATALYSTS OF CHANGE

A social or political upheaval does not just happen. It needs to be triggered. What were the catalysts of the 1973 election? The short-term trig-

---

[6] For example, the Conservative minister of commerce was strongly attacked by shopkeepers when he suggested a liberalization of shopping hours. For an analysis of the introduction of university legislation, see Pedersen, 1977.

[7] In 1971 the first academic electoral survey was conducted in Denmark, see Borre et al., 1976. The results from this survey as well as results from commercial opinion polls indicate that such feelings as a distrust in politicians, negative attitude towards public spending, the longing for "a strong man," etc. were running deep in the population as early as 1971.

[8] Even the Socialist Peoples' Party was being bruised by its institutionalized support of the government (1966–68); see Mader, 1979.

gering factor was the failure of the government to preserve its majority in an important division in the Folketing. The defection of the right-wing Social Democrat Erhard Jakobsen created this situation, which in turn led the prime minister to dissolve the Folketing—and the defector to form his own party, the Center Democrats. These events were, however, only the culmination of a long buildup of political tension that began on a night in January 1971, when a fairly unknown tax lawyer, Mogens Glistrup, declared on television that his income made him belong to the millionaire class, but that he did not pay any taxes. This statement landed as a bomb among the politicians, who, of course, knew that exploitation of tax loopholes was perfectly possible, but who were not able to control the reaction of the public. The public was deeply split on the issue between those who condemned the immorality of tax evasion, and those who saw the tax lawyer as a kind of freedom fighter against the entire state apparatus.

We will not follow in detail the ensuing buildup of political muscle by Mogens Glistrup.[9] Suffice it to say that tripartite government decided to let the police ransack the office of Glistrup, and to start a lawsuit against him. Thus he became highly visible in Danish politics. In 1972, when he was suggested as a Conservative candidate for the Folketing, the leadership of the Conservative party decided to block the nomination, and a few months later the rejected candidate formed his own party, the Progress party, and embarked upon an extremely vigorous campaign. In January 1973 the new party only gained 4 percent in the polls, but in April it reached its all-time high with 26 percent.

Personality matters in politics. It is evident that the personality and the campaign styles of Mogens Glistrup and Erhard Jakobsen were radically different from those of the other party leaders. At the height of their powers, these two politicians captivated their audiences by using heavy-handed satire, vitriolic ridicule, rambling play on words, and—mostly in the case of Mogens Glistrup—a peculiar *zünftigkeit*. The audience either loved it or hated it, and thus it worked. In contrast, other party leaders were inclined to use a vocabulary of moral indignation, political responsibility, and sometimes self-righteousness, a style that goes well with staunch party activists, but not with a mixed and volatile audience. The campaign, which started a year before the election, thus was conducted in terms of attack and defense, and the defenders of traditional Danish political values (the older parties) were often very much on the defensive. It is beyond doubt and well established by empirical research that the voters were being mobilized throughout 1973 to an extent without precedence

[9] For a good historical analysis of the genesis of the Progress party, see Hahn-Pedersen, 1981.

in Danish politics. It is also well established that the electoral decisions were to a considerable extent only made during the campaign itself, reflecting the short-term issues and fundamental issues whipped up by the highly efficient campaigners.[10]

FACILITATING CONDITIONS

It is difficult to envisage the electoral campaign, the swift breakthrough of new parties, and the extraordinary individual as well as aggregate volatility, unless one is familiar with a number of facilitating structural conditions that pertain to Danish politics.

First, one should remember that the electoral system provides an almost exact proportional representation of parties that pass the built-in threshold of representation. In order to gain representation, 2 percent of the valid vote is required, and this threshold has proven to be rather easy to overcome for new parties.[11] It is also fairly easy for new parties to participate in the electoral campaign, since new organizations only have to collect a number of signatures equivalent to 1/175 of the valid vote in the previous election in order to qualify as a party. Even more important in this respect is a set of legal regulations that ensures completely equal treatment in many ways during the campaign. Thus every party, irrespective of size and previous status, is, for example, given the same amount of free time and state support in the highly structured campaign on radio and television.[12] Since the newspapers are tending toward deemphasizing affiliation with particular parties and are increasingly providing opportunities for spokesmen of all parties to address the readers, and since the electronic media are pursuing editorial policies which tend to emphasize short-term conflicts and issues, it is a plausible hypothesis that the breakthrough of new parties is greatly facilitated in Denmark, when compared with conditions in other European countries.

BACK TO NORMALCY? OR PERMANENT REALIGNMENT?

Many Danish politicians back in 1973 expected the party system to return to its traditional four or five party format in a few years. Was Mr.

---

[10] See especially the analysis by Torben Worre and Steen Sauerberg in Borre et al., 1976: 9–49, 211–52.

[11] The threshold formula is more complicated, see, e.g., Johansen, 1979: 47.

[12] Danish radio and television is run by a public corporation; the parties are represented on its governing board along with representatives of various cultural and other organizations. On this organization and its policies, see, e.g., Skovmand, ed., 1975.

Glistrup and his Progress party not just a reply of Le Mouvement Poujade of the Fourth French Republic? Many convincing arguments could be made for the short lives of populist parties—and populism was the label that was quite often put on the Progress party as well as on the Center Democrats.

Predictions of a return to "normalcy" were also made by political scientists. Writing in 1974, Rusk and Borre thus foresaw that "some of the new parties will weaken and possibly disappear; others will regroup along the left-right dimension. Their most lasting effect will undoubtedly be to motivate the established parties to experiment and try new policies in the hopes of improving economic conditions" (Rusk and Borre, 1976: 159).

As with most predictions of political scientists, this proved to be slightly off the mark. If there is a " 'gyroscopic' tendency for parties to return in the long run to former levels of strength" (Borre, 1981: 62), it certainly looks like a long-winded process. A comparison of the election results of 1973 with those of the two latest elections suggests that the format of the party system of 1984 is essentially the same as in 1973 (see Table 10.2).[13]

The Communists have been ousted—for the second time—but another small Socialist party has regained a foothold. And the Justice party lost its

TABLE 10.2 Distribution of Seats in the Folketing in 1973, 1981, and 1984

Party	No. of Seats		
	1973	1981	1984
Communists	6	—	—
Left Socialists	—	5	5
Socialist People's party	11	21	21
Social Democrats	46	59	56
Radical Liberals	20	9	10
Center Democrats	14	15	8
Christian People's party	7	4	5
Justice party	5	—	—
Agrarian Liberals	20	20	23
Conservatives	16	26	42
Progress party	28	16	6
Total Number of Seats	175	175	175

[13] In Table 10.2 the parties have been ordered along a left-right dimension according to prevalent expert judgments, cf. Castles and Mair, 1984.

representation in the election of 1981. But apart from these minor changes, the picture is not qualitatively different from that of the 1970s. There is high fractionalization and high aggregate volatility, but there is also an astonishing equilibrating tendency, meaning that losses and gains for various competing and collaborating blocs of parties tend to cancel each other out.[14]

The intriguing question to ask about Danish party politics since 1973 is, how and why the new party system was able to sustain itself over so many elections? The following paragraphs will not provide an answer, but at best only some of the clues.

The simplest answer would consist in saying that those factors which caused the electoral uproar in 1973 are still operating in Danish politics. This answer may take us some way, but obviously it is not satisfactory, since one should not expect an explanation of sudden change to qualify also as an explanation of a situation of deadlock. A brief presentation of the arguments will indicate the limits and the possibilities of this line of thinking.

Since it is not easy for decisionmakers to affect long-term social factors in the short run, it would not be surprising if Danish politicians had been giving thoughts to possible ways to change the structural conditions of the party system, and thus indirectly affecting the party system. It would be tempting, especially for politicians from the defeated older parties, to aim at an electoral reform, by means of which the thresholds of representation and authorization could be raised.[15] By changing one of the major structural prerequisites of format change, one might expect, if not to recreate the old party system, then at least to weaken some of the new parties. Although the idea has been discussed several times since 1973, no attempt has been made to introduce a parliamentary bill. It is easy to understand why. Since restrictive measures are opposed by all minor parties; since most parties are minor parties which are periodically threatened by extinction; and since these small parties are to be found in the core as well as in the left and right peripheries of the new party system, any proposal advocating restrictive measures would immediately be killed in Parliament—the more so since the Progress party has been in opposition to such measures, even in its heyday. Consequently, the prediction is that the present electoral system will remain as a facilitating structure for high aggregate electoral volatility, for the representation of new parties, and for sustaining the life of even minor incumbent parties.

[14] For an extended discussion of patterns of cooperation and conflict in Danish politics before and after 1973, see Pedersen, 1981. Cf. also the brief presentation in Borre, 1980. Borre, 1985, discusses the pattern of electoral volatility until 1984.

[15] For a discussion of these concepts and theoretical problems related to minor parties, see Pedersen, 1982.

It has been suggested earlier that the turbulence in the 1973 election was related to the particular character of the electoral campaign and to the pattern of issues presented to the voters on that occasion. It is hard to envisage a repetition of this configuration of events, and evidence also demonstrates that subsequent elections have differed in tone and character. Electoral surveys have made clear that later elections have not to the same extent been "high-interest" elections. Still, on most indicators of political interest and activity, the voters have scored considerably higher than they did in 1971 (Borre et al., 1979; Borre, 1985). Political distrust and protest were still realities at the end of the 1970s. That a continuation of such attitudes may account partially for the relatively high level of activity in the electorate is plausible, but recent studies reveal a very complex pattern. Thus, apathetic distrust and alienation still seem to run deep among those voters who possess the least political resources, while on the other hand, the resourceful, well-educated voters are to a considerable extent characterized by activist distrustful attitudes (Damgaard, ed., 1980; Nielsen and Sauerberg, 1980). These findings are highly ambiguous, and they are in particular difficult to assess in a developmental perspective, the more so since analyses have not been extended into the 1980s.

An argument has been put forward that one should expect a high and sustained level of individual electoral volatility in a party system to which new parties have been added (Pedersen, 1983). In such a system, characterized by a distinction between old and new parties, the interparty competition will be different from the pattern of competition in a more consolidated party system. The newer parties will confront a distinct disadvantage. They will not yet have been able to build up a core of loyal voters, party members, and activists. Thus they will have to fight for their existence and their newly gained foothold for quite some time. Due to the composition of their electorate, they are able to appeal neither to partisan loyalty, nor to the self-interests of large social groupings. In this situation the new parties may feel tempted to conduct what has been termed "politics of outbidding" and "irresponsible opposition" (Sartori, 1976), but their leaders may as well try to politicize—and eventually monopolize—new, often narrow issues. The new parties are also prone to conduct their campaigning in a catchall style, to use broader-based appeals and other tactics intended to keep the floating voters alert and to attract them. This interpretation fits well with the observed tendency in the Danish electorate: a high degree of floating in and out of the smaller parties, less so in the older parties, and a resultant high aggregate volatility in the electorate. But this hypothesis can at best only partially account for the sustained existence of the new party system format.

Very few would doubt that short-term considerations and issue orientation play a greater role in politics than before 1973. But what is the status of those longer-term factors that accounted partially for the outcome of the 1973 election? Are they still operating, and what will their present impact be? This is probably *the* crucial question that has to be answered if one wants to predict the course of Danish politics. Some facts stand out: taxation levels, measured, e.g., in relation to GNP, increased throughout the 1970s, albeit a temporary leveling off was visible in the years immediately after 1973 (*Finansredegørelse*, Oct. 1981: 72); the number of public employees was steadily growing during the period, from 22 percent of the total labor force in 1970 to 32 percent in 1979 (*Statistisk Tiårsoversigt*). Long-term changes in the social structure are proceding at least at the same speed as in earlier decades, and one might add that unemployment is rising steeply from approximately one percent of the total labor force in 1973 to more than 10 percent at the beginning of the 1980s.

Not many would predict that such tendencies would produce apparent stalemate in the party system. Signs have also been detected of some underlying movements in the electorate. Thus some studies did suggest a gradual buildup of a polarized situation in which those who are active in the private sector of the economy are drifting more toward the non-Socialist parties, while the unemployed and especially the growing number who are employed in the public sector are more prone to vote for left-wing parties than was earlier the case.[16] On the other hand, support for the basic goals of present welfare policies may even be increasing in all categories of voters after a temporary decline in the early 1970s (Andersen, 1982). These and other indicators do, however, lend themselves to different interpretations, and they certainly do not suggest primacy for any particular prediction of future elections. It may be the case that the parties are still "suspended in the air," waiting for a new traumatic electoral experience. But it may as well be the case that recent structural trends will sustain an electorate that is relatively volatile, while at the same time a balance is preserved between and within the core parties and the peripheral parties.

CONCLUSION: ANY LESSONS FOR COMPARATIVE POLITICS?

We have discussed an intriguing phenomenon: the realignment in Danish politics around 1973. For all the intrinsic interest of this situation it is not irrelevant to ask now if anything can be learned from this exercise in terms of comparative theory?

[16] See, e.g., Andersen, 1979, and Andersen and Glans, 1981, who have made plausible a tendency toward political radicalization among the highly educated and among certain groups of public employees, in particular within the social service and the educational sector.

Evidently, not much, if Denmark 1973 was just an aberration, a unique situation in every respect. An interpretation like the present one runs the risk of exaggerating trends and relationships, thereby making the phenomena look more unique than they really are or simpler than they are. The reader may judge for himself and may wish to draw his own conclusions, but the author wants to make three theoretical comments, all of which can be read as warnings against too simplistic interpretations.

First, we have seen that the factors contributing to realignment were many. They could be grouped into at least four distinct categories. Some of these, like the long-term factors discussed earlier have been found to operate in most Western European systems, some of which have not experienced any electoral turbulence at all, for example, Austria, Switzerland, and Sweden. Other factors, in particular the personality factors, are probably unique. So is the lack of institutional safeguards against "intruders." In a certain sense the incumbent parties in Danish politics are institutionally unprotected. As we have seen, the electoral threshold is very low. The public subsidies to parties are among the lowest in Europe. "Equal treatment" in the electronic mass media gives a small party with a few hundred members the same access and coverage as, say, the party of the prime minister. The reader may wish to compare this institutional arrangement with that in France, as described by Frank L. Wilson later in this volume. The reader should, however, also be warned against stressing one or two such factors. The Danish realignment simply cannot be and should not be understood in terms of just one or a few explanatory factors. In particular, one has to warn against the fascination of many Anglo-Saxon scholars with the tax- and welfare-backlash *problematique*. It was not only angry taxpayers who revolted in 1973 because their interests had been given too little attention.

If the *explanans* of this discussion is complex, so is the *explanandum*, the changing format of the party system. But to what extent is the Danish development unique? It would not, of course, be theoretically interesting if it were completely different from others, nor if the opposite were the case. Fortunately, we are able to pinpoint the limits of variation. Comparisons with other European party systems have made it clear that the Danish 1973 election stands apart from other postwar elections in Europe in terms of the magnitude of aggregate volatility, the increase in fractionalization, and probably in most other conceivable quantitative indices.[17] But the difference is, after all, only one of degree. Evidently, Denmark with its critical election is the most pronounced case among several systems—primarily Norway and the Netherlands—that have experienced a consider-

---

[17] This point is argued at length in Pedersen, 1979, 1983.

able growth in the number of parties and, especially, in the volatility of the electorate. These systems, therefore, are of special theoretical interest for comparative typologists.[18] Denmark represents the borderline case, not only because of the quantitative aspect, the magnitude, but also because of the special configuration of change: the defeat of all incumbent parties in a single critical election.

The third and final theoretical point to be made in this conclusion has to do with the conceptual vocabulary used in the discussion. The reader will probably have noticed that the Danish case has been discussed by means of a rather simple terminology. An *explanandum*, the defeat of five incumbent parties in a single election, has been described, and a series of *explanatory factors* has been suggested. At best, the character of this essay is that of the hypothesis-generating case study. It is exactly this character that also accounts for the reluctance on the part of the author to make use of the more ambitious conceptual vocabulary advocated by the two editors of this volume. By framing the narrative in terms of linkage patterns, linkage failure, or just party failure, one may end up saying too little about the political phenomena under inspection. But there is also the risk that one says more than is warranted. Let me be a little more precise on these points.

I have not used the concept of linkage at all. This does not mean that this concept may not be useful for some purposes, including the purpose of comparative summarizing. But its analytical usefulness seems limited in connection with the study of a system like the Danish. With a great many parties; with a traditional pattern of minority governments which are forced to rule by negotiating and making compromises; and with a highly complex set of relationships between parties, interest organizations, and the state apparatus—in short with strong corporatist tendencies—it may conceal too much in a brief discussion to speak in terms of only four types of linkages or chains of connections.

If the concept of linkage provides too little mileage, the concept of failure easily takes us too far—and in the wrong direction. When the term appears in a few cases on the preceding pages, it is not used in a technical sense, but rather as a means to create stylistic variation. "Defeat" is the central term used both in the title of this essay as well as in the text, and this usage is deliberate. "Defeat" has the advantage of being an "objective" characteristic that can be attributed to a given party or to a group of parties. No one can deny that all incumbent Danish parties *were defeated* in December 1973. The party leaders and their followers at the time also *felt defeated*. Some of them even went as far as to blame the voters for

[18] See the extensive discussion of these systems in Sartori, 1976. Cf. also Lijphart, 1977.

their defeat. It was not until the subsequent post-mortems that some politicians started to ask whether their own party or other parties had *failed* in terms of strategy, tactics, or in the sense of not having met the expectations of the voters. This soul-searching was to a very high degree prompted by Mogens Glistrup, who found special pleasure in telling the leaders of the incumbent parties that they had failed—in that accordingly the older parties had become absolute relics.

To speak about a party's failure means that one attributes responsibility for some functional defects. This is a problematic venture, especially in a case like the present one when the very public debate is carried out in terms of failure. The scholar easily becomes a prisoner of political language. It is safer to stick to the neutral word "defeat," and then ask questions about the causes of defeat. This strategy does not preclude the possibility that some parties did indeed fail. But it makes it an open question for empirical research if defeat and failure are related in a simple and straightforward way.

REFERENCES

Almond, G. A. and S. Verba, 1963. *The civic culture*. Princeton: Princeton University Press.

Andersen, J. G. 1979, *Mellemlagene i Danmark*. Aarhus: Politica.

———. 1982. Den folkelige tilslutning til social-politikken—en krise i velfærdsstaten. In *Partier, ideologier, väljare*, ed. D. Anckar et al. Abo: Abo Akademi, 175–209.

———, and I. Glans. 1981. Socialklasser og partivalg i 70'erne. *Politica* 13: 5–45.

Andersen, P. C. 1975. *Kristen Politik*. Odense: Odense Universitetsforlag.

Bendix, P. 1974. Valget, som en politiker ser det. In *Decembervalget 1973*. Copenhagen: Schultz.

Borre, O. 1980. The Social Bases of Danish Electoral Behaviour. In *Electoral participation. A comparative analysis*, ed. R. Rose. Beverly Hills: Sage Publications, 241–82.

———. 1981. Den ustadige ligevægt—forskydninger i de danske partiers vælgerstyrke. *Politica* 13: 46–86.

———. 1985. Denmark. In *Electoral change in Western democracies*, ed. I. Crewe and D. Denver. London: Croom Helm, 372–99.

———. et al. (1976). *Vælgere i 70erne*. Copenhagen: Akademisk Forlag.

———. 1979. *Folketingsvalget 1977. Tillæg til Vælgere i 70erne*. Copenhagen: Akademisk Forlag.

Castles, F., and P. Mair. 1984. Left-right political scales: Some expert judgments. *European Journal of Political Research* 12: 73–88.

Dahl, R. A. 1970. *After the revolution*. New Haven and London: Yale University Press.

Damgaard, E. 1974. Stability and change in the Danish party system over half a century. *Scandinavian Political Studies* 9: 104–125.

Damgaard, E., ed. 1980. *Folkets veje i dansk politik*. Copenhagen: Schultz.

Eckstein, H. 1966. *Division and cohesion in democracy. A study of Norway*. Princeton: Princeton University Press.

Esping-Andersen, G. 1978. Social class, social democracy, and the state. Party policy and party decomposition in Denmark and Sweden. *Comparative Politics* 11: 42–58.

———. 1980. *Social class, social democracy, and state policy*. Copenhagen: New Social Science Monographs.

Finansredegørelse Oktober 1981. Copenhagen: Finansministeriet, Budgetdepartementet.

Fitzmaurice, J. 1981. *Politics in Denmark*. London: C. Hurst.

Hahn-Pedersen, M. 1981. *Historien om et nul. Mogens Glistrup og Fremskridtsbevægelsen 1971–73*. Odense: Odense Universitetsforlag.

Heidenheimer, A. J., H. Heclo, and C. T. Adams. 1975. *Comparative public policy: The politics of social choice in Europe and America*. New York: St. Martins.

Heisler, M. O. 1974. *Politics in Europe*. New York: David McKay.

Hibbs, D. A., Jr., and H. J. Madsen. 1981. Public reactions to the growth of taxation and government expenditure. *World Politics* 33: 413–35.

Jarlov, C., and O. P. Kristensen. 1978. Electoral mobility and social change in Denmark. *Scandinavian Political Studies* 1: 61–78.

Johansen, L. N. 1979. Denmark. In *European Electoral Systems Handbook*. ed. G. Hand et al. London: Butterworths, 29–57.

Kastrup, A. M., and I. Lærkesen. 1979. *Rindalismen. En studie i kulturmønster, social forandring og kultursammenstød*. Copenhagen: Reitzel.

Kirchheimer, O. 1966. The transformation of the Western European party systems. In *Political parties and political development*, ed. J. La Palombara and M. Weiner. Princeton: Princeton University Press, 177–200.

Lijphart, A. 1977. *Democracy in plural societies*. New Haven: Yale University Press.

Lipset, S. M. 1967. The changing class structure and contemporary European politics. In *A new Europe*, ed. S. R. Gaubard. Boston: Daedalus.

Lipset, S. M., and S. Rokkan. 1967. Cleavage structures, party systems, and voter alignments: An introduction. In *Party systems and voter alignments: Cross-national perspectives*. S. M. Lipset, and S. Rokkan. New York: Free Press, 1–64.

Mader, E. 1979. *SF under "det røde kabinet" 1966–1968*. Odense: Odense Universitetsforlag.

Nielsen, H. J. 1970. Voting age of 18 years. Adopted by the Danish Folketing, rejected by the popular referendum. *Scandinavian Political Studies* 5: 301–305.

Nielsen, H. J., and S. Sauerberg. 1980. Upstairs and downstairs in Danish politics: An analysis of political apathy and social structure. *Scandinavian Political Studies* 3: 59–78.

Ninn-Hansen, E. 1974. *Syv år for VKR*. Copenhagen: Det Schønbergske Forlag.

Paldam, M., and F. Schneider. 1980. The macro-economic aspects of government and opposition popularity in Denmark 1957–78. *Nationaløkonomisk Tidsskrift* 118: 149–70.

Pedersen, M. N. 1977. The Danish university between the millstones. *Minerva: A Review of Science, Learning and Policy* 15: 335–76.

———. 1979. The dynamics of European party systems: Changing patterns of electoral volatility. *European Journal of Political Research* 7: 1–26.

———. 1981. Denmark: The breakdown of a working multiparty system? *Working Papers*, November 1981, Odense University.

———. 1982. Towards a new typology of party lifespans and minor parties. *Scandinavian Political Studies* 5: 1–16.

———. 1983. Changing patterns of electoral volatility in European party systems, 1948–77: Explorations in explanation. In *Western European party systems*, ed. H. Daalder, and P. Mair. Beverly Hills: Sage Publications, 29–66.

Riis, O. 1969. Folkeafstemningen om 18 års valgret. *Økonomi og Politik* 43: 215–32.

Rose, R., and G. Peters. 1978. *Can government go bankrupt?* New York: Free Press.

Rusk, J. G., and O. Borre. 1976. The changing party space in Danish voter perceptions, 1971–73. In *Party identification and beyond*, ed. Budge et al. London: John Wiley & Sons, 137–61. Also published in *European Journal of Political Research* 2: 329–61.

Rustow, D. 1956. Scandinavia: Working multiparty systems. In *Modern political parties*. ed. S. Newmann. Chicago: University of Chicago Press, 169–93.

Sartori, G. 1976. *Parties and party system: A framework for analysis*. Cambridge: Cambridge University Press.

Skovmand, R., ed. 1975. *DR 50*. Copenhagen: Danmarks Radio. *Statistisk Tiårsoversigt*, various editions. Copenhagen: Danmarks Statistik.

Svensson, P. 1978. *De unges valgret*. Aarhus: Politica. Wende, F., ed. 1981. *Lexikon zur Geschichte der Parteien in Europa*. Stuttgart: Alfred Kröner Verlag.

Wichmann, J. 1977. *Fremskridtspartiet. Hvem og Hvorfor?* Copenhagen: Akademisk Forlag.

Wilensky, H. L. 1975. *The welfare state and equality*. Berkeley: University of California Press.

———. 1976. *The new corporatism, centralization, and the welfare state*. Beverly Hills: Sage Publications.

Wolinetz, S. B. 1979. The transformation of Western European party systems revisited. *West European Politics* 2: 4–28.

Worre, T. 1979. Forandringer i dett danske partisystems sociale grundlag. In *Dannsk Politik i 1970erne*, ed. M. N. Pedersen. Copenhagen: Samfundsvidenskabeligt Forlag, 68–82.

ELEVEN

Parties and Political Action Committees in American Politics

FRANK J. SORAUF

For most of the 1960s and 1970s it was commonplace to talk of the decline of the major American parties. While the operative noun varied sometimes—"decline" yielded to "decay" or "decomposition"—scholars widely shared a belief that the American parties were no longer the potent, dominant political organizations they had been a few generations earlier (Burnham, 1970; Broder, 1971). Recently, however, several scholars have noted signs of revival in the parties and warned that reports of their demise were premature (Pomper, 1980; Cotter et al., 1984). In a very short time, what had been a consensus on decline has turned to controversy.

The conventional case for the decline of the American parties, nonetheless, remains substantial. There are ample signs that the roles of the parties have shrunk over the last several generations and that they do not now play those roles with the vigor and authority they once did. To be specific:

1. The major American parties do not organize campaigns for elections as they once did. Their monopolies of information on the electorate, of manpower for the campaign, and of the avenues of communication in it have been broken by the new campaign specialists (Agranoff, 1976).
2. The parties can no longer sustain even the modest degree of discipline in American legislatures they once did. One study of party voting in the Congress identifies the years right after World War II as the time of the major decline in party cohesion in the House of Representatives (Turner and Schneier, 1970). The decline, moreover, has not been reversed.
3. Within the cognitions of American voters, too, the parties do not

I am indebted to too many people and organizations to mention all of them by name. I should, however, express my special indebtedness to my research assistants, Stephen Ansolabehere and David Linder, and my friend, Gerald Elliott.

count for as much as they did even in the later 1950s. The percentage of the American voters who identify with a political party has declined, and the percentage of independents rose from 22 percent in 1952 to 36 percent in 1976.[1] Even those loyalties that remain appear to do so in weakened, less effective form; straight party ticket voting, for example, has declined considerably in the past thirty years (Nie et al., 1976).

In short, the American parties have at least in part lost their dominant role in organizing American politics, both "within" the American voter and in the American electoral and legislative processes. Their hold on the loyalties of American voters and American policymakers is clearly not what it once was.

The recent challenge to the "decline of the parties" school focuses on the parties' new successes in raising money and rebuilding their organizations. It is undeniably true that the parties have begun to reassert themselves in the financial support of candidates. Between 1978 and 1984, for example, the net receipts of all committees of the Republican and Democratic parties increased three and a half times.[2] The strengthening of the national party organization, however, is more evident among Republicans. The renaissance of the Republican National Committee under the chairman of the later 1970s, William Brock, is generally acknowledged. The committee's ability to assist local parties and candidates has increased substantially in a very short period of time. Strengthening within the Democratic party has taken a somewhat different form. One sees in it a strengthening of the authority and voice of national party organs—stronger national officers and greater control over the selection of delegates to the party's national convention, for example (Longley, 1980). Finally, a comprehensive study of the American state and local parties suggests stronger organization in both parties than the conventional wisdom had supposed (Cotter et al., 1984).

Actually, there is little in the reports of decline and the reports of resurgence that is contradictory or incompatible. They may well both be correct, especially since they report on substantially different features of the parties. What appears to be simultaneous (or successive) decline and revival may be nothing more than their delayed adaptation to the major and

[1] The data come from the national surveys of the Center for Political Studies of the University of Michigan.

[2] There were, however, substantial differences in the magnitudes of the sums involved. The Democrats went from $26.4 million to $96.8 million, and the Republicans from $84.5 million to $300.2 million.

fundamental changes American electoral politics have undergone in the past half-century.

The slowness or failure to adapt of the American parties is hardly unique. Other parties have not found it easy to adapt to the loss of partisanship in the electorate, to the strengthening of nonparty groups, to great changes in the technologies of persuasion, and generally to a politics concerned with a lengthening agenda of issues. Indeed, the pattern of troubles is so widespread as to suggest a natural cycle in the lives of the parties in which they achieve their greatest influence in the early years of democracies and developing societies, only to lose it in the much greater political literacy, wider political involvement, and newer political agendas of those societies and economies as they mature.

There are, however, special American aspects to the problems of the American parties. Since they have been predominantly electoral parties, their challenges and losses have been electoral. (They have had very little membership to lose, for instance.) Their troubles center on the progressive inability of their activists and organizations—of the party "cadre"—to control the naming and election of candidates for public office. The ability of would-be candidates to court the public with their own resources has largely taken even the naming of presidential candidates out of the hands of the parties and their conventions. Moreover, because government regulation of the parties, party nominations, and campaign politics, especially their financing, is so pervasive in the United States, it gives a special dimension to party problems and limits the range of their responses. While those legal interventions do not in the long run cause the parties' problems, in the shorter run and in a more proximate way, they reinforce them and add an extra advantage to the alternative political organizations. The American legislation of the 1970s on campaign finance is only the latest in a long line of illustrations of that reality.

In recently confronting their problems, the American parties have faced a great adaptive choice. Were they to alter their essentially electoral role and become vehicles of issue and ideology? The national Democratic party started down that road with the reforms post-1968 and with the 1972 national convention and its presidential choice, George McGovern. Ideological membership organizations (the "clubs") had, in fact, begun to develop in both parties as early as the 1950s. By the 1980s, however, it is clear that both parties have renounced the ideological course. The membership organizations are in disrepair, and the Democrats have gradually pulled back from some of the reforms in the presidential nomination process in favor of return to electoral pragmatism (Price, 1984). Both parties now follow the path the Republicans chose in the 1970s: an attempt to strengthen the party for its traditional electoral role by mobilizing the new resources that role now requires. Once again two historically pragmatic parties have chosen the pragmatic course.

A REVOLUTION IN ELECTORAL POLITICS

More than most parties, the American parties will be challenged, even jolted, by changes in the electoral environment in which they function. Recently they have confronted a revolution in electoral politics taking place on at least three fronts. First, since World War II there has been a many-sided technological revolution in campaigning, rooted largely in the development of television, the computer, and opinion sampling. Television and the other media quickly became prime avenues of political communication, replacing much of the political contact, canvassing, and rallying that the older party organizations specialized in. Moreover, since television transmits personalities much more effectively than ideas or abstractions, it shifted the image of the campaign from the party and issues to the candidates. Scientific opinion polling came of age at about the same time, providing data on the loyalties, perceptions, and intentions of voters that the local party worker never could accumulate. And high-speed computers not only processed the survey data, but provided the means as well for organizing direct mail appeals of all political kinds, especially those for campaign contributions. Inevitably, the new technologies gave rise to a new race of technicians, the campaign consultants (Sabato, 1981).

At approximately the same time—the immediate postwar years—a second set of changes began: those in the loyalties and political perceptions of American voters. Better educated than previous generations, they were better informed and more aware of things political. In a sense they were also more sophisticated politically. Large numbers of voters reduced their dependence on the all-encompassing symbol of the political party, beginning to pick and choose among candidates and issues, splitting tickets in the polling booth, and dividing their loyalties among parties, individuals, and other political organizations. The result, of course, was a far more fluid, fragmented, independent, and selective electorate, an electorate far harder for the parties to mobilize than it was at the turn of the century or in the four or five decades after (Nie et al., 1976).

Finally, beginning perhaps a bit later—in the middle or late 1960s—the agenda of American politics expanded dramatically. To the traditional social and economic issues, the "gut" issues of American politics, we added concerns for racial and ethnic and sexual equality, for all aspects of the physical environment, for crime and punishment, for a lingering national involvement in Vietnam and then elsewhere in the world, even for sexual mores and preferences. Issues of equality, personal morality, and "life style" began to compete with those of economic well-being and security. Such a multiplication of issues and concerns in the American electorate doubtless reflected the erosion of consensus (or the erosion of ignorance) on a number of issues in American society. But whatever the reason, the result was an agenda too diverse and too divisive for the parties to embrace. Inevitably, it contributed to a greater issue concern in the electorate and to the appeal of the specialized, limited agendas of interest groups (Nie et al., 1976; Pomper, 1975).

In less than a generation, the implications of these changes for American electoral politics had become terribly clear. The parties lost their monopoly over some of the campaign functions and became technologically obsolete in others. The consequences for candidates were fully as fundamental. Their campaigns were less likely to be party led, party financed, and party staffed. They found themselves no longer in the barter economy of the traditional political party but in a cash economy where they could purchase the skills for the campaign from experts in the new knowledge and technology. They themselves, their smiles and their families, suddenly became the political message in the mass media. They were suddenly freed to run their own campaigns. They needed only the cash with which to do so.

So, the new campaign politics opened the door for new political organizations. The two major parties had long dominated American electoral politics, even to the virtual exclusion of minor parties. Interest groups, although they occasionally dabbled in electoral campaigns, largely limited their activities to policymaking politics in American legislatures and administrative agencies. But suddenly the American parties no longer could provide the resources for the new campaigns, and the way was clear for political organizations that could.

The Rise of Political Action Committees

Unlike political parties, not all political action committees carry their generic title in their names. The Committee on Political Education (COPE) of the AFL-CIO comes to mind, and so does the conservative Committee for the Survival of a Free Congress. Nonetheless, federal statutes regulating campaign finance are quite specific in defining them, even though they, too, do not use the phrase "political action committee." Political action committees are committees—other than party or candidate committees—that collect and spend resources (usually cash) to influence election outcomes. They influence them in two ways: either by contributing those resources to candidates (or to parties or other groups that will eventually give them to candidates), or by spending them "independently" to urge the election or defeat of a candidate. In the 1984 campaigns, for example, the PACs registered with the Federal Election Commission contributed $104.9 million to congressional candidates and spent another $4.6 million independently of any party or candidate's campaign to urge the election or defeat of those candidates.[3]

Although they did not become an object of media attention until the mid-1970s, PACs have been operating in American politics since 1943. In that year the Congress outlawed direct political expenditures by labor unions to parallel its much earlier ban on corporate spending. The Congress of Industrial Organizations (CIO) responded immediately by creating a separate fund, called simply the Political Action Committee, to raise campaign funds from its members. Shortly thereafter the CIO set up a sibling PAC, the National Citizen's Political Action Committee, to solicit political funds from outside its membership. In addition to being present at the creation, the labor movement presided over the maturing of the political action committee. The AFL-CIO's COPE, established in 1955 at the merger of those giant labor federations, is generally considered the prototype of the large and powerful political action committee.

The first thirty years of PAC development were modest ones. Some business, professional, and membership groups formed PACs, but the labor-based PACs dominated the movement. All that changed with the explosive growth of PACs in the 1970s (see Table 11.1). By whatever measure one prefers, their expansion was more than merely impressive. Between 1974 and 1984, the number of PACs in existence grew from 608 to more than 4,000; the sums they contributed to congressional campaigns grew more than eightfold from $12.5 million to $104.9 million. Since all sources of campaign funding grew in that period, perhaps the most accurate measure of PAC growth is in their share of contributions to general election campaigns for the Congress. From 1974 to 1984 that percentage climbed from 15.7 percent for general election candidates for both houses in 1974 to 29.1 percent in 1984.[4] While similar reliable data on PAC independent expenditures for the period before 1980 are not available, it seems beyond

[3] In addition, PACs also contributed $1.5 million to presidential candidates in the prenomination campaign and $17.4 million independently in the publicly funded presidential campaign after the nominating conventions.

[4] A word of warning is necessary here. These data on percentage of receipts are for the general election candidates only (although it does include their expenditures in primary campaigns). One can justify that shift in data base because it limits the computation of PAC contributions to the kinds of races that PACs are apt to contribute to; that is, it eliminates losing primary candidates who by and large have few prospects and very little PAC money.

TABLE 11.1   Growth of Political Action Committees, 1974–1984

	1974	1976	1978	1980	1982	1984
I Total number in existence	608	1,146	1,653	2,551	3,371	4,009
II Total contributions to congressional candidates (millions)	$12.5	$22.6	$35.2	$55.2	$83.1	$104.9
III Percentage of funds of general election candidates for Congress from PACs[a]	15.7	19.6	20.1	25.7	26.4	29.1

SOURCES: Data are from the reports of the Federal Election Commission. The data of III are adapted from Cantor, 1982.

[a] The PAC contributions to the general election campaigns for the House have consistently accounted for a higher percentage than for those for the Senate. In 1984, for instance, they were 37 percent of the receipts of House candidates, and 19 percent of those of Senate candidates. Note also that this percentage is limited to PAC contributions to general election candidates. The percentage drops if one computes it for all congressional candidates.

doubt that the $22.2 million figure for 1984 presidential and congressional elections is more than ten times greater than the total the PACs spent independently in 1976.

Among the 4,000 PACs in existence by 1984, there is an intimidating diversity. While they may all meet the operational definition of a PAC, they differ greatly in size, in vitality, in internal organization, in their strategies and tactics, in their relationships with contributors and recipients, even in their fundamental political goals. In differentiating among them it is best to begin with the six categories the Federal Election Commission has evolved. Those categories—labor, corporate, trade/health/membership, cooperative, corporations without stock, and nonconnected—embrace two closely related definitional criteria: the presence or absence of a parent organization to the PAC, and for those PACs so connected, the type or nature of the parent. The first five categories embrace the PACs with parent organizations; since the fourth and fifth (PACs of cooperatives and corporations without stock) account for so small a share of PAC expenditures—about 3 percent of all PAC expenditures in the 1984 federal elections—we will eliminate them from further discussion in the interests of simplicity. The sixth category (the "nonconnected" PACs) includes all of those without a parent organization, the so-called independent or ideological PACs. Thus the four categories of Table 11.2.

Within the PAC movement, growth has taken place at wildly different rates (see Table 11.2). Labor, having developed its PACs in the 1950s and 1960s, had relatively little "room" for expansion in the seventies and eighties. To a lesser extent that was true also for the trade/health/membership PACs. The most impressive growth, both in numbers and in expenditures, has been among corporate and independent (i.e., nonconnected) committees. In terms of relative strength, labor PACs have thus slipped considerably; what had been a dominant 44 percent of PAC contributions

TABLE 11.2 Growth of Political Action Committees, by Category, 1974–1984

	1974	1976	1978	1980	1982	1984
Corporate						
Number	89	433	784	1,204	1,469	1,632
Contributions to congressional candidates (millions)	(a)	(a)	$9.8	$19.2	$27.4	$35.3
Labor						
Number	201	224	217	297	380	394
Contributions to congressional candidates (millions)	(a)	$8.2	$10.3	$13.2	$20.2	$24.8
Membership						
Number	318	489	451	574	628	698
Contributions to congressional candidates (millions)	(a)	(a)	$11.3	$15.9	$21.7	$26.6
Nonconnected						
Number	(b)	(b)	165	378	746	1,053
Contributions to congressional candidates (millions)	(a)	$1.5	$2.8	$4.9	$10.7	$14.5

[a] F.E.C. data not available for these contributions in these years.
[b] The nonconnected PACs in these years were included in the Membership category.

to Federal candidates in 1974 was only 23 percent by 1984. On the other hand, corporate PACs more than trebled their contributions just between 1978 and 1984. Finally, while Table 11.2 shows major increases in the contributions of the nonconnected PACs, those figures understate their growth by not including independent spending. In 1984 they made independent expenditures of $19.1 million in the presidential and congressional elections; all other PACs of all other types spent $3.1 million.

The usefulness of the distinctions among types of PACs is clear on the face of it. (One may worry, though, that the trade/health/membership category is something of a catchall.) The value of the distinction between the connected and the nonconnected PACs may take some elaboration. Most PACs have been created by a prior, ongoing organization of some kind—a union, a corporation, a trade association. But a minority, about a quarter, belong to no such prior, affiliated organization; they have been set up as free-standing organizations, usually to promote a single issue or a broader ideology. The existence or absence of a parent organization is significant for a number of reasons. First, the parent organization is permitted by Federal law to pay the administrative and overhead expenses of the PAC from its own funds; thus all or virtually all of the funds the PAC collects can go for direct political purposes. The PACs without parents must pay all of their costs, including costs of solicitation, from their solicited funds. Second, the parent organization may control the internal operation of the PAC and set its goals and strategies. Put very bluntly, although the PAC's political money must be raised and kept separately, the parent organization may control the PAC and bend its purposes to those of the parent. Consequently, the connected and nonconnected PACs behave quite differently. We will deal with those differences later.

THE WHY AND WHEREFORE OF PAC GROWTH

Obviously, political action committees are superbly crafted for the new American campaign politics. They deal in the central political resource: cash. They are free to bypass the parties and forge electoral alliances with candidates and candidate organizations, alliances that suit the candidates who enjoy the independence of running their own campaigns but loath the inconvenience of raising money for them. And in their splendid variety, the PACs provide the narrow focus—in candidates, in issues, in priorities—that a large number of voters has come to want. It is probably no exaggeration to say that they are virtually the embodiment of the new electoral politics.

Indeed, the rise of PACs may even reflect the rise of a new structure of political constituencies. The old electoral constituencies, of course, are defined always in terms of geographical territory. American party organization, its forms largely described by the legislation of the states, still approximates those constituencies and the more detailed geographical units (i.e., the wards and precincts) that serve the governmental convenience in administering elections. But for the last generation or so, we have seen the divergence of electoral and political constituencies. Americans no longer live all of their lives in the compact confines of the local ward or neighborhood, or even of the congressional district. It is indeed the logical end point of the nationalization of American politics that voters may be politically closer to and more compatible with an issue constituency scattered all over the country. At the least they may find greater community in the work place, the trade or profession, than they do in the neighborhood. For such a shift from a geographical constituency to a functional or ideological constituency, the political action committee is similarly well adapted.

All of this is not to suggest, though, that the PACs are responsible for the weakness of the parties. Such an assertion would not wash either sequentially or conceptually. The decline of the parties was well under way—some might even say in an advanced stage—by the time of PAC expansion in the 1970s. More important, that decline happened by reason of fundamental changes in American life and politics and for the parties' inability to adapt to them. At the most, one can say that the decline of the parties created an opportunity, a vacuum, for the PACs and that the success and growth of the PACs merely underscored for the parties the harsh consequences of the changes afoot in electoral politics. To simplify greatly: changes in the American electorate, issue agendas, and campaign technology led in a number of steps to the decline of the parties' role in campaigns and to the creation of a new and central set of roles for the candidates themselves. Those changes put a new premium on cash as the means for securing the skills and goods of which campaigns are made, both by creating new campaign costs and by diminishing the availability of noncash resources to meet them.

Those developments in turn made the contributor of cash an increasingly important figure in campaign politics. But why didn't the individual contributor give his or her money directly to candidates? Or to a political party? Why increasingly through the intermediating agency of a political action committee?[5] The answer lies in the fact that in addition to the general influence of changes in electoral politics, there were more immediate,

[5] It should be clear, of course, that the great number of contributors do still give their contributions directly to the candidates for public office. Almost 55 percent of the contributions to congressional candidates in 1984 came from individuals other than the candidate himself or herself.

more proximate causes that favored the growth specifically of the PACs. Those proximate causes, both involving electoral law, are two: the Federal legislation on campaign finance of the 1970s, and the Supreme Court decisions in the same decade on the constitutional position of contributors to campaigns.

The Federal Election Campaign Act of 1971 (the FECA to insiders) and the amendments to it in 1974 and 1976 began a new era in the regulation of campaign finance in Federal elections. Among its numerous effects and consequences was the explicit legitimation of political action committees. The FECA was, in the words of a student of its effects, "the root cause of the PAC phenomenon" (Epstein, 1980a). It specifically authorized corporations and membership organizations to use their funds to create and administer a "separate segregated fund" to be used for political purposes. Whatever uncertainty may have lingered about the uses to which such separate funds might be put was removed by the Federal Election Commission's advisory opinion of 1976 deciding a number of issues brought to it by the PAC of the Sun Oil Corporation. Moreover, the amendments of 1974 also removed the statutory prohibition against the establishment of PACs by contractors dealing with the government of the United States. In short, the legal barriers to the formation of PACs by corporations and membership associations fell within the short span of five years (Epstein, 1980a; Alexander, 1980).[6]

It was not only the legislation pertaining to PACs that smoothed the way for their expansion. They were aided as well by legislation that gave them comparative advantages over their competitors.

1. In the aftermath of lavish individual spending—Clement Stone, the Chicago insurance magnate, had given more than $2 million to the 1972 Nixon campaign, for example—the Congress set lower contribution limits for individuals than for PACs. Individuals were limited to $1,000 per candidate per election and to an aggregate sum of $25,000 a year; PACs to $5,000 per candidate per election, with no aggregate limit.
2. While the limits the legislation imposed on the parties were in many ways more generous than those imposed on individuals and groups, it was the most stringent control the parties had ever experienced in campaign politics. The limits bore especially hard on state and local parties, and they were not relaxed until Congress in 1979 exempted

---

[6] The statutes are codified at 2 U.S.C. 431–442; for general administrative regulations, see 11 C.F.R., ch. 1. The major statutory references for the legislation of the 1970s are these: for 1971, P.L. 92–178 and P.L. 92–225; for 1974, P.L. 93–443; for 1976, P.L. 94–283; for 1979, P.L. 96–187.

their spending on campaign artifacts (buttons, brochures, signs, etc.) and registration and get-out-the-vote drives from expenditure limits (Kayden, 1980).

3. In 1974 Congress and the nation embarked on public funding for presidential election campaigns, one component of which was a requirement that candidates accepting public funds in the general election campaign had to agree not to accept private contributions. Major party candidates in 1976, 1980, and 1984 accepted public financing. The result was to move private funds to the more decentralized politics of congressional campaigns, an arena well suited to the specialized politics of PACs.

In short, the legislation of the 1970s had a series of important consequences, many of them largely unanticipated, that encouraged the PAC movement by discouraging individual and some party contributions to federal campaigns.

In the same decade, the Supreme Court of the United States twice added to American constitutional law in ways that protected the development of PACs. The more basic and extensive of the two decisions was in the case of *Buckley* v. *Valeo*, an across-the-board challenge to virtually every important section of the FECA and its amendments of 1974.[7] In *Buckley* the Court cloaked the giving of money to campaigns with the protections of the First Amendment. Political money became political speech. In the same vein it accepted only a single narrow ground for congressional regulation of campaign finance: preventing corruption or the appearance of corruption. The Court therefore struck down the limits on candidate expenditures, and while it upheld the limits on contributions to candidates, it made it very clear that Congress's power to regulate them was not without limit. It also struck down the FECA limits on independent expenditures and on candidates' use of their personal fortunes.

Just two years later, in 1978, the Court in *First National Bank of Boston* v. *Bellotti* overturned a Massachusetts law prohibiting corporate spending in referendum campaigns in the state, except where the financial interests of the corporation were directly involved in the referendum issue. A slim 5 to 4 majority of the justices held that such corporate activity enjoyed the First Amendment's protections, and moreover, that the corporation's rights were buttressed and supplemented by the public's right to

---

[7] 424 U.S. 1 (1976). The case was brought by an alliance of plaintiffs that embraced most of the American political spectrum. It extended from Senator Eugene McCarthy, a Democrat from Minnesota, to Senator James Buckley, a Conservative and Republican from New York. Among the organizational plaintiffs were the American Conservative Union, the New York Civil Liberties Union, and the Libertarian party.

hear political messages of the widest spectrum.[8] While *Bellotti* did not deal with PACs, it did suggest the possibility that Federal law prohibiting corporations and unions from making political expenditures directly from their treasuries—and thus requiring "separate segregated funds"—might not stand a future constitutional test. In any event, *Buckley* and *Bellotti* together extend a degree of constitutional protection that PACs have never before enjoyed. For the first time in American history there are clear and substantial constitutional as well as political limits to the power of the Congress to regulate the spending of money in election campaigns.

In sum, the growth of PACs in the 1970s resulted from both long-term and proximate causes. The fundamental changes in American electoral politics made way for new campaign mechanisms by demanding skills and resources that no existing political organization could provide. More immediate, proximate causes—largely the legal changes of the 1970s—opened new targets of opportunity for the PACs. That the congressional legislation and the judicial decisions of the decade helped push the political action committee to prominence seems beyond question. That such a consequence was largely unintended is one of the major political ironies of the era.[9]

The Life and Times of a PAC

Among the 4,000 PACs, there is no typical PAC. To identify even a modal type is no easy task. One can begin to do so, however, by going back to the four chief categories of the FEC, and by rejecting two of them. Since the modal PAC has a parent organization—with all that such parentage involves—the independent or nonconnected PACs can be eliminated as a special and very different type of PAC. Furthermore, the most substantial of the labor PACs are typically an integral part of a more extensive program of political action and mobilization. For the relatively separate, discrete PAC that operates under the aegis of a sponsoring organization, then, one looks to the corporate and association PACs. They will be the main point of reference in these paragraphs.

For all of their diversity, PACs share a striking organizational simplicity.

---

[8] 435 U.S. 765 (1978).

[9] The political coalitions supporting and opposing regulation of PACs have turned 180 degrees since 1971. In the initial stages of the new legislation, labor insisted on recognition for the legality and legitimacy of political action committees; conservatives and Republicans generally opposed that position until 1976 or so. By the time of the first attempts to limit PAC spending (such as the Obey-Railsback proposals of 1979), liberals and Democrats were the chief proponents.

Federal statutes specify very little—only that registered PACs have a treasurer and a bank account. They usually are governed by a board of trustees in some form. In corporate PACs that board is commonly appointed by the chief executive officer from upper-middle management; in associations, the elected officials usually choose it. The day-to-day administration of the PAC, and a good deal of its political direction, inevitably comes from the permanent staff of the parent organization. In the case of corporate PACs that often means personnel from the corporation's public or governmental affairs division; in the associations they come from the small permanent bureaucracy. (We know little about these PAC managers; as a new and important political elite, they warrant a great deal more study.) Contributors to the PAC very rarely participate in its governance or management, nor does there appear to be any substantial demand or movement for PAC democracy.

Nonconnected PACs are free to solicit whomever they wish, but Federal law limits the connected PACs to the solicitation of individuals in the parent organization. Association PACs may solicit only their members; many do so by including a voluntary PAC contribution line on the annual dues statement sent to members. They report greatly varying percentages of response, but the largest of them are in the 20 percent to 40 percent range. Corporations are free to solicit both management and stockholders; most stay exclusively with the former, and most indeed solicit only some of their management employees (i.e., only top management). They, too, report varying degrees of success in solicitation, with the success ratio generally declining as solicitation dips further and further down the ranks of management. Many well-run corporate PACs that solicit a half or more of their management employees receive contributions from less than one in three. Contributions of labor-union members to their PACs are often too casual—passing the hat in the union hall—for accurate counting. (Corporate and union PACs may also solicit each other's "natural" clienteles, but complex Federal requirements and unpromising prospects make such solicitations very rare.)

Aside from the decisions about raising the political funds, PACs face only one other set of decisions: how to spend them. The PACs with parent organizations spend largely or entirely in contributions to candidates. (In 1984 the corporate and association PACs spent $67 million in contributions to candidates for Federal office, but only $2 million in independent expenditures.) The allocations to candidates are usually made either by the board of the PAC or a committee of it. Since those boards or committees are composed wholly or largely of people inexperienced in politics, they rely at least in part on the expertise of others. That expertise may come from the PAC manager and other staff, or it may come from political consultants or the parent organization's Washington representatives. It may also come from other PACs; smaller corporate PACs, for example, rely on the research and advice of the Business-Industry PAC. While donors have no formal voice in the allocation of funds, few PACs ignore their views and some actively seek them. Donors, if dissatisfied, may refuse to contribute again, and as the PAC experience of the 1970s and 1980s lengthens, PACs are increasingly sensitive to the problem of dropouts (Sorauf, 1984–85).

The Realtors' PAC of the National Association of Realtors in the early 1980s can serve as a good and visible example of a large, effective association PAC. Approximately 180,000 (30 percent) of the 600,000 members of the association contributed to it, and the average contribution was around $30. Of the total receipts, some 60 percent were kept locally for state and local elections, and 40 percent went to Realtors' PAC for use in national elections. In the 1982 congressional elections it contributed $2.1 million to candidates and spent another $188,000 independently in the campaign, all of it in support of candidates and most of it in direct mailings. The management of the PAC was in the hands of one of the permanent vice-presidents of the association, Richard Thaxton. The elected presidents of the association appointed the members of its board in overlapping terms. Largely because the realtors are not a Federally regulated industry, their criteria for political assistance has no specific policy agenda; the Realtors' PAC looked generally for candidates supportive of a free enterprise philosophy. It also responded to recommendations from local realtor boards, many times even when those local contributors wanted to support a local congressional candidate, especially an incumbent, who might not fully meet the philosophical standards the board would prefer. (Conversely the PAC very rarely supported a candidate who had serious local opposition.) In making its decision, the Realtors' PAC used its own political and candidate evaluations. It had an experienced director and staff, and, untypically, it had a field staff of six posted all across the nation.

THE PACs: PRESENT AND FUTURE

For all their numbers and diversity, political action committees do have in common their mustering of resources to affect election outcomes. That is their public, active role in American campaign politics. Looked at from the vantage point of the individual, however, they are mechanisms or vehicles for political activity, means of working for political goals through collective action. Hundreds of thousands of Americans participate in politics through them, preferring to make their campaign contributions indirectly rather than directly to candidates or political parties. The reasons, even to the limited extent we know them, are significant, for they suggest just what kind of political organization the PACs are.

While the PAC movement does not enlist the sheer numbers of citizens that the parties do, it is clear that millions of Americans made contributions to the PACs registered with the FEC in the 1983–84 election cycle. We know that $288,000,000 was contributed to those PACs for the '84 elections, and reasonable estimates suggest that the average contribution over the cycle was probably less then $50. If one assumes it to be about $40, one comes up, by simple division, with 7.2 million "contributors." (With an assumption of a $60 average, the division comes to 4.8 million.) After making allowances for individuals making contributions to more than one PAC, one can safely suggest a total of between 5 and 6 million contributors. To these calculations, moreover, one must also add the completely unknown number of contributors to political action committees functioning exclusively in the states.[10]

One can sketch a rough picture of those PAC contributors with a bit of logic and some scraps of data. From the nature of their political act, we know they have chosen a somewhat passive form of political activity. Rather than make decisions about candidates and parties, rather than set their own political priorities, they have delegated those choices to the managers of the political action committee. That is, they have chosen a form of political activity that demands less of themselves—in time, in knowledge, in commitment—than almost any other. And indeed, compared with financial contributors to parties and candidates, they are by the measures of a 1982 national survey less active (see Table 11.3). Furthermore, their motives for giving through a PAC combine the nonpolitical with the political. Especially if the PAC is one sponsored by an existing organization, the contribution may simply express solidarity with one's fellow workers or with the parent organization. Or it may be intended to insure the approval of one's peers or superiors (Sorauf, 1984–85).

So, in the political action committee we appear to have a new kind of political organization for a new kind of less active political activist, one that draws also on nonpolitical motives and nonpolitical loyalties. Even

---

[10] Two notes on the mathematics of estimating average contributions may be in order. First, a survey of corporate PACs in late 1981 by the Business-Industry PAC and several associated organizations revealed an average contribution to corporate PACs of $161 over the two-year election cycle of 1979–80, or an average of $80–85 a year. Second, of the $140,159,259 that PACs reported receiving in that same cycle, only 12.5 percent ($17,528,542) came in contributions of $500 or more, a percentage very compatible with an average of $161.

TABLE 11.3 Contributors to Groups Compared with Contributors to
Candidates and Parties, 1982

	Gave Money to Groups	Gave Money to Candidates	Gave Money to Parties
Percentage who			
Went to political meetings	18	49	37
Were "very much" interested in the 1982 campaign	45	60	65
Followed government and public affairs "most of the time"	43	60	75

SOURCE: Data from the Center for Political Studies of the University of Michigan.

the political motives are expressed in most instances through prior loyalties to and association with the organization sponsoring the PAC. Because the parent organization may control the PAC and pay its overhead costs, the PAC is very much its creature. Moreover, PAC-parent linkages are reinforced by common loyalties and communities of interest. That partnership between PAC and parent organization makes possible new political relationships and new political strategies. Through the parent organization the PAC may extend its political influence beyond just supporting or opposing candidates. It may extend it back in time from the election to earlier voter education and mobilization, and forward in time to lobbying before legislatures and administrative agencies.

Organized labor offers the classic case of the PAC parent involved in voter education and mobilization before elections. The major labor organizations in the United States have long registered their members to vote, urged them to vote for labor-endorsed candidates, and then worked on election day to get out the labor vote. In considerable measure, of course, labor's emphasis on voter education and mobilization grew from three premises: the large number of potential voters involved, the high incidence of nonvoting among semiskilled and unskilled workers, and the common predisposition of working people to prefer Democratic candidates. The presidential elections of 1972 and 1980 may have shaken that third assumption, but labor nonetheless retains its deep commitment to voter mobilization.

The extent of that commitment is not easy to document. Federal statutes and the rules of the FEC consider registration and voter mobilization activities to be "nonpartisan" and thus not reportable as expenditures in the meaning of the FECA.[11] However, all organizations must report to the FEC all costs (beyond $2,000) of communications expressly advocating the election or defeat of a specific candidate. In 1982, organized labor accounted for more than half ($1.2 million of the $2.2 million total) of such communication costs reported to the FEC. Of the remaining million, the National Rifle Association accounted for more than $800,000. Beyond that, one pieces together bits and fragments of data. One well-informed scholar estimated that in 1976 organized labor spent some $9 million on behalf of the Carter candidacy in preelection mobilization of members in addition to $2 million on communication costs (Malbin, 1977).[12] Needless to say, these activities are well coordinated with the labor PACs' support of specific candidates. Indeed, many of them grow out of the same endorsement process.

It is even harder to arrive at estimates of similar activities by corporations and other membership organizations. Many corporations have for some time had voter registration and education programs, many of them administered by the same public or governmental affairs departments that administer the corporations' PACs. But they have tended to be lower key and more sedulously nonpartisan (or bipartisan) than similar programs within organized labor, if only because of the greater political heterogeneity of corporate employees. Trade and membership associations, on the other hand, are less apt to engage in registration programs and more apt to endorse candidates. In 1982, in fact, no corporation reported communication costs to the FEC. Obviously, these choices and differences reflect organizational imperatives. The dispersed, yet homogeneous, membership of a professional association, for instance, lends itself more readily to candidate support than to voter registration programs. But for all of these variations, the central point remains: none of these efforts begins to match the importance of voter mobilization by organized labor.

As PACs have grown up and aged, some observers have expected them and their parent organizations to commit more resources to the political mobilization of members and colleagues (Epstein, 1980b; Sorauf, 1980). Those expectations appear to reflect an implicit assumption about the political "maturing" of PACs: that as they develop they become politically more sophisticated, and that sophistication leads them to expand their political activities. To reconstruct the logic of such an assumption is to ex-

[11] 2 U.S.C. 441b (b)(2)(B).
[12] These data are computed from the *F.E.C. Index of Communication Costs: 1979–1980* (Washington: Federal Election Commission, 1983).

pose its leaps of faith. Perhaps the PACs and their sponsoring organizations have had a better sense of their limits, for those expectations have very largely been unfulfilled. What labor has attempted and accomplished requires a degree of political homogeneity, a similarity of political goals between organization and clientele, and a marriage of important political and nonpolitical interests that few other organizations can command. It is one thing to receive funds voluntarily from a subset of one's employees or members, but it is quite another to urge political action or choice on all of them. To look at the matter another way, if groups and their PACs aspire to mobilize voters the way parties do, they must achieve something of the dominant loyalties and cue-giving powers of the parties. None do yet, and only organized labor has come close.

Linkage in the other direction, toward the policymaking processes, is far more common. So common is it—or so common is it thought to be— that it gives rise to the major policy question surrounding the PACs: does financial support for legislative candidates "buy" their subsequent votes on legislation? While not every organization sponsoring a Federally registered PAC maintains a Washington office or representative, many do. And while not all of them coordinate closely the business of their PAC and the work of their Washington representatives, few leave them uncoordinated. All of this has become a media commonplace, and it is now the aspect of PAC operations that earns them their major visibility. While investigative journalism and public interest advocacy may select and overinterpret the nexus, they have not fashioned it out of whole cloth.[13] While most PACs do not seek a specific quid pro quo from candidates they support, they rarely contribute without any legislative goals at all. The least they seek with campaign contributions is what other political activists seek: legislative access and legislators of generally compatible views.

One need not, however, resort to anecdotal reportage to establish the electoral-legislative connection. It is apparent in the very strategies with which the PACs pursue campaign politics. In 1984, PACs gave $104.9 million to congressional candidates, and 71 percent of it ($74.8 million) went to incumbents. Only the nonconnected PACs gave as much as half of their funds to challengers and candidates for open seats (see Table 11.4). Furthermore, the PACs prefer highly placed incumbents to those of lesser place and status. In 1984, for instance, the House committee chairs running for reelection received 47.5 percent of their funds from PACs; all House in-

---

[13] Common Cause periodicals and flyers are certainly representative. See, for example, *Money, Power and Politics in the 97th Congress* (Washington: Common Cause, 1981). For examples of the best of journalistic reporting on the PAC-policy connection, see three articles in the *Wall Street Journal* by Albert Hunt, Dennis Farney, and James M. Perry (July 26, July 29, and Aug. 2, 1982).

TABLE 11.4   PAC Contributions to Incumbents in House and
Senate Races, 1984

Type of PAC	Amount (millions)	As Percentage of Contributions of All Candidates
Corporate	$27.5	78
Labor	$15.9	64
Nonconnected	$ 7.3	50
Membership	$20.9	79
Other	$ 3.2	86
TOTAL	$74.8	71

cumbents seeking reelection as a group received 43 percent from PACs. Furthermore, only the nonconnected PACs were willing to move outside of direct aid to candidates and spend independently to influence congressional races; they account for 67 percent of all the independent expenditures made by PACs in the 1980 congressional elections, for 84 percent in 1982, and for 60 percent in 1984. So it appears that PACs with parent organizations pursue their policy interests with a much more pragmatic strategy of legislative access than do PACs without parent organizations (Eismeier and Pollock, 1984). And one can even sharpen the point with an observation about corporate PACs. Among them there is a constant tension between control from company headquarters and control by the Washington office. All observers agree that those run from Washington are likely to follow a more bipartisan, incumbent-serving strategy than other corporate PACs (Handler and Mulkern, 1982; Sabato, 1984).

The ultimate in influence for any political organization results from linking both voter mobilization and policy politics to the electoral politics that separates them in sequence. In the American political experience it has been an elusive goal. Indeed, it defines the most elusive of all political organizations: the "responsible" political party, the party under whose aegis voter mobilization, control of nominations and elections, and policy influencing is linked into a single network of political influence. To achieve such linkages while mobilizing a majority of Americans has been a goal too difficult for the American parties to reach (Kirkpatrick, 1971). Groups and their PACs face a simpler task because they seek to mobilize smaller and more homogeneous populations. And yet the goal has largely eluded them, too; only the PACs of labor have even attempted it. The

American political action committees, in other words, have yet to achieve the political legitimacy and win the political loyalties necessary for such lofty aspirations. They remain organizations better suited to a far more limited political scope.

So, political action committees are in many ways the quintessential political organizations of their time. They have responded to an electoral politics in which large sums of money buy the new campaign skills and technologies, and they easily make alliances with the candidates who now run their own campaigns. At the same time, they suit a new kind of less active, less confident, even "less political" activist. Above all, they suit the purposes of interest groups that seek to extend their influence in the favorable environment of a more specialized and fragmented American politics. They have, in short, become instruments for the merging of electoral and interest group politics and, very possibly, for the creation of a new set of relationships between citizens and their elected representatives.

THE PRESENT AND FUTURE OF THE PARTIES

For more than a generation now, great changes have been abroad in American politics. And virtually every one of them has worked to the disadvantage of the American political parties and to the advantage of the emerging political action committees. The increasing political sophistication and specialization of interests—not to mention the greater organization of groups—has worked against them and in favor of organizations representing a more focused set of issues and commitments. New technologies and declining party loyalties have replaced their expertise and their role as both the medium and the message in the campaign; candidates have thus been freed to manage their own campaigns and find their own campaign resources. The explosion of group activity with the accompanying expansion of the political agenda has created a diverse politics that the parties find increasingly difficult to contain.

As the PACs wax and the parties struggle to adapt, it is easy to see the two of them locked in a deadly combat. They are, and yet they are not. Certainly the PACs have challenged the role, the influence, of the parties in campaign politics, but no more than that. They do not seek to replace the parties. They do not challenge the parties' monopoly of labels on the election ballot, and only some labor PACs have competed with their role in mobilizing an electorate. Rather, PACs exist as a parallel competitor of the parties and other political actors in the war of influence on electoral politics. In that sense they aim to supplement rather than supplant the parties. They create an additional avenue of representation in American politics, one more bond or link between citizens and public officials. Theirs is often a national constituency of particular, group-based interests that parallels the local electoral constituencies in which the parties have for so long been king.

At bottom, perhaps the most important characteristic separating the PACs and the major American parties is their number—two parties, but 4,000 PACs registered for national political activity. The PACs taken as a whole, therefore, have a flexibility, a variety, a choice that the two monoliths cannot provide. There are PACs whose agendas one might call "postmaterial," but there are many others whose goals are very material indeed. There are big PACs and little PACs, PACs with single-issue agendas and those promoting ideological world views. If it is the mission of the two major parties to aggregate interests, it is inevitably the role of PACs to represent a fragmented and fluid diversity of interests. Above all, the 4,000 PACs suggest how very difficult it is for the parties to represent minorities while they are at the same time building majorities.

So, two different kinds of political organizations compete at one central point in the organization of influence in American politics: the gathering of resources with which to contest the nation's elections. Campaigns in those elections have always been expensive. They were as expensive in the days of lavish noncash expenditures of party manpower as they are now in the expenditure of the cash the PACs (and other contributors) bring. Decades ago the parties had the rewards or incentives with which to recruit the campaign resources of the time; today they do not. Since both parties and PACs get their cash today from politically active individuals, the rise of PACs comes down ultimately to the reasons why individuals prefer to give their money to them rather than to the old, established parties. Why can the PACs recruit the necessary resources for campaigns more effectively than the parties? Group solidarity and commitment to an issue or ideology often have something to do with it. But more often the answer rests in the perception or expectation that the PAC offers the more effective route to policy goals. Parties thus are in a classic "catch 22"—they must appear effective and influential in order to raise the resources they need to become effective and influential.

In their responses to the challenges of the last several decades, the national Democrats and Republicans initially chose different adaptive paths. The Republicans began with increasing effectiveness to develop their fund-raising capacities and to mount programs of campaign assistance to candidates and to state and local party organizations. To simplify, they "joined" both the new cash economy and the technological revolution in campaigning that had earlier overwhelmed the parties. The Democrats, on the other hand, responded to pressures for representational equality and participatory democracy after the debacle of their 1968 convention. But after a decade or more of commitment to those directions, the national Democratic party departed from the issue politics and egalitarian norms of the 1970s, and about the same time began direct mail solicitations to try to catch up with Republican fund raising.

In all of this the inevitable question arises: are the parties destined to be nothing more than "Super PACs"? Not necessarily. The new direction only puts them back on the course of election-centered politics and electoral pragmatism. As successful electoral organizations, the parties may well recapture what they have lost of their role in coalition building and in becoming symbols and rallying points for majorities in the American electorate. Since they are present in virtually all American legislatures, a stronger electoral role may convert into policymaking discipline in the legislative process. Indeed, the central question for the parties in the next decade will be their ability to turn their electoral influence into policymaking discipline by building more unified and cohesive legislative parties. Can the Republicans in the 1980s, for example, convert their superior resources as a national party into cohesive support in the Congress for Republican programs? It is not clear that they have so far.

All of this is not to suggest that the parties will sharply diminish the PAC role in electoral politics. The PACs appear to have staked out a substantial place for themselves in it. Their growth depended on more than the weakness of the parties. Aside from the place they have made for interest group politics in election campaigns, they have to a considerable extent taken the campaign place of the large and influential individual contributors who dominated American campaign finance before the reforms of the 1970s. The parties, therefore, will not return to a monopoly of electoral politics. Even if they recapture their old electoral position, they will do so with new resources and new activists. Those changes will doubtless force changes in the parties themselves. We already have considerable evidence of the centralizing force of the new directions; fund raising appears to be easier and more efficient at national party levels. Moreover, as the parties enter a new competition for political money, they must develop new resource constituencies. As of now that would appear to be a problem especially for the Democrats. The price for them of an increased competitiveness in campaign finance may well be a stronger appeal to traditional monied sources and thus a gulf between the political liberalism of the party electorate and the centrism of an expanded group of party contributors.

Parties, PACs, and candidates have come to realize once again that influence in American politics flows greatly from electoral success. The recent changes in electoral politics—the fragmentation of groups, the issue differentiation, the candidate independence, the easy availability of new campaign skills—have heightened its importance. All of the contestants for influence in American politics—parties, groups, candidates—seem to accept two central propositions about it. First, control and influence in electoral politics is increasingly a necessary condition for influence elsewhere in the political process. Influence over policymaking, over legislatures and executives, is severely limited without it. And second, they seem to sense that the struggle among them is to a considerable extent a "zero-sum" battle in which any one of them wins influence largely at the expense of the others. With the political stakes so high, the competition is understandably intense.

REFERENCES

Agranoff, R. 1976. *The new style in election campaigns*. Boston: Holbrook.

Alexander, H. 1980. *Financing politics*. Washington, D.C.: Congressional Quarterly.

Broder, D. S. 1971. *The party's over*. New York: Harper and Row.

Burnham, W. D. 1970. *Critical elections and the mainsprings of American politics*. New York: W. W. Norton.

Canter, J. E. 1982. *Political action committees: their evolution and growth and their implications for the political system*. Washington, D.C.: Congressional Research Service of the Library of Congress.

Cotter, C. P., J. L. Gibson, J. F. Bibby, and R. J. Huckshorn. 1984. *Party organizations in American politics*. New York: Praeger.

Eismeier, T. J., and P. H. Pollock III. 1984. Political action committees: Varieties of organization and strategy. In *Money and politics in the United States*, ed. M. Malbin. Chatham, N.J.: Chatham House.

Epstein, E. M. 1980a. The P.A.C. phenomenon: An overview. *Arizona Law Review* 22: 355–72.

———. 1980b. Business and labor under the Federal Election Campaign Act of 1971. In M. Malbin, *Parties, interest groups, and campaign finance laws*. Washington, D.C.: American Enterprise Institute, 107–51.

Handler, E., and J. R. Mulkern. 1982. *Business in politics*. Lexington: Heath.

Kayden, X. 1980. The nationalizing of the party system. In Malbin, *Parties, interest groups, and campaign finance laws*. Washington, D.C.: American Enterprise Institute, 257–82.

Kirkpatrick, E. M. 1971. Toward a more responsible two-party system: Political science, policy science, or pseudo-science? *American Political Science Review* 65: 965–90.

Longley, C. H. 1980. National party renewal. In *Party renewal in America*, ed. G. Pomper. New York: Praeger, 69–86.

Malbin, M. 1977. Labor, business, and money—A post-election analysis. *National Journal* 9: 412–17.

Nie, N., S. Verba, and J. Petrocik. 1976. *The changing American voter*. Cambridge: Harvard University Press.

Pomper, G. M. 1975. *Voters' choice*. New York: Dodd, Mead.

——. 1980. *Party renewal in America: Theory and practice*. New York: Praeger.

Price, D. E. 1984. Bringing back the parties. Washington, D.C.: CQ Press.

Sabato, L. J. 1981. *The rise of political consultants*. New York: Basic Books.

——. 1984. *P.A.C. Power*. New York: W. W. Norton.

Sorauf, F. J. 1980. Political parties and political action committees: Two life cycles. *Arizona Law Review* 22: 445–63.

——. 1984–85. Who's in charge?: Accountability in political action committees. *Political Science Quarterly* 99: 591–614.

Turner, J., and E. V. Schneier. 1970. *Party and constituency: Pressures on Congress*. Baltimore: Johns Hopkins Press.

PART IV | Communitarian Organizations

TWELVE

The Failure of
Israel's Labor Party and
the Emergence of
Gush Emunim

MYRON J. ARONOFF

Gush Emunim (Bloc of the Faithful) is not only a product of significant changes in contemporary Israeli political culture but an active participant that is helping to shape those changes. It is a movement that has sought to achieve religious ends through political means, and that has justified extraparliamentary and illegal political actions through the evocation of religious sentiment and authority. As such, it provides contemporary illustration of such social science concepts as charisma, messianism, and revitalization movements. This analysis evaluates the importance of Gush Emunim in effecting as well as reflecting important changes in Israeli society, particularly in the context of the failure of linkage that resulted in the end of the dominant party system in Israel.

The main analytic focus of this analysis is on the process of institutionalization through which Gush Emunim passed from a spontaneous, charismatic, loosely organized extraparliamentary pressure group on the margins of the political system, to a well-organized and functionally differentiated network of related institutions which were incorporated within the national ruling establishment under the Likud governments (1977–84). Under the Labor-Likud National Unity Government formed after the 1984 election, Gush Emunim's influence diminished. Its political

I am grateful to the Joint Committee on the Near and Middle East of the American Council of Learned Societies and the Social Science Research Council which awarded me a grant from funds provided by the National Endowment for the Humanities and the Ford Foundation, and to Rutgers University which awarded me a Faculty Academic Study Program leave and grant that enabled me to conduct research in Israel for a year (1982–83). The essay is the first product of that research. I am also grateful for the helpful comments on an earlier draft of this essay by Professor Kay Lawson, Dr. David Somer, and the members of the Department of Political Science of Tel Aviv University to whom I presented a seminar based on the early draft. This earlier (and briefer) essay was published in Aronoff, 1984.

interests are expressed in the present Knesset primarily through the opposition parties Morasha and Techiya (which collectively have 7 of the
120 parliamentary representatives).

BACKGROUND

One of the most distinguishing features of Israeli society is that the major social, economic, and political institutions, and, to a certain extent, aspects of the political culture, were self-consciously created by the leaders
of the dominant voluntary associations of the Jewish community in Palestine. A newly created society such as Israel faces particularly acute challenges to the taken-for-grantedness of its visionary political culture from
the generation succeeding the founders. This is particularly so when the
society has undergone dynamic growth and diversification of its population, and of its social, economic, and political institutions. Inevitably, disparities arose between changing social realities and the structure of symbolic meanings expressed in the versions of the civil religion which were
dominant at different stages. Contradictions were exploited for partisan
political advantage as well as out of sincere ideological belief. With the
corruption of previously "sacred" creeds, attempts were made to revitalize and to reinterpret civil religion in the context of rapidly changing circumstances in order to regain a sense of coherence, meaning, and certainty. This is a study of one such revitalization movement.

The Israeli political system was dominated, both politically and ideologically, by the Labor party (in its various incarnations) for almost fifty
years. The political and ideological decline and loss of dominance culminated in the defeat of the party for the first time in the national elections
of 1977. The vacuum created by the erosion of the authority of the Labor
party, particularly in the last decade prior to its electoral defeat, provided
the general context which paved the way for the emergence of Gush Emunim (among other movements). Labor's historic partners in every coalition cabinet, the National Religious party (NRP, also known as Mafdal),
provided the more specific political and cultural context which gave birth
to the new revitalization movement.

The emergence of Gush Emunim as a potent force in Israeli politics can
only be understood in the context of the political and ideological vacuum
created by the failure of the Israel Labor party. Party failure in the context
of a dominant party system means the loss of both ideological and political dominance. Since the phrase "dominant party system" was first coined
by Duverger (1951), it has received sporadic and conflicting treatment by
scholars. Duverger never systematically developed his ideas on this subject

into a coherent conceptual framework. His main definition of a dominant party is:

> a party larger than any other, which heads the list and clearly out-distances its rivals over a certain period of time. . . . A party is dominant when it is identified with an epoch; when its doctrines, ideas, methods, its style . . . coincide with those of the epoch. . . . Domination is a question of influence rather than of strength; it is also linked with belief. A dominant party is that which public opinion *believes* to be dominant. . . . Even the enemies of the dominant party, even citizens who refuse to give it their vote, acknowledge its superior status and influence; they deplore it but admit it (Duverger, 1967: 308–309).

Political dominance in a multiparty system can be attained without an absolute majority if for numerical and/or ideological reasons no stable coalition can be formed without the participation of the dominant party.[1] Such was the case in Israel where Labor was dominant for a period of fifty years.[2]

Duverger adapted his notion from the concept of a dominant doctrine in the history of ideas. The significance of the implications of these intellectual origins has been generally overlooked. Ideological dominance need not be confined to situations in which an absolute majority of voters adhere to the official ideology of the dominant party. If that were the case, the phenomenon would be a very rare one indeed. Duverger suggests that dominance is achieved through the identification of a party and its leaders with an epoch.

In order to understand how a party can acquire (and lose) ideological dominance by becoming identified with an epoch, we need a conceptual framework which can relate the more specific ideology of the party to the general political culture. I conceptualize culture as a system of socially constructed and shared meanings embodied in enduring themes expressed symbolically through such forms as myth and ritual (Aronoff, 1980a, 1983). Ideology is the focused expression of shared meanings as they are related to specific socioeconomic and political interests. In addition to its

---

[1] Sartori (1976: 195) has criticized the notion of a dominant party, claiming that it "established neither a *class* nor a *type* of party system." Arian and Barnes (1974: 592), on the other hand, claim, "that the dominant party is *sui generis*." Sartori insists that the dominant party receive an absolute majority except in those countries that abide by a less-than-absolute majority principle. He disqualifies Israel on that basis. However, Arian and Barnes, and Blondel (1969) have cited Israel as a classic example of a multiparty dominant system. For an elaboration of this analysis, see Aronoff, 1981a.

[2] For analyses of the Labor party in various historical periods see Shapiro, 1976; Medding, 1972; and Aronoff, 1977, 1979, 1981a, and 1982.

greater focus and relationship to interests, ideology tends to be more rationally evaluated than other cultural forms such as civil religion (Aronoff, 1980b, 1981b). Civil religion is rooted in religion and incorporates aspects of religious symbol, myth, and ritual which are selectively used and transformed in the civil or political context. Ideology tends to be characterized by "secondary process thought," whereas civil religion tends to be more characterized by nonrational "primary process thought." Since the latter tends to be immune from rational criticism and scientific disconfirmation, it is often an important element in political control through cultural forms (cf. Bennett, 1982). These concepts will help to explain the emergence of a political/religious revitalization movement in the context of the conspicuous failure of a party which dominated Israeli society from its inception. The Labor party acquired ideological preeminence before it gained political dominance and lost the former before it lost the latter. Both Labor's leaders and its ideology were identified with the pioneering and visionary epoch which led to the establishment of the modern state of Israel. The leaders of Labor, and foremost among them David Ben-Gurion, played a crucial role in the articulation of a visionary civil religion and in the creation of the key institutions of modern Israeli society in its critical formative period. However, the endurance of dominant cultural forms depends on their effectiveness in providing models for the solution of various existential and societal problems. As they become less effective in resolving such problems—due to demographic, technological, socioeconomic and political changes—they lose their aura of immutability and are challenged and changed. Labor gave up the independent Histadrut school system because it hoped that the general national school curriculum would reflect the main Labor Zionist values. To a certain extent it did, albeit in a more diluted form. In 1953 a Jewish Consciousness program was introduced in the secular public school program, because it was felt that the general state schools, as opposed to the state religious schools, were failing to transmit important cultural values to the Israeli youth. In the long range, Labor failed to perpetuate its unique ideological worldview through the public school system.

On the other hand, the National Religious party (NRP), a religious Zionist party which has been a member of every coalition government, maintained control of the state religious schools. Thus the NRP, unlike Labor, continued to disseminate its values through the educational process and was thereby able to create the unique religious subculture in which the Gush Emunim was later to be born.

At the same time, Ben-Gurion articulated a new ideology of *mamlachtiut* [statism] which asserted that the state and its agencies, particularly Zahal, should become the pioneering vanguard to take the place of the Labor movement's agencies such as the Histadrut. This new ideology legitimized the transfer of important services from the Histadrut to the state, and also appealed to the wider non-Socialist constituency. However, it also planted the seeds of ideological discontent among those who resented the abandonment of the more traditional Socialism. The new nationalism failed to capture the fervent support of the masses. What it gained in scope, it lost in intensity of support. Ahad Ha'am, one of the early Zionist thinkers, prophetically feared "a hollow and sterile *etatism* which turns the means—the state—into the essence of national experience: this can happen when the national movement lacks spiritual and cultural dimensions" (Avineri, 1980: 21; 1981). Whereas the spiritual and cultural dimensions were central to early Zionist civil religion, they became the victims of processes of routinization, "normalization," and political expediency. In the ensuing years, Israel underwent a tremendous growth in population through a socially and culturally heterogeneous immigration which ranged from the survivors of the Holocaust in Europe to hundreds of thousands of Jews from the Islamic countries of North Africa and the Middle East. The dynamic growth and diversification of the economy were accompanied by a commensurate growth and complexity of government and its bureaucracy. The transfer of services from the Histadrut to the state decreased the dependence of the citizen on the Labor party (cf. Nachmias and Rosenbloom, 1978: 176). To compensate, the party built a strong machine, and patronage became the primary means for mobilizing support among the immigrants, particularly those from Islamic countries (Medding, 1972). The importance of the machine rose as the importance of ideology declined (cf. Lissak, 1974). At the same time, the development of increasingly oligarchic trends in Labor led to decreasing responsiveness of the leaders to the rank and file, and of the party as a whole to the public. Political apathy and alienation became widespread (Aronoff, 1977).

The economic boom and prosperity ushered in after the 1967 war was a mixed blessing. While most people prospered, it created a sense of relative economic deprivation among the poorest strata in Israel. It also brought about an unprecedented display of conspicuous consumption by the newly rich; and unabashed materialism and consumerism replaced the last remnants of egalitarianism and pioneering aestheticism of the previous era. This period was also characterized by a marked decline in party commitment and conversely by an increase in the proportion of the floating vote.

In the crisis which preceded the war of 1967, the opposition Herut party, led by Menachem Begin, was brought into the Government of National Unity as part of the Gahal alignment. Menachem Begin served in the government for three years, thereby acquiring considerable legitimacy among the public (cf. Levite and Tarrow, 1983). During these years, Labor and the opposition moved closer together on a number of policy issues, especially as the nationalist Herut expanded its alignment with the Liberals (Gahal) by joining with small moderate parties (including one that had split off from Labor) to form the Likud, and in doing so succeeded in projecting a more moderate image. Labor had long abandoned traditional Socialism for a complex form of mixed economy which Sharkansky calls "unfettered entrepreneurialism" (Sharkansky, 1979). Under Golda Meir, Moshe Dayan, and Yisrael Galili, Labor appeared to have become more hawkish, which also decreased public perception of the differences between it and the opposition.

The period between the 1967 and 1973 wars was one of political *immobilism* for the Labor party (Aronoff, 1977). Ideology was restricted to ritual discourse. Power and the resources that the party controlled, inertia, the conservatism of the electorate, and the ineffectiveness of the opposition maintained Labor's rule. Oligarchic control of the party resulted in a growing gap between the leaders and the public. The ossification of ideology and the politics of nondecisionmaking resulted in an enormous gap between sociopolitical reality and the meanings which ideology ascribed to it. The cumulative effect of this process crystallized through the catalytic "earthquake" of the Yom Kippur War.

The final years of Labor's rule were characterized by a major crisis of confidence in the credibility of the national party leadership, and the Labor party as a whole. The combination of mass public protests and internal criticism led to the resignation of Golda Meir and Moshe Dayan, and to the changing of the guard at the helm of the party and of the nation. The succession of Yitzhak Rabin in a bitterly divided government created a situation of weak national leadership. Public scandals rocked the party, including the "Yadlin Affair," the suicide of the minister of housing, and Prime Minister Rabin's resignation over his wife's conviction for an illegal foreign currency account. Public morale was at an unprecedented low point. Pressure from the United States about a Palestinian homeland, severe economic hardships, and social malaise contributed to, and symbolized, the failure of Labor (Aronoff, 1979).

ANTECEDENTS AND ORIGINS

On June 19, 1967, a few days after the war, the Israeli National Unity Government (which included Menachem Begin) adopted a position which expressed willingness to withdraw to the international borders with Egypt and Syria in exchange for peace treaties, normalization of relations, and demilitarization of the territories from which it was willing to withdraw. The future of the West Bank, the Gaza Strip, and the Palestinians were to be considered separately. This decision was communicated solely to the government of the United States (Rabin, 1979: 135). Since knowledge of the decision was highly restricted, it did not provoke opposition. In September 1967 at the Khartoum Conference, the Arab heads of state articulated a policy of "three no's": no peace with Israel, no recognition of Israel, and no negotiation with Israel. This dashed the hopes that were entertained by the Israeli government and people that their decisive victory would lead to peace. The total rejection of this possibility at Khartoum resulted in the hardening of the position of the Israeli government, and the beginning of the organization of a movement created to pressure the government to annex the territories which it had occupied during the war.

The Movement for a Whole Land of Israel (Tenuah Lemaan Eretz Yisrael Hashlema) was founded by a group of prominent politicians, intellectuals, and literary figures from different political party backgrounds who shared a common activist and nationalist orientation. In opposition to their demand for the annexation of the occupied territories, a less unified amalgam of diverse groups argued for the exchange of the territories for peace with Israel's Arab neighbors. Rather than present new ideas, both movements selectively revived and emphasized aspects of traditional Zionist ideology which had been generally ignored in recent years; and they gave new meaning to them in the dramatically changed context of the post-1967 period. The main contribution of these early precursors of Gush Emunim and its opposite Shalom Achshav [Peace Now], was "to give contemporary relevance to traditional beliefs" (Isaac, 1976: 4).

Just as the loss of its independent Socialist school system contributed to the undermining of Labor's ideological dominance, the establishment of a separate state religious school system in 1953 under the control of the National Religious party provided the framework for the development of a subculture from which Gush Emunim emerged. The leaders, activists, and supporters of Gush Emunim are overwhelmingly graduates of the extensive network of institutions of the state religious educational system and related institutions. The new generation of leaders of the National Religious party (Mafdal) and of Gush Emunim was trained in high school yeshivot (which combined secular and religious curriculums), especially those of B'nei Akiva. As Rubinstein (1982) observed, life in the single-sex religious boarding schools, like that of the agricultural schools of the Socialist camp of an earlier period, produced strong social bonds among those who emerged in the 1950s and 1960s as the new national religious elite (cf. Bar-lev, 1977).[3] This new generation of national religious leaders, their unity symbolized by the knitted skullcaps they all wear, saw themselves as leading a moral renaissance of the entire country.

The founder-leaders of Gush Emunim are all graduates of Yeshivat Merkaz Harav and are the disciples of the late Rabbi Zvi Yehuda Kook, interpreter and exegete of his father, Rabbi Abraham Isaac Kook, the first Ashkenazi chief rabbi of Palestine. Having come to the yeshiva to continue their higher religious education after the completion of their army service, they developed close social bonds with one another, and a reverent devotion to their teacher, Rabbi Kook. Rabbi Kook was considered to be naive and unrealistic by the veteran Mafdal leadership. Rubenstein suggests that the fact that Rabbi Kook was the complete opposite of the typical religious party hack may have made him attractive to his idealistic students. Rabbi Kook ascribed to the state mystical and holy authority as precursor of messianic redemption.

Most of the studies of Gush Emunim mention a speech given by Rabbi Kook at a reunion of his former students on independence day of 1967. In the midst of his lecture, Rabbi Kook dramatically altered his style of delivery as he told his students of how he sat in mourning when the United Nations resolution on the partition of the Land of Israel was announced. He lamented, "Where is our Schem? Where is our Jericho? Where is our Jordan?" Shortly thereafter, as his students participated in what they perceived to be the liberation of these integral parts of the historic Land of Israel, they interpreted their rabbi's speech as having been a case of true prophesy.

The wars of June 1967 and of October 1973 were important milestones in the development of Gush Emunim. Shortly after the 1967 war, a convocation of graduates of Yeshivat Merkaz Harav met and discussed issues related to the newly acquired territories. They decided to establish Yeshivot Hesdare (which combine higher religious studies and military training) which they hoped would be located by the army in the territories to prevent Israeli withdrawal from them. They asked hundreds of rabbis for their interpretation of religious law pertaining to the Land of Israel and whether it was permitted to withdraw from it for any reason. Whereas there were rabbinic opinions which specified conditions under which it was acceptable to return the territories (except Jerusalem) in exchange for peace, Rabbi Kook and those associated with him declared there were no authorized circumstances under which it was acceptable to sacrifice any part of the Holy Land.

---

[3] References to Hebrew sources—especially Rubenstein (1982) and Raanan (1980)—are paraphrased rather than translated quotations.

The October war of 1973 was called an earthquake in Israel. It was a traumatic event which catalyzed conditions which eventually led to major political changes. National morale was at an all-time low following the war. The unprecedented crisis of confidence in the government led to a proliferation of protest movements and demonstrations which, combined with internal party pressures, led to the resignation of Prime Minister Meir and Defense Minister Dayan (cf. Aronoff, 1977). In contrast to the triumphant self-confidence and ecstasy which resulted from the Six Day War, the post-Yom Kippur War period produced doubt and agony. Gush Emunim was a response to this general social malaise, and to the weakness of governmental authority resulting from this situation, which Gush Emunim both criticized and exploited (cf. Avruch, 1978–79).

After a series of preliminary meetings among the founding leaders, Gush Emunim was formally established at Gush Etzion at the end of the winter of 1974. Although originally established as a faction within the NRP, when the parent party joined the government formed by Yitzhak Rabin (after the resignation of Golda Meir) without succeeding in gaining their demand for a government of national unity including the Likud, Gush Emunim severed its official ties with the NRP. However, as I shall discuss shortly, the close symbiotic relationship which remained between Gush Emunim and the NRP was of considerable importance to both groups.

IDEOLOGY AND WORLDVIEW

Its complaint is that the state has veered from the self-confident and determined past that marked its earlier success. Instead, it has been overtaken by a lack of resolution and self-doubt. Defined in both secular and religious terms, willingness to sacrifice territorial integrity for vague promises of peace is both blunder and moral sin. The consequent policies supported by the movement are annexationist bordering on irredentism (Schnall, 1979: 139).

Although Gush Emunim is characterized by a unique religious political worldview, it has never clearly formulated a comprehensive general ideology. The basis for their worldview can be found in the teachings of Rabbi Abraham Yitzhak Kook as expounded and interpreted by his son Rabbi Tzvi Yehuda Kook. Further elaborations have been developed by the younger generation of rabbis trained by Rabbi Kook in his yeshiva. Rabbi Kook, the elder, saw in the modern Zionist movement the precurser and harbinger of the messianic process of redemption. The "liberation" of

Judea and Samaria was interpreted by Rabbi Kook, the younger, as ush-
ering in the next stage of the process of moral and spiritual redemption.
The true believers of Gush Emunim are completely convinced of the historical inevitability of this process (cf. Weissbrod, 1982).

They firmly believe in the mystical unity of the entire historic Land of
Israel and the Jewish people. Given the miraculous liberation of the very
heart of the Holy Land, Judea and Samaria, they believe it is the sacred
duty of every Jew to inhabit and repossess every portion of the ancestral
inheritance. The followers of Gush Emunim relate this mystical tie of the
people to the land to the central traditional Zionist value of settlement. In
so doing they claim to be the true successors of the pioneering Zionist settlement,[4] calling themselves a movement for the renewal of Zionist fulfillment. Sprinzak (1981: 37) observed: "It is apparent from all its operations and activities that it sees itself as a movement of revival, whose task
it is to revitalize historic Zionism that died out in the Israel of the fifties
and sixties."

Rubinstein (1982: 126–30) relates how Gush Emunim effectively manipulated key symbols of the earlier pioneering era, and timed some of
their demonstrations to coincide with important nationalist anniversaries
(e.g., the demonstration at Sebastia was held on Tel-Hai day). Even the
physical appearance of the Gush Emunim demonstrators hearkened back
to the veteran pioneers of a previous era: mustached men, women wearing
long hair in braids, shirttails out, sweaters tied around the neck, wearing
sandals, knapsacks on their backs, and weapons hanging at their sides.
Many observers of Gush Emunim have commented on its character as a
movement of sociopolitical reform and of cultural renewal which confronted an unacceptable reality by nostalgically returning to the sources
of what they considered to be good and beautiful in the Jewish and Zionist
past. However, no one has attempted to analyze it as a revitalization
movement, particularly of the messianic variety (cf. Wallace, 1956). Janet
O'Dea has come closest in her analysis of Gush Emunim as a type of religious sect, but I stress that it is more appropriately characterized as a
movement.

> The frame of reference in which the issue of the territories is perceived
> is determined by the deeply rooted prototype of "Jew versus world."
> . . . They have withdrawn from a world, which in the past oppressed
> them and in the present would press upon them intolerable compro-
> mises. Gush Emunim approaches mundane politics . . . with a
> "trained incapacity" to disentangle real from symbolic. . . . The fierce

---

[4] Raanan (1980: 133–62) elaborates the very substantial differences between the traditional labor-Zionist concept of settlement and that of Gush Emunim.

defensiveness of Gush Emunim is founded upon profound national, social and religious antipathy to the non-Jew, and equally upon fear of the possible unsettling or disintegrative effects of western culture (O'Dea, 1976: 46).

Given this worldview, it is not difficult to understand the movement's position on relations with the Palestinian Arabs. Although infrequently mentioned in their publications, their position is clear. As Sprinzak (1981: 36) has succinctly summarized, the Palestinians living in Judea and Samaria should be given the choice: to publically recognize the legitimacy of Zionism and enjoy full rights as citizens; to obey the laws without recognizing Zionism and enjoy all but political rights; or to immigrate to Arab countries (with economic incentives).[5]

Gush Emunim's attitudes toward democracy, the state, the rule of law, and modern thought are the subject of considerable controversy and disagreement among those who have written on the subject. Sprinzak is the most sanguine about Gush Emunim's respect for the secular institutional expressions of Israeli sovereignty. According to Gush Emunim, democracy is an acceptable system as long as it remains within a "proper" (as interpreted by Gush Emunim) Zionist framework. Even if a majority of the Knesset were to rule against settlement in Judea and Samaria, by definition this would be an illegitimate act which should be opposed at all costs. Rubinstein and Raanan, both of whom take a more engaged and therefore more polemic stance, express far greater anxiety about the threat which Gush Emunim poses to Israeli democracy. I shall return to this theme in my conclusion.

TACTICS

Ever since its formal founding in the spring of 1974, *Gush Emunim* has been marked by its extra-parliamentary style. The *Gush* was not prepared to confine itself to the framework of the law and the accepted rules of the Israeli political game. From the outset it adopted an extremist style of political action that included demonstrations, protests, unauthorized settlement and the like (Sprinzak, 1981: 38).

Whereas each of these tactics had been used individually and sporadically by previous groups, Gush Emunim developed them in combination systematically with such effectiveness that some observers conclude that

[5] Raanan (1980), A. Rubinstein (1980), Rubenstein (1982), Sprinzak (1981), and Weissbrod (1982) give extensive accounts of various aspects of Gush Emunim's ideology.

the rules of the political game in Israeli politics have been permanently altered. They became professionals who developed their own political style and special techniques over the years. They adapted their techniques to changing political conditions, the most important of which was the change from Labor governments, which were essentially hostile to their goals, to the governments dominated to the sympathetic Likud in 1977. They effectively exploited rivalries within the Labor governments (between Moshe Dayan and Yigal Allon and between Yitzhak Rabin and Shimon Peres), appealed to the hawks within Labor (Galilee, Hillel, Peres, and Yacobi), and received consistent support from the Mafdal ministers. From the beginning, they enjoyed easy access to many government ministers, members of the Knesset, and other high-ranking officials of government and other public agencies.[6]

A few weeks after the 1967 war, Kfar Etzion was established west of Hebron with the government's blessing at the initiative of a group of predominantly religious settlers, some of whom were members of the original settlement (which had been captured and destroyed during the war of independence) or their descendants. One of the settlers, Hanon Porat, became one of the most active and visible leaders of Gush Emunim. Another future top leader of Gush Emunim, Rabbi Moshe Levinger, led a group which celebrated Passover in a Hebron hotel in the spring of 1968. A series of events such as squatting and refusing to leave, negotiations with various cabinet members, and demonstrations forced the Labor governments first to agree to the establishment of a yeshiva in Hebron (June 1968), and later to allocate 250 housing units (March 1970), which led to the creation of an urban Jewish town, Kiryat Arba, on the outskirts of Hebron without the government ever having intended to do so.

Gush Emunim began its first phase of major protests against the interim agreements with Egypt and Syria in the spring of 1974, reached a peak with several mass rallies, and dwindled after the signing of the agreements. These activities were followed by large demonstrative marches in the territories, usually coinciding with school holidays to ensure a large contingent of religious youths. Such demonstrations created considerable excitement in religious neighborhoods. The festive atmosphere of the trips to the demonstration sites in Yehuda and Shomron and the national-religious ceremonies and rituals held there created the atmosphere of a continuous party for many of the youthful demonstrators. Even the encounters with the Israeli army, according to Rubinstein, took on the

---

[6] Rubenstein (1982: 81–82) gives detailed accounts of the extensive support received by Gush Emunim. For example, he estimates that approximately 350 families in Kiryat Arba are supported by public funds.

appearance of a gamelike hide-and-seek which ceased on the Sabbath and was renewed when the Sabbath was over.

The activity for which Gush Emunim is best known is the initiation of settlements across the "green line" (the armistice lines of 1948). The first such settlement established by Gush Emunim, Keshet in the Golan Heights, was actually initiated by members of a kibbutz movement affiliated with the Labor party. Thereafter, Gush Emunim took the initiative in forcing the government to recognize scores of settlements which had been established against the government's wishes. In almost all cases the government initially agreed to a seemingly modest demand, such as the establishment of a yeshiva in Hebron, which was over time expanded into an urban settlement. The government was similarly pressured to agree to the establishment of a camp for workers in the planned industrial zone east of Jerusalem (January 1975) which eventually expanded to become the town of Ma'alei Adumim. A similar camp for workers established east of Ramala in March 1975 became the settlement of Ofra. The most dramatic of all was the group led by Benny Katzover and Menachem Felix which attempted eight times to settle at Sebastia near Nablus, each time being forcibly evacuated by the army. The final confrontation forced the Rabin government to compromise and allow the settlement of Kadum. The same Gush Emunim leaders later forced the government to allow the establishment of a "field school" which became the settlement of Elon Moreh.

One of Menachem Begin's first acts after the victory of the Likud in May 1977 was to attend a ceremony in which a Torah scroll (containing the five books of Moses) was placed in the new synagogue at Kadum. He signaled his full support of the settlement efforts of Gush Emunim by declaring (with characteristically dramatic rhetoric) that, "we will have many more Elon Morehs." And yet the Likud government continued the previous government's practice of disguising settlements, especially by attaching settlers to military camps, some of which were set up especially for the settlers. The settlement which became Shilo was initially called an "archeological camp."

Rubinstein (1982: 74) notes that it was as if the governments wanted to establish settlements, but were afraid to do so. He claims that the disguised decisions and euphemisms for settlements were signs of weakness that were more self-deceptive than attempts to fool others. This weakness of government, he argues, increased the self-confidence and the missionary feelings of the Gush Emunim settlers. Although this conclusion blurs important differences between the motivations of and the conditions in the Labor and Likud governments, the general point is well taken. The internal strains within the Labor governments, particularly that of Yitzhak Rabin, severely weakened them and made them incapable of decisively resolving the conflicting external pressures (particularly from the United States) and internal pressures (from Gush Emunim). To a somewhat lesser extent, the same was true for the initial half of the Likud's first term in office. The liberal/moderate forces within the ruling coalition were initially weakened by the split in the Democratic Movement for Change when Professor Amnon Rubinstein led his faction into the opposition. With the resignation of Moshe Dayan (foreign minister) in October 1979 and Ezer Weizmann (defense minister) in May 1980, and with the former Liberal ministers within the Likud coalition following the hawkish Herut line, the forces of moderation were dealt a mortal blow, and the government thereafter was much more homogeneous. Gush Emunim no longer needed to engage in public demonstrations to accomplish its goals once there was a government dominated by Begin, Sharon, and Shamir.

However, before this happened, Gush Emunim was dealt a near-fatal blow by Sadat's famous visit to Jerusalem, the dramatic change in national perceptions of the possibility for peace which it precipitated, the Camp David accords, the peace treaty, and the autonomy plan. Gush Emunim failed to mobilize support for demonstrations against Sadat's visit, and the mass support it anticipated in support of its physical resistance to withdrawal from the town of Yamit in the Sinai failed to materialize (cf. Lewis, 1979). The establishment of Atzmona in the northern Sinai in March 1979 in protest against the peace treaty with Egypt was a desperately defiant act of a highly demoralized Gush Emunim. Ironically, it was during this period of greatest demoralization and low point of public support that Gush Emunim made its most dramatic strides in accomplishing its goal of creating new Jewish settlements in Judea and Samaria; and it did so with the complete cooperation and active support of the government, the army, and the Jewish Agency.

In the ten years of military occupation of the territories, the Labor government established twenty-four settlements on the West Bank with 3,500 residents, mostly in the sparsely populated lower Jordan Valley. Settlements established under the Likud governments in the first five years in office reflect the goals of Gush Emunim, that is, they are mainly in the heart of the most heavily Arab-populated areas. As of January 1985, there were about 114 Jewish settlements on the West Bank with a population of approximately 42,500 (Friedman, 1985: L17). On the Golan Heights there were thirty-five settlements with 10,000 residents; and in the Gaza Strip there were a dozen settlements with 1,000 residents in 1982 (Rabinovich, 1982: 3). Benvenisti estimated that the 1982 budget for development and building on the West Bank was $100 million. Given present rates of annual increase, he estimates that by 1990 there will be a Jewish population of 100,000 on the West Bank.

The settlements have been linked to each other and to Israel through extensive new networks of highways; and they have been linked to the Israeli national electric grid and water supplies. The West Bank has also been economically integrated with half the employed labor force working in Israel, more than half of which is employed in construction.

This extensive expansion of Jewish settlements on the West Bank was carried out at the initiative of Ariel "Arik" Sharon who served at the time as minister of agriculture and chairman of the Ministerial Committee on Settlements (and later became minister of defense) and Matityahu Drobles, chairman of the Settlement Department of the World Zionist Organization, with the active support of the military government and the extremely sympathetic chief of staff, Raphael Eitan, whose views are close to those of Gush Emunim. During the same period, Zahal was deployed more extensively on the West Bank.

Citing two critical military orders which laid the legal basis for creating and determining the boundaries of the Jewish regional councils and established the civilian administration for the territories, Benvenisti (1982) convincingly argues that a de facto dual society has been created: "There are two separate systems. One for Jews, now run by Gush Emunim and other settlers, and one for Arabs. . . . The pattern's establishment makes disengagement from the territories more expensive, and the progression is geometric. . . . In the end, disengagement may only come about through trauma or catastrophe" (Richardson, 1982: 7). This situation contributed to the polarization of Israeli politics which characterized the 1981 election campaign and the divisive war in Lebanon (Aronoff, 1984b).

POLITICAL SUPPORT: GUSH EMUNIM AND ITS ALLIES

Both Raanan (1980: 13) and Sprinzak (1981) have called Gush Emunim "the tip of the iceberg," which is based on a much broader sociocultural subsystem in Israeli society. As mentioned previously, the creation of a separate state religious school system under the control of the NRP resulted in the development of a new and distinct subculture in Israeli society, the renaissance of the "knitted skullcap" generation. The sociocultural environment of these national religious schools, yeshivot, youth movement, and associated institutions led to the emergence of newly synthesized and formulated values which were articulated by the new leaders of the Tze'irim (Youth) faction of the NRP and of Gush Emunim. This sociocultural base produced the leaders and activists of both the Tze'irim faction of the NRP and of Gush Emunim, and has remained their most important base of political support.

The relationship between Gush Emunim and the NRP has been complex; it was responsible for the success of the former, and significantly changed the religious as well as political character of the latter. The Tze'irim emerged in the 1960s from a young adult auxiliary of the NRP. It is composed primarily of native-born, urban, middle-class graduates of the aforementioned socialization system, particularly the B'nei Akiva high school yeshivot (Zuker, 1973). Having abandoned the kibbutz orientation of the youth movement, the faction emphasizes "the preparation of religious young people to fulfill key positions in the state," including the government, the army, and industry (Schiff, 1977: 63). Competing for the first time in internal NRP elections in 1968, the Tze'irim received 22 percent of the vote, which led to the entry of the faction's two main leaders, Zevulun Hammer and Dr. Yehuda Ben-Meir, into the Knesset, and eventually into government posts.

Gush Emunim was created by a small, homogeneous group of a dozen or so leaders who, in addition to sharing the general characteristics of the new religious elite, graduated during the same years from the Yeshivat Merkaz Harav in Jerusalem. They favored efforts within Mafdal to insist that a government of national unity be established which would include the Likud, in order to prevent withdrawal from the occupied territories. In spite of lively debates in the party's central committee, the traditional leadership of the NRP won out and the party joined a coalition with the Labor party. This decision led to the severing of the formal affiliation of Gush Emunim with the NRP. However, the informal relationship which remained was critical in shaping the development of both institutions. Like a rebellious teenager, Gush Emunim criticized and fought with its parent body, and yet continued to receive sustenance from it which enabled it to grow and to develop. Reciprocally, the parent party was reinvigorated by the youthful dynamism and religious/political revival and ideological reformulation which took place through the influence of the Tze'irim and their allies in Gush Emunim. The NRP placed Rabbi Haim Druckman, one of the top leaders of Gush Emunim, in the number two position on its list of candidates to the Knesset in the 1977 election, and it gained two additional seats in the Knesset.

The process of secularization, which has particularly affected the Oriental Jewish community in Israel, contributed to the decline in the NRP's share of the school population from 29 percent to 24.7 percent between 1968 and 1974. The NRP's long identification with the ruling Labor "establishment" detracted from its public image as well. As Isaac (1981: 85) perceptively observed, the territorial issue not only "gave the Mafdal renewed dynamism, it also threatened to split it." The issue has greatly increased ideological tension within the party. The creation of the Techiya

(Renaissance) party in 1979 by prominent leaders of Gush Emunim and secular ultranationalists (some of whom had left Prime Minister Begin's party in protest against the peace treaty with Egypt and others who were from the former Land of Israel Movement) split the Mafdal vote and created serious divisions within Gush Emunim. In the June 1981 election, Techiya received 44,700 votes which gave it three members in the Knesset, including Hanon Porat of Gush Emunim. "The absence of unity on an issue held by some religious members to be of central importance suggested that the religious bloc might lose its chief strength—a common definition of the targets of the state. The intrusion of what is simultaneously a secular-national issue into the religious domain has opened the religious parties to the same possibilities for fission and fusion that confront the secular parties" (Isaac, 1981: 85).

Sprinzak correctly stresses that much of Gush Emunim's influence, which has facilitated its achievements, has been based on its political support in the NRP. He adds, "Paradoxically, this also explains why there is little chance that Gush Emunim will become an adventuristic movement" (Sprinzak, 1981: 45). He argues that since Techiya failed miserably to realize its dream of creating a massive parliamentary opposition bloc to prevent the ratification of a peace treaty with Egypt, and since NRP funding and support have not been forthcoming to Gush Emunim since the establishment of Techiya, Gush Emunim members are having second thoughts about their involvement in Techiya.

Developments have led to a major rift between Gush Emunim and its most ardent backers in the NRP, Zevulun Hammer and Dr. Yehuda Ben-Meir, the leaders of the Tze'irim. An interview which Hammer, who is minister of education and culture, gave on an evening news program in September 29, 1982, sent shock waves through the Gush Emunim settlements. Hammer indicated that his political thought had been undergoing a change. He expressed regret that the nationalist emphasis on the Land of Israel had overshadowed the religious emphasis on the Torah, which had always been an important part of his party's mission. He expressed his desire to see more balance in the future (cf. Segal, 1982: 5). Reaction was immediate as several Gush Emunim settlements canceled the visits which Hammer had been scheduled to make—in effect declaring the minister *persona non grata*. Others did not cancel his visit, but gave him a cool reception, and subjected him to intensive cross-examination about his political positions. Rabbi Haim Durkman, M.K., said he was "astounded and taken aback"; and Rabbi Moshe Levinger called on Hammer to resign "in view of his about-turn and treason to the idea of Eretz Yisrael" (Honig, 1982: 1, 2).

Hammer's close ally Deputy Foreign Minister Yehuda Ben-Meir replied to the attacks on Hammer by launching an all-out attack on Gush Emunim. He charged that the Gush "would lead us to eternal war."[7] Although there have been attempts to smooth over differences, some observers feel the rift which has developed is irreversible. There are several explanations for these developments. Through the influence of Gush Emunim and the Tze'irim, the NRP's political policies became practically indistinguishable from those of the Likud, to whom it lost considerable electoral support. The creation of the ultranationalist Techiya further eroded support for the NRP, particularly among the militants in Gush Emunim. When the NRP's young Oriental leader, Aharon Abuhattzeira, broke away to create the ethnic Tami party, the party was further weakened, and consequently the NRP lost half of its Knesset seats in the 1981 election (Friedman, 1983). Its leaders are aware of the need to carve a new definitive niche for the NRP in the Israeli political arena. Hammer realizes that many (some say most) of the Gush Emunim activists who had been the mainstay of his support have left the NRP. He, therefore, needs to attract a new party constituency.

The war in Lebanon and its aftermath, including the massacre by Christians of Palestinians who were ostensibly under Israeli protection, has also profoundly influenced many religious as well as secular Israelis. Close associates of Hammer claim that he had been influenced by the high casualty rate suffered in the war by soldiers from the hesder yeshivot. A crack has appeared in the hawkish views of some of these nationalist religious youth. In television interviews, young hesder soldiers expressed for the first time the view that it might be worth making territorial sacrifices for peace. Knitted skullcaps appeared in a public protest demanding an investigation of the slaughter of the Palestinians by Lebanese Christian forces in the refugee camp. Rabbis Amital and Aharon Lichtenstein of Har Etzion Yeshiva (among others) brought Jewish ethics to bear in their condemnations of these events. Elhanan Noeh of the Hebrew University observed: "Yamit was perhaps the first indication that the all-embracing messianism has been undermined. The general religious community was not willing to go to Yamit. . . . Moreover, they were angry with Gush Emunim for pitting Jew against Jew. They weighed it in commonsense, nonmessianic terms. I think it was a turning point. The war in Lebanon perhaps continued the process" (Furstenberg, 1982: 9).

For all of these reasons, the unique symbiotic relationships between Gush Emunim and the National Religious party, and especially its Tze'irim faction, came to an end. Rabbi Haim Drukman left the NRP dur-

---

[7] Ben-Meir claims that, "the Gush is now advocating that Israel stay on in parts of Lebanon, because these are the lands of the biblical tribes of Naftali and Asher"; see Honig, 1982: 2.

ing the 10th Knesset, forming an independent Knesset faction called Matzad. During the 1984 election, he merged this faction with Poelei Agudat Yisrael to form Morasha which received two Knesset mandates. The breakdown of the symbiotic relationship between the NRP and Gush Emunim has contributed to the weakening of both. It contributed to the decline in the NRP's Knesset representation from twelve in 1977, to six in 1981, to four in 1984. It also led to the restriction of *direct* representation of Gush Emunim in the Knesset to parties in the opposition after the formation of the National Unity Government following the 1984 election.

Leadership and Organization

Whereas there has been striking continuity in the top leadership of Gush Emunim, there has been a marked differentiation and institutionalization of their spheres of activity. For example, in the beginning, Hanon Porat directed all settlement activity. In the summer of 1976, with the declining importance of demonstrations and the increasing importance of initiating settlements, Amana was established as the major settlement movement. Amana became the main institution through which Gush Emunim's settlement activities were sponsored. Several leaders of Gush Emunim found employment on Amana's full-time paid staff. As settlements were established, they elected secretaries to administer their affairs and representatives to regional councils. With the active support of the Likud governments, the number of settlements proliferated, and the regional councils were united under the Council of Jewish settlements in Judea, Samaria, and Gaza (Yesha) which has gained considerable political/administrative importance. Yesha has broadened Gush Emunim's authority and facilitated its bureaucratic incorporation into the institutions of the state.

Gush Emunim's main spiritual leader was the late and revered Rabbi Zvi Yehuda Kook. The former Chief Ashkenaiz Rabbi of Israel, Shlomo Goren, and Rabbi Moshe Zvi Neria are also influential spiritual leaders. The younger rabbis tend to combine active political roles with their religious functions. Two are Knesset members, while others, such as Moshe Levinger, concentrate their political activities outside of the parliamentary arena.

The decision of prominent leaders to run for the Knesset provoked heated debates in Gush Emunim; it was decided to allow individuals to do so, but not to officially affiliate the movement with any political party. In 1981, Hanan Porat (Techiya) was elected to the Knesset as was Rabbi Haim Drukman (NRP/Matzad). In 1984, Rabbi Eliezer Waldman

(Techiya), Gershon Shafat (Morasha), and Rabbi Haim Drukman (Morasha) entered the Knesset. There are reports that these top leaders meet to coordinate their activities. The most striking change in Gush Emunim's political fortunes has been that it has lost its previous position of influence which it had held in the Likud governments headed by Prime Ministers Menachem Begin and Yitzhak Shamir. The government formed after the 1984 election excluded the parties which had elected leaders of Gush Emunim.

MILITANCY REVIVED: RESISTANCE AND VIGILANTISM

Gush Emunim played an active leadership role in the Movement to Stop Retreat in the Sinai. Engaging in acts of controlled violence, members confronted Israeli troops in their vain efforts to prevent the withdrawal of Israel from the Sinai in compliance with the peace treaty signed between Israel and Egypt (Wolfsfeld, 1984).

The growth of vigilantism on the part of the Jewish settlers on the West Bank has been justified by the movement as a necessary means of self-defense. "These vigilantes are 'agents' of the Gush Emunim community as a whole. They carry out a strategy of control that is broadly discussed and supported" (Weisburd and Vinitzky, 1984: 82). The types of vigilante activity eventually escalated in degree of violence as well as in scope of activity.

On April 27, 1984, the first of a series of arrests took place which led to the trial and conviction of twenty-five Jewish settlers for membership in a terrorist organization and for having participated in six violent attacks on Arabs over a period of four years. Among those convicted were a number of prominent leaders and activists of Gush Emunim. The assaults included the planting of bombs that maimed two Arab mayors of West Bank cities in 1980; a machine-gun and grenade attack on the Islamic University in Hebron in July 1983 that killed three and wounded thirty-three, the planting of bombs on five Arab buses (they were disarmed before they exploded), and a plot to blow up the Dome of the Rock in Jerusalem (one of the holiest shrines in Islam).

Three of the Jewish settlers convicted of murder, Menachem Livni (the leader of the Jewish terrorist underground), Shaul Nir, and Uziah Sharabaf (son-in-law of Rabbi Moshe Levinger), were prominent in Gush Emunim. Gush Emunim spokesmen claimed that the Jewish settlers were forced to take up arms to protect themselves because of the "security vacuum" in the territories. They condemned the courts for refusing to allow the accused to explain their motives and called for a general pardon for the convicted. A number of prominent politicians of the ultranationalist right supported this demand.

When the parties linked to Gush Emunim are in the opposition they, and Gush Emunim, are considerably less restrained in their criticism of the National Unity Government's policies. The release of over one thousand Palestinian prisoners convicted of various acts of terrorism in exchange for three Israeli soldiers held by the PLO precipitated protests of outrage and increased pressures to pardon the convicted Jewish terrorists on the part of Gush Emunim and its political allies. The demonstrated willingness and ability of key elements within Gush Emunim to take armed action in pursuit of its policies constitutes a direct challenge to the authority of the government and to the rule of law. The sympathy and support which they have received from the more militantly nationalistic elements of the population indicate the extent to which they are the "tip" of a larger iceberg. The political implications of this development are discussed in the concluding analysis.

GUSH EMUNIM AS A REVITALIZATION MOVEMENT

In his classic essay on the subject Wallace (1956: 265) says, "A revitalization movement is defined as a deliberate, organized, conscious effort by members of a society to construct a more satisfying culture." He particularly stressed that the dissatisfaction with significant aspects of the cultural system, and the conscious effort to initiate broad cultural innovations, take the form of reviving what are thought to have been traditional cultural patterns. There are many different kinds of revitalization movements. Millenarian movements emphasize supernatural apocalyptic world transformation. Messianic movements emphasize the personification of a divine role in bringing about such world transformation. Charismatic movements center on leaders with unique qualities whom the followers consider to have been divinely inspired and/or selected.

Gush Emunim shares characteristics of all of the above types, but combines them to form its own unique corporate persona. It outspokenly rejects many significant aspects not only of modern secular Israeli culture, but also of religious orthodox positions as well. It rejects modern secular culture for its spiritual barrenness. It condemns the lack of Zionist fervor in the ultraorthodox community and the political pragmaticism and lack of vision of the veteran leadership of the national religious community. While drawing from the springs of Jewish mysticism in the Kabalah, its version of messianism and redemption deviates markedly from tradition in its concentration on nationalism and practical politics. As Raanan

(1980, ch. 6) points out, the "political theology" of Gush Emunim completely changed the priority of the three pillars of religious Zionist faith—the people of Israel, the Land of Israel, and the Torah of Israel—by stressing the primary importance of the Land, or Eretz Yisrael.

Raanan argues that Gush Emunim successfully crystalized around a wide range of frustrations which were felt deeply in many sectors of Israeli society: the failure of the "ingathering of the exiles" to bring more immigrants to Israeli's shores; the inability to realize the dream of the Greater Land of Israel; despair over the possibility of attaining peace; the continuation of anti-Semitism after the creation of the state of Israel; disappointment due to the gap between the myths of the "new Jew" and the new Israeli society as a "light unto the nations" and reality; and discouragement regarding the direction of the development of Israeli society and culture as it was influenced by postindustrial Western culture.

Gush Emunim capitalized on these frustrations, especially among the idealistic youth within a segment of the subculture of the national religious camp who had become disillusioned by what they perceived to be the failure of the leaders to practice the principles they preached.

Weber's concept of charisma is one of the most widely abused and misapplied concepts in the social science literature (Wilner, 1984). Therefore, it is with considerable care that I apply the term to the spiritual leader of Gush Emunim, the late Rabbi Zvi Yehuda Kook. At first glance he would appear to have been an unlikely candidate to become a charismatic leader; and in fact he became one only in the last stage of his long life. Even his former students admit he was barely articulate, and that both his speeches and writings were hard to follow. Yet he clearly cast a spell which created, first of all, a coterie of devoted disciples, and through them a much larger following. As in similar cases, the reciprocal relationship between the charismatic leader and his disciples is critical in explaining the mobilization and expansion of a revitalization movement. When Rabbi Kook died in 1982 at the age of ninety-two, he was mourned by hundreds of thousands. With the death of Rabbi Kook, the process of the institutionalization of charisma, which was already well underway, intensified. The leadership of Gush Emunim became more differentiated, each leader tending to specialize in one of the various spheres of activities carried on through the network of institutional frameworks which the movement had spawned.

CONCLUSIONS

Having begun as a movement on the margins of the political system, Gush Emunim was coopted and incorporated as an integral part of the ruling political establishment in Israel during the Begin era. It is difficult to evaluate exactly what the lasting impact of the movement has been and presently is on the political system. Opinions of scholars and politicians are sharply divided. Yitzhak Berman, the Liberal party leader who resigned from the second Likud government in protest against Prime Minister Begin's initial reluctance to appoint a judicial commission to investigate the massacre of Palestinians in the refugee camps in Lebanon, claimed that, "the spirit of Gush Emunim is steadily seizing control of the government, in the military and political spheres alike. The Gush Emunim concept that Israel is alone among the nations is gradually taking root among the government" (*Jerusalem Post Reporter*, 1982: 3).

The biblical prophesy of Balaam, "Lo, it is a people that shall dwell alone and shall not be reckoned among the nations" (Num. 23: 9) was, according to Labor party Knesset member, Rabbi Menachem HaCohen (in a personal conversation with me) a curse which Gush Emunim has elevated to a blessing. Janet O'Dea (1976: 39) claims the aforementioned passage is an expression of "the prototypical psychological, sociological and theological stance which underlies the movement." Yet Liebman and Don-Yehiya (1983–84) argue this orientation is part of a much broader new civil religion which they claim has gained dominance in Israel in the recent period. Whether this view has gained a dominant position or not may be debateable. However, there is no question that the orientation extends well beyond those identified with Gush Emunim. That this world-view was shared by key members of the second Likud government was vividly expressed by Prime Minister Begin in his letter of August 2, 1982, to President Reagan in which he compared Beirut to Berlin and Arafat to Hitler.[8] Therefore, it is questionable whether Gush Emunim can be credited or blamed (depending on one's political orientation) with influencing the government. It is more likely that they mutually reinforced a shared worldview (Aronoff, 1985).

Similarly, it is difficult to evaluate exactly how influential Gush Emunim was in persuading the second Likud government to implement its settlement policy.[9] Whereas Gush Emunim's influence in pressuring reluctant previous governments, both Labor and the first Likud government (which included Dayan and Weizman), was clearer, the second Likud appeared to pursue its own version of settlement. The reserves of idealistic Gush Emunim potential settlers had apparently been nearly depleted. Given the timetable which the previous Likud government had set itself, it could not rely on idealism alone to motivate sufficient numbers of people to settle

[8] The full text of the letter was published in *The Jerusalem Post* on Aug. 4, 1982, p. 8.
[9] Differing evaluations are given in Newman, 1985.

across the green line. Therefore, it engaged in a major promotion campaign to advertise the financial and other advantages of the new housing it built primarily in larger urban concentrations. Also, given the financial inducements of heavily subsidized apartments, and the fact that many of the new urban areas were close enough to major established urban centers for easy commuting, the number of nonideologically motivated "settlers" soon outnumbered their "pioneering" predecessors. Gush Emunim's single-minded obsession strengthened the resolve of a government which was strongly committed to the settlement of Jews in all of the Land of Israel.

Gush Emunim's influence in strengthening the self-confidence of the national religious subculture has clearly been significant. As the most radical expression of nationalist sentiment in the religious camp, it mobilized support for a more militant foreign policy, and, through its alliance with the Young Guard of the NRP, played an important role in placing religious Zionism in the forefront of leadership in the most crucial issues facing the nation. Gush Emunim has played an active part in moving the religious camp away from their defensive posture of self-segregation, and this has had profound social, cultural, and political consequences for the nation. Even though the leadership of the Tze'irim has moderated its stand, and a new movement of dovish religious Zionists called Netivot Shalom (Paths of Peace) has arisen as a counterbalance to Gush Emunim's hawkish stand, these phenomena also reflect the long-term influence of Gush Emunim in contributing to the new self-confidence of religious Jews in Israel.

The case of Gush Emunim provides support for both of Kay Lawson's hypotheses (in her essay in this volume) that alternative organizations emerge when major parties fail to provide acceptable forms of linkage; and that they endure when they succeed in providing the kind of linkage hitherto lacking in the political system. A summary evaluation of the impact of Gush Emunim on the Israeli political system must inevitably lead to the conclusion that the movement's influence was far greater than its numbers or Lawson and Merkl's classification of it as a communitarian organization might initially appear to warrant. It is not just that Labor had failed to respond to the communitarian demands of Gush Emunim's relatively narrow constituency of supporters. Had that been the case, Gush Emunim would never have had as significant an impact on the political system as it has had. Gush Emunim challenged and helped to undermine the authority of the already weakened and declining Labor government.

As Peter Merkl points out (in his concluding essay in this volume), the failure of a dominant party represents a major crisis for the entire political system. In such contexts, protest movements may constitute momentous challenges to the legitimacy of the establishment. Many factors contributed to the failure of the linkage system which, in different combinations of electoral, clientelistic, and directive forms, had maintained Labor dominance for fifty years. However, the *coup de grâce* was delivered by the militant illegal settlements and Gush Emunim's success in laying claim to be the new ideological heir of Labor as the vanguard of Zionist pioneering settlement. The ritual-like confrontations with the government over settlement dramatically conveyed to the public not only the weakness of the government, but also the bankruptcy of its ideological resolve. Gush Emunim provided a new ideological linkage which gave religious legitimation for a solution to a new policy challenge posed by the occupation of new territories in 1967 which appealed to a much wider public than that which identified with Gush Emunim as a movement. In so doing, Gush Emunim played a major role in strengthening the ultranationalist forces in the National Religious party which made the Likud the NRP's preferred partner, and ultimately led to serious electoral losses and internal fragmentation within the NRP.

Through collaboration with, and cooptation by the Likud government, Gush Emunim contributed a messianic, moral imperative which gave religious legitimation to the political settlement program of the Likud, and cloaked its leader, Menachem Begin, with a mantle of (folk) religiosity, thereby enhancing his electoral popularity. Gush Emunim contributed to the spread and acceptance of a new form of civil religion based on non-rational messianic nationalistic/religious myths.

However, as the militants of the movement pushed this ideology to its ultimate extremes by engaging in underground terrorist activities, they challenged the authority of the government with which those of their leaders who had been elected to the Knesset were aligned. One of the unintended consequences of such behavior was to make the Likud government, by then headed by Yitzhak Shamir, appear more moderate. This indirectly paved the way for the present National Unity Government. As the two major parties—with roughly equal electoral and parliamentary strength—moved toward each other to embrace in the new political center (which is substantially to the right of what constituted the center during the heyday of Labor dominance), they alienated their more militant former partners on opposite ends of the ideological continuum.

The July 1984 elections resulted in a stalemate between the two major blocs. The Labor alignment received forty-four Knesset seats and the Likud forty-one. The remaining thirty-five Knesset mandates were distributed among thirteen other parties. Parties supported by the militant members of Gush Emunim—Techiya (five), Morasha (two), and Kach (one; led by Rabbi Meir Kahane)—received a total of eight Knesset seats. Some Gush Emunim supporters cast their votes for the other religious parties, which received a total of ten Knesset seats, and the Likud. It is unlikely that they voted for the ethnic party, Tami (one), the four center parties (ten), or Labor, much less the two parties on the extreme left (six).

The electoral deadlock prevented either major bloc from forming a stable government without the support of the other. Given the extremely perilous economic situation and the agreement between the two main parties over the need to withdraw Israeli forces from Lebanon, a government of national unity was formed by dividing ministerial portfolios and responsibilities equally between Labor, the Likud, and their client parties. Whereas Labor incorporated two small center parties into its Knesset faction, it lost the leftist Mapam, which broke away from the alignment that it had formed with the Labor party in 1969. On the other side, the ultranationalist Techiya party, which had been a member of the previous Likud government, chose to remain in the opposition. Consequently, the parties and, with one important exception, the parliamentarians most directly representative of, and responsive to Gush Emunim are no longer in the government, and now belong to the small and ideologically highly polarized opposition. The important exception is the minister of commerce and industry, Sharon, who is strongly supported by Gush Emunim and is considered by them to be their most important patron in the present government.

Ironically, Gush Emunim's extremism has helped to replace the old dominant party system with a more competitive multiparty system led by two major party blocs on the left and right which are moving closer to each other in most important policy areas while remaining far apart on the most crucial one. Negotiations between Israel, Jordan, and representatives of the Palestinians do not appear likely in the near future. If and when they do take place, it is certain that Gush Emunim will play a volatile role in opposing any territorial concessions. If such an agreement were to be reached, militant elements within the movement would likely resort to armed resistance to prevent its implementation. The threat of possible civil war, even on a small scale, constitutes a serious constraint on any government which undertakes negotiations on this most crucial issue. This makes the Gush's influence considerably greater than merely an irritant to the United States or a "gadfly" in Israeli politics, as Merkl suggests. While Gush Emunim is not a serious contender as an alternative ruling party, its ideology has been adopted in a somewhat modified form by one of the two main political blocs which shares power in the present government. Whereas some Likud members and all Labor members of the government refuse to accept the more extreme demands of Gush Emunim, neither their views nor the threat by their more militant elements to disrupt civil order can be ignored. This may ultimately be Gush Emunim's most significant (and in the opinion of this writer, its more tragic) legacy.

REFERENCES

Arian, A., and S. H. Barnes. 1974. The dominant party system: A neglected model of democratic stability. *Journal of Politics* 36: 592–614.

Aronoff, M. J. 1977. *Power and ritual in the Israel Labor Party*. Amsterdam/Assen: Van Gorcum.

———. 1979. The decline of the Israel Labor Party: Causes and significance. In *Israel at the polls: The Knesset elections of 1977*, ed. H. R. Penniman. Washington, D.C.: American Enterprise Institute, 115–45.

———. 1980a. Ideology and interest: The dialectics of politics. In *Ideology and politics: The dialectics of politics*. Political Anthropology, vol. I, ed. M. J. Aronoff. New Brunswick: Transaction, 1–29.

———. 1980b. The creation and corruption of civil religion in Israel. A paper presented at the Burg Wartenstein Symposium No. 84 in Burg Wartenstein Castle, Austria, July 19–27.

———. 1981a. Dominant party democracy: The Israeli version. A paper presented at the annual meeting of the American Political Science Association in New York City, Sept. 3–6.

———. 1981b. Civil religion in Israel. *Royal Anthropological Institute News* 44: 2–6.

———. 1982. The Labor party in opposition. In *Israel in the Begin era*, ed. R. O. Freedman. New York: Praeger, 76–101.

———. 1983. Conceptualizing the role of culture in political change. In *Culture and political change*. Political Anthropology, vol. II, ed. M. J. Aronoff. New Brunswick: Transaction, 1–18.

———, ed. 1984a. *Religion and politics*. Political Anthropology, vol. III. New Brunswick: Transaction.

———. 1984b. Political polarization: Conflicting interpretations of Israeli reality. In *Cross-currents in Israeli culture and politics*. Political Anthropology, vol. IV, ed. M. J. Aronoff. New Brunswick: Transaction, 1–23.

———. 1985. Establishing authority: The memorialization of Jabotinsky and the burial of the Bar-Kochba bones. In *The frailty of authority*. Political Anthropology, vol. V, ed. M. J. Aronoff. New Brunswick: Transaction, 105–30.

Avineri, S. 1980. The relevance of Ahad Ha'am. *The Jerusalem Post International Edition*, May 4–10.

———. 1981. *The making of modern Zionism*. London: Weidenfeld and Nicholson.

Avruch, K. A. 1978–79. Gush Emunim: Politics, religion, and ideology. *Middle East Review* 11: 26–31.

Bar-Lev, M. 1977. The graduates of the Yeshiva High School in Eretz-Yisrael: Between tradition and innovation. Ph.D. diss., Bar-Ilan University (Hebrew).

Bennet, W. L. 1982. Culture, communication, and political control. In *Culture and political change*. Political Anthropology, vol. ii, ed. M. J. Aronoff. New Brunswick: Transaction, 39–52.

Benvenisti, M. 1982. The West Bank and Gaza data base project interim report no. 1. Jerusalem: The West Bank Data Base Project (mimeo.).

Don-Yehiya, E. 1981. Origins and development of the Aguda and Mafdal parties. *The Jerusalem Quarterly* 20: 49–64.

Duverger, M. 1967. *Political parties*. Trans. B. and R. North with a forward by D. W. Brogan. London: Meuthen. (Originally published in French in 1951 as *Les partis politiques* by Armand Colin in Paris.)

Friedman, M. 1983. The NRP in transition—Behind the party's electoral decline. In *The roots of Begin's success: The 1981 elections*, ed. D. Caspi, A. Diskin, and E. Gutmann. London: Croom Helm, 141–68.

Friedman, T. 1985. Jewish settlers are put at 42,500. *New York Times*, Feb. 10: L17.

Furstenberg, R. 1982. Ferment in the yeshiva. *The Jerusalem Post*, Oct. 1: 9.

Goell, Y. 1981. Gush country *and* Patriots and pragmatists. *The Jerusalem Post International Edition*, Feb. 1–7: 9, 22; Feb. 15–21: 14–15.

Green, J. D. 1984. Religion and countermobilization in the Iranian revolution. In Aronoff, 1984a: 85–104.

Honig, S. 1982. NRP concerned as Hammer reveals his changing views *and* Gush Emunim tells Hammer: don't visit. *The Jerusalem Post*, Oct. 1: 1; Oct. 5: 2.

Horowitz, D. and M. Lissak. 1978. *Origins of the Israeli polity*. Chicago: University of Chicago Press.

Isaac, R. J. 1976. *Israel divided*. Baltimore: Johns Hopkins University Press.

———. 1981. *Party and politics in Israel*. New York: Longman.

Jerusalem Post Reporter. 1982. "Gush" taking over the government, Berman charges. *The Jerusalem Post*, Oct. 14: 3.

Levite, A., and S. Tarrow. 1983. The legitimation of excluded parties: A comparison of Israel and Italy. *Comparative Politics* 15: 295–397.

Lewis, A. 1979. The peace ritual and Israeli images of social order. *Journal of Conflict Resolution* 23: 685–703.

Liebman, C. S., and E. Don-Yehiya. 1981. The symbol system of Zionist-Socialism: An aspect of civil religion. *Modern Judaism* 1: 121–48.

———. 1982. Israel's civil religion. *The Jerusalem Quarterly*, 23: 57–69.

———. 1983. *Civil religion in Israel*. Berkeley: University of California Press.

———. 1984. The dilemma of reconciling traditional, cultural, and political needs: Civil religion in Israel. In Aronoff, 1884a: 47–62.

Lissak, M. 1974. The political absorption of immigrants and the preservation of political integration in Israel. A paper presented at the International Political Science Association Round Table on Political Integration, Jerusalem, Sept. 9–13.

Medding, P. Y. 1972. *Mapai in Israel*. Cambridge: Cambridge University Press.

Nachmias, D., and D. H. Rosenblum. 1978. *Bureaucratic culture: Citizens and administrators in Israel*. New York: St. Martins.

Newman, D. ed. 1985. *The impact of Gush Emunim: Politics and settlement in the West Bank*. London: Croom Helm.

O'Dea, J. 1976. Gush Emunim: Roots and ambiguities, the perspective of the sociology of religion. *Forum* 2: 39–50.

Raanan, T. 1980. *Gush Emunim*. Tel Aviv: Sifriat Poalim (Hebrew).

Rabin, Y. 1979. *The Rabin memoirs*. Boston: Little, Brown.

Rabinovich, A. 1982. Rate of settlement to drop to one per year, WZO says. *The Jerusalem Post*, Sept. 20: 3.

Richardson, D. 1982. De facto dual society. *The Jerusalem Post*, Sept. 10: 7.

Rubenstein, A. 1980. *Mi Herzl Ad Gush Emunim Ubechazera* [From Herzl to Gush Emunim and back]. Tel Aviv: Schocken (Hebrew).

Rubenstein, D. 1982. *Mi L'Adoni Eli: Gush Emunim* [On the Lord's side: Gush Emunim]. Tel Aviv: Sifriat Poalim (Hebrew).

Sartori, G. 1976. *Parties and party systems*, vol. I. London: Cambridge University Press.

Schiff, G. S. 1977. *Tradition and politics: The religious parties of Israel*. Detroit: Wayne State University Press.

Schnall, D. J. 1979. *Radical dissent in contemporary Israeli politics*. New York: Praeger.

Segal, M. 1982. Education Minister Zevulin Hammer talks to Mark Segal about the aftermath of the Beirut massacre. *The Jerusalem Post*, Oct. 15: 1.

Shapiro, Y. 1976. *The formative years of the Israeli Labor party: The organization of power 1919–1930*. Beverly Hills: Sage Publications.

Sharkansky, I. 1979. *Whither the state?* Chatham, N.J.: Chatham House.

Sprinzak, E. 1981. Gush Emunim: The tip of the iceberg. *The Jerusalem Quarterly* 21: 28–47.

Wallace, A.F.C. 1956. Revitalization movements. *American Anthropologist* 58: 264–81.

Weisburg, D., and V. Vinitzky. 1984. Vigilantism as rational control: The case of Gush Emunim settlers. In *Cross-currents in Israeli culture and politics*. Political Anthropology, vol. IV, ed. M. J. Aronoff. New Brunswick: Transaction, 69–87.

Weissbrod, L. 1982. Gush Emunim ideology—From religious doctrine to political action. *Middle Eastern Studies* 18: 265–75.

Wilner, A. R. 1984. *The spellbinders: Charismatic political leadership*. New Haven: Yale University Press.

Wolfsfeld, G. 1984. Political violence and the mass media. *The Jerusalem Quarterly* 131: 130–44.

Zucker, N. L. 1973. *The coming crisis in Israel: Private faith and public policy*. Cambridge: MIT Press.

THIRTEEN

When Parties Fail:
Ethnic Protest in
Britain in the 1970s

PETER PULZER

What is political failure? It lies in the eye of the beholder. The system under which mass unemployment came to Germany in the early 1930s was
judged a failure; the systems under which the same phenomenon came to
Britain and the United States were not. A sentence of failure on parties depends on the job they are expected to do. They may fail individually

- because they no longer satisfy the claims of their particular clientele
- because they no longer manage to aggregate, or adjudicate between,
  the competing claims of their subclienteles
- because their clientele is disappearing and they are unable to recoup
  from elsewhere
- because new clienteles are arising which existing parties fail to accommodate.

But parties can also fail collectively because they are collectively associated with system instability, incompetence and/or corruption. The Weimar Republic or the Fourth French Republic are obvious examples of this.
Or they may fail collectively in a more incremental and less spectacular
way: each, during its own term of office, fails to deliver widely expected
outputs in the policy areas that determine mass electoral response, the
most important of which is generally economic management.

Whatever the form of failure, unless it results in a coup d'etat or a mass
repudiation of a pluralistic, party-competitive polity, the outcome will be
an erosion of the traditional parties' electoral support. They will be replaced by one or more of (a) hitherto small parties, claiming to provide
traditional benefits, only more competently; (b) new parties, with similar
claims; (c) parties (whether new or hitherto small), raising new issues; (d)
a withdrawal into apathy, marked by declining electoral turnout.

The evidence for limited party failure in Britain over the past twenty
years is unambiguous. Turnout has dropped, though unevenly. The major

parties' share of the vote has dropped fairly consistently. The share of the minor parties peaked at 25 percent in the two general elections of 1974, and though it dropped again in the general election of 1979, it was still above the level of the 1960s. In 1983, following the formation of the Social Democratic party, it reached a new peak of 30 percent (see Table 13.1).

To explain this phenomenon, I want to test a number of hypotheses, which are not necessarily mutually exclusive:

1. That there have been social-structural changes in the population that deprive the traditional parties of their natural constituency and increase the electorally mobile and volatile part of the population
2. That the traditional parties have failed to deliver on bread-and-butter issues
3. That the traditional parties have (for whatever reason) ceased to be broadly based and ideologically eclectic so as to be able to appeal to independent voters
4. That the change in the economic environment and in Britain's world position has brought new issues and concerns to the fore

All of these are plausible hypotheses, though to verify them is not necessarily to establish their significance.

1. As in all advanced economies, the traditional occupations in the pri-

TABLE 13.1

Year	% Turnout of Registered Electors	% of Votes Cast for Con. + Lab.	% of all Electors Voting Con. + Lab.
1951	82.5	96.8	80.8
1955	76.8	96.1	73.8
1959	78.7	93.2	73.3
1964	77.1	87.5	67.5
1966	75.8	89.8	68.2
1970	72.0	89.3	64.4
Feb. 1974	78.1	74.9	58.5
Oct. 1974	72.8	75.0	54.7
1979	76.0	80.8	61.0
1983	72.7	70.0	50.9

mary and manufacturing sector in Britain are diminishing; the service sector, demanding higher educational qualifications and greater occupational and physical mobility, is expanding. The group loyalties and subcultures derived from the impact of the industrial revolution are breaking down.

This is of significance since most observers agree that class (both objectively and subjectively measured) is much the most important partisan divisor in twentieth-century Britain, and much the most reliable predictor of electoral choice. If class cohesion is declining, we may expect class voting to decline, and this indeed has happened since the 1960s (Särlvik and Crewe, 1983: 87; Rose, 1980, passim; Franklin, 1985, passim; *The Economist*, London, June 18, 1983: 34–37).

2. The failure to deliver on bread-and-butter issues is much more difficult to quantify. It is well known that on such standard indicators as per capita growth GNP, rate of inflation, unemployment, share of world market, Britain has performed less well than most advanced industrial countries.

Relating this poor performance with electoral response is not easy. Discontent is quite consistent with high rates of growth (e.g., France); low rates of growth may be quite tolerable to some nations, and some survey evidence suggests that the British are quite satisfied with their standard of living (Forester, 1977: 158–61). The indirect evidence for dissatisfaction with government performance is the increasing frequency with which governments are turned out of office. But since we cannot use as proof what we want to prove, this evidence does not get us very far. What is demonstrable is that the degree of antigovernment swing at any time—whether in the direction of the main opposition party or toward minor parties—correlates highly with the performance of the economy (Goodhart and Bhansali, 1977: 43–106; Miller and Mackie, 1973: 263–79, for a more skeptical view; Butler and Kavanagh, 1980: 24–25, 29). This becomes relevant when we consider the fluctuations in ethnic protest voting.

3. Contrary to what might be expected, and contrary to the experience of most West European countries, there is no doubt that both major parties have moved away from the vote-maximizing "catchall" concept. Both—and particularly the Labour party—have identified more closely with their "core" class constituency and have become ideologically more sharply delineated. If we consider this development side by side with the decline in the relative size of the "core" social groupings, it becomes evident that the potential clientele for new political parties or nonparty political activism is further increased.

4. On the one hand, we may expect that the environmental and libertarian issues, generally identified as "postindustrial," would increase in

salience; on the other, that as Britain ceases to be a world power, the pressures making for national homogeneity and political unity diminish.

That new issues, and new (or previously weak) parties, articulating new concerns, came to the fore in the 1970s, is the starting point of this discussion. But what is far from self-evident is which is cause and which effect in these developments. Did the traditional parties decline primarily because they were insensitive to new policy demands, thus leaving the field to rival parties? Or did the new parties, with their new policy demands primarily fill a vacuum created by traditional parties' incompetence in "valency" issues? Were the nonmajor parties' voters of the 1970s symptom or cause of the minor earthquake that shook the British party landscape, the rumblings of which are far from dead? I shall attempt to answer these questions in the light of the electoral fortunes of the Scottish National party, the Plaid Cymru in Wales, and the National Front. I shall not discuss the Liberal party, the largest of the vehicles of party protest—though I shall bring it in for comparative purposes—nor the Social Democratic party, which was founded only after the 1979 election.

The decline in the popularity of the two major parties has been moderate, but unambiguous (see Table 13.1). As old-established parties, with a long history of officeholding, they are, as Rose and Mackie point out in their essay, well placed for persistence in the political system. Indeed, every one of Rose and Mackie's criteria for survival, except proportional representation, applies in Britain. Nor has Britain been subject to the kind of developmental crisis or regime failure that has a seismic effect on the party structure (LaPalombara and Weiner, 1966: 14–19). As in France, the pattern of institutions has also helped to sustain the existing party alignment: in France it is the primacy of the executive, in Britain the association of Parliament with national sovereignty, in both countries the electoral system (Rose and Mackie, in this volume). It is therefore not surprising that major party support in Britain has been eroded rather than undermined, illustrating an acceleration of discontent rather than a collapse of legitimacy. All three nonmajor parties, whatever the difference between them, demonstrate that though class may constitute the principal cleavage in British electoral behavior, it is not the only one. There is, in addition to class, a (generally weak) center-periphery dimension to party allegiance and also a religious one, which to some extent overlaps with it (Pelling, 1967; Morgan, 1963; Guthrie and McLean, 1978; Miller, 1977: 175–82). The Conservative party is the party of Crown and church, of state and Empire. It is a predominantly English party and its heartland is the counties of southern England. It is, or used to be, predominantly Anglican, i.e., Episcopalian, in its religious following: the Church of England was "the Conservative party at prayer." The other Protestant churches—

Free Churches or Nonconformists—were predominantly anti-Conservative: before 1914 that meant Liberal, thereafter Liberal or Labour. Their geographical concentration was peripheral: southwestern England, northern England, and Wales. The Presbyterian Church of Scotland also tended toward Liberalism. Catholics (7 percent of the English population, 14 percent of the Scottish) are mainly descended from Irish immigrants. For reasons that reflect both memories of the home-rule struggle and their originally low socioeconomic status, they were overwhelmingly Liberal before 1914 and have been overwhelmingly Labour since.

These nonclass cleavages, secondary though they are, explain the special dimensions of Scottish and Welsh politics and of anti-immigration politics in England.

Scotland

Widespread electoral support for the Scottish National party, reaching 30 percent in the October 1974 general election and peaking at about 36 percent (according to opinion polls and municipal elections) in the mid-seventies was a new phenomenon. But the SNP, in existence since 1934, is not; neither is the demand for some form of Scottish self-government.

Before the union of England and Scotland in 1707, Scotland had been a separate state and even within the Union retained some of the attributes of statehood. The Church of Scotland remained the established church and its General Assembly was, in the absence of a separate parliament, the nearest thing to a national representative institution. The Scottish legal, educational, and (until 1974) local government systems have also remained separate. Within the unitary British state the functional devolution of Scottish affairs has proceeded steadily. The cabinet post of Secretary (now Secretary of State) for Scotland was created in 1885; by 1939 the Scottish Office was located in Edinburgh and it has become responsible for the administration in Scotland of most United Kingdom legislation. The effect of this separation of institutions is ambiguous: on the one hand, it satisfies the feeling that Scotland should not be treated as one more bit of the United Kingdom, on the other, it invites the argument that some form of self-government is the next logical step.

Developments on the noninstitutional level have pushed Scotland in the opposite direction: toward greater integration in the United Kingdom. As economies become first nationalized, then internationalized, more and more Scots are employed by firms owned and run from outside Scotland. The effect of this integration has also been ambiguous: when it appears, on balance, to benefit the welfare of Scots, it is accepted; when not, it is resented.

The campaign to give institutional form to Scottish national aspirations dates from the end of the nineteenth century. Between 1889 and 1920, there were eight votes on Scottish home rule in the House of Commons; that in 1913 showed a majority in favor. Scottish aspirations were articulated by the non-Conservative parties—Liberal between 1885 (when the majority of adult males first had the vote) and 1914, Liberal and Labour in varying proportions since then.

The Scottish home-rule cause got some halfhearted support from the Liberal party before 1914 and from time to time quite strong support from sections of Labour (Keating and Bleiman, 1979). What Labour principally had to offer Scotland was the redistributive benefits of centralized planning, decked out with subsidy machines like the North of Scotland Hydro-Electric Board and the Scottish Development Agency, as well as various regional investment incentives that favored Scotland disproportionately, though not exclusively. Except in the period between 1929 and 1959, the Conservatives have polled fewer votes and held fewer seats than would be predicted from class structural data (Miller, 1981: 210). There is thus a distinct Scottish dimension to British politics, but until the late 1960s the main British parties were able to absorb this.

The question therefore arises why the SNP suddenly took off in the late 1960s. We may consider three classes of explanation: (1) that the case of Scottish home rule suddenly became more popular; (2) that the cause of Scottish home rule enjoyed more intense, even if not more widespread, support; (3) that votes for the SNP were an expression of general dissatisfaction with the existing parties, for which sympathy with home rule was a necessary condition, but not a sufficient one.

The first explanation is the least likely. Regular survey figures measuring the support for home rule are available only since 1965. They produce an average level of support, with very little fluctuation of 22 percent for full independence; 40 percent for devolution without full independence; 22 percent for more responsibility, short of devolution; 16 percent for the status quo (Miller, 1981: 99–101). It is a reasonable assumption—though no more—that these levels applied for some time before. Fluctuations in SNP support cannot therefore be attributed primarily to fluctuation in support for independence or devolution.

For the third explanation there is some circumstantial evidence. Though the SNP had fought general elections and by-elections before the 1960s, occasionally scoring respectable polls, its consistent rise began in the early 1960s exactly at the time when the Liberal party was making spectacular gains in England. Had the Liberals in Scotland been better organized, they might have succeeded in heading off the SNP revival: indeed, in the 1964 and 1966 general elections they gained a total of six rural seats, their best holding since 1929. However, the Liberals had no base in urban Scotland, which is where the second SNP surge, that of 1967, culminating in the epoch-making by-election victory at Hamilton, took place—again coinciding with Liberal successes in England. Combined with widespread local government victories in 1968, this gave the SNP what it had always previously lacked: credibility.

Having pinpointed the timing of the SNP's rise, we can now look at the second potential explanation, viz. that home rule was more intensely, even if not more widely demanded. By the early 1970s three additional factors were added to the existing demand for home rule:

a. In response to SNP successes the government appointed a Royal Commission on the Constitution (the Kilbrandon Commission), which reported in 1973, recommending a Scottish parliament but reduced Scottish representation at Westminster. This made the constitutional position of Scotland a central issue in British politics.
b. The discovery of North Sea oil, a Scottish share of which might make an independent Scotland more viable economically, as well as providing an emotive rallying cry.
c. Proposed British membership of the Common Market, which raised the question whether Scottish interests were best represented by London, both in negotiation and after.

Oil, devolution, and the Common Market were thus all in the air in the first of the 1974 elections, when the SNP gained 22 percent of the vote and seven seats out of seventy-one a voting share similar to that of the Liberals in England. But in the second 1974 election the SNP rose to 30 percent and eleven seats, whereas the Liberals in England declined. From this time on, the SNP and English Liberal curves diverge, and the SNP curve is more clearly related to developments on the home-rule front.

Of the three additional home-rule factors, that of EEC membership was disposed of by the referendum in 1975. The SNP advised a "no" vote, but few electors, according to opinion polls, took their cue from the SNP on this issue (see Table 13.2). Fifty-eight percent of Scots voted "yes," compared with 68 percent in England.

The oil factor remained unresolved. Here (see Table 13.2) more electors took their cue from the SNP, though of these only a minority accepted the SNP platform that all oil revenues from the Scottish sector of the North Sea should be devoted to Scotland.

The big one was the devolution question. Devolution became an issue

TABLE 13.2   Party Preferences on Selected Issues

	Party Preferred on Issue					
	Con.	Lab.	Lib.	SNP	DK	
Nationalization	35	22	4	5	35	100%
Social services	22	32	2	5	39	100%
Wage controls	28	31	3	3	35	100%
EEC membership	20	31	3	9	37	100%
Oil	13	17	3	26	40	100%
Devolution	15	21	7	30	27	100%

SOURCE: Miller, 1981: 125. Used with the author's permission.

because of the SNP, though the SNP did not favor it. Its policy was independence. The party that offered devolution was Labour—because it was in power from 1974 to 1979, and above all because Scotland provided a disproportionate number of Labour seats and devolution was judged the only way of saving them. That is why Labour's devolution proposals ignored two of the Kilbrandon proposals: fewer Scots MPs at Westminster and proportional representation for the devolved assembly. The Conservatives, most of whose instincts were antidevolution, also offered an assembly, but without specifying the details.

The changing fortunes of the SNP and Labour in Scotland from then on were a direct function of the fortunes of the Labour government's devolution plans. There were four phases:

1. Support for the SNP rose to a peak in late 1975, when the government published its White Paper, *Our Changing Democracy*, which proposed veto powers for the Secretary of State over assembly decisions.
2. Support for the SNP declined throughout 1976 as the government produced improved proposals, culminating in the Scotland and Wales Bill, which included referendum provisions.
3. Support for the SNP surged once more when the bill was defeated by the votes of dissident Labour MPs at Westminster in February 1977.
4. Support for the SNP subsided slowly in the second half of 1977 while the government prepared a new bill, and fell rapidly when it passed in mid-1978.

The fact that the bill passed only subject to an amendment requiring a "yes" vote of 40 percent of registered electors had little immediate effect on opinion, as polls suggested that this hurdle would be cleared.

In each of the above phases it seemed as though issues determined partisanship: voting intentions reflected the parties' intentions. In the run-up to the referendum, the relationship was reversed: the referendum was not on self-government or devolution as such, but on the Labour government's Scotland Act. Though neither main party was unanimous, and there were a number of "yes" and "no" crossparty umbrella organizations, Labour was for and the Tories against. As Referendum Day (March 1, 1979) approached, the commanding "yes" lead melted away: opposition to the act among Conservative identifiers rose from 54 percent in early January 1979 to 79 percent, Labour support remained steady at 66 to 68 percent. As a consequence, the "yes" vote was 51.6 percent and since the turnout was only 63.8 percent, this constituted 32.9 percent of registered electors, well short of the act's 40 percent requirement. (Table 13.3 shows the distribution of partisan support for devolution.)

In the general election two months later, the Tories under Mrs. Thatcher defeated Labour, but Scotland bucked the trend. In England there was a Conservative lead of 10.5 percent in Scotland a Labour lead of 10.1 percent—a difference of 20.6 percent instead of the 8 percent one would predict on class criteria alone. The SNP dropped to 17.3 percent and lost eleven of its thirteen seats. In one sense these Scottish voting figures are a continuation of the trend observable since 1977, which identified Labour as the agent of Scottish political aspirations. Yet Labour had conspicuously failed to deliver: if the election had been primarily on the constitutional issue, one might have expected the SNP to benefit. What the election showed was that home rule is *an* issue in Scotland, not *the* issue. It was a British election, fought on British issues, but their impact had a Scottish dimension. The election was about jobs and prices, and job security gained in salience as one moved north from London. In the three southernmost regions of England, the swing to the right was 6.4 percent. In the three northernmost regions it was 4.0 percent. In Scotland it was 0.7 percent. There was, therefore, still a Scottish dimension to British politics, but it had reverted to its pre-1970 agenda. The results of the 1983 election merely confirmed this reversion. Support for the SNP dropped further, to 11.8 percent, and the SDP-Liberal Alliance, with 24.5 percent asserted itself as the principal third force in Scotland. Labour's lead over the Conservatives fell by 3.4 percent to 6.7 percent, but this underscored even more the contrast with England, where the Conservative lead rose by 8.6 percent to 19.1 percent (see Table 13.4).

There remains the question of who voted for the SNP and why. The SNP

TABLE 13.3   Support for Constitutional Change in Scotland and Wales, 1975–1979 (in percent)

A. Scottish Referendum Voting Intention by General Election Voting Intention, 1976–1979

		Con	Lab	SNP	All
Yes	Oct. 76	61	62	76	65
	Feb. 77	55	59	82	64
	Apr. 78	46	66	84	63
	Jan.–Feb. 79	28	47	84	45
	8–11 Feb. 79	32	56	86	49
	15–16 Feb. 79	24	53	75	44
No	Oct. 76	21	18	14	16
	Feb. 77	28	17	12	19
	Apr. 78	47	24	11	27
	Jan.–Feb. 79	60	34	8	20
	8–11 Feb. 79	52	30	7	33
	15–16 Feb. 79	54	25	6	30
Don't Know	Oct. 76	18	20	9	19
	Feb. 77	17	24	6	17
	Apr. 78	9	11	2	10
	Jan.–Feb. 79	12	19	8	20
	8–11 Feb. 79	15	13	6	17
	15–16 Feb. 79	22	22	19	26

B. Welsh Referendum Voting Intention by General Election Voting Intention, 1976–1979

		Con	Lab	Lib	PC	All
Yes	Dec. 76	16	28	27	69	27
	Mar. 77	14	27	23	79	27
	May 78	21	54	25	63	41
	Feb. 79i	20	41	27	73	33
	Feb. 79ii	7	27	19	85	22
No	Dec. 76	58	33	47	13	40
	Mar. 77	73	48	57	12	53
	May 78	67	30	58	10	41
	Feb. 79i	63	40	50	9	46
	Feb. 79ii	87	58	67	12	65
Don't Know	Dec. 76	26	39	26	18	33
	Mar. 77	13	25	20	8	21
	May 78	13	16	17	27	18
	Feb. 79i	17	19	23	18	21
	Feb. 79ii	6	14	13	6	13

SOURCE: Balsom and McAllister, 1979: 408–409. Used with the permission of Oxford University Press.

TABLE 13.4   Labour Lead over Conservatives in Scotland and in the
United Kingdom at Four General Elections (in percent)

	Scotland	United Kingdom	Difference
Feb. 1974	3.8	−0.7	+4.5
Oct. 1974	11.6	3.4	+8.2
1979	10.1	−7.0	+17.1
1983	6.7	−14.8	+21.5

is a party of opinion, not of interest. The principle it speaks for is fairly evenly supported throughout the Scottish population, as Table 13.5 shows: we should therefore expect SNP support to be equally evenly spread. However, this is not so. Factors other than support for independence or devolution also determine support for the SNP. Two groups stand out as deviant: the young and the Catholics. Those under twenty-five were slightly more prodevolution and independence, but heavily more pro-SNP in October 1974. Catholics, though average in their support for home-rule platforms, were heavily underrepresented in support for the SNP. This suggests that the SNP shares the general characteristics of new or rapidly expanding parties: it can appeal most easily to the least integrated and least organized elements in society. The young obviously fall into this category; Catholics, with their elaborate urban subculture and historic links with Labour machine politics, equally obviously do not.

This raises a further, and for my argument crucial, question about the forces influencing SNP voting: is the rise of the SNP primarily a response to a specific issue demand, or is it—partly, and possibly predominantly—a Scottish variant of a trend common to the whole of Great Britain, that of dissociation from the traditional major parties? There is ample and well-known evidence that the proportions of British electors who identify strongly with one of the main parties halved between 1964 and 1979 (Särlvik and Crewe, 1983: 334-36). There is strong evidence that those who switched to the Liberal party in England in 1974 (when it won 20 percent of the vote) did so less because they were attracted to Liberal policy platforms than because they were dissatisfied with those of the existing main parties (Alt et al., 1977: 366–67; Miller et al., 1977: 93–94). There is parallel evidence that the SNP vote in Scotland also consisted of these elements. The fact that the three surges of third-party voting were simultaneous in England and Scotland (1962–63, 1967–68, 1972–73) supports the hypothesis that SNP was a Scottish surrogate for British third-party voting.

TABLE 13.5A   Scottish Voting by Social Indicators, 1974 (in percent)

	Con	Lib	Lab	SNP	Dnv
BY CLASS					
Among middle class	36	12	19	26	7
Among working class	10	3	50	24	13
BY OCCUPATION					
Higher managerial	37	11	11	37	3
Lower managerial	35	10	16	29	9
Skilled nonmanual	36	5	26	27	7
Other nonmanual	24	10	30	26	10
Skilled manual	12	3	39	33	12
Other manual	11	4	52	20	14
BY TRADE-UNION CONTRACTS					
Respondent in a trade union	11	6	46	26	11
Someone else in household					
in a trade union	16	5	36	32	11
Neither	31	8	26	22	13
BY INCOME LEVELS					
Level 1 (lowest)	24	9	29	22	16
2	17	8	35	27	12
3	21	6	41	23	10
4	20	6	34	29	10
5 (highest)	30	9	23	29	9
BY HOUSE TENURE					
Owned, no mortgage	49	7	14	19	11
Mortgaged	28	12	17	33	10
Rented privately	27	9	23	24	16
Rented from council	11	5	49	24	12
BY RELIGION					
Among Church of Scotland	28	8	28	27	9
Among other Presbyterians	23	4	25	31	15
Among Catholics	10	2	69	11	8
Among Anglicans	39	11	15	19	16
Among no religious denominations	14	7	36	28	16

SOURCE: *The Scotsman* (Edinburgh), Oct. 15, 1975.

TABLE 13.5B   Devolution, Age, Sex, Religion, Education, and
House Tenure

	Percentage in favor of	
	Devolution	Independence
Age		
Under 25	75	30
25–29	67	26
30–34	69	29
35–44	69	19
45–54	62	19
55–64	65	16
65–74	58	14
75 plus	55	19
Sex		
Male	72	25
Female	61	19
Religion (sect)		
Church of Scotland	68	19
RC	63	20
None	65	30
Anglican	56	15
Religiosity		
Very much so	63	16
To some extent	68	16
Not really	67	22
Education		
Academic further	68	10
Other further and academic school	78	20
Other further	69	23
More than minimum	63	23
Minimum	61	23
Tenure		
Owned	62	20
Mortgaged	73	21
Private rented	70	20
Council	63	22

SOURCE: Miller, 1981: 112. Used with permission of the author.

There is only one major snag to accepting this hypothesis in its entirety. The chief characteristic of the British Liberal party is that it has a vast range of policies that relatively few of its voters know of or care for. Everyone knows what the SNP stands for: in that respect it is a different kind of party. The advantages of that are obvious, but the disadvantages should be equally obvious. Not only do specific policies arouse opposition, they attract only if they seem important, even crucial, to voters. At no time was that true of the Scottish electorate. Home rule of one kind or another was very important to relatively few Scots—about 10 percent according to opinion poll responses (Miller, 1981: 103) and fairly important to a good many more. The majority of electors thought general economics issues the most important, and did not judge the SNP competent on them (see Table 13.2).

I conclude, therefore, that the demand for some form of self-government was a necessary condition for the rise of the SNP, and in the brief period of the devolution debate (1975–79) it helped to determine the level of support for it. But it was never a sufficient condition, first because many supporters of self-government failed to switch their vote to it, and second because a predisposition to dislike or distrust the main parties was at least an equally important condition.

WALES

There are both similarities and differences in the reasons for the rise of nationalist feeling in Wales and Scotland. Welsh national sentiment has a weaker institutional base than Scottish, but a stronger cultural one. Wales came under the authority of the English Crown and Parliament in 1536, but had no previous history of independent statehood and next to no separate administrative and representative institutions thereafter. What survived in Wales, but not in Scotland, was the native Celtic language, and what constituted the principal rallying cry for the nationalist revival in the nineteenth century was the need to defend that language against the impact of industrialization and greater ease of communication. In 1901, half the population of Wales spoke Welsh and 15 percent no English; in 1971 only 21 percent spoke Welsh and virtually no one was ignorant of English. Since then the decline has been largely halted. The Welsh-language predominates in the rural areas of the north and west; it is uncommon in industrial south Wales, where two-thirds of the population lives.

An equally important cultural factor is the strength of religious nonconformity. In the mid-nineteenth century, Nonconformist churches outnumbered the Anglican Church by 5 to 2 and still do so by about 2 to 1 today.

Nonconformity was a bastion of the Welsh language and therefore against the supremacy of London. One of its principal demands was the disestablishment of the Anglican Church in Wales; one of its principal cultural weapons is the demand for the closure of public houses on Sunday (Butt Philip, 1975: 52–57, 124–53).

The noninstitutional factors undermining regional distinctiveness, already noted in Scotland, are much more in evidence in Wales. Communications with neighboring parts of England are easier than between the different parts of Wales and the main centers of English population are much closer to Wales than to Scotland. In the districts closest to England, over a quarter of the population are English-born, a phenomenon noticeable even a century ago. Perhaps the most striking example of the fragility of Welsh national cultural institutions is the University of Wales, founded in 1893. As late as the 1930s, nearly 90 percent of its students were Welsh born; now it is under 40 percent (Butt Philip, 1975: 62).

All of this suggests that the political atmosphere of Wales is less separatist than that of Scotland, but more strongly peripheral. This is reflected in the party representation of Wales, which has been overwhelmingly non-Conservative since 1885. In this century it has been unusual for the Conservatives to win more than 30 percent of the Welsh vote, and the deviation from a class-based prediction has been even greater than in Scotland. In the mid-1960s, i.e., before the nationalist parties' main takeoff, the Conservative share of the vote among the various occupational groups was as shown in Table 13.6 (Butler and Stokes, 1969: 126–27). The Liberal party before 1914 established itself as the advocate of church disestablishment, teetotalism, and home rule. The fruits of this were the Sunday Closing Act of 1881 and the Welsh Church Act of 1920. On home rule nothing happened.

The Labour party, as the party of central economic planning, was less keen on home rule, though its Welsh section occasionally passed resolu-

TABLE 13.6   Conservative Voting Shares of Occupational Groups in Great Britain, 1963–1966 (in percent)

	Wales	Scotland	Great Britain
Managerial and professional	58.0	79.8	74.5
Other white collar	41.9	61.6	60.0
Skilled manual workers	15.2	30.5	33.0
Other manual workers	13.5	29.9	28.5

tions in favor of it. Labour governments took some steps in favor of devolution, creating the Council for Wales in 1949 and the Secretary of State for Wales in 1964. But neither of these had significant powers, certainly not compared with their Scottish equivalents.

The partisan vehicle of Welsh nationalism, the Plaid Cymru, founded in 1925, is similarly ambivalent on self-government. While the claim for self-government has been a consistent part of its platform, it is evident that what mattered most was the maintenance of a traditional culture, and for this a choir was more use than a parliament. The principal grievances of Welsh nationalists since World War II have centered on the husbanding of resources—to oppose the flooding of Welsh valleys to create reservoirs for supplying English conurbations and the buying up of country cottages as holiday or retirement homes by the English, to promote more Welsh-language programs on radio and television and bilingual road signs and public notices. The linguistic demands have met with some success, the others not. Yet even the language and cultural question is a source of weakness as well as strength to the Welsh nationalist movement. Most Welshmen now do not speak Welsh, most Welshmen like to drink beer even on Sundays, and the Plaid and its campaigns threaten the dictatorship of the minority. This emerged clearly in the devolution debate of the 1970s.

Up to the mid-sixties, Plaid Cymru had, like the SNP, scored the occasional respectable vote in parliamentary elections, mostly in Welsh-speaking rural Wales. It had not shared in the minor-party upsurge of the early sixties from which both English Liberals and SNP benefited. Then, in 1966, it provided a bombshell by winning a by-election at Carmarthen, followed by two near misses in industrial constituencies in the south. There is little doubt that the Carmarthen victory provided some of the impetus for the SNP's Hamilton success and from then on, Welsh and Scottish nationalism were bracketed as a political phenomenon and a constitutional challenge. The Kilbrandon Report recommended elected parliaments for both Scotland and Wales. But though it could be argued that Wales had led the field in electing nationalist MPs, it was Scotland that caused the problem. Without Scottish nationalism, the Labour government would not have offered Wales devolution: Wales was included for symmetry.

The reasons for this we have seen in the ambiguity of Welsh nationalism, in its priority for nonconstitutional aims, the divisive role of the language, and the porousness of the frontier with England. There was a halfheartedness about the referendum campaign compared with Scotland and this extended to the impact of the party. Plaid Cymru and the Liberals campaigned for a "yes" vote, though the devolution offer fell short of what they demanded, the Conservatives for a "no" vote. But though the official Labour line was for devolution, the party was in fact divided and a number of prominent Labour MPs campaigned for a "no" vote, including Neil Kinnock, now leader of the Labour party. Plaid Cymru's electoral progress in the mid-1970s, exactly paralleling that of the SNP and including the penetration of hitherto "stony fields," such as industrial towns in the south, masked the low priority that separate institutions had for most Welsh people. Support for the assembly declined as the campaign progressed, exactly as in Scotland, but from a lower peak (see Table 13.3b). The outcome was a humiliation for the devolutionists. The turnout was only 58.8 percent. The "yes" vote was 20.3 percent. In no county, not even the Welsh-speaking ones, did the "yes" vote exceed 34.4 percent, though the level of the "yes" vote did correlate with the level of Welsh speaking (see Table 13.7). In the four counties of the industrialized south, the "yes" vote ranged from 20.2 percent to 12.1 percent or 12 percent to 7 percent of registered electors. Only 32 percent of Labour supporters followed their party's lead (Foulkes, Jones, and Wilford, 1983: 206).

Welsh devolution is now dead, in a way that Scottish devolution is not. Since the referendum, there have been two developments that illustrate the strengths and weaknesses of traditional loyalties. The weakness is seen in the 1979 election that brought Mrs. Thatcher to power. This still left Labour ahead in Wales, but only by 17.1 percent. The regionally based anti-Conservative bias was not eliminated, but it has greatly diminished. The Conservatives won eleven of the thirty-six seats, which equaled the highest number in this century. In rural Wales the Conservatives' vote rose by 10.5 percent and they did particularly well in former strongholds of Nonconformist radicalism. As in Scotland, the 1983 election merely confirmed

TABLE 13.7   Welsh Speaking and Referendum Vote

County	%Welsh Speaking	%Yes in Referendum
Gwynedd	64.7	34.4
Dyfed	52.5	28.1
Powys	23.7	18.7
Clwyd	21.4	21.6
West Glamorgan	20.3	18.7
Mid Glamorgan	10.4	20.2
South Glamorgan	5.0	13.1
Gwent	1.9	12.1

this trend. The Labour lead over the Conservatives, which had been 32.7 percent as recently as 1966 and 16.4 percent in 1979, is now only 6.5 percent. That makes it lower than in Scotland for the first time in modern electoral history. On the other hand, the Plaid Cymru vote stabilized at 7.8 percent (-0.1 percent compared with 1979), largely because its two incumbent MPs improved their share of the poll. The results of these two elections suggest that the referendum defeat has weakened, though not eliminated, the ethnically determined peculiarities of Welsh party politics, particularly outside the old industrial areas (see Table 13.8).

In contrast, the continuing cultural strength of Welshness was shown in 1981 when the Conservative government announced the creation of a second commercial television channel and the leader of *Plaid Cymru*, Gwynfor Evans, said that unless it was an all-Welsh language channel he would go on a hunger strike. The government capitulated: on its own chosen ground, Welsh nationalism is undefeated.

THE NATIONAL FRONT

Although the National Front's organization covers the whole of Great Britain, its electoral impact is restricted to England. Formed in 1967, it brought together a number of previously rival bodies that aimed at furthering the aims of extreme nationalism, of which the most important were the League of Empire Loyalists, the British National party, and the Greater Britain Movement. These in turn may be regarded as the successors of a series of ultranationalist, imperialist, and xenophobic organizations going back to the beginning of the century—the British Brothers League, founded in 1902 to combat East European Jews in immigration, Mosley's British Union of Fascists in the 1930s, and the post-1945 Union Movement, also led by Mosley.

It may be asked what a party of this kind has in common with either the

TABLE 13.8 Labour Lead over Conservatives in Wales and in the United Kingdom at Four General Elections (in percent)

	Wales	United Kingdom	Difference
Feb. 1974	20.9	-0.7	$+21.6$
Oct. 1974	25.6	3.4	$+22.2$
1979	16.4	-7.0	$+23.4$
1983	6.5	-14.8	$+21.3$

SNP or Plaid Cymru. True, all three are "nationalist." While both the SNP and Plaid Cymru have members or supporters with extreme ethnocentric views, and while some Scottish or Welsh nationalists (always disavowed by the SNP and the Plaid) advocate violence, there is no doubt that the SNP and the Plaid accept a pluralistic social and political structure and competitive party politics, while the National Front does not. It can be properly classified as an extremist party in the sense that its outlook is monist, fundamentalist, and conspiratorial, and as an extremist party of the right in that it advocates an authoritarian state under charismatic leadership, national self-sufficiency with crossclass solidarity, and differential access to resources and power in accordance with a discriminatory ideology.

As with the SNP and the Plaid, the distinctiveness of the program risks repelling more supporters than it attracts. In the British political culture, an addiction to violence and intolerance is a drawback. The norms of British public life favor moderation, free speech, and nonviolence; while everyday behavior may not live up to these norms, the norms enjoy wide acceptance. The National Front's most militant opponents have exploited this vulnerability, calling themselves the Anti-Nazi League. Survey evidence suggests that 90 percent of electors would not consider voting for a National Front candidate even if he seemed well placed under the British plurality system (Harrop and Zimmerman, 1977: 12–13). This contrasts with the greater attractiveness of the SNP and the Plaid, whose generalized patriotism made it easy for discontented voters to desert their own party without having to cross over to the enemy, and which are more attractive for "tactical" voting.

We have now to examine the principal components of National Front ideology and to ask to what degree, if any, these are instrumental in attracting support. They are

1. Biological determinism, entailing a hierarchy of races and genetically justified male dominance
2. Anti-Communism and antiliberalism
3. Anti-internationalism, entailing opposition to all supranational organizations, including the EEC and the Commonwealth ("a bastardized ant-heap")
4. A belief in a Zionist world conspiracy
5. Implacable hostility to all nonwhite immigration, and the advocacy of enforced repatriation of all nonwhite immigrants, and their descendants, already in Britain (Taylor, 1982: 64–81, esp. 76).

The National Front supports the often-observed phenomenon that the smaller a party is, the greater its output of theoretical materials. Most of the ideological literature it produces, however, is intended for the committed membership: its purpose is to integrate rather than convert. Its popular publications concentrate overwhelmingly on race and are filled with horror stories about the consequences of colored immigration. Its image is therefore that of a single-issue party, although its belief system is, as we have seen, multifaceted.

The level of its electoral following, and that of its predecessors and rivals, is more difficult to measure than that of the SNP, Plaid Cymru, and Liberals. Shortage of funds and the lack of a systematic organization mean that the NF and its cousins fight elections on a haphazard basis. If we assumed that an NF or NF-related vote is a specific response to a perceived threat from immigration, we should expect it to correlate with the following events:

1. The race riots in Nottingham and London (Notting Hill) in 1958.
2. The main wave of colored immigration in the late fifties and early sixties, peaking in 1960 when there was a net inflow of 100,000 from the New Commonwealth.
3. Immigration waves of Asians with British passports from East Africa: Kenya in 1967; Uganda in 1972; Malawi in 1976.
4. Enoch Powell's "rivers of blood" speech of 1968, warning of the consequences of permitting further immigration.
5. The 1981 riots in Brixton, Liverpool, and elsewhere.

In part it could be argued that the major parties were quick to preempt antiimmigrant electoral attractiveness by passing restrictive legislation, thus limiting the NF's appeal, but yielding to some of its arguments. Similarly, a number of Conservative candidates and MPs, though not as a rule the leadership, have endorsed antiimmigrant stands. On the other hand, the major parties also sponsored antidiscrimination legislation, which is, of course, anathema to the NF.

Some isolated NF successes at by-elections (8.2 percent in Uxbridge, West London, in 1972; 16.0 percent in West Bromwich, near Birmingham, in 1963) have coincided with peaks in Liberal voting. The peak which the NF achieved in municipal elections in 1975–77 coincided with the SNP-Plaid peak already noticed, but its best year, 1976, also coincided with publicity over the Malawi Asians' arrival. But even the NF's peaks have been scattered. In 1976 it scored between 10 percent and 20 percent in three cities with high immigrant populations (Bradford, Leicester, and West Bromwich) but failed to make headway in others with similar density. In 1977 it scored between 10 percent and 20 percent in ten constituencies in the Greater London Council elections. An aggregate data analysis of this election showed that a high proportion of manual workers was the only characteristic that correlated strongly with a high NF vote: a high level of immigration, or of unemployment or other forms of deprivation did not correlate (Whiteley, 1979: 370–80; Steed, 1978: 282–93). The reason for this is that high NF votes were concentrated in the north-eastern quadrant of London, i.e., the old London docks area, the principal arrival point for immigrants and the principal stronghold of both the British Brothers League and the British Union of Fascists. In other strongly working-class and high immigration areas of London, e.g., Brixton, Brent, Southall, the NF polled poorly. It could therefore be argued that the success of the NF in the 1977 G.L.C. election was the revival of a local tradition rather than a new phenomenon.

In 1979 the NF vote fell, as did that of all minor or protest parties in Britain. In Greater London it scored 2.1 percent, compared with 4.2 percent in October 1974 and 5.3 percent in the G.L.C. election. In the area of its best performance in the G.L.C. election, there was an exceptionally high swing to the Conservatives of 13.1 percent in 1979, over twice the national average. However, it would be rash to conclude that many working-class Labour defectors used the NF as a way station to the Conservatives (Husbands, 1984: 254-55).

As far as the attitudes of NF supporters are concerned (based on a sample of young white males in East London), the overwhelming characteristic is hostility to colored immigrants. There was also majority disapproval of Common Market membership (but not much greater than in the control sample), and stronger minority support for violent protest than in the control sample; on the other hand, there was a rather low level of support (one-third) for anti-Semitic views (*New Society*, April 27, 1978: 186–93; Harrop, England, and Husbands, 1980: 271-81). One curious aspect of protest voting is that the NF and the Liberal party, despite their obvious ideological antagonism, appear to be competing for a section of the same protest vote: at least some of the fluctuation in NF support—but probably not more than 2 percent—can be attributed to Liberal intervention or withdrawal in a given constituency (Butler and Kavanagh, 1975: 351; Steed, 1978: 284–85). The NF's successes during the 1970s were obtained almost exclusively in urban, indeed metropolitan, areas. In this respect it differs from many contemporary and earlier parties of the radical right that have flourished in small-town and rural environments, suburbs, or retirement communities. Its almost entirely plebeian character and its inability to recruit any elite or opinion-guiding public figure severely limited its constituency. If there is a more diffuse, nationalist-authoritarian sentiment in provincial England, it would have to be tapped by a more respectable force, like the American New Right, directed against trade unions and left-wing intellectuals rather than immigrants. For the moment, it looks as though it would be hard for such a force to compete against Mrs.

Thatcher's Conservative party. The NF therefore failed to achieve the necessary prerequisite of a protest movement of the radical right, that of mobilizing the generalized feeling of cultural and political malaise and national pessimism which was undoubtedly in the air.

The evidence—granted its patchiness—is that NF voting has many of the characteristics of SNP and Plaid voting. There is no evidence that the hostility to colored immigration has fluctuated significantly in the past twenty years, though the intensity of this can be briefly affected by particular incidents. There is no evidence that any other issue attracts casual support to the NF, as opposed to hard-core committed members. There is some evidence that the curve of NF support has run parallel with that for other protest parties and that some of the NF vote is interchangeable with that for other protest parties, but that the cutoff point for NF support is much lower than that of other protest parties: not more than 5 percent nationally, in all probability.

GENERAL CONSIDERATIONS

In their introduction to this volume, Kay Lawson and Peter Merkl say "it may be that the institution of party is gradually disappearing, slowly being replaced by new political structures more suitable for the economic and technological realities of twenty-first-century politics." This proposition is quite frequently advanced in an American context. According to Frank Sorauf, "Political life in the United States without the guiding dominance of two assertive political parties is not unthinkable," and Walter Dean Burnham has talked of "a critical re-alignment to end all critical re-alignments" (Sorauf, 1980: 408; Chambers and Burnham, 1975: 308).

There is little sign of such a development in Britain or anywhere else in Western Europe. To be sure, party loyalties are less intense than before, and subcultures and encampments give fewer cues to individual behavior. There is no lack of pressure groups and single-issue coalitions, and in Britain, at least, such lobbies, at times very powerful ones, date back to the middle of the nineteenth century. Nor is it difficult to collect vast crowds these days on at least some issues—disarmament and nuclear energy spring to mind most readily. But that is not the same as saying that such movements have replaced parties on an American scale. The principal reasons for that are organizational and cultural. Parties have greater historical strength in Europe, including Britain. The technological facilities for cheap mass-mailing and mass-telephoning are less widespread in Europe, and one suspects that there would be greater antipathy to such campaign methods than has been experienced in America. Given the greater salience of parties in British public life, then, it is not surprising that party failure leads in the first place to more parties.

The evidence I have presented here suggests that it was the decline of the traditional parties that caused the rise of the newer parties, not the other way round. Of the various factors that have been adduced for the decline of traditional party loyalties in the developed world, some at least seem to apply to Britain in the 1970s. "Postindustrial" values appear to have little to do with it, except insofar as a new search for personal identity, expressed in the revival of cultural tradition and a sense of ethnic allegiance, falls into that category. A more familiar factor is boredom or tiredness with a cartel of existing parties, which between them carve up interest representations in an immobile pattern and bar access to new concerns or even new types of individuals. While this cartel has never, in Britain, reached the dimensions of the West German Parteienstaat or Italian Partitocrazia, one symptom of this alienation, the failure to pass party identification on to the next generation is evident (see Peter Merkl's concluding essay). Both the SNP and the National Front appealed disproportionately to younger voters, to a degree that cannot be explained by a disproportionate attractiveness of their programs to these age groups.

The ebb and flow of protest voting over the past two decades has been strikingly well synchronized, which seems to confirm that it is in the defects of the established parties rather than in the merits of the nonestablished that we have to seek our explanation.

The first peak, that of 1962–63, affected the Liberals in both England and Scotland and the SNP. It did not affect Wales, probably through lack of opportunity. The National Front had not yet been founded, but one of its predecessors, the British National party, polled quite well.

The second peak, that of 1966–68, also affected the Liberals, but most of all the Plaid Cymru and the SNP, both of whom entered Parliament and local government at this stage. The third peak, at the approach of the 1974 general election, affected all minor parties, bringing them by-election and local government gains; and in contrast with the earlier peaks, they consolidated these gains at the general elections, giving them unprecedented parliamentary representation. The fourth peak, that of 1976–77, affected all three ethnic protest parties, but not the Liberals who at that time were supporting the Callaghan government in Parliament.

Not only did these surges coincide, they were to some degree interchangeable. The SNP and Plaid votes often came in places where the Liberals had previously done well and were on occasion inhibited by surviving Liberal strength. Conversely, in 1983 the SDP/Liberal Alliance did exceptionally poorly in SNP and Plaid strongholds. There are even indications that, at the margin, National Front and Liberal votes were interchangeable, but it will not do to suppose that all we have here is an undifferentiated protest vote, randomly attributable to any candidate. To assume this would imply that the parties' policies had no effect at all on their ability to attract votes.

As far as we can tell, the demands for some kind of political autonomy in Scotland and Wales have a long history and have varied little in extent or intensity; the same applies to hostility to colored immigration. As long as other parties could effectively articulate these special claims, there was no reason why low SNP/Plaid/NF support should not coexist with quite high levels of nationalist consciousness. What happened in the 1960s and 1970s was that declining partisan allegiance and weak governmental performance by both main parties made previously marginal parties more attractive. Once these had irrupted into electoral competition, the major parties felt obliged to respond with concessions to their policy demands.

That these demands played some part in electoral fortunes is shown by the timing of the ethnic protest surges. These did indeed coincide with troughs of the government parties' popularity, but only approximately so. The Labour Government's lowest ratings occurred in 1975 and 1977; however, the National Front's vote peaked in 1976, presumably in response to the Malawi Asians' scare, while the SNP's curve followed the fortunes of the government's devolution plans as much as of its macroeconomic management.

Other interpretations of these protest votes, particularly those of the mid-seventies, have also been advanced. At one level the protest is generalized: it is against the failure of macroeconomic management. At another, the generalized protest has a local dimension: it is against the failure of Labour to fulfill its role as the advocate of relatively deprived regions and inner cities. At yet another it is also against the dissonance between political practice and popular needs: in Scotland and Wales it is a vote against overgovernment and bureaucratic insensitivity and a vote for locality, community, and politics with a human face; in the inner cities it is a cry of disillusionment by working-class voters, especially the young and unskilled, with a Labour party that has lost touch. These last hypotheses are plausible and attractive, but they are hardly verifiable and must remain speculative.

CONCLUSION

Which, if any, of the hypotheses we started with have been supported by the evidence?

1. The principal reasons for "party failure" in Britain appear to be the

growing secularization of the electorate, the diminution of the traditional parties' natural constituency, and the poor performance of the British economy. The first two are beyond the control of politicians: they could, at best, hope to compensate for them by high-quality economic management, which they increasingly failed to do in the 1960s and 1970s.

2. The character of the failure is therefore general, rather than related to specific policy areas; it has so far damaged the parties, but not, to any noticeable degree, confidence in the parliamentary system of government.

3. The electoral gains by minor parties have in the main coincided with points of special unpopularity of the governing party and the unattractiveness of the opposition, rather than the rise in popularity of the minor parties' special concerns.

4. There is no evidence that demand for the distinctive policies espoused by the minor parties has significantly risen during the period under review.

5. However, the rise of the minor parties put these policies higher on the agenda: fear of further electoral losses obliged both parties to offer concessions, especially to the Scottish and Welsh electorates.

6. Although class accounts for the principal cleavage throughout Great Britain, periphery-center conflicts, enhanced in Scotland and Wales by national identity, provide a further cleavage, traditionally to the benefit of the Liberal and Labour parties.

7. Failure in macroeconomic management is particularly injurious to deprived regions, which in Britain include Wales and (preoil) Scotland; a party that emphasizes the national/regional/peripheral dimension of politics therefore becomes an attractive substitute for major parties that had previously tried to articulate that dimension.

8. Nationalism in Scotland is directed primarily to state-institutional ends, in Wales to cultural-linguistic ends. Support for nationalism in Wales is therefore more stable, but constrained by the unattractiveness of the language claims.

9. Support for the National Front is also related to general perceptions of party failure, but its narrower policy demands and extremist image repelled a greater proportion of electors than nationalism in Scotland and Wales.

10. The rise of ethnic protest parties in Britain was a consequence, not a cause, of the weakening of the traditional class parties. Once they had irrupted into electoral competition, their claims, for which there had long been latent demand, increased in political salience. However, these claims had high priority for only a minority of the relevant electorates, and are liable to be displaced again by more traditional issue conflicts.

REFERENCES

Alt, J., I. Crewe, and B. Särlvik. 1977. Angels in plastic: The Liberal surge in 1974. *Political Studies* 25: 366–67.

Balson, D., and I. McAllister. 1979. The Scottish and Welsh referenda. *Parliamentary Affairs*, Autumn, 408–409.

Bochel, D., D. Denver, and A. Macartney. 1981. *The referendum experience: Scotland 1979*. Aberdeen: Aberdeen University Press.

Butler, D., and D. Kavanagh. 1975. *The British general election of October 1974*. London: Macmillan.

———. 1980. *The British general election of 1979*. London: Macmillan.

Butt Philip, A. 1975. *The Welsh question: Nationalism in Welsh politics*. Cardiff: University of Wales Press.

Chambers, W. N., and W. D. Burnham. 1975. *The American party systems: Stages of political development*. New York: Oxford University Press.

Forester, T. 1977. Do the British sincerely want to be rich? *New Society*, 28 April.

Foulkes, D., J. Jones, and R. A. Wilford. 1983. *The Welsh veto. The Wales Act 1978 and the referendum*. Cardiff: University of Wales Press.

Franklin, M. N. 1985. *The decline of class voting in Britain: Changes in the basis of electoral choice*. Oxford: Oxford University Press.

Goodhart, C.A.E., and R. J. Bhansali. 1970. Political economy. *Political studies*, March.

Guthrie, R., and I. McLean. 1978. Another part of the periphery: Reactions to devolution in an English development area. *Parliamentary Affairs*, Spring.

Harrop, M., and G. Zimmerman. 1977. Anatomy of the National Front. *Patterns of Prejudice*, July–August.

———, J. England, and C. Husbands. 1980. The bases of National Front support. *Political Studies*, June.

Husbands, C. 1984. When the bubble burst: Transient and persistent supporters of the National Front. In *British Journal of Political Science*, October.

LaPalombara, J., and M. Weiner, eds. 1966. *Political parties and political development*. Princeton: Princeton University Press.

Miller, W. L. 1977. *Electoral dynamics in Britain since 1918*. London: Macmillan.

———. 1981. *The end of British politics? Scots and English political behaviour in the seventies*. Oxford: Oxford University Press.

———, B. Särlvik, I. Crewe, and J. Alt. 1977. The connection between SNP voting and the demand for Scottish self-government. *European Journal of Political Research*, June, 93–94.

Morgan, K. O. 1963. *Wales in British politics, 1868–1922*. Cardiff: University of Wales Press.

The National Front and the young: A special survey. 1978. *New Society*, April 27.

Pelling, H. 1967. *The social geography of British elections, 1885–1910*. London: Macmillan.

Rose, R. 1980. *Class does not equal party: The decline of a model of British voting*. Glasgow: Centre for the Study of Public Policy.

Särlvik, B., and I. Crewe. 1983. *Decade of dealignment: The conservative victory in 1979 and electoral trends in the 1970's*. Cambridge: Cambridge University Press.

Sorauf, F. J. 1984. *Party politics in America*, 5th ed. Boston: Little, Brown.

Steed, M. 1978. The National Front vote. *Parliamentary Affairs*, Summer.

Taylor, S. 1982. *The National Front in English politics*. London: Macmillan.

Whiteley, P. 1979. The National Front's vote in the 1977 G.L.C. elections: An aggregate data analysis. *British Journal of Political Science*, July.

FOURTEEN

The National Democratic Party of Alabama and Party Failure in America

HANES WALTON, JR.

Nearly all scholars agree that one of the crucial indicators and symptoms of major party decline in contemporary twentieth-century America is voter turnout. Voter turnout is steadily decreasing and has reached the point where little more than half those eligible to vote take part even in presidential elections. Scholarly observers of this decline have noted that in terms of actual numbers and percentages, the potential voters are "not supporting one candidate or party or the other. Rather these people are withdrawing from the electorate. . . . The American electorate of the late twentieth century is a 'turned-off' electorate" (Crotty and Jacobson, 1980: 3–7; Fishel, 1978: xi–xxviii).

When an effort is made to analyze the reasons for this continuous decline in turnout, a variety of answers is suggested. For some, the problem lies in the new technology of politics; for others the decline is related to registration barriers; still others stress split-ticket voting, the increased salience of issues, and the role of the media as causes for the decline. (Rusk, 1974: 1028–49; Rosenstone and Wolfinger, 1978: 22–45; Hadley, 1978, passim; Wolfinger and Rosenstone, 1980, passim; Crotty and Jacobson, 1980: 20).

However, when one shifts from a search for national causes to regional explanations, it is often easier to pinpoint the reasons for the decline. In the South, for example, it is clear that the registration practices initiated to halt and limit "Black Reconstruction" were one of the prime causes for the decline in turnout. Southern whites wanted to regain control of the region's politics after the implementation of the Fifteenth Amendment, and did so by instituting "stiff registration standards [that] allowed them constitutionally to disenfranchise blacks . . . and to again assume the political reins within their states" (Crotty and Jacobson, 1980: 20).

The end result of this activity was not only a decline in turnout but also the decline of the major parties in each of the southern states. The Republican party was literally destroyed as a competitive political organization, and the Democratic party survived in only a very modified form. Political parties ceased to be key political institutions in the South for more than half a century.

THE THEORIES OF PARTY FAILURE AND THE NDPA

There are four theories advanced in this volume about party failure: (1) Lawson's idea that failure is related to linkage breakdown, (2) Merkl's belief that failure is due to lack of competition and a perception of a crisis of ungovernability, (3) Rose's and Mackie's notion that bad or incorrect voluntary choices made by party leadership between external and internal goals lead to failure, and finally (4) the idea that failure need not be permanent, but can lead to rejuvenation and regeneration and replacement. Each of these theories is useful for one or more of the studies included in this volume. However, what is surprising here is that all four theories in combination offer a better and much more comprehensive and systematic picture of what happened in the case of the NDPA than any single theory. Thus, we shall look at the NDPA in light of those four theories.

Kay Lawson's theory that the major party's failure "to provide acceptable forms of linkage" between the citizen and the state is what usually gives rise to an alternative organization correctly describes what occurred in Alabama. And the Lawson/Merkl definition of a communitarian organization as an "organization that is formed by members of an ethnic or religious community in an effort to protect their rights in a larger society" more than aptly describes and characterizes the NDPA and its emergence in the state of Alabama.

Yet the special circumstances surrounding the NDPA do not stop there. In Alabama, there was a lack of political competition because it was essentially a one-party state (it still is today); therefore blacks had very few options and alternatives in terms of political entities except to form and fashion a new political organization to challenge the government which governed without their input and participation and involvement. Professor Merkl's thesis fits these realities well. A lack of political competition gave the activists who formed the NDPA no other choice but to develop a new and viable political alternative. Thus, both Merkl's and Lawson's theories, which are seemingly different, adequately cover different aspects of the NDPA's case.

Rose's and Mackie's theory—that party failure can result when party leaders make poor voluntary choices between external and internal goals—helps to further clarify what happened to the Alabama Democratic party. When the leaders of this party fashioned it as an organization that would preserve and maintain a segregated society, such a choice inevitably led to a political climate in which the question of an alternative organization could be raised. Ultimately, the choice or path taken by the regular or major party led to its own demise and failure.

And finally, the theory advanced by Frank Wilson further explains the NDPA situation and particularly what is happening to the regular Democratic party in the state. The party has and is currently undergoing rejuvenation, regeneration, and replacement. It has been forced to move from its stance as a party of whites which stood for white supremacy to a party which includes blacks and some of their aspirations. Needless to say, the party now invites black support, and permits some black leadership. Basically speaking, the party has allowed its original goals and objectives to be significantly modified and changed, and in so doing is now approaching Wilson's contention that parties can, after their failure, regenerate and replace themselves.

In conclusion then, all four theories when taken in combination can dramatically explain the nature and scope and significance of party decline and failure and the emergence of the NDPA in Alabama. Each theory offers special insights and together they provide a comprehensive picture of the situation in Alabama that will more than adequately guide the reader through the specifics of this case study.

The Failure of Political Parties in Alabama

To approach and understand the demise and failure of the major parties in a single southern state, Alabama, one must be able to grasp the irony of the situation. And to do that, two pertinent questions must be asked and answered. First, how did the major parties set into motion the forces and counterforces that led to their own decline and transformation in the state? Second, when did this decline start and when did it stop—or seem to stop? To begin with, one must appreciate the fact that the major parties in the state in no way consciously planned for their own decline or transformation. They planned for success, continuation, hegemony, and the perpetuation of strongly held values about white supremacy. Yet in the process of pursuing these goals, they set into motion the very forces that would insure their own decline.

Voter turnout and participation in Alabama from 1824 to 1860 were very high and at times exceeded the level achieved in the nation as a whole (see Figure 14.1). However, in 1861 Alabama seceded from the Union in order to maintain the institution of slavery, and things changed drasti-

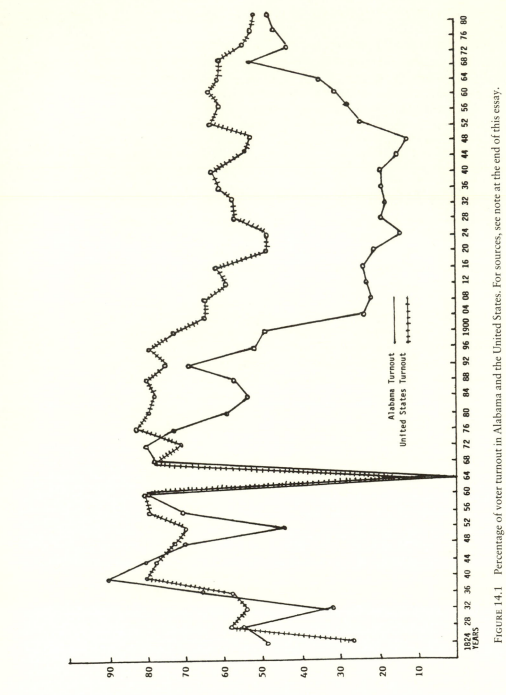

FIGURE 14.1   Percentage of voter turnout in Alabama and the United States. For sources, see note at the end of this essay.

cally. The question of slavery had become a central political issue for both major parties. Each state party formulated its own posture and stand on the issue, and the ensuing political and military conflict altered the nature and pattern of political parties in the state. V. O. Key described Alabama party evolution during this period as follows: "In the debates over secession a party realignment occurred. The slave holders of the black belt became Democrats and eventually carried the state for secession, but the northern and southeastern whites went along reluctantly" (Key, 1949: 45).

The new political equation wrought by the conflict brought blacks in as new political participants by 1868 and political participation in Alabama was once again high, as shown in Figure 14.1. Four years later, in 1872, it had increased to such a point that the rate of participation in the state again exceeded that in the nation as a whole. However, two years later, whites regained control of the state government and by 1876 political participation had begun to decline. Of these times, Rayford Logan writes, "So determined were most white Southerners to maintain their own way of life that they resorted to fraud, intimidation and murder in order to reestablish their own control of the state government" (Logan, 1965: 21).

According to Logan, "White rule was restored [in Alabama] in 1874 . . . not even the presence of Federal troops was able to prevent the achievement, by force, of 'home rule' " (ibid.). As Senator Pugh of Alabama said, "no power—no public opinion, state, federal or military force—could stop whites from preventing Negroes from voting." For the senator, this steadfast determination to deny blacks the right to vote was a "gift of God" (Logan, 1965: 77).

Speaking of all the southern states, Key noted, "Force and threat of force had put the whites in power. Within 10 or 15 years after 1867 the . . . enfranchisement of the Negro was largely undone, and undone by veritable revolution" (Key, 1949: 536). It was a revolution of extralegalism and violence, augmented by legal techniques and devices, as white legislators "contrived devious electoral procedures to nullify the efforts of blacks who still had the inclination to vote" (ibid.). The black-belt whites reestablished themselves and the Democratic party in power. And as they did so, voter turnout steadily declined. Except for a brief rise in turnout in 1892, the year of the populist revolt in the state (see Gaither, 1977: 104–10), political participation continued to fall under the weight of the first stage of disfranchisement (see Figure 14.1).

The second stage of disfranchisement came in 1901 when Alabama adopted a new constitution explicitly designed to take all blacks off the voting rolls. In accomplishing this, the new constitution eliminated numerous white voters as well, a fact that caused some serious opposition to its adoption. Nevertheless, the new constitution was ratified by a narrow margin, after which voter turnout (both black and white) was even more depressed. The pattern of declining participation continued until the 1965 Voting Rights Act took effect in the state. The herculean efforts of isolated black leaders and legal victories by civil rights groups were able to raise voter turnout and participation only in a minimal way in the state (Brittain, 1959: 196–99, and 1962: 127–38).

The disfranchisement of blacks was not intended to cause the decline of white political participation, but such was its effect. Although, as C. Vann Woodward has pointed out, it was widely believed that disfranchisement would "enable white men to divide freely on fundamental issues," in practice removing blacks from the rolls hastened the demise of the lively and competitive two-party system Alabama had maintained prior to 1860 (Woodward, 1951: 348).

The decline of two-party competitiveness in Alabama had begun well before the campaign to disfranchise blacks was undertaken. The first serious crack in the two-party system was the emergence of a strong third party, the Populist party, during the recession crisis of the 1880s. Following the war, the Republican party took a strong lead in two successive presidential elections (1868 and 1872). But by 1876, thanks in large measure to the politics of disfranchisement, both Republicans and Populists had nearly disappeared from state politics, and the Democratic party had assumed the position of dominance it was to maintain without serious interruption for over seventy years.

In 1948, the national Democratic party took a more liberal stance on the issue of civil rights, a development that prompted Alabama Democrats to switch their allegiance to the new splinter group of Democratic segregationists, the Dixiecrats. In 1964, and 1972, when the national Democrats took increasingly more progressive stands on the rights of black Americans, white Alabama Democrats again turned in large numbers to available alternatives—to the "Free Electors" or to the Republicans in 1964, to the American Independent party in 1968, and back to the Republicans in 1972 and 1980 (see Figure 14.2).

In sum, the disfranchisement tactics of Alabama's Democratic party— and the failure of the state's Republican party to offer an alternative stance on the racial issue—meant that shortly after the Civil War, party politics in Alabama was dominated by the ideology of white supremacy. As the party more strongly associated with this doctrine, the Democrats were soon able to create a noncompetitive party system, a single-party state. However, such a party system, based on a single issue, generated very low political participation. Furthermore, it was a party system dependent on an electorate quite erratic in its partisan loyalties—support of

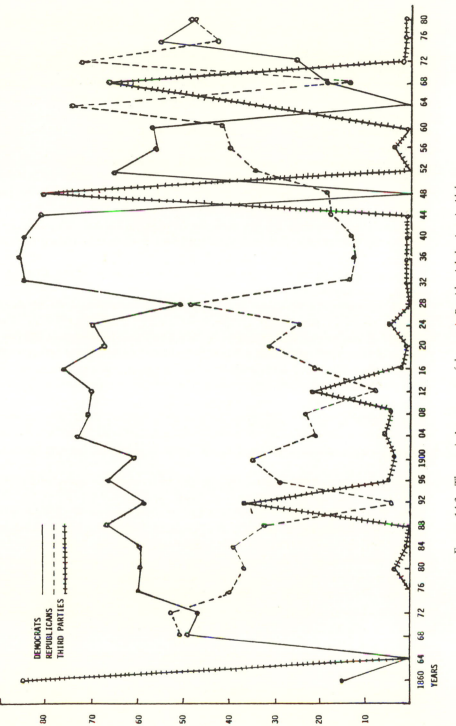

FIGURE 14.2   The parties' percentage of the vote in Presidential elections in Alabama.

the national party was a function of commitment to the ideology of white supremacy. Whenever the national party's stance on this issue wavered, instant realignment in favor of a third party of the Republicans could and did take place. Combined, these factors ensured major party failure in the state.

However, the state's behavior and its shifting role in presidential politics is only part of the story. When the analysis shifts from national to state and local elections, the capacity of the above factors to function as depressants of political participation and harbingers of party failure becomes even more pronounced. In Figure 14.3, the actual votes cast in the Democratic gubernatorial primaries from 1922 until 1982 are juxtaposed with the total voting age populations. What immediately stands out is how few persons voted from 1922 until 1950, even though the number of whites of voting age and the total voting age population steadily increased. Had blacks been able to vote, and had they voted, political participation would, of course, have been far greater.

The same pattern—of depressed political participation as a result of black disfranchisement—is apparent in trends in black registration from 1867 through 1980 (see Figure 14.4). With the adoption of the 1901 constitution, black registration fell precipitously, then increased only slowly and erratically until 1947, when the white primary was abolished, at which point it began the steady upward trend that continues today.

This situation is further illuminated and illustrated in Figure 14.5, which juxtaposes the turnout in Democratic gubernatorial primaries with the percentage of blacks registered to vote in the state from 1922 until 1982. For the first two decades, the percentage of blacks registered to vote remained significantly below one percent. In fact, although the group shows one percent, the actual percentage of blacks registered to vote stood at about one-half of one percent in 1946. And between 1922 and 1946, turnout in gubernatorial races remained almost constant at 19.5 percent. On the other hand, the moment the percentage of registered black voters began rising, turnout increased, to the point where in 1966—one year after the passage of the Voting Rights Act—the two lines in the graph nearly meet. In short, throughout the forty-four-year period from 1922 to 1966, the party was able to limit the electorate to a narrow elite of white voters. But once these tactics of repression were eliminated by Federal intervention, the entire system all but exploded with participation.

At the same time that the ruling white Democrats were suppressing voter registration and participation, they were also restructuring the party organization in a fashion to ensure continued white dominance. This remaking of the major party's organizational structure evolved gradually in a piecemeal fashion; eventually, it encompassed setting requirements for

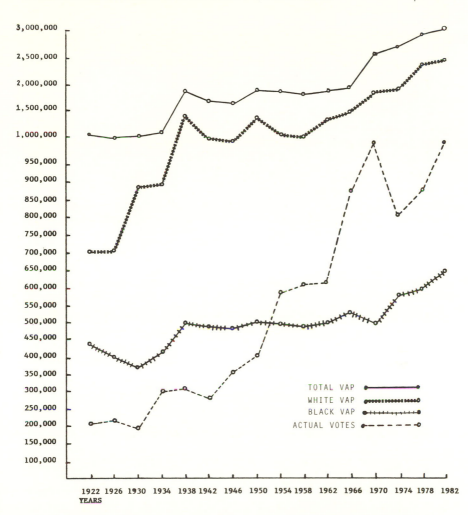

FIGURE 14.3 Total voting age population (VAP), white voting age population, black voting age population, and voter turnout in the Democratic gubernatorial primaries, 1922–1982.

membership and officeholding, as well as restructuring the party's relationship to the state's governmental machinery. In a series of votes, directives, and other actions, the party's State Executive Committee succeeded in preventing blacks from joining the party and from holding office. The latter ban was accomplished by requiring all prospective state elected officials to file political candidate forms that contained a "white only" clause (Brittain, 1957: 206). In case any further discouragement was re-

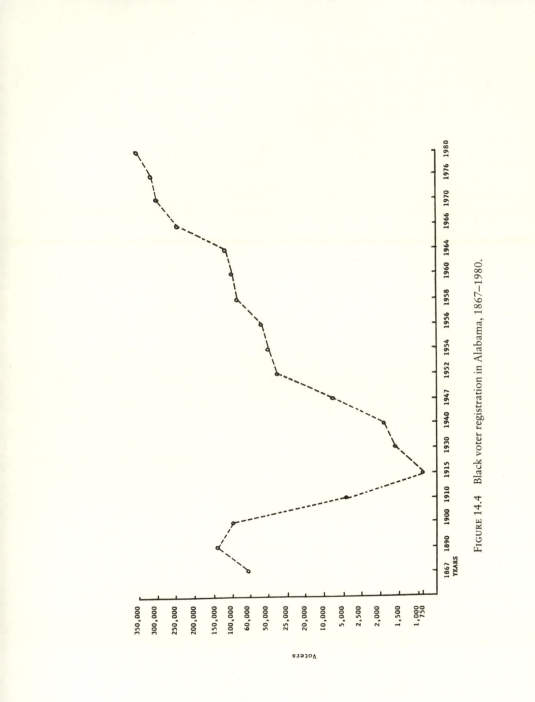

FIGURE 14.4 Black voter registration in Alabama, 1867–1980.

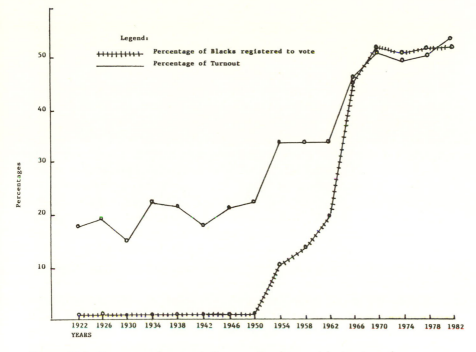

FIGURE 14.5 Percentage of turnout in Democratic gubernatorial primaries and percentage of blacks registered to vote, 1922–1980.

quired, the Executive Committee adopted as the party's emblem a crowing rooster saying "White Supremacy for the Right"; in addition, the party's constitution required all members to promise to uphold racial segregation and the principles of white supremacy. It was not until January 22, 1966, that the committee, under pressure from Alabamian blacks and the National Democratic party, changed its slogan to "Democrats of the Rights" (Walton, 1972: 149–50). Even then, the change was essentially cosmetic, since blacks were still not invited into the party's organizational structure.

The party's techniques—if they may be termed such—for leadership recruitment were equally faithful to the principles and rhetoric of white supremacy. When these procedures came under severe attack from outsiders, the party's response was to elevate their most unrepentant white supremacists to positions of leadership—the rise of George C. Wallace in state politics is a case in point. Ultimately, the party elevated this ardent segregationist to a position of such power and esteem within the state that he was able to undertake a personal effort to capture, refocus, and change the policies and direction of the national Democratic party. His efforts, although they ended in failure, endured from 1964 through the presidential primaries of 1976, and were not without considerable impact on both national parties and their leadership.

Not suprisingly, the party used the state's governmental machinery to reinforce white supremacy and its own place in power. To begin with, its elected leaders made certain that the registration process was party controlled. Three persons in each county were appointed to the County Registration Board by the governor and two state officials, for terms of four years, but could be removed "by same without reason given" (Lewinson, 1963: 222–23). This meant that if any county board appeared "too friendly," admitting what the state party leaders considered to be too many blacks to the rolls, its members could be removed without any justification. In addition, each county had an elected probate judge whose own involvement in matters of registration gave him the power to counteract the impact of any board that showed signs of violating the principles of white supremacy.

Similar techniques and devices were developed for primary regulations, state election procedures, and the entire legislative and judicial system that undergirded and managed the process. In fact, even the state's congressional delegations were pressed into service to ensure that no serious substantive attacks came from outside the state to alter the patterns of Alabama politics (Key, 1949: 345–85). And while the legal and organizational edifice was being carefully structured, quasi-political organizations like the Ku Klux Klan and the white citizen councils were developed to assist and aid the major party in its control over the state's political process. Many high-ranking major party leaders simultaneously held positions of authority and power in these quasi-political organizations.

However, just as preventing black citizens from voting had the effect of weakening overall political participation, so restructuring the party and its role in government in order to maximize implementation of the principles of white supremacy had unexpected negative results. The party focused so ardently on maintaining the dominance of white Alabamans that it neglected to meet the economic and social needs of its supporters. At the same time, party leaders remained oblivious to the major shifts in public opinion that were taking place on the racial issue. In a time when the civil rights revolution and the black social revolution were shifting from protest to politics, and when national civil rights politics was dramatically changing the "southern way of life," the state party leadership persisted in attempting to revive and shore up the practices of the past. The net result was short-term success in maintaining white supremacy, coupled with undeniable failure in addressing the state's major economic and social problems and in responding to the more egalitarian spirit of the times.

THE COMING OF THE NATIONAL DEMOCRATIC PARTY OF ALABAMA

When parties fail, other organizations emerge, first to expose and propagandize the weaknesses of the major parties, second to attempt to place their own representatives in power. Even when these new organizations do not succeed in the latter part of their mission, they often have considerable success in the former. This has been particularly true of black political parties, as Samuel D. Cook has noted: "Black political parties have been agents and vehicles of creative dissent and social change. They have challenged the established political order, noted its hypocrisy, insensitivity and neglect, and proclaimed a higher, richer and more inclusive public good, the American Dream and Creed" (Walton, 1972: 7).

The National Democratic Party of Alabama (NDPA), formed in January 1968, provided just such a challenge. The very existence of this new black political party proclaimed the failure of the promises and policies of the regular state party. Furthermore, the creation of the NDPA disrupted the traditional patterns of linkage between the citizens of Alabama, the regular state party, and the National Democratic party. According to Hardy T. Frye, it was the emergence of NDPA that stimulated moderate white leaders in the regular party to pull away from that organization, dominated as it was by the supporters of Wallace, and from the Alabama Independent Democratic party (AIDP). Like the NDPA, the AIDP challenged the regular state party at the 1968 national convention and won some seats and considerable recognition (Frye, 1980: 71–80).

Furthermore, by issuing such challenges at the national convention and in congressional races, the NDPA was able to play an important part in the series of protests that inspired the national party to set up the McGovern–Fraser Commission and ultimately to adopt, on that commission's recommendation, guidelines that had the effect of seriously altering the old relationship between the state parties and the national party, strengthening the latter at the expense of the former.

Finally, the creation of the NDPA forced black leaders and voters to reconsider their own patterns of participation. Now, instead of the unsatisfactory alternatives of abstaining, voting for the candidates of a weak minority party, or giving the Wallace faction their support, they had the options of supporting the NDPA or the AIDP. In short, the coming of the

NDPA forced a realignment of the electorate and set in motion a new configuration in state politics.

The primary goal of the NDPA was to increase political participation in the state, and particularly black participation. This twofold purpose is apparent in all the party's founding documents, in legal documents as the party pursued its ends through the courts, in conventions and congressional challenges, in all the extant speeches of its leaders, in its newspaper, *The Eagle Eye*, and in its platforms. In each of these documents the party promised to assure full political participation for all citizens of the state. The party's constitution stressed the same overriding principle: "all voters in the State of Alabama have the right to vote for any and all major candidates for the highest offices in our land . . . any breach or obligation of this right is an *inexcusable violation of the public trust*, regardless of the financial, political or social station of the persons who have allowed such a situation to exist in fact" (Walton, 1972: 257).

The party was eminently successful in meeting this objective. Once it entered the electoral process in Alabama, political participation increased dramatically in the state. Figure 14.6 makes clear the huge increase in turnout for congressional, presidential, and gubernatorial elections in 1968 and thereafter. The increases in 1968 are unparalleled in state history, and the level of voting that this pivotal year established has continued for nearly two decades, with only slight decreases.

The data in Table 14.1 suggest the dimensions of the NDPA contribution to these improved rates of turnout. It is, of course, possible that those who voted for the NDPA in the 1968, 1970, 1972, 1974, 1976, 1980, and 1982 elections would have been stimulated to vote even if that choice had not been available, but such a supposition, given the continuing segregationist tone of major party politics, strains our credibility. It seems far more reasonable to assume that the NDPA vote not only captured but inspired the surge in voter turnout that took place in these seven elections.

The NDPA did more than increase black voting turnout in the state. As Earl and Merle Black have noted, the mobilization of blacks by a black third party in a state that emphasized white supremacy had the effect of stimulating more whites to register and vote in an effort to counteract and limit the political advances of blacks (1973: 421–45; see also Boykin, 1973: 51–56).

Furthermore, the party offered its own supporters considerably more than an alternative at the polls. The existence of the party stimulated large numbers of Alabamans who hitherto had no persuasive reason to participate in their state's party politics to offer themselves as candidates, serve as party activists, and/or make financial contributions to the new party. In other cases, the creation of the new black party stimulated those who had

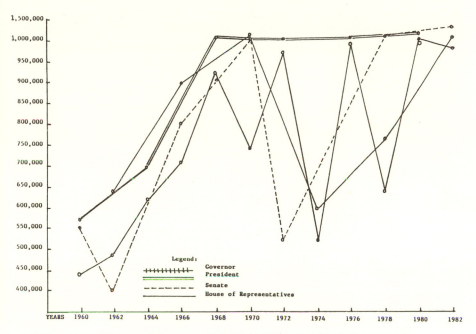

FIGURE 14.6 The general election vote in Alabama for president, senator, congressman, and governor, 1960–1982.

offered such services to the regular state Democratic party to leave that party and make their contributions to the NDPA.

Moreover, the party also provided Alabama's black voters with an important new political ideology: racial consciousness and racial pride. Like black parties elsewhere, it "fostered the notion and ideal of self-help, self-propulsion, group consciousness and solidarity and political sensitivity, awareness and appreciation" (Cook, quoted in Walton, 1972: 7).

Although the NDPA was a black party, it was not an exclusively black party: "Although NDPA had a mostly black constituency, they viewed themselves as a progressive third party and included white members. Describing NDPA, however, the statewide news media continued to emphasize the mostly black nature of the party and this projected the idea that NDPA was only concerned with issues relating to blacks" (Frye, 1980: 162). The party fought this projected image as a distortion of its real efforts and argued that it was a party for all the people of Alabama. However, the preachings of the party's leadership did not match their political rhetoric during campaigns, when the party called openly for black unity at the polls, thereby giving the media and the voters good reason to see the

TABLE 14.1   The NDPA Vote, 1968–1982 (Number of votes, percent of statewide turnout)

Year	Congressional Votes	%	Senatorial Votes	%	Presidential Votes	%	Gubernatorial Votes	%
1968	83,818	9.2	72,699	8.0	54,144	5.2		
1970	67,228	9.1					125,000	12.5
1972	37,610	4.0	31,421	3.0	37,815	3.8		
1974	6,416	1.2						
1976	1,021	.1						
1978	0							
1980	1,743	.2	2,973	.2				
1982							4,693	.004
Total	197,836		107,093		91,959		129,693	
Mean	32,973	4.0	35,698	3.7	45,980	4.5	64,846	6.25

SOURCE: *Guide to U.S. Elections.* Washington, D.C.: Congressional Quarterly, 1976, 861, 866, 871, 876; the 1982 gubernatorial returns were sent to the author by Secretary of State Don Siegelman. Clerk of the House of Representatives, *Statistics of the presidential and congressional elections, 1968, 1972, 1976, and 1980.* Washington, D.C.: Government Printing Office, 1968–80.

party as an all-black entity concerned with essential black issues. Nevertheless, the party's occasional insistence that it was also open to whites, while at the same time stressing race consciousness and the need for black power to offset white power, had the effect of encouraging the old-line black political elite and moderate whites to work together more effectively in Alabama politics than had previously been the case.

Indirectly, the NDPA also provided some momentum for the emerging Republican party in the state and contributed to a somewhat modified stand on civil rights issues among the regular Democrats. Worried by the emergence of this new party and attracted by the ever more conservative stances the national Republican party was taking on civil rights issues and the enforcement of civil rights legislation, conservative whites, particularly those from the black-belt areas of the state, began to move into the state Republican party. The loss of some supporters to the Republicans, and others to the NDPA, forced the state Democrats to change their own tune—for the first time, the party leadership was ready to bring at least a "token" number of blacks into the regular party organization (Seagull, 1975: 88–95; see also Cosman, 1966).

Thus the NDPA was able to stimulate a return to a more competitive party system as well as add a new ideology and consciousness to the state's political culture. But perhaps its most significant role was in realigning and splintering the conservative white political base in the black-belt counties. As Key observed, it was the black-belt whites who were responsible for secession, disfranchisement, the defeat of populism, and the adoption of segregationist policies in all the southern states. It was in such counties that the NDPA concentrated its greatest efforts and had its greatest electoral successes. Figure 14.7 shows the overwhelming number of black elected officials (county, judicial, law enforcement, and education officials) in ten such counties, as compared to the remaining counties in the state. The vast majority of black officials are to be found in the black-belt counties organized and dominated by the NDPA: the remaining few come primarily from the urban areas of the state. In one such county, Green County, the NDPA took full control of every political office (on the other hand, there are still several black-belt counties that have very few or no black elected officials).

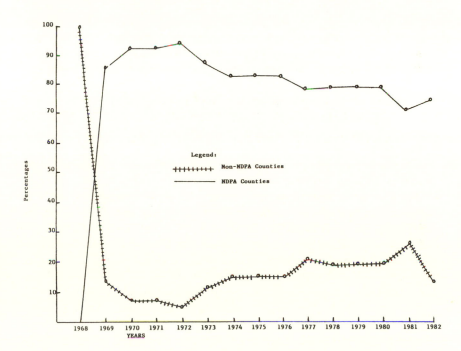

FIGURE 14.7   Percentage of black elected county officials in NDPA-dominated counties and in non-NDPA organized counties.

Thus, even today—long after the party has become nearly dormant in statewide politics, and white control of state legislative offices continues relatively undiminished—the NDPA is able to maintain control over the local politics of several black-belt counties. This in turn means that the black struggle for political power in Alabama has been able to establish a base for future action in the black-belt counties. The power and influence of conservative black-belt whites in Alabama is on the decline, and it can reasonably be expected that Alabama will soon follow the lead of other southern states, where, as Bullock and Henry have noted, "The long established pattern of heavily black districts electing the South's most conservative legislators has been broken" (1981: 22).

A fourth role played by the NDPA is that of reforming and possibly "liberalizing" the state Democratic party and its practices. To begin with, the increase in the number of black Democratic delegates to national conventions—and the shifting balance between the national Democratic and Republican parties on this matter—can be almost directly attributed to the various convention challenges of the NDPA. For one hundred years prior to 1968, the Alabama Democrats had never sent a black delegate to the national convention, whereas the Republicans fairly often seated one to three members of the "Black and Tan" delegations that routinely appeared to challenge that party's regular state delegation. But as a response to the 1968 NDPA convention challenge, the regular state Democratic party included three blacks in its delegation. By 1972, the time of the NDPA's second challenge, the number had risen to ten. In 1976, a year when no NDPA challenge was offered, the number dropped to six, but rose again in 1980 when once again the voices of black dissent were heard (see Table 14.2).

Moreover, the NDPA's continuing efforts to demonstrate to the national party that the regular state party was an illegal organization, discriminating against blacks and failing to provide an adequate representation of the national party within the state of Alabama, have had the effect of forcing the regular party to extend leadership positions in the regular state party's organization and to permit black candidates to file and run on the regular party ticket. That the party's more moderate white leadership was able to bring about these changes during the era of Wallace domination of that organization is a testimony to the strength of the NDPA challenge.

The NDPA has also forced a complete turnaround in the stated policies of the regular party. Over the years, the old party had elevated to leadership only those candidates who promised, promoted, and professed "segregation now and segregation forever" and white supremacy as a way of life. In 1962 the man who symbolized that stance for the state and the na-

TABLE 14.2 The Number of Black Delegates from
Alabama to the National Democratic and Republican
Conventions: 1868–1984

Year	Black Delegates at Democratic Convention	Black Delegates at Republican Convention
1868	0	0
1872	0	1
1876	0	2
1880	0	2
1884	0	1
1888	0	2
1896	0	1
1900	0	1
1904	0	3
1908	0	3
1912	0	0
1916	0	1
1964	0	0
1968	3	0
1972	10	1
1976	6	1
1980	17	0
1984	23	0
TOTAL	59	19

SOURCE: Walton, H., Jr. 1975. *Black Republicans: The politics of the black and tans* (Metuchen: Scarecrow Press, 170–76, and *Guide to Black Politics, 1972, 1976, 1980*. Washington, D.C.: Joint Center for Political Studies, 1972, 1976.

tion was George C. Wallace. Yet twenty years later, Wallace had completely disavowed his earlier position and taken one diametrically opposed (Harris, 1983: A3; see also Frady, 1978, passim).

These dramatic reforms have had the effect of weakening the NDPA, which is no longer the only organization to welcome black candidacies and deplore the politics of segregation. In that sense, these reforms help account for the failure of the party thus far to make its mark in statewide politics. However, such Pyrrhic victories are, in the American electoral context, one of the few ways to achieve at least a measure of success in third-party politics.

Summary and Conclusions: Insights from a Case Study

As Cook has noted, "it is perilous . . . to evaluate black political parties in terms of normal standards. . . . Black political parties are, after all, expressions of radically abnormal conditions and consequences—basic defects in the political system. They have had a special mission—correction of those fundamental deficiencies" (1972: 6). However, even in the context of "radically abnormal conditions," the achievements of the NDPA have been impressive, as numerous authors discussing recent southern politics have been quick to point out. Of the NDPA's participation in the 1968 contest, Donald Strong has said, "(it) made a respectable showing for a brand new party. It ran candidates for Congress in all eight districts. In three of these it managed to poll around ten percent of the vote. Its banner district was the Fifth, where its nominee, William Branch, outpolled the Republican nominee, won a majority in two counties in the district, and finished second with 23 percent of the total vote" (1972: 464). And Bass and Devries flatly affirm. "The presence of NDPA allowed blacks to get on the ballot in the 1960s in counties where the regular Democrats had blocked them, and the NDPA presence helped spark reform of the state Democratic Party" (1972: 77).

Moreover, when one compares the impact made by the party in Alabama with the impact made by black voters in Georgia or in other southern states where no such party existed, the depths and degree of influence of the Alabama party stand out. In Georgia, for example, only one black-belt county is presently under black political control and the majority of black elected officials do not come from the traditional black-belt counties. White politicians are still in control of these areas and have given up very little, if any, political control (Walton, 1988: chs. 4 and 5). Similarly, in South Carolina, where there were two black political parties, no county is controlled completely by blacks (Walton, 1974: 86–95, and "Legislative Issue," 1983: 6–32). Throughout the South, blacks trying to gain political power have been forced to face one stumbling block after another. The absence of strong black political parties comparable to the NDPA has meant that in state after state, black-belt whites have given up very little of their political power.

To put it differently, the Voting Rights Act enabled blacks to enter the political system and gain political office in the South, but usually only in the urban and near-urban areas and not in the backbone of the region, the black-belt counties. The major exception has been in the state of Alabama, due to the existence of the NDPA. The success of this party, formed less than twenty years ago, in accomplishing this goal takes it far beyond the level of accomplishment customarily associated with strong third parties. Such parties often have the opportunity to effect considerable change in the systems in which they form, even when they never succeed in wrestling power from failing or faltering major parties. They bring new issues to the fore, and force the major parties to accommodate points of view hitherto ignored or scorned. Black political parties in today's South are well placed, both geographically and historically, to achieve those standard ends. But the case of the NDPA suggests further that if they seize their opportunities, and focus their efforts on the rural areas where black voters are most strongly concentrated, they may be able to initiate a process of political change that will go far beyond the traditional functions of third-party politics. They may ultimately be able to destroy the base of white supremacist power altogether, and bring about a significant realignment of power throughout their states. They may succeed in altering the balance of southern political power forever.

NOTE ON SOURCES FOR THE FIGURES

Since the data for the various graphs were scattered through a variety of sources, I list here the major works from which the raw data was taken.

Figure 14.1. Sources: 1975. Bureau of Census. *Historical statistics of the United States colonial times to 1970—Part 2.* Washington, D.C.: Government Printing Office, 1071–72. Bureau of Census. 1980. *Statistical abstract of the United States, 1980.* Washington, D.C.: Government Printing Office, 502, 516, 517.

The percentage of voter turnout in Figure 14.1 was drawn directly from *Historical statistics of the United States: Colonial times to 1970—Part 2.* This section was prepared by Walter Dean Burnham, Department of Political Science, Massachusetts Institute of Technology. He used as his data base to calculate these turnout percentages free white males, twenty-one years and over, from 1824 to 1868; black males and white males both were used from 1872 (Mississippi, Texas, and Virginia did not participate in the 1872 election) to 1920, when women were added. However, there is one exception to this procedure. Several states gave women the right to vote earlier than 1920 and in the years when this occurred for the particular state in question, sex-related adjustments were made. The final adjustments were made for citizenship which became a universal prerequisite for voting in the 1928 election. Prior to this requirement, Burnham made adjustments for those states where aliens were permitted to vote. (For a complete explanation of his technique see pp. 1067–69. The tables with the turnout percentages are on pp. 1071–72.)

Figure 14.2. Sources: 1975. Bureau of Census. *Historical statistics of the United States: Colonial times to 1970—Part 2*. Washington, D.C.: Government Printing Office, 1077–80. Bureau of Census. 1980. *Statistical abstract of the United States, 1980*. Washington, D.C.: Government Printing Office, 501–502.

Figure 14.3. Sources: Heard, A., and D. Strong. 1950. *Southern primaries and elections, 1920–1949*. Tuscaloosa: University of Alabama Press, 9–20. Price, M. 1957. *The Negro voter in the South*. Atlanta: Southern Regional Council, 5. Walton, H., Jr. 1972. *Black political parties*. New York: Free Press. Bartley N.V., and H. D. Graham. 1978. *Southern elections: Precinct data, 1950–1972*. Baton Rouge: Louisiana State University Press. Bureau of Census. 1980. *Statistical abstract of the United States, 1980*. Washington, D.C.: Government Printing Office, 502, 514, 516, 517, 519.

Figure 14.4. Sources: Lewinson, P. 1963. *Race, class and party*. New York: Russell & Russell, 216–18. Gomillion, C. G. 1957. The Negro voter in Alabama. *Journal of Negro Education*, 26: 281–82. Bureau of Census. 1980. *Statistical abstract of the United States, 1980*. Washington, D.C.: Government Printing Office.

Figure 14.5. Sources: Heard A., and D. Strong. 1950. *Southern primaries and elections, 1920–1949*. Tuscaloosa: University of Alabama Press, 9–20. Walton, H., Jr. 1972. *Black political parties*. New York: Free Press. *Guide to black politics 1972, 1976, 1980*. Washington, D.C.: Joint Center for Political Studies.

Figure 14.6. Sources: Scammons, R., and A. McGillivary, eds. 1960–81. *American votes series, 1960, 1964, 1972, 1980*. Washington, D.C.: Election Research Center.

Figure 14.7. Sources: *National roster of black elected officials, 1970–82*. Washington, D.C.: Joint Center for Political Studies. *Black elected officials in the South, 1969*. Atlanta: Voter Education Project.

REFERENCES

Bass, J., and W. Devries. 1972. *The transformation of southern politics: Social change & political consequence since 1945*. New York: Basic Books.

Black, E., and M. Black. 1973. The changing setting of minority politics in the American Deep South. *Politics* 3: 42–45.

Boykin, M. 1973. Black political participation in Greene County, Alabama. *Politics* 3: 51–56.

Brittain, J. M. 1957. Negro suffrage and politics in Alabama since 1870. Ph.D. diss.: Indiana University.

———. 1959. The return of the Negro to Alabama politics: 1930–1954. *Negro History Bulletin* 22: 196–99.

———. 1962. Some reflections on Negro suffrage and politics in Alabama—Past and present. *Journal of Negro History* 47: 127–38.

Bullock, C. S., and K. S. Henry. 1981. The impact of increased black political participation: Legislative voting in the South. *Civil Rights Research Review* 5: 22–31.

Cook, S. D. 1972. The politics of the success of failure. In *Black political parties: An historical and political analysis*. New York: Free Press.

Cosman, B. 1966. *Five states for Goldwater.* Tuscaloosa: University of Alabama Press.

Crotty, W. J., and G. C. Jacobson. 1980. *American parties in decline.* Boston: Little, Brown.

Fishel, J., ed. 1978. *Parties and elections in an anti-party age.* Bloomington: Indiana University Press.

Frady, M. 1978. *Wallace.* Cleveland: New World.

Frye, H. T. 1980. *Black parties and political power: A case study.* Boston: G. K. Hall.

Gaither, G. 1977. *Blacks and the populist revolt: Ballots and bigotry in the "New South."* Tuscaloosa: University of Alabama Press.

Hadley, A. T. 1978. *The empty polling booth.* Englewood Cliffs: Prentice-Hall.

Harris, A. 1983. An Old South governor rises again, vowing "Mercy and Justice." *Washington Post,* Jan. 18: A-3.

Key, V. O. 1949. *Southern politics.* New York: Vintage Books.

"Legislative Issue." 1963. *Living in South Carolina* 35: 12–32.

Lewinson, P. 1963. *Race, class and party.* New York: Russell & Russell.

Logan, R. W. 1965. *The betrayal of the Negro: From Rutherford B. Hayes to Woodrow Wilson.* New York: Collier Books.

Rosenstone, S. J., and R. E. Wolfinger. 1978. The effects of registration laws on voter turnout. *American Political Science Review* 70: 22–45.

Rusk, J. G. 1974. The American electoral universe: Speculation and evidence. *American Political Science Review* 68: 1028–49.

Seagull, L. 1975. *Southern Republicanism.* Cambridge, Mass.: Schenkman Publishing Company.

Strong, D. 1972. Alabama: Transition and alienation. In *The changing politics of the south*, ed. William C. Havard. Baton Rouge: Louisiana State University Press.

Walton, H., Jr. 1972. *Black political parties: An Historical and political analysis.* New York: Free Press.

Walton, H., Jr., and W. Boone. 1974. Black political parties: A demographic analysis. *Journal of Black Studies* 5: 86–95.

———. 1975. *Black Republicans: The politics of the black and tans.* Metuchen, N.J.: Scarecrow Press.

Walton, H., Jr., and W. Boone. Forthcoming. *The Carter vote in Georgia: An election data analysis.*

Wolfinger, R. E., and S. J. Rosenstone. 1980. *Who votes.* New Haven: Yale University Press.

Woodward, C. V. 1951. *Origins of the New South, 1877–1913.* Baton Rouge: Louisiana State University Press.

FIFTEEN

Stealing Congress's Thunder:
The Rise to Power of a
Communist Movement
in South India

RONALD J. HERRING

INTRODUCTION: PARTY FAILURE AND PARTY SUCCESS

The purpose of this essay is to analyze the reasons for the success of a Communist party in South India. It became what is often considered the first freely elected Communist government in the world. The core argument is that the Communist success was in large part the counterdynamic to the failure of a then-hegemonic nationalist movement transformed into a political party—the Indian National Congress. To simplify, the argument stresses the inability of conservative forces within the Congress—because of their class base, organizational constraints, and dominant (Gandhian) ideology—to address issues of exploitation along both class and caste lines. This inability spawned an organization of radicals within the same umbrella Congress which, because of alternative tactics and ideology, created effective linkages to the mass political energy of the socially and economically oppressed. These radicals, eventually forming themselves into a Communist party, achieved significant political success—at the polls and in public policy. Their successes, by changing the caste and class structures, eroded the very basis for Communist strength—namely, widespread moral outrage at the inequalities and indignities of the old order. Congress failed because it built its linkages through that old order and thus could not create new linkages with those whose subordination supported the old order. The competition between these political forces—and shifting allies—has structured the party system of one of India's most volatile states.

The notion of party failure is a complex one, always relative to some arbitrary standard. By arguing that the Congress party failed in Kerala, I refer to several related indicators. First, the Congress failed to prevent the emergence of the first Communist state government in India, despite its vigorous anti-Communist actions at the local and national levels. Second, the state-level Congress failed to effect national Congress policy objectives for fundamental social transformation, particularly in the agrarian system. But this failure was characteristic of the national Congress party as well; however, on the national level, the Congress was able to fail and yet retain the allegiance of outcaste and depressed sectors, through symbolic politics and manipulation of patron-client networks, and remain the hegemonic party, despite rampant factionalism and splits after 1967. In the same 1957 elections which brought the Communists to power in Kerala, the Congress party captured almost three-fourths of the seats in the national Parliament. In 1967, the electoral hegemony of the Congress in the states was severely shaken—by Communists both within and outside Kerala and by other parties. By 1977, Indira Gandhi's hold on the national Parliament was broken and the Congress was routed at the federal level and in the states.[1] Though the Congress has returned to power, it is no longer the party it was in the time of Nehru, either in terms of assured dominance in the center or states, or in terms of cohesion and "institutionalization" of the party itself (see Rudolph and Rudolph, 1981).

Like many nationalist movements which attempt the transition to a centrist umbrella political party after independence, the Congress has spawned splinters, and thus new political parties, to both its right and left. The puzzling question concerns the reasons for the remarkable success of one of those groups—the Communist party in Kerala. An enduring puzzle for students of Indian politics has been the continued mass electoral appeal of the Congress despite its failure to deliver on longstanding commitments to social justice and social transformation. Surely one answer to that question is that the Congress has remained, in much of India, "the only game in town"—the only credible governing party (cf. Michie, 1978). The development of a leftist party as an alternative viable governing force in Kerala suggests one set of conditions for the emergence of credible challenges to Congress hegemony, and some ironic constraints.

The plan of this essay is to analyze the dialectical relationship between the development of the Congress party and that of the Communist party, emphasizing the period before the Communists' electoral victory in 1957. This dialectical relationship had profound consequences for the internal development and tactics of each party, and has shaped the party system of the state. Those who eventually formed the state unit of the Communist

[1] On the issues in the 1977 election, and outcomes, see Weiner, 1978. On the success of leftist oppositional parties in other states, Brass and Franda, eds., 1973. For a detailed portrait of the Congress party's style of mobilization and the exercise of hegemony before the unraveling of the late 1960s, Weiner, 1968; Kochaneck, 1968.

party (in 1940) were recruited into politics by the Congress during the anticolonial struggle of the 1920s and 1930s; the conflict between right and left *within* the Congress established the pattern of conflict (and some cooperation) that became a defining characteristic of the party system of Kerala. A central conflict between the political mobilization and linkage strategies centers on the issue of social transformation; the Congress has largely chosen to work through existing structures of power, the Communists to overturn them. Precisely because those structures of power disadvantaged so many, so extremely, a radical party with appropriate political theory, tactics, and organization became a structural potential, though by no means an inevitable outcome.

STEALING CONGRESS'S THUNDER: PEASANT AND OTHER POLITICS

The title of this essay is borrowed from an article written by Wolf Ladejinsky in 1951, describing how the American-induced land reform in Japan "stole communist thunder" and produced conditions of rural social stability and conservatism.[2] Ladejinsky was the intellectual force behind that, and other, Asian land reforms; he spent his last years in India. Ladejinsky, like Barrington Moore, Jr., Doreen Warriner, Gunnar Myrdal, and Samuel Huntington, concluded that the possibilities for radical land reform in India had passed; such policies became a structural impossibility given the distribution of political power in rural areas in independent India (Hart and Herring, 1978: 233–41). Official proclamations from Delhi have elaborately documented the failure of land reforms nationwide since the 1950s (Herring, 1983: ch. 5). Kerala state constitutes an important exception to that rule: between 1970 and 1980, the system of rentier landlordism was abolished, land was distributed to the tenants, and almost half of the agricultural land in the state changed hands (Herring, 1980).

The agrarian issue illustrates a major theme: the Communists fought for and eventually delivered what the Congress only promised with regard to rural redistributive policy, and in the process created powerful linkages to radical agrarian classes. The Communists could make those linkages precisely because they lacked the ideological and class-based constraints

[2] Ladejinsky's article was picaresquely entitled "The Plow Outbids the Sword in Asia: How General MacArthur Stole Communist Thunder with Democratic Land Reforms, Our Most Potent Weapon for Peace," *Country Gentlemen* (now *Farm Journal*), June 1951. A year later came a companion piece, "Too Late to Save Asia?" For more on the theme, see McCoy, 1971.

which rendered the Congress—in Kerala and elsewhere—incapable of overturning the rural social structure as so often promised. The analysis is then focused on the political theory, tactics, and social bases of the competing political parties as explanations for success and failure.

The importance of agrarian politics derives from economic structure—the overwhelming majority of Indians live in rural areas and derive their livelihood in ways connected to the land. Jawaharlal Nehru termed the land question the central issue in building a democratic and dynamic republic. Because the Indian constitution is federal, and allocates to the states responsibility for land reform, the directives of the Congress-dominated center (Delhi) have been only imperfectly, if at all, translated into law by Congress-dominated state governments. There has been persistent handwringing in Delhi over the failure of conservative state-level elites affiliated with the Congress to translate central policy into results on the ground; part of this concern, explicitly articulated by Indira Gandhi, is that the failure of land reforms, and the consequent increasing disparities in life chances in rural India, produce political instability and the opportunity for radical parties to mobilize the rural poor. A great deal of Indian politics is peasant politics; as Bhabani Sen Gupta has argued, "land relationships happen to be the strongest determinant in political alignments at the state level" (1972: 290). Though Communist leaders attribute a great deal of their success to mobilization of a radical peasant movement, there are other crucial issues on which the Communist party may be said to have stolen Congress's thunder in the political process, to be discussed throughout.

Kerala is a state of about 25 million people on the southwestern coast of India. It is widely recognized for having the highest literacy rate in India and, despite falling below the national mean per capita income, the highest Physical Quality of Life Index rating (a measure which equally weights progress in terms of literacy, life expectancy, and infant mortality) (Mencher, 1980; Morris and McAlpin, 1979). It is also one of the most intensely politicized states. The area has historically had among the highest percentages of "untouchables" in India, and the richest land: until recently, gross value of product per acre was more than 200 percent of the All-Indian average. The combination of very productive land and extremely high rates of landlessness and "untouchables" (which are highly intercorrelated) produced uniquely wide inequalities of wealth, standing, and opportunity.

The present state was formed in 1956 from three distinct regions; regional differences and history are important explanatory factors in the argument that follows. Of particular importance is the history of party competition in Malabar, the northernmost region. First, the Communist party struck its deepest organizational roots in Malabar. Moreover, the more radical of the two Communist parties (after the split in 1964) retains its major organizational and electoral strongholds in Malabar, and the more radical factions of the undivided party originated there. Equally important for this analysis, Malabar was under *direct* colonial rule as part of the Madras presidency; the other two regions, Travancore and Cochin, were under indirect rule through maharajas until Independence. The Malabar region thus evidenced direct competition within the anticolonial national movement between those who became leaders of the Indian National Congress and those who founded the Communist party in the state. Finally, the Malabar region offers evidence for an ideal type of explanation for the development of a radical mass-based political party: a structural niche for a party with the social theory and organizational capacity to convert those objective conditions into political power.

Malabar and the Origins of a Radical Peasant Movement

Malabar under colonial rule became in many ways the archetypal disintegrating agrarian system, earning, as one colonial officer said, "the unenviable reputation of being the most rack-rented place on the face of the earth" (Varghese, 1970: 78). With the introduction of colonial law, particularly the imposition of a legal system based on the absolute notion of land as private property, traditional overlords were able to evict tenants and raise rents according to the familiar rule of "what the market would bear," enforced by the police powers of a colonial state (Koshy, 1976: 51–69; Kurup, 1981; Paulini, 1978: ch. 1). These practices were quite at variance with norms of the traditional "moral economy" (cf. Scott, 1976; Popkin, 1979: ch. 1; Parameswaran, 1951: 8–16). The result was a series of quite serious agrarian uprisings, beginning in 1836, peaking in 1841, and continuing sporadically throughout the nineteenth century. The simmering agrarian revolt exploded in 1921 in the Moplah (Mappilla) Rebellion, one of the most intense uprisings in Indian colonial history (Hardgrave, 1977; Pannikar, 1979; Radhakrishnan, 1980; Namboodiripad, 1952: 122–30).

The Moplah Rebellion illustrated the structural unity of landlordism and colonial rule. The colonial government was quite explicit in its recognition of dependence on the landed elite for continued hegemony (cf. Sen, 1955: 55), and the landlords reciprocally depended on the colonial state's machinery to quash challenges to their local authority. Understanding this structural unity is crucial for understanding the divergence in support bases for Congress and Communist programs: conservative groups within the Congress came to oppose, with varying resolve and militancy, one leg of the agrarian power structure—colonial rule—but were unwilling to attack the other—landlordism as a social institution. The radicals within the nationalist movement, on the other hand, came to oppose with increasing militancy both landlordism and the colonial state, perceiving this linkage to be crucial for the success of the independence struggle. A member of the Congress left, who later became a Communist leader, noted: "Not only was the peasantry the most numerous section of the Indian people, but it was in the villages that imperialism had its most reliable ally—the feudal landlords. The police *thana*, functioning in close collaboration with the big landlords, was the center of imperialism's oppressive machinery" (Namboodiripad, 1976: 183). The Moplah Rebellion, and later outbursts of peasant militance, were denounced and abandoned by Gandhi and Congress conservatives; the radicals supported, nurtured, and organized around these social impulses, with incrementally increasing, though uneven, organizational development and tactical success (Paulini, 1978: ch. 1–3; Radhakrishnan, 1980).

Differences in ability to address expressed grievances and organize around radical programs are rooted in both the social theories and the social bases of the contending groups which later became the Congress party and the Communist party. The Moplah rebels were branded indelibly with the mark of violence and class conflict, tactics repeatedly disavowed by All-India Congress leadership and by Mahatma Gandhi in particular. Moreover, the Congress connection with local notables rendered an alliance with peasant radicalism impossible practically. Gandhi's theory of exploitation was more palatable to landed elites: landlordism *as usually practiced* was indeed exploitative, Gandhi argued, not from an "inherent necessity," but rather because of the moral defects of certain landlords (defects which were corrigible through suasion and enlightenment). Gandhi's theory of "trusteeship" explicitly allowed for maintenance of traditional class divisions and privileges, though optimally with reforms in the moral economy of the overlords.[3] Gandhi himself recognized that the Congress represented "no immediate menace" to wealthy merchants, landlords, and industrialists (Thorner, 1980: 47). Indeed, given the colonial state's periodic reformist impulses, landlords sometimes found it ad-

---

[3] On Gandhi's conservative position on peasant movements, Dhanagre, 1975; on landlords, Gandhi, 1966: 233–40, 248–50; on "Trusteeship," Gandhi, 1970. Bhabeni Sen Gupta, 1972: 289, also notes the importance of Gandhi's retreats from peasant militancy, and treats the weakness of the peasant movements on the All-India level (ch. 8). For an expansion of the treatment of landlordism as a social system, Herring, 1984.

vantageous to keep a hand in politically through the Congress (McLane, 1978: 211).

Tactically and philosophically, the Indian National Congress was not a revolutionary movement, but rather a reformist and anticolonial one. In the developing leftist analysis, the abuses of landlordism were not simply manifestations of aberrant, morally deficient landowners. Rather, landlordism was perceived in structural, systemic terms: a social system propped up by force ultimately guaranteed by colonial rule. In this analysis, landlordism was a multifaceted institution inextricably intertwined with caste indignities (which were more severe and extreme in Kerala than elsewhere, as suggested in Vivekananda's characterization of Kerala as "the madhouse of India"), economic exploitation, political inequality, and imperialism: a social system which land tenure reform alone could not resolve.[4]

The leftists did use land tenure reform (security of use-rights and rental controls) as a mobilizing issue, but not as an end in itself; rather, they employed a continuous ratchet-effect strategy. As the colonial government made minimal concessions (such as the Malabar Tenancy Act of 1930), the leftists mobilized for extension of the concessions to lower layers of the peasantry and simultaneously organized both for effective implementation of the limited relief provisions and against the multifaceted social manifestations of landlordism (cf. Radhakrishnan, 1980; Koshy, 1976: 110–16; Herring, 1983: ch. 6).

The combination of economic exploitation and social oppression of the agrarian underclass arguably produced unique conditions for the revolutionary force born of what Barrington Moore, Jr. (1978), has termed "moral outrage." The outrage was generated not only by the continuing presence of debt bondage, slavery, and serfdom at the very bottom and by deterioration of traditional security and economic rights in the middle, exacerbated by the world depression of the 1930s, but also by the extreme manifestations of noneconomic inequality. Peasants of the lower orders were degraded and humiliated by such practices as "untouchability," which prevented certain groups from using public roads, entering temples, approaching "clean caste" members, covering certain parts of their bodies with clothing, using certain water supplies, etc. The rural poor were subjected to severe oppression such as sexual exploitation of women and brutal beatings, as well as to petty significations of inferior status, such as not being allowed to wear shoes or long dhotis (cf. Saradamoni, 1980; Aiyap-

---

[4] For an expanded view of this perception, and its concrete implications, see the following works of early Communist activists and party leaders: Gopalan, 1973: ch. 8, 9; Krishnan, 1971: 44 et passim; Namboodiripad, 1968: 97 et passim; 1981.

pan, 1965; George, 1975: 17 et passim; Pillai, 1967; Rajendran, 1978: 8–29; Pandian, 1980).

The organizational culmination of local protests was the formation of local units of the Kerala Karshaka Sangham (peasant association), beginning in Malabar in 1935. The district-level Malabar Sangham was formed the following year. The radicals of the Congress patiently organized, village by village, building in each one a volunteer defense committee, and establishing study groups and reading rooms. Leading Congress Socialists wrote plays with radical content, and dramatic presentations aided in mobilization. Two of the most important plays criticizing landlordism had the telling titles of "Arrears of Rent" and "Drinking of Blood" (Paulini, 1978: 160–68; Fic, 1970: ch. 2; Gopalan, 1973: ch. 8).

These organizational linkages were aided by the enormous respect for learning, and relatively high literacy rate, in Kerala. Naturally enough, school teachers and students were important in spreading the message, and their respect in village society enhanced their efforts. The great leader of peasant movements, A. K. Gopalan, began his professional life as a village schoolteacher (Gopalan, 1973; cf. Niranjana, 1977). Communist party elder E.M.S. Namboodiripad gives perhaps the best summary of the fusion of mobilizing agents and issues: "It is the combination in one person of the office bearer of the Village Congress Committee, the leader of the Teachers' Union, and the organizer of the Kisan Sangham (peasant association) that made the anti-imperialist movement strike deep roots in the countryside" (Namboodiripad, 1968: 156).

As will become apparent in the following section, the mobilization of the peasantry was a major source of cleavage within the Congress. The conservative Congress leadership, locally and nationally, had deep reservations about militant peasant movements under the aegis of the Congress. The leftists in the Congress in Kerala had no such reservations and built a powerful peasant movement around issues of economic exploitation and social indignities that was linked organizationally to the nationalist movement and to the burgeoning trade-union movement. Their success contrasts sharply with efforts in many other parts of the subcontinent and provided a solid political base for the eventual emergence of the Communist party.

COMPETITION AND CLEAVAGES WITHIN THE ANTICOLONIAL MOVEMENT: THEORY AND TACTICS

Radical leadership within the independence movement in Kerala in no sense appeared on the scene with a Leninist organization or theory; quite the contrary. The leaders who founded the Communist party were drawn into politics by the anticolonial fervor sweeping Kerala and by the organization and educational efforts of the Congress. In their biographies and autobiographies, the most consistent theme is one of movement from political naiveté through groping with various levels of understanding of society, largely learned through practice, certainly not from texts. Leaders of the party's organizational and political work, such as A. K. Gopalan and Krishna Pillai, neither claimed nor were accorded status as theoreticians, but rather first and foremost as political activists.

The indigenous development of Kerala's radical leadership produced two important legacies: first, the radicals were not hamstrung by rigid adherence to any European theory of revolution. Second, their *implicit* theory grew from practical struggle for social change in escalating opposition to that of the Congress conservatives with whom they contested for popular allegiance. If there is any single strand to that ideology which should be emphasized, it is the rejection of the Gandhian notion that societal transformation can take place without economic structural change, class conflict, and violence. Their view of society was explicitly conflictual and their view of power was structural: dominating classes, foreign and domestic, maintain their privileges ultimately by force, and it is demonstrated potential to use force which will produce change. Moreover, militant opposition to an existing configuration of power will typically provoke violence from the organs of the state—usually the police, sometimes the army—and that force must be met with all the militance popular organizations can muster.

Though the radicals entered politics in part because of inspiration from Gandhi and the existing anticolonial activists, fundamental differences emerged very early. An open split occurred in 1920, when the conservatives, having been outvoted on the issue of land tenure reform, walked out of the Congress session discussing policy (Namboodiripad, 1968: 129; Hart and Herring, 1979: 256–57). Krishna Pillai, one of the eventual founders of the Communist party in Kerala, talked in terms of "the Congress of the rich and the Congress of the poor"; if one's allegiance were to the latter, work among the peasantry was essential (Krishnan, 1971: 19; cf. Pillai. 1977).

In the growth of a mass movement under Congress leadership, issues of social reform evoked considerable passion, mobilization, and conflict. Indeed, E.M.S. Namboodiripad began as a social reformer in his own caste association (of Namboodiri Brahmins), and has stressed the role of organizations for caste uplift as vehicles for the antiimperialist struggles of the 1920s and the class-based movements of the peasantry in the 1930s and 1940s (Namboodiripad, 1968: 116, 120; 1976: 21ff.). Such movements began in Kerala before the turn of the century (cf. Saradamoni, 1980: chs. 1, 4, 5; Namboodiripad, 1968: 112–13; Rajendran, 1974: ch. 3; Nossiter, 1982: 77–83). Because low caste status was associated closely with political and economic disabilities, more so in Kerala than in other areas, such movements inevitably clashed with dominant political and economic, as well as social, groups—and thus with the colonial state.

The social reform component of the nationalist movement exhibited certain dynamics similar to those of the more strictly economic campaigns such as land reform, tax reduction, and wage struggles. For example, in the famous Guruvayoor temple-entry agitation of 1931, the objective was to remove an important caste-based social disability imposed on the lower orders of Hindu society—the prohibition against entering temples. Congress militants were prominent in the movement, which aroused considerable mass involvement and extensive suffering from police repression. Gandhi called off the agitation when it threatened to escalate into large-scale violence. In defiance, radicals in the Kerala unit of the Congress (the KPCC) called for independent mass protests; as in earlier retreats called from above, the result was disillusionment with the conservative national leadership among local activists (Krishnan, 1970: 18, 21–22).

Among the tactics which the conservative national Congress leadership considered legitimate, civil disobedience was the most aggressive, and dangerous. As Gandhi noted, the danger of mass mobilization was great, for it was "no easy task to restrain the fury of a people incensed by a deep sense of wrong." Despite his fears of escalation into violence, well-grounded in previous experiences, Gandhi explicitly recognized that "to do nothing is to invite violence for a certainty" (in Thorner, 1980: 45).

The cleavage on issues of both tactics and policy between conservatives and leftists intensified in the early 1930s, in Kerala and in the national movement. The Karachi meeting of the national Congress in 1931, dominated by the leftists, resolved to support radical economic change, including the nationalization of industries. The formal organizational manifestation of the growing right/left split was the formation of the Congress Socialist party (CSP) within the umbrella Congress in 1934. The Declaration of Independence of the Congress proclaimed the "inalienable right of the Indian people, as of any other people . . . to enjoy the fruits of their toil and have the necessities of life." For CSP activists, winning this inalienable right depended not only on expulsion of colonial masters, but also on reforms in economic patterns which could be won only through organized struggles by workers and peasants. Since the majority of Indians were workers and peasants, even the attainment of political freedom narrowly defined required organizations of these classes; when the notion of freedom is expanded to include an "inalienable right to the fruits of their toil" and the "necessities of life," the movement cannot be restricted to working within the existing economic and social structure. The Socialists in the Congress thus came to define the goals of the independence movement in terms of economic structural change, whereas the Gandhians viewed the goals in terms of moral and social purification and regeneration.

The creation of a Congress Socialist party thus formalized a longstanding cleavage between the "Congress of the rich" and the "Congress of the poor." The latter continued work among the peasantry, and in the nascent trade-union movement, whereas the former concentrated on issues such as "harijan (untouchable) uplift" (Krishnan, 1971: 22). Not only did Gandhi fear and distrust organizations of workers and peasants, but Gandhians in the national leadership resisted bringing such organizations into the Congress. Indeed, in 1933 the Congress temporarily disbanded its mass organizations (Thorner, 1980: 62). These conservative sections in the national organization met powerful resistance from Nehru and the CSP, but the political vector sum was typically compromised by concessions to Gandhi and the Gandhians. Moreover, leftist strength in the national Congress in terms of ideology was frequently vitiated by rightist control of the organizational machinery. Unlike the situation in other parts of India, in Kerala the Congress radicals controlled the organizational apparatus, largely because of the strength of the mass movements they led. In 1934 the Kerala leftists outvoted the conservatives on an official resolution expressing "lack of confidence in the efficacy of the Gandhian principles of truth and non-violence in the fight for *swaraj* (self-rule)" (Hart and Herring, 1977: 200).

The organized trade-union movement preceded and moved in parallel with the organization of the peasantry. Though the industrial base of Kerala was minimal, the militance of the working class was of great importance in the growth of radical popular movements. As the organizations of peasants and workers assumed increasing importance in the anticolonial struggle, the political strength of the leftists in the Congress improved. Moreover, the leftists fielded an impressive network of cadres totally committed to political work, in marked contrast to what A. K. Gopalan called "Sunday Congressmen" such as the advocates of Calicut who appeared only occasionally to address a rally (Krishnan, 1971: 25). This organizational work was of particular importance in providing some security for those who risked a great deal by confronting the colonial state. Mass protests and militance inevitably produced mass arrests, and martyrs, and the socialists organized relief and support for the families of victims, as well as a network for legitimizing and memorializing sacrifices (cf. Niranjana, 1977; George, 1975; Krishnan, 1971: 80 et passim).

Development of the Socialist movement outside Malabar illustrated again the provision by the conservative national leadership of an important niche for a more radical movement. National Congress policy was that areas under "indirect rule" i.e., controlled directly by traditional rulers such as the maharajas under the British, should be spared agitation. This perspective derived from the single-issue focus of dominant Congress strategy—national independence; any protests against princely rulers could alienate them and weaken the nationalist cause. Gandhi believed the princes were tractable more through suasion than political protest. In Kerala, the radicals in the Congress bitterly opposed the policy that the Congress flag should not be raised in the princely states (which constituted about two-thirds of contemporary Kerala) (cf. Krishanan, 1971: 44 et passim).

By proposing and supporting more radical positions on both the establishment of popular government in the princely states and social reform, the CSP was able to form linkages with both student groups and the emerging working-class movement; the organized working class of Alleppey had demanded representative government as early as 1921, long before there was an organized socialist party (George, 1975: 8). As importantly, the long *jathas* (protest processions) organized in support of the movement in Travancore by the Malabar CSP began building concrete political connections over an extended area—the entire region within which Malayalam is spoken—laying the base for the subsequent successful political movement for a linguistically homogeneous Kerala State, which succeeded in 1956, largely under Communist leadership.

The response of the princely administration in Travancore to these movements was one of brutal repression. As in Malabar, the tactics of the socialists involved concrete linkage of political and economic demands and close collaboration with and support for local leaders of militant groups. Police repression created martyrs, and underlined the socialist claim that the bosses could be moved only through militance. The concessions won through such struggles, even if minimal, reinforced the confidence of mass organizations in their own potential power, and in the leadership of socialists. An archetypal case of these dynamics was the bloody month-long general strike of 1938 in Alleppey, a center of early working-class organization. Significantly, the workers raised both the tricolor flag for national independence and the red flag of revolution; purely economistic demands were linked to demands for release of political prisoners held by the government. Concessions on both kinds of demands strengthened the popular movement and its identification with CSP leadership (Krishnan, 1971: 52–55; Namboodiripad, 1952: 136–46).

The leftists themselves were not well read in Socialist theory, but were deeply impressed (as was Nehru) by the dramatic economic progress of the Soviet Union, a recently poor and agrarian nation, at a time when the capitalist world was sinking into a severe depression (Nehru, 1946: 14, 304 et passim; Namboodiripad, 1976: 157; Krishnan, 1941: 27–28). Whereas the conservatives in the Congress endorsed certain social reforms, these were largely limited to social reform within Hindu society—prohibition, reducing caste barriers, uplift of "untouchables," etc.—and tactically restricted to moral suasion and education. The socialists argued two points: social reforms would not cure all that was wrong with India from the perspective of those at the bottom, and social reforms themselves were difficult to achieve without organizational work among depressed classes and tactical support for the expressed demands of those classes across a spectrum of issues.

The great strength of the Socialist program was the linkage of demands for representative government—with neither British nor princely overlords—to specific economic grievances—land taxes, rents, debts, wages, etc.—and social reforms such as removal of caste disabilities; this permitted both the extension of the movement below the educated middle class which dominated the early Congress movement (Kochanek, 1968) and staying power under repression. Indeed, repression itself contributed concretely to the Socialist cause. The jail terms and beatings of militants not only demonstrated their resolve and commitment to the mass public, but allowed access to militants from other areas with new ideas, experiences, and ideologies. It was in jail that Krishna Pillai, the eventual "founder of the Communist Party" in Kerala first read of the Russian revolution (through John Reed's famous account) (Krishnan, 1971: 14). E.M.S. Namboodiripad, who clearly deserves comparable status as a founder of the party, has claimed "it will not be an exaggeration to say that the seeds of the left-wing Congress and the Congress Socialist Movement in Kerala, were laid in the Cannanore jail" (1976: 133).

The demonstrated dedication and comprehensive transformational program of the leftists were especially attractive to the youth of Kerala, who were becoming disillusioned with the compromising and backtracking of national Congress leadership. In the words of the young Socialist leader Krishna Pillai, that leadership "would not project any worthwhile policy or programme calculated to enthuse and inspire the younger generation who had rushed headlong into the battle for national liberation with no personal motives other than freedom for their motherland" (Krishnan, 1971: 27). With organizational work among the peasantry, the youth, and the working class, the CSP developed undisputed leadership of the mass political energy in Kerala. As Bhabani Sen Gupta has rightly remarked, "there are actually only two majorities in India, the young and the poor, both dominating the rural universe; what happens to these two majorities is bound to shake the Indian polity . . ." (1972: 291).

THE FORMAL CREATION OF
THE COMMUNIST PARTY IN KERALA

By the late 1930s, radicals within the Congress movement had achieved a great deal. They had formed an autonomous organization—the Congress Socialist party—and their leadership had come to dominate the organization of the state-level Congress itself. Peasant associations, a student federation, and trade unions were well established under the leadership of the CSP or their allies. The conflicts with the conservatives in the Congress had sharpened. Indeed, the conservatives found it necessary to respond by forming their own organization—the Kerala Congress Gandhi Sangh—though it largely failed to attract mass support or gain organizational strength.

Organizationally and ideologically, it became increasingly difficult for the leftists to remain within the Congress. From 1938 onward, the Kerala Pradesh Congress Committee (KPCC), controlled by the leftists, began a massive program of "physical and political training" for some three thousand volunteers who became the backbone of the five hundred or so village Congress committees. A rent strike by the tenantry was successfully conducted in Malabar in 1938–39, in direct opposition to the Gandhian tactical position. Late in 1939, the national Congress Working Committee dissolved the Socialist-dominated KPCC (Namboodiripad, 1968: 158–59). Simultaneously, further strains were produced by the radical agrarian agitations led by Socialists in Malabar which appeared to create trouble for the Congress government of Madras, elected on a radical platform in 1937 but unwilling in practice to address the grievances of the Malabar peasantry.

War in Europe added to these well-developed conflicts. The leftists in Kerala supported an open struggle against India's being dragged into a war among imperialist powers. The conservatives within the national Congress held that the war was indeed imperialist, but could be supported under certain conditions (most importantly a promise of complete independence). Leftists around Nehru worried that total opposition to the war effort would harm nations such as China, and perhaps even India itself (Nehru, 1946: 331–63; Thorner, 1980: 82–90; Namboodiripad, 1968: 169).

These strains culminated in a decision by the leadership of the Kerala CSP to declare itself the Communist party of Kerala on January 26, 1940.

Virtually the entire left within the Congress joined the new party. Since the Communist party of India was then banned by the colonial government, the Congress members who formed the Communist party in Kerala retained their primary membership in the Congress (Fic, 1970: 22). The Communists immediately began to mobilize militant opposition to the war effort, again outflanking the Congress. At that time, the Communists viewed the war as "an attempt of antagonistic imperialist groups to repartition the world among themselves" (Namboodiripad, 1952: 151). Thus, any participation by India on behalf of Britain was to be opposed. When the Soviet Union was invaded on June 22, 1941, the Kerala Communists, in accordance with the international Communist position, turned a *volte face* which is widely seen as a source of the party's subsequent weakness on the national level: they declared the war supportable as one which "would decide the future of the Soviet Union and through it of world socialism" (ibid.).

This famous reversal put the Congress and the Communists on opposite sides in a curious way; as Congress activists were jailed for their opposition to the war after Gandhi's "Quit India" ultimatum in 1942, the Communists were released from jail and allowed to operate openly. The Communists have since agonized about the loss of credibility entailed in the switch of lines, and admit that the party put itself in opposition to the deep antiimperialist sentiments of the Indian people. But the common portrayal of the Indian Communists as unfortunate puppets of Moscow is misleading; had militant fascism been able to destroy socialism in the Soviet Union, Communists in the colonial world would have lost an important ally. Still, there were immediate political costs; as the first Communist Chief Minister, E.M.S. Namboodiripad (1968: 171–72) noted, "the Communists who had always been regarded to be the fighters appeared as compromisers" and, more seriously, "a new generation of anti-imperialists grew who genuinely believed that the Communist Party was a paid agent of British imperialism."

More proximate damage was the desertion of many leading leftists who formed the Kerala Socialist party in 1942 and began competing with the Communists for control of mass organizations—trade unions, student and peasant associations. Whereas not a single member of the CSP had dissented from the decision to form a Communist party, many could not accept what was perceived to be the party's subordination of Indian interests to Moscow (Fic, 1970: 26–28; Namboodiripad, 1952: 152–54; 1968: 172; Krishnan, 1971: 95ff.).

Despite the fracturing of leftist unity, the position of the Communist party from 1942–45 had advantages. Since the Communists could operate above ground, and Congress activists were jailed, the party was able to recover and expand its peasant and working-class organizations. Moreover, party activities on price controls, food rationing, the Grow More Food campaign, and famine relief built popular support (Thorner, 1980: 93). A Kerala Communist leader noted: "By every criterion of organizational strength of any political party—such as funds collected from the people, the number as well as the quality of work of cadres, the circulation of the Party organ, the average sale of political pamphlets and other publications, etc.—the Party created epoch-making records" (Namboodiripad, 1968: 175).

Despite the desertion of the Socialists in 1942, the Communists retained the strongest base in the mass organizations of workers, peasants, and students, and, as even their critics admitted, the most extensive, disciplined, active, and dedicated network of local-level cadres. Despite the symbolic liability of perceived collaboration with the British while Congress activists languished in jail (as Nehru charged, "they were on the other side in 1942"), the hardships of the war years gave the Communists new opportunities to demonstrate commitment to alleviation of the daily difficulties of ordinary people—from inflation to cholera.

Fracturing of leftist unity at the elite level and the formation of the Socialist party proved to be serious blows to the electoral prospects of both the Congress and the Communists. The Kerala Socialist party itself eventually fractured and added to the instability of Kerala politics, which have been among the most unstable in India. Though Socialist parties have joined coalitions with the Communists, they have also refused to do so at critical junctures—such as 1954 and 1960. It was the predominantly leftist character of the Congress movement in Kerala, as demonstrated by the organizational dominance of the CSP, which denied the Congress electoral hegemony in Kerala after independence comparable to that established elsewhere.

THE FIRST COMMUNIST STATE GOVERNMENT: 1957

From 1947 until 1957, Kerala had no unified state politics or government. Malabar was incorporated into the Tamil-majority state of Madras (now Tamilnadu), whereas Cochin and Travancore were merged into one state. During that period, the state's Congress exhibited the characteristics implied by Sen Gupta's characterization of the party as one of the "weakest and most fragmented in the country" (1972: 175). In Travancore-Cochin there were ten ministries in nine years, all but one Congress-led: the exception was a ministry of the Praja Socialist party supported by Congress. Internal intrigues and personal/communal rivalries doomed each of these governments (Fic, 1970: 31–51); the Socialist government fell when it pushed leftist programs, including land reform, too far for the Congress (cf. Oommen, 1975: 32).

Congress's failure to form stable governments in the period between 1947 and 1956 is in part attributable to the electoral strength of the leftists—Socialists and Communists—but is also a failure of programatic cohesion. As an umbrella party, the Congress locally contained warring factions and communities, a microcosm of the extremely plural society which produced it. E.M.S. Namboodiripad noted that "many genuine democrats" wanted to "give Congress a chance," and opposed Communist agitations against the new government; but what those "genuine democrats" received instead of government was "mutual squabbles on the issue of dividing the loot" generated by control of the state. The result was widespread disgust with Congress ministries, which rival Congress factions used to bring down successive governments (Namboodiripad, 1968: 193; cf. Fic, 1970: 31ff.).

The phenomenon of an independence movement losing its vision with the attainment of independence, and subsequently lapsing into corruption, factionalism, and support of the status quo is not unusual. But in Kerala the independence struggle was predominantly a struggle for social change, which implied redistribution of power, wealth, and privilege; the Congress could not deliver. Indeed, there were historical precedents which presaged this outcome. When the Congress campaigned nationally for limited representative government under the British in 1937, it was on a radical agrarian and labor program. Once in power, Congress governments found that right-wing control of the party machinery largely thwarted the promises hammered out elegantly by the Nehru faction. In 1938, Nehru wrote to Gandhi a prescient observation on the Congress ministries in power: "They are trying to adapt themselves far too much to the old order and trying to justify it. . . . What is far worse is that we are losing the high position that we have built up, with so much labor, in the hearts of the people. We are sinking to the level of ordinary politicians" (in Thorner, 1980: 71).

When the first elections in the integrated state of Kerala were held, the Congress had already shown itself incapable of governing in Travancore-Cochin, despite its position as the most successful party at the polls. Second, the Congress governments had shown themselves unwilling to promote or even support a redistribution of power and privilege to the peasantry and working class, despite continuing resolutions in that direction from the national Congress leadership. Indeed, just as the Karachi Congress session of 1931 and the radical Congress election manifesto in 1937 had added legitimacy to the program of the left, and embarrassed the Congress when disregarded by Congress politicians in practice, developments of the independent period further legitimized the Communist program. The Indian constitution contains a number of powerful provisions concerning social justice, and in 1955, at the Avadi meeting of the Congress, came the resolution pledging work toward "a socialist pattern of society."

The political process which resulted in the formation of a Malayalam-speaking state of Kerala also produced considerable conflict and popular mobilization; the Communists emerged from that struggle as champions of deeply felt popular aspirations. The demands for reorganization of states from the patchwork of British administrative units provoked widespread agitation and violence in India (Brecher, 1959: 181–86). Though the Congress movement had organized itself along the lines of linguistic protostates, better to carry on grass-roots mobilization, Congress leadership in independent India found the demands for reorganization of states along linguistic lines troubling on grounds of national integration.

The collective identity of the Malayalam-speaking people is strong, expressed in legends of origin, special cultural practices, and vigorous literary traditions. The CPI had formulated a proposal for Aikya (United) Kerala in the 1942–45 period and led continuing agitations for a Malayalee state. When that was achieved, on November 1, 1956, after the examination of the States Reorganization Commission from Delhi, the Communists were in a solid position to campaign for the following elections on the basis of past accomplishments and a program of radical social change for the future.

In the campaign, the Communists excoriated the Congress for inept governance and suppression of legitimate popular demands. Their manifesto stressed industrial development with increased funds from Delhi, wage increases, nationalization of foreign-owned plantations, decentralization of administration, sweeping agrarian reforms, and a "new police policy" to prevent the police from suppressing peasant and working-class agitations. These planks, with the exception of the new police policy, did not differ fundamentally from announced policies of the national government and Congress party. Indeed, Nehru's support for "a socialistic pattern of society" embarrassed local red-baiting Congress leaders who argued that India could never be a Socialist society (Fic, 1970: 69). As the eventual chief minister stressed, the Communist view of state government was that the party could not create revolution in one state, but could simultaneously ease the immediate hardships of the oppressed and demonstrate the hypocrisy of Congress leaders by implementing fairly radical Congress promises (Namboodiripad, 1959; Herring, 1983: ch. 6).

In the 1957 elections, the Communists stood alone, as the Socialist parties refused to cooperate. Nevertheless, the Communists won 60 seats of the 126 in the assembly, polling 35 percent of the popular vote. With 5 Independents whom they had supported, the Communists thus had an absolute majority in the legislature and formed a ministry headed by E.M.S. Namboodiripad. The Congress received 37 percent of the vote, and 43 seats; the two Socialist parties, 14 percent of the vote and 9 seats.

The Communist party ministry did not last its full term, but its twenty-eight months of rule were far longer than that of typical preceding governments. The government pushed its program very hard, but met stiff resistance from Delhi and the courts, particularly on agrarian reforms. The Congress launched a "liberation struggle," vowing "to paralyze the administration," striking particularly hard on the issue of educational reform and the agrarian legislation. The opposition created a "law and order" problem, aided significantly by contributions from abroad, and demanded dismissal of the government by Delhi. Nehru vacillated, almost certainly embarrassed that Socialist programs which he supported were the object of so much vituperation by the state-level Congress party. Finally he ordered the government dismissed on July 31, 1959.[5] Significantly, the Congress president at the time was Indira Gandhi.

The following elections demonstrated how popular the Communist government had been, despite the "liberation struggle." The Communists increased their share of the vote to 39 percent, polling more than 1.2 million votes more than in the 1957 elections. However, with the other parties aligned against it, the CPI won only 26 seats. The Congress saw its percentage of the vote fall to 34.5, lower than the Communist percentage for the first time; yet it won half of the assembly seats and formed yet another short-lived coalition ministry with the Praja Socialist party (which contributed the Chief Minister) and, incongruously, the Muslim League.

The very strong showing of the Communists in the 1960 elections demonstrated that the 1957 victory was more than a dual response to the unpopularity of the preceding Congress regimes and a cashing in of credit gained in the subnationalist struggle for a linguistic state: the Communist programs, particularly their agrarian reforms, evoked considerable mass support. Indeed, the scuttling of the agrarian reforms by the courts and subsequent Congress ministries provided an issue for intensified mobilization of the rural poor, and further polarization between the parties of the "haves," led by the Congress, and those of the "have nots," led by the Communists (cf. Gopalan, 1973: ch. 27; Paulini, 1978: 258–62; Koshy, 1976: 229–32; Herring, 1983: ch. 6). The longstanding Congress promise

[5] On the politics of the ministry, Sen Gupta, 1972: ch. 7; Overstreet and Windmiller, 1959: 548–51; Fic, 1970: chs. 4, 5; Namboodiripad, 1959 and 1968: 206–18; Herring, 1983: ch. 6; Paulini, 1978: 231–45; Gopalan, 1973: ch. 27; Lieten, 1979; Nossiter, 1982: 140–67.

of "land to the tiller," legislated by the Communist party, remained a central issue of political conflict and rural violence into the 1970s.

THE RESULTANT PARTY SYSTEM OF KERALA: FACTIONS, SPLITS, AND COALITIONS

The dominant dynamic in the party system of Kerala has been closely contested competition between the dominant parties—the Congress and the Communists—with neither able to rule without allies in unstable coalitions. A second important dynamic is the continuous formation of factions in the dominant parties, particularly the Congress, precipitating splits and thus further fragmentation of the party system. By the 1970 elections, sixteen parties were fielding candidates; by 1982, twenty-two.

Both dominant parties split in 1964. From the Congress, a splinter group, largely representing Christian landed interests—the Kerala Congress—split off with a solid, though small, regional base. That splinter later split into three parties in the 1970s. The main body of the Congress likewise split along with the national division between Indira Gandhi's faction and the "organization" (or Congress-O, which failed to take hold in Kerala in a serious way). Subsequent labyrinthine realignments centered on cooperation with or opposition to Indira Gandhi during the Emergency. There are now three parties claiming the Congress label, and three claiming that of the Kerala Congress. Analysis of the tactical twists and turns of these "parties" suggests that they are all more properly termed community- or personality-based factions, born more of convenience and opportunism than of program, held together more by patronage potential than by ideology or organizational cohesion.[6]

The Communist party likewise split in 1964 into what are usually, and correctly, called right and left wings. The right Communists retained both the original designation (CPI) and a majority of the top leadership. The left wing is called the Communist party of India-Marxist, or CPI-M, or, usually, simply the Marxists; it retained the allegiance of the most militant activists and the primary loyalty of the mass base, particularly the agrarian organizations. The right Communists were acutely embarrassed in the first election after the split, winning only three of one hundred seats contested; seventy-five of their candidates lost their deposits, having received less than 6 percent of the votes cast. The left Communists, in marked contrast, became the strongest single electoral party in the state, though by a

---

[6] The account of alliance behavior and outcomes is amalgamated from *Proceedings of the Kerala Assembly*, official election reportage, publications by the major political parties, newspaper accounts and the author's field research in Kerala (1973; 1979–80; 1983).

narrow margin. The further splintering of the national communist movement in 1968—the formation of the Communist party of India (Marxist-Leninist)—did not significantly affect the Kerala Communists, though ultraleftist factions remain in evidence (Hardgrave, 1973, 1975; Sen Gupta, 1972: 199).

Among the shifts in coalition strategy, one caused great bitterness and produced the longest lasting government in Kerala's history: the alliance between the right Communists and Indira Gandhi's Congress, led by the CPI, beginning in 1970. That coalition was born in the dissolution of the United Front government, dominated by the CPI-M with Namboodiripad again the chief minister, which had united Communists and Socialists from 1967 to 1969. Given the intense, historically rooted bitterness between the Communists and the Congress, and the overwhelming electoral success of the leftist front, that odd marriage requires some explanation.

There was always a deep division in the Communist movement on the importance of progressive elements and programs represented by the Congress, and thus on the extent to which tactical alliances were legitimate.[7] The debate after 1969 centered on Indira Gandhi's radical redistributionist claims (the "garibi hatao," or "abolish poverty" campaign), just as in the early period of independence the issue was whether or not to "strengthen Nehru's hand." Given the history of Congress performance, particularly in state governments, and the slipping of Congress hegemony in the 1967 general elections, it was clear that Indira Gandhi needed to revive the image of Congress as a force for social justice (Koshy, 1976: 246ff.). The consideration of partial alliance with the right Communists must be seen in the context of other nominally leftist symbolic gestures by Indira's Congress: the abolition of annuities for former rulers of "princely states," the nationalization of banks, renewed rhetoric on the need for land reform, and so on. In Kerala, the Congress needed allies desperately, as it had been almost eliminated from the state assembly in 1967 (9 of 133 seats) by the alliance of other parties against it. The CPI not only had new presumptive evidence of the progressive character of the Congress after the 1969 split, but was clearly fearful of being dominated within the left by the mass base of the CPI-M. Indeed, the CPI is sometimes referred to as a "mushroom party"—possessing an attractive top but virtually no roots, particularly in the villages.

The second important characteristic of electoral performance of the major parties in Kerala is the low correlation between percentage of the

[7] For a compendious, and unrelentingly hostile, treatment of the national Communist movement in India, see Overstreet and Windmiller, 1959, especially chs. 12 and 13. Also, Sen Gupta, 1972: chs. 2 and 3. On the connection between national Communist politics and the Kerala party, see Fic, 1970; Paulini, 1978.

vote and strength in the assembly. For example, in 1967 the Congress received 36 percent of votes cast, but only 6.8 percent of the assembly seats; in 1960, the CPI polled 39 percent of the votes but only 23 percent of the assembly seats. There is, of course, nothing surprising about this result, given the dynamics of coalition behavior in a parliamentary system lacking proportional representation, but it does add to two pressures which have become characteristic of Kerala politics. First is the pressure to register intensely held positions outside normal electoral channels; when the Communists were excluded from power in the assembly in 1960, despite their strong electoral showing, because of the electoral coalition forged to deny them power, the rural poor mounted massive protests to support the CPI's agrarian reforms (which were being vitiated in the new assembly). Second, there is significant pressure to form electoral alliances to prevent the other dominant party from forming a government. By 1980, even the left Communists were willing to form coalition fronts with Congress splinter parties to prevent the Indira Congress from forming a government. The result is dilution of the common programs of the coalitions to the least common denominator, detracting from both the clarity of issues for the voters and the possibility of coherent political will in the resultant government. These dynamics are a direct result of the indecisive competition between blocs led by the Congress and the Communists over the decades and seem to be embedded in the party system for the foreseeable future.

ECOLOGICAL DETERMINANTS OF PARTY SUCCESS AND FAILURE: THE IRONY OF SUCCESS

Donald Zagoria (1971) has argued that Communist electoral support in India is heavily determined by ecological-demographic conditions: the Communists do well in areas characterized by agrarian crisis, identified by high population/land ratios, high rates of tenancy, and a large percentage of the agrarian population with subviable plots of land. Kerala indeed represents the agrarian crisis of India in extreme form; historically, the area has had the lowest per capita availability of land, the highest rates of tenancy, and the largest proportion of landless laborers—the most depressed agrarian class (Hart and Herring, 1977; Herring, 1983: ch. 6). The Malabar region exhibited these characteristics in extreme form, and spawned the most extensive and radical agrarian movement in South India.

K. G. Krishna Murthy and G. Lakshmana Rao (1968: ch. VI) have demonstrated that the Communists received their strongest electoral support in Kerala in areas characterized by a high ratio of landless agricultural laborers to cultivators, the weakest support in areas where the cultivators dominate; Congress support is the mirror image. Indeed, the conservative argument for land reform internationally, from Japan and Taiwan and Vietnam through El Salvador, has been that small rural propertyholders are likely to ignore the appeals of the Communists and support conservative regimes (Ladejinsky, 1951; McCoy, 1971). This understanding has long perplexed leftists in the formulation of agrarian strategy; at least since Lenin there has been a fear that agrarian reform will simply turn a radical class into a conservative one. Gunnar Myrdal has explicitly argued this case for India as a whole: piecemeal reforms have strengthened the political and economic power of middle sectors of the peasantry, decreasing the potential for radical land reforms (1968, 2: 1367).

There are two important implications of this analysis. First, a radical party may be victimized by its own success—the land reforms of the Communists not only established a newly landed, and presumably proproperty, class, but also removed the most extreme forms of "moral outrage" which propel radical movements. That is, the ecological niche which generated potential support for the Communists disappears as the Communists gain sufficient power to reform the system but do not have sufficient power to control the state or fundamentally remake society. The fruits of past Communist success may indeed sow the seeds of future failure (cf. Krishnaji, 1979; Herring, 1980; Mencher, 1980).

Similar dynamics appear to apply to social groups other than the tenantry. Organizational work and militance, nurtured for decades by the Communists, have produced remarkable gains in wages, benefits, and working conditions for laborers in both industry and agriculture relative to productivity and relative to conditions elsewhere in India. But with a militant and well-protected labor force, how are the Communists, when they govern, to prevent capital flight and capital strikes, much less attract new investment as they have tried fervently to do? Underemployment has long been particularly severe in Kerala; capital strikes and capital flight aggravate that situation. The excruciating dilemma for the Communists is that prolabor policies may ironically redound to the disadvantage of the most depressed classes, precisely because the state government does not have the power to control the broader arena within which economic dynamics operate, nor the power to preside over any but a capitalist system.

The second implication of Communist success is that conservative parties are capable of learning. Symbolically, the Congress in Kerala has increasingly espoused radical policies. After sinking the first Communist agrarian reform from the state and national levels, and then substituting a pale shadow to respond to vigorous peasant protests, the Congress presented itself as the champion of land reform in the 1970s. The United Front land reforms, legislated by an explicitly anti-Congress coalition, were implemented by a Congress-backed government (albeit haltingly and in response to threats from the CPI-M and the radical agrarian left); ironically, the state-level Congress—the historical opponent of "land to the tiller"—received at least partial credit for finally accomplishing a goal proclaimed by the national Congress in 1931 and 1937 and codified by the Congress Agrarian Reform Committee in 1949, but legislated only under Communist regimes (Herring, 1983: 153–216).

But politics is not entirely symbolic; there is an organizational learning process as well. The various splinter factions of the Congress have sponsored local and statewide organizations of peasants, workers, and students—and most recently, even of agricultural laborers, the largest single occupational category (and most depressed class) in the state. If the Communists can no longer advocate further redistribution of a virtually constant economic pie without losing support of the small farmers who hire laborers, then the only remaining strategy is to advocate expanding the pie instead in a quasi-corporatist strategy. But this the Congress can offer as well, and has historically preferred it to redistribution. Moreover, the Congress can offer it with somewhat better prospects, since the Communists have no friends in Delhi, where the resources for development must be sought.

The conclusion is that the notion of ecological niche contributes to the understanding of party success and failure, but is too static to capture the dynamics of change. Moreover, the ecological/structural perspective tells us very little about the process of translating objective conditions into political action. Kerala, and Malabar in particular, presented a structural niche for a radical party: a configuration of extreme insecurity, exploitation, and social oppression which, once politicized, could be answered only through radical tactics and strategy. The Congress, for reasons of ideology and class base, could not answer and would not mobilize those inchoate radical social forces (Herring, 1984).

The structural conditions stressed by Zagoria and others thus provide the necessary but not sufficient conditions for "moral outrage" (Moore, 1978). Structural conditions spawning exploitation, indignity, and insecurity are a necessary condition for mass-based, sustained moral outrage, but are not sufficient. Extreme misery and insecurity may, and often do, produce nothing more than quiescence, whether from fear of repression or through legitimating ideologies which explain those conditions as warranted, inevitable, or immutable. The least secure and most exploited may turn to organized militance, but may alternatively seek limited, often illusory, security through identification with and loyalty to patrons whose patronage powers are guaranteed by continuance of the existing order. Such dependence through patronage networks has been a major source of Congress strength among the poorest classes, in Kerala and throughout India (Frankel, 1972; Michie, 1978; Weiner, 1968).

Why widespread moral outrage develops spontaneously in some conditions and not others is a complex problem. In Malabar there were peasant insurrections long before there were Communists. But for sporadic jacqueries to develop into a coherent, sustained movement requires leadership and organization. The radicals in the Congress were uniquely able to respond to the inchoate bitterness and anger of the oppressed sections of the population, to build organizations among them, and to carry on continuous education linking local outrage to the understanding that the entire system was responsible: it was not that a given landlord or capitalist was evil, but rather that the logic of these systems generated insecurity and poverty. The Kerala Communists proved willing to investigate, learn from, and mobilize the outrage of the peasantry and to link their potential energy to the small, but radical, working class. In doing so, they built alternative networks of partial security and self-help among the peasants and workers, offering an alternative to the patronage systems of dominant elites. The Congress largely accepted and mobilized through those networks, and certainly did not threaten to destroy their material base—traditional inequalities of wealth and power.

In explaining the success of Communists in Kerala relative to other areas, structural variables take us only so far; it is clear that the leftists in Kerala developed a remarkable group of leaders, and that there was nothing automatic about this development. Namboodiripad admits that in the first conflict in the Congress between supporters of landlords and supporters of tenants, he voted with the landlords (casually noting that he was, after all, a scion of a Brahmin landlord family). When he inherited the family property, he had to deal with tenants as both landlord (who evicted "three or four" tenants) and Socialist leader mobilizing on the slogan: "death to landlordism." Namboodiripad sold the family estate and donated the proceeds to launch the Communist newspaper (Namboodiripad, 1976: 75–76, 195–98). Though Namboodiripad provides an explicit account of his transformation from aristocratic offspring to Communist out-caste, it is difficult to explain the conversion of Kerala's Communist leaders generally. Their dedication and integrity were truly remarkable; it says a great deal that Krishna Pillai died of a snake bite in the mud hut of a landless laborer or that A. K. Gopalan lived much of his life in ill health because of periodic malnutrition and abuse in prison.

But whatever the origins, the leadership of the left in Kerala proved to be a rare political asset. It is noteworthy that the left in Kerala has produced a number of leaders of national stature, in marked contrast to the Congress. They understood, like Mao Zedong, the importance of the peasantry, while Communists in some other parts of India remained urban-centered and dedicated to rigid European theories of revolution. Their political tactics began with concrete investigation of the grievances of the majority of the population; the Congress, beginning from an elite and middle-class base, did indeed expand to encompass ever lower orders of Indian society (Kochanek, 1968), but the aggregation of interests was an additive process in which full commitment to those at the bottom was precluded by the preexisting organizational strength of those at the top. The leadership of the left shared the moral outrage of the lower orders, and dedicated themselves uncompromisingly to redress; the conservatives in the Congress knew that the political expression of that outrage was a threat to the society they wished to rescue from foreign domination.

The notion of ecological niche is thus crucial for explaining the success of a radical political party—and its political limits—and the failure of a compromising umbrella party. Limits are born partly of success; Namboodiripad identifies two critical factors in the success of the revolutionary movement—antiimperialism and the peasantry. The colonial state is gone, and the tenantry has become propertied through agrarian reforms which abolished landlordism. Extreme social indignities imposed on the lowest orders have been removed. The Communists retain considerable support because of their uncompromising commitment to the poor, but the means to achieve greater social justice are no longer so clear, and moral outrage is no longer so dominant, widespread, or focused a force. Simultaneously, social forces opposed to redistribution have been augmented by the process of redistribution. The former tenants, now landed proprietors, are no more eager to surrender their land or pay higher wages to the landless laborers than were the landlords—and they are both more numerous and better connected in the villages than were the rentiers. Most people in Kerala remain poor, but it is no longer clear what the Communists can do for them (Herring, 1985).

The final sense in which the Communists may have become victims of their success is less measurable, but important. Just as Nehru warned Gandhi in 1938 that Congress activists in power were "sinking to the level of ordinary politicians," some Communist leaders who struggled through the dark years of repression and struggle worry that a new generation of party members lacks the commitment of their predecessors (e.g., Gopalan, 1973: 263; Krishnan, 1971: 72). In many parts of Kerala, a generation of young people has matured in a milieu in which the road to political success lies through the Communist party, just as it does through the Congress party in much of India.

It would thus be extremely surprising if the Communist party, having become both legitimate and successful, did not attract its share of opportunists, hacks, and time-servers. To the extent that this is true, a major source of Communist success is jeopardized. That source is the intangible character of commitment of local-level cadres; it is captured nicely in the following description of the CPI of the 1950s by a leading Malayalam daily (*Mathrubhoomi*) which supports the Congress:

> Deep-rooted in the soil of Kerala and tended by constant care and attention of its activists is the Communist party of Kerala. In every remote village there are Communist activists who are closest to the most downtrodden of the people and who have identified themselves with these sections. It might be that he goes about like a vagabond. But in his village, he keeps contact with all individuals. And he takes the message of the party to every heart. He has an objective which keeps him inspired. And to achieve that objective he devotes his self-sacrificing endeavors. The better tomorrow may perhaps be a mirage, but to him it is the complete truth. And the means to achieve his aims he finds in the Communist party. The party is his body and soul (Sen Gupta, 1972: 182–83).

There was a time when much the same could be said of Congress activists, many of whom eventually founded the Communist party. That level of commitment is a rare political commodity, difficult to maintain in the absence of burning moral issues with clear solutions, and in the presence of electoral politics-as-usual—compromised, tactically expedient, more oriented toward winning elections and holding positions than to social revolution. The Congress has held national power, and largely abandoned its aspirational, transformational tenets. The Communists have the opposite problem: unlikely to attain national power, and unable to work a Socialist revolution in one state, they find it difficult to formulate a program which regenerates the surging movements of earlier decades and separates them decisively from the "ordinary politicians" Nehru and Gandhi viewed with such unease.

REFERENCES

Aiyappan, A. 1965. Social revolution in Kerala village. Bombay: Asia Publishing.

Brass, P. R., and M. Franda, eds. 1973. Radical politics in South Asia. Cambridge: MIT Press.

Brecher, M. 1959. Nehru: A political biography. London: Oxford University Press.

Dhanagre, D. N. 1975. Agrarian movements and Gandhian politics. Agra: University Press.

Fic, V. M. 1970. Kerala: Yenan of India: Rise of communist power, 1937–1969. Bombay: Nachiketa.

Frankel, F. R. 1972. India's green revolution: Economic gains and political costs. Princeton: Princeton University Press.

Gandhi, M. K. 1966. Socialism of my conception, ed. A. T. Hingorani. Bombay: Bharatiya Vidya Bhavan.

———. 1970. My theory of trusteeship, ed. A. T. Hingorani. Bombay: Bharatiya Vidaya Bhavan.

George, K. C. 1975. Immortal punnapra-vayalar. New Delhi: Communist Party of India.

Gopalan, A. K. 1973. In the cause of the people: Reminiscences. Bombay: Orient Longman.

Hardgrave, R. L., Jr. 1973. The Kerala communists. In Brass and Franda, 1973.

———. 1975. The Communist parties of Kerala: An electoral profile. In Electoral politics in the Indian states: Party systems and cleavages, ed. M. Weiner and J. O. Field. Delhi: Manohar.

———. 1977. The Mappilla rebellion, 1921: Peasant revolt in Malabar. *Modern Asian Studies* 11: 1.

Hart, H. C., and R. J. Herring. 1977. Political conditions of land reform: Kerala and Maharashtra. In *Land tenure and peasant in South Asia*, ed. R. E. Frykenberg. Delhi: Orient Longman.

Herring, R. J. 1980. Abolition of landlordism in Kerala: A redistribution of privilege. *Economic and Political Weekly* 15: 26.

———. 1983. Land to the tiller: The political economy of agrarian reform in South Asia. New Haven: Yale University Press.

———. 1984. Structural niches, agents and issues of horizontal mobilization in Kerala. Workshop on Status, Class and Dominance, New Delhi, 1983.

———. 1985. From moral economy to marshallian dilemmas: Redistributive policy and landless laborers after the land reforms in Kerala (South India). Paper given at the American Political Science Association meeting, New Orleans.

Government of India, periodic, Election Commission. *Election commission reports*. New Delhi.

Government of Kerala, periodic, Secretariat of the Kerala Legislature. *Synopsis of the proceedings of the Kerala legislative assembly*. Trivandrum.

———. 1977a. Department of Public Relations. *Kerala election reportage, 1977*. Trivandrum.

———. 1977b. Planning Board. *Statistics for planning*. Trivandrum.

Kochanek, S. A. 1968. The Congress party of India: The dynamics of one-party democracy. Princeton: Princeton University Press.

Koshy, V. C. 1976. The politics of land reforms in Kerala. Ph.D. diss., Jawaharalal Nehru University, New Delhi.

Krishna Murthy, K. G. and G. Lakshmana Rao. 1968. *Political references in Kerala*. New Delhi: Radhakrishna Prakashan.

Krishnan, T. V. 1971. *Kerala's first communist: Life of "Sakhavu" Krishna Pillai*. New Delhi: Communist Party of India.

Kurup, K.K.N. 1981. *William Logan: A study in the agrarian relations of Malabar*. Calicut: Sandya.

Ladejinsky, W. 1951. The plow outbids the sword in Asia: How General MacArthur stole Communist thunder with democratic land reforms, our most potent weapon for peace. *Country Gentleman* (now *Farm Journal*), June.

Leiten, G. K. 1979. Progressive state governments: An assessment of the first Communist ministry in Kerala. *Economic and Political Weekly* 14: 1.

McCoy, A. 1971. Land reform as counter-revolutions: U.S. foreign policy and the tenant. *Bulletin of Concerned Asian Scholars* 3: 1.

McLane, J. R. 1978. *Indian nationalism and the early Congress*. Princeton: Princeton University Press.

Mencher, J. P. 1980. The lessons and non-lessons of Kerala: Agricultural labourers and poverty. *Economic and Political Weekly* 15: 41–43.

Michie, A. N. 1979. Agricultural policy and political viability in rural India. *Comparative Political Studies* 12: 3.

Moore, B., Jr. 1978. *Injustice: The social bases of obedience and revolt*. White Plains, N.Y.: M. E. Sharpe.

Morris, M. D., and M. B. McAlpin. 1980. Measuring welfare in South Asia. ssrc/icssr Conference on South Asian Political Economy. New Delhi, Dec. 12–16.

Myrdal, G. 1968. *Asian drama: An inquiry into the poverty of nations*. New York: Random House.

Namboodiripad, E.M.S. 1952. *The national question in Kerala*. Bombay: People's Publishing House.

———. 1959. *Twenty-eight months in Kerala: A retrospect*. New Delhi: People's Publishing House.

———. 1968. *Kerala: past, present and future*. Calcutta: National Book Agency.

———. 1976. *How I became a communist*, trans. P. K. Nair. Trivandrum: China.

———. 1981. Once again on castes and classes. *Social Scientist* 9: 12.

Nehru, J. 1946. *The discovery of India*. New York: John Day.

Niranjana. 1974. *The stars shine brightly: Saga of the kayoor martyrs (Chirasmarane)*, trans. Tejaswini Niranjana. New Delhi: People's Publishing House.

Nossiter, T. J. 1982. *Communism in Kerala*. Berkeley: University of California Press.

Oommen, M. A. 1975. *A study of land reforms in Kerala*. New Delhi: Oxford and IBH.

Oommen, T. K. 1976. Problems of building agrarian organizations in Kerala. *Sociologia Ruralis* 16: 3.

Overstreet, G. D., and M. Windmiller. 1959. *Communism in India*. Berkeley: University of California Press.

Pandian, M.S.S. 1980. Caste and class in upper cloth riots, South Travancore, 1820–1860. *Mainstream*, March 1.

Pannikar, K. N. 1979. Peasant revolts in Malabar in the nineteeth and twentieth centuries. In *Peasant struggles in India*, ed. A. R. Desai. Bombay: Oxford University Press.

Parameswaran, S. 1951. Peasant question in Kerala. Bombay: People's Publishing House.

Paulini, T. 1978. Agrarian movements and reforms in India: The case of Kerala. Ph.D. diss., University of Stuttgart.

Pillai, T. S. 1967. *Two measures of rice*. Bombay: Jaico.

Popkin, S. L. 1979. *The rational peasant*. Berkeley: University of California Press.

Radhikrishnan, P. 1980. Peasant struggles and land reforms in Malabar. *Economic and Political Weekly* 15: 50.

Rajendran, G. 1974. *The ezhava community and Kerala politics*. Trivandrum: The Kerala Academy of Political Science.

Rudolph, L. I., and S. H. 1981. Transformation of Congress party: Why 1980 was not a restoration. *Economic and Political Weekly* 16: 18.

Saradamoni, K. 1980. *Emergence of a slave caste: Pulayas of Kerala*. New Delhi: People's Publishing House.

Scott, J. C. 1976. *The moral economy of the peasant*. New Haven: Yale University Press.

Sen, B. 1955. *Indian land systems and land reforms*. Delhi: People's Publishing House.

Sen Gupta, B. 1972. *Communism in Indian politics*. New York: Columbia University Press.

Throner, D. 1980. *The shaping of modern India*. New Delhi: Allied.

Varghese, T. C. 1970. *Agrarian change and economic consequences: Land tenure in Kerala 1850–1960*. Bombay: Allied.

Weiner, M. 1968. *Party building in a new nation: The Indian national congress*. Chicago: University of Chicago Press.

———. 1978. *India at the polls: The parliamentary elections of 1977*. Washington, D.C.: American Enterprise Institute.

Zagoria, D. S. 1971. The ecology of peasant communism in India. *American Political Science Review* 65: 144–60.

PART V | Antiauthoritarian
Organizations

SIXTEEN

The Limits of Organization and Enthusiasm: The Double Failure of the Solidarity Movement and the Polish United Workers' Party

ZVI GITELMAN

Communist parties that have come to power not through authentic revolutions, but as a result of the force of Soviet arms, have had a difficult time establishing their legitimate right to rule in the eyes of those over whom they would rule. The genuinely revolutionary Communist regimes—the Soviet, Chinese, and Yugoslav ones are the primary examples—accumulated authority in the course of the struggle for power, first against invading foreigners and then in civil wars against domestic political opponents. In the course of the struggle for power, a political infrastructure was established, adherents were won over, and a persuasive claim to rulership was staked out. By contrast, the derivative Communist regimes of most of Eastern Europe came to power either on the bayonets of a liberating Red Army or as the result of intricate political maneuvering made possible by the presence of Red Army forces. If power was more easily seized by the derivative regimes, or on their behalf, legitimacy was more painfully acquired, if at all. Most of the Communist elites in Eastern Europe have based their rule more on power than on authority, and they have long struggled to shift the balance more in the direction of authority (Gitelman, 1971). The Hungarians have been perhaps the most successful in this endeavor, and the Poles the least. In fact, the events in Poland in 1980–81 can be seen not only as a failure to gain authority for the Communist system, but also as a near loss even of power by the Polish United Workers' party (the Communist party). Authority seemed to fall into the hands of

I would like to thank the Center for Russian and East European Studies, the University of Michigan, and Margalit Tal, for their assistance.

the Solidarity movement, which had started as a trade-union movement but rapidly expanded its role into that of a general political movement. However much authority Solidarity might have gained, its power was quite fragile. In a situation where the party has no authority and was seemingly losing power, and where Solidarity had authority but only intermittent and obstructionist power, it was left to the military, then enjoying both power and authority, to step into the breach. But since civilian, i.e., party, control of the military is a cardinal principle of Soviet-type systems, military rule must be temporary if the Communist character of the system is to be preserved. The military can be returned to its proper role only if the party regains its own. Therefore, the Polish party will be engaged in a desperate struggle at a minimum to regain a monopoly of political power, and, optimally, to establish its authority. At the present time, the prospects for the party's establishment of authority are dim. Even its monopoly of power is challenged by remnants of Solidarity, both underground and above ground, by some elements of the Catholic Church, and, as the murder of Father Jerzy Popieluszko showed dramatically, even by some elements within the security services (and perhaps by their supporters in the USSR). The conditions listed by Frank Wilson elsewhere in this volume for survival and revival of political parties do not apply to the Polish United Workers' party. There seems to be little reason to believe that Poland will follow the French pattern analyzed by Wilson. Rather, the Polish party's failure will prove to be a long-term one, but, at the same time, it is difficult to imagine an alternative which will be viable in the long run.

Since the starting point of the Polish Communist system was similar in time and circumstances to that of others in Eastern Europe, why has this particular regime proved weaker than the others, undergoing major crises in 1956, 1968, 1976, and the early 1980's? The weakness of the Polish United Workers' party (PUWP) derives from both long- and short-term factors. Throughout its history, first as a small, illegal, and quite powerless party, and then as the ruling party, the PUWP has been dogged by its identification with the historic national enemy, Russia. In a profoundly Catholic country, it has stood for atheism. In a country with strong traditions of anti-Semitism, Jews have been overrepresented in its ranks and in its leadership. Nationalistic feelings run strong in a country which has lost its independence on several occasions and which has served as a parade ground for the armies of larger and more powerful nations. Yet, the Communist movement has stood for internationalism and, at times, for the subordination of Polish national interests to Russian ones. Some of the early leaders of Polish communism thought the idea of reconstituting Poland a reactionary and illogical one, ignoring the most powerful sentiment in Polish society, irrespective of class.

It might be objected that the Romanian and Hungarian Communist parties had similar long-term disadvantages. Why have they not experienced a party crisis such as the Polish one? First, in neither country was there an alternative authority structure, like the Polish church, which could make a credible claim to represent the historic nation, its beliefs and values. Second, each of these parties did succeed in building authority, the Romanians through national self-assertion which established them as the legitimate embodiment of the nation-state, and the Hungarians through sustained economic prosperity., relative to the other Socialist countries, and through a parallel relative political relaxation. Third, the Polish party historically had serious internal difficulties which were greater than those of other parties (see Lewis, 1982; Dziewanowski, 1976). Factionalism and ideological deviation have been endemic to the party. It is the only party in the history of the Communist movement to have been officially disbanded. This decision was taken by the Comintern in 1938 following the party's prolonged internal crisis. After the war there were the confrontations between the "Muscovite" and "native" Communists, i.e., those who had returned from refuge in the USSR and had been molded in the Stalinist image, and those who had remained on the home front. There was a conflict between those who wanted to adopt the Soviet model in all its details, and those who generally supported Gomulka's idea of a "Polish road to socialism." In 1956 there was a struggle between the neo-Stalinist Natolin faction of the party and its liberal ("revisionist") counterpart, the Pulawy group. Throughout the 1960s, a variety of factions tugged and pulled the party in various directions. Finally, in recent years the Polish party had looked bad in comparison with sister parties in the region. While Hungarian, Bulgarian, and, to a lesser extent, Czechoslovak and East German Communist leadership could point to economic achievements and political stability as indicators of their successful strategies, a major effort by the Polish leadership to establish authority on the basis of economic achievement was sabotaged by a combination of poor planning and execution by the Poles, on the one hand, and Western economic crisis, on the other.

Having come into power as a result of a workers' revolt against steep price increases announced just before Christmas of 1970, Edward Gierek was seemingly determined not to repeat Wladyslaw Gomulka's mistakes. Reacting to Gomulka's blithe disregard of the consumer and his conservative economic policies which kept the economy relatively insulated from Western involvement, Gierek tried simultaneously to increase investment and consumer consumption on an unparalleled scale. This could be accomplished by increased productivity of inputs, rather than in their quantities, as well as by unprecedented, massive imports of foreign credits, licenses, and products. Between 1971 and 1975, total trade turnover increased 165 percent, with imports from the West increasing by 452 percent and exports growing by 167 percent. The gap between imports and exports would be made up by credits. By 1974 Poland's trade with the West was nearly equal to that with the countries in the Council for Mutual Economic Assistance (CMEA). But her hard currency debt was rapidly mounting, from $7 billion in 1975 to $14 billion in 1979, to about $27 billion in 1981. The gains between 1971 and 1975 were extremely impressive, however. For example, half of Poland's industrial capacity had been installed between 1971 and 1975. This rapid growth seems to have enjoyed wide approval in Polish society, as real income grew by about 7 percent a year, and popular consumer items, such as automobiles, became widely available for the first time. Thus, the political strategy of the PUWP was to accumulate authority by offering material incentives to political compliance and gaining respect and admiration for its economic successes (Gitelman, 1981).

The bubble burst when the Western economies, buffeted by dramatically rising energy costs, went into recession. Unwilling to take Polish exports at a time of domestic belt-tightening, and reluctant to extend further aid and credits to Poland, the Western economies could no longer foot the bill of the ambitious political-economic strategy of First Secretary Gierek and his colleagues. The strategy was crippled by domestic developments as well. The labor force did not increase rapidly enough, the financial system remained rigid, and long-term agricultural and administrative problems remained unsolved and, in many instances, unaddressed (see Baka, 1977; Terry and Korbonski, 1980). The result was an end to economic growth and prosperity, the frustration of rapidly rising consumer expectations, a growing and highly variegated movement of political dissent, and the leadership's unsuccessful attempt, largely by exhortation, to maintain its authority while moving away from material incentives. The years of prosperity might have drawn the party closer to the working class, and certainly created a fairly large group of state and party officials who benefited materially from the leadership's policies. But when the crunch came, the working class was unwilling to extend much political credit to the leadership, which remained with the Socialist nouveau riche and the professional party *apparatchiki* as the social base of its support. This proved to be insufficient to maintain the party's power, let alone to build its authority. The basic failure of the party, then, was that while it claimed to be the "vanguard of the proletariat" and to speak in its name, it had failed to institutionalize its role as the leader of society and to build institutions which could link effectively the working class to the party. As Kay Lawson points out in Chapter 2, "alternative organizations emerge when major parties fail to provide acceptable forms of linkage" between the state and its citizens. The failure of the Polish party to provide this linkage gave rise to an alternative political force, the Solidarity movement, which challenged the party directly, beginning in 1980.

"Overinstitutionalization" and the Relationship between the PUWP and the Proletariat

Samuel Huntington's well-known argument holds that "The primary problem of politics is the lag in the development of political institutions behind social and economic change" (Huntington, 1968: 5). Social and economic modernization lead to a great expansion in political participation, but if the strength of political institutions does not expand concomitantly, political disorder and "decay" result. Stability depends on the institutionalization of participation. Institutionalization is the process whereby organizations and procedures acquire "value and stability" (ibid: 12). While Huntington and others often associate stability with value, in Eastern Europe, at least, these two are separable, and one of the fundamental problems of Eastern European polities is that their institutions are stable—perhaps too stable— but are without value. That is, the institutions endure and are not changed very much, but they do not acquire authority, they are not valued for their own sake. Institutionalization has outstripped participation and mobilization, since these are highly ritualized, *pro forma*, and lacking the sense of efficacy, voluntarism, and responsiveness (Sharlet, 1967; DiFrancesco and Gitelman, 1984). The result is what Mark Kesselman calls "overinstitutionalization," a state when "institutions are better at holding the line than responding to change" (Kesselman, 1970: 24).

Both the PUWP itself, as well as the institutions linking it to the working class, represent failures of institutionalization and are examples of "overinstitutionalization." In both instances, stability, in the sense of organizational forms being preserved, was achieved without value being infused into these forms. Overinstitutionalization forced the working class to go outside the party and the officially sanctioned linking institutions and form Solidarity as the valued institution of the working class. The ultimate failure of Solidarity is also a failure of institutionalization, but this time value was gained quite rapidly, though organizational stability was not achieved, even before external force was used to dissolve the movement. Again, Lawson's generalization is very apt for the Polish case. She points out that alternative organizations to parties, though they may provide what might be called the "missing linkage," may not endure because of factors far beyond their control.

The PUWP has never succeeded in establishing its authority and has ruled largely on the basis of power. In the one post-1947 election which had any meaning at all, that of January 1957, the PUWP won just 51 percent of the vote, and that only because of the irony that the then Primate of Poland, Stefan Cardinal Wyszynski, urged the faithful not to vote against the party lest this bring about a Soviet intervention and an erasure of the gains seemingly won in the upheaval of 1956. As we shall see, public opinion polls conducted in 1980–81 showed that of all the major institutions of the Polish state and society, it was the PUWP which was trusted and valued least. It is a cliche of Polish politics that while the party might represent the *pays légal*, it is the church which stands for the *pays réel*.

The party, whose cells are present in every factory and economic enterprise of any significance, is supposed to be a major link between elites and masses. To the extent that the party is ineffective in performing this role, that linkage is weakened or nonexistent. But there are other mechanisms to provide this linkage. The trade unions are the most prominent among them, but the events of 1980 showed how ineffective they are. In 1956, because workers were disenchanted with the party and the unions, they spontaneously established workers' councils. The Leninist reflex of the party to distrust any spontaneous activity resulted in the emasculation of these councils through the creation of the Conference of Workers' Self-Management (KSR) in 1958. The KSR includes the workers' councils, the official trade unions, the party, the technical organization (STO), and the youth organization of the party. Thus, the councils were diluted and outvoted by organizations controlled by the party. Both the councils and the KSR achieved organizational stability and persisted, but neither achieved value in the eyes of the workers. Empirical studies, even by party sociologists, showed that as early as 1963 and 1965, councils and KSRs were seen as having little influence and importance (Widerszpil, 1965; Jarosz, 1967; Owieczko, 1966, 1967). A typical feeling was that "The workers' council does not inform the workers. . . . Everything takes place behind the workers' backs. . . . No one asks me about anything; only a small group has any influence. . . . KSR representatives do not inform or associate with the workers" (Owieczko, 1967: 21). A perceptive journalist and researcher noted that the party committees in the factories tended to ignore the work crews, the trade unions busied themselves with organizing canteens or supplying workers with fruit, potatoes, and Christmas trees, and the KSR was ineffective since most of its members "are employed in management and are persons holding permanent positions in the sociopolitical organizations [primarily, the party], their activity is identified in the minds of the work crew with the activity of the administration, and generates a belief that their interests are not being represented" (Maciag, 1973: 127).

When he assumed power in 1971, Edward Gierek acknowledged these problems and set about rectifying them by changing the institutional structures linking elites and masses and changing the style of leadership. Aside from an administrative reorganization which abolished one level, the *powiats*, and resulted in a greater centralization of political power, the institutional arrangements remained largely unchanged, with no accretion of value to them. The more populist style of the leadership was generally praised until it showed its inadequacies in 1976 when a major rise in prices announced by a leadership obviously out of touch with the mood of the country had to be rolled back within hours of outbursts of violence (Gitelman, 1977).

Once again, the party leadership failed to draw the obvious conclusions. Instead of reforming and revitalizing the linking institutions, they allowed them to fall into disuse. The number of workers' councils dropped precipitously as fewer enterprises bothered to elect them. By 1978, out of 30,000 enterprises, fewer than 10,000 had any form of self-government. In those councils that remained, the proportion of workers declined. Empirical studies showed that only a small proportion of workers were aware of the councils' activities, and only a minority had the feeling of co-ownership of their workplaces (Maziarski, 1978: 3). Not until 1978, twenty years after the establishment of the KSRs, was the first national meeting held of their representatives. At the second such meeting, held a year later, it was admitted that workers were kept uninformed of controversial matters, that decisions were not only made secretly but were kept from the workers, and that many enterprise administrators felt that in times of economic difficulties there was no place for the development of workers' self-government (Winiarski, 1978: 28–29). Sociological studies continued to show that the KSRs were being dominated by the white-collar employees, that they were the tools of the enterprise administration and that their mission was seen as boosting production. A study of sixty-two WOGs (conglomerates of enterprises) showed that the KSRs almost never exercised their rights in the appointment of directors and that in many cases the KSRs existed "only on paper" (Sadurski, 1979: 16). Thus, in the decade since it had come to power following the breakdown of party-proletarian communication and relations, the leadership of the PUWP had not succeeded in altering that relationship and failed to infuse value into the institutions linking it with the Polish working masses.

The Maturation of the Polish Working Class

Like all countries of the region except Czechoslovakia, Poland was a predominantly agricultural country before World War II, though it has a significant industrial base, working class, and workers' movements and parties. The advent of Communism brought with it extensive industrial growth and mobility out of the peasantry into the proletariat, resulting in rapid urbanization. The number of industrial workers more than doubled between 1950 and 1970. In the latter year, workers and their families and dependents constituted nearly half the Polish population, while in 1930 about 60 percent had been dependent on agriculture for their subsistence. The working class has a high proportion of manual workers and of women. It is a relatively youthful group: in 1968 nearly 30 percent of all those employed in industry and construction were less than twenty-four years old (Jarosinska and Kulpinska, 1974: 137); in 1973, 46 percent of all workers were between thirty and forty-nine years old (Maziarski, 1978). By the late 1970s, nearly 8 million of the 11.7 million people employed in the socialized economy were classified as workers. As the working class grew in size, its educational levels rose. About 47 percent, and a higher proportion in the older cohorts, have only elementary education, but a quarter of the working class has secondary education, nearly 20 percent have advanced vocational training, and 7 percent have higher education (Kuzinski, 1979: 15–17). This is no longer the proletariat of the 1950s—newly arrived from the countryside, with little education and class consciousness—but second- or third-generation urban dwellers with a fair amount of education and considerable class consciousness.

The class consciousness and political sophistication of the working class grew as the result of a cumulative learning experience. The workers made a political revolution in 1956, only to see it eroded by Wladyslaw Gomulka, the great hope of party "revisionists" and workers alike, who, once firmly in power, proceeded to roll back most of the gains made in 1956. In 1970 the workers had the heady experience of forcing the party to remove Gomulka, who had betrayed their hopes, and to replace him with Gierek, pledged to pay closer attention to the needs of workers and consumers and to bring the party and the population closer together. The gap of understanding was never really breached, as the 1976 outbursts showed. The workers had been neutralized in the party's struggle against intellectuals in 1968 and had been largely uninvolved in the issues that agitated the intelligentsia ever since. But when the dissident intellectuals reached out to the workers by forming a committee for the defense of the workers punished for protesting the 1976 price rises, they found a responsive proletariat. It seemed as if the workers had learned that as long as the mass social force of the working class was kept apart from the reformist intelligentsia, the party could control both. The intelligentsia, for its part, had come to respect not only the raw power of the working class, but also its growing political sophistication and its openness to new ideas.

In the upheavals in Hungary and Poland in 1956, and in Czechoslovakia in 1968, it had been the intelligentsia, particularly that part of it which was active in the Communist party, that had shown the way to reform. Pressures for political change emanated largely from the intelligentsia, while the working class seemed most interested in short-term economic changes, and the peasantry remained largely uninvolved. In all three instances, the intelligentsia provided programmatic direction, the working class the large-scale activity, a dissident wing of the party the political legitimacy: political change came about when all of these forces were brought together by some catalyzing event. In March 1968 the PUWP was able to crush a dissident intelligentsia by isolating it from the working class and by holding its own ranks together, despite the challenge to Gomulka's leadership by General Mieczyslaw Moczar and his "Partisan" faction. On the other hand, the toppling of the Gomulka regime in 1970 was accomplished by the workers alone. In the latter half of the 1970s, especially after the worker protests of 1976, an active, pluralist, and vociferous dissident movement emerged in Poland, ironically at just about the time that Soviet dissent was being systematically repressed. The dissidents ranged from nationalists who wanted to restore the prewar system, to neo-Stalinists; from Catholic intellectuals to the Communist "revisionists," some of whom had been active in 1956 and 1968. Dissident activity was widespread and in the open, in contrast to the Soviet dissident movement which was concentrated in a few of the largest cities and generally hidden from public view. Huge amounts of written material were produced by all shades of the Polish dissident movement. In contrast to the furtive *samizdat* of Soviet dissenters, the Polish groups were able to disseminate their materials quite easily, and there was even a dissident publishing house established, though it operated in a somewhat clandestine manner (Bromke, 1978).

One of the best known of the dissident groups was KOR, formed originally to help defend those workers persecuted for their part in the 1976 price riots and to aid their families. Among the KOR activists were veteran dissenters such as Jacek Kuron, former lecturer at Warsaw University and coauthor of a 1964 "Open Letter to the Party" in which the bureaucratization of the system was sharply criticized. In September 1977, KOR expanded its activities to include the defense of civil rights generally, and it became known as the Committee for Social Defense (KSS-KOR). Its periodical, *Robotnik*, was aimed at the working class. By 1978 workers' groups had formed in Katowice and in the Baltic area, calling for the formation of "free trade unions" on a national scale.

THE EROSION OF THE PUWP AND THE RISE OF SOLIDARITY

Every Communist party is challenged by the contradication between two of its most sacred myths. On the one hand, the party is supposed to be one of the working class and for that class. On the other hand, the party is supposed to include within its ranks "the leading elements" of society. As the latter have come to include more and more educated, white-collar people, it has become progressively more difficult to reconcile the working-class character of the party with its desire to include "the leading elements." Typically, the level of education within the party is far higher than that in the population as a whole, and all the ruling European parties have a significantly higher proportion of white-collar members than are in the population as a whole. For this reason, periodic drives have been launched to recruit more blue-collar workers to the party, and at party congresses there are almost always announcements that a very high proportion of the recent recruits to the party are drawn from the blue-collar ranks. Even the casual observer will note that the proportion of workers among the recruits is always considerably higher than the proportion of the workers in the party as a whole, and so the question is, what happens to all those workers who are recruited? The Polish case provides the answer, and illustrates the problematics of worker representation in the Communist party.

The journal of the PUWP, *Zycie Partii*, is full of reports of successful recruitment of workers in the 1970s. In the Czestochowa area the proportion of workers grew from 51.4 percent to 59 percent between 1975 and 1979 (Gryfiel, 1979: 4–5). Similar trends were reported in Lublin (Kruk, 1979: 6–7), Olsztyn (Bialecki, 1975: 10–11), Kutno (Biedrzycki, 1975: 27), and many other places. This does not mean that greater numbers of workers spontaneously flocked to the ranks of the PUWP. Most of them were actively recruited. In the open atmosphere of 1981, it was admitted that many workers were reluctant, and even ashamed, to join the party, and that basic party organizations were assigned membership quotas for which they had to account (Osobka, 1981: 29). Small wonder, then, that "Greater numerical participation of workers in the party may have given the organization a more respectable social profile, but did little to boost its image as a vehicle for blue-collar interests. According to a poll commissioned by the party in 1976, only one in every five industrial workers thought that the party represented their interests." (*Pravda*, 1982: 178).

Perhaps because of such attitudes, the proportion of workers who quit or were expelled from the party was very high. This explains the disparity between the proportions of workers recruited into the party and those who are in its ranks. There is simply a high rate of turnover among the proletarian members of the PUWP (De Weydenthal, 1977: 344–45). When one looks at party membership from the perspective of social class, one finds that in the early 1970s, 40 percent of all engineers and of teachers, and 44 percent of technicians, belonged to the party, but only 13 percent of the blue-collar workers and 4 percent of the farmers did so (ibid.). Moreover, as one goes up the party hierarchy, the number of workers diminishes. While constituting about 46 percent of the membership, workers made up only 10 percent of the central leadership and 2 percent to 3 percent of those who spoke at plenary sessions of the Central Committee (Kolankiewicz, 1982: 54).

The people who really run the party are, of course, the *apparatchiki*, the full-time employees of the party who make their livelihood in it. Kolankiewicz estimates that in recent years there have been 11,600 full-time apparatchiki. Though of working-class origin, they rarely have manual labor experience themselves. They have obtained higher education, but mainly in administration or politics, "which did not make them easily employable elsewhere." Rather, it made them more responsive to their superiors, upon whom promotion depended, than to the organizations they are supposed to serve. "It led to a filtering and distortion of information to make it more acceptable to their masters, but in the process this stifled the critical voice of the grass roots, thus creating an 'apparat party' " (ibid.: 58). As Alex Pravda points out, "By blocking attempts to articulate workers' real interests, the party apparatus further reduced the credibility of the party as a representative organization and inadvertently promoted the cause of blue-collar radicals" (1982: 179). The apparatus also aroused resentment as it became increasingly obvious that it enjoyed access to material benefits unavailable to the rest of the population. In an attempt to improve the quality of the party administration (*Zycie Partii*, 1975: 11–12), Gierek had offered incentives of power and privilege which many of the apparatchiki were able to transform into prosperity. As early as 1978 there were calls for the exposure of the benefits the *apparat* was enjoying, even by those who thought that inequalities were inevitable and even acceptable in a Socialist society.[1] By 1979 the official party journal quoted a sardonic remark, "We have a reversal of the situation in the capitalist system. Over there, property leads to power. Here, power leads to property. And that is unacceptable" (*Zycie Partii*, 1979: 49). In the open atmos-

---

[1] See discussions in *Polityka* during the first half of 1978.

phere of 1980–81, there were many more revelations about the corruption pervading the party and government. The party tried to turn these to its advantage by using charges of corruption to discredit the old leadership, thus setting them up as a scapegoat for discontents who were threatening to topple the new leadership. In May 1981 it was announced that criminal investigations had been launched against 4 ex-ministers, 7 deputy ministers, and 7 former regional officials of state and party. Altogether there were 102 cases opened against top- and middle-level officials. Gierek and his son, former prime ministers Jaroszewicz and Babiuch, and other high officials were charged with the abuse of their positions and power. The most notorious case was that of the director of Polish television, Maciej Szczepanski, who was accused of having built private villas for himself, equipped with a collection of 900 pornographic films, among other amenities. When he tired of these domestic delights, he would betake himself to Paris and other playgrounds of the capitalist world (*Kultura*, 1981: 143). Charges of using public funds for the construction of private homes were brought against 3,422 people by the spring of 1981. Those charged included 3 former secretaries of the party Central Committee, 23 first secretaries of the provincial party committees, 34 other secretaries of those committees, 18 ministers, 56 vice-ministers, and so on (*Kultura*, 1981: 101–102). Small wonder that resentment of inequalities and special privileges for the elite became a central theme of the Solidarity movement. "The resentment of conspicuous consumption by the power elite found a prominent place in the workers' grievances," and demands for redistribution of social welfare benefits, leveling of wages, and limitations of privileges were prominent in Solidarity's appeals and program (Bielasiak, 1983).

A second source of resentment, mostly from party members themselves, was the lack of democracy within the PUWP. On one hand, the party tried in the mid-1970s to improve the quality and activity of its membership. In the 1970s the number of those expelled from the PUWP amounted to 38 percent of the number recruited into its ranks. Most of those expelled were blue-collar workers (Kolodziejczyk, 1979: 7). The most frequent causes of expulsion were "economic crimes" (i.e., abuse of position for personal gain), alcoholism, and "hooliganism." Abuse of power and suppression of criticism were less frequently cited causes of expulsion (J. F., 1975: 25–26).[2] On the other hand, this "quality control" did not induce the leadership to allow more leeway to the presumably improved

---

[2] In 1974, 68,480 party members and candidate members were removed from the rolls. For 1979 figures, see the report by Stanislaw Pawlek, "Kontrola warunkiem sprawnego kierowania," *Zycie Partii*, 1979: 2–3.

rank and file. As the first secretary of the Bydgoszcz area party organization put it:

> It seems to me that in the past it was forgotten all too often that the
> main idea of a Socialist state must be the conjunction of the desires
> and undertakings of the citizens with the activities of the administra-
> tion . . . the people do not want and do not approve of bureaucratic
> centralism . . . and they are right, for it always arises from the rulers'
> mistrust of the popular masses. [It results in] an impenetrable mys-
> tery, turning the function of government into some sort of magic act,
> available only to a selected few . . . (Bednarski, 1981).

As early as 1977, a group of academics, all of them orthodox party members (one of them served as minister of justice in the martial law regime),
reported to the party that political participation was seen as "illusory window dressing" and that there was a "widespread disbelief in the possibility that the individual citizen can exert any influence on things . . . on the
activities of party and social organizations . . ." (RFE, Aug. 25, 1981: 10).
Party activists charged that there were two categories of members, those
who could be criticized and those who could not, and that party meetings
were ritualized affairs lacking a democratic exchange of ideas and opinions. Moreover, the "election" of party secretaries was rigged to such an
extent that people who had failed to get a majority of votes in a secret ballot were then announced as the winners (*Zycie Partii*, 1981: 26–28).
These discontents had long festered among some party members, but it
was only with the general crisis in the party and the system that they could
be relatively freely expressed.

The Rise of Solidarity and the Disintegration of the PUWP

When on July 1, 1980, the Polish government introduced a new price
system for meat and meat products, work began to stop in several large
industrial plants, as workers demanded compensatory wage increases.
Fearful of a repetition of 1970 and 1976, the government ordered factory
managers to negotiate. However, work stoppages spread, with KSS-KOR
acting as an information exchange, as "the only source of news about the
strikes for both Poland and the outside world . . . helping to transform the
strikes from a scatter of local disputes into a self-aware and coordinated
movement of national protest" (Ascherson, 1981). By mid-August, under
the leadership of Lech Walesa and others, an Inter-Factory Strike Committee (MKS) had been formed at the scene of one of the largest strikes, the

Baltic city of Gdansk. Advised by KSS-KOR, in mid-August the MKS issued a list of sixteen demands, soon to expand to twenty-one, that went beyond the conventional demands of trade unions. Among other things, they included a guarantee for freedom of expression and the abolition of censorship, access by all religious groups to the mass media, abolition of privileges for the security organs, and publication in all mass media of news about the strikes and the establishment of the strike committee (*New York Times*, 1980). The number of plants associating themselves with the demands grew within two days to 156, and later to 600, and MKS formed in other cities. The demands served as the basis for negotiations between the workers and a succession of government representatives. In September, a national coordinating commission of the strikers was formed, and "Solidarity" was chosen as the name of the entire movement (De Weydenthal, 1980).

In September the Solidarity movement formulated statutes, later legalized by the courts, which set forth its aims. Among other things, the statutes stated that "The Union does not propose to play the role of a political party . . . it acknowledges that the PUWP plays a leading role in the state." However, the "Union is independent of the administrative agencies of the state and of political organizations." Thus, it was a union free of the political tutelage which characterized the official unions. It also claimed the right to pass judgment on "projects and regulations affecting the life of working people . . . workers' participation in management, social legislation . . . as well as other essential questions affecting working people" (RFE, Nov. 7, 1980: 21ff.). The ideological amalgam behind the movement was expressed as "The nation's best traditions, Christianity's ethical principles, democracy's political mandate, and Socialist social thought—these are the four main sources of our inspiration" (RFE, July 22, 1981: 3).

When a government team negotiated an agreement with Solidarity on August 31, 1980, the new trade-union movement agreed that it would "defend the social and material interests of employees" but did "not intend to play the role of a political party. . . . Recognizing that the PUWP plays the leading role in the state and without undermining the actual system of international alliances," the unions "seek to insure for the working people suitable means of control, of expressing their opinions and of defending their interests" (Gdansk Protocol in Ascherson, 1981: 284–85).

However sincerely Solidarity may have pledged not to play the role of a political party, it soon expanded its activities in a way that was interpreted by the PUWP, perhaps justifiably, as an attempt to compete directly with the PUWP and to become something more than a conventional trade union, even in the Western conception of that institution. This role expansion was not necessarily the result of a deliberate plan by either the KOR intelligentsia or the workers of Solidarity, but may have resulted from the rapid growth of Solidarity into a mass movement, ultimately including some 10 million people (nearly a third of the total population). As the PUWP degenerated and disintegrated, with about a third of its own members simultaneously holding membership in Solidarity, a power vacuum was increasingly perceived. What could be more natural than for this dynamic social force, geographically and socially widespread, to fill the vacuum? The country was in dire economic straits and seemed to be without an effective leadership to lead the way out. As the distinguished sociologist Stefan Nowak points out, the Solidarity unions were not "instrumental associations only. . . . They are . . . communities with their own self-fulfilling emotional value. The speed of their development testifies also to the degree of frustration, in the social vacuum of the preceding period, of the need felt by so many people to belong to and to feel the support of others" (Nowak, 1981: 53). Solidarity was not simply an organization or a trade union, but a movement. Ironically, it seemed to be becoming what the party should have been—a dynamic social and economic movement of, by, and for the working class. As early as November 1980, some Western observers saw that "Solidarity has increasingly become identified in the public mind with a broad concept of social self-organization. . . . The original proletarian and syndicalist character of the organization seems to be undergoing dramatic transformation. . . . For many people, Solidarity has become an avenue toward their own self-assertion, a social institution symbolizing pluralization of political life and serving as an outlet for participation in public life" (De Weydenthal, 1980a: 10). By January 1981, the Soviet party newspaper *Pravda* expressed agreement with this view, albeit from a different perspective, when it spoke of "anti-Socialist forces . . . which for the most part operate under the cover of the Solidarity trade union, [that] are urging organizations of that . . . union to assume the role of a kind of counterweight to the official bodies of power, to become a political organization" (*Pravda*, Jan. 7, 1981). Solidarity had become primarily an "anti-authoritarian organization," directing itself to "the masses." Yet, it also displayed some characteristics of what are called in this volume "supplementary organizations" since it claimed to try to gain "supplementary representation" for the workers who were being so poorly represented by the party or other official organizations.

In the course of the turbulent year 1981, a political war was fought between Solidarity and the PUWP. All the pulling and tugging that went on between them made it ever more clear that Solidarity was intent on broadening its legitimate concerns and operations and the party was determined to narrow them. A climax was reached in the fall when the national congress of Solidarity declared that "We are society's sole guarantor. Therefore, our union has recognized as its basic duty the initiation of all immediate and long-term actions aimed at saving the country from collapse and society from poverty, despair, and self-destruction." Solidarity now described itself as "an organization which combines features of a trade union with those of a wide social movement" (Brumberg, 1981: 19). At the same time, party secretary Stanislaw Kania was insisting that the "party as a whole cannot be pushed out to a position of marginal importance because the party is a leading force of the working class and the nation, the force that carries a historic responsibility for the country's destiny" (Radio Warsaw, Sept. 3, 1981). If once party and church had vied for the role of "society's guarantor," it was now Solidarity and the party that were competing for it. Solidarity made this clear by adopting a program at its October congress which included demands for cuts in military expenditures, an economic reform of major proportions, a reform of the judiciary and the penal system, a reform of the educational system, and comprehensive restructuring of political institutions so that they would be accountable to the public. Solidarity also called for the establishment of a Social Council for the Economy which would have veto power over government decisions (De Weydenthal, 1981).

Solidarity's character as a social movement was also reflected in its evolving structure. The movement was formed "from below" and the subnational groupings and their leadership retained autonomy and independent power throughout. The National Commission had 69 of its 107 members elected at the national congress, but the 38 others were regional chairmen put on the commission on an ex officio basis. The other central body was the audit commission. Below these there were regional organizations electing general assemblies of delegates who, in turn, chose executive boards and their presidia. From the very beginning there were tensions between the national and regional organizations and considerable debate over the delineation of the regional branches.[3] The program of the movement clearly stated that "Structurally, our union has not yet assumed its final form. . . . Our labor union faces the great problem of streamlining the structure of those [branch] sections and [regional coordinating] commissions, and of finding the correct relationship between the basic authorities of the union—the regional and national authorities—and the branch and trade union sections" (RFE, July 22, 1981: 21). These issues were never completely resolved, and in the year or so of Solidarity's national activity, there was no clear trend toward centralization. The central lead-

[3] For a description by a sociologist who was herself involved, on behalf of the MKS in the Gdansk negotiations and the formation of the national movement, see Jadwiga Staniszkis, "The Evolution of Forms of Working Class Protest in Poland: Sociological Reflections on the Gdansk-Szczeczin Case, August, 1980, *Soviet Studies*, 33.

ership expended considerable efforts at coordination of policy lines and activities. While this weakened the movement's ability to deal with its opponents in the period of open, legal operation, it may have allowed the movement to survive better once it was driven underground.

The spontaneous formation and dizzying growth of Solidarity highlighted the internal weakness of the PUWP and stripped away the façade of unity and strength that had covered internal rot for many years. The editor of *Polityka*, Mieczyslaw Rakowski, a man long considered a "liberal" within the party but now a leading member of the martial law regime, gave an unusually candid interview three months after the imposition of martial law. "[The Party] disintegrated, I agree. . . . Who could deny that it went bankrupt, intellectually and politically, that it was unable to organize the society, to get the country out of the disaster, even to defend the state? In the end . . . we are the ones to be blamed, not Solidarity" (Rakowski, 1982).

The symptoms of party disintegration were highly visible in 1981: internal conflict, leadership turnover, mass defection of members. In a desperate attempt to undercut Solidarity and hold on to power, the party leadership that succeeded the disgraced Gierek group claimed to go along with the *odnowa*, or renewal, process, and to apply it within its own ranks. Party leader Kania stated in the fall of 1980 that "A new situation has arisen in the country. There is a need for a new approach to the party's tasks. . . . It is no longer possible to use the old methods. . . . In our party, in all its units, there is no need to search persistently for new and better approaches . . . for renewal, and we shall do it, but only on Socialist grounds. . . . The much needed renovation of social life can only be a Socialist innovation, and the leading force in the process will be the Polish United Workers' Party" (Radio Warsaw, Oct. 4, 1980). Kania was whistling in the dark. The party leadership did not initiate any reforms at all, but was sometimes reluctantly dragged along by initiatives emanating from Solidarity. At the grass roots, however, there was a struggle between those who wanted the party to join actively the process of odnowa, and those, mainly from the apparat, who wanted the party to resist it. Aside from the open criticism of past party practices, the clearest manifestation of a desire for renewal was the emergence of the "horizontal" movement, whereby party organizations at the same level in the hierarchy linked up with each other in order to check the power of the apparat. Originating in the Torun area, and paralleling the regional organization of the Solidarity movement, the horizontal party associations were an expression of the idea of self-management and a departure from the Leninist idea of democratic centralism. As such, this "represented a collective response to the stultifying inertia and organizational paralysis of the middle-level party apparatus, whose only reflex appeared to be to look upwards and wait for directives that never came" (Kolankiewicz, 1982: 63).

The idea of horizontal associations was opposed by both the Polish and the Soviet party leaderships. The Soviet press warned that "It's no secret that in this complicated crisis atmosphere by no means all of the Communists, and not even all party organizations . . . have displayed the necessary political maturity. . . . There was confusion, lack of initiative, and outright connivance with the activity of . . . KOR and other anti-Socialist forces." The conservative Warsaw party leader, Stanislaw Kociolek, was quoted approvingly: "In the party itself there are unhealthy phenomena that are shaking its ideological foundations and the principle of democratic centralism" (Losoto and Sklarov, 1981: 11). Throughout the summer of 1981, the Soviet and East European presses voiced anxiety about "reformist tendencies" and "ideological confusion" in the PUWP. In June the Central Committee of the Soviet Communist party sent a letter, made public, to its Polish counterpart in which the criticism was very explicit. "Endless concessions to the anti-Socialist forces . . . have led to a situation in which the PUWP has retreated step by step under the onslaught of counterrevolution, which relies on the support of imperialist subversion centers abroad. . . . No actual steps have been taken to combat [the counterrevolutionary threat] so far. . . . The situation within the PUWP itself has . . . become a matter of special concern" (*Pravda*, June 12, 1981: 2).

Kania attempted to walk the thin line between the pressure for reform generated within Poland, and the pressure to halt it coming from the Soviet Union. The only result was that the party was perceived by both Poles and the Soviets as indecisive and lacking in initiative, indeed, unable to control events. Within the party, the lack of a clear line led to conflicts among various levels in the organization, and among ideological groups on all levels. Both those who disagreed with the line of their particular group, as well as those who were simply waiting for a single line to emerge, lapsed into passivity regarding party work or left the party altogether. It seems to have been largely the reformers who left the party— after all, they had somewhere to go—thus leaving the field to the more conservative elements. Party leaders spoke of the "internal disintegration of some sectors of the party's ranks" (Mokrzyszczak, 1981). Indeed, in the fifteen months between July 1980 and September 1981, 380,500 party members were expelled or "lapsed," 219,800 resigned, but only 33,000 new people joined (De Weydenthal, 1981a). Workers accounted for between 60 and 72 percent of those who left the party. Even many of those who remained in the party had joined Solidarity, whether to hedge their bets or because they genuinely believed that there was no intrinsic conflict in being a member of both. One million party members were also Solidarity members. In several places, workers demanded that party activities be removed from work premises, that party functionaries be taken off the featherbedded payrolls of the enterprises, and that people simply leave the ranks of the party.

This grass-roots turbulence was reflected at the highest levels of the party. Eighty percent of the delegates to the Extraordinary Congress of the PUWP, held in July, were freely elected by regional conferences, and 20 percent of them were Solidarity members. Only 18 of 146 members of the Central Committee were reelected, and the new politburo, which had only 3 holdovers out of 14 members, had a Solidarity member on it (Lewis, 1982: 146). The Central Committee included only 8 of the 49 provincial (*wojewodstwo*) party secretaries, and only 2 of 7 central party secretaries were included. Though the congress failed to define a new political line, its composition showed that in terms of personnel there was a process of "renewal" going on. There was a revolt against the people who had led the party until that point, though there was no clear consensus on where the new people should take the PUWP.

Opinion polls vividly expressed disenchantment with the party and enthusiasm for Solidarity. Opinion polling had been going on ever since the late 1950's and provided quite a reliable gauge of the public's attitudes toward the government and party (Huszczo, 1977). A review of opinion polling in the late 1970s concludes that "for the Poles today it is the nation, its history and present that are most important. The nation is seen as a federation of families. By contrast, everything that lies between the family and the nation—and above all, the institutional structure (political organizations, trade unions, state administration)—arouses no feeling of identification at all" (Mink, 1981: 157). In 1980–81, national samples were asked about the degree of trust they had in Polish institutions. In May 1980, 94 percent said they had a high degree of trust in the church, 90 percent in Solidarity, 89 percent in the military. But only 56 percent had much trust in the official trade unions, only 42 percent in the police, and only 32 percent in the PUWP, the least trusted institution (Siemienska, 1982: 15). By November 1981, trust in all institutions had declined somewhat, perhaps because of the political confusion of the year. The church and the army slipped only very slightly, but the percentage of people expressing high trust in Solidarity declined to 55, and that for the party was down to 12.[4] While in 1980 a third of the population favored "strengthening the role of the party in the administration of power," only 20 percent favored that by the end of 1981. In the latter period over 60 percent of the general population, and even 46 percent of party members, favored

---

[4] Information supplied by Dr. Raymond Taras who was in Poland at the time.

limiting the party's role (Mason, 1982: 10–11). Again, Solidarity's popularity also showed a decline, though it remained far more trusted than the party: at the end of 1980, 58 percent of the population, and even 45 percent of party members, "decisively supported" the national activities of Solidarity, but by December 1981, this had slipped to 33 percent of the population (ibid.: 9). Polls reflected a growing sense that Solidarity might have gone too far, that it ought to seek some compromise with the party and government, and that it had gone beyond the boundaries of a trade-union movement. This trend was probably accelerated after the imposition of martial law when, after initial resistance, there was a growing sense that Solidarity could not present a viable alternative after it had been forced underground. The trend may have reached a peak on November 10, 1982, when Solidarity's calls for a general strike went largely unheeded. Confident that it had destroyed the Solidarity threat, the martial law regime released Lech Walesa from confinement. The underground Solidarity leaders, tacitly acknowledging the new atmosphere, called off future strikes on the grounds that the situation had changed for the better. Since opinion data was not released, one cannot tell what kind of shift had occurred in public perceptions of the situation, of Solidarity and of the party. While the popular assessment of Solidarity may have been that it would be ineffective, at least in the short run, there is no reason to believe that the public's evaluation of the party had changed. A realistic reconciliation with present reality could occur without any greater respect for, or trust in, the party accompanying it.

Martial Law: A Coup against the Party?

On December 12, 1981, a "state of war" was declared by the Polish government, allowing it to ban public meetings, suspend civil liberties, and impose regulations which would curb political and economic activities. This was the first such instance in Communist history, and it had been preceded by another "first." Wojciech Jaruzelski, who had been minister of defense, was the first professional military officer to become a prime minister (February 1981), the first prime minister to retain the defense portfolio, and the first officer to become first secretary of the party (October 1981). One man, perhaps the most popular of the top leaders in 1980–81, concentrated within his hands the three main levers of power, something not even Stalin had done. But this was not a personal coup, for it was accompanied by an expanding political and even economic role for the military as a whole. Army personnel had been deployed throughout the country to help in the "equitable distribution" of goods, and military officers had been promoted to important political positions. General Florian Siwicki had been made a deputy member of the politburo, and General Tadeusz Dziekan was made head of the important cadres (personnel) department of the party's Central Committee. Four generals had ministerial posts, and the representation of the military in the party Central Committee doubled between 1980 and 1981 (Korbonski, 1981). Jaruzelski had justified the "influx of military personnel" into party bodies on the grounds of "the need of the moment and [the recognition that] people have confidence in people in uniform" (RFE, Nov. 11, 1980).

Jaruzelski's move recalled a parallel one taken by Marshal Jozef Pilsudski, the national hero of Poland, when he seized power in May 1926 after the political parties had failed to bring political stability and economic growth to the country. In both instances, the image was that of the man on horseback, the national hero rising above petty partisan squabbles to save the nation from the mess made by the politicians. The military represented the national, not the partisan, interests, and was the only incorruptible institution. Although this was a fairly frequent occurrence in the third world, it had also happened in France (De Gaulle). Some Western social scientists see it as evidence of political immaturity or lack of political development. In the Communist system, it was not only unusual but ominous. One Western analyst asserted that "The overshadowing of the Party by the army struck at the roots of the Communist system" (Johnson, 1982: viii). Another thought that Jaruzelski's appointment as party secretary had already "represented a basic shift of power within the regime away from the Party toward the armed forces." "Are we at the beginning," he asked, "of a realignment of relationships in the communist system, with the Party declining in authority and being replaced by the forces of coercion—the army and the security apparat?" (Brown: 11, 17). Jaruzelski was acutely aware of the unprecedented nature of his move, and apparently highly sensitive to the question of the party's role, especially since it could not but be foremost on the minds of the Soviet leaders. In his announcement of material law, Jaruzelski said, "We do not seek a military coup, a military dictatorship. . . . Over the long term, none of the Polish problems can be solved by the use of force. The Military Council of National Salvation does not substitute for the constitutional organs of powers. Its sole task is to protect law and order in the state and to create executive guarantees that will make it possible to reestablish order and disciplines. . . . A special place is set aside for the party. Despite the mistakes and bitter defeats, the party continues to be an active and creative force in a process of historical transformations." But he seemed to make the party's future rule conditional on extensive changes within it. "If the party is to exercise its leading role effectively . . . it must rely on honest,

modest, and courageous people. . . . That is what will determine the authority of the party in society" (*Trybuna Ludu*, Dec. 14, 1984). In the
coming months, Jaruzelski was to reaffirm the "party's leading role" on
the "basis of our political system" and to reject proposals to dissolve the
party and recognize it under a different name. He denied that the party
had "fallen apart," despite some "profound cadre changes" and the fact
that "Over the past 18 months, 53 percent of political workers have left
the party apparatus for various reasons." Nevertheless, the party "will not
remain a convalescent patient forever" (ibid., Feb. 25, 1982).[5]

As of this writing there is little sign that the patient is recovering, though
its rival, Solidarity, also seems moribund. The fate of the latter illustrates
that, as Ross Johnson puts it, "mass enthusiasm is no substitute for organization" (Johnson, 1982: 51). But the conditions of the PUWP demonstrates that organization without mass enthusiasm cannot sustain a political party forever, even if it has a monopoly of power. Who but Leninists
should have understood that "consciousness" and "spontaneity" are *both*
necessary for a successful movement.

REFLECTIONS ON A DOUBLE FAILURE

The case described above involves the failure of a party in power and
the failure of a social and political movement which rose alongside it and
challenged it. The PUWP failed because it had power but little authority.
Solidarity failed because in the short time it had, it could not translate authority into sufficient power. Into this stalemate stepped the armed forces
which, more than any other governmental or political body, enjoyed both
power and authority, as well as, apparently, the blessing of the Soviet
leadership. In the three major political crises of Communist East Europe,
the central issue has been the Communist party's monopoly of political
power and control. In Hungary in 1956 the threat to the party came from
the revival of non-Communist parties which were to be tolerated by a reformed Communist party. In 1968 in Czechoslovakia, the Communist
party itself approved the legitimation and institutionalization of pluralistic politics, where the ruling party would have to prove itself worthy of
power, or give it up. By contrast, the Polish party paid lip service to odnowa but resisted Solidarity's increasing attempts to share power. In all
three instances, military force was the only effective means of maintaining

---

[5] Earlier, the *New York Times* reported that "the authorities are sensitive to any suggestion that the party's power is on the wane. The press had tried to create an impression that
party meetings are being held all around the country to thrash out policy" ("Army is in Control in Poland but Party is Not Counted Out," Dec. 29, 1981).

the exclusive position of the party in its Leninist conception. In Hungary and Czechoslovakia, Soviet military force was used, but in Poland it was the domestic military that intervened to save the party from eclipse, and perhaps to save the nation from Soviet intervention.

This was not, then, a military *coup d'état*. Jaruzelski fused several roles in his person, and it is not absolutely clear in which role he was acting—probably in all three at once. This was a move, not against the party, but to save the party. A government which had five prime ministers in a year, a party which had three first secretaries and had experienced such tremendous membership turnover could be said to have lost power well before the military assumed it. The military preempted Solidarity's power; it did not take away the party's, for there was little to take away. In terms of roles, the PUWP failed to play its role successfully. Solidarity expanded its role to the point where it threatened the party directly, and, by implication, the Soviet Union and its allies in Eastern Europe. Jaruzelski tried to solve both problems by fusing his roles and filling the power vacuum. Even if he is sincere in his declared intention of holding power only so long as the party needs in order to regroup and reestablish itself—and in late 1985 he took the first step by giving up the prime ministership—he may find himself unable to restore clearly civilian party rule. For PUWP rule has always been based on power, and it never succeeded in translating that power into authority, i.e., the kind of rule that would allow it to chart the course of Poland without the explicit or implicit threat of military force, whatever its source. In this sense, the PUWP has been a failure, not only in 1980–81, but throughout its history.

REFERENCES

Ascherson, N. 1981. *The Polish August*. Middlesex: Penguin.

Baka, W. 1977. Doskonalenie systemu planowania i zarzadzanie w Polsc e. *Nowe Drogi* 6.

Bedrzycki, J. 1975. Iniciatiwy i zamierzenia. *Zycie Partii* 4: 27.

Bialecki, Z. 1975. Warunki zaangazowanie. *Zycie Partii* 3: 10–11.

Bielasiak, J. 1983. Inequalities and the politicization of the Polish Working Class. In *Communism and the politics of inequalities*, ed. D. Nelson. Lexington, Mass.: Lexington Books.

Bromke, A. 1978. The opposition in Poland. *Problems of Communism* 27.

Brown, J. F. N.d. The significance of Poland. RFE, internal paper.

Brumberg, A. 1981. Solidarity's dilemma. *The New Republic* Nov. 25.

De Weydenthal, Jan B. 1977. Party development in contemporary Poland. *East European Quarterly* 11: 244–345.

———. 1980a. Workers and party in Poland. *Problems of Communism* 29.

De Weydenthal, Jan B. 1980b. Poland's new unions gain a place in the system. RFE, RAD, BR/277, Nov. 20.

———. 1981. Solidarity's national congress: Stage two. RFE, RAD, BR/291, Oct. 19.

———. 1981. Polish party calls for special powers for government. RFE Situation Report, Dec. 22.

DiFrancesco, W., and Z. Gitelman. 1984. Soviet political culture and "covert participation" in policy implementation. *American Political Science Review* 78.

Dziewanowski, M. K. 1976. *The Communist party of Poland*. Cambridge: Harvard University Press.

J.F. 1975. Owocny rok partinej kontroli. *Zycie Partii* 5: 25–26.

Gdansk Protocol, translated in Ascherson, 1981: 284–85.

Gitelman, Z. 1971. Power and authority in Eastern Europe. In *Change in Communist Systems*, ed. C. Johnson. Stanford: Stanford University Press.

———. 1977. Development, institutionalization, and elite-mass relations in Poland. In *Political development in Eastern Europe*, ed. J. Triska and P. Cocks. New York: Praeger.

———. 1981. The world economy and elite political strategies in Czechoslovakia, Poland and Hungary. In *East-West relations and the future of Eastern Europe*, ed. M. Bornstein, Z. Gitelman, and W. Zimmerman. London: George Allen and Unwin.

———. 1982. Politics on the output side: Citizen-bureaucrat interaction in the USSR. Paper delivered at the American Political Science Association meeting, Denver.

Gryfiel, J. 1979. Unocnienie sil partii. *Zycie Partii* 3: 4–5.

Huntington, S. P. 1968. *Political order in changing societies*. New Haven: Yale University Press.

Huszczo, A. 1977. Public opinion in Poland. In *Public opinion in European Socialist systems*, ed. W. Connor and Z. Gitelman. New York: Praeger.

Jarosinska, M., and J. Kulpinska, 1974. Transformation of the social structure in the USSR and Poland. Moscow-Warsaw, 1974.

Jarosz, M. 1967. *Samorzad robotniczy w przedsiebiorstwie przemyslowym*. Warsaw: PWE.

Johnson, A. Ross. 1982. *Poland in crisis*. Santa Monica: RAND Note N–1891 AF, July.

Kesselman, M. 1970. Overinstitutionalization and political constraint: The case of France. *Comparative Politics* 2.

Koladziejczyk, T. 1979. Skreslenie—problem niepolojecy. *Zycie Partii* 8: 7.

Kolankiewicz, G. 1982. The politics of "Socialist renewal." In *Policy and politics in contemporary Poland*, ed. J. Woodall. New York: St. Martins Press.

Korbonski, A. 1981. The dilemmas of civil-military relations in contemporary Poland: 1945–1981. *Armed Forces and Society* 8.

Kruk, W. 1979. Formy, metody i warunki dzialania. *Zycie Partii* 3: 6–7.

Kultura (Paris). 1981. 6: 143.

Kuzinski, S. 1979. Przemiany spoleczno-demograficzne. *Zycie Partii* 5: 15–17.

Lewis, P. G. 1982. Obstacles to the establishment of political legitimacy in Communist Poland. *British Journal of Political Science* 12: 144–45.

Losoto, O., and Yu. Sklyarov. 1981. Poland—April, May. *Pravda*, May 21. Trans. in *Current Digest of the Soviet Press (CDSP)* 33: 11.

Maciag, Z. 1973. Organizacja partyjna, zwiazkowa i mlodziezowa. *Zeszyty naukowe UJ* (Krakow).

Mason, D. 1982. Solidarity, Socialism and public opinion. Paper delivered at the American Political Science Association meeting, Denver.

Maziarski, J. 1978. W imeniu robotnikow. *Polityka* 21: 3.

Mink, G. 1981. Sondage, soudeurs, opinion publique et pouvoir politique en Pologne à la fin des années soixante-dix. *Revue Etudes Comparatives Est-Ouest* 12: 157.

Mokrzyszczak, W. 1981. In *Trybunu Ludu*, Nov. 28–29.

Na temach presy regionalnej. 1979. *Zycie Partii* 1: 49.

New York Times, Aug. 18, 1980.

Nowak, S. 1981. Values and attitudes of the Polish people. *Scientific American* 245: 53.

Osobka, W. 1981. In *Zycie Partii* 2: 29.

The outline of solidarity's program. 1981. RFE, RAD, BR/210. July 22.

Owieczko, A. 1966. Dzialalnosci i struktura samorzadu robotniczego w opinii zalog fabrycznych. *Studia Socjologiczne*, 3.

———. 1967. Samorzad robotniczy w przedsiebiorstwie przemyslowym a zaloga. *Studia Socjologiczno-Polityczne* 22.

Pravda, A. 1982. Poland 1980: From "premature consumerism" to labour solidarity. *Soviet Studies* 2: 173.

Pravda, June 12, 1981, p. 2. Trans. in *CDSP* 33: 1.

Provocational demands. 1981. *Pravda*, Jan. 2. Trans. in *CDSP* 33: 11.

Radio Warsaw, Sept. 3, 1981. Quoted in J. B. de Weydenthal, Polish leadership presents its stand on self-management. In RFE, Situation Report, Sept. 8, 1981.

Report of the team of technical advisers to the PUWP Central Committee's First Secretary July 1977. Quoted in RFE, RAD, BR/241, Aug. 25, 1981.

Rothschild, J. 1966. *Pilsudski's coup d'etat*. New York: Columbia University Press.

Sadurski, W. 1979. Demokracja w fabryce. *Polityka* 15: 16.

Sharlet, R. 1967. Concept formation in political science and Communist studies: Conceptualizing political participation. *Canadian Slavic Studies* 1.

Siemienska, R. 1982. Mass-authority relations in the Polish crisis. Paper delivered at the American Political Science Association meeting, Denver.

Sprawniej i skutecznej. 1975. *Zycie Partii* 2: 11–12.

The statutes of the independent self-governing solidarity labor unions. 1980. RFE, Polish Situation Report 20, Nov. 7.

Terry, S. M., and A. Korbonski, 1980. The impact of external economic disturbances on the internal politics of Eastern Europe: The Polish and Hungarian cases. In *The impact of international economic disturbances on the Soviet*

Union and Eastern Europe: Transmission and response, ed. E. Neuberger and L. D'Andrea Tyson. New York: Pergamon Press.

Trybuna aktywisty. 1981. *Zycie Partii* 2: 26–28.

Trybuna Ludu, 1981.

Widerszpil, S. 1965. *Sklad Polskiej klasy robotniczej*. Warsaw: PWN.

Winiarski, L. 1979. Z pozycjii gosdpodarzy. *Zycie Partii* 3: 28–29.

SEVENTEEN | Independents and Independence: Challenges to One-Party Domination in Taiwan

LIANG-SHING FAN
AND FRANK B. FEIGERT

> The employment of ultimate, comprehensive, and legitimate physical coercion is the monopoly of states, and the political system is uniquely concerned with the scope, direction, and the conditions affecting the employment of this physical coercion (Almond, 1965: 395).

In this analysis, we examine two separate but parallel strains of activity, each representing a substantial challenge to the Kuomintang or Nationalist party government of Taiwan. We shall be concerned with the development of these strains, which stem from the deliberate exclusionary policies of the ruling party and the responses of the government to these challenges to its legitimacy.

Unlike Rose and Mackie, we argue that failure is not the disappearance of a major party, but an inability of the existing party system to accommodate to stress, internal and external. Miller (1955: 527–29) has suggested that (living) "systems respond to continuously increasing stress first by a lag in response, then by an overcompensatory response, and finally by catastrophic collapse of the system." While we are not suggesting that Taiwan is in immediate danger of collapse, it provides a fertile ground for testing whether Miller's thesis is applicable to political as well as living systems.

The internal stress referred to derives, in part, from external stress, the failure of the Kuomintang (KMT) on the international scene, as the party has become increasingly the object of criticism for the diplomatic isolation of the Republic of China (ROC). Further internal stress, as we discuss below, derives from allegations of abuses of power. In an authoritarian system such as that found in Taiwan, this may lead to the use of repression against critics of the regime. In the eyes of the critics of the KMT, we have occasion to see an application of Acton's thesis that "all power corrupts; absolute power corrupts absolutely." Finally, for some time there has been stress based on the questions of KMT legitimacy and whether Taiwan should be an independent and sovereign nation, neither laying claim to the territory controlled by the People's Republic of China, nor being claimed by that government.

One movement we discuss involves political independents, known as Tangwai [Those Outside the Party], who challenge the KMT electorally, even though they are legally forbidden from coordinating their activities, since this would constitute an illegal party. The other, known as the Taiwan Independence Movement (TIM) challenges the legitimacy of the KMT government, and seeks to remove the domination of the Taiwanese system by "mainlanders," those who came uninvited to the island with Chiang Kai-shek.

These movements defy ready categorization. Each is distinctly antiauthoritarian, as the editors have organized the case studies in this volume. Yet, there is also a strong tendency toward political environmentalism in their concern for greater egalitarianism. As such, they represent, in a very real sense, "the determination of their members to take direct, personal action in the struggle to bring about change," as Lawson and Merkl state in their Introduction. Further, they can also be described as somewhat communitarian, given the questionable integration of the majority native population in the island's official politics, as we shall demonstrate.

BACKGROUND

Taiwan has been under martial law since 1947. A better context for what Lawson refers to as "directive linkage" could not exist. The KMT is decidedly concerned with the maintenance of "control over the behavior of citizens. At all levels, from grass roots to national office, the party is an agent of education, or of coercion, or of both."

Returned to Chinese control by the Japanese in 1945, Taiwan was virtually ignored by the KMT for two years, while Chiang Kai-shek and his armies were concerned with resisting the Communist insurgency. Settled some three hundred years before by fishermen from Fukien province, Taiwan had gradually developed a culture which was relatively distinct from those on the mainland. For instance, even though the written language remained the same, the spoken language was quite incomprehensible to mainlanders, being comprised of eight tones, while Fukien province retained a five-tone dialect and Mandarin, the official language, was and is based on four tones. Although certain similarities remained, there are many cultural differences. The essential point is that, at least from the 1895 cession of Taiwan to the Japanese until 1945, there was little attention paid to the people of Taiwan by the various ruling governments on the mainland (Kerr, 1974).

When the Japanese left, a KMT governor general was appointed, but integration of the Taiwanese into Chinese life was less than quiet. In the account of one leader of the independence movement: "For eighteen months they looted our island. The newcomers had lived all their lives in the turmoil of civil war and of the Japanese invasion. They were carpetbaggers, occupying enemy territory, and we were being treated as a conquered people" (Peng, 1972: 61).

Probably the signal event in the development of an independence movement took place on February 28, 1947, when army troops were sent ashore and killed an unknown number of people following a protest incident at the Tobacco Monopoly Bureau in Taipei. Estimates of the deaths vary widely, from "hundreds" (McBeath, 1978: 17) to the several hundred mentioned in initial Western press reports, to ten thousand (Fairbanks, 1982: 379) to "ten to twenty thousand" (Peng, 1972: 70). Some corroboration of the higher figure is given by a former American consular official (Kerr, 1965) then stationed on the island. Many of those killed were part of the island's political, economic, and social leadership. These events, known collectively as "Two Twenty-eight," are part of the lore of the island, never mentioned in texts or the press, but apparently known to most if not all native Taiwanese, and discussed only among trusted friends and family. From these events early in 1947 through this writing, Taiwan has been in a continual state of martial law. This is even longer than the martial law rule in South Korea and is, indeed, the longest in modern political history. In recent years the focus of martial law has shifted from concern with dissident native Taiwanese to fear of subversion by the People's Republic of China. Moreover, the KMT tries to associate the Taiwanese Independence Movement with subversion by the PRC, although there is no reason to assume that the PRC favors such a policy (Chen, 1977).

When his armies were defeated on the mainland, a rout took place, and Chiang Kai-shek took up "temporary residence" on Taiwan in order to resist further Communist expansion and to prepare for the eventual "liberation" of the mainland, part of the official mythology explaining the presence of the KMT and mainlanders on the island. It might be added, parenthetically, that American political leaders and the press were part and parcel of this line of reasoning through the 1950s (Liebling, 1964). Arriving with Chiang were a great many mainlanders from most if not all of the provinces. In 1947 there were some 6.5 million people living on Taiwan (Executive Yuan, 1977: Table 18) while there are presently some 18 million. Of these about 2.5 million or approximately 15 percent are classified by the government as "mainlanders," whether or not they were born on the mainland itself. The distinction is based on the time when one or one's ancestors arrived on the island. Although this has been downplayed in recent years ("we are all Chinese"), registration or identification cards still list different provinces for mainlanders.

There is some quarrel over the extent to which there are differences between mainlanders and Taiwanese. Socialization studies, however, have shown that there are some significant differences between the two groups in subjects studied, cultural values held, and opportunities of a political, social, or economic nature (Marsh, 1968; Wilson, 1968, 1970, 1974; Appleton, 1970, 1976, 1976–77). This is all the more testimony to the distinct lives led by Taiwanese and mainlanders, inasmuch as "The KMT-controlled school system teaches Chinese mainland history, geography, and culture—but doesn't teach the students anything about their own homeland" (Shutt, 1982: 13; see also Martin, 1975).

In governing Taiwan, the KMT has had virtually unchallenged rule since the imposition of martial law in 1947 and Chiang's 1949 arrival. In fact, the KMT has often been confused with the very government of Taiwan, at least by its leaders, transferring such symbols as flag and anthem from party to nation. The KMT claims that even though no new party is allowed, Taiwan is by no means a one-party state because there are two other parties, the Democratic Socialist and Chinese Youth parties. Brought to Taiwan by the KMT, they receive monthly subsidies from the Nationalists but, because of internal squabbling over how to allocate these monies, they have split into three to five factions each. If one defines a party in terms of the likelihood of its winning office, neither would qualify.

In the 1960s, a group of mainlanders and some native political leaders tried to form a meaningful opposition, to be known as the Chinese Democratic party, but the leader, Lei Chen, was quickly jailed on a charge of harboring a Communist agent on the staff of his *Free China* monthly.

Taiwanese have become increasingly active in a political sense in recent years, especially since the 1971 expulsion of the Republic of China from the United Nations and other international organizations, and the 1972 Nixon visit to Beijing. Non-KMT political candidates have stood successfully for elective offices at several levels, including the Provincial assembly, mayor or magistrate of cities and prefectures (counties), and local councils. Even though they are separate and independent candidates as required by law, they have coordinated their activities as Tangwai. This has resulted in significant pressure for the KMT, culminating in the now-famous "Kaohsiung incident" of 1979, to which we address ourselves further, below. As a result of this incident, major Tangwai leaders are now in jail, convicted of "treason." More detailed analysis of this and related events is provided in the latter part of this paper, but we first turn our attention to the movement for independence.

THE TAIWAN INDEPENDENCE MOVEMENT (TIM)

It must be stressed, at the outset, that there is no necessary or functional linkage between the two movements, although the ROC government has attempted to make this connection. The Tangwai movement implicitly challenges the legitimacy of the KMT, whereas TIM openly challenges the legitimacy of both the party and the government, however much they are the same. Challenges to authority are seen as "subversive," a synonym in the rhetoric of the ROC for attempted Communist influence.[1]

The TIM (also known as the Formosan Independence Movement; see Peng, 1972) has essentially two physical bases—one in the United States where symbolic leadership is accorded Peng Ming-min, and in Taiwan itself, where it necessarily exists as an underground movement. Peng, a former legal adviser to the ROC delegation to the United Nations and head of the department of political science at prestigious National Taiwan University, was arrested and charged with sedition in 1964. In 1970 he escaped from prison to Sweden and eventually to the United States, where he is hiding.

In discussing TIM, the early history of several independence movement activities must be discussed, in order to clarify both their present position and the responses of the ROC regime. The massacre of February 28, 1947, had virtually eliminated the intellectual elite of Taiwan except for a few who escaped to a number of other countries, including the People's Republic of China. Thomas Liao and a group of friends established the Formosan Democratic Independence party in 1950, and it evolved into a Provisional National Congress of the Republic of Formosa in Japan. A provisional government-in-exile was established on February 28, 1956 (the date clearly was not chosen randomly) with Liao as its first president. However, a lack of both financial support and competent leadership led to a split. Younger members, under the leadership of Ong Joktik established a radical group called Taiwan Chinglian (Youth) Associates in 1960. Liao's favorite nephew in Taiwan was arrested and sentenced to death by

---

[1] In Chinese terms, "Tai Hun maotsue" (put a pink hat on someone).

the ROC regime. His sister-in-law was also sentenced to fifteen years imprisonment on the charge of treason, and Liao's assets were confiscated. Lacking a following and tempted by the promise that his relatives' prison sentences would be reduced and his personal assets returned, Liao betrayed the independence movement of which he was leader and returned to Taiwan in 1965.

Although the movement did not die out in Japan, major activities gradually shifted to the United States and a group of young graduate students in that country (King, 1974). The earliest leaders were Ciu Shebing in Wisconsin, Edward Chen in Philadelphia, and Tsai Tongrong on the West Coast. In 1966 a united front was born, known as United Formosans in America for Independence (UFAI). A parallel organization (UFEI) was also established in Europe. On January 1, 1970, a worldwide united front was created, known as the World United Formosans for Independence (WUFI). This organization embraced UFAI, UFEI, UFYI (Japan), the Committee for Human Rights in Formosa (Canada), and the Freedom League of Formosa (an underground resistance movement in Taiwan). Tsai Tongrong, the first president, was succeeded in 1972 by his former teacher, Peng Mingmin. The current president is George (Changhon) Chang, who has been active in leading various revolutionary and propaganda activities in the United States.

In a long-term movement such as this, one must expect many splinter groups, given ideological and personal conflicts. The WUFI currently holds the allegiance of the majority of Taiwanese who are active. It has at its disposal a twice-weekly newspaper, the *Taiwan Tribune*, published in New York, with a worldwide distribution.

In 1980, the independent Magistrate of Taoyuan, Hsu Hsin-liang, who had defeated the KMT candidate in 1977 by a two to one margin, was removed from office by the Control Yuan and exiled from Taiwan with his family members. He and a group of supporters publish a popular weekly, *Formosa*, after a magazine by the same name which was banned in Taiwan.[2] His group consists mainly of newcomers to the United States, and they align themselves rather more closely to the Tangwai in Taiwan.

The WUFI and other allied groups have at least two objectives in common. The first is the complete political independence of Taiwan, without any attachment to the People's Republic of China. The second is to rid the island of the KMT regime controlled initially by Chiang-Kai-shek and now by his son, Chiang Ching-kuo (WUFI, 1981). Through various activities,

---

[2] The monthly magazine was issued only five times in Taiwan. It was a popular vehicle for dissidents, reaching the unusually high circulation of over 100,000 copies per issue within three months. The government banned it by accusing it of inciting the "riot" in Kaohsiung, of which we have more to say below.

and generally avoiding the factionalism which characterized the movement at an earlier time, TIM has grown in membership. This has come largely through a growing number of new immigrants to the United States, including graduate students situated at various American universities and elsewhere throughout the world. The KMT and the regime in Taiwan apparently consider this movement to be of sufficient threat that they have attempted both to infiltrate it and blame it for various activities, such as the letter bomb which injured Taiwan's then governor, later vice-president Hsieh.

POLITICAL INDEPENDENTS: TANGWAI

As the official party on Taiwan, the KMT has gone virtually unchallenged in any formal sense. The two minor subsidized parties appear on the ballot only occasionally, electing their candidates quite rarely, and then in local elections for the most part. Such challenges as there may be come from the Tangwai, who might be considered Independents in the American sense, were it not for the fact that there have been recent attempts at coordination of their campaigns. We have compiled such data as are available to trace the success of the KMT, the two minor parties, and the Tangwai.

Before proceeding, some cautionary notes are in order. First, the data we have available show the election of local representatives and executives, as well as representatives to the Provincial Assembly. There are no comparable data for the election of national officeholders, nor is it really possible that one could find such. The president, under the ROC Constitution, is nominated and elected every six years by the National Assembly, a body which is often compared to the U.S. electoral college. However, during the "Period of Communist Rebellion" declared in 1948 and not since withdrawn, there have been no elections to this body. Although there have been no general elections, there have been supplementary elections in Taiwan and on the ROC-controlled islands of Quemoy and Matsu. These elections added no more than 50 seats to an assembly with an allocated total in excess of 3,000. Today, after the last "general election" in 1947 on the mainland, there are fewer than 1,200 surviving mainland members. The average age of its members, most of whom "represent" mainland provinces under Communist control, is over seventy.

The presidential election is held every six years, and the nominee of the National Assembly is unopposed. Chiang Kai-shek was elected five times. In the first free elections there was some token opposition to *peihsieng* (accompany) him, but in later elections this luxury had to be foregone. Under the terms of ROC election procedures, the president must obtain a stipulated minimum percentage of the total seats in the National Assembly. Shrinking numbers, based on simple attrition through death, made this impossible. Chiang Kai-shek's son, first elected in 1978, is the only other president elected by the National Assembly since its inception.

Leadership of four of the branches of the national government, the Executive, Legislative, Examination, and Judicial Yuans, devolves from presidential appointment powers under the ROC Constitution. Hence, except for the election of native representatives to the Legislative and Control Yuans[3] there is little opportunity for non-KMT emergence in the national political arena, given the total dominance of the National Assembly by the KMT (see Table 17.1).

There is yet another difficulty in examining these data, and that is that they are clearly incomplete. One might wonder at the delays inherent in compiling data for post-1962 elections, such that their results could not be made official by 1975, the last date for which we have official sources for local elections. Related to this is the problem of veracity, as illustrated by the presence of election data for pre-1945 years. These elections were conducted on the mainland by the KMT, and the only likely participants might have been the few Taiwanese who had fled their island which was then under Japanese rule. One might also inquire why, given the opportunity to compile such data, party-relevant figures were not aggregated by the government for earlier elections for local representatives. Inexplicably, the data are available at the county level, but not officially aggregated as they were for later elections. Yet another example shows the problematic nature of interpretation using official data. This is illustrated by the nature of two reports for the 1962 elections for local representatives (see Table 17.2). The first, published eleven years after the election, is sharply at variance with the second, published a year later, the latter showing a decrease in the proportion of elected Tangwai, as well as 2,765 fewer persons elected.

Given these problems, what lessons can be drawn from the data? The first is that there is seemingly a base of support for nonparty candidates below which they seldom pass. In and of itself, this is somewhat remarkable, given the extent to which the KMT has come to dominate Taiwanese

---

[3] There are five Yuan or branches in the ROC government. The Legislative, Executive, and Judicial Yuans are close enough in function to our own not to warrant further explanation. The Examination Yuan might be likened to a combination of the Civil Service and the College Entrance Examination Board, administering the mandatory examinations for governmental as well as student placement in the national university system. The Control Yuan is charged with handling the impeachment of governmental officials.

TABLE 17.1 Composition of the Taiwan Provincial Assembly

Year	Total Seats (N)	KMT Party (%)	China Youth Party (%)	China Democratic Socialist Party (%)	Nonparty (%)
TAIWAN PROVISIONAL PROVINCIAL ASSEMBLY					
1951	55	78.2	1.8	—	20.0
1954	57	84.2	—	—	15.8
1957	66	80.3	1.5	—	18.2
TAIWAN PROVINCIAL ASSEMBLY					
1959	66	80.3	1.5	—	18.2
1960	73	79.5	—	—	20.5
1963	74	82.4	1.4	—	16.2
1968	71	84.5	—	—	15.5
1973	73	79.5	—	—	20.5
1977	77	72.7	—	—	27.3[a]
1981	77	76.6	—	—	23.4[a]

SOURCE: The data were kindly provided by the Speaker of the Taiwan Provincial Assembly.

[a] The term "Tangwai" was being widely used to describe the solidarity, if not formal organization, of these members during the campaigns.

society.[4] The base of support is variable, from office to office, as one might expect. There are far fewer local-level executives than legislators, as one would expect given the greater importance of that office, and the tight control otherwise exercised by the central government and the KMT over the Taiwanese political system. Hence, the election of local executives as Tangwai has considerable symbolic importance.

The source of nonparty support is not revealed by the data and merits separate attention. For the most part, those counties with a high level of Taiwanese as compared to mainlander population give the greatest electoral support to the independents. Mainlanders are typically concentrated in the largest cities, Taipei and Kaohsiung, with something of a presence (but far from a majority) in the smaller industrial cities of the island.

[4] In a recent election, the KMT claimed a total membership in excess of 1.5 million on an island of 18 million people. However, most of the Tangwai's leaders were once considered among the intellectual elite of the KMT, an important fact for the future of Taiwan.

TABLE 17.2   Election Results for Local Officials

Year	Total Offices (N)	KMT Party (%)	China Youth Party (%)	China Democratic Socialist Party (%)	Nonparty (%)
MAYORS AND MAGISTRATES					
1943[a]	21	90.5	—	—	9.5
1946	21	95.2	—	—	4.8
1949	21	90.5	—	—	9.5
1953	21	81.0	4.8	—	14.3
1957	20	85.0	—	—	15.0
•					
•					
•					
1977[b]	20	80.0	—	—	20.0
1981[b]	19	78.9	—	—	21.1
COUNCILLORS OF COUNTIES AND MUNICIPALITIES					
1939–40[a]	814	63.0	—	0.4	36.5
1941–42[a]	860	60.0	0.2	—	39.8
1943–44[a]	928	70.8	—	—	29.2
1947	1,025	64.1	—	0.1	35.8
1950	929	62.3	0.1	0.2	37.4
1953	907	73.9	0.2	0.6	25.4
1957	847	73.9	0.1	0.6	25.4
1962	850	73.5	—	0.4	26.1
CIVILIAN REPRESENTATIVES OF TOWNSHIPS, HSIANGS, AND CITIES UNDER DIRECT COUNTY JURISDICTION					
1942–44[a]	5,926	41.2	[c]	[c]	58.8
1947–48	5,678	45.4	0.1	[c]	54.6
1950–51	5,260	43.6	[c]	[c]	56.4
1953–54	4,776	49.3	[c]	[c]	50.6
1957–58	4,721	53.3	—	[c]	46.7
1962[d]	6,522	67.0	[c]	[c]	32.9
or	3,757	72.1	—	0.1	27.8

SOURCES: Department of Civil Affairs, Taiwan Provincial Government, Republic of China, *Statistics on Civil Affairs*, Nos. 2 (1973), 3 (1974), and 4 (1975).

[a] Elections conducted on the mainland for Taiwan natives by the ROC government.

[b] Selected newspaper reports, and *Newsweek* (Asia Edition), Dec. 5, 1977:9.

[c] Less than 0.1%.

[a] The first set of figures was reported in *Statistics*, No. 3 (1974), Table 20; the second set was published in *Statistics*, No. 4 (1975), Table 20.

Why do candidates choose to run as Tangwai, when the rewards inherent in belonging to the KMT are manifest? Nonparty members are basically denied any possibility of promotion to positions of importance and almost all school teachers, civil servants, and officers in the armed services belong to the KMT. Our data give no direct answer to this question, but it is our impression that nonparty candidates use their campaigns, at some personal risk, to publicize their implicit criticisms of the KMT and to make various allegations of abuses of power.

A recent example of such activity was the 1977 "Chungli incident," which caused considerable embarrassment to the regime. Starting as a protest against alleged balloting irregularities by a KMT election official, the incident grew to a full-scale riot. An estimated ten thousand persons stormed and burned the Chungli police station and twelve police riot-control wagons.[5] In that particular election, Hsu-Hsin-liang, to whom we referred earlier as the successful candidate for magistrate of Taoyuan County, had also been openly critical of the KMT, even though he had been one of its most trusted members until 1976. Both his campaign and the violence at Chungli were at sharp variance with traditional election practices in Taiwan.[6] Events similar to those in Chungli took place in seven other cities that night, but reports of these incidents were confined to local press accounts, and did not receive coverage in either the official or "independent" newspapers (for a useful discussion on this distinction, see Jacobs, 1976).

Since 1977, Tangwai have developed greater unity, informally organizing and coordinating their campaigns. The KMT has attempted both explicit and implicit intimidation, without apparent success. The recognition of the People's Republic of China by the United States in December 1978, has provided a further rallying point for Tangwai coordination. The survival of Taiwan is a matter of crucial importance for all its residents, regardless of whether they are natives or mainlanders. Open criticism of the KMT leadership has emerged that blames them for the near-complete political isolation of Taiwan. At this writing, only thirteen nations, mostly small Latin American countries, plus South Africa, Saudi Arabia, and South Korea maintain relations with Taiwan. However, the

[5] McBeath (1978: 17), mentions "hundreds of Taiwanese" in his account. However, the unexpected live television broadcast reports of the incident used the higher figure in describing the violence.

[6] A book sharply critical of the KMT and its election practices, ironically entitled *Long Live the Election*, was quickly printed, quickly confiscated by the Garrison Command after distribution had started, and just as quickly "pirated" in New York, where it was made widely available to the Chinese community. The young author, a Taiwan-born mainlander, was later elected to the Taipei City Council, becoming the first mainlander Tangwai to be elected.

American recognition of the PRC, announced by President Carter just a few days before a scheduled election, gave the ROC an excuse to declare an emergency and indefinitely postpone supplementary elections for the National Assembly, the Legislative Yuan, and other offices. During 1978–79, Tangwai used informal leadership conferences in order to achieve more unity. Some measure of the public support they have received can be seen in the circulation of their monthly magazine—100,000 copies, at the rather expensive price of NT$100 (U.S. $2.50). About 2,000 subscriptions were sold in the United States as well, for $50 per year.

The growing strength of Tangwai did not go unremarked by either the authorities or the general public. On December 10, 1979, Tangwai leaders staged a Human Rights Day demonstration in Kaohsiung. Police refused to allow the more than 30,000 demonstrators to walk through the main street, and a clash took place, during which all key Tangwai leaders were arrested and charged with sedition (Kaplan, 1981). Following what is now known as "the Kaohsiung incident," the mother and two daughters of one of the jailed leaders were murdered in their home. As of this writing no one has yet been convicted of the crime.[7]

With well over thirty key Tangwai members sentenced and jailed, supplementary elections were conducted for the Legislative Yuan and National Assembly in 1981. Elections were also held for the Taiwan Provincial Assembly and the city councils of Taipei and Kaohsiung. The Tangwai made a strong showing, as Table 17.1 demonstrates, despite the fact that most of their leaders were then in jail. Some of the wives of these leaders stood for election, and were elected by overwhelming margins. According to a study published in Taiwan (Lin, 1982), even though the KMT won fifteen of the nineteen mayorships and magistrate positions, and 75 percent of the Taiwan Provincial Assembly and city council seats of Taipei and Kaohsiung, the total Tangwai vote exceeded 43 percent. This result was obtained despite the fact that the Tangwai, lacking formal organization and media coverage of any sort, were forced to rely entirely on campaign speeches and word of mouth to communicate their positions.

Besides their own electoral activities, the Tangwai are likely to profit from the changing balance of power between native Taiwanese and mainlanders in the KMT at both the municipal and provincial levels of government. All nineteen mayors and magistrates are now native Taiwanese. Even in the larger cities of Taipei and Kaohsiung, where mainlanders are

---

[7] As it happened, his wife was visiting Lin in jail when the incident took place. One of the three daughters survived the attack, and later came to the United States with her mother, where she is being treated. Bruce Jacobs, an American political scientist cited in this work, was detained in Taiwan for three months under suspicion. The ROC government has recently announced that, although he is now in the United States, he is an "alleged suspect."

concentrated, Taiwanese won large majorities: forty-eight of the fifty-one city council seats in Taipei and thirty-seven of forty-two in Kaohsiung. The Democratic Socialist and Chinese Youth parties, clearly identifiable as mainlanders in origin, received only 0.1 percent and 0.08 percent of the vote respectively, and elected no members. Taiwanese also won seventy-six of the seventy-seven seats in the Provincial Assembly, the sole exception being a guaranteed seat for women which was won by a mainlander.

Similarly, advantages accrue to the Tangwai from the activities of native Taiwanese in the Legislative and Control Yuans. Taiwanese occupy only a few seats in these two bodies, but they are typically young and outspoken. Mainlanders in the Legislative Yuan are mostly in their late seventies and most in the Control Yuan are eighty years or older. There is potential for significant change in these branches of the government, since the older members do not always attend sessions, and Taiwanese Tangwai members, sometimes with the cooperation of Taiwanese KMT members,[8] can effectively block KMT-supported actions by simple quorum calls.[9]

CONCLUSION

We have traced in broad outline the two major movements which challenge the continued one-party dominance of the Republic of China by the KMT. Both movements threaten the legitimacy of the government, the presence of which has never been voted upon by the people of Taiwan. The continuance of a distinct ethnic identity, despite attempts by the regime to impose other values, fosters the two movements, providing a climate for further instability.

As we have suggested, there are distinct cultural differences between Taiwanese and mainlanders. Despite protestations by the government that "we are all Chinese," the distinctions are made and continued. Formally sanctioned by the government through identity cards and representation in the National Assembly, the distinctions are informally and even more powerfully realized through the electoral process. Almond has suggested some possible reasons for these phenomena: "The totalitarian political culture gives the appearance of being homogeneous, but the homogeneity is synthetic. . . . [I]n view of the thorough-going penetration of the

---

[8] Despite strong party organization, KMT party discipline is not nearly as strong as, for instance, that found in British political parties.

[9] The KMT has recently been debating the meaning of a quorum—one-fifth of the original 700-plus seats, or one-fifth of the current 400 seats. The first option is not possible, and the second option would make the small Taiwanese bloc, Tangwai and KMT, a force with which they would have to reckon.

society by a centrally controlled system of organization and communications, and the special way in which coercion or its threat is applied, the totalitarian system, in contrast to the others, tends to be non-consensual" (Almond, 1956: 403). As we have had cause to see, it is evident that the nonconsensual political system can overreact to stress, providing yet further bases for its critics to raise charges to which an "overcompensatory response" (Miller, 1955: 527) may be likely.

To what extent has the KMT penetrated Taiwanese society, such that these responses would be unlikely? This is a difficult question to answer. A pro-KMT argument might suggest that their domination of the political scene reflects an increasing recognition by the populace that the official party is best able to provide that which the country needs—effective leadership and national unity. A counterresponse might be that the KMT, as the ruling party under martial law, has had a long time to develop and implement some of the classic techniques of machine and dollar politics, offering material rewards to those who cooperate.[10] For those who fail to cooperate, either in the electoral sense or by representing a threat through the independence movement, threats of physical coercion can be employed. These range from visits by the Garrison Command for intimidation purposes[11] to the use of troops to put down political demonstrations, to the jailing of particularly troublesome Tangwai.

At a partisan level, the most recent elections aside, one might believe that the KMT has become increasingly powerful. Taiwan has become increasingly isolated from the rest of the world in a diplomatic if not economic sense. The ROC, it can safely be said, is a pariah in the international community, maintaining relations with less than two dozen countries, although it trades with well over one hundred. As if further demonstrations were necessary, the recent nine-point peace overture by the PRC, and their reactions to arms sales to Taiwan by the United States, may be taken as indicative of the international isolation of the ROC. In this sense, the regime has appealed to all residents to identify more clearly with the KMT, and to eschew Tangwai politics and politicians. Yet, this clearly has not

[10] A suggestive example of this problem, one which greatly embarrassed the KMT, was the recent Taipei County Assembly election of their speaker, in which the speaker-elect was arrested for buying each vote for U.S. $5,000. With canceled checks as evidence, the KMT-controlled government was forced to indict the speaker-elect. See various issues of the *Far East Times* (March 1982). He was sentenced to one-and-a-half years in jail in April 1982.

[11] By way of further illustration, L. S. Fan visited Taiwan in the summer of 1980 for three days. The day after he left, his uncle was visited by two security agents. Of a much more serious nature was the July 1981 murder of Professor Chen Wen-cheng of Carnegie-Mellon University, following thirteen hours of interrogation by the Taiwan Garrison Command about his activities in the United States. The official government position on this was that Professor Chen "fell" from a building.

happened. Rather, the Tangwai blame the KMT for Taiwan's tenuous position in world affairs. And TIM offers independence as the means of resolving the issue, believing that Beijing has neither the ability nor the desire to achieve hegemony by force.

One might also inquire whether the activities of Tangwai, if not the TIM, actually serve the KMT's purposes. It is notable, in this regard, that Tangwai have not been outlawed. However, inasmuch as the Tangwai lack a formal organization, since such is not allowed, it would be difficult at best for the ROC to make such a move, at least in the legal sense. In the practical sense, it would risk another Kaohsiung incident, which it might not be able either to afford or contain. Much is made by the ROC government of the appearance and necessity of practicing "democracy" as it is known in the West. Comparisons are constantly made in Taiwan's press with their own practice of democracy as compared to the monolithic state of the PRC. Indeed, their press is fond of pointing out that Taiwan has a higher rate of voter participation than does the United States.

Hence, some semblance of political pluralism can serve to enhance the image, if not the reality, of Taiwan as a consensual state, while the KMT leaders attempt to develop their own version of democracy, adapted to their own needs and conditions. "Our political mind is facing various challenges from different aspects. Nonetheless, our duties are assigned to make it move toward our goal. We have to pay more attention to the growth of American democratic ideas, but we furthermore need to absorb them in order to create 'our own' at a higher level" (Tsao, 1978: 46).

The ROC exists in a situation of stress, thanks to its role in the international community as well as to the growth of the Tangwai and TIM movements. Its response has been to employ practices widely considered antithetical to democracy. Given the recent increase in domestic disorders and electoral repudiation of the ruling party, such practices appear to be as repugnant to the native population as to Western observers. It remains to be seen whether the TIM and Tangwai movements will continue to grow and prosper, at the expense of the KMT, or whether the latter will find new means to reassert its hegemony over the Taiwanese political system.[12]

EPILOGUE

Further and more formal challenges to the party system of Taiwan took place in 1986. The Tangwai organized as a new party, the Democratic

[12] Li (1981) provides varying viewpoints about Taiwan's future. Tien (1982) contains more updated opinions on this subject by scholars concerned with Taiwan's and China's future.

Progressives, in contests for the Legislative Yuan and the National Assembly. This party could have been banned from the ballot, since it lacked formal recognition. Possibly because it was seeking accommodation with dissident elements, the Kuomintang-controlled government allowed the DPP to appear on the ballot. The DPP received 30 percent of the vote and twelve of seventy-three seats in contests for the Legislative Yuan, as well as 25 percent of the vote and eleven of eighty-four seats for the National Assembly. True Independents, not associated with the DPP, received 7 percent and 6 percent of the vote and two and eleven seats, respectively. Hence, opposition is becoming more formalized in the Republic of China, while the KMT maintains firm control of the government.

REFERENCES

Almond, G. A. 1956. Comparative political systems. *Journal of Politics* 18: 391–95.

Appleton, S. 1970. Taiwanese and mainlanders on Taiwan: A survey of student attitudes. *China Quarterly* 44: 38–65.

———. 1976. The social and political impact of education in Taiwan. *Asian Survey* 16: 703–20.

———. 1976–1977. Survey research on Taiwan. *Public Opinion Quarterly* 40: 468–81.

Chen, K. C. 1977. Peking's attitude toward Taiwan. *Asian Survey* 17: 903–18.

Executive Yuan. 1977. *Statistical yearbook of the Republic of China.* Taipei: Directorate-General of Budget, Accounting, and Statistics.

Fairbanks, J. 1982. *Chinabound.* New York: Harper and Row.

Jacobs, J. B. 1976. Taiwan's press: Political communications link and research resource. *China Quarterly* 68: 778–88.

Kaplan, J. 1981. *The court-martial of the Kaohsiung defendants.* Berkeley: Institute of East Asian Studies, University of California, Research Papers and Policy Studies No. 2.

Kerr, G. H. 1965. *Formosa betrayed.* Boston: Houghton Mifflin.

———. 1974. *Formosa: Licensed revolution and the home rule movement, 1895–1945.* Honolulu: University of Hawaii Press.

King, A. M. 1974. A short history of the Formosan independence movement. *Independent Taiwan,* 34.

Li, V. 1980. *The future of Taiwan: A difference of opinion.* White Plains, N.Y.: M. E. Sharpe.

Liebling, A. J. 1964. The rubber-type army *and* The rubber-type army: A postscript. In *The press.* New York: Ballantine Books.

Lin, C. 1982. Studies of Taiwan area voter behavior. *Far East Times* (Chinese), Jan. 29.

Marsh, R. M. 1968. The Taiwanese of Taipei: Some major aspects of their social structure and attitudes. *Journal of Asian Studies* 27: 571–84.

Martin, R. 1975. The socialization of children in China and on Taiwan: An analysis of elementary school textbooks. *China Quarterly* 62: 242–62.

McBeath, G. 1978. Taiwan in 1977: Holding the reins. *Asian Survey* 18: 17–28.

Peng Ming-min. 1972. *A taste of freedom: Memoirs of a Formosan independence leader.* New York: Holt, Rinehart and Winston, Inc.

Shutt, A. 1982. The Two Taiwans. *Christian Science Monitor*, April 7.

Tien, Hung-Mao, ed. 1982. *China, Taiwan, and the United States.* Boston: Olgeschlager, Gunn and Hain, Inc.

Tsao, Jiun-han, 1978. The acceptability and adaptability of American democratic ideas to the Chinese political mind: A cross-cultural analysis. *American Studies* 8: 21–46.

Wilson, R. W. 1968. A comparison of political attitudes of Taiwanese children and mainlander children on Taiwan. *Asian Survey* 8: 988–1000.

———. 1970. *Learning to be Chinese.* Cambridge: MIT Press.

———. 1974. *The moral state.* New York: Free Press.

WUFI. 1981. Statement on the position of the people of Taiwan concerning Taiwan-China relations. (English translation), Oct. 5.

EIGHTEEN

Political Party Failures and Political Responses in Ghana

JON KRAUS

Since the early 1960s the West African country of Ghana has experienced three failures of political party regimes, each overthrown in a military *coup d'état*. Despite the varying composition and political orientations of the successor military regimes, new and adapted forms of civilian political organization and representation have emerged within these military regimes and struggled for recognition, resources, and power. The persistent failure of political party regimes raises the central question of why they have failed and in what senses. This involves, first, an assumption that the elimination of political regimes in which political parties were active constitutes a failure and, second, an assessment of the extent to which the roles and behavior of the political parties were significant in the failure of the regimes. Political party regime failure also poses the question of what alternative organizations or groups came into existence to seize political roles, or transformed themselves by undertaking political activities, and to what extent these groups or organizations can or seek to perform crucial political roles that political parties normally assume.

The seizure of executive political power by military officers or mixed military-civilian groups clearly preempts a central role that political parties play as institutions that compete for power in order to hold governmental office. However, political groups and organizations in Ghana in nonparty regimes have sought to play almost every other role, including openly competing with a military regime for power, as is occurring again in the 1980s in Ghana. There has been little systematic analysis of these political groups. What have been the origins, character, and leadership of these groups? Do they represent largely the leadership remnants and networks of previous parties? Have they reflected simply existing economic, social, and political structures, formal and informal, of power in society? Or have nonparty environments permitted social classes or groups not normally mobilized in political party regimes to organize for resources and power? Can they articulate the interests of membership groups, aggregate broad ranges of interests and claims? Are political parties really replaceable for organizing power and eliciting and mobilizing popular support? Or are these alternative political groups simply parties in inception, unable to assume their genuine guise in a hostile environment?

This essay will address these major questions regarding political party failure and the sources and character of alternative political organizations which assume political life in the absence of parties in the case of Ghana. Ghana has had six political regimes since independence, three civilian political regimes in which political parties played predominant roles, each succeeded by a military regime of some kind. Kwame Nkrumah and the Convention People's Party (CPP) came to power in Ghana in 1951, led it to independence in 1957, eliminated the combined United Party (UP) thereafter, and ruled until 1966 when the regime was overthrown. There was a competitive party system until about 1959–60 and, in effect, a single-party system after 1960, though there is significant debate concerning the significance and viability of the CPP after 1960 (Apter, 1972; Bretton, 1966; Owusu, 1970; Zolberg, 1966). The National Liberation Council (NLC) government came to power in 1966, led by a military-police council. The NLC justified its seizure of power by Nkrumah's and the CPP's dictatorship, promised to restore economic health and democratic civilian rule, and substantially liberalized political life and pressure group activity, permitting political parties, elections, and civilian rule in 1969. The competitive elections of 1969 were won by Dr. Kofi Busia's Progress party (PP), which included many of the most important leaders of the previous opposition party to Nkrumah's CPP. It won 59 percent of the vote and 105 of the 140 seats against several other parties (Kraus, 1970: 218–20; Twumasi, 1975). The most important opposition party, the National Alliance of Liberals (NAL), was led by Komia Gbedemah, one of Nkrumah's former top CPP leaders (who had fled the country in 1961) and a broad range of ex-CPP leaders and rank and file.

In January 1972, the PP government and regime were overthrown by Colonel I. K. Acheampong and a group of junior officers who established the National Redemption Council (NRC; after 1975 renamed the Supreme Military Council, SMC) government. The NRC/SMC took a much less tolerant view than its NLC military predecessor toward political parties and most quasi-political organizations, and opposed a restoration of civilian rule, especially one in which parties would play a major role. After a sustained conflict between 1977 and 1979 with a wide variety of social and political groups which arose to oppose it, the SMC gave way, briefly, to two successor military regimes which, ultimately and reluctantly, permitted the restoration of parties, elections, and civilian rule: SMC II (July

1978, to June 1979; led by Gen. Fred Akuffo), and the radical populist Armed Forces Revolutionary Council, which erupted from a military mutiny in June 1979, led by Fl. Lt. Jerry Rawlings.

In September 1979, President Hilla Limann and the People's National party (PNP) came to power, with the PNP having 71 of 140 parliamentary seats and Hilla Limann 62 percent of the presidential vote in the second, runoff poll (36 percent in the initial poll) (*Legon Observer*, July 13, 1979; *West Africa*, Oct. 15, 1979: 1909). Limann's PNP was a direct lineal descendant of Nkrumah's CPP, the party finances and machinery run directly by many members of the CPP old guard, while its assembly members and most of its cabinet officers were drawn from a younger post-CPP generation. The two main opposition parties were direct descendants from Busia's Progress party and its leadership: the Popular Front party (PFP), led by Victor Owusu, with its core support areas in the Ashanti and Brong/ Ahafo regions, and the United National Convention (UNC), whose ex-PP leaders had sought a broader base than the former PP. Limann's PNP government lasted a month less than its civilian PP predecessor, only twenty-seven months, and was overthrown on December 31, 1981, by a small group of nonofficer military elements, active and retired. The effort was led by a radicalized Fl. Lt. Jerry Rawlings (the AFRC leader), who formed a civilian-military Provisional National Defense Council (PNDC) government in 1982. The PNDC was significantly different from prior military regimes in that, first, its leadership had formed a number of political organizations before the coup (e.g., Rawlings's June 4th Movement) and, second, it made major efforts to develop new civilian political organizations as a base for the regime and in order to carry through major political-economic changes. However, other political and politicized organizations also arose and mobilized heavy and sustained opposition to PNDC policies, its new political organizations, and the regime itself.

Despite successive party "failures," it is clear that the careers of these major political parties persisted through three civilian and military regimes, the CPP/NAL/PNP and the UP/PP/PFP and UNC. In the face of regime disruptions and structural political changes (i.e., new regimes), each was linked to its predecessors by objective factors (personnel, organizational networks) and subjectives ones (ideas, widely perceived identities)(see Rose and Mackie, below, on party careers).

This essay will offer a number of theoretical explanations for the failure of political party regimes and then test these on the three different party regimes in Ghana, especially on the most recent Limann/PNP regime of 1979–81. Second, it will explore and assess the major characteristics of the alternative political organizations and groups which have arisen during the nonparty military regimes, in particular those under the Rawlings/

PNDC regime which seized power in December 1981. It is important on both topics to deal with previous political party regimes and alternative political organizations under military rule, first, because there has been considerable continuity of political organizations under party and non-party regimes and, second, because previous forms of organization, behavior, and party failures help to explain both the causes and character of subsequent political organizations and the relationships between socio-economic and political power under these regimes.

FAILURE OF PARTY REGIMES

Political party regimes overthrown in military coups clearly failed, at least in ensuring their own survival. However, the sources of these failures may not necessarily be found in the deficiencies of the party system or political party behavior. We shall assess different types of political, economic, and military explanations of regime failure and test these on the three civilian political party regimes in Ghana in order to isolate to the extent possible the contributory roles of different factors and of political parties and party systems in particular. A number of explanations have been offered for the failure or weaknesses of political party systems or regimes generally.

Hypothesis 1. System crises. During certain crucial historical junctures, most frequently those in which countries confront fundamental socio-economic and political changes, countries may experience simultaneous "crises" or conflicts regarding the legitimacy of authority, political participation, identity (subjective basis of membership in a political community), and penetration (extent of central government control over subnational political institutions). "Crises" may be regarded as serious threats to, or irreversible changes in, the functioning of a political regime (Grew, 1978: 10–11). It is argued that when these "crises" are experienced simultaneously rather than sequentially (as was the case in most currently industrialized countries), the "load" or pressure on a political system tends to increase government repression and restrict sharply the activities and roles of political parties. This undermines a system in which parties play crucial roles in selecting and holding accountable political leaders, articulating and drawing together for representation public interests, and linking in a consensual way individuals and communities to the government (see LaPalombara and Weiner, 1966: 399–418; Grew, 1978: 15–24; Binder et al., 1971: 62–67). These acts constitute a failure of a competitive party system and may contribute to the regime's loss of power.

Hypothesis 2. High participation-low institutionalization. The achievement of political community in modernizing societies involves the extensive integration of subsocieties and the assimilation of new social and economic classes. The rapid expansion of political participation is likely to be politically destabilizing where organized and institutionalized political parties have not developed prior to this expanded participation, generating violence and low legitimacy. Low levels of participation weaken parties relative to other social forces and institutions (Huntington, 1968: 401–402).

Hypothesis 3. Political structures. Certain structures in political regimes—e.g., concentrated presidential authority and high levels of bureaucratization—tend to reduce the salience, power, and representational capabilities of political parties, leading to reduced capacity or stunted growth in activities (Lawson, 1976: 147–48, 172–73).

Hypothesis 4. Party origins. Parties formed outside the system tend to have a low commitment to existing political institutions and norms. Mass nationalist and revolutionary parties, often external, tend to claim a monopoly on legitimacy and political offices.

Hypothesis 5. Autocracy and corruption. Where political parties and party leaders act to reduce their accountability to broad public and salient interest groups and to employ political offices for private or narrow group benefits, the party system loses legitimacy and support among excluded groups.

Hypothesis 6. Ethnic and class monopolization. Party systems with low organized participation lead to parties where leadership reflects established class and/or ethnic socioeconomic power. Upper-class or narrow ethnic monopolization of party and government offices will tend, in the face of crises in the political economy, to lead to sharply reduced legitimacy for the parties and party systems among excluded classes and ethnic groups.

Hypothesis 7. Economic crises. Severe economic depressions, or economic mismanagement crises, sharply reduce support for incumbent parties in most systems. In monocrop or mineral-dependent export economies, sharp external world market price fluctuations may generate recurring economic crises, increasing political conflict and reducing the legitimacy of a party system perceived as ineffective.

Hypothesis 8. Military praetorianism. Military coups occur for a number of major reasons, including authoritarianism, poor economic performance, corporate military grievances, and class conflicts. Initial interventions tend to politicize and exacerbate factions in the military. Thus, military coups tend to recur against party regimes for much less substantive reasons than the first time.

The coming into existence of political parties does not mean that there exists a set of institutions, rules, and norms institutionalized at the level of behavior and belief, commanding broad consent among political party followers and equivalent meaning at national and local levels, as observers of Ghanaian politics have noted (Apter, 1972: 185–233, 241–70; Austin, 1964: 119–26, 209–33). In 1949, Ghana (then the Gold Coast) consisted of a large number of minimally integrated traditional states, many culturally and linguistically distinct, within the loose colonial administrative grid. The impact of the penetration of capital, a market economy, and secular institutions was highly skewed regionally and ethnically and altered but did not wholly erode these traditional political units and the social norms which they embodied. Thus, there has persisted strong particularistic local and ethnic loyalties and norms sustaining local-ethnic solidarities and, in the 1950s, chiefs and traditional councils with significant social and political power.

Under these circumstances, the propriety and legitimacy of political parties and a political party system as agencies for eliciting consent and pursuing public purposes has been questioned preceding or during every political party regime. A major connotation of political parties to many in Ghana, as elsewhere historically, has been that they are factious, socially and politically divisive, and self-interested, animating social disruptions and conflict (Sartori, 1976: 3–29).

This was a major argument raised against Nkrumah's CPP, which penetrated and captured local power through local council and parliamentary elections, often in conflict with chiefs and councils (in southern and central Ghana), sometimes in alliance with them (in northern Ghana, the least modernized area, where the social basis for an educated commoners' party had not been created). The populist CPP, and the idea of party generally, was often perceived as a profound threat to chiefly power, tradition, and the social order. Party divisiveness was raised as a rallying cry by aggrieved ethnic communities and states, and political dissidents employed ethnicity (or tribal ties) to mobilize anti-CPP electoral support (Austin, 1864: 246–75). Opposition groups often referred to themselves as movements of the people, not parties, e.g., the National Liberation Movement in Ashanti, which opposed "stranger" groups controlling their power and resources.

In 1968 as the NLC military prepared to retire, opposition to political parties as divisive, excessive, nonrepresentative, and self-interested was raised anew in newspaper articles and in petitions to the Constitutional Commission recommending outlawing parties. But the merchant/professional bourgeoisie which dominated the Constitutional Commission considered parties as bound up with representative democracy (Ghana, 1968d: 106–108). Antagonism to political parties and a party system was raised more vigorously in 1976–78 by the Acheampong military government, as it sought to stave off rising political opposition to persistent military rule, by its proposal for "Union" or national government, with no parties but with military-police participation. A political party system, Acheampong argued, "brings in its trail division, hatred, sectional and tribal interest. . . . A Party Government is not really representative of the people" (Ghana, 1977: 140, 143). Acheampong formed an Ad Hoc Committee on Union Government to sound out public opinion and propose an appropriate constitutional form. Despite the probable self-serving character of much testimony, some animus could be rallied against parties: between 75 percent and 85 percent of the individuals and organizations submitting written or oral testimony favored government without parties (Ghana, 1977: 61). The somewhat fraudulent referendum in March 1978 provided the military government with a narrow majority for Union Government. However, a public opinion poll in Kumasi, Ashanti in July–August 1977, in the midst of the "Unigov" debate, found that Union Government (without parties) was supported by only 10.5 percent of respondents, while 13.9 percent favored continued military rule, 27.2 percent a one-party state, and 29.7 percent a multi-party state, favored by a plurality at all educational and occupational levels (N = 905, Osei-Kwame, 1978).

THE NKRUMAH/CPP REGIME (1951–66)

The Nkrumah/CPP regime experienced severe and simultaneous crises in political legitimacy, political participation, national identity, and penetration (Hyp. 1). As a mass nationalist, external party (Hyp. 4), much of its national leadership appears to have had a relatively low commitment to a competitive party system. And any tentative commitment to a parliamentary system the British imposed was sharply reduced by these crises. Ethnic cleavages were sharply politicized as political participation expanded rapidly in the preindependence period (1949–56), leading to high ethnic-regional-communal demands (which the CPP partly accommodated, partly embraced), breakaway parties based on ethnicity (Ashanti National Liberation Movement, NLM, Ewe Togoland Congress party, TCP) and religion (Muslim Association party); there were other parties based on regional (Northern People's party) and ethnic grievances. These posed a sharp challenge to CPP rule before independence and to the CPP's coherence as a party. The CPP as a populist, commoners' nationalist party, with broad membership and a widespread, locally rooted party organization, had fragile roots. Local political dissidents from within challenged the CPP and capitalized on local, ethnic, and regional grievances, which led to a severe erosion in CPP political strength between the 1954 and 1956 elections. Demands for a federation and threats of secession were raised (Austin, 1964: chs. 5–7; Kraus, 1970: 158–71). Three of the five opposition groups were external in origin and had political movement rather than party characteristics. The CPP government responded with repressive measures and material and status inducements to the opposition, and with higher government-party penetration of the regions and local areas in the postindependence period with the appointment of district commissioners, who soon challenged the CPP members of Parliament for local power and influence.

By 1960 a de facto one-party system was in effect, and at the national level power was increasingly concentrated in the presidential office (Nkrumah) under the 1960 Constitution. The decline of the opposition reduced the CPP constituency party as a center of activity. Concentrated presidential power (Hyp. 3) and increased regime authoritarianism after 1960 tended to reduce established party roles, generating structural atrophy, although many backbench MPs persisted in their established roles of vigorously articulating and representing constituency and other public interests.

After 1960, Nkrumah claimed the CPP's role was to serve as mass mobilizer of collective energies in behalf of establishing Socialism in Ghana, but the reality was different. The desire for change, which required conflict within the omnibus CPP, was constrained by Nkrumah's need for order. Party activism became ritualized; party linkages and controls over auxiliary groups (of trade unions, cocoa farmers, youth) were used to mobilize support in a narrowly controlled fashion (Jeffries, 1978: 58–101; Kraus, 1979a: 127–36; Beckman, 1976: chs. 6, 8). Nationally, a careerist party was fashioned through manipulation, patronage, and fear to buttress Nkrumah's dictatorship, and local party satrapies, penetrated from the center, helped to maintain social order (Owusu, 1970; Apter, 1972: 372–86; Kraus, 1970: 168–77).

This decline of the party contributed to the more immediate forms of behavior between 1961 and 1966 that prompted the military overthrow of the regime in 1966. The authoritarianism permitted increased nonaccountability of CPP leaders and high levels of corruption (Hyp. 5): import licenses were manipulated for private profit (Ghana, 1964, 1965, 1967a); state corporation resources were massively diverted to private CPP elite purposes (Ghana, 1967, 1968, 1968a, 1968b, 1969–70a, 1970; Levine, 1975); and the CPP leadership came to be widely, and accurately, regarded as corrupt (Ghana, 1968c, 1969, 1969–70). Although not perceived in these terms then, the party in power could turn its leadership (ministers,

TABLE 18.1 Ghana: Economic Indicators

Year	Regime	Cocoa Production (tonnes)[a]	Average World Price (£ per tonne)	Percentage Change in World Price	Real Average Cocoa Producer Price Index (1963–64 = 100)	Real Govt. Minimum Wage Index (1963 = 100)	Average Rate of Inflation (%)
1957	Nkrumah/CPP Govt.	264	243	48.7			1.0
1958		207	347	+42.7			0
1959		255	281	−19.0			2.8
1960		317	222	−21.0		120.0	1.0
1961		432	177	−20.3		113.0	6.4
1962		410	167	−5.6	130.0	104.0	8.6
1963		422	205	+22.8	113.0	100.0	4.5
1964		421	188	−8.3	100.0	90.0	10.8
1965		538	138	−26.6	83.4	66.4	26.1
1966	Coup 2/66	401	193	+39.9	43.8	58.3	13.5
1967	Ntl. Librn. Cncl., 1966–9/69	368	238	+23.3	52.5	68.6	−8.5
1968		415	320	+34.5	69.1	67.9	8.3

1969	Busia/PP Govt. 9/69–1/72	323	415	+29.7	68.7	63.5	7.0
1970		403	306	−26.3	73.4	61.2	3.7
1971		413	232	−24.2	70.8	56.0	9.3
1972	Coup, 1/72	454	270	+16.4	64.7	68.1	10.0
1973	Acheampong/SMC	407	585	+116.7	78.6	57.1	17.5
1974		340	990	+69.2	75.1	73.2	18.4
1975		376	723	−27.0	79.3	75.2	29.7
1976		396	1,399	+93.5	65.2	48.1	53.3
1977		320	2,994	+114.0	52.2	33.4	116.3
1978	Coup, SMC II	271	2,006	−33.0	43.9	25.6	73.7
1979	AFRC mutiny	265	1,727	−13.9	50.3	16.7	53.9
1980	Civ. rule 9/79	296	1,270	−26.5	49.3	16.6	50.1
1981	Limann/PNP	258	1,114[b]	−12.3	32.8	15.4	116.0
1982	Rawlings/PNDC	225			50.7	12.6	22.3
1983		178				9.9	128.8
1984		E150				11.5	27.7

SOURCES: Gill and Duffus, 1981: 27; Ghana, CBS, 1976: 106; Ghana, 1967[b]: 31; Ghana, CBS, 1977–82.
[a] Calendar year 1960-Cocoa crop year 1959–60.
[b] Average January–November prices.

MPs, district commissioners, city council members, administrators of state corporations) into a new upper class, a state bourgeoisie, whose control over state power provided high salaries, enormous perquisites (cars, multiple houses: an instant rentier class was created), privileged access to state resources (loans, import licenses, contracts), and the widespread illegal diversion of scarce public wealth into private hands. At the same time, potentially politically significant classes (peasant cocoa farmers, wage workers, petty-bourgeois teachers and civil servants) increasingly felt their interests unrepresented, their material well-being undermined (Ghana, 1967). The cocoa producers' real price index (1963 = 100) fell from 130 to 44 or 66 percent during 1961–65; real minimum wages were almost halved from 1960 to 1965 (see Table 18.1). The sharp 33 percent fall in world cocoa prices between 1963 and 1965 exacerbated economic conditions severely, generating inflation, consumer shortages, and discontent (Hyp. 7). Cocoa revenue shortfalls made more pronounced the inadequacies of economic policies and their implementation, with ineptly organized and overambitious state investment and state corporate programs, financed with medium-term supplier credits (Killick, 1978).

In conclusion, system crises (Hyp. 1), rapidly expanding political participation that generated legitimacy challenges (Hyp. 2), and the external, mass nationalist character of the CPP (Hyp. 4) contributed most heavily to the demise of the competitive party system. These in turn animated the authoritarianism and corruption of the Nkrumah CPP regime (Hyp. 5), a source of the atrophy of the CPP itself (Hyp. 3), which, rendered more vulnerable by the impact of falling world cocoa prices and poorly implemented economic policies, led most directly to the military overthrow of the single-party system in 1966.

Busia/Progress Party (PP) Regime (1969–72)

The Busia/PP government that came to power after the 1969 election, with a comfortable parliamentary majority of 105 of 140 assembly seats, was overthrown by a faction of the military in January 1972, less than two and a half years after its formation. The Busia/PP government did not confront the simultaneous crises of legitimacy, political participation, national identity, and state penetration that the Nkrumah regime did (Hyp. 1), nor the rapid expansion of participation (Hyp. 2). No major regions or their representatives sought federation or secession or resisted the government with violence and intimidation, as occurred between 1954 and 1957. The new parliamentary institutions created did not involve a high concentration of power which reduced the capacities of parties to represent constituents and groups (Hyp. 3). The regime remained relatively liberal, although showing some indications of autocratic behavior. Nor did the parties emerge external to the system (Hyp. 4): the parties and party leaderships drew upon preexisting groups and emerged within the bosom of the constituent assembly and of a constitution of their own making.

The rapid demise of the Busia/PP regime must be found in explanations involving ethnic and/or class monopolization of power through parties; autocratic and corrupt behavior; a sharp economic decline; and praetorian military behavior.

The Progress party (PP) did possess some strong strains of both class and ethnic dominance which led a number of important groups to feel themselves without representation. The PP leadership had two major sources which helped to determine its leadership, character, and structural linkages to society. First, it drew upon the leadership of the old opposition parties under the Nkrumah regime: the Ashanti NLM, the northern NPP (the most thoroughly linked with traditional authority structures), and the Ghana Congress party (of the merchant-professional class bourgeoisie), which together had become the United party in 1958. While some of these leaders had joined the CPP, many had fled abroad or been jailed. They reappeared with renewed status as opponents of the Nkrumah dictatorship, and the military NLC (1966–69) government hoisted them into prominence as economic and political advisers, heads of state corporations, and members of the Constitutional Commission and Constituent Assembly. The other major source of new party leadership was the younger generation of lawyers, senior civil servants, state managers, and businessmen generated by Nkrumah's ambitious economic and educational programs. The old political leaders formed an important network to which these rising lawyers and businessmen attached themselves, a network lubricated by illegal money (Ghana, 1976: 2–38). Higher education and wealth became important publicly sanctioned symbols of social status and accomplishment, aggressively expressed to further discredit the CPP "verandah" and "socialist boys" and CPP populism (see Price, 1974). The PP leadership was overwhelmingly from the bourgeois-professional class—lawyers, businessmen, corporate managers, and a handful of ex-senior civil servants and university teachers—as were the leaders of the other political parties. Some 55 percent of the party's MPs were university graduates and almost a quarter were lawyers, as were a third of the PP government ministers.

Nonetheless, the links of PP leaders to established ethnic-regional bases, the banning of most ex-CPP leaders and persisting CPP unpopularity, the ex-UP (now PP) leaders' prior championing of important interests (trade unionists in Sekondi, cocoa farmers) during the Nkrumah regime, and their public visibility under the NLC combined to enable this party to develop a national base. Power attracts, and the prospects of the PP's electoral victory brought many new leaders and constituencies into its ranks in a bandwagon effect. It won 59 percent of the vote, 75 percent of the assembly seats, popular majorities in six of nine regions, and all or a majority of seats in seven regions (Kraus, 1970: 219). The PP in 1969 looked like the national party that the CPP had been, a significant change from the 1954 and 1956 elections.

Despite this broad base, eight cabinet posts (44 percent) went to leaders from Ashanti and Brong regions, another four (22 percent) to closely allied leaders from the eastern region; thus 67 percent of cabinet seats went to members from regions with 42 percent of the population. The PP excluded the Ewe from the cabinet (Ewe formed the core NAL support). And the leaders of the PP occasionally expressed themselves in terms of Ashanti chauvinism, which further nurtured popular suspicions of ethnic favoritism. The PP came to be identified as dominated by Ashantis and the ethnically related Brongs.

The PP leadership, representing Ghana's merchant-professional bourgeoisie, also came to possess a class aura for some that it did not initially have. Party leaders pursued numerous economic policies (e.g., transfer of foreign businesses to Ghanaian ownership) which sustained their class interests generally and their own in particular, and responded with substantial antagonism to the grievances of the organized working class, lower-level civil servants, and small farmers, despite PP rural development policies (Jeffries, 1978: 102–65; Kraus, 1979, 1979a: 136–47; Shepherd, 1978; Ghana, 1976, 1979).

Bourgeois domination of the PP government was not much mitigated by popular pressures flowing through the PP since it and the other major parties were essentially patron parties and election machines, without strong, local activist bases (see Dunn, 1975; Peasah, 1975; Twumasi, 1975). The PP and other party leaders were linked to the electorate in several ways: first, by their constituents' acceptance of their status and capabilities— "the best brains," the PP proclaimed of its leaders; and second, by the money and local ethnic-community identifications upon which the PP's successful election machinery was built. These leaders were also initially linked to some of the many associational groups which arose or were regenerated after 1966 in a burst of renewed associational activity. They were able to establish themselves as leaders or spokesmen for many modern associational groups, as well as some rural groups of food and cocoa farmers, canoe fishermen, market women, cooperatives, and the many local or regional development committees all over the country (Chazan, 1982; Twumasi, 1975; Chambas, 1980: chs. 4–5). The representation was often elitist and patron-client in character, and many groups became disenchanted by the PP's failure to represent their interests.

In 1970–71, PP government leaders began to behave in autocratic ways when confronted with relatively mild challenges and accusations (Hyp. 5). The party refused to hold local council elections while in office, dominating them by appointing PP members to "management committees." Prime Minister Busia harshly rejected a Supreme Court decision requiring the government to rehire fired workers. The government banned a small pro-Nkrumah party and passed legislation against any party showing Nkrumah's picture; it harassed the opposition press; and, in the face of union demands for increased minimum wages, it passed legislation to dismantle the Trades Union Congress (TUC), freeze its assets, and abolish contracting-out check-off. Union-government disputes over collective agreements and strikes severely antagonized wage workers, who launched repeated strikes "from below." Colonel Acheampong, who seized power in 1972, cited all these abuses and appealed, with some success, to these aggrieved groups.

The Busia/PP government would undoubtedly have experienced less erosion of its support had it not confronted a sharp 44 percent decline in average world cocoa prices in 1970–71, upon which it depended for about 60 percent of its export earnings and a substantial portion of budget revenue. This compelled it to adopt a somewhat "austere" budget in July 1981, reducing perquisites for civil servants and the military, enacting a policy to require university students to pay a room-and-board fee, reducing the military's size and equipment, spurning any minimum wage increase, and keeping the same producer price paid to cocoa farmers (the real price eroded from 73.4 percent to 65 percent of its 1963 level in 1971). The government climaxed these generally necessary austerity measures with a severe devaluation of the cedi in December 1971, which increased the dollar cost of imports by 90 percent, sharply cutting the real earnings of all urban consumers. The leaders of the PP were less able to legitimate their austerity measures because of their visibly elite consumption patterns, their aura of class privilege, and the widely noted corruption (Ghana, 1976, 1979).

Within three weeks of the devaluation, a small group of military officers, led by Colonel Acheampong and three of his serving majors, overthrew the Busia government, with virtually no military resistance. It has been argued that the economic crisis had not prompted a loss of political legitimacy but set the stage for the military to intervene primarily on behalf of some corporate grievances (loss of perquisites, declining officer autonomy) and to serve the ambitions of some who had been bypassed in the rapid promotion jumps accorded those officers associated with the 1966

coup (Bennett, 1973). This thesis understates the sense of political grievance and perception of class and ethnic monopolization of government resources felt by important Ghanaian groups. Nonetheless, the poor economic performance, which was exacerbated by external commodity price
declines, was crucial to the NRC's claim to legitimacy (Hyp. 7). The NRC
military did launch some new policies of economic nationalism in its first
several years which broke from those of the Busia government. The clear
ambitions of Colonel Acheampong, the narrow basis of the coup leadership, and the alacrity with which other officers scrambled for places on the
new military council, however, suggest strongly that the Ghanaian army
had started on its route to praetorian interventionism (Hyp. 8).

LIMANN/PEOPLE'S NATIONAL PARTY GOVERNMENT (1979–81)

The return to civilian rule in late 1979 occurred in the context of an utterly devastated economy, enfeebled and corrupt state bureaucracies, and
the collapse of military institutions, which gave rein to military praetorianism—all of which contributed significantly to the Limann/PNP regime's
early demise. The economy had experienced hyperinflation of over 100
percent for several years, an absolute decline in food and agricultural export production, disinvestment in productive and infrastructural facilities,
soaring budget deficits, and systematic shortages throughout the 1970s of
essential consumer goods, spare parts, and capital goods imports. Well
over 5 percent of Ghana's 12.4 million population had left the country to
seek jobs and survival elsewhere, among them many of Ghana's most
skilled and educated workers and professionals. The military disintegrated after the mutiny-coup of lower-level officers, noncoms, and pri-
vates against their senior officers in June 1979.

Civilian resistance to continued military rule had been led by Ghana's
professionals, students, and many politicians associated with Busia's PP
and the opposition NAL/Justice party. After the removal of Acheampong's
government in 1978, these groups and others agitated for party-based
elections. Parties were hurriedly formed in early 1979. Elections and the
return to civilian rule were postponed briefly after the AFRC mutiny-coup,
led by Fl. Lt. Jerry Rawlings, which ruthlessly purged many senior military officers and civilian leaders of state corporations and carried out a
populist housecleaning of many state institutions, a necessary task but one
which further enfeebled their capacities.

The 1979 election witnessed the renewed expression of the two-party
partisanship of previous elections, although in 1979 ex-CPP leaders were

at the center of party leadership of the PNP as they had not been in 1969 with the NAL (they had been banned). The PNP was a reborn CPP, with the ex-CPP old guard controlling the party but ineligible for election and many new members of the merchant-professional bourgeoisie becoming MPs. The Popular Front (PFP), led by Victor Owusu (UP in the 1950s, PP in the 1960s), was a revived PP. The PNP was the only national party, winning seats in all regions, 71 of 140 parliamentary seats, and returning to the CPP fold southern and much of northern Ghana (with a northerner as presidential candidate). The PFP reverted to a predominantly Ashanti and Brong party, winning twenty-nine of their forty-two assembly seats in these regions. Dr. Hilla Limann, the PNP presidential candidate, a Sissala from the northern region, a diplomat and political unknown who was vaulted into candidacy by his uncle (ex-CPP leader Imoru Egala), won 35.8 percent of the vote on the first round, against Victor Owusu's (PFP) 29.9 percent, and 62 percent on the second round. Discontent with these old party groups was sufficient to provide significant popular support and assembly seats for several other parties: the United National Convention (UNC), led by ex-PP and ex-NAL leaders and with Ga and Ewe support (thirteen seats); and the Action Congress party (ACP) of ex-Colonel Frank Bernasko, which gathered Fanti support in southern Ghana (ten seats).

The overthrow of the Limann/PNP government can be explained by four factors: most important was economic failure—poor external markets were compounded by floundering policies, both of which made worse the economic disaster the PNP inherited (Hyp. 7); nonaccountability, corruption, and autocracy within the governing PNP (Hyp. 5); these two factors stimulated popular perceptions of elite and class monopolization of access to scarce resources (Hyp. 6); and the interventionist tendencies of a fragmented military no longer controlled by its officer corps (Hyp. 8).

The inability of the Limann/PNP government to revitalize a terribly depressed economy quickly eroded its legitimacy. Early economic efforts sensibly sought to reactivate underutilized productive facilities and to mobilize aid and foreign capital to renew investment; scarce foreign exchange was allocated to priority sectors and wage demands contained. However, prices for Ghana's exports declined sharply between 1979 and 1981: average world cocoa prices dropped by 26.5 percent in 1980 and a further 12.3 percent in 1981 (overall, −35.5 percent, see Table 18.1). Although cocoa export volume rose somewhat in 1980–81, it dropped to a twenty-year low in 1981–82. A smaller crop and lower prices led to an estimated 40 percent decline in Ghana's 1981 export earnings and a 32 percent drop in its exports, which exacerbated shortages and black marketing. Two strategic policies proved devastating. The Limann government was extremely reluctant to devalue the grossly overvalued cedi, which reduced any incentives to produce for export (and led to high levels of smuggling) and undervalued imports. The maintenance of price controls at the ex-factory level meant profits went to traders and smugglers, not the producers. Gradual removal of retail price controls increased goods on the market but at prices most Ghanaians considered criminal. The absence of consumer goods in the rural areas made farmers less willing to produce for urban markets. The real prices cocoa farmers were paid (in 1980, 33 percent of the 1963 price; in 1981, 14 percent) induced them to switch to food production.

The decision of MPs to vote themselves salaries of $18,000 per year, roughly thirty-eight times the minimum wages, led to a popular outcry, numerous strikes, and the collapse of the government's ability to hold down wage increases. The government had to triple minimum and other wages, which led to an enormous budget deficit in 1981. Inflation, which had been slowed from 74 percent in 1979 to 54 percent and 50 percent in 1980 and 1981, rocketed back to 121 percent in 1981, leading to genuine desperation among Ghanaians on how to feed themselves (see Table 18.1). The government's agricultural program never got off the ground. The promise to "flood the market" with imports (to restock *empty* store shelves) proved impossible. The political response to demands for equitable allocations was to distribute some scarce commodities through MPs for their constituencies, a program as inefficient as it was guaranteed to raise suspicions of favoritism and corruption (*West Africa*, Dec. 28, 1981: 3098).

Initially, the new political system did not appear nonresponsive. A vigorous National Assembly whose members were drawn from local constituencies scrutinized the PNP government of President Limann and had ample powers to do so. The minority UNC joined the PNP in a quasi-alliance in order to increase prospects for the PNP's success and thus stave off renewed military intervention.

However, the performance of the PNP and other parties gave rise to the perception of their nonaccountability, corruption, ineffectiveness, and, to a lesser degree, PNP autocracy. From the PNP's inception, its internal structure of power impeded its responsiveness and accountability to the public. The PNP Central Committee and regional organizations were dominated by ex-CPP old guard leaders who had provided the finances and organizational network for the PNP's victory. Limann was a weak president, and control over the PNP rested in the hands of two competing factions of ex-CPP leaders, one headed by Nana Okutwer Bekoe, the national chairman, the other by Imoru Egala, Limann's uncle, who by early 1980 was accusing Bekoe of corruption. This semipublic struggle appears to have centered on efforts to control patronage and contracts. Several left-wing factions of the PNP publicly criticized the self-interest and bourgeois proclivities of the old guard. Factional conflict burst spectacularly upon the public scene in late 1981 when some PNP leaders sued the PNP's leading officers for failing to render accounts and for corrupt activities. An out of court settlement required the resignation of the PNP's officers and inspired the belief that PNP corruption was being hushed up.

The opposition parties also presented a public face of absorbed self-interest and disarray. Repeated attempts in 1981 to form a united opposition foundered on the unwillingness of the top leaders to accept secondary positions in a unified party.

Accusations of corruption against PNP leaders were heard during their first months in office, persisted in charges of diversion of goods and contracts, and climaxed in the PNP's last months in power. A National Assembly investigation was underway into a possible kickback in a contract for printing Ghana's currency. Most spectacular was the demand made in a London lawsuit by an Italian businessman resident in South Africa that he be reimbursed for a loan of $980,000 that he had made to top PNP leaders shortly after Limann took office. The funds were subsequently divided among these leaders. Corruption charges simply compounded the widespread view that the political elite feathered its own nest, indifferent to public suffering.

The generally nonauthoritarian Limann government engaged in some authoritarian behavior with delegitimizing consequences. Recently won press freedoms were eroded by PNP control of the press commission. Strikes were regarded as illegal; several strikes and worker demonstrations led to massive government dismissals and prolonged public disputes. Accurate suspicions of antiregime plots by ex-AFRC leader Rawlings and AFRC sympathizers led to repeated arrests of military personnel, secret trials, and the sustained harassment of Rawlings and his allies (Kraus, 1982).

Political corruption and the high salaries, new cars and other imported goods possessed by the MPs, reanimated a recurring Ghanaian belief that access to economic resources was dominated by the political elite (Hyp. 6). The widening gap in incomes, wealth, and the capacity to survive in an extremely depressed hyperinflationary economy between the mass of Ghanaians and the privileged few (among them party leaders) was increasingly a source of rankling popular grievance.

Lastly, the Limann government failed in its efforts to rebuild officer control and hierarchy within the Ghana military following the AFRC mutiny and lower ranks domination between June and September 1979. Despite sustained intelligence surveillance, the highly popular Rawlings and a small core of ex-military men successfully sought out nonofficer allies and launched a coup on December 31, 1981, to remove the Limann/PNP government. The politicization and interventionist tendencies of the military were crucial in permitting the coup (Hyp. 8). There was little officer support for the coup, and few significant efforts to stop it. Many officers perceived that they had insufficient authority to prevent the collapse of military hierarchy, which would result from Rawlings's coup. Many disappeared, fearing a repetition of attacks against officers as occurred in June 1979. The military was no longer a coherent institution, only a collection of armed men, many ready to throw off the restraints of civilian power.

RESPONSES TO PARTY FAILURES

There was substantial continuity in the political parties, party leadership, and (to a lesser degree) patterns of partisanship under the three party regimes. Equally, there has been great continuity in the types of groups which have become politically participant under military regimes to articulate group and popular interests, bargain with governing authorities, and seek a measure of power. The dismantling of political parties under Ghana's military regimes has not meant a total falling off of political participation. It has eliminated national political organs (e.g., the legislature) which could publicly hold government leaders accountable, and curtailed the formal linkages that bound groups of partisans together. However, the assumption that substantive political participation has not occurred under military regimes in Ghana and in some (but not all) other African states has confused formal party structures and voting with purposive political activity designed to influence public policy and its implementation.

Several types of politically participant groups have been regularly active in Ghana (Chazan, 1982). The first involves voluntary organizations of an interest group type, whose membership is multiethnic and linked by common interest, occupation, and/or status. They originated in Ghana's substantial early economic development and labor force and class differentiation. Two factors which explain persistent participation under all regimes in Ghana in contrast with many other African states are, first, there is a relatively large merchant-professional-managerial bourgeoisie and working class; and second, members of this bourgeoisie and the working class formed substantial associations prior to independence, with norms of the right to participation and representation, which have persisted, intermittently reinforced in postindependence democratic regimes. Important groups include the Ghana Bar, medical, architects, engineers, surveyors, pharmacists, and accountants associations (all linked through the Association of Recognized Professional Bodies or ARPB); Ghana Trades Union Congress (TUC), with seventeen unions and over 700,000 members in 1980; Ghana National Association of Teachers (GNAT; NUGS (students); chambers of commerce, manufacturing, and mining; diverse contractors associations; Christian Council; Catholic Bishops Conference; and a huge range of others representing such varied occupations as market women, rice and cocoa farmers, timber producers, canoe fishermen, lorry owners, traditional healers, butchers, nurses. A second type of participation groups people locally and ethnically. These are the local ethnic, improvement, "youth," and development associations, virtually all devoted to local improvement, a just share in resources, and redressing grievances (see Chambas, 1980; Dunn, 1975; Twumasi, 1975; Austin, 1964). Many such groups have established branches in urban areas among ethnic or local migrants, who provide crucial linkages in enhancing access to funds, knowledge, and government ministries.

Apart from trade unions and market women, the associations of the merchant-managerial-professional bourgeoisie tend to be more active and influential than others and include members of an alternative political elite (e.g., lawyers in the GBA). Moreover, in a largely nonliterate society, those with advanced education, wealth, and knowledge of how government works are looked to by local youth and ethnic groups to promote their home town interests, giving them a source of potentially mobilizable support.

Both types of groups were normally concerned, among themselves and in relations with government, to advance their members' interests but were also periodically mobilized to demand political leadership changes and to challenge the governments and their policies. Military governments which sought to regulate wide ranges of economic activity could not ignore such groups.

Levels of group political activities, group-military government relations, and military government responses to group demands were, in part, determined by the character of prior regimes, the relationship of the diverse groups to these regimes, and the goals of military regime leaders. The overthrow of all three party regimes was prompted in part, and justified, by their failing economic policies and ineffective or unjust representation of salient group interests. The role of nonparty group political activities under the three military regimes is analyzed below, particularly the attempt of the populist Rawlings/PNDC government to create new participant institutions as the major bases for regime support, representation, and radical change.

POLITICAL PARTICIPATION UNDER
THE NLC AND NRC/SMC GOVERNMENTS

The NLC military legitimized its coup against the Nkrumah/CPP by its promise to restore economic growth, full freedoms, and democratic government. It removed the CPP's coercive monopoly over most associational groups, permitting a vigorous revival of national and local associational activity. It tended to regard group demands as legitimate and to bargain with the groups, although constrained by severe economic problems.

Structurally the NLC involved a military-police-senior civil servant government, but it sought support from politically and economically salient groups. The NLC favored members of the merchant-professional bourgeoisie and ex-UP opposition leaders in its appointments, for example, to the Political Advisory Committee. But NLC recognition of the role of associations and local and regional groups was fully conveyed in the composition of the 150-member Constituent Assembly: farmers, market women, and chiefs' organizations each selected nine representatives, associational groups and some statutory bodies (judiciary, universities) another fifty-five.

There was continuous political bargaining and organizing by groups and their leaders to increase their political and organizational power. The GBA, which had become moribund under Nkrumah, reasserted itself with vigor, ensured passage of Article 51 of the Constitution which provided professional associations with full autonomy to govern their professions, and secured GBA representation on important judicial and police committees (Luckham and Nkrumah, 1975: 103, 112–13). The TUC reorganized itself into a vigorous union movement. It engaged in conflicts with the NLC over wages, layoffs, and strikes, and persuaded the NLC to respect its autonomy and give it representation on a wide range of state committees (Kraus, 1979: 266–82). Other important groups campaigned to influence public policies in behalf of their interests and power: chiefs for control of local government institutions (which local development associations contested) and traditional institutions and conflicts; cocoa farmers for representation on the Cocoa Marketing Board, higher prices and subsidies, and restoration of their marketing association; businessmen and merchants for increased access to import licenses, credit, and an NLC decree (1969) to reserve for Ghanaians important segments of business (Pinckney, 1972; Ghana, 1967; Kraus, 1970: 193–98). In the 1969 election many of the newly revived improvement and youth associations were crucial building blocks for local party organization and leadership (Twumasi, 1975).

The NRC/SMC (1972–79), which sought to hold power indefinitely, permitted associations but restricted their activities, engaged in little consultation, was coercive in its bargaining, and tried (unsuccessfully) to compel groups to control their members' activities in behalf of government goals and SMC power. Initially the Acheampong/SMC government sought to legitimize its seizure of power by appealing to the grievances of a wide range of groups (NUGS, trade unions, GBA, cocoa farmers, civil servants, businessmen), reversing Busia/PP austerity measures, and soliciting group enthusiasm for populist policies of nationalization and self-reliance. However, many groups soon found the SMC deaf to their representations, determined to maintain control over policies, coercive in policy implementation (e.g., NUGS, unions), and quick to designate groups as scapegoats for its economic mismanagement (e.g., market women, businessmen). Rural groups found SMC economic policies served a narrow wealthy elite, permitted vast corruption, and excluded the participation of representative local groups (Shepherd, 1978; Chambas, 1980: 153–60, 199–208 on rural youth group protests). The TUC was an exception, since it saw in the old PP regime a class enemy; the SMC provided the unions with a wide variety of benefits and maintained support through wage increases (Silver, 1978; Kraus, 1979a).

Between 1976 and 1978, intolerable economic conditions and SMC authoritarianism animated a broad range of groups, led by lawyers, professionals, and students, to mobilize their associations to assume an explicit political role. These groups launched a sustained public attack upon SMC rule—by strikes, demonstrations, and denunciations of SMC competence and legitimacy—and ultimately forced the Acheampong regime from power, a unique event in Africa. The leadership of lawyers and professionals, an alternative political elite, and students was crucial; they had independent economic bases, high social status, a tradition of liberal norms, and organizational competence. Hyperinflation had developed, with prices rising almost 100 percent between January and June 1977. Real wages and real cocoa farmers' incomes sank drastically (see Table 18.1). There were incredible scarcities of all essential goods. The GBA demanded that the Acheampong regime restore civilian rule. University student protests on food and discipline spilled over into anti-SMC protests, drawing police and military repression. The SMC set up an ad hoc committee to canvass Ghanaians on a proposal for a nonparty Union Government in which the military and police would participate. In late June 1977, the GBA, joined by other professional groups in the ARPB, made a public demand that Acheampong and the SMC hand over power to a transitional civilian government by July 1, or they would launch a strike. The professionals struck for nineteen days, compelling the SMC to seek political legitimacy by a promise to restore civilian rule (Union Government) in two years and to consult public opinion and voters on its program, which partially reopened a public political process.

In the campaign preceding the March 1978 referendum on Union Government, there developed a broadly based agitational movement against continued SMC rule, led by lawyers, professors, university and some secondary students, and two broad fronts of ex-politicians with extensive links to rural groups: the PP and NAL-supported People's Movement for Freedom and Justice (PMFJ) and the narrowly PP-led Front for the Prevention of Dictatorship (FPD) (Chazan and Levine, 1979). Although their rallies and demonstrations were disrupted or forbidden, opposition transmitted itself widely, broadening from an intraelite conflict to one involving local groups throughout Ghana. The SMC employed its economic and coercive resources so blatantly that the Christian Council and Catholic Bishops Conference entered the fray in behalf of freedom of speech and against military coercion, disseminating their message and news of events through churches and the Catholic *Standard* newspaper. The SMC apparently manipulated the referendum results for a 54 percent victory, promptly banned all political associations, and jailed its opponents. It now confronted renewed lawyer and student strikes, plus a vast upsurge in ostensibly nonpolitical but disruptive worker strikes. Senior officers removed Acheampong from power in July 1978, reiterating a promise to establish a nonparty Union Government by July 1979. They now faced an extraordinary upsurge in strikes, demonstrations, and protests, some seeking party elections (conceded in December), others by workers, junior employees, and groups demanding wide-ranging investigations into corruption and mismanagement in state institutions (Ghana, 1979a).

POLITICAL PARTICIPATION UNDER THE RAWLINGS/PNDC GOVERNMENT

The regime of Fl. Lt. Jerry Rawlings and the PNDC was animated by years of perpetual crisis in Ghana's economy—soaring inflation, shortages of food and other items, general impoverishment, vast disparities in wealth, and the Limann/PNP government's incapacity to deal with these multiple crises. In 1982–83 Ghana experienced something akin to a revolution, driven by furious popular perceptions of the persistent misappropriation of public resources—directly and indirectly (e.g., nonpayment of taxes)—by the private and state bourgeoisie through party and personalist linkages to state institutions and resources. Economic mismanagement and the diversion of public resources have been demonstrated for years by commissions of inquiry and, again, under the PNDC by Citizen Vetting

Committees (CVCS) and National Investigation Committees (NICS) (*West Africa*, April 5, 1982: 925–26). Democracy under its latest Limann/PNP guise had, in part, the putrid odor of class privilege and corruption (*West Africa*, May 10, 1982: 1251–53).

Rawlings seized power this second time (the first time under AFRC in June 1979) to "return power to the people" and to recreate a moral economy, with just prices. Rawlings's sincerity was not initially doubted, even if his methods and competence were. The Rawlings/PNDC regime undertook to attack the structures of power, institutions, and norms which had sheltered privilege and corruption and disenfranchised the common man: senior state managers and their presumed competence; the law and its technicalities, courts and lawyers; the *kalabule* (corrupt trade) of businessmen and black marketeers; centralized government; distorted priorities in government expenditures. It was initially a populist revolution.

Rawlings fostered participation by laboring to construct a political coalition of organized support on several key pillars: junior officers and lower ranks of the military; workers and common people in People's Defense Committees (PDCs) and Workers' Defense Committees (WDCs) in neighborhoods, villages, and work places; unionized workers; independent technocrats; university and secondary students; and radical political activists as the organizers. Rawlings's regime sought to foster a direct participatory linkage between citizens and local political action organizations, replacing the intermittent participatory linkages through the former parties (whose local caucuses did choose parliamentary nominees), the electoral linkages through national elections of MPs who were too little responsive to local constituencies, and the clientelistic linkages of "big men" with top political leaders and national bureaucracies (see Lawson, above, on forms of linkages). After the AFRC had withdrawn from power in 1979 and Rawlings had been dismissed from the military, he had formed the June 4th Movement to organize these strata in order to hold the PNP leaders accountable. But he had attracted only a small core of activists, including ex-student leaders, ex-military personnel, and union dissidents, and established linkages with other small leftist organizations.

The core political support bases Rawlings tried to develop once in power possessed some strengths but also profound weaknesses for the economic and political rejuvenation he sought. These shortcomings were apparent in the exceptionally narrowly based and unrepresentative character of the PNDC itself, the ruling body. It was initially composed of Rawlings himself, an able ex-general reinstated as Chief of Defense Staff, two nonofficer servicemen (an AFRC loyalist and a radical northern sergeant), an ex-NUGS (student) leader who was secretary of the June 4th Movement, a dismissed ex-trade unionist, and a liberal activist, once-defrocked priest.

Rawlings sought to broaden the regime's representative character somewhat in his selection of ministers (called secretaries): of the initial twenty,
four were from the opposition parties; another four were from the left
wing of Limann's PNP; the rest were technocrats, professors, and one ex-
officer. Several other ex-officers were PNDC advisers, the most important
of whom was the radical Capt. Kojo Tsikata, who controlled the intelligence services and the regime's security guard. The tumultuous quality of
populist rule and policy in the PNDC's first year engendered such conflicts
within the PNDC itself and its initial group support that by December
1982, only two PNDC members remained, Rawlings and the AFRC loyalist;
a PNDC secretariat member noted that "the PNDC is no more functioning."
Between 1983 and 1985, Rawlings tried to broaden the class and group
representation on the PNDC, but in 1985 it was still largely composed of a
narrow group of loyalists. In a society where ethnicity is politically highly
salient, Rawlings's appointments of key leaders has inspired the perception of regime domination by the minority Ewe people.

The construction of popular participant institutions as a regime base
has generated many problems and some successes but probably alienated
more people than it has attracted. The PNDC has specifically sought to recruit the common people, the working class, and the young; it initially
spurned and attacked many established associational groups.

Although the regime is largely civilian, the military is Rawlings's irre-
ducible base of support; not the hierarchical army and the officers' corps,
but the junior officers, noncoms, and other ranks. Rawlings wants a
people's army based on equality and mutual respect, not one based on
hierarchical fear relationships which governments employ to repress the
people (*West Africa*, Feb. 4, 1980: 189–92). Rawlings's successful appeal
to the military's lower ranks is political and based on four major experiences: the degraded living conditions which enlisted men and junior officers have shared with all Ghanaians in recent years; the extreme rank consciousness and social distance between officers and other ranks, which
constitutes a class cleavage; the corruption of senior officers under
Acheampong's SMC; and the June 1979 mutiny and AFRC rule, where the
lower ranks and junior officers took over the military, beat and arrested,
then purged, many senior officers, and participated in new senior officer
selections.

Rawlings has sought to have the military acquire some political consciousness and to participate with PDCs in implementing politically crucial
regime policies, including price controls, the prevention of smuggling,
food transport, distribution of essential commodities, and support for
PDCs. Several critical contradictions have defeated his design. His appeal
for the reassertion of lower-ranks and junior officer power involved fun-

damental attacks against military hierarchy and discipline and created severe antagonism between officers and enlisted men. Rejection of officer
authority or fear of anti-PNDC sentiment prompted enlisted rank arrests of
officers all over Ghana in 1982 and some killing of officers. Fearing for
their lives or demoralized, many officers left their posts, retired, fled into
exile, or bided their time, some with plots. The creation of PDCs within
military ranks increased enlisted rank power. Second, these undisciplined,
angry, armed, and poor soldiers have repeatedly employed violence and
intimidation against civilians, sometimes in their zeal to support price or
border controls, other times to steal cars, goods, or food, still others for
political ends (the killing of three high court judges). Military violence in
1982–83 was endemic, incited widespread fear, and was the single most
important source of widespread opposition to the regime (Pellow, 1982;
West Africa, July 19, 1982: 1855–57). Lastly, Rawlings's populist beliefs
and political needs made him slow to reestablish military authority to restrain the violence; in 1982–83 most senior officers were incapable of doing
so. In consequence, while some units of the military are zealous PNDC supporters, the military is a violent, unreliable, and highly counterproductive
base for PNDC authority and thus a dangerous source of opposition.

However, by 1984, substantial officer authority over the military had
been reasserted and violence reduced and punished. The activity of the PDCs
declined. Service commanders became the PNDC's link to the military.

In response to Rawlings's appeals, PDCs and WDCs organized themselves all over Ghana, in urban neighborhoods, villages, and work places,
one thousand in Ashanti region alone. They were designed to be an alternative to parties, an egalitarian source of power and direct representation,
with representatives from the local level elected to district, regional, and,
eventually, national PDC bodies; this design was never implemented. Asserting popular power at the local levels and work places, they scrutinized
institutions and managers for abuses and corruption, removed managers
and selected new ones, vigorously oversaw implementation of price and
rent control laws, educated members on PNDC policies (or interpretations
of them), conducted trials of malefactors and imposed fines (a power not
theirs, said the PNDC), organized voluntary labor and self-help projects,
and regularly mobilized demonstrations in behalf of PNDC policies and
against PNDC opponents. When University of Ghana students demonstrated against PNDC rule in 1983, the university WDC countered them and
sought to close the university. When the Ghana Bar and ARPB demanded
the resignation of the PNDC government in July 1982, and the creation of
a transitional government with broad representation, some PDCs demonstrated against the Bar and ARPB in major cities, invading lawyers' chambers, closing down masonic and other lodges. When local magistrates'

courts have ruled in behalf of landlords to expel tenants, PDCs have prevented their eviction and in some cases beaten magistrates and closed down the courts (*West Africa*, Feb. 21, 1983: 487–88).

The PDC/WDC organization was set up energetically in 1982–83, with regional and national coordinating committees and an overall National Defense Committee. Membership on the NDC and regional PDC coordinating committees was drawn from radical activists, many of whom were members of small, linked leftist groups, e.g., the June 4th and New Democratic movements and the Revolutionary Guards, some with roots and experience dating back to the Nkrumah movement. The NDC was severely purged of some radical factional supporters of Sgt. Akata-Pore after the November 1982, quasi-coup attempt against Rawlings. Although guidelines were elaborated for the organization and procedures of PDCs, with rules for selecting local leaders, zealousness and local power relationships have often dictated not only who leads, but PDC behavior. Originally, membership was to be confined to common people and junior employees. In 1983 Rawlings said all could join. The interim National and Regional Coordinating Committees were extremely busy in 1982–83 organizing radicalizing activities and trying to settle deadlocked disputes between workers and managers whom PDCs were trying to remove. Despite the apparent importance of the PDCs to radical change in Ghana, they were not given legally defined powers. The PDCs were certainly far more active and autonomous than local party branches, more horizontally linked to one another, able to initiate radical actions and to pressure the government. The PDCs were not strongly controlled from above, and this has increasingly been seen as a problem. The regime's radicals worked to coordinate PDC/WDC support for PNDC policies, set up PDC leaders cadre training, recruited them for lower-level offices, and mobilized urban PDCs for their own policy preferences.

The consequences of PDC activity have been varied. Certainly PDCs sharply increased the level and consciousness of class conflicts in Ghana. The more activist PDCs zealously elaborated the populist ideology of the rights and capacities of the common man and woman and the exploitive proclivities of Ghana's merchant-managerial-professional bourgeoisie. Their antagonism to authority in many places was so great that some public institutions and corporations operated at much lower levels. Many managers were extremely reluctant to exercise authority while under sustained scrutiny. Although PDCs have uncovered many abuses and corrupt activities, they have also been socially and sometimes physically coercive in initiating or implementing policies and stigmatizing others as "class enemies." They have their share of opportunists, who abuse popular prerogatives and engage in the black market with goods "liberated" from market women and others. In addition, organized popular power can make crucial economic reforms difficult, as when mid-1983 government policies permitted 50 percent to 400 percent increases in food prices and generated widespread popular protests.

The PDCs/WDCs have constituted in limited senses a dual structure of power, with a capacity and willingness at regional levels and in cities to challenge state officials. When the Rawlings government reversed its economic policies in mid-1983, most PDCs continued to support the government. But the IMF-sanctioned policies—massive devaluation, gradual removal of consumer subsidies, reduced government spending—created immediate losses in real wages and salaries that were not relieved by the doubling of the minimum and some other wages. Real government minimum wages declined in 1983 to 9.9 percent of their 1963 value (see Table 18.1). These problems were compounded by Ghana's worst drought, severe food shortages, and, hence, terrible inflation in 1983 (128 percent), which declined again in 1984 (28 percent).

Suddenly PDCs at regional and some urban levels began to challenge Rawlings and the PNDC, saying he was abandoning the revolution, creating "antipeople" policies. Government's attempts to remove a minister of trade who favorably allocated goods to the PDC's Peoples Stores (alternative distribution units, which have collapsed) brought sharp PDC pressures; the minister was reinstated, briefly. Rawlings started to search for allies among the middle class, some of whom he appointed to the PNDC. He also instituted a crackdown on dissident or corrupt PDC regional centers; in 1984, centers in two regions were raided, the leaders arrested. Rawlings sought more secure bases of support and was troubled by volatile PDC behavior and attacks on Ghana's very limited economic policy choices as well as casualness in policy implementation. Could the PDCs, but not populist legitimacy, be curbed?

In December 1984, Rawlings moved to subordinate the PDCs more fully: the national headquarters was dissolved, and the PNDC secretariat put in charge; all PDCs/WDCs were henceforth to be called Committees for the Defense of the Revolution (CDRs), and PDCs were told unequivocally that they were subordinate to state officers at every level. The PDCs/CDRs are by no means dead, but insofar as the new decree is effective, their autonomous power and legitimacy have been constrained sharply. Moreover, by 1984 most had lost their zeal and had been watered down by mass, ritualistic enrollment. Nonetheless, they persist, as do WDCs and the Public Tribunals, now being extended to district levels in some areas.

The university student organizations (in NUGS) moved from initial enthusiastic support for the PNDC to a refocus on student interests to total opposition by mid-1983. On coming to power, the PNDC suspended university classes and sought student participation in reconstruction task forces. Under its officers, NUGS became a fervent PNDC supporter. However, by April 1982 most students were anxious to return to the universities and did so. Students became more critical of military and PDC abuses. An essentially anti-PNDC slate of officers won the heavily contested NUGS election in mid-1982. The leaders of NUGS began to protest critical food shortages, military violence, two-year National Service, and new university governing boards which imposed PNDC and WDC nominees. By May 1983, criticisms had turned into support for other group demands that the PNDC resign and combative protests (*West Africa*, July 19, 1983: 1654–55). Universities were closed.

Soon after the PNDC came to power, the leader of the TUC and individual trade unions were attacked for failing to represent the workers. Ghana's union movement has been fairly democratic since 1966. Caught between the pressures of successive government and rank-and-file workers on wage demands and strike issues, union leaders became decidedly cautious but fought to maintain union autonomy. Wage gains fell far behind inflated prices. Dissident unionists, supported by some WDCs and the PNDC, coercively removed existing union leaders in April 1982. Interim Management Committees in each union and the TUC undertook to reorganize the unions and hold elections. While submitting to some PNDC pressures and supporting the PNDC and its populist policies, interim union leaders insisted that unions must maintain their autonomy; they denied an accord with the PNDC on a wage freeze, claiming their right to retain collective bargaining. Union elections in 1983 saw the return to power of a number of prior union leaders or their lieutenants. Unions have not permitted the WDCs to take over their functions. New union and TUC leaders have bargained insistently with the government for worker interests, as in May–June 1983 and 1984 for wage increases, in 1984–85 against price increases and layoffs. The ability of Rawlings to retain worker support will depend on the state of the deteriorating economy and his willingness to give unions a stake in the regime. The depressed economy in 1982–83 and the lifting of price controls have severely alienated the union movement, and the slight economic recovery in 1984–85 has in no way increased the impoverishing level of real wages (see Table 18.1).

Another PNDC institution that permits limited public participation are the Public Tribunals, composed of persons appointed by the PNDC rather than judges (although lawyers have chaired the tribunal boards, and some PDC heads have been tribunal members). The tribunals, which have jurisdiction over a wide variety of criminal and political offenses, have tended to replace the courts, are open to the public, and permit counsel for the accused, who have had the right of appeal since 1984. They are guided "by the rules of natural justice," not "legal technicalities," and have been boycotted by the GBA lawyers. Initial evidence indicates the tribunals have dispatched cases swiftly, declined to acknowledge evidence of police coercion, and imposed harsh penalties (*West Africa*, Oct. 25, 1982: 2772–73). This public justice is effective and not necessarily inequitable. Plans to extend tribunals to local levels will increase participation in them and their abuse.

The PNDC has encountered strong opposition from other politically participant groups. Foremost among them have been the GBA and the ARPB, which have criticized publicly press censorship, military brutality and violence, illegal property seizures, denials of civil liberties, violation of the courts, operations of Public Tribunals, incitement to class conflict, and authoritarian departures from the rule of law. The GBA and ARPB have repeatedly demanded that the PNDC turn power over to a broadly representative transitional government, which would recreate democratic institutions. The GBA and ARPB have been joined in these protests and demands by the Christian Council, Catholic Bishops' Conference, university students, and some ex-politicians; the opposition of many businessmen and politicians to PNDC rule has been vigorous but more covert.

Political participation has grown more violent as the social order unravels, with groups battling one another. The opposition forces, led by the GBA and ARPB, seized upon the tough 1983 budget and the PNDC's non-publication of the judicial inquiry into the murder of three high court judges to mount a series of protests in May–June 1983 and an attempted strike to force out the regime, as in 1977–78. The strike failed, because important groups refused to strike. The PNDC brought in truckloads of "workers," paid in food and cash, who violently attacked the TUC, a church conclave, and students. Following a coup attempt against the PNDC on June 19, 1983, the regime began to make selective arrests of opposition figures. Other political opposition has taken quieter forms. Pastoral letters have been read in churches throughout Ghana denouncing regime abuses and requesting the resignation of the PNDC. Organized market women, who form the backbone of the retail distribution system in Ghana and who have been harassed constantly for selling above control prices, reduced their services. Cocoa farmer groups refused the PNDC's request that they accept lower prices; the regime has had to increase prices drastically. Food farmers protested price controls by refusing to send food to urban markets and appear to have reduced production.

Since the major conflicts of mid-1983, the PNDC has moved toward greater moderation in its policies and behavior, controlling military violence and reducing the mobilization of class conflicts. In addition, its partial reemphases on market mechanisms and prices to restimulate agricultural and industrial production have eased its need to use coercive direct controls, thereby inducing greater agricultural production. In turn, the level of concerted resistance has declined, in particular among some traditional leaders, the churches, and students. The GBA and ARPB continue in their opposition and refusal to cooperate.

The Rawlings/PNDC attempt to create a broadly based participatory alternative to party democracies has been fostered both by the ineffective and inequitable economic policies of civilian regimes and by the collapse of Ghana's economy. But Ghana's desperate scarcities of economic essentials and foreign exchange have prompted intense group and individual competition, legal and illegal, for scarce resources, preeminently food. Skilled persons and others have fled the society, though perhaps a million Ghanaians (8 percent of the population) were expelled from Nigeria to Ghana in early 1983. Past governments have pursued inflationary fiscal and monetary policies and price controls to stave off popular dissidence. The Rawlings government initially sought legitimacy through its sanction of direct participation in decisions at some levels and (unsuccessful) extensive state-military economic interventions to provide basic necessities at prices the common man could afford. But by mid-1983 it understood that the economic reforms necessary to reverse the profound economic breakdown required ending expensive subsidies on essential commodities, sharply curtailing government expenditures, and permitting prices to producers to rise as incentives for production. The immediate effect of adopting these policies in March–April 1983 (as part of an agreement with the IMF and foreign governments for large loans) has been to increase dramatically the cost of living for Ghanaians, especially the urban worker and lower-middle class which constitute the core of PNDC support and PDC/CDR membership. It was only organized and manipulated support from some PDCs and its populist legitimacy with the unions that enabled the PNDC to adopt these policies in the face of protests. That populist legitimacy has now eroded. The PNDC is also pursuing genuine reforms in government decentralization, tax assessment and collection, and restructuring education.

The appeals by the PNDC for political participation by the common person were very popular among a significant segment of Ghanaians whose political participation had not been central to political life previously. The democratic ethos in southern and central Ghana is supportive of institutions such as PDCs/CDRs, although they severely violate deference norms. Despite the broad organization of PDCs/CDRs and the participation of other groups, the regime's sharp insecurity, activism, uncontrolled violence, and radical populist ethos did not emphasize procedural regularities and norms of fairness which would have inspired public confidence and encouraged the persistence of the PDCs as institutions. However, without these or other strongly participant institutions that are open to the common person, Ghana's merchant-managerial-professional bourgeoisie or the military would dominate political life. Military participation is hated and feared by Ghanaians. Ironically, it has appeared to increase as popular mobilization has slowed.

CONCLUSION

Recent party regimes have failed for several major reasons: sharp economic declines (Hyp. 7), caused by falling export prices and poor economic policies, which in turn have sharpened perceptions of ethnic/class monopolization of power and state resources (Hyp. 6) and corrupt and nonaccountable elite behavior (Hyp. 5); and the development of a praetorian military (Hyp. 8), which is symptomatic of a broader collapse of the state's authority and capabilities.

However, political participation has persisted under military regimes. As noted, early economic development and labor differentiation generated class strata—a merchant-professional bourgeoisie, urban workers—which developed associations that reflected liberal and populist values and means for pursuing their interests prior to postindependence attacks against liberal norms (the CPP). A relatively egalitarian traditional culture (in southern Ghana), associational development to promote interests, preindependence and later electoral politics, and the broader dissemination of liberal norms have engendered a relatively participant political culture. Divergent strands of Ghana's political culture are crystallized in the political and class conflict in Rawlings's Ghana. The lawyer-professional-church-student and also union opposition represent the more liberal culture, emphasizing the law, individual liberties, institutional independence, and traditional democratic institutions (e.g., parties); Rawlings's PNDC and the PDCs/WDCs represent the more populist ethos, now animated by profound economic scarcities and inequalities. The populist ethos is not without regard for democratic participation in Ghana. Thus, the PNDC government and PDCs have been dictatorial and democratic, manipulatory and spontaneous, popular and despised, weak and potentially strong, idealistic and cynically concerned with power. However, the tensions between participatory demands from below and government desires to construct and implement a nonpopulist economic policy were resolved in 1984–85 in terms of a state decision to curtail PDC/CDR demands and noncompliant activities. Ritual participation replaced reality. The PNDC is less attentive to the known needs of consumers and wage workers—indeed, ignoring the TUC and its representations—as it seeks to induce economic reconstruction by reducing economic controls and sending market signals (higher prices) to producers in agriculture and industry. It is thus more open to the grievances of those with capital and managerial power. Politicized interest groups persist in their representations but are often unheard by a government with few linkages with these groups and intent on increasing its relative autonomy in order to implement its economic reconstruction goals.

References

Apter, D. 1972. *Ghana in transition*. Princeton: Princeton University Press.
Austin, D. 1964. *Politics in Ghana*. London: Oxford University Press.
————, and R. Luckham, eds. 1975. *Politicians and soldiers in Ghana, 1966–72*. London: Frank Cass.
Beckman, B. 1976. *Organizing the farmers: Cocoa politics and national development in Ghana*. Uppsala: Scandinavian Institute of African Studies.
Bennett, V. P. 1973. The motivations for military intervention: The case of Ghana. *Western Political Quarterly* 26: 659–74.
Berg, E. 1971. Structural transformation versus gradualism: Recent economic development in Ghana and the Ivory Coast. In *Ghana and the Ivory Coast*, ed. P. Foster and A. Zolberg. Chicago: University of Chicago Press, 187–230.
Binder, L., S. Coleman, and J. La Palombara. 1971. *Crises and sequences in political development*. Princeton: Princeton University Press.
Bretton, H. 1966. *The rise and fall of Kwame Nkrumah*. New York: Praeger.
Chambas, M. 1980. The politics of agricultural and rural development in the Upper Region of Ghana. Ph.D. diss. Cornell University.
Chazan, N. 1982. The new politics of participation in Tropical Africa. *Comparative Politics* 14: 169–89.
————, and V. LeVine. 1979. Politics in a "non-political" system: The March 30, 1978, referendum in Ghana. *African Studies Review* 22: 177–207.
Crisp, J. 1979. Union atrophy and worker revolt: Labour protest at Tarkwa goldfields, Ghana, 1968–69. *Canadian Journal of African Studies* 19: 267–93.
————. 1981. Rank and file protest at the Ashanti Goldfields Corporation, Ghana, 1970–72. *Labour, Capital and Society* 14: 48–62.
Dunn, J. 1975. Politics in Asunafo. In Austin and Luckham, 1975: 164–213.
Ghana. 1964. *Report of commission of enquiry into alleged irregularities and malpractices in connection with the issue of import licenses*. Akainyah Commission.
————. 1965. *Report of commission of enquiry into trade malpractices in Ghana*. Abraham Commission.
————. 1967. *Report of committee of enquiry on the local purchasing of cocoa*.
————. 1967a. *Summary of the report of commission of enquiry into irregularities and malpractices in the grant of import licenses*. Ollennu Commission.

———. 1967b. *Report of commission on structure and remuneration of the public services in Ghana.*

———. 1968. *Report of commission into affairs of Ghana timber marketing board and Ghana timber co-operative union.*

———. 1968a. *Report of commission into manner of operation of the state housing corporation.*

———. 1968b. *Report of commission of enquiry into Ghana cargo handling company.*

———. 1968c. *Report of the Sowah commission: Assets of specified persons.*

———. 1968d. *Proposals of the constitutional commission for a constitution for Ghana.*

———. 1969. *Report of the Jiagge commission: Assets of specified persons.*

———. 1969–70. *Report of the Manyo-Plange (assets) commission: Assets of specified persons.*

———. 1969–70a. *Interim and final reports of commission of enquiry into Accra-Tema city council.*

———. 1970. *Report of commission to enquire into affairs of Sekondi-Takoradi city council.*

———. 1973. *Speeches and interviews by Col. I. K. Acheampong.*

———. 1976. *Report of Taylor assets committee.*

———. 1976a. *Final report of the committee of enquiry into trade malpractices, (Aschkar group of companies).*

———. 1976b. *Report of the Joe Appiah committee of enquiry into the affairs of R. T. Briscoe (Ghana) Limited.*

———. 1977. *Report of the ad hoc committee on Union Government.*

———. 1978. *Proposals of constitutional commission for a constitution for the establishment of a transitional national government for Ghana.*

———. 1979. *Report of the Taylor assets committee.*

———. 1979a. *Report of the committee of Inquiry into the civil service strike of November, 1978.*

Ghana, CBS. 1965, 1966. (Central Bureau of Statistics). *Economic Survey.*

———. 1976. *Economic Survey, 1969–71.*

———. 1972–82. *Statistical Newsletter(s).*

Gill and Duffis. 1981. *Cocoa market report,* No. 298, Nov.

Grew, R., ed. 1978. *Crises of political development in Europe and the United States.* Princeton: Princeton University Press.

Huntington, S. P. 1968. *Political order in changing societies.* New Haven: Yale University Press.

Jeffries, R. 1978. *Class, power and ideology in Ghana: The railwaymen of Sekondi.* Cambridge: Cambridge University Press.

Killick, T. 1978. *Development economics in action.* New York: St. Martins.

Konings, P. 1978. Political consciousness and political action of industrial workers in Ghana: A case study of valco workers at Tema. *African Perspectives* 2: 69–82.

Kraus, J. 1970. Arms and politics in Ghana. In *Soldier and state in Africa,* ed. C. Welch. Evanston: Northwestern University Press, 154–221.

Kraus, J. 1979. Strikes and labor power in Ghana. *Development and Change* 10: 259–85.

———. 1979a. The political economy of industrial relations in Ghana. *Industrial relations in Africa*, ed. U. Damachi et al. New York: St. Martin's, 106–68.

———. 1982. Rawlings' second coming. *Africa Report* 27: 59–66.

LaPalombara, J., and M. Weiner, eds. 1966. *Political parties and political development*. Princeton: Princeton University Press.

Lawson, K. 1976. *The comparative study of political parties*. New York: St. Martin's.

———. 1978. Constitutional change and party development in France, Nigeria, and the United States. *Political parties: Development or decay*, ed. L. Maisel and J. Cooper. Beverly Hills: Sage Publications, 145–78.

Legon Observer, issues 1979–81.

Levine, V. 1975. *Political corruption: The Ghana case*. Stanford: Hoover Institution.

Leys, C. 1974. *Underdevelopment in Kenya*. Berkeley: University of California Press.

———. 1979. Capital accumulation, class formation, and dependency: The significance of the Kenyan case. In *Socialist register, 1978*, ed. R. Miliband and J. Savile. London: Merlin Press.

Luckham, R. 1976. The market for legal services in Ghana. *Review of Ghana Law* 8: 7–27.

———. 1978. Imperialism, law and structural dependence: The Ghana legal profession. *Development and Change* 9: 201–43.

———, and S. Nkrumah. The constitutional assembly. In Austin and Luckham, 1975: 88–125.

Osei-Kwame, P. 1978. Ghanaian views on government. *West Africa*, March 6: 428–30.

Owusu, M. 1970. *Uses and abuses of political power*. Chicago: University of Chicago Press.

Peasah, J. A. 1975. Politics in Abuakwa. In Austin and Luckham, 1975: 214–32.

Pellow, D. 1982. *Kalabule out, Warabeba in*: Coping in revolutionary Ghana. Paper given at the African Studies Association Meeting, November.

Pinkney, R. 1972. *Ghana under military rule, 1966–1969*. London: Methuen.

Price, R. 1973. The pattern of ethnicity in Ghana. *Journal of Modern African Studies* 11: 470–75.

———. 1974. Politics and culture in contemporary Ghana. *Journal of African Studies* 1: 173–204.

———. 1975. *Society and bureaucracy in contemporary Ghana*. Berkeley: University of California Press.

Rothchild, D. 1979. Comparative public demand and expectation patterns: The Ghana experience. *African Studies Review* 22: 127–48.

Sartori, G. 1976. *Parties and party systems*. Cambridge: Cambridge University Press.

Scalfani, J. 1977. Trade unionism in an African state: The railway and ports Workers' Union of the TUC (Ghana). Ph.D. diss., Brown University.

Shepherd, A. 1978. Rice farming in the northern region. *West Africa*, April 9: 54–55.

Silver, J. 1978. Class struggles in Ghana's mining industry. *Review of African Political Economy* 12: 67–86.

Stepan, A. 1978. *The state and society: Peru in comparative perspective*. Princeton: Princeton University Press.

Twumasi, Y. 1975. The 1969 election. In Austin and Luckham, 1975: 140–63.

Wallerstein, I. 1966. The decline of the party in single-party African states. In La Palombara and Weiner, 1966: 201–14.

West Africa (London), weekly.

Zolberg, A. 1966. *Creating political order: The party-states of West Africa*. Chicago: Rand McNally.

PART VI | Major Parties
Do Not Always Fail

NINETEEN

When Parties Refuse to Fail:
The Case of France

FRANK L. WILSON

In recent years, journalists and scholars often have pointed to a purported decline of political parties in Western democracies. The seeming weakness of democratic political parties contributes to a new crisis of survivability of Western democracy as it enters the new postindustrial period (Bell, 1976; Benjamin, 1977; Brzezinski, 1971; Hancock and Sjoberg, 1972; Huntington, 1974; Lindberg, 1976; Touraine, 1972). Economic, social, and political changes accompanying the advent of this new period seem to raise doubts as to whether or not the democratic institutions which developed during the industrial period of development can survive in the postindustrial era (Berger et al., 1975; Berger, 1979; Crozier, 1975). Some of the features of the new era seem to undermine especially the political party systems that have provided the foundation for modern representative democracy. Thus, some scholars have questioned the viability of democracy with weakened parties:

> The development of political parties in the nineteenth century went hand-in-hand with the expansion of the suffrage and the increased responsibility of governments to their citizens. Parties made democratic government possible. Throughout the twentieth century, the strength of democracy has varied with the strength of the political parties committed to working within a democratic system. The decay of political party systems in the industrialized world poses the question: How viable is democratic government without parties or with greatly weakened or attenuated parties (Crozier, 1975: 165–66)?

We have seen in this volume that there are many kinds of party failure. As Merkl points out in his concluding chapter, the principal concern is not with the "normal" alterations in parties' voting strength nor with the

The author expresses his appreciation to the American Philosophical Society for a fellowship which made possible interviews with ecologists and others in the spring of 1982. Professors Kay Lawson and Mark Kesselman provided very useful suggestions on an earlier draft of this chapter.

gradual decline and replacement of once major parties. The cause for anxiety is the seemingly sudden crumbling of established major parties and the disruption of stable relationships between voters and these parties. He explains such party failure in systemic terms with reference to the nature of the overall party system. On the other hand, Lawson suggests that the parties' failure to maintain the linkage between their publics and the polity is related to party decline, and to the rise of new, political organizations. Both interpretations, however, imply broader concerns about the impact on parties (and democracy) of new socioeconomic and political developments of our contemporary era.

An important feature of the new period is the expansion or even the explosion of political participation in Western democracies. In part, the higher levels of participation are the natural consequence of rising educational levels since, generally speaking, the better educated are more likely to become politically involved than are those who have little formal education. But the participation explosion is also fueled by the emergence of newly politicized groups: women, racial or linguistic minorities, and youth. In the past, these social categories were either barred from political participation by formal discriminatory restraints or abstained from involvement due to social and political conventions. Now the old impediments are disappearing and these social categories are aggressively directing their demands at the political system. The sudden entry into political activity of once passive groups threatens to overburden the existing representative institutions, especially political parties. Lacking attachments to the old parties, these new participants often look for alternative forms of political expression.

The established political parties fail to attract these new participants. Perhaps more critical, they are unwilling or unable to incorporate the issues that concern the newly mobilized citizens. Noting the massive politicization of the late 1960s and 1970s, Berger (1979: 27) points to the parties' failure: "That this surge of collective activity and new high levels of participation nowhere led to political transformation or even to major reform but only to dead ends and deadlocks is principally due to the political parties: . . . in general, to the parties' incapacity to translate new aspirations into political projects."

It is not only the extent but also the nature of the new participation that is menacing to the established patterns of party politics. First, many of the new participants as well as old participants have resorted to unconventional means of political participation (Barnes and Kaase, 1979). Parties and other existing political structures are unresponsive, so those concerned with new issues resort to direct action or protest politics to press their demands. Even the traditional middle classes, perceiving themselves as the silent and neglected majority, turn to unorthodox means of mass political action. Second, the new activists often focus on single issues that serve well to mobilize masses for collective action but lack the continuity and breadth needed to institutionalize new representative groups.

Some argue that another explanation of the decline of Western political parties is found in the emergence of alternative forms of representation based on social functions rather than on party ideologies or geographic constituencies. Lehmbruch (1982), Schmitter (1979), Winkler (1976), and others (Berger, 1981; Harrison, 1980) see the emergence of new forms of corporatism in advanced industrialized democracies. In part, the corporatist trend is promoted by the response of political elites to the overloading of government with excessive demands. Corporatism is a means of responding to these demands or channeling them into new patterns of policymaking capable of controlling the otherwise "implacable pursuit of self interest" (Schmitter, 1981: 288). The shift of policymaking powers to corporatist bodies contributes to the decline of parliament and its constituent elements, the parties. The trend toward corporatism may enhance governability, at least temporarily, by increasing the state's ability to channel growing demands (Schmitter, 1981: 285–327), but it does so at the cost of the decay of the principal representative bodies, parliament and the parties.

The combined effects of the participation explosion, the new forms of political involvement, and the trend toward corporatism are the decomposition of political party systems in advanced industrial democracies. Thus, we are alleged to be in a new era of democratic politics when some of its fundamental supports are decaying. In the United States (Broder, 1972), Britain (Kavanagh, 1977; Finer, 1979; Smith and Polsby, 1981), and other democratic countries, commentators have seen evidence of party decay in declining voter turnout rates for national elections, reduced party discipline, and lower rates of party identification and involvement. Citizens seem to be turning from the established parties to spontaneous citizen action groups, single-issue groups, and new political parties to express their political feelings. Many analysts, sharing E. E. Schattschneider's (1842: 1) view that "political parties created democracy and . . . modern democracy is unthinkable except in terms of the parties," see party decline as threatening the existence of modern representative democracy.

When party decay is viewed as organizational weakness, loss of power, and replacement by alternative forms of representation, France, at first thought, might appear to be an excellent example of political party decay. The party system there has been plagued by fragmentation, indiscipline, disorganization, and polarization. Laymen and political scientists alike have regarded French parties with disdain. The events of May 1968, with a student revolt and a workers' general strike, are often cited as the prototype of the revolt that other Western democracies might expect if decay continues and other opportunities for effective participation do not develop (Crozier, 1974: 128–36; Touraine, 1972). Earlier, at the end of the 1950s, the public's mistrust of the parties and its disgust with their machinations resulted in the overthrow of the Fourth Republic under the threat of a military coup and the installation of a new regime based on a powerful president determined to remain aloof from the old parties. The French party system—shaken by the parties' loss of political influence and by a series of defeats to its major components—was in tatters. Party membership declined sharply for nearly all parties; important schisms weakened several major parties; the traditional parties and the party system itself lacked the confidence and support of the French public.

However, most French parties have recently undergone important transformations, resulting in the emergence of a substantially new and revitalized party system by the beginning of the 1980s (Wilson, 1982). By 1980 French parties were much stronger and more vital than at any time since the immediate postwar period. The major parties adapted quickly to the new demands of presidential politics: they abandoned old and stodgy techniques in favor of new political approaches and strategies. Public confidence in the parties was restored; party organizations were stronger and more active; parties played a significant part in the political process even as it became more presidential; and they seemed to be more capable of fulfilling the linkage function assigned to them by democratic theorists (Wilson, 1979; Lawson, 1981).

The French pattern of party revitalization runs counter to the claimed decline of parties in Western democracies. While other democratic party systems seem threatened by new forms of rival political organizations, the French party system refused to fail. It has succeeded in surviving successive challenges from a variety of alternative political organizations in the 1960s and 1970s to maintain its predominance. This essay will explore how French parties fended off threats from political clubs in the 1960s and from a variety of citizen action groups and miniparties in the 1970s. The parties either absorbed and dominated these alternative organizations or pushed them to the margins of French politics. Based on the French experience, I suggest that major parties are better able to resist the challenges of alternative groups and organizational decay when:

1. They have newly modernized organizational structures.
2. The most salient political issues are those they have traditionally articulated.

3. A strong sense of class identity persists as a basis of political cleavage.
4. The political institutions (centralized decisionmaking and electoral system) foster a few strong parties rather than numerous minor parties.
5. The polity is accustomed to political turmoil by minor groups and no longer takes it seriously.

Those who claim to see a general trend toward party decline and toward the replacement of parties by alternative political organizations are correct to express deep concern about the potential effects of such trends on Western representative democracy. The alternatives, whether in the form of new citizen action groups, miniparties based on ethnicity or specific issues, or corporatist interest groups, are unlikely to carry out the role that parties traditionally have filled of combining varied interests into meaningful programs for political action and of responding quickly to changes in the public's needs and priorities. Therefore, it is useful to explore why and how the French party system has deflected the challenge from rival political groups. It is possible that the French parties' experience may aid us in better understanding the vulnerability or resistance of parties elsewhere to threats from alternative political organizations in those countries where parties appear to fail.

The Political Club Movement of the 1960s

The first challenge to the French political parties came early in the 1960s at a time when the parties were indisputably in a state of advanced decay. Membership figures for all parties were dropping, and those members who remained were less involved in party activities. In many parties, once active local units ceased to function and leaders had difficulty reviving them even for election campaigns. The public held the parties responsible for the stalemate and failure of the Fourth Republic. President Charles de Gaulle's antiparty rhetoric and supraparty stance found a receptive audience among French citizens from all points on the political spectrum.

In 1962, de Gaulle defied the traditional parties in pushing a questionable constitutional referendum to shift the presidential election from an electoral college to direct popular vote. When the parties responded to this challenge and censured the government, de Gaulle declared war on them and soundly thrashed them in the referendum and in the subsequent National Assembly elections (Goguel, 1965). In the wake of these defeats, the traditional parties of the right and center—the moderates, Christian Democrats, and Radicals—began to disintegrate. The left-wing parties—the Socialist SFIO and the Communist party—refused to adapt to the new political setting, fearful that any change might cause the loss of the ever-smaller core of party faithful. Their leader still clung to the hope that this "Gaullist parenthesis" would soon end and give way to the return of politics as usual in the style of the Third and Fourth republics. Even the successful new parties of the Fifth Republic, the Gaullists and Valéry Giscard d'Estaing's Independent Republicans, were still only skeletal organizations based on de Gaulle's personal appeal and on a few well-established notables.

In this general setting of decaying old parties and new parties not yet fully born, a new political phenomenon appeared, the political club movement (Cayrol and Lavau, 1965; Lavau, 1965; Colard, 1964–65; Mossuz, 1970; Olivier, 1967; Wilson, 1971a). In the early 1960s, a large number of political clubs appeared spontaneously in several parts of France with essentially the same goal: promotion of a reformed left-wing alternative to Gaullism. Among the most prominent were the Club Jean Moulin and Citoyens 60 in Paris, the Centre Tocqueville in Lyon, and the Cercle d'Action Politique de Toulouse. These clubs devoted more attention at first to political reflection than to overt political action. They prided themselves on their modernity and on the fresh ideas that they could bring to the declining parties of the traditional left. The clubs hoped their ideas would encourage the transformation and unification of the left. In contrast to the rigid and stodgy parties of the left, the political clubs looked very attractive. The press quickly characterized them as *force nouvelles* and *forces vives* in contrast to the decaying old parties.

Because of the popularity of the clubs compared to the unpopularity of the parties, politicians began to form "clubs" to organize their supporters rather than parties. Francois Mitterrand, on his way out of a small and dying party, organized the Convention des Institutions Republicaines. The small Unified Socialist party (PSU), hopelessly divided despite its title, spawned a number of "clubs" as various disaffected leaders or factions prepared to leave it. The "clubs" were little more than miniparties spun off by decaying parties. In other cases, parties created clubs to attract new adherents who were uninterested in the old parent parties. Even the right picked up on the political club fad as Valéry Giscard d'Estaing turned to the club format to further his ambitions; he organized his followers into clubs called Perspectives et Réalités. These party-clubs imitated the original clubs in form but did not adopt their style of political reflection and party reform. They soon fell victim to the same vices they condemned in the older parties: disunity, domination by discredited leaders from the

Fourth Republic, excessive ideological commitments, personal rivalries, individualism, and sectarianism.

Gradually, some of the original clubs, like the Club Jean Moulin, deepened their political involvement. The desire to reform the left led several of them to become involved in the 1965 presidential election campaign. They played a key role in Gaston Defferre's abortive plan to build a "grand federation" of the center-left and then in the creation of the Federation of the Left between Socialists, Radicals, and clubs (Wilson, 1971b). As a result of these political engagements, the original goals of political reflection and party reform were superseded by the desire to popularize the federation. The clubs continued to urge the development of the federation along lines they thought responded to the changing political and social environment, but no longer appeared as disinterested party reformers but rather as partisan supporters of the federation. They were caught up in the ideological debates and personality conflicts that they had earlier criticized in the parties they set out to reform. Within the federation, the clubs gradually lost ground to the parties. Despite the dynamism and innovative ideas of the clubs and the parties' general decline, the parties remained better organized than the clubs, and they could mobilize more committed activists than could the clubs. The clubs lacked seasoned militants who were ready to press for their ideas in the protracted negotiations with party leaders. Thus, the clubs started out with the goal of reforming the parties but eventually were engulfed by the parties. The few clubs which resisted this politicization or withdrew from politics soon disappeared. By the end of the 1960s, the challenge of the political clubs to the parties' hegemony as representative bodies had ended. Even in their weakened and discredited condition, the parties had fended off the political club movement's threat to their preeminent political role.

THE CHALLENGES OF THE 1970S

By 1970, the French party system had begun to revive (Wilson, 1979). The Gaullists and, to a lesser degree, the Giscardians were developing mass, well-structured parties which broke with the usual pattern of weak, poorly organized right-wing parties in the past. On the left, the Socialist and Communist parties were reformed more slowly but eventually quite thoroughly during the 1970s (Johnson, 1981; Brown, 1982). The development of four major parties paired into coalition on the left and right undercut the small, centrist parties which have usually dominated French politics. The fact that there were four major parties helped to deter splintering since the large parties represented a broad range of options and, in most cases, at least one of the four would pick up on the grievance of nearly all groups. Consequently, parties of the far left and far right faltered as the four main parties developed. During this period of party revival, the major parties fended off challenges from a succession of alternative political organizations threatening directly or indirectly the parties' representative role: from ethnic nationalist groups, from ecology and environmental protection movements, and from organizations seeking to defend the interests of apparently declining sectors of the middle class.

THE POLITICS OF ETHNIC NATIONALISM IN FRANCE.   In 1966, a noted observer (Brinton, 1968: 19) of French politics wrote: "Not even in Brittany . . . where several hundred thousands have Breton, a Celtic tongue, as their natural speech . . . is there a genuine separatist movement. . . . Breton nationalism is surely . . . no menace to present-day French unity." Yet, almost as this observer wrote these words, Breton nationalists were turning to terrorist bombings to dramatize their claims for greater autonomy or outright secession. The Bretons were soon followed by equally or even more violent Corsican nationalist movements. In addition, more pacific nationalist organizations became active in Alsace, Occitanie, and the French portions of Basquelands, Catalonia, and Flanders (Beer, 1980).

This is not the place to examine in depth the reasons for the resurgence of ethnic nationalism in France.[1] Clearly, the hard-line assimilationist policies usually attributed to the Jacobin traditions of postrevolutionary France have not removed the cultural and linguistic bases for ethnic nationalism (Krejci and Velimsky, 1981: 155–64). A 1978 poll found that 35 percent of the population in France speaks a regional language as well as or sometimes in preference to French. Fears that these linguistic and associated cultural traits might be destroyed, perceptions of economic discrimination against areas inhabited by ethnic minorities, anger over the despoliation of natural resources by outsiders, and the inspiration or contagion of ethnic nationalist movements elsewhere in the world combined to breathe new life into French nationalist causes long thought to be fully assimilated.

The revival of ethnic nationalism in France involved a complex of cultural, economic, sentimental, and political dimensions. However, the political impact of the ethnic minorities in France on the overall political system was less than the impact of similar movements in other industrialized democracies. Elsewhere in Western Europe, the renewed ethnic national-

[1] For discussions of the causes of ethnic revival in France and elsewhere see Beer, 1980: 28–39; Esman, 1977; Jacob, 1980; and Foster, 1980.

ism contributed to political party decay, governmental instability, and political uncertainty. For example, in Belgium and Britain, nationalist parties undermined traditional party loyalties, weakened the effectiveness of those parties, and provoked governmental instability as coalitionbuilding became more complicated and as minority governments replaced stable majority government. In Spain, Basque separatists and Catalonian autonomists threatened to destroy the fragile democracy established after Franco. In France, no less intense ethnic nationalist revivals seemed to have had much less political impact.

Two types of organizations have developed out of ethnic revival in France. The ethnic organizations enjoying the largest audiences are those that are cultural in nature and that seek to maintain and promote the folklore, costumes, dances, traditions, and especially the languages of the various ethnic communities. These associations generally restrict their activities to cultural issues and avoid overt politics. They have been successful in attracting mass memberships and in developing broad popular support for cultural preservation among most of France's ethnic minority groups. The second type of ethnic organization is the more explicitly political movement seeking greater autonomy or even outright independence for the ethnic homeland. These politically oriented ethnic associations have had much less success in attracting followers. In Alsace, Occitanie, and the French portions of Basque lands, Catalonia, and Flanders, minuscule political nationalist movements, often with less than a hundred members each, exist alongside very popular ethnic cultural associations. The Union Democratique Bretonne (UDB), the largest Breton nationalist movement, had only 400 members at its peak in 1973 (Berger, 1977: 169). Organizations seeking to perpetuate Breton culture, however, thrive. Only in Corsica do the ethnic political organizations seem to have attracted significant followings. In the mid-1970s, the principal Corsican nationalist organization mobilized as many as 5,000 for its conferences and rallies (Savigear, 1980). Corsican nationalists alone were able to persuade a significant portion of their regional population to express sympathy for greater autonomy.[2]

Some have suggested that the new ethnic awareness would result in the trade-off of old party ties for new ethnic-based party loyalties (Berger, 1972: 169–76). There is evidence of this in Scotland where many Scots traded, at least temporarily, old attachments to the Labour party for allegiance to the Scottish Nationalist party. In Flemish Belgium, many vot-

---

[2] A 1975 poll of Corsicans found 31 percent favorable to more autonomy and 2 percent wanting independence for Corsica. The overwhelming majority (61 percent) wanted Corsica to remain a department like all the rest of France. *Sondages*, 3–4 (1976): 57–58.

ers shifted from the Socialist party to Flemish nationalist parties. But there is no evidence of such a trade-off in France. In a party system often noted for its fluidity and vulnerability to the rise of "flash" parties, ethnic-based parties have been electoral flops. While there have been a few isolated cases of ethnic party candidates making semirespectable showings in local by-elections, ethnic parties in all regions have failed to have any impact on national or local elections. Periodically, ethnic parties have presented candidates in their elections but they invariably have been ignored by the voters.[3] In the 1974 presidential election, there were two candidates identified principally as federalists and as advocates of greater autonomy for ethnic regions: Guy Heraud and Claude Sebag. Together, they won only 60,000 votes (0.24 percent of the votes cast), with no sign of support even in ethnic regions (Beer, 1980: 56–58).[4] In the 1979 European Parliament elections, supporters of ethnic and regional autonomy presented a list but could not raise enough funds to mount a campaign or even to pay the deposit so that ballots could be prepared. In Corsica, where about one-third of the adult population has expressed sympathy for greater Corsican self-government, this potential reservoir of support fails to vote for nationalist candidates in national elections. Similar problems exist in Brittany. In 1973, a major Breton nationalist party presented candidates in twenty-six of the region's thirty-two districts but still garnered only a disappointing 2.3 percent of the votes cast (Reece, 1977: 221–22). Alsatian, Basque, Occitanian, and other ethnic candidates do worse. Even calls for abstention which permit the nationalists to claim not only those who heed their calls but also those who go fishing instead of voting have not yielded results. For example, in 1981 the Corsican nationalist parties joined in condemning candidates for all the parties as typical "clan" politicians and called for abstention on the second ballot of the legislative election. But this appeal fell on deaf ears and there was no significant increase in the percentage of Corsicans not voting.

The revival of ethnic nationalism in France has not spilled over into partisan politics. Ethnic parties have been unsuccessful at the polls. None of the established major parties has moved to advocate the cause of greater ethnic autonomy. The parties out of power have often made ambiguous pledges of greater decentralization of political power in general but show

---

[3] In Corsica, nationalist parties resorted to chicanery to inflate their electoral strength, without much success. In the 1973 legislative elections, in one district a nationalist party won 3.4 percent of the vote by running a candidate with the same last name as the Leftwing Radical candidate, a well-known local mayor who ultimately won the seat. In 1978, similar tactics gave a nationalist candidate 7.2 percent of the vote in a district where the nationalist's last name was the same as the Gaullist candidate who was the major and incumbent deputy.

[4] In the 1981 presidential election there was no candidate linked with ethnic causes.

little consistent support for the causes of specific ethnic movements. The major parties have not felt the need to do so since there is no threat to their electoral bases in minority regions from ethnic parties. Ethnic parties appeared, challenged the traditional parties, but failed to win public backing.

While ethnic nationalism does not pose a threat to French parties, it does present a serious problem to security forces trying to maintain law and order. In Brittany and Corsica, small but dedicated groups have turned to terrorism and insurrection to press their demands for independence. Breton terrorists blew up the national television transmission tower in Brittany in 1974 and bombed a part of the Versailles palace in 1978. Between 1975 and 1980, the number of separatist-linked bombings in Corsica averaged approximately 300 a year (Savigear, 1980). A handful of terrorists is not a menace to the party system but does create a police problem.

THE ECOLOGY MOVEMENT. Another sociopolitical challenge to political parties in Western Europe has been the ecology movement. In some ways, the threat of the ecologists is greater than that of ethnic minorities. The ecologists have a nationwide appeal rather than one focused on specific regions and peoples. In addition, the ecologists have preferred a new, comprehensive worldview instead of adapting the old political ideologies—especially of the left—as have the nationalist organizations. While this new ideology is often incomplete and vague, it emphasizes the need for humans to live in harmony with nature. It includes a notion of how nations ought to interact with each other as well as how national governments ought to act with respect to their own people. The ecologist view rejects the development and growth impulses of most older ideologies and urges steps for controlling economic and demographic growth. Ecologists offer a model for an alternative society in which forests are valued more than jobs. As one prominent French ecologist indicated in an interview with the author, "Our movement tries to define a global policy in economic problems touching our contemporary society. Our goal is to create some propositions for a society not based simply on production and consumption." With a new ideological perspective, the ecologist movement offers one of the few available alternatives to the timeworn and seemingly unpopular ideologies of the established parties. In some European countries, especially West Germany and Belgium, the ecologists have become important political movements rivaling the parties for followers and electoral support.

In France, the ecologist movement has attracted a large following. Although there is a relatively small core of militants committed to an alternative society, the movement also mobilizes farmers opposed to projects that will cut up their land, city dwellers concerned about the noise and pollution of expressways or airports, residents who fear the dangers of living near a nuclear energy plant, and young people opposed in principle to anything nuclear. The diverse political and economic orientations of this following and the sometimes bitter competition of several different ecological groups impede unified action. But the various ecological groups have assumed political importance. French ecologists pursue their objectives through traditional interest group politics in pressuring elected officials to pay more attention to environmental concerns. When these methods fail to produce satisfactory results, as they often do, the ecologists organize demonstrations and protests to oppose and if possible to block government actions they deem inappropriate. Much of the ecologists' political action is at the local level where they try to prevent the new construction of airports, highways, and other public and private projects damaging to the environment. The ecologists have targeted France's large and rapidly expanding nuclear energy projects for special opposition (Nelkin and Pollak, 1981).

Beyond these traditional political approaches, the French ecologists have mounted electoral challenges to the existing parties. Ecologists believe that the established parties have not picked up the environmental issues despite what they perceive to be growing public concern. They feel that only by creating an electoral challenge that will demonstrate the public's attention to ecology can those concerned with the environment force the parties to address their issues. The first electoral challenge from the ecologists came in 1974 with the presidential campaign of René Dumont. One of twelve candidates, he finished sixth with 338,000 votes (1.32 percent of the votes cast). In the 1977 municipal elections, the ecologists made a major effort to attract voter support. Overall, the ecologist candidates did not win as many votes as did Dumont three years earlier, but ecologists were absent from the ballot in most municipalities. In cities with populations over 30,000, the ecologists took 2.9 percent of the vote even though they were not represented in most of these cities (Lancelot, 1977; Goldey and Bell, 1977). In Paris, the ecologists won 10.1 percent of the vote; in one Parisian suburb, the ecologist list took 27.1 percent of the vote on the first ballot. This good showing in local elections in Paris, its suburbs, and larger cities encouraged many to see a political swing favoring the ecologists for the 1978 parliamentary elections. However, these elections were very disappointing to ecologists. They fielded candidates in approximately 40 percent of the districts but won only 2.04 percent of the vote (Jaffre, 1980: 57; Bridgport, 1978). In the 1979 election for the European Parliament, the ecologists hoped to profit from the disarray and division of both the right and the left and from the adoption of proportional representation for the European election to win a political foothold. Their electoral strength rose significantly to 4.38 percent of the vote, but they failed to surmount the 5 percent barrier required for seats and for the reimbursement of the ballot deposit and printing costs. In the 1981 presidential election, Brice Lalonde, leader of the Amis de la Terre, represented the ecological movement.[5] He hoped ambitiously for 15 percent of the vote but ended up with 3.87 percent, exceeding 5 percent of the vote only in five departments.[6] In the legislative elections held a month later, the ecologists suffered another sharp setback. Fielding approximately the same number of candidates in 1981 as in 1978, the ecologists dropped from 2.04 percent of the total votes cast in 1978 to only 1.08 percent in 1981.

The ecologist movements lack strong organizations and large memberships. The largest group, Amis de la Terre, claimed only 5,000 members nationwide in 1979. The other principal groups, SOS-Environment and Mouvement Ecologique, claimed far fewer members but larger numbers of "sympathizers." The Mouvement Ecologique, the most political of the ecologist groups, had only 20 people in Paris who were actually involved in the work of the organization, and it could muster only about 400 volunteers for election campaign efforts. The ecologists can mobilize large numbers of people when these people feel that their interests are endangered by a pending building project, but they have not been able to turn these people or others into a large body of reliable political workers.

The French parties have not really felt threatened by the ecology movement. Pressure from the ecologists may have contributed to the addition of a few lines of rather vague promises to protect the environment to the programs of the major parties. They have not changed the parties' basic priorities, and the environmental concerns expressed in programs are soon forgotten once the election is over. For example, the Socialists called for an immediate halt to nuclear testing while they were in opposition. Once Mitterrand was elected, he imposed a moratorium on nuclear tests in order to conduct a thorough review of the program and safeguards. But this "review" lasted only five days before testing was resumed (McBride, 1982).

In part, the electoral system has protected the French parties from ecologist pressures. The two-ballot majority system precludes small parties without allies from winning legislative seats. To be present on the decisive

[5] Lalonde faced a rival ecologist in a bitter precampaign and ultimately gathered the required 500 sponsoring signatures only with the aid of an established party, the Center for Social Democrats (Giscardian).

[6] His strongest showing was in Essone where he had 5.35 percent of the votes cast.

second ballot, candidates must win at least 12.5 percent of the *registered* vote. This is an obstacle that no candidate from an unaffiliated minor party—ecologist, nationalist, or otherwise—has succeeded in overcoming since 1967. The sporadic nature of rising and falling electoral support for ecologists has also diminished the threat to the parties. There is no clear trend of rising public support for the ecologists to alarm the established parties. Instead, the ecologists do well in one election only to falter in the next. They did well in the 1977 municipal elections and declined in the 1978 National Assembly elections; the ecologist candidate did well in the 1981 presidential election but his fellow ecologists did very poorly a few weeks later in the National Assembly elections. With such a pattern of uncertain support for the ecologist movement, parties see little need to do more than make a few symbolic gestures toward the environmental issue.

Finally, the ecologists' impact on the established parties is reduced by the diversity of their voters. In a tight election, the ecologists might hope to influence the outcome if they could direct their first-ballot voters to support the party or candidate who made the most convincing pledges to protect the environment. For example, in the 1981 presidential election, the 4 percent won by the ecologist might have made the difference on the second ballot. Ecologist leaders, however, felt that their voters would not follow their directions on how to vote on the second ballot. To avoid splitting the movement, they declined to make a choice and the ecologist vote split with 53 percent voting for Mitterrand, 26 percent for Giscard, and 21 percent abstaining.[7] In the aftermath of the 1981 elections, French ecologists struggled to maintain their followers and to unify their movement while "greens" across the Rhine and elsewhere flourished.

THE MIDDLE-CLASS REVOLT. Another challenge to established political parties during the 1970s came from disgruntled middle-class voters who revolted against high taxes, government intervention in their economic and private affairs, and the deterioration of morality in the "permissive society." In Denmark, the antitax Progress party of Mogens Glistrup swept onto the political scene for the first time in 1973 and took 15 percent of the vote to become the second largest party in the Danish parliament (Nilson, 1980). By the end of the decade, with its leader convicted of tax evasion, the party still controlled 11 percent of the Danish vote. A parallel antitax party in Norway had somewhat less success but still cut into the support of traditional parties and found its way into the Storting. In Britain, the ratepayers' revolt is credited with an important contribution to the Liberal party's electoral surge in the mid-1970s (King, 1979).

[7] SOFRES poll reported in *Le Nouovel Observateur*, June 1, 1981.

These electoral shifts on the part of the traditional middle class accentuated the fragmentation of party systems (Wolinetz and Mayer) and raised concerns about overall political stability in these and other countries. In addition, the revolt of the middle classes, traditionally the heart of support for Western democracies, dealt an important symbolic blow to political stability in Western Europe (Bechhofer and Elliott, 1976).

France seemed another likely spot for a middle-class revolt. During the Fourth Republic, small shopkeepers rallied to the demogogic appeals of Pierre Poujade and further undermined that tottering regime (Hoffman, 1956; Bourne, 1977). In its first national election, the Poujade movement won 2,500,000 votes (11.6 percent of the total vote) and 52 seats in the National Assembly. Fifteen years later, the threat of a similar middle-class revolt remained. Small merchants and artisans still made up 8 percent of the working population at the end of the 1960s. They often felt themselves severely disadvantaged by the rapid modernization of French industry and commerce. Discount stores and supermarkets were threatening the existence of the small shops and specialty stores of the traditional middle class. The government's policies favoring economic modernization ignored the small enterprises while often providing subsidies and tax breaks to modern, large industries. In addition, the *patente* tax placed a heavy financial burden on artisans and small shopowners. The government perceived these small, independent businesses as a declining sector of the economy; the traditional middle classes felt betrayed and struck back.

In 1969, a cafe owner, Gerard Nicoud, forged the CID-UNATI[8] to pressure government for action to protect the small shopkeepers (Lefranc, 1976: 234–39). Motivated by the apparent success of mass protest such as that of the Events of May 1968 in provoking government response, Nicoud and his followers organized boycotts, hunger strikes, and demonstrations which ended in violence, kidnapped and took hostage civil servants, bombed or burned supermarkets, and engaged in other militant action (Berger, 1981). At one point, Nicoud succeeded in rallying 30,000 protesters in the streets of Paris to protest government failure to respect the interests of small shopkeepers and artisans. His organization presented candidates for the local chambers of commerce and artisan chambers, winning control of many of them early in the 1970s.

The French middle-class revolt of the 1970s did not become the electoral challenge that similar movements presented in Denmark or Norway, or that the earlier Poujadist movement did in France. The Gaullist and Giscardian governments moved quickly to alleviate some of the shopkeep-

[8] Actually, a merger of two groups: Centre d'Information et Defense–Union Nationale des Artisans et des Travailleurs Independants.

ers' greatest complaints. A law was passed that prevented the construction of new supermarkets or discount stores without the approval of local committees composed largely of local merchants. As one observer noted, "it was rather like placing the decision on opening of new pubs in the hands of the Plymouth Brethren (Wright, 1978: 181)."[9] The government assessed new taxes on supermarkets to raise retirement funds for small merchants. Another reform replaced the patente with a *taxe professionelle* which shifted more of the burden to larger enterprises; small shopkeepers paid 62 percent less than with the patente and artisans got off with 53 percent less than under the old tax (Berger and Piore, 1980: 114). Government decrees restricted the use of advertised "loss leaders" and disguised book discounts by barring publishers from printing a set price on book jackets.[10] These reforms took much of the radicalism out of the French middle-class revolt. Shopkeepers left the streets to return to business. Nicoud tried to reshape his declining CID-UNATI into a more typical businessmen's association, but internal divisions and competition from the older established associations prevented success. By the end of the decade, Nicoud was in jail and his movement nearly dead.

Others tried to translate the middle-class revolt into election politics but with no success. Jean Royer, the author of the legislation limiting supermarket construction, ran for the presidency in 1974. His campaign emphasized the themes of the middle-class revolt: high taxes, bureaucratic excesses, and the permissive society. But he failed to win the support of the traditional middle class. He finished fourth in a field of twelve first-ballot candidates, taking 3.2 percent of the votes cast. His appeal was regionally based rather than drawn from the traditional middle class. Royer was mayor of Tours and he finished first in his home city with 35 percent of the vote. He did well in his department and in surrounding departments. But the farther one moves from Tours, the less his vote (Lancelot and Lancelot, 1975: 150). Another attempt to draw the middle-class revolt into politics during the 1979 European parliamentary elections also failed. A list presented by two conservative deputies and Pierre Poujade campaigned on the need to restore traditional values, fight technocracy, and defend private property and free enterprise. It attracted only 283,000 votes na-

[9] The new law reduced the construction of new supermarkets by 30 percent in its first year. Later, when the climate that produced the legislation had moderated, supermarket operators learned to get around these committees through political and judicial maneuvers; see Keeler, 1982.

[10] The Mitterrand government recently reversed the law on printing the price of books but only to better protect small book dealers. The price now must be printed on the book and discounts are limited to only 5 percent in contrast to the 15 percent to 25 percent offered earlier by discounters such as FNAC and the hypermarchés.

tionwide (1.3 percent of the votes cast). In the 1981 presidential election campaign, several precandidates appeared to base their hope on middle-class discontent, including one former national leader of CID-UNATI. None of these candidates even made a serious effort to gather the necessary sponsors to actually qualify for the ballot. The principal white-collar worker union also talked of running its own presidential candidate because it felt neglected by all the major parties. Eventually it too withdrew and remained apolitical during the 1981 campaign.

The Gaullist and Giscardian governments' prompt responses to the most pressing concerns of the traditional middle class vitiated the radical protest movement developing among the shopkeepers. The growing rivalry between Gaullists and Giscardians after 1974 triggered a bidding war between these two parties as they both made extensive promises to the small entrepreneurs, making it unnecessary for them to shift their votes to new parties. The established parties no doubt remembered the Poujadist electoral precedent and sensed the danger of the middle-class revolt to their political preeminence. They reacted quickly and foreclosed the possibility of a new party attacking them within their usual middle-class bailiwicks.

The Parties' Refusal to Fail

The French party system avoided the disruptions and weaknesses that plagued parties elsewhere in Western democracies during the 1970s. It was not that the French parties did not face challenges from alternative political organizations. There have been French versions of the ethnic nationalist movements, ecological groups, and middle-class rebellions that imperilled party systems in Belgium, Britain, Denmark, Norway, West Germany, and elsewhere. The French parties fended off these rivals more successfully than parties in other Western European countries seem to have been able to do.

A MODERN PARTY SYSTEM. One explanation for the vitality of the major parties is the relative youth of the current French party system. While the current parties have antecedents in the past, they are comparatively recent creations. The party system of the 1970s was radically different from that system which dominated and destroyed the Fourth Republic. Emerging out of the 1960s and 1970s, the major parties have been better able to adapt to the new demands of these decades than have been European parties formed or reformed in the 1940s or before. These French parties were not decaying or stagnant; they were still in the act of emergence or reformation. In other European countries, those dissatisfied with the party system might turn to alternative organizations; in France the dissatisfied activists were engaged in party reform or in the creation of new parties. During the 1970s, French parties experienced rapid growth in membership and profited from a swing to partisan identification on the part of many French voters who in the past avoided expressing sympathy for a specific party (Cameron, 1972).

Each of the four major French parties experienced major transformations during the 1970s. The Gaullist party, now known as the Rally for the Republic (RPR), is the creation of successive political leaders—Pompidou and then Chirac—who have seen it as a means to further their own political ambitions and who have crafted the party to pursue them (Lawson, 1981; Charlot, 1971; Wilson, 1973). Despite the fact that the party is commonly labeled after General de Gaulle, it bears little resemblance to the Fourth Republic party founded and presided over by de Gaulle. The RPR claims its Gaullist legacy but certainly is not bound by the political goals or ideas of de Gaulle. Pompidou and then Chirac felt free to adjust the party's positions according to their own interpretations of the current political situation. They altered the organization and even the party's name to reflect new orientations. They brought new people into the party and replaced leaders, often with their friends. The frequent renewal of the Gaullist party organization and leadership has given it a sense of dynamism that attracted conservative party reformers who otherwise might have been tempted by alternative political organizations (Schonfeld, 1980a, 1980b).

The Gaullist party's modernization stimulated rival parties to undertake their own efforts at renewal (Lawson, 1981). The Giscardian party, the Republican party (PR), is also a recent creation, although it can trace its lineage to various Third and Fourth Republic conservative parties. The PR emerged with a distinctively new, although somewhat fragile doctrine and organization in the mid-1960s (Colliard, 1971). During the 1970s, its leaders attempted to solidify its organization and define more clearly its positions, often in direct response to the issues of the 1970s. Giscard wanted to give his party and his regime the image of moderate reform by advocating decentralization, women's rights, youth rights, and concern for the environment. The concrete results were often more symbolic than real: permitting the election of a mayor in Paris; cancellation of a planned Parisian expressway; creating a ministry of women's affairs; lowering the voting age. But the reforms did deflect some moderates who otherwise might have joined alternative political organizations championing these causes.

On the left, the parties were also in flux. The Socialist party (PS) began extensive internal reform and revitalization at the beginning of the 1970s (Johnson, 1981; Lieber, 1977; Brown, 1982). Under the leadership of François Mitterrand, the PS recommitted itself to a radical Socialist ideology and forged an alliance with the Communist party. It renewed its leadership ranks, although not as extensively as did the Gaullist party (Schonfeld, 1980b). It recruited many of those who earlier had been involved in the political clubs. It attracted many of the isolated leftist sympathizers who in the past had joined fringe parties like the small Unified Socialist party (PSU) or who had remained out of politics because of their contempt for the old SFIO Socialist party.

The Communist party (PCF) had more problems in the 1970s. For most of the decade, the PCF flirted with Eurocommunism and charted an independent course from Moscow (Tiersky, 1974; Stiefbold, 1977; Fauvet, 1977). It joined with the Socialists and the small Leftwing Radical party in drafting a Common Program to be fulfilled when the left came to power. This moderate course failed to increase the Communist electoral base. Thus, the PCF returned to a more revolutionary stance and to the Kremlin's fold at the end of the decade (Wilson, 1978; Aviv, 1979).

The various party reforms of the 1970s responded only imperfectly to the specific issues and challenges raised by would-be alternative organizations. It is not clear that all or even most of the changes in the established parties were the appropriate adaptations for the decade or the future. Nevertheless, the movement in these major parties was important enough to monopolize public political attention. The politically alert citizens were preoccupied with the changes in these parties which dominated the news and relegated the news of ecologists, ethnic nationalists, and middle-class rebels to the back pages of the newspapers except when these groups engaged in violence.

THE LEFT VERSUS THE RIGHT. A second and related explanation of the French parties' refusal to fail is the critical importance of the conflict between the left and the right. Throughout the 1970s, the overriding political question was whether or not the revived and reunited left would be able to wrest power out of the hands of the Gaullists and Giscardians. Every political contest from 1971 through the 1981 presidential election was a battle between the left and right, with the growing prospect for a victory of the left. Other issues, whether new or old, were secondary to the central questions of whether or not alternation in power was possible or desirable. The stakes were high in such a rotation between the right and left because the two blocs represented dramatically different economic, social, and political philosophies. The preoccupation with the left-right battle drew attention away from the challenges of alternative organizations at election times. With the stakes in each election high and the contests close, voters were disinclined to trade off their ties to the major parties in order to support a new minor party even if it represented ethnic nationalist or ecological interests with which the voters sympathized. Nor could middle-class rebels risk voting for an antitax party when voting for a minor party might make possible a victory by the anticapitalist Socialists and Communists.

The electoral manifestations of the various alternative political bodies were most successful in gathering votes when it was clear that the election would in no way affect the national political balance between the major parties. The best election showing for the ecologists came in the 1979 election for the European Parliament. Coming soon after the right had turned back decisively the left's latest challenge in the 1978 National Assembly election, there was no chance that the European parliamentary election would in any way affect the domestic political situation in France. Turnout was low; the right and left blocs were divided internally; public interest was lacking; and the ecologists scored their all-time high of 4.4 percent of the vote. In municipal and cantonal elections and, to a lesser degree, in parliamentary by-elections, voting for ecologists or regional candidates was greater than in national elections because the overall political balance was not at stake.

Until 1981, the intensive competition between left and right always resulted in the victory of the right. The left had not held power since the 1930s. In other European countries, left-wing parties have held power for extended periods and demonstrated what they can and cannot do. Those dissatisfied with the performance of both left-wing and conservative parties because they neglected new issues tended to turn to alternative political organizations. In France, the left had not had an opportunity to disillusion anyone by its conduct in office. It made promises to decentralize government to the benefit of ethnic nationalities, to reevaluate the nuclear energy program, and to provide relief for the small merchants against the competition from large commercial firms. Even though these promises were sometimes vague or contradictory, they gave hope that the victory of the left would result in greater attention to these causes. Most of those interested in such issues thus slipped into one side or the other of the basic left-right political division.

PARTIES AND THE PERSISTENCE OF CLASS CONFLICT IN FRANCE. A third explanation of the French parties' immunity to the threats of the 1970s is found in the persistent problem of integrating the French working class. In many parts of Western Europe, the working class seemingly has been well integrated into society. Working-class parties have shared in shaping the existing social institutions. Whether genuinely integrated, or deluded into a false sense of belonging as neo-Marxists contend, workers in many European societies rarely view politics from the perspective of class versus class confrontations. Nor are they encouraged to do so by their trade unions or parties. With class warfare not a fashionable explanation, those still finding themselves dissatisfied with the status quo must search for alternative explanations for their disadvantaged condition. Some seek an answer in ethnic nationalism that sees patterns of economic and social discrimination or internal colonization. Others, dissatisfied with the status quo orientation of the principal left-wing parties and with the ineffectiveness or sterile ideological debates of the far left fringe parties, focus their reformist impulses on the environmental issues. Middle-class elements, no longer fearful of working-class attacks on their major interests, can afford to engage in their own radicalism to protest taxes or press for other vested interests.

In France, however, class conflict continues to be a principal political theme (Marceau, 1977; Vaughan, 1980). The working class remains poorly integrated (Gallie, 1980) and left-wing parties were excluded from power until 1981. Despite the egalitarian rhetoric, the distribution of income in France is more unequal than in any other European industrial democracy (Sawyer, 1976). There is evidence to suggest that a political and economic consensus may exist at the mass level in France (Duhamel, 1978). But left-wing political elites still resist what they view as efforts to smother working-class consciousness through the imposition of a false national consensus. Trade unions and left-wing parties keep the class warfare rhetoric alive; they resist all "class collaboration" which might reduce class tensions and hence diminish the revolutionary potential of the workers. Since class politics remains alive in France and the established parties remain the vehicles for that political struggle, alternative political organizations have had a more difficult time in reaching center stage in French politics. Further, since the left was excluded from power between 1958 and 1981, the dissatisfied of all types could turn to the established left-wing parties for solutions to their problems since these parties were unsullied by the compromises that are an inevitable part of governing.

THE EFFECT OF POLITICAL INSTITUTIONS ON PARTY DURABILITY. A fourth explanation of the strength of the French parties during the 1960s and 1970s is found in the institutional patterns of the Fifth Republic. We have seen already how the electoral system prevented the small parties emerging out of the new political forces from electing public officeholders. The two-ballot system prevented them from even playing the role of "spoilers." To the extent that the small parties had had a spoiler effect, it was as tools of the major parties. Thus, a Giscardian party provided nominating signators to the ecologist presidential candidate in 1981 in the hopes that an ecology candidate would draw votes away from the Socialist candidate. Similarly, in 1978 and 1981 there were rumors that the PCF had put up phony ecologist candidates in the National Assembly election in districts where they feared the PS might replace the Communist as the largest party of the left.

The highly centralized political system and the strength of the executive under the Fifth Republic further reduced the impact of the alternative political organizations. The issues that the new groups raise may be popular ones, but the government has the ability simply to ignore the issue when it chooses to do so. The government is secure from worrisome parliamentary inquiry or censure. It can use its control of television and radio to minimize or distort coverage of threatening alternative political groups. This aloofness of the government from pressure coming from alternative groups is easily illustrated in the case of environmental groups' protest against nuclear energy facilities. In both France and Germany, government plans for expanding nuclear energy capabilities came under attack during the 1970s by local residents and environmentalists (Nelkin and Pollak, 1981). In Germany, mass protests led to greater government concern for public involvement in decisions on plant sites and eventually to a moratorium on the construction of new plants. In France, to the contrary, similar mass protests had little effect on government plans. The siting decision remains the near exclusive prerogative of the centralized bureaucracy. Plant construction continued despite the protests and plans were developed for a nuclear waste treatment center in France that no other European country would approve because of domestic political pressures. The nuclear energy development plan continued under the Socialists, presumed to be more hostile to nuclear energy, with only a brief pause to "reevaluate" the previous government's programs. The French system is simply better insulated from the pressures of immediate public opinion than is the case in most other Western European countries.

THE DEJA VU FACTOR: A TRADITION OF PROTEST POLITICS. Fifth, there is a long tradition of political protest in France which immunizes the political system against the wave of new mass actions. One of the reasons for the startling impact of alternative political groups such as the middle-class antitax revolt, national minority groups, ecologists, and others in Western Europe was the fact that such mass action was unconventional and unexpected. In Belgium, Britain, Denmark, and elsewhere, it was not normal for groups to take to the streets in protest against government policies. Such unusual political approaches attracted public attention to the issues and the groups that used them in most European countries. There was often public soul-searching as to why such events were happening to disturb the normally tranquil pattern of politics. Ameliorative action was often forthcoming to restore political peace. In France, however, such protest tactics are normal and expected aspects of the political game (Hoffmann, 1974: 111–44). Alternative political groups, which in other European countries quickly dominated the political scene because of their dramatic actions, shared the stage in France with dozens of other established and spontaneous groups protesting against one form of perceived governmental abuse or another. Long experience in facing such mass actions made the French political system and parties less vulnerable to alternative organizations which used these tactics.

The French parties and government have developed a response to such challenges from alternative organizations or other potential rebels which has been described as the "feather quilt strategy" (Berger, 1972). They absorb blows from discontented elements even when these protests take the form of low-level violence. Such protest action is not unusual and special riot police are well trained and effective in handling it. There is no panicky reevaluation which might affect government policy or party programs. The government and major parties may slightly modify their stands to acknowledge the issues raised, but rarely are these changes anything more than cosmetic adjustments. They simply wait for the challengers or dissidents to tire and to dissolve because of their internal divisions. The "feather quilt strategy" has worked well in France. The new alternative political organizations lack the internal strength and unity for the prolonged political struggle the parties impose on them.

Of course, there is the risk that the unrest will spread and turn to broader revolt as in May 1968, thus tearing the quilt and scattering the feathers. Indeed, the Events of May 1968 are often cited as the prototype of the anomie and political uprising that will accompany party failure in postindustrial democracies. This uprising was spontaneous. All major parties—even the nominally revolutionary Communist party—were left on the sidelines of the most important French social and political upheaval of this century.

To infer from the "Events" that the French parties had failed is unjustified for several reasons. First, such revolts are a regular feature of French politics and occur periodically regardless of the health of the political parties. The Events of May are part of a tradition of protest that has been well defined by Hoffmann (1974: 111–44). They are the latest episode of the French tendency toward periodic revolt after docilely accepting the status quo that was described over a century ago by Tocqueville. Second, in earlier revolts, political parties have always been left on the sidelines by the spontaneity of the movement and by the rush of events. For example, no party or group of parties controlled the outburst of enthusiasm—and vengeance—at the Liberation in 1944–45. Similarly, the Popular Front parties were overwhelmed by the spontaneous and uncontrolled outburst of their followers in 1936. The revolt of May 1968 was no more a precursor of the future postindustrial crisis of democracy than it was a reenactment of past revolutionary dramas (Aron, 1969).

Third, although the parties were not involved directly in the revolt, the largest demonstrations during the Event were those organized by the established political parties: the massive march in Paris and elsewhere on May 13 organized by the left-wing parties and trade unions, and the equally massive rally in support of de Gaulle on May 30, organized by the Gaullist movements. Indeed, Hoffmann (1974: 164) argues that it was the absence of organized parties that ultimately condemned the revolt to failure: "In the last analysis, the rebels had good fists, stout lungs, but no adequate political weapons. . . . What the rebels really needed was the support of the one true, massive and coherent opposition force: the French Communist party. But the party turned against them."

Fourth, even though the parties were largely absent from the street action of the Events, they were the ultimate beneficiaries. The immediate winner was the Gaullist party which capitalized on reaction against the revolt to win the first single-party majority in five French republics. Ultimately, the Socialist party profited from the Events in the radicalization of its doctrine and in the recruitment of large numbers of militants who were politicized and mobilized by the Events and then later turned to the PS as the means for effective political action.

SUMMARY

To summarize, French parties resisted the challenge of alternative political organizations because (1) the major parties were themselves reforming or emerging; (2) the central political issue of the 1970s was the battle between left and right in which the alternative organizations had no part; (3) class confrontation remained important in France and encouraged citizens to identify with the established vehicles for class conflict rather than to turn to alternative political organizations unrelated to the class issue; (4) the centralized and aloof pattern of policymaking insulated the political system from the alternative groups and their issues; and (5) the tradition of political protest made the new groups of the 1970s seem little different from a long history of other groups advocating mass action.

There is often the sense, more implicit then explicit, that the trend of party decline is both inevitable and irreversible. Thus, Berger (1980: 18) writes that the weakening of Western European parties is the product of "political shifts that have been long in the making and that no forseeable set of decisions or constellation of circumstances would reverse."[11] And Huntington (1975: 191) suggests that "political parties are a political form peculiarly suited to the needs of industrial society and that the movement . . . into a postindustrial phase hence means the end of the political party system as we have known it." However, the French experience suggests that party decline is not irreversible and not necessarily linked to postindustrial phenomena. French parties were in a state of decline in the 1950s and early 1960s before the advent of postindustrial society. The French party system displayed then most of the same symptoms now attributed to the decay produced by postindustrial trends: declining memberships and reduced partisan identification on the part of the general electorate; lower turnout for elections; lack of public trust in the parties or in their leaders; vulnerability of the system to new "flash" parties; stagnant party organization and weakened discipline. At the time, observers regarded the French party system as a deviant case, not as an omen of what lay ahead for other European parties.

This was not the first period of party decay in French democratic history. In 1799, the parties' violent disputes were held responsible for *l'anarchie* which brought Napoleon Bonaparte to power; in 1851, it was *le desordre* of the parties that led to Louis Napoleon's ascent; in 1940, the revolt against *la decadence* of the parties paved the way for the fascist rule of Pétain and Laval; and in 1958, *l'immobilisme* of the parties brought down the Fourth Republic (Serfaty, 1968: 91). Each time the decay of parties produced a political vacuum, old parties revived and new ones emerged to fill the need for electoral competition as democracy was reinstituted. The party system revived again after the decay of the 1950s, and the present party system has greater coherence, strength, and resiliency than ever before. The French experience clearly demonstrates that party revival as well as party decay can occur in societies moving toward the postindustrial model.

This revitalization of the French party system runs counter to the purported trend of party decay, even though French society seems to be undergoing the same socioeconomic changes that are elsewhere linked with the postindustrial era and party decline. The cycle of decline followed by renewal in France was unrelated to postindustrial changes. The

[11] Earlier in this article, she states that party stagnation is not inevitable and points out briefly that the parties still possess important resources (pp. 27–28). But the rest of the article stresses the theme of irreversible party decadence.

decline came from specific weaknesses in the institutional framework of government, from the frailties of the parties themselves, and from specific political problems facing France during the 1940s and 1950s. Revival came as new parties and reform-minded and ambitious party leaders faced the expanded electoral challenges of the Fifth Republic (Wilson, 1980). While the party system still has its weak points and some of the transformations are still incomplete, there is no indication that the parties are slipping back into decline, despite continuing socioeconomic changes toward the postindustrial pattern.

The French experience of party decline and revival suggests an alternative explanation to the problem of party decay in other European democracies. If parties in other countries are in decline, and in my view the decline is not as self-evident as is often believed, it may be appropriate to view this as part of a normal process of party decline and regeneration/replacement produced by problems and developments that are country-specific. This may be a more accurate explanation of current developments in Western European party systems than the notion of a general trend toward new political forms in the postindustrial era.

REFERENCES

Anderson, M. 1974. *Conservative politics in France*. London: George Allen and Unwin.
Aron, R. 1969. *The elusive revolution: Anatomy of a student revolt*. New York: Praeger.
Aviv, I. 1979. The French Communist party from 1958–1978: Crisis and endurance. *West European Politics* 2.
Barnes, S. H. and M. Kaase. 1979. *Political action: Mass participation in five Western democracies*. Beverly Hills: Sage Publications.
Bechhofer, F. and B. Elliott. 1976. Persistence and change: The petite bourgeoisie in industrialized society. *Archives Européenes de Sociologie* 17.
Beer, W. R. 1980. *The unexpected rebellion: Ethnic activism in contemporary France*. New York: New York University Press.
Bell, D. 1976. *The coming of the post-industrial society: A new venture in social forecasting*. New York: Basic Books.
Benjamin, R. W. 1977. *Government and collective goods in postindustrial society*. International Studies Occasional Paper No. 15.
Berger. S. 1972a. Bretons, Basques, Scots, and their European nations. *Journal of Inter-Disciplinary History* 3.
———. 1972b. *Peasants against politics*. Cambridge: Harvard University Press.
———. 1977. Bretons and Jacobins: Reflections on French regional ethnicity. In Esman, 1977.

————. 1979. Politics and antipolitics in Western Europe in the seventies. *Daedalus* 108.

————. 1981. *Organizing interests in Western Europe: Pluralism, corporatism, and the transformation of politics*. Cambridge: Cambridge University Press.

————, and M. J. Piore. 1980. *Dualism and discontinuity in industrial societies*. New York: Cambridge University Press.

————, G. D. Feldman, G. Hernes, J. LaPalombara, P. C. Schmitter, and A. A. Silver. 1975. New perspectives for the study of Western Europe. *Social Science Research Council Items*, 29: 34–37.

Bourne, D. 1977. *Petit bourgeois en revolt? Le mouvement Poujade*. Paris: Flammarion.

Bridgport, J. 1978. The ecologist movement in the French general election 1978. *Parliamentary Affairs* 31.

Brinton, C. 1968. *The Americans and the French*. Cambridge: Harvard University Press.

Broder, D. S. 1972. *The party's over: The failure of politics in America*. New York: Harper Torchbook.

Brown, B. E. 1982. *Socialism of a different kind: Reshaping the left in France*. Westport, Conn.: Greenwood Press.

Brzezinski, Z. 1971. *Between two ages: America's role in the technetronic era*. New York: Viking.

Cameron. D. R. 1972. Stability and change in patterns of French partisanship. *Public Opinion Quarterly* 36.

Campbell, P. 1965. *French electoral systems and elections since 1789*. Hamden, Conn.: Anchor Books.

Cayrol, R., and G. Lavau. 1965. Les clubs devant l'action politique. *Revue Française de Science Politique* 15.

Charlot, J. 1971. *The Gaullist phenomenon: The Gaullist movement in the Fifth Republic*. New York: Praeger.

Colard, D. 1964–65. Le Phénomène des clubs. *Politique* 7–8.

Colliard, J.-C. 1971. *Les Républicains Indépendants, Valéry Giscard D'Estaing*. Paris: Presses Universitaires de France.

Crozier, M. 1974. *The stalled society*, trans. Rupert Swyer. New York: Viking.

————, S. P. Huntington, and J. Watanuki. 1975. *The crisis of democracy: Report on the government of democracies to the Trilateral Committee*. New York: New York University Press.

Duhamel, A. 1978. Le consensus social. In *L'Opinion française en 1977*, ed. J. Jaffre. Paris: Presses de la Fondation Nationale des Sciences Politiques.

Esman, M. J., ed. 1977. *Ethnic conflict in the Western world*. Ithaca, N.Y.: Cornell University Press.

Fauvet, J. 1977. *Histoire du parti communiste 1920–1976*. Paris: Fayard.

Finer, S. E. 1980. *The changing British party system, 1945–1979*. Washington, D.C.: American Enterprise Institute.

Gallie, D. 1980. The ideology and workers' conception of class inequality in France. *West European Politics* 3.

Goguel, F., ed. 1965. *Le référendum d'octobre et les élections de novembre 1962*. Paris: Armand Colin.

Goldey, D. G., and D. S. Bell. 1977. The French municipal elections of March 1977. *Parliamentary Affairs* 30.

Hancock, D. M., and G. Sjoberg, eds. 1972. *Politics in the post-welfare state: Responses to the new individualism*. New York: Columbia University Press.

Harrison, R. J. 1980. *Pluralism and corporatism: The political evolution of modern democracy*. London: George Allen and Unwin.

Hoffmann, S. 1956. *Le mouvement poujade*. Paris: Armand Colin.

———. 1974. *Decline or renewal? France since the 1930s*. New York: Viking.

Huntington, S. P. 1974. Post-industrial politics: How benign will it be? *Comparative Politics* 6: 163–91.

———. 1975. The United States. In Crozier, 1975.

Jacob, J. E. 1980. Ethnic conflict in contemporary France. *Contemporary French Civilization* 5.

Jaffre, J. 1980. The French electorate in March 1978. In *The French National Assembly elections of 1978*, ed. H. R. Penniman. Washington, D.C.: American Enterprise Institute.

Johnson, R. W. 1981. *The long march of the French left*. New York: St. Martins.

Kavanagh, D. 1977. Party politics in question. In *New trends in British Politics: Issues for research*, ed. D. Kavanagh and R. Rose. Beverly Hills: Sage Publications.

Keeler, J.T.S. 1982. Corporatist decentralization and commercial modernization in France: The Royer Law's impact on shopkeepers, supermarkets and the state. Paper presented at the 1982 annual meeting of the American Political Science Association.

King, R. 1979. The middle class revolt and the established parties. In *Respectable rebels: Middle class campaigns in Britain in the 1970s*. New York: Holmes and Meier.

Krejci, J., and V. Velimsky. 1981. *Ethnic and political nations in Europe*. New York: St. Martins.

Lancelot, A. 1977. Le rouge et le vert: Les élections des 13 et 30 mars 1977. *Projet*, 116.

Lancelot, M.-T., and A. Lancelot. 1975. A cartographic approach to the presidential election, May 1974. In *France at the polls: The presidential election of 1974*, ed. H. R. Penniman. Washington, D.C.: American Enterprise Institute.

Lawson, K. 1981. The impact of party reform on party systems: The case of the RPR in France. *Comparative Politics* 13.

Lefranc, G. 1976. *Les organisations patronales en France*. Paris: Payot.

Lehmbruch, G., and P. C. Schmitter, eds. 1982. *Patterns in corporatist intermediation*. Beverly Hills: Sage Publications.

Lieber, N. I. 1977. Ideology and tactics in the French Socialist party. *Government and Opposition* 12.

Lindberg, L. 1976. *Politics and the future of industrial society*. New York: David McKay.

Marceau, J. 1977. *Class and status in France: Economic change and social immobility*. Oxford: Oxford University Press.

Mayer, L. 1980. A note on the aggregation of party systems. In *Western European party systems*, ed. P. H. Merkl. New York: Free Press.

McBride, S. 1982. Plutonium in paradise. *Christian Science Monitor*, March 11.

Mossuz, J. 1970. *Les clubs et la politique en France*. Paris: Armand Colin.

Nelkin, D., and M. Pollak. 1981. *The atom besieged: Extraparliamentary dissent in France and Germany*. Cambridge: MIT Press.

Nilson, S. S. 1980. Norway and Denmark. In *Western European party systems*, ed. P. H. Merkl. New York: Free Press.

Olivier, V. 1967. *Les clubs politiques en France*. Aix-en-Provence: Presse de l'Université d'Aix-en-Provence.

Petrolla, R. 1980. Nationalist and regionalist movements in Western Europe. In *Nations without a state: Ethnic minorities in Western Europe*, ed. C. R. Foster. New York: Praeger.

Reece, J. E. 1977. *The Bretons against France: Ethnic minority nationalism in twentieth century Brittany*. Chapel Hill, N.C.: University of North Carolina Press.

Savigear, P. 1980. Corsica and French state. In *Nations without a state*, ed. C. R. Foster. New York: Praeger.

Sawyer, M. 1976. Income distribution in OECD countries. *OECD Economic Outlook, Occasional Studies*, July.

Schattschneider, E. E. 1942. *Party government*. New York: Holt, Rinehart, and Winston.

Schmitter, P. C. 1981. Interest intermediation and regime governability in contemporary Western Europe and North America. In *Organizing interests in Western Europe*, ed. S. Berger. New York: Cambridge University Press.

———, and G. Lehmbruch, eds. 1979. *Trends toward corporatist intermediators*. Beverly Hills: Sage Publications.

Schonfeld, W. R. 1980a. La stabilité des dirigeants des partis politiques: Le personnel des direction nationales du Parti Socialiste et du mouvement gaulliste. *Revue Française de Science Politique* 30.

———. 1980b. La stabilité des dirigeants des partis politiques: La théorie de l'oligarchie de Robert Michels. *Revue Française de Science Politique* 30.

Serfaty, S. 1968. *France, De Gaulle, and Europe*. Baltimore: Johns Hopkins University Press.

Smith, G., and N. Polsby. 1981. *British government and its discontents*. New York: Basic Books.

Steifbold, A. E. 1977. *The French Communist party in transition: PCF-CPSU relations and the challenge to Soviet authority*. New York: Praeger.

Tiersky, R. 1974. *French Communism 1920–1972*. New York: Columbia University Press.

Tocqueville, A. de. 1965. *The old regime and the French Revolution*, trans. S. Gilbert. Garden City, N.Y.: Doubleday.

Touraine, A. 1972. *The post-industrial society*. New York: Random House.

Wilson, F. L. 1971a. *The French democratic left, 1963–1969: Toward a modern party system*. Palo Alto, Ca.: Stanford University Press.

———. 1971b. The political club phenomenon in France. *Comparative Politics* 3.

———. 1973. Gaullism without de Gaulle. *Western Political Quarterly* 26.

———. 1978. The French CP's dilemma. *Problems of Communism*.

———. 1979. The revitalization of French parties. *Comparative Political Studies* 12.

———. 1980. Sources of party transformation: The case of France. In *Western European party systems*, ed. P. H. Merkl. New York: Free Press.

———. 1982. *French political parties under the Fifth Republic*. New York: Praeger.

Winkler, J. T. 1976. Corporatism. *Archives Européenes de Sociologie* 17.

Wolinetz, S. B. 1979. The transformation of Western European party systems revisited. *West European Politics* 2.

Wright, V. 1978. *The government and politics of France*. New York: Holmes and Meier.

TWENTY

Do Parties Persist or Fail?
The Big Trade-off
Facing Organizations

RICHARD ROSE AND
THOMAS T. MACKIE

> If things are going to stay the same, there will have to be some changes made.
>
> Giuseppe di Lampedusa, *The Leopard*

What does it mean to speak of the failure of a political party? To say that a party has failed, in the sense of ceasing to exist as an organization, does not mean that the voters who formerly supported it have disappeared, or that its leading politicians have abandoned party politics; they may remain active under new labels. If the statement means only that nonelectoral organizations are becoming more important as representative or linkage organizations in a political system, this is more precisely described as an indication of the rise of extraparty movements. If the statement means that parties are decreasingly significant electorally, it does not follow that parliaments (or committees in the United States Congress) have discarded the practice of using parties to organize government. To suggest that parties cease with the collapse of a regime is misleading, for modern French, German, Italian, and Austrian experience demonstrates that parties can persist through three or more regimes, notwithstanding interruptions by dictatorship and occupation. To say that parties fail in a normative sense is to imply criteria very different from functional definitions.

To speak of the success of parties is also ambiguous. At a minimum, it may only mean that a party persists, maintaining an organization to contest elections. If elections are regarded as central to the success of a party, then at any given election more parties will fail than succeed, by not winning office or by seeing their vote decline (Rose and Mackie, 1983). Within a national party system, the norm is for one party to establish a hegemonic position, winning far more than its arithmetic share of elections; the complement is that most parties will "fail to succeed," being confined to opposition. However, if success is defined as the achievement of programmatic or ideological goals, the concept becomes more complex, for any large party will almost invariably be divided about its principal goals, and whether or not they have been achieved. In the case of nationalist parties, success in achieving independence threatens a postindependence split, as the initial unifying goal is replaced by controversy about what to do next.

As the paradoxical epigraph from Lampedusa emphasizes, adaptation is a necessary condition of survival. In a dynamic political environment a party that avoids change is threatened with electoral failure. Parties must necessarily adapt to changes in the larger social environment if they are to sustain electoral support. Parties do not exist *in vacuo*, but represent groups and interests in society. The longer the time span observed, the greater the pressures on parties to adapt, as groups and interests alter through the process of societal change. In the past century war, technology, and economic growth have transformed every Western society. Intergenerational change forces a renewal of electoral support, and of a party's leadership. To remain in a fixed position in a dynamic environment is to change relative to the party system.

Because parties are organizations, all of their activities must be viewed in terms of two very different contexts; an introverted concern with what happens within the party qua organization, and an extroverted concern with changes in the larger political environment of which the organization is but a part. A party could define success in terms of electoral victory, have members keenly interested in achieving success, and win popular support in consequence. Alternatively, a party could define its mission as propagating a set of goals, and regard success as remaining true to its principles, however few votes it wins. Tension arises from differences between a party's internal goals (e.g., to propagate and achieve programmatic measures) and external events (e.g., the majority of the electorate may reject its programmatic goals). The big trade-off facing parties is the need to strike a balance, which may vary across time and between parties, between introverted and extroverted goals.

Ideas of failure and success are relative; they only have meaning when judged by explicit criteria. The focus of this essay is upon the careers of parties, that is, what happens to a party through the years; do parties persist or disappear? The term *persistence* is employed to describe parties that continue qua organizations, albeit in forms that can include marginal adaptation or even structural change in the face of disruption. Parties that *disappear* cease to contest elections and leave no legacy to a successor party. The two concepts provide an empirical basis for evaluating the careers of parties. They are also relevant to other criteria, for a party that disappears from a nation's political system would be said by most standards to have failed, and a party that persists, while not necessarily successful in winning elections or achieving programmatic goals, has met a precondition for success, survival.

The Institutionalization of Political Parties: The Precondition of Persistence

Before a political party can persist, it must exist. This is true whether the new group is postmaterialist, populist, ethnic, or a splinter or action group supplementing an established party. The establishment of a party organization is a process; a particular date, such as the foundation meeting, is only one point in time in a process of previous political activity often extending for many years. For example, the founding meeting of the British Labour party, held in London on December 19, 1900, was preceded by fifteen years of elections in which candidates had fought for seats in Parliament as representatives of Labour as a class; almost two decades were required before the Labour party in its present institutional form was established in 1918.

Every country's political history is full of the record of political groups that *might* have become political parties nominating candidates and seeking votes nationwide. But far more groups prefer to remain pressure groups or factions or *correnti* within established political parties than organize to fight elections, and run the risk of being embarrassed by a low popular vote (McAllister, 1981). Moreover, the success of the few groups in becoming established as party organizations should make it more difficult for groups subsequently to enter the electoral arena, because the great bulk of the vote will already have been mobilized.

To become institutionalized—that is, to merit recognition as an established political party—a group of politicians must do three things: (1) create a crosslocal organization to contest elections nationwide; (2) nominate candidates to fight national elections; and (3) continue to nominate candidates at successive elections. A party that nominates candidates at only one election is not institutionalized but ephemeral; a group that does not nominate candidates is a pressure group; and one that is not crosslocal is likely to be supporting an individual personality. We must distinguish between parties that seek to become institutionalized and fail, and those that do become institutionalized.

To test whether and to what extent parties succeed in becoming institutionalized or are ephemeral, we must examine a universe of countries with a long record of holding competitive free elections. The universe of analysis here consists of nineteen Western nations for which full results of elections from their national beginnings are presented in *The Interna-*

tional Almanac of Electoral History (Mackie and Rose, 1982): Australia, Austria, Belgium, Canada, Denmark, Finland, France, Germany, Iceland, Ireland, Italy, Luxembourg, the Netherlands, New Zealand, Norway, Sweden, Switzerland, the United Kingdom, and the United States. In all these countries, competitive nationwide elections have been held since the First World War, and in twelve countries since the nineteenth century.[1]

Reviewing electoral competition in many countries for periods of up to a century provides a very substantial data base for testing hypotheses about the conditions in which parties become institutionalized. Nationwide competition between parties extends back to 1828 in the United States, and to 1831 in Belgium. The average number of elections held in the 19 countries examined here is 28; the range is from 41 elections in Belgium to 13 in Luxembourg. In all, 369 parties have contested at least one national election and secured at least one percent of the vote. An average of 19 parties has contested elections within a country, but only 7 contested the latest national election. Hence, a substantial proportion of parties have either failed to become institutionalized, or have not persisted intact.

An institutionalized party must continue from election to election; operationally a party is judged to have become institutionalized if it fights more than three national elections. A group that fails to do this is not an established political party, but an ephemeral party. A total of 369 parties can be judged for their capacity to become institutionalized; an additional 32 must be excluded from analysis here for they have been founded so recently that there was not the opportunity to fight a fourth election as of December 31, 1983.[2]

Among would-be political parties, failure to become institutionalized is widespread: 42 percent of all parties examined here were ephemeral, fighting no more than three national elections. Of the 142 ephemeral parties, 61 fought only one election, 48 fought two elections, and 33 fought three. A total of 195 parties have persisted to fight at least four elections.

The complex of national, organizational, and individual factors affecting specific actions by a specific party at one moment in historical time means that we should think of factors *affecting*, rather than determining, the careers of parties. The presence of conditioning influences is some-

---

[1] Three countries in the *Almanac* are excluded because competitive elections have not yet been institutionalized: Greece, Portugal, and Spain. Japan has been excluded because of inadequate documentation of its pre-Second World War party system in a language known to the authors, and Israel because the state was only founded in 1948.

[2] Of the thirty-two untried parties, twenty-seven have yet to win as much as 10 percent of the vote in any election contested. The exceptions are the Belgian Socialistische Partij and Parti Socialiste, the Union pour la Démocratie Française, the Dutch Christen Democratisch Appel, and the British Social Democrats.

times but not invariably associated with a predictable outcome. Association between conditioning influence *a* and outcome *x* is here measured by the correlation statistic lambda.[3] When correlations are substantially less than 1.00, an association is neither necessary nor sufficient cause; it indicates a *tendency* for a given influence to affect a party's career. The less the association between conditioning influences and party careers, the greater the scope for voluntary choices by party leaders in circumstances of uncertainty.

Four factors increase the chances of a nascent party becoming institutionalized.

Origin at the founding of competitive elections. Of parties that contested the first nationwide competitive elections (n = 68), 78 percent succeeded in fighting at least three more elections. The novelty and uncertainties of testing an untried political process were not handicaps. Of those parties that came later, 53 percent succeeded in becoming institutionalized (lambda: 0.04).

Contesting elections under proportional representation. Of parties created in proportional representation systems (n = 161), 60 percent succeeded in becoming institutionalized, thanks to the low barrier for achieving parliamentary representation that characterizes proportional representation. Of parties created in first-past-the-post plurality systems, 41 percent succeeded in becoming institutionalized.[4] Ephemeral parties are more likely under first-past-the-post systems because of the greater difficulty in converting a substantial number of votes into any seats (McAllister and Rose, 1984) (lambda: 0.12).

Based upon organized social group. Of the 265 parties that drew electoral support from voters already institutionalized into major social organizations—class, religious, or agrarian—64 percent succeeded in becoming institutionalized. By contrast, of parties making a catchall appeal to the electorate (Kirchheimer, 1966), without regard to their preexisting institutional commitments, 42 percent became institutionalized. Founding a party upon an organized social group offers greater chance of institutionalization than attempting to create a party without a social base (lambda: 0.11).

Initial success in winning votes. Of the 132 parties that never secured 5.0 percent or more of the vote, 35 percent became institutionalized. By contrast, among those that secured 5.0 percent of the vote at least once, 76 percent succeeded in becoming institutionalized. That there is a rela-

[3] For details on the calculation of lambda, a statistic appropriate for relationships involving nominal variables, see N. Nie and C. H. Hull et al., 1975: 225–26.

[4] For a vigorous rebuttal of the "sociology of politics," see Sartori, 1969: 93–94.

tionship between the ability of a party to win votes and its ability to become established is hardly surprising. What is noteworthy is that the association is imperfect (lambda: 0.30) rather than invariant. Almost one-third of all parties unable to win 5.0 percent of the vote did succeed in becoming institutionalized, and nearly one-quarter of parties polling above the 5.0 percent threshold were ephemeral.

Parties that do not become institutionalized are of two different sorts: those that make no impact upon electoral competition, and those that flash across it like a meteor. Of the ephemeral parties, 61 percent leave no impact, never winning as much as 5.0 percent of the vote. By contrast, 55 parties make a fleeting impact, securing at least 5.0 percent of the vote at least once in their brief career. Precisely because it is new, a flash party can make a disproportionate impact with a limited vote. For example, the Poujadists registered an impact on party competition in the last days of the Fourth Republic by winning 11.7 percent of the vote in 1956, and George Wallace's American Independent party made a big impact upon the 1968 presidential race with 13.5 percent of the vote. Flash parties are not infrequent: they account for 16 percent of all parties examined, although their brief life means that they do not appear so often in electoral lists.

Three factors increase the likelihood of the appearance of flash parties.

The novelty of competitive elections. The less established electoral competition is, the less mobilized the electorate, and thus, the greater the likelihood of a party making an impact and disappearing. Among flash parties, 87 percent appeared before the Second World War. In the post-1945 era, dozens of parties have been formed, but they are less likely to be flash parties. Of the ephemeral parties founded before 1945, 47 percent were flash parties; of the ephemeral parties founded since 1945, only 19 percent have been flash parties (lambda: 0.21).

A catchall electoral appeal. The lack of a well-organized social base of support can be a temporary asset, enabling a party to win voters who are not mobilized by established institutions, or have become demobilized. Among flash parties, 61 percent have been catchall parties, compared to 28 percent for all other parties (lambda: 0.16). Whereas parties with a defined social base can prosper by adding floating voters to a persisting core, catchall parties are vulnerable because they have no persisting core to compensate for the loss of floating voters.

National context. Of the fifty-six flash parties identified in nineteen different countries, ten occurred in the United States, almost one-half the total of twenty-three parties competing in American elections. Flash parties constitute eight of nineteen parties in Iceland, eight of sixteen in Luxembourg, five of twenty-four in Australia, and six of thirty-nine in Germany. Together, these five countries account for two-thirds of all flash parties.

The presence of a large number of flash parties in the oldest party system examined, the United States, is striking, especially as it is not only a phenomenon of a nascent party system, but also of the mature twentieth-century system, e.g., the 1912 Bull Moose Progressives, the 1924 La Follette Progressives, George Wallace in 1968, and John Anderson in 1980.

The logic of labeling parties as ephemeral is that they make a brief intervention in a continuing party system, then disappear, leaving little trace of their unsuccessful effort to become institutionalized. Of the ephemeral parties, 61 percent ended their career by disappearing without a link with a successor party. By contrast, only 23 percent of parties that succeeded in becoming institutionalized disappeared. Of the noninstitutionalized parties, 43 percent appeared from nowhere, being founded without links to any prior party. The remaining 57 percent can best be described as falling stars, usually being created as the result of a split in an established party, then falling out of sight after an election or two.

INTRODUCTED AND EXTROVERTED PRESSURES ON PARTY CAREERS

Once a party becomes successfully institutionalized, its problems commence anew. Having demonstrated that it is an established organization, a party then needs to make a career. Whereas the process of becoming institutionalized need occur only once, the career of a party is a continuing process. Each election is another step in a party's career; an election is likely to produce as many defeated as victorious parties.

To speak of a party's career is to eschew the normative evaluation of success vs. failure and to concentrate attention upon the empirical record of a party's activity in the course of half a century or more. A party's career can take many different forms, both electorally and organizationally, and the two can interact. The analysis of shifts in electoral favor is marginal analysis, concentrating upon movements or the absence of movements of a few percent in votes (Rose and Urwin, 1970; Maguire, 1983). But the career of a party qua organization concerns structural continuity or discontinuity. For a party to cease to exist as an organization is a nonincremental nominal change. Because a party is an organization not an organ, it has no natural life span. While this means that it may persist for centuries (e.g., the British Conservative party or the American Democratic party), it also means that an established party can split (e.g., the British Liberals and successive Australian anti-Socialist parties) or disappear (e.g., the American Whigs or the German Zentrum) on short notice.

Every established organization, not least a political party, must deal with two different but interrelated sets of pressures, those arising from its internal organization, and pressures from its external environment. To ask which is more important in the career of a party is to miss the point: every party must be both introverted *and* extroverted.

In order to maintain a party as an organization, its leadership must be introverted, responding to pressures within as a necessary condition of maintaining the internal cohesion necessary for survival. This requires instrumental activity relevant to the organization (e.g., raising money, organizing meetings, recruiting and nominating candidates) and also expressive activity (e.g., affirming symbols and values that unite supporters). Debates about party programs attract much attention and consume a great deal of time because they are both instrumental and expressive. A program identifies actions that the party might take in office, and affirms the party's commitment to specific values and principles. Party programs also reflect its instrumental nexus with organized interests, e.g., trade unions, business groups, farmers' associations, and churches. Winning an election is not the sole end of party activity; within the organization it may be viewed as a means to the end of enacting a program that satisfies the members' material and symbolic concerns.

In order to maintain the party in the face of electoral competition, its leadership must also be extroverted. To win a constant number of votes in a society that is changing requires positive political action, including the adaptation of practices and principles that had been considered more or less fixed within the party. Adaptation is forced upon party leaders as a condition of electoral survival, for no party can "freeze" the world of which it is a part (Lipset and Rokkan, 1967). Even when a party appears relatively static in its position, it is not frozen; the absence of movement represents a temporary equilibrium resulting from the tension between internal and external pressures. Introverts within a party will emphasize commitment to a party's established symbols and practices; change can be a threat to established cohesion. By contrast, extroverts within the party will emphasize the importance of winning more votes; refusal to change will be seen as a threat to a party's electoral future. It is possible for both sets of pressures to point toward an agreed course of action, but this is by no means certain.

The big trade-off always facing leaders of parties is simply stated: how much weight should be given to external as against internal pressures? The choice is not to be conceived in either/or terms. By definition, if a party is to continue, it must maintain some organizational cohesion. But equally, it must maintain enough relevance to the electoral environment to win some votes. The choice facing politicians is typically a matter of degree, not kind: whether to emphasize the principles that maintain cohesion more and risk gaining fewer votes, or emphasize principles in hopes of winning more support from uncommitted voters. While the trade-offs of party politics cannot be calculated as precisely as the quantities of economics, they do conform to an essential economic proposition, namely, that a party cannot expect to have more of everything.

A stable equilibrium is relatively easy to maintain in a world in which the costs and benefits of choice are relatively constant. Party leaders then know what the alternatives for choice are; the question is how much they should alter their behavior to move up or down a particular preference curve. As Figure 20.1 shows, logically a party may trade a little cohesion for a few more votes, it may trade a lot of cohesion for a lot of votes, or vice versa. If circumstances are very favorable, the trade-off curve will move outward, increasing the base from which it starts. In very unfavorable circumstances, the curve moves closer to the point of origin. In the course of several elections, a party will show at least a little movement up and down this preference curve, seeking more votes by adapting its principles until the internal strains thus produced force the leaders to reaffirm traditional commitments, even at the cost of losing votes, which would then create pressures to reverse direction.

When the environment of parties alters, politicians must adapt if only, as Lampedusa notes, in order to maintain the same relative position. The pressures to change can be favorable to party cohesion. If, for example, a party's principles are made *more* relevant by changes in the environment (say, it is identified with opposition to inflation, or with military defense), it can simultaneously enjoy both electoral success and cohesion. When a preference curve shifts in a party's favor, the choice facing its leaders is between competing goods: whether to maintain its principles at the preexisting level of cohesion and see its vote rise, whether to refine its principles, trading off surplus votes for more cohesive principles, or whether to gain a big increase in votes at a relatively low cost in terms of principles.

Alternatively, changes in the external environment can put major

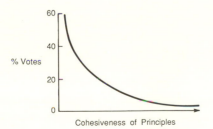

FIGURE 20.1   The trade-offs facing party leaders.

strains on party cohesion by shifting its preference curve in an unfavorable direction. If changes in the society and economy make it harder for a party to win votes by reaffirming established principles, then leaders will have to make changes that risk conflict with introverted partisans without actually gaining votes, or alternatively, remain consistent with the wishes of most committed supporters, and face a continuing loss of votes. For example, when the number of farmers in a society is contracting, a farmers' party faces pressure to appeal to nonagricultural interests, but doing this risks disrupting the cohesion of the established organization by diluting what appeals to the party's most committed supporters.

Whether the environment is stable or unstable, the basic logic remains: party leaders can normally choose a little more cohesion and a little less electoral success, or they can choose a little more electoral success and a little less cohesion. Because parties have multiple goals, their leaders must constantly be making trade-offs. As long as the terms of trade are within established and acceptable parameters, the party leaders can adapt their behavior, balancing different pressures. But there is no assurance that a party will always be able to maintain both internal cohesion and electoral strength. When countries suffer major disruptions, such as defeat in war or the overthrow of a regime, there is a prima facie assumption that discontinuities in the political system will be reflected in discontinuities in the party system.

The career of a political party is defined by *how* it persists as well as by whether it persists. A party that persists by adapting its behavior may be unchanged in nominal form, but adaptation necessarily involves substantive alterations. The British Labour party of Michael Foot was not the same as the Labour party of Harold Wilson, nor was Wilson's party that of Keir Hardie. Neil Kinnock's goal is to make the party he now leads different from the party that Michael Foot led to electoral disaster. The Italian Christian Democratic party of the 1980s is not the same as the party in the cold war era of the 1940s, and the Republican party of Ronald Reagan is not the same as the Republican party of Abraham Lincoln.

To say that a party ceases to exist can be true in the organizational sense, but it overlooks the genealogical continuities that create a legacy between as well as within party organizations. A split causes the demise of one party, but it does so by creating two parties, each of which may claim to be the heir of their common antecedent. If two parties merge, the result may be the organizational demise of the partners to the merger, but the resulting institution is hardly new in the sense of being independent of preexisting parties. The complete mobilization of the electorate through generations of universal suffrage has created a situation in which new parties are as likely to gain votes by inheritance as by appeals *de novo*. With no new section of the population to mobilize for the first time, a so-called new party can simply be a different combination of preexisting political groups.

The career of a political party can take any one of four different courses. At one extreme, a party may persist intact without any organizational change. A second alternative is that a party can persist with only marginal modifications, keeping the same name but occasionally losing a splinter group or incorporating elements from another party. The third and most complex alternative is that a party can be disrupted. Structural changes may result in the disappearance of its name, but organizationally it leaves a readily discernible legacy, because the party has become merged in another party, has split into two parties, or is closely linked by subjective identification with a successor party. At an extreme, a party can disappear without leaving any discernible legacy. From the foregoing, we would expect parties to vary substantially in their careers. The historical record in the *International Almanac* makes it possible to see which career patterns are most and least common (see Table 20.1).

Persists intact (33 percent). A party that fights elections from decade to decade under the same name, without any splinters or incorporating another party by merger, can be said to persist completely intact. Almost

TABLE 20.1   Alternative Careers of Political Parties
in Western Nations

	Number	%
Persists intact	64	33
Persists with marginal modifications	43	22
Structural change:		
Merger	(26)	(13)
Split	(11)	(6)
Subjective legacy	(6)	(3)
TOTAL	43	22
Disappears	45	23
TOTAL	195	100

SOURCE: Calculated from data for nineteen Western nations in Mackie and Rose (1982), for institutionalized parties contesting at least three elections and securing a minimum of one percent of the vote in at least one election.

one-third of political parties can claim to persist completely intact from their foundation. The category includes such well-known and electorally successful parties as the Canadian Conservatives and the New Zealand National party and such lesser parties as the Danish Radicals and the Dutch Staatkundig Gereformeerde Partij. For a party to persist intact is not evidence that it remains unchanged; the opposite is the case. To persist for decades without any organizational alteration is evidence of continuing and successful adaptation to external challenges in ways that maintain internal integration. This "happy" trade-off is the desire of nearly every party leader—but the careers of most parties show that it is difficult to sustain indefinitely.

Marginal modifications (22 percent). A party can continue fighting elections from decade to decade under the same name yet from time to time undergo marginal modification as a consequence of losing a splinter group, or alternatively, through the accession of a lesser party in a merger. For example, the Democratic party in the United States has had a substantial number of breakaway groups, both to the right (states' rights parties) and to the left (Henry Wallace's Progressive party). Yet its organizational core has continued intact. Similarly, the British Conservatives have persisted while absorbing a variety of groups breaking away from the Liberal and Labour parties since 1885. Modification through merger can be an advantage when the terms are unequal, that is, the group being incorporated augments the receiving party without swamping it. An occasional split may have advantages, insofar as the group that splits off is small and its departure substantially reduces the conflict between internal and external pressures.

Structural change (22 percent).

1. *Merger* (13 percent). If two parties join in a merger, the new party contains the organizational assets of two predecessors. Insofar as the merger is well conceived, then such structural change may be the best way for some parties to respond to external pressures that they cannot meet separately. For example, in the Netherlands, separate Catholic and Protestant parties, confronted with declining confessional loyalties, have combined to form a Christian Democratic Appeal. Parties that have fought enough elections to become institutionalized without winning as many votes and seats as leaders might like can seek to further their political goals by merger with a larger party. In Norway, the Social Democratic Workers party split from the Labour party in 1919 when the latter joined the Third International, but after the former fought two elections as a weak competitor and the Labour party left the International, the Social Democrats merged back into the Labour party in 1927.

2. *Splits* (6 percent). If a party splits, the old party organization ceases

to exist, but two (or more) parties result. The frequency of established parties splitting is relatively low: only 12 of 195 parties examined here had their careers terminated by a split. Belgium offers a rich example of party splits. In the face of linguistic conflicts between French and Flemish speakers in the past twenty years, the formerly bilingual Christian Democrats, and Liberal and Socialist parties have each split into two separate monolingual parties. Insofar as there are strong conflicts between internal and external pressures, the most suitable way for groups at loggerheads to respond may be for each to form its own party organization.

3. *Subjective identification* (3 percent). The intervention of a war or the imposition of authoritarian rule may put a party into suspension, and its assets may be sequestered. Subsequently, a party may be founded that claims lineal descent from an older party, and gives evidence that this is the case, having some of the same leaders, appealing to similar groups within the electorate, and invoking continuity with the past. For example, in Ireland a Republican party calling itself Sinn Féin has appeared at three different times to contest a series of elections. While the intervening periods often emphasize splits within the Republican movement, the claim of the organizers of each successive Sinn Féin party is that it and it alone is the "true" heir to the original party that achieved Irish independence. Similarly, the Christian Democratic party of postfascist Italy claims descent from the pre-Mussolini Partito Popolare. The DC's initial postwar leader, Alcide de Gasperi, was the last political secretary of the Popular party.

Disappears (23 percent). A party disappears if, and only if, it ceases to contest elections and leaves no identifiable successor through splits, merger, or subjective identification. Insofar as this is the case, then a party has failed completely. The Nazi party of the German Third Reich is a conspicuous example of complete failure; its leaders and organizational assets have been dispersed, and no successor party claims to be its heir.

Empirical analysis supports the big trade-off model of the careers of political parties. The theory emphasizes the conflicting pressures upon parties from internal and external sources. Given such pressures, we would expect most political parties to be incapable of remaining completely intact organizationally. This is the case: 67 percent of all established parties undergo some form of organizational change during their career, ranging from marginal modification to complete disappearance. Yet it can also be said that 78 percent of all parties demonstrate at least some degree of persistence. Most parties do not remain completely intact, but a degree of continuity is demonstrated even in the face of splits and mergers. The fourfold differentiation of party careers avoids the false dichotomy between persistence intact and complete disappearance. These alternatives are end points on a continuum; they are not the only possible career that a party organization can have. The median party is not at an extreme; it has experienced marginal modification.

TESTING THE CAUSES OF DIFFERENCES IN PARTY CAREERS

In the face of such variable outcomes, we should not ask whether parties persist or disappear, but rather *why* do some parties persist whereas others disappear? The process that determines which parties persist and which fail to persist could reflect any one of a great variety of theoretical rationales. A simple Darwinian theory of the survival of the fittest would postulate that at the first national election a large number of parties would appear, each testing how much support it could gain in an unprecedented and therefore uncertain competition; the parties that won a significant amount of support would then persist, and those that did not would fail. At the other extreme, a public choice theory might assume that before each election, politicians would review their assets, and form election-specific parties that would maximize their current net appeal. Institutionalist theories could postulate that parties would persist as long as there was not a major system shock, like repudiation of the constitution or a change in the electoral system, causing all established parties to collapse in the face of a systemwide shock, and new parties to emerge.

To ask which theory best explains the persistence or failure of parties is to assume what remains to be proven, namely, that the careers of parties are more or less fully determined by one or two factors. But the conflicting pressures described above face party leaders with *choices*: what trade-off do the leaders want to risk in conditions of considerable uncertainty? A choice of trade-offs implies a degree of voluntarism reflecting the values and knowledge of party leaders. Sartori (1969: 93) emphasizes: "The greater the range of politics, the smaller the role of 'objective factors.' All our *objective certainties* are increasingly exposed to, and conditioned by, *political uncertainty*."

To merit testing here, a theory must first of all specify contingent circumstances in which some parties should persist, and others disappear. It cannot assume away evidence of failure by stipulating that all politicians are rational, and act upon rational expectations. Such an assumption begs the question posed by the big trade-off model: under what circumstances is it rational for some politicians to maintain their organization, and other politicians to accept disruption or risk disappearance?

Logically, two different types of influences may affect the careers of political parties: characteristics of a national party system and characteristics of types of parties. Under the first heading are such influences as the introduction of proportional representation or the fall of a constitutional regime, affecting all parties within a country whether left or right, religious or secular. Under the second heading are such influences as a working-class or agrarian base that may affect only one party within a nation, but all parties of the same type in many nations.

CHARACTERISTICS OF PARTY SYSTEMS

The importance of early origins. The best known theory of the careers of parties, developed by S. M. Lipset and Stein Rokkan (1967), starts by considering the historical emergence of a series of political cleavages—church vs. state; national vs. local or peripheral identities; industrial vs. agricultural economy; and industrial workers vs. the urban middle class—out of which a nationwide competitive party system emerges. While the introduction of nationwide party competition occurs at different points in time among Western nations, analytically it represents the crossing of a common threshold. Because parties are seen as based on established group cleavages within society, they can be expected to persist at least as long as the groups themselves are significant in size in a society.

In developing their theory, Lipset and Rokkan argue that the early establishment of a party gives it a distinctive competitive advantage. A party that starts with the founding of electoral competition is able to mobilize voters who have no prior electoral commitment. By contrast, parties created subsequently will often have to demobilize voters from the ranks of other parties as a precondition of mobilizing them as supporters. Furthermore, an established party becomes an organization with an interest in survival for its own sake. The result is described as "the freezing of the major party alternatives." Lipset and Rokkan (1967: 50; italics in the original) conclude: *"The party systems of the 1960s reflect, with few but significant exceptions, the cleavage structures of the 1920s."* The importance attributed to early institutionalization as a positive factor in the survival of parties is not unique to party politics; for example, Wilensky (1975) concludes that the early institutionalization of a welfare state program is the most important factor determining the contemporary size of a program.

Older parties are more likely to persist. The Lipset-Rokkan hypothesis can be empirically tested by making comparisons between the careers of parties that originated: (a) with the founding of the regime and afterwards; (b) with the introduction of universal suffrage or afterwards; and (c) with the introduction of proportional representation, a major system shock in most Western party systems.

Parties organized at the foundation of competitive elections are in fact *less* likely to persist intact than parties founded later (see Table 20.2). Whereas 15 percent of founding parties have persisted intact, 39 percent of parties founded subsequently have remained intact. The median founding party has undergone structural change, whereas the median postfoundation party has simply undergone a minor modification.

One reason why an older party can be handicapped is that an old party mobilizes voters under established rules; a party can be successful *because* the electorate is narrowly defined, or because of a distinctive bias in an electoral system. The introduction of universal suffrage or of proportional representation can be a system shock disrupting parties institutionalized under an earlier system. Once again, the age of a party is a handicap, not an asset. Even though a party has the opportunity to mobilize support prior to the introduction of universal suffrage, it is less likely to persist intact (see Table 20.3). Only 8 percent of parties founded prior to the introduction of universal suffrage persist intact, as against 40 percent of those founded after the electorate has already been mobilized.

Changing the rules for counting votes also has a positive effect upon the ability of a party to persist intact. Only 14 percent of parties founded before the introduction of proportional representation have survived intact, compared to 67 percent of parties founded after the introduction of proportional representation (see Table 20.4). The association is reasonable, for proportional representation gives a party seats in approximate proportion to its number of votes. Under PR there is little incentive to merge with another party; in a first-past-the-post system, where the threshold of electoral success is much higher, the rewards and penalties for getting more votes are much greater.

In the historical context of the twentieth century, the older a party, the

TABLE 20.2   Founding Parties Are Less Likely to Persist Intact

Career	Founding Party (N = 53) %	Postfoundation (N = 142) %
Intact	15	39
Marginal modification	28	20
Structural change	40	15
Disappears	17	25

Lambda = 0. 09.

TABLE 20.3   Parties Founded before Universal Suffrage Are Less Likely
to Persist Intact

	Preuniversal Suffrage (35) %	Postuniversal Suffrage (157) %
Intact	8	40
Marginal modification	26	21
Structural change	60	13
Fails	5	22

Lambda = 0.15.

TABLE 20.4   Parties Founded before Proportional Representation Are
Less Likely to Persist Intact

	Founded pre-PR (60) %	Post-PR (97) %
Intact	15	44
Marginal modification	22	19
Structural change	45	8
Disappears	18	29

Lambda = 0.17. (Excludes thirty-eight parties contesting elections in countries without proportional representation.)

greater the likelihood it has been subject to the major system shocks of
war, the overthrow of a constitutional regime, or both. In the extreme case
of Germany, parties founded in the Wilhelmine Reich have since seen Germany ruled by three different constitutional regimes, and twice subject to
military defeat. Even countries that have not experienced a regime change
have been impacted twice by world war. The First World War administered major shocks to social systems and political values. The Second
World War made military occupation a fact of life in Continental Europe;
political organization then took the form of armed resistance to an occupying army instead of electoral organization (cf. Urwin, 1972: ch. 1). Ger-

many, Italy, Austria, Finland, and France have each adopted a new regime at least once after military defeat.

There is a clear tendency for parties to be substantially altered by the shock of world war. Only 12 percent of parties founded before the First World War have remained completely intact, as against 35 percent of parties of interwar foundation, and 59 percent of parties founded since 1945 (see Table 20.5). The median party founded before the First World War has since been disrupted by structural change; by contrast, the median party founded between the wars has experienced only marginal modification, and the median post-1945 party has persisted completely intact.

The likelihood of a party disappearing when a regime fails is substantial (see Table 20.6). When a party was founded before a regime collapsed, in 42 percent of all instances it disappeared, compared to 17 percent of parties contesting elections under a regime that has persisted. Where a regime has collapsed, the median party has undergone structural change. Where no collapse has occurred, the median party has experienced marginal modification.

On all tests, the Lipset-Rokkan theory of older parties being more likely to persist is rejected. Parties that were created at the beginning of the regime, before universal suffrage, before the introduction of proportional representation, before the First World War, or before the creation of the current regime are less likely to persist intact. The metaphor of the freezing of party alternatives is inappropriately rigid. It is introverted, assuming that the environment will maintain a constant and low ambient temperature precluding any prospect of the demobilization of voters. It seeks

TABLE 20.5 World Wars Make It More Difficult for Parties to Persist Intact

	Foundation		
	Pre-1914 (76) %	Interwar (65) %	Post-1945 (54) %
Intact	12	35	59
Marginal modification	26	21	17
Structural change	41	11	9
Disappears	21	32	15

Lambda = 0.17. (The interwar period includes the two world wars; that is, it extends from August 1914 to May 1945.)

TABLE 20.6   The Collapse of a Regime Makes Parties More Likely to Disappear

	Regime Persists (150) %	Regime Collapses (45) %
Intact	39	13
Marginal modification	23	18
Structural change	21	27
Fails	17	42

Lambda = 0.10.

to impose a fixed and unalterable structure upon the ebb and flow of party competition.

The positive insight in the Lipset-Rokkan analysis is the emphasis on the *continuity* of parties. Older parties are less likely to disappear completely than newer parties (see Table 20.2–6), that is, not to leave any legacy. Older parties have usually disappeared in name but not entirely in substance; they have merged their assets with another party, or bequeathed an identification to another party, or have generated two new parties by a process of splitting. To point to the continuity between one part of an older party and another part of a newer party is not so much a demonstration of the success of the older party as of the necessary persistence of electoral blocs and combinations of politicians who continue to fight elections even though their previous party has disappeared.

The appropriate metaphor for viewing the role of party politicians and voters emphasizes adaptation, such as the cybernetic concept of steering. The environment can be visualized as a sea, sometimes made turbulent by unexpected or unwelcome changes. Within a sometimes tempestuous environment, politicians and voters must be prepared to abandon one ship and change to another if they wish to reach their desired haven, and may even be under great pressure to keep afloat (Oakeshott, 1951: 22; Deutsch, 1963).

CHARACTERISTICS OF PARTIES

The capacity of parties to respond to system shocks is a variable, not a constant. The influence of system changes upon parties is one of degree, but it is by no means determinant. Therefore, we must also consider differential characteristics of parties *within* a given party system as influences upon party careers.

The persistence of parties is a function of their social base. A political party exists to organize electoral support from election to election. Insofar as its electoral support is also organized on a persisting basis, then its chances of continuation should be enhanced. Insofar as the social group that provides the electoral base of a party is diminishing (e.g., farmers) or has disappeared (e.g., an ethnic minority that has seceded or been expelled), then the party is pressured to change structurally, or risk disappearance. Insofar as a party lacks any social base at all, being dependent upon a catchall appeal to whatever voters are floating loose at the moment (Kirchheimer, 1966), then it is most likely to swing between electoral extremes, with structural change or disappearance the result of an extreme downward turn.

Party organization and social organization can be viewed as two complementary aspects of a network of social relationships. The conventional Socialist model of a party is that it is a working-class party drawing support from voters whose lives are more or less enclosed within a network of linked and overlapping institutions: the party, the trade-union movement, cooperative societies, and cultural associations. Parties of religious adherents, especially Catholic parties, are similarly one part of a network of parochial relationships organized nationwide and meant to affect nonpolitical as well as political activities. Farmers' parties, too, reflect the importance of relationships within a network of associations between farmers as producers, as neighbors in rural communes, as participants in rural cooperatives, and so forth. The existence of a single-interest claim means that a party need not restrict its activities to electoral competition; its institutions can continue between elections.

Arguably, a stable social base is a better guarantee of the persistence of a political party than ideological consensus. The greater the importance of ideology within a party, the greater the risk that ideological discussion will lead to ideological disputes, and then to splits. An ideological party may be so guided by introverted signals derived from its principles and goals that it tends to ignore changes in the external environment, thus failing to adapt. Social cohesion is a unifying influence. People who disagree about issues and political principles can still vote together if they work together, pray together, or farm in the same community. Social loyalties can be used to maintain a party's cohesion in the face of political differences.

Changes in social structure result in parties relying upon a "crescive" or a "contracting" social base. A party whose social base of support is increasing in the population has a crescive base, for example, a labor party in a society with an increasing proportion of the electorate belonging to trade unions. Parties relying upon groups declining in size in society have a contracting base. When viewed in terms of annual percentage rates, social changes may appear slight, but when compounded across decades and generations, their cumulative effect upon parties can be great.

In the twentieth century, three social groups linked with political parties have tended to contract. There has been a decline in the rural population, implying a demise or contraction of agrarian parties; a decline in religious practice, implying the contraction or demise of confessional parties; and an increase in economic affluence and nonmanual employment, implying a contraction of Communist or Socialist parties identified with the working class. The crescive cleavage linked to parties has been the rise in trade-union membership. However, in the extreme case of Sweden, union membership is so widespread that instead of dividing the electorate, elections can divide union members. It could be hypothesized that the general diffusion of affluence in the postwar era has increased pressures on Socialist and Communist parties to split, because divisions between the haves and have-nots may divide manual workers into prosperous and less prosperous, or advantaged and disadvantaged.

Although affecting the likelihood of a party becoming institutionalized, the social bases of parties have very little influence upon a party persisting intact (see Table 20.7). Only agrarian parties show a tendency to be influ-

TABLE 20.7   The Effect of Social Bases of Support upon Party Persistence

	Working Class (44) %	Religion (36) %	Middle Class (23) %	Agrarian (29) %	Language (10) %	Catchall (68) %	Total (195) %
Intact	34	47	39	7	40	34	33
Marginal modification	40	6	9	24	40	17	18
Structural adaptation	18	28	22	28	0	20	21
Disappears	9	19	30	41	20	29	28
Lambda	0.02	0.00	0.00	0.08	0.00	0.00	0.00

NOTE: The number of parties recorded in the first six columns total more than 195 because an individual party may have more than one social base. Fifteen of the 195 parties included in the table have multiple social bases.

enced by their social base; they are less likely to persist intact and more likely to disappear. This is consistent with the contracting size of the agricultural vote. Working-class parties are no more likely to remain intact, nor are they more likely to split. Notwithstanding declining church attendance, religious parties do not show any particular tendency to disappear.

The independence of a party's career from its social base is shown by the fact that catchall parties resemble the universe of parties. They are slightly more likely than average to remain intact or to disappear, but the differences from the overall patterns are statistically negligible. The leaders of catchall parties appear to use the flexibility of their electoral base to adapt to external pressures with as much success as parties whose well-defined social base may restrict adaptability as well as stabilize votes.

The more successful a party is in electoral competition, the greater its likelihood of persistence. Party competition necessarily differentiates parties, for every election produces lots of losers as well as one or more winners. This is true whether victory is measured in terms of winning a government office, or winning additional votes. The two definitions are not identical. In parliamentary systems, coalition government is the norm, and bargaining between parties in Parliament rather than the election outcome often determines who governs.

Winning a share of power in government is conventionally defined as a mark of success, but it can also strengthen conflicting pressures within a party, altering the balance between internal and external forces. When a party enters office, its field of action is changed fundamentally. The internal life of the party organization is no longer the sole or immediate concern of the party's leaders; instead, the pressures of government are likely to come first. The pressures of office, institutionalized by large bureaucratic ministries with established program commitments enacted by predecessors, often force party leaders to act in ways that would not occur in opposition. In office, party leaders can learn that there are "some things stronger than parties" (Rose, 1984: ch. 8).

The greater the pressures of the external environment upon the party-in-government, the greater the potential risk of conflict if the party organization outside government is concerned with what government does, as well as with who governs. There is the risk of frustration, if leaders do not follow policies laid down in opposition. Two familiar sayings sum up the conflicts: the ministerial view that "Socialism is what a Socialist government does," and the activist fear, "There may be Socialists in office, but never a Socialist government." The problem is not distinctive to the left. Right-wing ideologues supporting a Reagan government can note contradictions between what Ronald Reagan has said and what President Reagan does—and the same is true of the speeches and actions of Margaret Thatcher's government in Britain.

Participation in government does make a difference to the careers of parties. Those parties that are often in government are less likely to disappear; only 13 percent do so, compared to 34 percent of parties that are rarely in government (see Table 20.8). But parties in government do not maintain sufficient agreement on the rewards of office to remain completely intact; 69 percent of parties that are often in office have undergone either marginal modification or structural change. For a party rarely in office, there are two major alternatives. If it is sensitive to internal pressures, it remains intact though its success in achieving government office is low; alternatively, it disappears because it has little reason to persist.

Winning votes has more influence than winning office upon the career of a political party (a lambda of 0.14 as against a lambda of 0.04; see Tables 20.8 and 20.9). Parties that never win as much as 10 percent of the vote at one national election are much more likely to disappear; 47 percent in this category do so as against 4 percent of parties that win at least half the vote in at least one election. But the vote needed to persist may not be large. Among parties that win at least 10 percent of the vote once, there is at least a 90 percent probability of not disappearing compared to a 53 percent probability for parties which never cross this low threshold of popular support. But parties that poll few votes can still remain intact: 39 percent of parties that never win as much as 10 percent of the vote remain completely intact, compared to 36 percent of parties that win at least 50 percent of the popular vote once.

TABLE 20.8   Participation in Government Makes Parties Less Likely to Disappear

| | Participation in government | | |
	Often (55) %	Sometimes (46) %	Infrequent or Never (94) %
Intact	31	32	34
Marginal modification	29	32	13
Structural change	27	22	19
Disappears	13	13	34

Lambda = 0.04. (Often in government = 50 percent or more of the time; sometimes = 10 percent to 49 percent; infrequent or never = less than 10 percent of the time.)

TABLE 20.9 Winning Votes Reduces a Party's Risk of Disappearing

	Highest % share of vote ever won					
	1–9 (70) %	10–19 (44) %	20–29 (25) %	30–39 (16) %	40–49 (18) %	50+ (22) %
Intact	39	32	40	25	6	36
Marginal modification	4	30	28	9	50	36
Structural change	10	23	20	50	44	23
Disappears	47	16	12	6	6	4

Lambda = 0.14.

THE IMPORTANCE OF VOLUNTARISM

The most striking feature of the careers of parties is their variability. Whatever the control used in examining the universe of parties, a substantial number persist completely intact or with marginal modifications; a substantial fraction undergo structural change yet leave an identifiable legacy; and a lot disappear. Variability contrasts with the Lipset-Rokkan model of a party system determined by a unique configuration of crises, and more or less "freezing" thereafter. It also contrasts with a Downs (1957) model of competition generating a stable equilibrium between parties competing for votes with sufficient success so that each maintains its position as a vote-mobilizing organization. As the essays by the editors of this volume emphasize, the careers of parties reflect a multiplicity of influences and can have a variety of outcomes.

Tests of the causes of variability are most significant for what they reject. First of all, the idea that parties are determined by social structure which causes their fortunes to wax and wane with social change is conclusively rejected. There is no association between a party's social base and its career. Second, the theory that parties originating at the founding of a system are most likely to persist by being frozen into a system is conclusively rejected. Older parties are less likely to persist intact than parties established after the formative crises of a political system.

What then best explains the weak association between hypothesized determinants of a party's career and observed empirical outcomes? The answer is voluntarism, the actions of party leaders. By definition, the big trade-off facing parties is a choice. Since politics is about the articulation of conflicting views, politicians may disagree about the relative weight to be given internal as against external pressures upon the organization. Party officials are likely to put maintenance of the organization first, even at some cost in electoral support. Ideologues, too, will tend to be oriented toward goals within the party, whatever the cost to the party's electoral fortunes. By contrast, politicians who see seats in Parliament and participation in government as an end in itself, and a party as but a means to this end, will tend to stress the importance of winning votes as a precondition of winning office. Office may be sought for micromotives (jobs for party leaders) as well as macromotives (to carry out a party program). The important point here is that party leaders concerned with government will put external pressures first, even to the extent of being prepared to see the party's distinctive positions merged in an electoral alliance or a coalition government. As Wilson's case study of France in this volume shows, many French politicians have shown themselves far more adaptable than would be allowed for by simple deterministic theories.

The big trade-off model emphasizes that competition takes place *within* parties as well as between them (Rose, 1964). Within a party, there is competition between those who put internal goals first, and those who give first priority to electoral and governmental pressures. The art of party leadership is to balance conflicting pressures in order to maintain a party intact and have it reasonably successful in electoral competition.

To speak of trade-offs by party leadership is to move a long way from the deterministic language of the sociology of politics. It is to realize that in party politics the biggest choices are in fact open, not predetermined. The will of party leaders is often grossly exaggerated vis-à-vis the more or less intractable problems of government. When party leaders are in office, the external pressures of government tend to count for more than the wants, intentions, and choices of individual incumbents. But in the direction of parties, the choices of party leaders are of first importance, extending far beyond effects upon competition for marginal votes. The voluntary choices of party leaders affect the career of the party itself. They determine whether the party persists completely intact or with marginal modifications, undergoes structural change, or disappears.

REFERENCES

Deutsch, K. W. 1963. *The nerves of government.* New York: Free Press.
Downs, A. 1957. *An economic theory of democracy.* New York: Harper and Row.
Hogwood, B. W., and B. G. Peters. 1982. *Policy succession.* Brighton: Harvester Press.

Kirchheimer, O. 1966. The transformation of the Western European party systems. In *Political parties and political development*, ed. J. LaPalombara and M. Weiner. Princeton: Princeton University Press, 177–200.

Lipset, S. M., and S. Rokkan. 1967. Cleavage structures, party systems and voter alignments: An introduction. In *Party systems and voter alignments*, ed. Lipset and Rokkan. New York: Free Press, 1–64.

McAllister, I. 1981. Party organization and minority nationalism. *European Journal of Political Research*, 9: 237–55.

———, and R. Rose. 1984. *The nationwide competition for votes: The 1983 British election*. London: Frances Pinter.

Mackie, T. T., and R. Rose. 1982. *The international almanac of electoral history*. London: Macmillan, and New York: Facts on File.

Maguire, M. 1983. Is there still persistence? Electoral change in Western Europe, 1948 to 1979. In *Western European party systems: Continuity and change*, ed. H. Daalder and P. Mair. Beverly Hills: Sage Publications, 67–94.

Nie, N., and C. H. Hull. 1975. *SPPS: Statistical package for the social sciences*. New York: McGraw-Hill.

Oakeshott, M. 1951. *Political education*. Cambridge: Bowes & Bowes.

Punnett, R. M. 1981. *Alternating governments: The inefficient secret of British politics?* Glasgow: University of Strathclyde Studies in Public Policy No. 93.

Rose, R. 1964. Parties, factions and tendencies in Britain. *Political Studies* 12: 33–46.

———. 1984. *Do parties make a difference?* London: Macmillan, and Chatham, N.J.: Chatham House.

———, and D. W. Urwin. 1970. Persistence and change in Western party systems since 1945. *Political Studies* 18: 287–319.

———, and T. T. Mackie. 1983. Incumbency in government: Asset or liability? In *Western European party systems*, ed. H. Daalder and P. Mair. Beverly Hills: Sage Publications, 115–37.

Sartori, G. 1969. From the sociology of politics to political sociology. In *Politics and the social sciences*, ed. S. M. Lipset. New York: Oxford University Press, 65–100.

Urwin, D. W. 1972. *Western Europe since 1945*. London: Longmans.

Wilensky, H. 1975. *The welfare state and equality*. Berkeley: University of California Press.

PART VII | Conclusions

TWENTY-ONE

The Challengers
and the Party Systems

PETER H. MERKL

Every major democratic election leaves in its wake large numbers of disappointed voters who believe that the party of their present or former allegiance has "failed" them. Whether *their* party won or lost—and parties of course advance or decline simply in the natural course of politics—it may indeed have failed in its linkage to some of the groups that had constituted its basis of support, as Kay Lawson explains in chapter 2 of this book; or it may be "failing" because of the recent systemic changes in advanced democracies that are often referred to as the "decline of parties." Their sharp disappointment constitutes the normally occurring emotional detritus of democratic politics. Such "failure," however, has rarely involved the permanent decline or disappearance of a particular major party or the basic realignment of a party system. Like old soldiers, it seems, old parties just about never die no matter how often they may have disgraced themselves. Worse yet, they do not even seem to have the decency to fade away in accord with long-range, secular erosion processes at their particular base (Dalton, Flanagan, and Beck, 1984: 95–96, 130–32). Instead, they hang on tenaciously to their strategic positions in the party system, taking advantage of the voters' inertia and lack of viable options and perhaps attracting new groups of supporters to make up for those whom they have alienated. Given this tenacity, or "nonfailure" of the established parties in defending the ramparts of the system against all challenges, we need to turn our attention not just to today's linkage problems but also to how the challengers have fared in different kinds of party systems.

The recent growth of alternative forms of political action and of linkage failure of the kind described in these chapters can be viewed from several points of departure. One is from the point of view of the established parties, the defenders of the system. This can be from the perspective of the stability of the established party system, such as the governing parties and their form of "party government" or it could be from that of the strength and unity required to get into power at the next elections or soon thereafter. But it could just as well be from the perspective of the challengers or of groups of dissidents from the established parties; there is only a formal line of distinction between dissident factions pushing for their policy preferences from within a party or their secession and agitation as an alternative movement outside it—such as new or neglected old minorities, or rebellious new generational groups such as those that have been described as examples of the "new politics" (see Inglehart, 1977; Baker, Dalton, and Hildebrandt, 1981: ch. 6).

There is also the perspective of systemic change: protest movements and attempts at founding new parties are hardly new,[1] but this time the rise of a new political agenda, of new groups and problems, coincides crucially with a weakening, or at least a transformation, of modern party politics and of government itself. The new politics, or postindustrial politics, has a distinctive agenda, much of which is shared by many of the alternative groups examined in this book, environmental issues, feminism, questions of cultural (ethnic or religious) identity, disarmament, and of increased citizen participation in governmental decisionmaking (Dalton, Flanagan, and Beck, 1984: 19–20, 54–56, 66–67, 109–10). On the other hand, the once-central role of parties and the representative process in democratic states has been shrinking and increasingly been shared by such rival agenda-setters as interest groups and the media. We need to remind ourselves that the role of parties in modern government is itself not much older than a hundred years in most advanced democracies and that the parties in this period have undergone a great deal of change in form and political role (see Lawson, 1980: 3–4). In view of this protean character of parties, the rise of new forms of political action should not surprise us, nor need we put it beyond the pale of legitimacy. Government itself, by the same token, has changed tremendously in the last fifty years alone, greatly expanding its role in society and delegating many policy functions that are, or were once, under democratic control to a bureaucracy grown vast over the years, or to neocorporatist interest intermediation beyond the electoral process. Is it any wonder that many groups of citizens affected by the ever-growing reach of "irresponsible" government are developing alternative channels and procedures for being heard?

---

[1] However, there are notable differences, for example, between the new kind of ethnic movements, say of Scotland and Wales, or of Brittany, and the older nationalist irredentism of Ireland or Eastern Europe. The adherents of contemporary ethnic or nationalist movements in democratic countries are generally more interested in asserting their individual ethnic identity than they are in preserving or recreating an ethnic folk society, and more likely to be content with increasing economic opportunities for their kind than to aim at taking over the entire state.

Kinds of Party Failure

It is important for the comparative study of the case studies before us to define major party failure so as to exclude extreme interpretations. This investigation is not meant to explain the normal wax and wane of majority voting from one election to the next, or the equally normal process by which a governing party or coalition gradually loses its support and, eventually, its grip on power. This by itself is not what we mean by party failure, although the phenomenon we are concerned with may indeed speed the drop in the vote of any established party. Our kind of major failure presumes one of two likely scenarios. One is the presence of a stable relationship between a certain clientele of an established party such as, say, Scottish voters—and perhaps members as well—of the Labour party, or young (under twenty-five) Labour voters in Edinburgh, and their party in power or in the opposition. When the Labour party suddenly loses the loyalty of a substantial part of such a group over critical issues, these voters become available for either the major established rival parties, the Conservatives or Liberals, or for an alternative movement such as the ones discussed in these essays. To speak with Albert O. Hirschman, they have made their choice among "exit, voice, and loyalty" and chosen to exit, possibly after prolonged efforts at "voicing" their discontent and being unable to elicit a satisfactory solution from their party.

Whether the dissidents go to the opposition or to an alternative movement depends, of course, also on the opposition party (or parties) which may make a well-calculated effort to woo them by offering them a modicum of what they seek, in this case recognition of their quest for Scottish home rule. If the Conservatives or resurgent Liberals had succeeded in intercepting the Scottish nationalist voters of 1974 from among the traditional following of Labour, it would have been only a case of the normal fluctuations between the established two major British parties, as indeed it turned out to be five years later.

The other scenario presumes only a likelihood of continued voter allegiance, say, among the sons and daughters of the traditional clientele of an established party against a background of salient social change. The most obvious such kind of change is generational: the party "fails"—perhaps because of the inflexibility of its leadership or of its older members, or simply for lack of consensus among disparate constituencies—to appeal to the young generation in as convincing a manner as it did to its older clientele in the past. Given the passage of time and notable achievements of past struggles, for example, working-class parties, and perhaps all social movements, have a way of resting too long on their laurels, convinced that they have won the most important battles in the world and slow to realize that their pride and loyalty are not necessarily hereditary. The young, moreover, may already have experienced a very different kind of society, already beyond the concern with the battles won and focusing instead on new issues and new complaints. Upward social mobility may also have placed the young in a higher social bracket than their elders—perhaps advancing from unskilled to skilled labor or from blue collar to the "service classes"—or it may have eroded the hard and fast class and occupational barriers of old and introduced a much more fluid and diversified form of stratification that no longer lends itself to the simple dichotomies of the old militant slogans (Dalton et al., 1984: 29–30).

Another way of looking at the failure of the major parties, as Peter Pulzer shows in his contribution on the ethnic parties of Great Britain, fastens upon such signs of voter alienation as the declining turnout at elections over the last three decades (see Dittrich and Johansen, 1983: 95–114) or the shrinking percentage of the vote for both Labour and the Conservatives. With the latter, of course, comes a concomitant increase of the voting share of minor parties, at least in the popular vote which in Great Britain, thanks to the electoral law, is translated into only a negligible share of the seats in the House of Commons. It is worth mentioning that since 1945 there has almost always been a parliamentary majority for either Labour or the Conservatives even though neither of them ever commanded a majority of the popular vote. Even before the recent onslaught by minor parties, in other words, the established major parties have usually been shielded from failure by the extreme distortions of the single-member plurality—or first-past-the-post—system of voting. American parties have benefited from the same electoral law and even lower turnout. In the Federal Republic, under a different electoral law and high turnout, there have also been signs of electoral alienation from the major parties (see Kaltefleiter, 1980: 597–608).

Since a mere switch from Labour to the Conservatives, or even the Liberals, as we have said, is only normal fluctuation, flocking to a new or alternative group implies also the failure of the other established parties to attract the dissidents of the first-named party. With many of the alternative movements described here, such as the West German Greens, the Italian Radicals, or the Swiss citizen initiative groups, it is indeed the whole party system that has failed. Social and cultural change appears to have produced a whole new stratum of educated, white-collar and professional, service occupations, including their student acolytes, who have a distinctive, postmaterialist mentality, and value issues of life style more than those of class and status (Dalton et al., 1984: 106–109). In large part, it may be the issues of their ardent interest that the established parties are not willing to accommodate, possibly because they clash head-on with commitments to other important constituent groups. Typical examples of this have been the problems of the West German and Swedish Social Democrats to reconcile labor-union support for nuclear energy with the virulent opposition to nuclear plants within their own ranks. The antinuclear dissidents, at least in the Federal Republic, had nowhere to go except into new protest groups and, eventually, to the Greens.

The other part of the motives for alternative action lies in the participational revolution that has swept many European countries since the late sixties. Regarding West Germany, for example, Jutta Helm reports the mushrooming of citizen initiatives, between 1970 and 1973 alone, to the point where their participants outnumbered the members of all the political parties (see Helm, 1980: 576). A whole generation thirsting for political action found itself denied access by restrictive rules of the game, by collusion of the established parties—perhaps another kind of party failure—and by the longstanding shift of governmental functions to the bureaucracy and to corporatist interest intermediation.

Party Failure in Different Party Systems

The phenomenon of major party failure obviously has a different impact on different kinds of party systems. If one or both parties of an essentially bipolar system like that of the United States suffers a lapse of the kind we described, the result is often a third party which faces an enormous uphill battle against restrictive rules of the game and well-established habits of mind on the part of the voters: somehow it always seems more promising to battle it out within the party or switch to the opposition than to vote for a third party, no matter how persuasive its stand on issues. Worse yet, a moderately successful third party is very likely to have its issues taken up by one or both of the major parties which may deprive it of its reason for being.[2] A similar process of self-correction may well be

---

[2] While the rise and decline of the National Democratic Party of Alabama (NDPA) described by Hanes Walton, Jr., is a typical third-party story, this was not true of such earlier southern developments as preceded the NDPA. The suppression of black voting and political representation—and incidentally, the competition of Alabama Republicans and Populists as well—during the decades between the 1870s and the 1940s instead appears to have been the replacement of one "exclusionary party system," under slavery, with another which gave the white supremacists a state and regional monopoly at the expense of the responsiveness of the party system to most popular needs other than racial domination. The Dixiecrats, Free Electors, and American Independent party of 1948, and the 1960s and the 1970s, were more typical third-party reactions to the changes in the national party system, if not stories of third-party success.

at work in most bipolar systems, although it hardly suffices to explain all the likely paths of alternative action.

On the other hand, the United States offers an extreme example of party failure in the sense of the parties' general decline in the minds of the voters, in their role in organizing campaigns, and in legislative discipline, as Frank Sorauf has explained above in this book. Since their electoral role has always been particularly important—as compared to the membership organization of European parties—they were also particularly affected by the revolution in communications, and the changes in the American electorate and in the agenda of politics which became, in Frank Sorauf's words, "too diverse and too divisive for the parties to embrace." This resulted, among other things, in alternative organizations other than national third parties taking up issues ignored or neglected by the two major parties: political action committees appeared to maximize the impact of geographically scattered voters, interests, and opinion leaders and their funds on selected policy issues and candidates. The upshot appears to be a pattern of politics dominated by the individual candidates, individually organized and financed, leaving to the parties little more than the role of beacons of symbolic identification for politicians and voters. American parties have been adapting to their diminished role, moreover, and are developing centralized fund-raising operations quite similar to some of the more effective PACs. Nevertheless, they are rather unlikely to recoup their former position on the political stage. The weakness of the established parties may actually make it easier for future third parties or alternative grass-roots movements, such as the peace movement or antinuclear energy organizations, to flourish. The same circumstance may also encourage regional or local grass-roots rebellions within the remaining party organizations, such as the one described by Raffaella Nanetti above, which really deserves to be compared with the one-party-dominant systems below, rather than related to alternative action in bipolar situations. The remainders of the Chicago Democratic machine may offer an unusual setting for it, but the dynamics of internal rebellion and renewal are universal. There is also the perpetual need for asserting the power of local minorities through pressure groups, neighborhood associations, and other kinds of grass-roots action.

Great Britain, on the other hand, differs in the nature of the original, bipolar game in that the third, the Liberal party, has survived all these years even without the reinforcement of a functional role in the bipolar system, as a coalition party in the government like the West German FDP. In fact, the Liberals experienced a notable period of resurgence in the early 1970s which at times made them a competitor of SNP, Plaid Cymru, and the National Front, although they seemed to enjoy no more hard-core support than did the two major parties. In this context, the ethnic parties, the British National Front, and, most recently, the Social Democratic party (SDP) seem more typical of the alternative, third-party type that flourishes upon the failure of the major parties to address ethnic home rule, the immigration issue, and other concerns. The leftward march of Labour and the rightward development of the Conservatives had clearly left a void asking to be filled by a party more responsive to the concerns of moderate constituents of both parties. If the Labour party overcomes its crisis and the defeat of 1983, and once more appeals to its dissidents of the center, the SDP may conceivably suffer the fate of most third parties in the United States. In the meantime, the example of the SDP is particularly noteworthy because of its alliance with the Liberals without which it would face an even bigger electoral hurdle. The encouragement by Liberal leaders like David Steel gives the 1981 foundation of the SDP a strong overtone of cooptation by an established organization, if hardly an established major party. This element and the patent interest to win elections have to be weighed against the more third-partyish aspects of the SDP clientele of voters and members. As Geoffrey Pridham has described it, even its timid and deliberately vague policy positions place the SDP not very close to the oppositional stance of continental alternative parties and movements.

Across the fluid line of distinction between these "two-party" systems and bipolar systems featuring three to five parties, we find the impact of alternative movements, at least under certain specifiable circumstances, far more serious. The March 1983 election in the Federal Republic of Germany, for example, was widely (and mistakenly) expected to produce a deadlock and crisis in the party system: the two major parties, SPD and CDU/CSU seemed to be neck and neck, but neither one capable of a clear majority. The perpetual coalition party, the FDP, had just painfully severed its alliance with the SPD and was not expected to poll the required 5 percent of the popular vote for representation in the Bundestag. In its place, according to some public opinion polls, the alternative Greens had a strong chance to enter Parliament and to blackmail whichever major party would try to form a minority government. The Greens had left no doubt about their intransigence regarding issues ranging from the stationing of new missiles to shutting down all nuclear plants and major freeway, canal, and airport construction projects. The elections, fortunately, turned out differently: both the FDP and the Greens made it over the 5 percent hurdle. This enabled the FDP to continue in coalition with the CDU/CSU in the government majority while the Greens missed out on being in a position to dictate policies to the government. But there had been plenty of reason to expect a stalemate: the Greens, or Alternatives, had already produced analogous stalemate situations in two state elections (Hamburg and Hesse) in 1982 (see Cerny, 1987).

The reader may object, to be sure, that the impact the Greens had on the West German party system owes as much to the inability of either major party to poll a majority and, perhaps, to the internal crisis of the FDP as to any special attribute of the Greens. This is true, although we need to remember that without the legerdemain of British electoral law, neither Labour nor the Conservatives have ever polled 50 percent or more since 1945, and the same has been true with rare exceptions of all European parties. Moreover, the intransigence of the Greens shows that they are no ordinary party but a typical example of the new-issue politics that have been described in several of these essays. Many of the alternative citizens' initiatives that preceded the Greens were far more willing to compromise. On the other hand, other less successful West German third parties such as the NPD or the Moscow-leaning, Communist DKP have not shown any willingness to compromise with the established parties either, except perhaps in the few city councils where they are represented.

The case of the Swedish Environmentalists' failure in 1982 resembles the German situation in that the two halves of the five-party system were evenly matched and neither one seemed likely to control a parliamentary majority. The Environmentalists, according to public opinion polls, were expected to poll enough votes to enter the Riksdag and there to hold at ransom whichever bloc, the Social Democrats or the three bourgeois parties, would form a minority government. As in West Germany, the alternative with its determined issue politics seemed to challenge the basic left-right cleavage of Swedish politics per se. On the other hand, none of the other Swedish parties, not even the Communists, is as intransigent as the extreme wings in the Federal Republic. If the Environmentalists had succeeded in the manner anticipated, there might have been an unexpected bargain struck across the great divide between the two blocs. Even in Germany, for that matter, there were voices in both the major parties proposing to overcome the likely impasse with a grand coalition of SPD and CDU/CSU despite the widespread uneasiness about such a political cartel of the major parties.[3] The case of France offers the other side of the coin, so to speak, in that here the established Socialists (PS), Communists (PCF), Gaullists (RPR), and Democratic Union (UDF) easily turned back the challenges of right-wing populism, ecologists, and insurgent nationalists. Among the reasons cited by Frank Wilson above, perhaps none is more

[3] Between 1966 and 1969, such a grand coalition under Chancellor Kurt Georg Kiesinger (CDU/CSU), and Vice-Chancellor Willy Brandt (SPD) governed the Federal Republic, leaving only the FDP on the opposition benches and the right-wing NPD and left-wing Extraparliamentary Opposition (APO) outside to criticize the government.

important than that the drama of the left-right confrontation—in fact, the eventual triumph of Mitterrand's PS over the ruling right-wing coalition—simply stole the show from all the other attempts at opposition with the possible exception of the Corsican nationalists. While in Sweden and West Germany, in other words, the left-right polarization seemed to lose salience in the face of the environmentalist challenges, in France it clearly remained the most dramatic show at the center of the political stage. The faltering of the right and, after decades of Gaullist and Giscardian dominance, the triumphant upsurge of the left must have robbed the small oppositional fringe of much of its appeal for the time being, although some of these parties may perk up again as France tires of Mitterrand's reign.

COMPLEX MULTIPARTY SYSTEMS

As we move from the bipolar two- or three-to-five party systems to complex multiparty systems, the impact of major party failure and of the new-issue politics tends to become more diffuse. The presence of socially based or cultural-ideological subcultures defeats the cleansing function of fluctuations, or floating votes, between the major antagonists and replaces it with complex patterns of exchanges among three or more parties.[4] The recent Italian elections, for example, have exhibited a major shift from the polarized confrontations of the 1970s, between Christian Democratic coalition governments and a Communist-led potential "new majority," to depolarization in 1983 which cost both sides dearly in present or future voting support. The Communists (PCI) had already lost some of their newly gained edge in 1979 and were unable to regain their momentum in 1983.[5] The Christian Democrats lost a crucial one-seventh of the 38 percent to 40 percent of the vote they had had for four decades. The beneficiaries of this depolarization were nearly all the small parties, including a new Pensioner's party and regional movements such as the Liga Veneto. Even Bettino Craxi's Socialists (PSI), who have been hoping for a Mitterrand-type (polarized) landslide in their favor for years, gained a little from the depolarization; the same held true for a number of the usual small government coalition parties: the Republicans, Social Democrats,

---

[4] Such exchanges are not unknown in bipolar systems either: in West Germany in 1980, for example, former CDU/CSU voters were observed switching to the FDP which in turn lost some of its supporters to the Greens (who also benefited from defections among the SPD).

[5] The local and regional elections of 1985 meanwhile confirmed the depolarizing trend. There is much evidence for the assumption that the voters found them too timid and halfhearted to be a convincing alternative in 1983. This appeared to offer only a *mezz' alternativa* (Rossanna Rossanda).

and Liberals. We have to assume that the increased vote for these "pygmies" of the party system also represents a return of voters to whatever issues they are identified with, and that "issue politics" can stress old issues as well as new ones. In the case of regional parties such as the Liga, the Union Valdotaine, or the South Tyrolean People's party, the issues also involve local and regional complaints that had for too long taken a back seat to the pressing national confrontations of right and left.

For the traditional Italian ruling party, the Christian Democrats (DC), there is an additional twist to their defeat in that, under General Secretary Ciriaco DeMita, the party had just attempted to reform itself along lines of a new emphasis on issues rather than the old clientelistic course of protecting small business and local interests. In the process, the DC may well have alienated its old friends at the same time that its new concern for issues was put forth more convincingly by the rival Republicans, Social Democrats, and Liberals who had the distinct advantage of not having to aggregate the diverse group interests of a large party. Unlike the electoral laws of Great Britain and France, or the minimal hurdles of Swedish and West German elections, moreover, Italian electoral law allows even the smallest and newest party an opportunity to survive. Some, like the Republicans, have done so ever since the end of World War II with no more than 2 percent to 3 percent of the national vote and a few local strongholds. Compared to these "old" small parties, the Radicals (RP) of Angelo Panebianco's essay differ mostly by their modern communications skills and by their curious mixture of elitism and democratic radicalism. Their record in the political battles of recent years is living proof of how a pygmy party can get the better of the establishment of giant parties by skillful manipulation of the media and of the public at large on an issue of broad support.

Much as we may marvel at these successes, however, the RP has neither been a threat to the existing party system nor can the established parties be said to have "failed" in a way clearly pointing to the RP. They did, of course, turn a deaf ear at the time to each of the particular causes promoted by the Radicals, such as divorce and abortion, but even this usually from a reasonably accurate sense of what their own supporters would accept. The Radicals succeeded in second-guessing the leadership of the established parties mostly from a shrewd perception of changing national majorities and thanks to the persuasive opinion leadership of Radical leader Marco Panella. Theirs has been an extraordinary high-wire act that could probably not be repeated indefinitely with ever-new issues. As Panebianco has pointed out, it may already have met up with its own inherent limitations when Panella tackled the issue of world hunger. A noble, self-sacrificing do-gooder issue, world hunger may not be able to sustain a level of support comparable to the *piccolo divorzio* in the competition among other issues in hard times. Even if it should fail to convince a majority of Italians, however, the Radical championship of the hungry masses of the third world forms an inspiring contrast to the lack of such moral leadership in many advanced countries of the Western world. If Marco Panella can arouse the conscience of even a plurality in a relatively poor country like Italy, what could a president of the mighty United States do if he were to use his moral suasion to help right the balance of justice in the world? The remarkable public opinion leverage of the Radicals clearly appeals to an idealistic and, of course, postmaterialist streak in Italian minds that other politicians have ignored in the past because the battle for materialistic needs was, and is, far from won in Italy. The advancing secularization of Italian politics, moreover, may entail also, along with many other changes, a secularization of once otherworldly concerns toward the suffering in this world.

The spectacular loss of one-fourth to one-half of the votes of each of the five established Danish parties in 1973 is a textbook case of the effects of various long-range and short-range factors, as Mogens Pedersen has shown above. Denmark is an extreme example of volatility among several European countries including, for example, the Netherlands and other formerly more segmented societies that are in the process of losing the social bases of their party systems (Dalton et al., 1984: 236, 271–88; Lijphart, 1975: ch. 10). Many Western European systems have been subject to the same erosion of social bases if not yet to comparable political upheavals, possibly because their party leadership is coping better with the ensuing challenges. To speak with Hans Daalder, "Even if one regards with Rokkan the party systems of the 1960s as mainly a reflection of cleavage structures of another era, this does not gainsay their evident ability to handle a host of new issues and changes . . ." (Daalder and Mair, 1983: 18). In Denmark in 1973, several long-simmering revolts seem to have burst into flames simultaneously: not just a taxpayers' revolt against bureaucracy and the welfare state, but also a rebellion against political and cultural elites, political parties and institutions, and a populist reaction against presumably excessive sexual and social liberation. The charismatic personality and clever tactics of Progress party leader Mogens Glistrup, who has meanwhile been sentenced to imprisonment, only showed up the weakness of the established leadership.

Encouraged also by the heavy preoccupation of the media with particular issues rather than parties, the revolt propelled no less than five challengers—the Communists and the Justice party among them had been in the Folketing in earlier decades—into Parliament. Glistrup's Progress party was the largest of the new-issue parties but accounted for less than half of the newly won seats. The moralistic Christian People's party and the populist Centrists together won almost as many seats as the Progress party. It is illuminating to compare the 1981 election results with those of 1973 and the situation before the electoral earthquake: by 1981, the Social Democrats and Socialist People's party together had nearly recovered their pre-1973 stand and the Conservatives (with twenty-six of their thirty-one pre-1973 seats) had also recouped much of their 1973 losses. Only the Radical Liberals (down two-thirds) and Agrarian Liberals (down one-third) have been unable to reverse their decline. As for the challengers of 1973, the Centrists and Christian People's party have more or less retained their gains while the Progress party has been slipping and will probably slip more now that its leader is in prison for tax evasion. The Justice party and the Communists lost their 1973 representation altogether, although there is now a Left-Socialist party that may well have picked up the Communist votes. The upshot of all this seems to be a considerably more fragmented right and a weakened left—that is, without Communists or Left Socialists—that is farther from a majority than ever. A series of Danish minority governments of Social Democrats alone, or with the Agrarian Liberals, since 1973 has dramatized the situation with its reliance on ad hoc issue coalitions in the Folketing (Thomas, 1982).

How do these Danish developments fit into our theory of major party failure and the challenge of new-issue movements? The failure of the established parties to rise to the challenge of long- and short-range changes hardly requires further comment, although we may be left to wonder at what point the "old" party leadership should have realized that it needed to adapt to the cumulative, if often disharmonious, new trends. What is very clear is that the "failure" of the old parties antedated and obviously was not the result of the rise of Glistrup or of the other new movements. The latter moved into the limelight merely as the misfortunes of the various established parties seemed to leave a vacuum of issues and leadership for them, although their initial successes seem to have accelerated the decline of the old parties.

It is instructive to recall at this point the reasons cited by Frank Wilson for the vigorous triumph of the French parties against all challengers: (1) The comparative "youth" of the French party system, with three of the four major parties having been newly organized or reborn in the 1970s. Dissatisfied political activists thus could be absorbed with the renewal or reforms of their respective party. (2) A considerable increase in party identification among French voters and surging memberships in the same decade. (3) The intense left-right competition and eventual left victory which also meant the triumph of a working class that, unlike that of other Western European countries, had not yet been completely integrated into

French society. By comparison, left-right polarization was low in Denmark—where the workers are well integrated and the Communist party (DKP) plays a negligible role—and began to increase again only toward the end of the 1970s. (4) There are institutional safeguards in France such as the electoral system (*scrutin uninominal*) and the admixture of strong presidentialism and government centralization which evidently protect the established parties better from challengers than does the Danish system of proportional representation with a 2 percent minimum of the vote for representation. The governing parties in France usually control television and radio and hardly need to worry about parliamentary opposition. Danish parliamentary government, by way of contrast, has been so weak all along that the politicians have learned to cope with the problems by way of minority governments and ad hoc legislative issue coalitions.[6] Wilson's final conclusion, on the other hand, that one should view party failure more as a cyclical phenomenon—of which France has had its share, for example, in 1940 and 1958 but not now—is appropriate but may fail to explain the long-range trends at work in Denmark and in many another country (cf. Pedersen, above).

The example of Israel fits in quite well with the multiparty systems of Western Europe in which a strong left-right cleavage—the religious emphasis being more important in Israel than property or entrepreneurial definitions of the right wing—asserts itself above the seeming proliferation of small parties. Before the Likud coalition under Menachem Begin was formed in 1977, the country was dominated by the Socialist Mapai/Alignment and its coalitions with the National Religious party (NRP) and others, until social and generational change and, according to Myron Aronoff, a loss of ideological faith led to Mapai's decline. From 1977 on, the NRP went with Likud, and smaller right-wing groups helped to flesh out an ample governing majority which has held together with impressive discipline through various crises (Seliktar, 1982). The impact of the Gush Emunim on the NRP was part of the process of fragmentation of this party. But it was not likely to be destabilizing in numbers or because, like the ecological parties of Sweden and West Germany, it might occupy the position of the balancer between two evenly matched blocs neither of which has a majority. The leverage of this group is more likely to be limited to the Likud bloc itself and may be an irritant for the United States because of its irrepressible settlement policies. Its position on the political spectrum of Israeli parties thus makes it a gadfly rather than an alternative or

---

[6] Wilson's further point that the French have learned to cope with protest because it has always been endemic (and his example of protests against nuclear plants) are very illuminating but perhaps less relevant to Denmark than they may be in comparison with Germany.

competitor. It would make little sense to look for "party failure" in the sense of a failure of the government parties to satisfy or absorb the clientele of Gush Emunim. Any party should have the right to refuse to accommodate extreme demands of whatever description. On the other hand, the Gush Emunim as a "revitalization movement" on issues with the power to inspire important parts of the Likud bloc may have extraordinary leverage either to push the government into extreme positions from which there is no graceful way to retreat or to break up crucial coalition partners such as the NRP.

ONE-PARTY DOMINANCE OR MONOPOLY

As we compare competitive and de facto noncompetitive systems, ignoring for the time being the possibility of internal or factional competition within the one dominant party, we can expect party failure and new challengers to play entirely different roles. Competition among parties, after all, is supposed to supply the corrective mechanism that takes care of most new or unsatisfied group demands as a matter of course. In a noncompetitive system, however, whether it is a democratic, one-party dominant one like India (see also Sartori, 1976: 192–201) or a dictatorial one like Poland or Taiwan, a "failure" of the dominant party is a major crisis for the entire system, that is, if it is a party regime and not a military dictatorship. Protest movements, by the same token, have to be seen in a different light. Their role may seem either frustratingly inconsequential, incapable of budging the well-entrenched establishment, or it may be a momentous challenge to the legitimacy of the establishment, a David undermining Goliath more effectively by his mere presence than he could with an electoral landslide. This impact may be obvious with dictatorial one-party states, but it can also play a role with one-party dominant systems,[7] as we shall see.

The rise of the Communist party of India (CPI) to power in Kerala in 1957 raises many relevant questions, beginning with that of the levels of government. The impact of Congress failure and CPI triumph in one state clearly posed no threat to the national dominance of the Congress party, although it may conceivably have heralded developments in other parts of India as well. To understand the nature of the "failure" of the Congress, we also need to remind ourselves of its character as the quintessential,

[7] While party dictatorships may seem an obvious category, one-party dominant systems are not. We shall consider as one-party dominant only systems in which the national domination of one party has been the rule since 1945, even though opposition parties exist and are permitted to function.

broad independence movement which united political strains and groups ranging over a large spectrum until after independence when many of them either formed their own parties or factions or were absorbed by the ubiquitous clientelistic networks. The Congress remained dominant—except for one brief lapse between Indira Gandhi's constitutional dictatorship and her triumphant return to power—as a faction-ridden, clientelistic umbrella organization that retained its hold over the rural masses through "symbolic politics," to speak with Ronald Herring, and by manipulating patron-client networks. Its original promise of fundamental transformation of Indian rural society was lost among the hard facts of landlord dominance except in places like Kerala where the CPI "stole Congress thunder," by mobilizing the rural masses for radical reform. As Herring shows in Kerala, conservatives and radicals had already been polarized within Congress, and after independence the radicals formed their own fractious leftist movements, leaving the state Congress party weak and chiefly dependent on landlords and other right-wing supporters. Despite its own divisions, the Kerala CPI was a constant embarrassment to the national Congress which, at least under Jawaharlal Nehru, still advocated many of the Socialist reforms the CPI was carrying out against fierce resistance by the state Congress party.

Later splits and the reluctant implementation of the legislated land reforms by the state Congress party under pressure from all sides detract only in minor ways from the conclusion that Congress failure and CPI triumph are closely related. The CPI, too, eventually met its fate when its reforms began to weaken its own base. On the other hand, as Herring also emphasizes, the presence of unusually competent and dedicated leadership on the radical side and its absence on the conservative side create parallels to the systems we discussed earlier. This factor, however, was subject to the same cycles as the achievements of the reforms: the best leaders took on national careers or simply got old or out of touch, while mediocrities and opportunists may have been attracted by the erstwhile success of the party. The "bite of failure" among the state Congress, by the same token, may have helped that party to improve and to renew itself with notable effect.

In the Indian case, as in many others, a certain immobility prevents free-floating competition at the national level. Outside of Kerala and a few other places, the CPI and Congress are firmly tied to long-established clienteles that keep them by and large from drastic increases or losses. The kind of social change that has eroded the social bases of the Danish party system in a postmaterialist direction is still a long way off, although major social changes are proceeding apace, creating new and reinforcing old cleavages that support the party system. That the "old" CPI was more successful in Kerala than elsewhere had a great deal to do with such crucial imponderables as the local circumstances and traditions of agrarian rebellion as well as the uneven distribution of leadership talents between radicals and conservatives. The many other smaller Indian parties—regional, religious, ideological, or socioeconomic in emphasis—are also capable, at least in some instances, of capitalizing on lapses of the Congress. Such capability, moreover, might even topple the dominant party if it suffered a crisis comparable to that of Indira Gandhi's fall and brief replacement by a coalition of five small parties. In this case, the Congress party, or rather her faction of it, eventually came back in triumph as the five parties under Morarji Desai quarreled and were perceived to be unable to cope with India's enormous problems. But the temporary lapse and division of the Congress could just as easily have initiated a disastrous and terminal loss of cohesion and legitimacy that would have spelled the end of the Indian republic.

How does the Indian example compare with the case of the Sanrizuka movement in Japan? Here, too, there is a dominant party, based on a vast clientelistic network and there are a number of small opposition parties of ideological or religious emphasis, though Japan's party system lacks the regional angle of India. Instead, the Narita airport movement drew together in one place local farmers and village representatives, New Left pacifists, antinuclear demonstrators, and many who wished to protest the oppressiveness of Japanese laws and the unresponsiveness of the bureaucracy and the existing political process. The closest analogy to Sanrizuka are perhaps the citizen initiatives of continental Europe, especially those described by Robert Sorensen, above, and perhaps with a strong admixture of antinuclear plant protests and the current peace movement in Western Europe. There are some important differences in practice, as David Apter's account makes clear: considerable numbers of Japanese militants were living there more or less permanently, in huts and self-built strongholds, who next to the farmers formed the cadres of resistance augmented by large numbers of students, and left-wing groups from the outside. Unlike the rather transitory phenomenon of European nuclear plant protests or the occupation of controversial construction sites—including the runway expansion of Frankfurt airport—the Narita airport site and its farms nearby have the rebel occupation permanently implanted, and the authorities have not expelled it from there. The element of physical control of a locality, whether temporary or permanent, is an important feature of twentieth-century protests (except for terrorists), and directly puts the police or army in defense of the monopoly of the modern state against defiant rebels (see also Merkl, 1980a: 163–64). Control of the area also preoccupied the European labor struggles of more than a hundred years of lockouts and sit-down strikes and inspired European labor and Socialist movements, with demonstrations and vigilante action, to strive for a "control of the streets" contested violently by the police and, later, by fascist paramilitary groups. This struggle for turf, of course, tends toward symbolism and symbolic exaggerations such as equating the struggle against the Narita airport with a struggle against U.S. imperialism, Vietnam, Japanese militarism, and a nuclear holocaust.

What is drastically different from our Indian example is the New Left character of the Narita airport movement, an element it shares with some of the current protest movements of Western Europe and the United States. Even though the Japanese New Left sects also had links in many cases to dissident offsprings of the latter, their involvement at Narita had little to do with the primary, "materialistic" forces of the industrial or agrarian class struggle, but a great deal to do with the postmaterialistic values of the environment. To be sure, the farmers involved may remind the reader of the small farmers and laborers of Kerala, but Japanese small farmers are relatively well-off, after decades of rice price supports and high returns on other farm produce. They are "small-scale agro-businessmen," to use Apter's phrase. If anything, the old Narita and Chiba province farmers bring a note of village nostalgia and solidarity against the outside usually associated with the Japanese radical right which is, however, not too incongruous a pose for the educated New Left.

As long as the government is eager to buy out the farmers and compensate them for their losses with land and other material incentives, their resistance has been limited to nonmaterialistic, deeply felt traditionalist elements. Whether protest under these circumstances becomes violent is strictly a matter of the native culture—that is, at what flashpoint are the farmers ready to resort to extreme means—and of reactions to police repression. That heavy-handed police action anywhere, with any public, can produce counterviolence is easy to demonstrate from examples ranging from student demonstrations in many countries to labor unrest and military occupations (Merkl, 1986: ch. 11). In the Sanrizuka case, violence and self-chosen martyrdom evidently came easy to the farmers, and the poor judgment of the riot police helped to fan the flames into a conflagration lasting many years. Among the citizen initiatives of Switzerland, Austria, or West Germany, such resort of farmers or small-town people to violence is rare, except where violent police action may trigger it. In Zürich, brutal repression of youth demonstrations by the police and exceptional authoritarianism on the part of the city council produced prolonged, but rather nonviolent agitation among the city's youth over the closing of a youth center. Austria and West Germany also have had occasional incidents of local violence, such as in cases where villages have been forced to merge with others or were incorporated in a town against their will during the local territorial reform of a few years ago. The resistance of citizen initiatives is usually nonviolent. Violence has been present in big-city confrontations in Hamburg or Berlin or where local controversies, such as those concerning the building of nuclear plants, have attracted violent militants from far away who welcome the opportunity to battle the police. These elements, not the local farmers, may be the equivalent of some of the violent New Left groups in the Sanrizuka movement.

So where did the Liberal Democrats or any other Japanese party fail? Apter mentions that some of the militant farmers had been bosses or local officials of the Liberal Democrats or the Socialist party which may indicate a failing of sorts. But in principle no specific party failure was involved other than that of the smaller opposition parties that would not take up this cause. The Liberal Democrats, at least in providing for a new and modern airport for Tokyo, obviously had to serve the overriding interest of the nation and its economy, even if this conflicted with the desires of the local farmers. And there was no way the government could avoid becoming the target of a concerted attack by the New Left groups of the entire country. The entire conflict was a tragedy, but—aside from subjective perceptions—hardly an unusual one, or without precedent in other developed or developing nations. Yet this is not to deny its impact on Japanese politics which will never be the same again after the farmers of Chiba and Narita stood up to the authoritarian state. That state, in turn, may well advance a few steps toward the destination some Western governments have already reached—democratic ungovernability.

PROTEST MOVEMENTS UNDER DICTATORSHIPS

The case study of Ghana forms a convenient link between one-party-dominant systems and dictatorships. As Jon Kraus has explained above, there have been three civilian and more-or-less competitive party regimes each followed by military rule. The first was dominated by Kwame Nkrumah and his Convention People's party (CPP) which insisted on a monopoly after 1960 and progressively faded away even before it was replaced by the military National Liberation Council in 1966. In 1969, electoral competition returned with Kofi Busia's Progress party (PP) and its victory over Nkrumah's successors and their National Liberation Alliance, only to be overthrown once more in 1972 by another military council, the National Redemption Council (NRC). After prolonged military rule and further coups, Milla Limann's People's National party (PNP) ushered in another competitive period, in 1979, which signified a comeback of the successors of Nkrumah's CPP over two successor parties of Busia's PP. At first glance and interrupted by frequent military intervention, we can speak here of a bipolar system that has been operating, off and on before Fl. Lt. Jerry Rawling's latest coup of 1981, for three decades.

Professor Kraus points out the ways in which Ghanaian party regimes may have failed to perpetuate themselves, each in its own way. The requirements of party success in a country such as Ghana are obviously so complex and varied that they make their equivalent in Western democracies seem easy by comparison. A successful Ghanaian party—and probably the major parties in many other third world countries as well—must be extremely careful not to exclude any ethnicity, locality, or socioeconomic group from fair representation and consideration in its ranks. It must maintain its organization but without offering major incentives that might suggest corruption. Furthermore, it needs to aim at effective economic development and national integration, and ward off any challenge to its rule from the military. How can a party regime expect to gain lasting popularity in the face of "an utterly devastated economy, enfeebled and corrupt state bureaucracies, and collapsed military institutions," as Kraus describes Ghana in 1979? As compared to our democratic cases, however, party failure in Ghana and comparable semidemocratic regimes has been more likely to lead to a military takeover than to the growth of alternative political action. In a way, we could even speak of the military takeover—usually by rather modernized, well-educated, and technocratic officers though rarely free of ulterior motives (Nordlinger, 1977: 34–53, 68–70)—as a kind of alternative, if not very political, action. Frequently, social forces dissatisfied with the vagaries of partisan politics, and its inevitable favoritism and corruption, actually prevail upon the military to intervene. Once the military is ensconced in power, on the other hand, there may be new favoritism, new corruption, and new economic mismanagement which, for example in the late seventies in Ghana, once more generated popular pressure for a return to civilian, partisan rule.

The case of Ghana is particularly noteworthy in that there is an on-again, off-again bipolar party system at work between the successors of Nkrumah's CPP (NAL, PNP) and of Busia's PP (PFP), even though various contending military elements continually intervene in their interaction. Political participation through mass and interest group organizations, moreover, evidently continues at lower and regional levels and may take on the role of a mobilized opposition to the military or to dictatorial tendencies in a ruling party whenever appropriate. Ghana's first military government, the NLC, appreciated these group structures and used them to give itself a broad, popular basis, as did the partisan revival of 1979 (after the military rule of the NRC/SMC of 1972–79 had restricted their activities). FL. Lt. Jerry Rawling's coalition of lower officer ranks with union-ized workers, students, and a network of local communities finally united the contending elements, although the resulting organization is rife with violence and corruption and unlikely to produce a cohesive, partylike ef-fect. The People's Defense Committee (PDC) network has been an egali-tarian, populist "alternative" to party control only in the sense that it at-tempts to purge managers, local officials, and professional people—for protesting Rawling's PNDC rule as well as for corruption or mismanage-ment. It would be more appropriate simply to call it a new, and rather well-organized, grass-roots party in rapid evolution and evidently a re-placement for the disintegrating military hierarchy and the two parties that preceded it. In this sense the PNDC/PDC is indeed a response to the fail-ure of the latter and of military rule.

The case of the KMT, the independents, and the Taiwan Independence Movement is a simpler one in that this mixture of one-party dominance and dictatorship is based on a pattern of historic conquest and ethnic domination by mainlanders—including the KMT-subsidized, tiny Demo-cratic Socialist and Chinese Youth parties—over the native Taiwanese. The KMT has hardly "failed" as yet, although by the 1970s, it has found it prudent to tolerate Tangwai independents.[8] As the KMT gerontocracy is shrinking in numbers by natural attrition, and the Tangwai become in-creasingly organized, the crucial time of testing of the KMT political ma-chine may well be near. When the test comes, it will clearly show whether the KMT leadership has been able to meet the political challenge of lasting accommodation and/or amalgamation with the natives. Coercion and vi-olent showdowns are unlikely to solve the problem which depends also, among other things, upon Taiwan's international role and possible mode of accommodation with the People's Republic of China (PRC).

Imagining the likely implications of a complete merger of Taiwan with the PRC—for heuristic purposes only since such a merger would be an ex-treme solution in a range of possible ones—also provides a transition to the case of Poland. The Polish United Workers' party (PUWP), like the Communist parties of other Communist party states, is supposed to oc-cupy the central, energizing role in the entire system, monopolizing both authority and power (see also Sartori, 1976: 230–32). As Zvi Gitelman points out in his essay above, however, the PUWP has always had a crucial

---

[8] According to news reports, the process of Taiwanization has begun: in the legislative elections of late 1983, all but half a dozen of the seventy-one winners were Taiwanese-born, including those of mainlander parents. A Taiwanese, Lee Teng-Hui, was also nominated as vice-president and presumable successor to ailing Kuo-Mintang president Chiang Ching-Kuo. The party itself now claims to be substantially "rejuvenated" and to consist of three-fourths Taiwanese.

lack of the legitimacy that its Soviet, Chinese, and Yugoslav sister parties had gained from their struggle against foreign invaders and domestic enemies. In the crisis of 1980–81, as the mushrooming Solidarity trade-union movement defied state and Communist strictures upon independent unionism, it also gathered momentarily the political legitimacy that had always eluded the PUWP. Worse yet, masses of local PUWP members actually joined Solidarity and, by the time of the Extraordinary Party Congress of 1981, the party had suffered a loss of more than 600,000 members on top of its chronic failure to maintain a substantial working-class following. The Communist local periphery was uniting to rise against the loyalist party core. The initiatives emanating from Solidarity toward *odnova* (renewal) of grass-roots democracy within the party, anticorruption drives against high-living Gierek appointees, and criticism of economic mismanagement finally threatened—in the form of the "horizontal movement"—to overcome the authoritarian Leninist principle of vertical links between local branches and the central *apparat*.

As Professor Gitelman points out, the failure of PUWP must also be viewed against the background of the earlier failures of the Hungarian (1956) and Czechoslovak (1968) Communist parties to maintain the orthodox communist monopoly against liberal pluralistic patterns. The PUWP did not fall into the same error, but tried to hold out against the intellectuals of KOR and Solidarity whose role, by 1981, began to evolve increasingly from an independent trade union into a broad social mass movement of ten million, soon to be seconded by a rural solidarity movement of similarly massive proportions. In these extreme circumstances— by that time Solidarity too had overshot the mark and was declining in popular favor—the faltering party fell, exhausted, into the arms of General Jaruzelski who, as defense minister, general secretary of PUWP, and prime minister of the state, was given sweeping powers unprecedented for a military man in a communist system. His imposition of martial law in December 1981, while forestalling Soviet military intervention and further "anarchy," also signified the final collapse of the PUWP's normal role in the governance of the communist system, reducing communist power *sans* authority to its most barefaced extreme, simple coercion. The Polish case not only leaves no doubt about the disastrous consequences of party failure in a one-party state, but it also seems to negate the possibility of meaningful internal renewal from inside or outside the only legal party. Military dictatorship, whether from the outside or from within, is hardly a propitious, nurturing environment for odnova. What all these dictatorial systems have in common, of course, is the absence of a popular, self-regulating mechanism such as the role elections perform in pluralistic systems. The institutional channels in Ghana, Taiwan, and Poland have made it nearly impossible for abuses to be corrected without overthrowing the state.

INSTITUTIONAL CHANNELS FOR DISSENT

It may be a long distance from Taiwan to Central Europe, but mention of institutional barriers to opposition or dissent should remind us that a new or dissenting group in West Germany, Italy, or Switzerland is not quite as assured of a hearing as the democratic nature of these political systems might lead us to expect. When citizen initiatives first began to gather in West Germany to oppose planning decisions, nuclear plants, and environmental policies, they had to face the fact that neither the state constitutions nor the Basic Law permits initiatives or referendums for any purpose outside of territorial changes.[9] The peace movement of the 1950s discovered that it was not possible to launch a plebiscite against West German rearmament (Drummond, 1982: 224), and the current agitation against nuclear missiles and for the creation of "nuclear-free zones" likewise found itself stymied by the constitutional prohibition of plebiscites. The Federal Republic must be a rare example of this abstention from forms of direct democracy among Western constitutional democracies.

The reason for this anomaly lies in the German past. The framers of the Basic Law and dominant political leaders of the early years all felt a deep-seated distrust of the masses and their political passions. These German masses, in their opinion, had voted for or at least supported the Hitler regime and, under the rather permissive democratic constitution of the Weimar Republic, abused initiative and referendum and other democratic rights with disastrous consequences. Plebiscitary campaigns repeatedly had brought political conflict to a fever pitch. Because of their fear of the people's voice, the founders of the Bonn Republic went out of their way to create a stable form of party government that could, if necessary, be operated without and even against popular consent and, for short periods of time, also, without a parliamentary majority.[10] Instead of the people, the established parties received a monopoly of political power which was

[9] The article in the Basic Law authorizing changes in state boundaries, Article 29, has not been used since the formation of the state of Baden-Württemberg in the early 1950s. Provisions in state constitutions and local government statutes (*Gemeindeordnung*) requiring plebiscites for incorporations, annexations, and local boundaries were revoked in order to frustrate protests against the local territorial reforms in the various states.

[10] The framers of the Basic Law undertook to safeguard a government in office both against a willful president and a possible combined majority of the extreme left and extreme right, evidently remembering the fateful flaws that had ruined the Weimar Republic in the early thirties.

made even more independent of popular support by a generous arrangement of public campaign finance about two decades later. There resulted, then, the West German *Parteienstaat*, a political system run almost exclusively by political parties in executive, legislature, and even in important aspects of administration and judicial appointments (constitutional courts).

For the local citizen initiatives of the 1970s, the Greens, and, for that matter, for any other group of the "new politics" agenda, the Parteienstaat severely limited access to the making of important public decisions. Even within the parties in power, it was often very difficult to get a hearing for minority points of view, such as those of pacifists, feminists, or ecological factions. Given traditions of party discipline, minorities simply had to accept the majority point of view or "exit" from their party. From the outside and at the lower levels of government, it was even more difficult to break into the charmed circle of party politicians, established planners and administrators, and interest groups with privileged access. Citizen groups upset about plans for the construction of nuclear plants, highways, or about "urban renewal" projects that involved the destruction of historic monuments and familiar, old neighborhoods had no recourse other than lawsuits that might lead nowhere or determined *alternative political action* against the bulldozers and the premature decisions behind them. This was the origin of the local citizen initiatives that eventually grew into a national movement of distinctive style and a greatly expanded program of new issues, such as the ones set forth by the Greens:

1. Prevention of NATO rearmament with Pershing II and Cruise Missiles and of deposits of poison gas and other chemical and biological weapons in the Federal Republic. This is connected to the long-range goal of an atom-free zone and neutral belt in Central Europe.
2. A stop to the nuclear plant program; immediate closing of all such plants and development of alternative energy supplies.
3. Immediate steps against further destruction of the forests, pollution of lakes and rivers, and poisoning of the soil.
4. A stop to the monster construction projects of the [Frankfurt airport] West runway, Erding [Munich] airport, Rhine-Main-Danube Canal, fast breeder and nuclear processing plants, and hot reactors, as well as diversion of these resources toward alternative energy, sulphur emission treatment, etc.
5. Transformation of the economy toward decentralized and alternative production and technologies; shorter working hours and

other steps against unemployment and a reduction of social services.

6. Prevention of further reductions in democracy and fundamental
rights, and the development of an alternative democratic culture
that helps to realize the will of the people and foregoes the use of
violence.

7. Equal rights and opportunities for women and men in all aspects
of economic, political, and social life.

8. A stop to cable development, media monopolies, private radio
and television; retention of the public character of, and access for
social movements to, the media.

(From a resolution of the Green Congress of November 1982, in
Hagen.)

This list of Green concerns clearly has lost most of its traces of local antecedents. For the sake of completeness, in fact, we should add the em-
phatic Green statements about the exploitation of the third world, the
treatment of such domestic minorities as gays and gypsies, and the evils of
an overindustrialized society. All of these are issues that could hardly be
pressed any more by lying down in front of bulldozers. Given the limits to
constitutional dissent in West Germany, they compelled the dissenters to
become a national party and to seek election to national office.

The new Radical party of Italy, to be sure, faces no constitutional ban
on plebiscites. Nevertheless, its issue concerns—which overlap considerably with those of the West German Greens—clearly were not getting a
public hearing in a system dominated by the *partitocrazia* and *trasformismo*, and the pervasive influence of parties and interest groups on the
media and the bureaucracy, until the RP developed its own ingenious leverage which consisted of well-aimed one-issue crusades, the judicious use
of civil disobedience, its own media (such as Radio Radicale), and the
hitherto neglected referendum. It became the "party of the referendum"
because it had learned to persuade majorities of voters to support many of
its "new politics" issues, such as divorce, abortion, disarmament, opposition to nuclear plants, and to legal and judicial abuses. Concentration on
one national issue at a time supplied the Archimedean fulcrum that helped
Marco Panella and a tiny minority to unhinge the resistance of the "giant"
parties of the country to taboo reforms. And the referendum became the
perfect instrument to make these one-issue majorities prevail against the
party-dominated Parliament.

The West German and Italian cases gain further depth from comparison
with that of the Swiss civic action groups described by Robert Sorensen
above, as long as we bear in mind the different levels of government.

Switzerland does not share the West German ban on plebiscites, nor have initiative and referendum been unusual channels to resolve public controversies on a wide range of issues. In fact, direct democracy on all three levels is often cited as a major reason among several why Swiss parties have been declining as a means of political expression, at least in the electoral turnout for the national Parliament. Even if their electoral turnout is also rather low, national referendums repeatedly overturned unpopular legislation passed by the "grand coalition" of the four major parties. Why then did not the local groups involved simply resort to a local initiative to overturn obnoxious decisions passed by unresponsive bureaucrats and party politicians in municipal councils? Professor Sorensen points to "a particular understanding of citizen participation and democracy" and a desire on the part of the civic action groups to "act as gadfly" rather than as a replacement of the normal process of representation. But he also mentions the genuine popular satisfaction with the system and the consensualism characteristic of "amicable agreement" in Switzerland, implying a kind of "interest group pluralism" that, by trying to keep all groups happy, may well have created a thicket of selective participation impenetrable to newcomers and outsiders.

Local government in Switzerland, moreover, is dominated by "powerful localist forces"—shades of James Madison's *Federalist* paper No. 10— that consult in well-institutionalized ways with local interest group representatives. The local officeholders, bureaucrats, and organized interests very likely dominate the media as well and can frustrate most efforts at launching an effective initiative campaign within the local jurisdiction that would vote on it. Sorensen documents the actual rise of the number of initiatives in recent years along with the spreading malaise about how poorly the system works. He also mentions the growth of local ad hoc committees outside of parties and interest groups instead of the use of initiatives or referendums in the 1970s, especially with respect to "quality of life" issues that are deemed to be more amenable to lobbying and direct pressure on government officials. Not only is the volume of concerns much larger now, it would appear, but their nature often calls for an "end run" around the quintessential Swiss procedures of direct democracy.

Several reasons could explain this avoidance of the initiative process: perhaps the ad hoc groups are not sure their concerns are likely to receive majority support at the polls and hence they follow the example of other special interest groups who also prefer to avoid the polls. Another reason might be the low turnout and the likelihood of opposition at the polls by equally determined groups. And third, it may be difficult to cast life-style issues in the form of an initiative text, or even a law, whereas proper attitudes of the government officials are easier to achieve. Finally, and this point seems borne out mostly by direct observation, the local jurisdiction for an initiative rarely coincides with the public that is most affected by many of the typical civic action concerns, such as historic preservation or public construction projects. Hence, an initiative on such a subject would very likely be treated with indifference and probably defeated by what is essentially the wrong electorate.

CONCLUSION

This survey of various forms of alternative political action in different kinds of political systems has tended to focus on the differences rather than on what such protest movements may have in common. Most striking among these differences, of course, is the presence or absence of meaningful political competition. In exclusionary or dictatorial systems, organized protest is important, but it seems to follow a different rationale than in the advanced democratic systems we discussed at the beginning. This is not to say that the more competitive systems are competitive on all levels and in all areas, i.e., they too may present some settings similar to the monopolistic party or hegemonic military state.

In the advanced democratic and industrialized societies today, however, forms of alternative action strikingly reflect the dilemmas of life and politics of these societies. For one thing, they reflect the new life style, or post-industrial concerns, of individuals in today's society, such as their desire for autonomy, dignity, and freedom even from the role structures of the human family. This manifests itself also in issues of personal identity—ethnic, sex-, or age-related—and of the humanization of everyday labor, housing, and the social, cultural, and natural environment.

The ever-more complex interrelationship between governmental activities and everyday life, including economic production and services, furthermore, has created a gigantic overload for government at a time when most political systems already suffer from severe structural problems, or from a degree of overorganization tying together administration, parties, and interest groups, that would make it difficult even under the best of circumstances to rise to the challenge. The result has been that large numbers of groups of people affected by social change and by governmental action or inaction have resorted to self-help, in a manner of speaking. And since they have often spurned the established parties and institutional channels for one reason or another, their hectic activities often give the exaggerated impression that entire political systems are in danger of destabilization. Perhaps, further dramatic increases of this kind of alternative political action—and we have only selected a few, not always representative examples in this book—might reach a point at which the stability of a system is in doubt. As for now, such fears appear unjustified.

In fact, the rise of the current crop of protest and single-issue movements in the advanced democratic countries must be seen also against the changing roles of political parties. Parties and the representative process no longer play quite the dominant role in democratic systems that they once did. They have increasingly abandoned important policymaking areas to interest groups, bureaucratic planners, or neocorporatist interest intermediation—or failed to claim them when they came into focus. At the same time, the media and other agencies have taken over much of what used to be the parties' functions of political communication and agenda-setting. Thus the thrust of much of the contemporary protest, especially of ecological parties and citizen action groups or single-issue movements, confronts an insensitive, technocratic bureaucracy or powerful interest brokers rather than the parties or party systems. In this sense and to this extent, then, the protest may signify a crisis of democratic government rather than a mortal threat to parties.

But there is also another kind of distress abroad between the established parties and their challengers, rightly or wrongly: a sense of frustration and malaise has been spreading both among the activists involved and the many people who have responded with apathy and nonparticipation to the crisis of ungovernability they perceive. Their sense of alienation, moreover, is mirrored in the desperate defensiveness of many supporters of the establishment who are frightened by the unorthodox, unconventional behavior of the alternative challengers. Together, these three groups no longer see democratic government as working *comme il faut*, and their distorted visions of it make governmental malfunctioning and protest or direct civic action more real than, perhaps, they ought to be in a well-ordered, democratic society.

REFERENCES

Baker, K. L., R. J. Dalton, and K. Hildebrandt. 1981. *Germany transformed: Political culture and the new politics*. Cambridge: Harvard University Press.

Browne, E. C., and J. Dreijmanis. 1982. *Government coalitions in Western democracies*. New York: Longman.

Cerny, K., ed. 1987. *Germany at the polls: The 1980 and 1983 Bundestag elections*. Durham, N.C.: Duke University Press.

Daalder, H., and P. Mair, eds. 1983. *Western European party systems: Continuity and change*. Beverly Hills: Sage Publications.

Dalton, R. J., S. Flanagan, and P. A. Beck, eds. 1984. *Electoral change in advanced industrial democracies: Realignment or dealignment?* Princeton: Princeton University Press.

Dittrich, K., and L. N. Johansen. Voting turnouts in Europe, 1945–1979. In Daalder and Mair, 1983: 95–114.

Helm, J. 1980. Citizen lobbies in West Germany. In Merkl, 1980a: 576–96.

Inglehart, R. 1977. *The silent revolution: Changing values and political styles among Western publics.* Princeton: Princeton University Press.

Kaltefleiter, W. 1980. A legitimacy crisis of the West German party system. In Merkl, 1980a: 597–608.

Lawson, K., ed. 1980. *Political parties and linkage: A comparative perspective.* New Haven: Yale University Press.

Lijphart, A. 1975. *The politics of accommodation: Pluralism and democracy in the Netherlands.* Berkeley: University of California Press.

Mazmanian, D. 1974. *Third parties in presidential elections.* Washington: D.C.: Brookings Institution.

Merkl, P. 1980a. *The making of a stormtrooper.* Princeton: Princeton University Press.

———, ed. 1980b. *Western European party systems: Trends and prospects.* New York: Free Press/Macmillan.

———, ed. 1986. *Political violence and terror: Motifs and motivations.* Berkeley and Los Angeles: University of California Press.

Nordlinger, E. 1977. *Soldiers in politics: Military coups and governments.* Engelwood Cliffs, N. J.: Prentice-Hall.

Ranney, A., and W. Kendall. 1956. *Democracy and the American party system.* New York: Harcourt, Brace.

Sartori, G. 1976. *Parties and party systems: A framework for analysis.* New York: Holt, Rinehart.

Seliktar, O. 1982. Israel: Fragile coalitions in a new nation. In Browne and Dreijmanis, 1982: 283–314.

Thomas, A. H. 1982. Coalitions and minority governments. In Browne and Dreijmanis, 1982: 109–41.

NOTES ON CONTRIBUTORS

DAVID E. APTER is Henry J. Heinz II Professor of comparative political and social development at Yale University. His most recent book is *Against the State: Politics and Social Protest in Japan*. He is presently at work on two volumes. The first, *Mao's Republic*, will be based on interviews with Chinese soldiers who participated in the Long March. The second, *Rethinking Development: Modernization, Dependency and Post-Modern Politics*, is a study of what appears to be the worldwide inadequacy of the modern state.

MYRON J. ARONOFF is professor of political science and anthropology at Rutgers University. He is the author of *Frontiertown: The Politics of Community Building in Israel* and *Power and Ritual in the Israeli Labor Party*, and has edited five volumes of *Political Anthropology*. He is presently working on a study of cultural and political change in Israel.

LIANG-SHING FAN is professor of economics at Colorado State University. His articles have appeared in *The American Economic Review, Rivista Internazionale di Scienze Economiche e Commerciali*, and *Future of Taiwan*. He is presently studying contemporary Chinese economic reforms.

FRANK B. FEIGERT is professor of political science at North Texas State University. His work, largely on U.S. parties and voting, includes *The American Party System and the American People* (with Fred Greenstein), now in its third edition. He is currently writing a book on Canadian elections.

ZVI GITELMAN is professor of political science and former director of the Center for Russian and East European Studies at the University of Michigan. His most recent book is *Becoming Israelis: Political Resocialization of Soviet and American Immigrants*. He is currently working on bureaucratic encounters in the USSR and on the impact of Hungarian reforms on Poland.

RONALD J. HERRING is professor of political science at Northwestern University. His field work in India, Pakistan, Sri Lanka, and Bangladesh has been primarily concerned with agrarian political economy. He is the author of *Land to the Tiller: The Political Economy of Agrarian Reform in South Asia*, among other works, and is presently interested in domestic-international linkages in the determination of development policy, beginning with liberalization in post-1977 Sri Lanka.

JON KRAUS is professor of political science at the State University of New York, Fredonia. He is author and editor of *Radical and Reformist Military Regimes* and author of numerous articles on African political economy. Kraus is currently working on two projects: a book on the political economy of trade unionism in Ghana and an essay on the conditions under which military regimes are succeeded by civilian government in Africa.

KAY LAWSON is professor of political science at San Francisco State University. Her recent work includes editing *Political Parties and Linkage: A Comparative Perspective* and writing *The Human Polity: An Introduction to Political Science*, as well as various articles on U.S. and French party politics. She is presently writing *The Possibility of Politics*, a study of the feasibility of democratic politics in modern democracies, using France and the U.S. as her examples.

THOMAS T. MACKIE is lecturer in politics at the University of Strathclyde, Glasgow, Scotland. He is the coauthor and editor of *The International Almanac of Electoral History*, the *Europe Votes* series, and *Unlocking the Cabinet*.

PETER H. MERKL is professor of political science at the University of California, Santa Barbara, a former member of the steering committee of the Council for European Studies, and currently president of the Conference Group on German Politics. Recent publications include *Political Violence Under the Swastika: 581 Early Nazis*, *The Making of a Stormtrooper*, and a symposium, *Political Violence and Terror: Motifs and Motivations*.

RAFFAELLA Y. NANETTI is professor of urban planning and policy at the University of Illinois at Chicago. A former visiting fellow at Nuffield College, Oxford, and a Fulbright Senior Research Fellow, she has published extensively in the area of decentralization policies and neighborhood planning, with an emphasis on urban planning in Chicago.

ANGELO PANEBIANCO is professor of political science at the University of Bologna and the author of *I partiti politici italiani fra centro e periferia* and *Modelli di partito: Organizzazione e potere nei partiti politici*, among other publications.

MOGENS N. PEDERSEN is professor of political science at Odense University. His articles on party systems have appeared in *Comparative Political Studies*, *SPS*, and in *Western European Party Systems: Continuity and Change*. He is currently interested in inter-Scandinavian comparisons.

GEOFFREY PRIDHAM is reader in European politics at the University of Bristol. He is the editor of *The New Mediterranean Democracies: Regime Transition in Spain, Greece and Portugal*, and of *The Theory and Practice of Coalitional Behaviour: An Inductive Model*. He is presently at work on several projects related to political parties and the party system in Italy.

PETER PULZER is Gladstone Professor of government and public administration and Fellow of All Souls, Oxford. His recent publications include the third edition of *Political Representation and Elections in Britain*, and contributions to *Party Government and Political Culture in West Germany*, and to *Democracy and Elections*. He is currently working on a study of the German party system.

RICHARD ROSE is director of the Centre for the Study of Public Policy at the University of Strathclyde, Glasgow, Scotland. His numerous publications include *Voters Begin to Choose, Do Parties Make a Difference?, The International Almanac of Electoral History, Electoral Behaviour, The Problem of Party Government*, and *Politics in England*.

DONALD SCHOONMAKER is professor of politics at Wake Forest University. He is the author of *German Politics* and of several articles on the West German political system. He is currently working on two manuscripts: a book-length analysis of the Greens and a study of the political imagination of Heinrich Böll.

FRANK J. SORAUF is professor of political science at the University of Minnesota. His recent publications include the fifth edition of *Party Politics in America* and several articles on political action committees. His current research remains in the area of American campaign finance.

ROBERT C. A. SORENSEN is professor of political science at Middlebury College in Vermont. His research interests are in the area of grass-roots activism and participation in new social movements, particularly in Switzerland and the Federal Republic of Germany.

EVERT VEDUNG is professor of government at Uppsala University, Sweden. His recent publications include *Political Reasoning, Politics as Rational Action*, and *Energy Policy Evaluations 1973–1981*. He is currently working on problems of implementation and evaluation of public policies, particularly in the field of energy.

HANES WALTON, JR., is Fuller E. Callaway Professor of political science at Savannah State College. His works include *Black Political Parties: An Historical and Political Analysis, Black Politics: A Theoretical and Structural Analysis*, and *Invisible Politics: Black Political Behavior*. He is currently at work on a new book, *The Black Voter*.

FRANK L. WILSON is professor of political science at Purdue University. He is the author of the *French Democratic Left, Political Parties in Fifth Republic France*, and numerous articles on French politics. He has recently completed *Interest Group Politics in France*.

INDEX

anarchism, 52–53
Austria, 277, 533, 536, 550, 577–78

Bahro, Rudolf, 55, 64
Beer, Samuel, 42–43, 46
Ben-Gurion, David, 312
Berger, Suzanne, 42–43, 46, 111n, 123, 504, 511, 517–18, 525, 527
Brandt, Willy, 45–46, 56
bureaucracy, 562, 565, 584, 587; in Denmark, 264; in France, 524; in Ghana, 487; in Japan, 198, 204–6, 214–15, 220, 223; in Poland, 429, 433; in West Germany, 44, 47, 52–53

Chiang Kai-shek, 448–49, 454
China, People's Republic of, 447–51, 457–58, 461, 580
citizen initiative groups, 582–87; in France, 513–14; in Japan, 199, 203–6, 214, 576–78; in Switzerland, 585–86; in West Germany, 54–57, 62, 565, 568
civil disobedience, 584; in Italy, 111, 127; in Switzerland, 149–63; in West Germany, 54, 63, 66. *See also* nonviolent resistance
colonial legacy, in India, 393–95, 398–99, 403, 414, 575
Communists, 7, 9, 232, 553; in Denmark, 258–59, 262, 273; in France, 508–9, 521–26, 568–69; in India, 389–415, 574–76; in Italy, 115–20, 129–35, 569; in Japan, 198, 200, 208; in Poland, 421–43; in Sweden, 77–79, 82–84; in Taiwan, 449–50, 453; in West Germany, 58
consensual (nonmajoritarian) democracy, 138–43, 163–64, 257, 585
consociational democracy, 117–18, 137n, 149
counterculture, in France, 513–14; in Japan, 203; in Switzerland, 163–65; in West Germany, 50, 54, 58

Dahl, Robert A., 50, 141
decentralization, in France, 512–13, 520;

in Great Britain, 344–45, 351–52; in India, 406; in Sweden, 77, 82, 94, 102–3; in West Germany, 49–50, 67
de Gaulle, Charles, 507–8, 520, 526
democratization, 176, 178–79; in Poland, 437–39; in Sweden, 101–2; in Switzerland, 158, 160; in Taiwan, 461; in West Germany, 45–49, 52–53, 56, 67, 69
Denmark, 8, 21–23, 31, 79, 99–100, 232, 257–81, 516, 519, 524, 536, 544, 571–75
direct democracy (initiative), 11, 582–86; in Denmark, 266–67; in France, 507; in Great Britain, 352; in Italy, 111, 133; in Switzerland, 137–39, 145–49, 165–69; in West Germany, 44, 52–53, 67n, 69
disarmament, 54, 112, 562, 584
Duverger, Maurice, 124, 310–11

economic growth (limits to), in France, 513; in Poland, 423–24; in Sweden, 77, 94–101; in West Germany, 47, 50–52, 56, 59, 68–69
electoral law, effect of, 537, 548, 564, 570, 573; in Denmark, 258–59, 272; in France, 515–16, 523–24; in Great Britain, 231–32, 237; in Sweden, 92–93, 105–6; in West Germany, 57
electoral realignment, in Denmark, 261–63, 266, 272–73, 277; in Great Britain, 230–31, 250–51; in Israel, 334; in the U.S., 369, 372, 378, 385
electoral volatility, 231–33, 250–51, 259, 272–75, 277, 571

farmers, as party supporters, 540, 546, 552–53; in Ghana, 474–76, 480, 484–85; in Japan, 197–213, 216–17, 219–20, 576–78. *See also* peasant associations
feminism, 6, 562, 583–84; in Denmark, 269; in Italy, 125–26, 130; in Sweden, 77, 102, 104; in West Germany, 52
France, 10, 67, 100, 111, 133, 273, 277, 340, 441, 503–22, 533, 536–38, 550, 557, 569, 572–73

LIBRARY OF CONGRESS CATALOGING-IN-PUBLICATION DATA

When parties fail.

Bibliography: p.   Includes index.
1. Political parties. I. Lawson, Kay. II. Merkl, Peter H.
JF2011.W54 1988   324.2   87–22566
ISBN 0–691–07758–4 (alk. paper)   ISBN 0–691–10242–2 (pbk.)